The Brownings' Correspondence

Volume 14
September 1846 – December 1847
Letters 2616 – 2716

Florence, 1846

The Brownings' Correspondence

Edited by
PHILIP KELLEY & SCOTT LEWIS

Volume 14

———

September 1846 – December 1847
Letters 2616 – 2716

Wedgestone Press

The editorial work on this volume was supported by a grant from the Division of Research Programs of the National Endowment for the Humanities, an independent United States federal agency.

The printing of this volume was supported by a grant from the Division of Research Programs of the National Endowment for the Humanities, an independent United States federal agency.

∞ The paper used in this publication meets the requirements of American National Standard for Permanence of Paper for Printed Library Materials, ANSI Z39.48-1984.

Copyright © Browning Letters, John Murray, 1998
Copyright © Editorial Matter, Wedgestone Press, 1998

All rights reserved. No part of this publication may be reproduced, stored in a retrieval system, or transmitted, in any form or by any means, electronic, mechanical, photocopying, recording or otherwise, without the copyright owners' prior permission.

Published by
Wedgestone Press

Distributed by

In the United States and Canada

Wedgestone Press
P.O. Box 175
Winfield, KS 67156-0175

Outside the United States and Canada

The Athlone Press
1 Park Drive
London NW11 7SG

British Library Cataloguing in Publication Data

A catalogue record for this book is
available from the British Library
ISBN 0–485–30034–6

Library of Congress Cataloging-in-Publication Data

Browning, Robert, 1812–1889.

    The Brownings' correspondence.

    Correspondence written by and to Robert and Elizabeth Barrett Browning.
    Vols. 9– edited by Philip Kelley & Scott Lewis.
    Contents: v. 1. September 1809–December 1826, letters 1–244—v.2. January 1827–December 1831, letters 245–434 — [etc.] — v. 14. September 1846–December 1847, letters 2616–2716.
    1. Browning, Robert, 1812–1889 — Correspondence. 2. Browning, Elizabeth Barrett, 1806–1861 — Correspondence. 3. Poets, English — 19th century — Correspondence. I. Browning, Elizabeth Barrett, 1806–1861. II. Kelley, Philip. III. Hudson, Ronald. IV. Lewis, Scott. V. Title.
    PR4221.A4   1984   821'.8   84–5287
    ISBN 0–911459–09–X (v. 1)

    ISBN 0–911459–25–1 (v. 14; alk. paper)

Manufactured in the United States of America.

Contents

Illustrations	vi
Cue Titles, Abbreviations and Symbols	vii
Chronology	x
THE CORRESPONDENCE	
1846: Letters 2616–2646	1
1847: Letters 2647–2716	93
Appendix I	
Biographical Sketches of Principal Correspondents and Persons Frequently Mentioned	357
Appendix II	
Checklist of Supporting Documents	361
Supporting Documents: Index of Correspondents	374
Appendix III	
Contemporary Reviews of the Brownings' Works	375
Appendix IV	
EBB's Letters to Her Sister Henrietta	405
Appendix V	
The Brownings in 1847	408
List of Absent Letters	413
List of Collections	414
List of Correspondents	415
Index	417

Illustrations

Florence *frontispiece*
Pencil and chalk sketch, by Charles Hayter, 31 July 1846.
From the editors' file.

FACING PAGE

Collegio Ferdinando, Pisa
Photograph, ca. 1955.
Reproduced from *The Life of Elizabeth Barrett Browning*,
by Gardner B. Taplin (New Haven, 1957).   146

4222 (now 6) Via delle Belle Donne, Florence
Photograph of the Brownings' first Florentine residence, 1972.
From the editors' file.   147

Palazzo Guidi, Florence
Photograph of the Brownings' second and fifth Florentine residence, viewed from Via Mazzetta, 1972.
From the editors' file.   147

1881 (now 21) Via Maggio, Florence
Photograph of the Brownings' third Florentine residence, 1972.
From the editors' file.   147

1703 (now 8) Piazza Pitti, Florence
Photograph of the Brownings' fourth Florentine residence, 1972.
From the editors' file.   147

EBB to Her Sisters Arabella and Henrietta
Letter 2701, [13 September 1847].
From the editors' file.   306

Palazzo Guidi, Florence
Photograph, viewed from Piazza San Felice, ca. 1955.
Reproduced from *The Life of Elizabeth Barrett Browning*,
by Gardner B. Taplin (New Haven, 1957).   307

Rev. James Stratten
Oil painting, date unknown.
Reproduced from *Paddington Chapel* (London, 1913).   358

Hope End Mansion
Water-colour and pencil by Arabella Moulton-Barrett, 1831.
Courtesy of Mary V. Altham.   407

Cue Titles, Abbreviations & Symbols

Adrian	"The Browning-Rossetti Friendship: Some Unpublished Letters" by Arthur A. Adrian, *PMLA*, 73 (1958)
Altham	Mary V. Altham, Babbacombe, England
Berg	The Henry W. & Albert A. Berg Collection, The New York Public Library, Astor, Lenox and Tilden Foundations
B-GB	*Letters of the Brownings to George Barrett*, ed. Paul Landis (Urbana, 1958)
BL	British Library, London
Browning Collections	*The Browning Collections. Catalogue of Oil Paintings, Drawings & Prints; Autograph Letters and Manuscripts, Books ... the Property of R.W. Barrett Browning, Esq.* (London, 1913). Reprinted in Munby, *Sale Catalogues*, VI (1972), 1–192
Carlyle	*The Collected Letters of Thomas and Jane Welsh Carlyle.* Duke-Edinburgh edition, ed. Charles Richard Sanders, *et al.* (Durham, North Carolina and London, 1970–)
Checklist	*The Brownings' Correspondence: A Checklist*, comps. Philip Kelley and Ronald Hudson (New York and Winfield, Kansas, 1978)
Chorley	*Letters of Mary Russell Mitford*, second series, ed. Henry Chorley, 2 vols. (London, 1872)
Christie's	Christie, Manson & Woods, auctioneers, London
DNB	*Dictionary of National Biography*
Duke	Duke University, Durham, North Carolina
EB	*Encyclopædia Britannica*
EBB	Elizabeth Barrett Barrett / Elizabeth Barrett Browning
EBB-HSB	*Elizabeth Barrett to Mr. Boyd. Unpublished Letters of Elizabeth Barrett Browning to Hugh Stuart Boyd*, ed. Barbara P. McCarthy (New Haven, 1955)

[vii]

Cue Titles

EBB-MRM	*The Letters of Elizabeth Barrett Browning to Mary Russell Mitford, 1836–1854*, ed. Meredith B. Raymond and Mary Rose Sullivan, 3 vols. (Winfield, Kansas, 1983)
EBB-RHH	*Letters of Elizabeth Barrett Browning, Addressed to Richard Hengist Horne, with Preface and Memoir*, ed. S.R. Townshend Mayer, 2 vols. (London, 1877)
Eton	Eton College Library, Eton College, Windsor, England
Garnett	R. & E. Garnett, *Life of W.J. Fox* (London, 1910)
GM-B	Gordon E. Moulton-Barrett, Mobe Sound, Florida
Goethe	Goethe- und Schiller-Archiv, Stiftung Weimarer Klassik, Weimar, Germany
Harvard	Harvard University, Cambridge, Massachusetts
Heydon	Peter N. Heydon, Ann Arbor, Michigan
Huntington	Huntington Library, San Marino, California
Huxley	*Elizabeth Barrett Browning: Letters to Her Sister, 1846–1859*, ed. Leonard Huxley (London, 1929)
LEBB	*The Letters of Elizabeth Barrett Browning*, ed. Frederic G. Kenyon, 2 vols. (London, 1897)
L'Estrange (2)	*Life of Mary Russell Mitford*, ed. Alfred Guy Kingham L'Estrange, 3 vols. (London, 1870)
Lilly	The Lilly Library, Bloomington, Indiana
LRB	*Letters of Robert Browning Collected by Thomas J. Wise*, ed. Thurman L. Hood (New Haven, 1933)
LVC	*Letters from Robert Browning to Various Correspondents*, ed. Thomas J. Wise, 1st. Ser., 2 vols. (London, 1895–96). 2nd Ser., 2 vols. (London, 1907–08)
Maynard	John Maynard, *Browning's Youth* (Cambridge, Massachusetts, and London, 1977)
Mitford	Mary Russell Mitford, *Recollections of a Literary Life, or Books, Places, and People*, 3 vols. (London, 1852)
NL	*New Letters of Robert Browning*, ed. W.C. DeVane and K.L. Knickerbocker (New Haven and London, 1950)
NYPL-Ms	Manuscript Division, New York Public Library, New York
OED	*Oxford English Dictionary*
Powell	Thomas Powell, *The Living Authors of England*, (New York, 1849)
RB	Robert Browning
RB, Sr.	Robert Browning, Sr., RB's father
Reconstruction	*The Browning Collections: A Reconstruction*, comps. Philip Kelley and Betty A. Coley (London, New York, Waco, Texas, and Winfield, Kansas, 1984)

Cue Titles

RWEMA	R.W. Emerson Memorial Association, Harvard University, Cambridge, Massachusetts
Scotland	National Library of Scotland, Edinburgh, Scotland
SD	Supporting Document—any pertinent item other than a letter to or from EBB or RB. SD's originating in the period covered by any volume of this work are cited therein, in checklist format, with extracts of such material as relates directly to the poets.
Smalley	"Joseph Arnould and Robert Browning: New Letters (1842–1850) and a Verse Epistle," by Donald Smalley, *PMLA*, 80 (1965)
Smithsonian	Archives of American Art, Smithsonian Institution, Washington, D.C.
Taplin	Gardner B. Taplin, *The Life of Elizabeth Barrett Browning* (New Haven, 1957)
TTUL	*Twenty-two Unpublished Letters of Elizabeth Barrett Browning and Robert Browning Addressed to Henrietta and Arabella Moulton-Barrett*, ed. W.R. Benet (New York, 1935)
Verney	Sir Ralph Verney, Claydon House, Middle Claydon, Buckingham, England
Yale	Yale University, The Beinecke Rare Book and Manuscript Library, New Haven, Connecticut
[ ]	Square brackets indicate material inserted by editors
⟨ ⟩	Angle brackets denote some irregularity in the manuscript. The absence of a note indicates that the information within the brackets is a conjectural reconstruction caused by seal tear, holes or physical deterioration of the manuscript
⟨...⟩	Angle brackets enclosing ellipsis show an actual omission caused by a defect or physical irregularity in the manuscript. Except in the case of text lost through seal tears, holes, etc., the nature of the irregularity is indicated by a note. This symbol appears on a line by itself if lost text exceeds half a line
⟨★★★⟩	Angle brackets enclosing triple stars indicate the lack of a beginning or end of a letter
| |	Vertical bars are used before and after a word which, though not physically obliterated, is a word of uncertain transcription
...	Ellipses indicate omissions from quoted material in notes and supporting documents, but in the actual texts of the Brownings' correspondence they merely reproduce the writers' style of punctuation

Chronology

1846 19 September: EBB & RB travel from London to Le Hâvre, accompanied by EBB's maid Elizabeth Wilson and Flush, EBB's spaniel.

20 September: Rest in Le Hâvre till 9 p.m. departure for Rouen.

21 September: 1:00 a.m. Brownings depart for Paris, arriving mid-morning, to the Messagerie Hotel; note to Mrs. Jameson; visit from her 9:00 p.m. Barretts leave 50 Wimpole Street and go to Little Bookham, Leatherhead, Surrey, while Wimpole Street is being refurbished.

22 September: Mid-morning visit to Mrs. Jameson.

23 September: Move to Hotel de la Ville de Paris.

25 September: EBB & RB walk along Les Champs Élysées.

28 September: Evening departure for Orleans via Chartres. Mrs. Jameson and her niece Gerardine Bate accompany the Brownings, Wilson, and Flush to Pisa.

30 September: Travel by day from Orleans to Bourges.

October: EBB's "A Woman's Shortcomings," "A Man's Requirements," "Maud's Spinning," "A Dead Rose," "Change on Change," "A Reed," and "Hector in the Garden" published in *Blackwood's Edinburgh Magazine*.

1 October: Travel by day from Bourges to Roanne via Nevers.

2 October: Travel by day from Roanne to Moulins.

3 October: Travel overnight from Moulins to Lyons.

5 October: Travel by boat from Lyons to Avignon.

8 October: Day excursion from Avignon to Vaucluse and back.

10 October: Travel by day from Avignon to Aix.

11 October: Travel from Aix to Marseilles; embarked at Marseilles 5 p.m.

12 October: Arrive at Genoa 7 p.m.

13 October: Leave Genoa at nightfall.

14 October: Land at Leghorn 8 a.m. and on to Pisa, staying at the Hotel Peverada (Le Tre Donzelle).

18 October: Brownings take up residence in Collegio di Ferdinando.

Chronology

7 November: Mrs. Jameson and Gerardine Bate leave Pisa for Rome via Florence.

23 December: EBB sends "The Runaway Slave at Pilgrim's Point" to James Russell Lowell.

1847 23 January–1 February: EBB & RB nurse Wilson.

February: EBB's brother, Charles John ("Storm") leaves England for Jamaica, not to return until after their father's death in 1857.

21 March: EBB's first miscarriage.

20 April: Brownings arrive in Florence, Hotel du Nord.

22 April: Brownings take rooms in Via delle Belle Donne, 4222 (now 6).

23–30 April: Mrs. Jameson and Gerardine Bate visit the Brownings.

21 May: The Brownings' marriage settlement witnessed by Compton John Hanford.

14 July: Brownings go to Vallombrosa to escape the heat of Florence.

19 July: Brownings return to Florence to Via delle Belle Donne.

20 July: Brownings move to Palazzo Guidi, Piazza San Felice.

12 September: EBB & RB celebrate their first wedding anniversary. It coincides with the Florentine celebration of the Grand Duke's granting a Civic Guard.

19 October: Move to Via Maggio, 1881 (now 21).

29 October: Move to Piazza Pitti, 1703 (now 8).

The Brownings' Correspondence

Volume 14
September 1846 – December 1847
Letters 2616 – 2716

2616. EBB to George Goodin Moulton-Barrett

[London]
Thursday & friday– [17–18 September 1846][1]

My dearest George I throw myself on your affection for me & beseech of God that it may hold under the weight– Dearest George, go to your room & read this letter! and I entreat you by all that we both hold dearest, to hold me still dear after the communication which it remains to me to make to yourself and to leave to you in order to be communicated to others in the way that shall seem best to your judgement .. And oh, love me George, while you are reading it. Love me—that I may find pardon in your heart for me after it is read.

Mr Browning has been attracted to me for nearly two years– At first and for long I could not believe that *he* (who is what you know a little), could care for such as I, except in an illusion & a dream. I put an end (as I thought) briefly to the subject– I felt certain that a few days & a little more light on my ghastly face, would lead him to thank me for my negative, and I bade him observe that if my position had not been exceptional, I should not have received him at all. With a protest, he submitted,—and months passed on so. Still he came continually & wrote, & made me feel (though observing my conditions in the form) made me feel with every breath I drew in his presence, that he loved me with no ordinary affection. But I believed that it would be a wrong to such a man, to cast on him the burden of my sickly life, & to ruin him by his own generosity– He was too good for me, I knew, but I tried to be as generous. I showed him that I was altogether bruised & broken,—that setting aside my health, which, however improved, was liable to fail with every withdrawing of the sun, .. that the common advantages of youth & good spirits had gone from me .. that I was an undone creature for the pleasures of life, as for its social duties.

His answer was .. not the common gallantries which come so easily to the lips of men .. but simply that *he loved me*—he met argument with fact. He told me .. that, with himself also, the early freshness of youth had gone by, .. & that throughout it he had not been able to love any woman—that he loved now for the first time & the last. That, as to the question of my health— he had been under the impression when he first declared his attachment to me, that I was suffering from an incurable injury on the spine, which would prevent my ever standing up before his eyes. If *that* had been true, .. he bade me tell me how it should have operated in suppressing any pure attachment of a soul to a soul. For his part, he had desired under those circumstances, to attain to the right of sitting by my sofa just two hours in the day as one of my brothers might—and he preferred, of deliberate choice, the realization of such a dream, to the brightest, which should exclude me, in

[1]

the world.—— But he would not, he said, torment me– He would wait, if I pleased, twenty years, till we both should grow old, & then at the latest, .. too late, .. I should understand him as he understood himself now ... & should know that he loved me with an ineffaceable love. In the meanwhile, what he asked, I had it in my power to give. He did not ask me to dance or to sing, .. but to help him to work and to live .. to live a useful life & to die a happy death—*that* was in my power.

And this was the attachment, George, I have had to do with, & this, the man. Such a man!– Noble he is—his intellect the least of his gifts! His love showed itself to me like a vocation. And I a mere woman, feeling as a woman must, & in circumstances which made every proof of devotion sink down to the deepest of my heart where the deep sorrow was before. Did he not come in my adversity? When I had done with hope, did he not come to me– Call to mind the sorrow & the solitude, & how, in these long years, the feeling of personal vanity had died out of me, till I was grateful to all those who a little could bear with me personally. And *he*, such a man! Why men have talked to me before of what they called love,—but never for *any one*, could I *think* even, of relinquishing the single life with which I was contented. I never believed that a man whom *I* could love, (I having a need to look up high in order to love) .. could be satisfied with loving *me*. And yet *he did* .. does. Then we have one mind on all subjects—& the solemner they are, the nearer we seem to approach. If, poets, we are together, still more we are Christians. For these nearly two years we have known each other's opinions & thoughts & feelings, weakness & strength, as few persons in the like position have had equal opportunities of doing. And knowing me perfectly, he has entirely loved me—! At last, I only could say .. "Wait till the winter. You will see that I shall be ill again– If not, I will leave it to you." I believed I should be ill again certainly. But the winter came, mild & wonderful—I did not fail in health—nor to *him*.

I beseech you, George, to judge me gently, looking to the peculiar circumstances, .. & above all, to *acquit him wholly*. I claim the whole responsibility of his omission of the usual application to my father & friends—for he was about to do it .. anxious to do it—& I stopped him. That blame therefore belongs to me. But I knew, & *you know*, what the consequence of that application would have been—we should have been separated from that moment. He is not rich .. which w^d have been an obstacle——. At any rate, I could not *physically bear* to encounter agitating opposition from those I tenderly loved,—& to act openly in defiance of Papa's will, would have been more impossible for me than to use the right which *I believe to be mine*, of taking a step so strictly personal, on my own responsibility. We both of us comprehend life in a simpler way than generally is done, and to live happily according to our conscience, we do not need to be richer than we are. I do beseech you, George, to look to the circumstances & judge me gently, & see that, having resolved to give my life to one who is in my eyes the noblest of all men & who loves me as such a man can love,—there was no way possible to my weakness but the way adopted with this pain. The motives are altogether different from any supposable want of respect & affection where I owe them most tenderly. I beseech you to understand this— I beseech you to lay it before my dearest Papa, that it is so– Also, to have *consulted any one of you*, would have been ungenerous & have involved you in my blame. I have therefore consulted not one of you. I here declare that everyone in the house is absolutely ignorant & innocent of all participation in this act of my own. I love you too dearly, too tenderly, to have done you such injustice. Forgive me all of you for the act itself, for the sake of the love which came before it .. & follows after it—for never (whether you pardon or reproach me) will an hour pass during my absence from you, in which I shall not think of you with tenderest thoughts.

It appears right to say of dear M! Kenyon, to whom I ever shall be grateful, that he has *not any knowledge of these circumstances*– It appears right to say it, since M! Browning is his friend.

And I think it due to myself, to observe, that I have seen M! Browning only in this house & openly .. except the day of our meeting in the church of this parish in order to becoming his wife in the presence of the two necessary witnesses. We go across France, down the Seine & Rhone to Pisa for the winter, in submission to the conditions considered necessary for the reestablishment of my health, & shall return in the next summer. As soon as he became aware that I had the little money which is mine, he wished much that I would leave it with my sisters, & go to him penniless– But this, which I would have acceded to under ordinary circumstances, I resisted on the ground of my health—the uncertainty of which seemed to make it a duty to me to keep from being a burden to him .. at least in a pecuniary respect.

George, dear George, read the enclosed letter for my dearest Papa, & then .. breaking gently the news of it—give it to him to read. Also if he would deign to read this letter addressed to you, .. I should be grateful .. I wish him in justice, & beseech him in affection, to understand the whole bearings of this case. George, believe of me, that I have endeavoured in all this matter to do right according to my own view of rights & righteousness– If it is not your view, bear with me—& pardon me. Do you all pardon me, my beloved ones, & believe that if I could have benefitted any of you by staying here, I would have stayed– Have I not done for you what I could, always? *When* I could. Now I am weak. And if in this crisis I were to do otherwise than what I am about to do, there would be a victim without an expiation, & a sacrifice without an object– My spirits would have festered on in this enforced prison, & none of you all would have been the happier for what would have [been] bitter to *me*. Also, I should have wronged *another*– I cannot do it.

If you have any affection for me, George, dearest George, let me hear a word—at Orleans—let me hear.[2] I will write– I bless you, I love you– I am

your Ba–

Address: George Goodin Barrett Esq.re / 50 Wimpole Street.
Publication: B-GB, pp. 148–154.
Manuscript: Pierpont Morgan Library.

1. This letter is postmarked 19 September 1846, the Saturday the Brownings departed for Italy.
2. In a letter written to her sisters from Roanne (letter 2621), EBB describes her reaction to letters she received at Orleans from George, as well as from her father.

2617. EBB TO MARY RUSSELL MITFORD

[London]
Friday [18 September 1846][1]

My dearest friend I have your letter & your prophecy,—& the latter meets the event like a sword ringing into its scabbard. My dear dearest friend I would sit down by your feet & kiss your hands with many tears, & beseech you to think gently of me, & love me always, & have faith in me that I have struggled to do the right & the generous & not the selfish thing,—though when you read this letter I shall have given to one of the most gifted & admirable of men, a wife unworthy of him. I shall be the wife of Robert Browning. Against *you*, .. in allowing you no confidence, .. I have not certainly sinned, I think—so do not look at me with those reproachful eyes. I have made no confidence to any .. not even to my & his beloved friend M.r Kenyon—& this advisedly, & in order to spare him the anxiety & the responsibility. It would have been a wrong against him & against you to have told either of you—we were in peculiar circumstances—& to have made you a party, would have exposed you to the whole dreary rain—without the shelter *we* had– If I had loved you less—dearest Miss Mitford, I could have told you sooner.

And now .. oh, will you be hard on me? will you say .. "This is not well."?

I tell you solemnly that nothing your thoughts can suggest against this act of mine, has been unsuggested by *me to him*– He has loved me for nearly two years, & said so at the beginning. I would not listen—I could not believe even. And he has said since, that almost he began to despair of making me believe in the force & stedfastness of his attachment. Certainly I conceived it to be a mere poet's fancy .. an illusion of a confusion between the woman & the poetry. I have seen a little of the way of men in such respects, and I could not see beyond that with my weary, weeping eyes, for long.

No. 2617 [18 September 1846]

How can I tell you on this paper, even if my hands did not tremble as the writing shows,[2] how he persisted & overcame me with such letters, & such words, that you might tread on me like a stone if I had not given myself to him, heart & soul. When I bade him see that I was bruised & broken .. unfit for active duties, incapable of common pleasures .. that I had lost even the usual advantages of youth & good spirits—his answer was, "that with himself also the early freshness of youth had gone by, & that, throughout his season of youth, he had loved no woman at all, nor had believed himself made for any such affection—that he loved now once & for ever—he, knowing himself—— That, for my health, .. he had understood, on first seeing me, that I suffered from an accident on the spine of an incurable nature, & that he never could hope to have me stand up before him. He bade me tell him, what, if that imagination had been true, what there was in that truth, calculated to suppress any pure attachment, such as he professed for me? For his part, the wish of his heart had been *then*—that by consenting to be his wife even so, I would admit him to the simple privilege of sitting by my side two hours a day, as a brother would: he deliberately preferred the realization of *that dream*, to the brightest, excluding me, in this world or any other."

My dear friend, feel for me. It is to your woman's nature that I repeat these words, that they may commend themselves to you & teach you how *I* must have felt in hearing them—*I* who loved Flush for not hating to be near me .. I, who by a long sorrowfulness & solitude, had sunk into the very ashes of self humiliation– Think how I must have felt to have listened to such words from such a man. A man of genius & of miraculous attainments .. but of a heart & spirit beyond them all!——

He overcame me at last. Whether it was that an unusual alikeness of mind .. (the high & the low may be alike in the general features) .. a singular closeness of sympathy on a thousand subjects, .. drew him fast to me—or whether it was *love simple* .. which after all is *love proper* .. an unreasonable instinct, accident .. 'falling', as the idiom says .. the truth became obvious that he would be happier with me than apart from me—and I .. why I am only as any other woman in the world, with a heart belonging to her. He is best, noblest—— If you knew him, YOU should be the praiser.

I have seen him only & openly in this house, observe—*never elsewhere*, except in the parish church before the two necessary witnesses.[3] We go to Italy .. to Pisa—cross to Havre from Southampton .. pass quickly along the Seine, & through Paris to Orleans—till we are out of hearing of the dreadful sounds behind. An escape from the winter will keep me well & still strengthen me—& in the summer we come back .. if anyone in the world will receive us– We go to live a quiet, simple, rational life—to do work "after the pattern in the mount"[4] which we both see .. to write poems & read books, & try to live not in vain & not for vanities–

In the meanwhile, it is in anguish of heart that I think of leaving this house *so*– Oh—a little thread might have bound my hands, from even working at my own happiness– But all the love came from *that side*! on the other .. too still it was—not with intention .. I do not say so—yet too still. I was a woman & shall be a wife when you read this letter. It is finished, the struggle is——

As to marriage .. it never was high up in my ideal, even before my illness brought myself so far down. A happy marriage was the happiest condition, I believed vaguely—but *where were the happy marriages*? *I*, for my part, never could have married a common man—and never did any one man whom I have had the honour of hearing talk love, as men talk, lead me to think a quarter of a minute of the possibility of being married by such an one. Then I thought always that a man whom *I* could love, would never stoop to love me– That was my way of thinking, years ago, in my best days, as a woman's days are counted—& often & often have I been gently upbraided for such romantic fancies—for expecting the grass underfoot to be sky blue, & for not taking M! A or B or C for the "best possible" whatever might be.

We shall not be rich—but we shall have enough to live out our views of life—& fly from the winters in Italy.

I write on calmly to you– How little this paper represents what is working within in the intervals of a sort of *stupour*.

Feel for me if not with me my dear dear friend– *He* says that we shall justify by our lives this act,—which may & must appear to many, .. as *I* say .. wilful & rash. People will say that he is mad, & I, *bad*—with my long traditions & associations with all manner of sickness. Yet God judges, who sees the root of things–[5] And I believe that no woman with a heart, could have done otherwise .. much otherwise– You do not know *him*.

May God bless you—I must end. Try to think of me gently—& if you can bear to write to me, let me hear .. at Orleans—Poste Restante.

Here is the truth—I *could not* meet you & part with you now, face to face.

Tell me of M! Buckingham– I shall be as faithful as ever to anything you will tell me– Why that man must be a wretched villainous man,—after your inexpressible goodness to him! No *friend*–

May God bless you my dear dear kind friend——

Your most affectionate
EBB

Wilson goes with me, of course. And the last commission she has is to settle with Rolandi for you.[6] God bless you–

Publication: EBB-MRM, III, 187–190.
Manuscript: Wellesley College.

1. Dated by EBB's reference to her marriage the previous Saturday (12 September) and her impending departure to Italy, which took place on Saturday, 19 September.

2. EBB's erratic handwriting reflects her emotional distress during her last few days in 50 Wimpole Street.
   3. EBB's maid Elizabeth Wilson and RB's cousin James Silverthorne.
   4. Cf. Hebrews 8:5.
   5. Cf. I Samuel 16:7
   6. i.e., for EBB's gift subscription for Miss Mitford with the foreign bookseller (see letter 1601, note 4).

2618. RICHARD HENGIST HORNE TO EBB & RB

[London]
22 September 1846[1]

Offered for sale by Raphael King, London, Catalogue 24, 1935, item 15. 3 pp., 8vo. Horne writes to RB: "You have got the flower of all time—whose leaves are touched already with a bright futurity. And she has got the one most worthy of her."

   1. The letter was not concluded until 4 October 1846. The original is in the private collection of Peter N. Heydon.

2619. E.F.R. PALMER TO EBB

6. Western Cottages.
25 Sept [1846][1]

My dear Friend.

Allow me sincerely to congratulate you on your marriage, and to express the hope that by

"The Bridegroom of Heaven.
To Thee, now a Bride, His best blessing be given."–[2]

My first intimation of the happy event was by "The Daily News"– If you did not like to tell me yourself, I think our mutual friend, dear Fanny might have told me, that I might have had the opportunity of offering you some testimony of my regard & affection– My Mother also joins in cordial wishes for your happiness, and we do trust that in your new sphere, renovated health & strength may be your appointed portion.

In the midst of all the joy & happiness that surrounds you, may I request the favor of an occasional kind thought towards an admiring and affectionate friend like myself. And if you would not think it an intrusive impertinence, will you allow me to offer my compliments to M.r Browning, & believe me to remain

Y.r obliged & affectionate
E. F. R. Palmer–[3]

Address, on integral page: M.[rs] Robert Browning / Obliged by Miss Barrett.[4]
Publication: None traced.
Manuscript: Mary V. Altham.

    1. Year based on internal reference to the Brownings's recent marriage.
    2. We have been unable to trace the source of this quotation.
    3. We have been unable to identify this correspondent. The original letter is in the possession of a descendant of EBB's sister Henrietta, so we conclude that the letter was not forwarded to Italy, but that its contents were relayed in one of Henrietta's letters. Western Cottages was located in the vicinity of North End Road, Hammersmith, and the descriptions of occupants entered in the 1841 and 1851 censuses were primarily of labourers or domestics. This fact, the handwriting, and the tone of the letter suggest that the correspondent was probably in service. Fanny, the "common friend," cannot be identified with any certainty; however, one possibility is Fanny Dowglass, who was in England at this time.
    4. Presumably EBB's sister Henrietta.

2620. EBB TO ARABELLA MOULTON-BARRETT

Hotel de la ville de Paris. Paris–
Saturday [26 September 1846][1]

My beloved Arabel I write to you after a thousand thoughts .. (for I have not heard a breath of any of you yet) but the strongest brings me still to writing to you– I believe that *you* at least, you & my dearest Henrietta, would rather hear from me than not hear– So without a word more of *feeling* .. leaving all the grief & the doubt on one side, .. I hurry on blindly to let you hear the whole story of me, which seems to me to run in a whole circle of years rather than days, .. so strange it all is, & full of wonder.

    After the Havre passage which was a miserable thing in all ways, there was nothing for it but to rest all day at Havre– We were all three of us exhausted either by the sea or the sorrow, & Wilson & I lay down for a few hours, & had coffee & what else we could take—this, till nine oclock in the evening when the diligence set out for Rouen. Four hours by the diligence, we thought,—& then to rest, till the middle of the next day when we meant to go by the Paris railroad. In the diligence we had the coupé to ourselves .. we three .. & it was as comfortable & easy as any carriage I have been in for years—now five horses, now seven .. all looking wild & loosely harnessed, .. some of them white, some brown, some black, with the manes leaping as they gallopped, & the white reins dripping down over their heads .. such a fantastic scene it was in the moonlight!—& I who was a little feverish with the fatigue & the violence done to myself, in the self controul of the last few days, began to see it all as in a vision & to doubt whether I was in or out of the body.[2] They made me lie down with my feet up– Robert was dreadfully anxious about me—& after all, he was the worst, I believe, of any of us– Arrived at Rouen,—through some mistake or necessity of form, we were allowed to remain if we pleased, but were forbidden to keep any part of our luggage. The luggage was to go by the railroad on to Paris directly– What was to be done? So I prevailed over all the fears, that we should continue our route, after a rest of twenty minutes at the Rouen Hotel .. coffee & the breaking of bread,—& you would have been startled, if in a dream you had seen me, carried in & out, as Robert in his infinite tenderness would insist on carrying me, between the lines of strange foreign faces & in the travellers' room, .. back again to the coupè of the diligence which was placed on the railway, .. & so we rolled on towards Paris. It was a night's travelling, & the daylight was at ten or eleven a.m. when we were deposited in the Messagerie Hotel, in a great noisy court—taking & not choosing that Hotel .. taking it for being the nearest, & meaning to remain there, for that day & the next, on account of the necessities of the passport, which the Mayor of Havre promised faithfully to let us receive in time for an early departure– For me, I was quite satisfied with our accommodations in this hotel—but they were small & not over convenient, & the light & the noise, my two enemies, poured in upon us on all sides. Still we had good coffee, & everything was clean, & everybody courteous to the top of courtesy—& while I lay resting, Robert went to speak to M:rs Jameson according to her address & the agreement of us both that her goodness to me deserved some passing look or sign, if we could give no more– She was not at home. He left a note .. "Come & see your friend & my wife EBB—"[3] .. nearly as brief as *that*—, & signing it RB. Never thinking of either of us she stood for some moments, she told us afterwards, in a maze .. wondering what these things could mean– In the meanwhile, it was night .. or nine in the evening at least .. & he was so thoroughly worn out with the anxiety, agitation, fatigue, & effect of the sea voyage together with that of having scarcely eaten anything for three weeks, that he quite staggered in the room, & was feverish enough to make me talk of sending for a physician, & in default of it, to entreat him to go & lie down where he could not be disturbed .. I promised to receive M:rs Jameson myself .. imagine with what terrors– She came with her hands stretched out, & eyes opened as wide as Flush's .. "Can it be possible? is it possible? You wild, dear creature! You dear, abominable poets! Why what a ménage you will make!– You should each have married a 'petit bout de prose'[4] to keep you reasonable. But he is a wise man .. in choosing *so* .. & you are a wise woman, let the world say as it pleases!—& I shall dance for joy both in earth & in heaven, my dear friends." All this in interrupted interjections! She was the kindest, the most cordial, the most astonished, the most out of breath with wonder!——& I could scarcely speak—looking "frightfully ill" as she has told me since. So she would not stay .. I was to rest, she said, for the first thing, .. & never to think (for the second) of travelling all night in that wild way any more—also I was to prevail on Robert to go with me to her apartment at the Hotel de la Ville de Paris, in the morning, when we could talk about Italy & the rest.

Which was done as she said. We went to her in the morning. She received us both as the most affectionate of possible friends could .. *kissing Robert*, embracing me .. professing to be as delighted as she was astonished, praising us for our noble imprudences which were oftener successful, she said, even in this world, than the chiefest of worldly wisdoms .. in short, nothing could be more cordial & more cheering. May God bless her for all the good she did me—& does me—for we did not leave her *so*. She persuaded us to remove from the Messagerie to her Hotel, induced us to take the apartment above her own in the same (this same Hotel) a cheap, yet delightful suite of small rooms, .. furnished with very sufficient elegance .. dining room, drawingroom, two bedrooms, & a room up higher for Wilson .. as quiet as in the midst of a wood, nearly, & in the best situation, or one of the best, in Paris– She persuaded us to settle here for a few days, in order to rest, both of us, & manage the passport business, & wait for herself, .. she promising to go with us to Pisa, .. travel with us, .. & help him to take care of me. You may think how grateful we are! I am! & *he* is, still more, perhaps .. if possible,—for it lifts from him a good half of the anxiety about moving me from one place to another, which, well as I bear it all, is felt by him too much at moments. Now he is well .. I thank God .. & I am well .. living as in a dream, .. loving & being loved better everyday .. seeing near in him, all that I seemed to see afar, ... thinking with one thought, feeling with one heart, .. & just able to discern that (if it were not for what I have left behind, .. with the dreadful, dreadful looking for the letters at Orleans perhaps, ..) I should be the happiest of human beings .. happiest through *him*– He loves me better he says than he ever did—& we live such a quiet yet new life, it is like riding an enchanted horse. We see M.rs Jameson at certain hours, but keep to ourselves at others. We breakfast quietly, & spend the morning, .. have bread & butter at one, (& coffee) then dine with her at the Restaurants .. walking there, .. ordering our own dinner at our own table in Parisian fashion, & walking home afterwards. The distance is short, being understood .. & I do not at all dislike it. M.rs Jameson & Robert talk .. he pouring out rivers of wit & wisdom .. (it is wonderful),—& she the agreeable, cultivated, fervid & affectionate woman I but half guessed her to be. I in the meanwhile, sit silent, & enjoy or suffer, as God lets me– Oh never, never believe that I can forget you, or love you less, my dearest dearest all of you, .. my own Arabel, do not think so!– I *never do*, even while I feel that as far as any human choice can be wise & happy, .. made under such circumstances .. I mean, as far as I could have a right to choose at all, .. I have done well, & received full compensation for the past sorrows of my life. He is *perfect*—far too good & too tender for me—far too high & gifted– To hear him say that he is happy because of me, overwhelms me with a mixture of wonder & of shame.

He *will* carry me up stairs, & make me eat too much—our chief disputations are on such points: & for the rest, we have broken no peace yet—we sit through the dusky evenings, watching the stars rise over the high Paris houses, & telling childish happy things, or making schemes for work & poetry to be achieved when we reach Pisa- This, if the good spirits & hopes take the pre-eminence.

And everybody cries out that I look well—the first fatigue has passed .. & the change, & the sense of the Thing Done (resuming the place of a painful resolution) & the constant love & attention of every moment .. have done me good—for *they* touch me, besides the pain & fear. I am quite capable of travelling .. quite. And on monday, we set out again—Mrs Jameson & Gerardine her niece,[5] Robert & I & Wilson. We go to Chartres, because a visit to the cathedral there is necessary for a book she is completing,[6] & we can only go by Diligence- Thence by railroad to Orleans—(oh my letters, how you frighten me at this distance!) & slowly onwards to Marseilles. You shall hear again. Robert has told Mrs Jameson to call me Ba .. & I am to call her *Aunt Nina* which is her favorite name for relation or friend. I tell you this nonsense to let you see how we are on familiar terms- She writes little notes to us, nearly every morning, sent up stairs by Gerardine for a post, beginning .. "Dear friends, how are you today, & where will you go?" You comprehend why I repeat such foolishnesses to you. She has taken us once to the Louvre .. I, trembling for fear of meeting somebody too dear! And, by the way, I have not written a word to Jane [Hedley]- Dont tell her how long I have been here, not daring to give her a sign .. although Robert & I walked up the *Rue Champs Elyssées* only yesterday.

The glance of the Louvre was a mere glance—the divine Raphaels .. unspeakable, those are. Mrs Jameson on one side of me, & Robert on the other, were learned equally .. & I, the ignoramus, between!- He & I have seen nothing of course, comparatively, of Paris wonders,—but we shall return here some day, & see & hear. The colouring & life everywhere are very striking, .. & the magnificence of the city, as a city, infinitely beyond London-

Mrs Jameson spoke to Lord Normanby[7] (the English ambassador) about the wrong done to us in our passport at Havre—for we have not yet received it—& he instantly said that he knew Mr Browning by reputation & would be happy to give us another which should put us to no trouble whatever. It was graciously said, & quickly done- And now the mayor & his devices are to be defied-

My dearest, dearest Arabel .. my beloved all of you .. my heart goes out to you .. I love you .. I bless you in the name of God- Forgive me that I have caused you this pain, .. oh, I beseech you– Kiss dearest Trippy for me, & say so too. My excuse is in *him*– If he were as another man in anything, I should have less an excuse– I wish you heard him talk of you all .. how he grieves to have offended where he would give up all (except *me*) to conciliate– Wishing, he was, this morning, that you or dearest Henrietta were with us here, & hoping for *me*, that, one day, he might have you with us, as his sister & mine– You would love him & hold me justified, if you knew him— such a pure, tender, religious spirit, .. apart from the secular attainments & the specific genius– He rises on me, higher and higher–

Now this is a long letter– Write me one I beseech you—& direct to Posta Restante, Pisa.–

May God bless you– Tell dear Minny not to follow me with too hard thoughts. *No woman*, beloved as I have been by *such a man*, could have acted much otherwise in the same circumstances– Is Stormie very angry? & George?

Dear Henrietta will understand why I do not write to her today—it shall be for another day– I love her—I love *you*–

I am your own attached
Ba

Do you think, Arabel, that dearest Papa will forgive me at last?——
Answer

Wilson likes everything—& we try to make her comfortable in change for her great services– Oh, that day, Arabel when I left you!——

Arabel, Henrietta, dearest ones, both of you write to me.

Publication: None traced.
Manuscript: Berg Collection.

1. The only Saturday during the Brownings' stay in Paris fell on 26 September 1846.
2. Cf. II Corinthians 12:2.
3. Mrs. Jameson had arrived in Paris on the 18th, three days earlier than the Brownings. For her account of meeting and travelling with the Brownings on their journey to Pisa, see SD1272-74, SD1276, SD1283-1284, and SD1289-1290.
4. "A little bit of prose."
5. Gerardine Bate (afterwards Macpherson, 1831-78), the eldest daughter of Mrs. Jameson's sister Louisa; see letter 2388, note 6.
6. Mrs. Jameson was collecting material for a book that would be entitled *Sacred and Legendary Art* (1848). In a letter to Lady Byron, dated 28-29 September [1846], Mrs. Jameson wrote: "While travelling with these friends I am obliged to put all my own convenience & all selfish projects out of the question" (SD1276). They apparently did not stop in Chartres.
7. Constantine Henry Phipps, 1st Marquis of Normanby (1797-1863), had been appointed ambassador to Paris the preceding month, which post he held until 1852. From 1854 until 1858, he was minister to the Court of Tuscany in Florence.

No. 2621 2 October 1846 13

2621. EBB TO ARABELLA & HENRIETTA MOULTON-BARRETT

Written at Roanne[1]
Oct 2– 1846.

I thank & bless you my dearest dearest Henrietta & Arabel .. my own dearest, kindest sisters!– What I suffered in reaching Orleans, & at last holding all these letters in my hands, can only be measured by my deep gratitude to you, & by the tears & kisses I spent upon every line of what you wrote to me .. dearest & kindest that you are. The delay of the week in Paris brought me to the hour of my death warrant at Orleans—my 'death warrant' I called it at the time, I was so anxious & terrified. Robert brought in a great packet of letters .. & I held them in my hands, not able to open one, & growing paler & colder every moment. He wanted to sit by me while I read them, but I would not let him– I had resolved never to let him do that, before the moment came—so, after some beseeching, I got him to go away for ten minutes, to meet the agony alone, & with more courage *so*, according to my old habit you know– And besides, it was right not to let him read––– They were very hard letters, those from dearest Papa & dearest George– To the first I had to bow my head– I do not seem to myself to have deserved that full cup, in the intentions of this act—but he is my father & he takes his own view, of course, of what is before him to judge of. But for George, I thought it hard, I confess, that he should have written to me so with a sword. To write to me as if I did not love you all .. *I*, who would have laid down my life at a sign, if it could have benefitted one of you *really* & essentially:—with the proof you should have had life & happiness at a sign. It was hard that he should use his love for me to half break my heart with such a letter—— Only he wrote in excitement & in ignorance– I ask of God to show to him & to the most unbelieving of you, that never, never did I love you better, all my beloved ones, than when I left you—than in that day, & that moment. I ask Him too to bless you from Himself, my own beloved sisters, for the good & blessing & *tears* your writing brought me, when I read last the kindness & faith of it.

Now I will tell you—Robert who had been waiting at the door, I believe, in great anxiety about me, came in & found me just able to cry from the balm of your tender words– I put your two letters into his hands, & *he*, when he had read them, said with tears in his eyes, & kissing them between the words—"I love your sisters with a deep affection– I am inexpressibly grateful to them– It shall be the object of my life to justify their trust as they express it here." He said it with tears in his eyes. May God bless you—bless you!–

Dearest Henrietta & Arabel, .. how I suffered that day—that miserable saturday .. when I had to *act a part to you*—how I suffered! & how I had to think to myself that if I betrayed one pang of all, I should involve you deeply in the grief which otherwise remained my own. And Arabel to see through it, notwithstanding!- I was afraid of her—she looked at me so intently, or was so grave .. my dearest, dearest Arabel! Understand both of you, that if, from the apparent necessities of the instant, I consented to let the ceremony precede the departure by some few days, it was upon the condition of not seeing him again in that house & till we went away. We parted, as we met, at the door of Marylebone Church—he kissed me at the communion table, & not a word passed after. I looked like death, he has said since. You see we were afraid of a sudden removal preventing everything,[2]—or at least, laying the unpleasantness on me of a journey to London *previous* to the ceremony, which particularly I should have hated, for very obvious reasons. There was no elopement in the case, but simply a private marriage,—& to have given the least occasion to a certain class of observations, was repugnant to both of us. And then, he was, reasonably enough, afraid lest I should be unequal to the double exertion of the church & the railway, on the same morning: and as he wished it, & had promised not to see me, I thought it was mere cavilling on my part, to make a difficulty. Wilson knew nothing till the night before. What I suffered under your eyes, you may guess—it was in proportion to every effort successfully made to disguise the suffering. Painful it is to look back upon now- Forgive me for what was expiated in the deepest of my heart.

With your letters at Orleans, I had one from dearest M.̲ Kenyon, in reply to those which we had written to him at the last. Nothing could be more generously & trustingly kind—& to poor Robert it was a great relief, as the verdict of a friend whom he loved & looked up to on many grounds- I will transcribe to you what M.̲ Kenyon says, .. *for you*—you will understand how it is of great price to us. "My dearest EBB I received your & your husband's letters yesterday. To speak briefly as I must, I sympathize in all you have both been thinking & feeling, & in all you have done. Nothing but what is generous in thought & action could come from you & Browning— And the very peculiar circumstances of your case have transmuted what might have been otherwise called "Imprudence" into "Prudence," & apparent wilfulness into real necessity.—— To speak personally of you both, .. I know no two persons so worthy of each other; & to speak personally TO you both, be assured that out of your own households, you can have no warmer & more affectionate well-wisher than I am. It is a pleasant vision to me to think that, if I live, I may hereafter enjoy your joint society & affection, as hitherto I have derived happiness from each of you singly- .... Altogether I am not only delighted that you, my dearest cousin, should have so virtuous, & highminded a protector, but if the thing had been asked of me I should have advised it, albeit glad that I was not asked for the reason which I have given. Saying God bless you both, I am obliged to close abruptly &c... Most affectionately yours always & ever J. Kenyon." The one or two sentences omitted, (for I have not room) are in harmony with all the rest- Dearest, kindest M? Kenyon! how I love him better than ever!- Also I had kind notes from Miss Mitford, Nelly Bordman & M? Jago, who sent me the prescription for the draughts with ever so many good wishes. Nelly wishes to be let go to see you sometimes, Arabel, .. which for my sake you will not say 'no' to. She loves me, & is worthy of love. I wrote to Jane when I was in Paris .. or rather about to leave it—but to Bummy I have not written yet. When the fatigue gives me half an hour I will do it, be sure. I thank you for those letters you speak of having written for me. Did you get my long letter from Paris? And Trippy, my short note from Havre? Oh, dear Trippy—let her not think hardly of me. No one can judge of this act, except some one who knows thoroughly the man I have married. He rises on me hour by hour. If ever a being of a higher order lived among us without a glory round his head, in these later days, he is such a being. Papa thinks that I have sold my soul for *genius* .. mere genius. Which I might have done when I was younger, if I had had the opportunity, .. but am in no danger of doing now. For my sake, for the love of me, from an infatuation which from first to last has astonished me, .. he has consented to occupy for a moment a questionable position- But those who question most, will do him justice fullest—& we must wait a little with resignation. In the meanwhile, what he is, & what he is to *me*, I w^d fain teach *you*- Have faith in me to believe it. He puts out all his great faculties to give me pleasure & comfort, .. charms me into thinking of *him* when he sees my thoughts wandering .. forces me to smile in spite of all of them- If you had seen him that day at Orleans- He laid me down on the bed & sate by me for hours, pouring out floods of tenderness & goodness, & promising to win back for me, with God's help, the affection of such of you as were angry- And he loves me more & more- Today we have been together a fortnight, & he said to me with a deep, serious tenderness .. "I kissed your feet, my Ba, before I married you—but now I would kiss the ground under your feet, I love you with a so much greater love." And this is true, I see & feel. I feel to have the power of making him happy .. I feel to have it in my hands. It is strange that anyone so brilliant should love *me*— but true & strange it is .. & it is impossible for me to doubt it any more- Perfectly happy therefore we should be, if I could look back on you all without this pang- His family have been very kind. His father considered him of age to judge, & never thought of interfering otherwise than by saying at the last moment .. "Give your wife a kiss from me" .. this, when they parted. His sister sent me a little travelling writing desk, with a word written .. "EBB, from her sister Sarianna"- Nobody was displeased at the reserve used towards them, understanding that there were reasons for it which did not detract from his affection for them & my respect.

I told you that Mrs Jameson was travelling with us, & that we had seen a great deal of her in Paris. She repeats, of Robert, that she never knew anyone of so affluent a mind & imagination combined with a nature & manners so sunshiney & captivating– Which she well may say .. for he amuses us from morning till night,—thinks of everybody's feelings, .. is witty & wise, .. (& foolish too in the right place) charms cross old women who cry out in the diligence "mais, madame, mes jambes!"[3] .. talks latin to the priests, who enquire at three in the morning whether Newman & Pusey are likely "lapsare in erroribus"[4] (you will make out *that*) & forgets nothing & nobody ... except himself .. it is the only omission. He has won Wilson's heart I do assure you—& by the way, Wilson is excellent & active beyond what I could have expected of her. Most affectionate & devoted she has been to me throughout, & now she is not scared by the French, but has learnt already to get warm water & coffee & bread & butter. We applaud Wilson very deservedly. And she desires me to name her to you, & to regret properly that she was "forced to leave your things in such disorder." Also she is a little afraid of dear Minny, lest Minny sh.^d be angry with her. Let dear Minny forgive her if she can—because the blame was all mine, you know, & Wilson's part was simply the consequence of her attachment to me & her unwillingness to leave me to my trial alone. By the way, what does George mean by speaking of "Arabel or Minny my *accomplices*"? Does he not believe me when I have spoken the very contrary of such a thing?—or is it that dear Minny has spoken too gently of me to be unblamed? For my Arabel, I know her as I love her, .. & do not ask how she spoke.

But I think .. think .. of the suffering I caused you, my own, own Arabel, that evening!– I tremble thinking of you that evening—my own dearest dearest Arabel!– Oh—do not fancy that new affections can undo the old. I love you now even *more*, I think. Robert is going to write to you from Pisa, & to Henrietta also– He loves you as his sisters, he says, & wishes that you were with us, & hopes that one day you will be with us, .. staying & travelling with us, .. exactly as I do myself. And I must not forget to tell you that Mrs Jameson said the other day to me, .. "Well, it is the most charming thing to see you & Mr Browning together! If two persons were to be chosen from the ends of the earth for perfect union & fitness, there could not be a greater congruity than between you two–" Which I tell you, because I think it will please you to hear what is an honest impression of hers, though far too great a compliment to me– (The only thing she objects to, is his way of calling me "Ba" .. which I like: & which she never will talk him out of, I am confident, because he likes it as well–) And for the rest, if he is brilliant & I am dull, (socially speaking) *Love makes a level*—which is my comfort.

Two separate (not following, of course) nights we have passed in the diligence;—& I have had otherwise a good deal of fatigue which has done me no essential harm. I am taken such care of,—so pillowed by arms & knees .. so carried up & down stairs against my will, .. so spoilt & considered in every possible way. Also the change of air does me good– I am able to do more—& when we get to our rest at Pisa, the fatigue will leave no trace, I think, except of good. You would stare however to see me thrown abroad out of all my habits, ..! I seem to be in a feverish dream. Tomorrow we take the railroad to Lyons, & the next day embark on the Rhone. At Avignon, we pause a day & go to Vaucluse to hunt Petrarch's footsteps.[5] Today I have not been allowed to stir from this bed where I write, because last night we were travelling—& there has been a table brought close to it (foreign fashion, Arabel!) for Robert to dine on & to make me dine– Mrs Jameson & Gerardine dine by themselves in their own room today, much in the same way.

I am so glad that you are in the country—do write—do write .. & tell me everything, & tell me if you like Little Bookham. Half of my soul is with you .. May God bless you my own beloved ones. Give my best love to dear Mr Boyd, to whom I shall write in time– And let Mrs Martin understand the same– And do *you* feel & know, that as for *me* .. for my position as a wife .. it is *awfully happy* for this world. He is too good & tender, & beyond me in all things—& we love each other with a love that grows instead of diminishing. I speak to you of such things rather than of the cathedral at Bourges, because it is of these, I feel sure, that you desire knowledge rather.

I am going to write to Papa—& to George—very soon, I shall. Ah— dear George would not have written so, if he had known my whole heart— yet he loved me while he wrote, as I felt with every pain the writing caused me. Dear George—I love him to his worth– And my poor Papa!– My thoughts cling to you all, & will not leave their hold. Dearest Henrietta & Arabel let me be as ever & for ever

Your fondly attached Ba–

Does Stormie like the new house? my dearest Stormie.

Flush is very gracious, & behaves perfectly—but moans & wails on the railroad, when the barbarians insist on putting him into a box.

May God bless you, dearest all of you– I hope dear Trippy is with you.

I meant you to have the letters an hour after I left Wimpole Street– It was very unhappy—I grieve for it. As to going to Bookham, I *had* thought of that once—but the wrong to you w^{d} have been greater, to have spoilt & clouded the new scene, instead of allowing it to be a resource to you– Be happy, my dearest ones– I will write, be sure–

Address: Angleterre / Miss Barrett / The Rectory / Little Bookham / near Leatherhead / Surrey.
Publication: TTUL, pp. 1–12.
Source: Transcript in editors' file.

1. EBB made this notation on the reverse of the envelope.
2. The Barrett family household was temporarily relocated to the Rectory in Little Bookham, Surrey, while 50 Wimpole Street was redecorated. This move precipitated the Brownings' marriage and departure to Italy.
3. "But, madam, my legs!"
4. "To lapse into error."
5. The fountain, or spring, of Vaucluse, near Avignon, is the source of the river Sorgue, and was immortalised by Petrarch. Vaucluse is referred to by EBB in *Casa Guidi Windows*, I, 1111-18, and by RB in "Apparent Failure," line 12.

2622. EBB to Mary Russell Mitford

Moulins
Oct. 2. [1846]¹

I began to write to you, my beloved friend, earlier, that I might follow your kindest wishes literally .. & also to thank you at once for your goodness to me .. for which may God bless you. But the fatigue & agitation have been very great, & I was forced to break off .. as now I dare not revert to what is behind—I will tell you more another day. At Orleans, with your kindest letter I had one from my dearest generous friend M! Kenyon, who, in his goodness, does more than exculpate .. even *approves*—he wrote a joint letter to both of us. But oh, the anguish I have gone through!- You are good—you are kind .. I thank you from the bottom of my heart for saying to me that you w^d have gone to the church with me. *Yes—I knew you would.* And for that very reason I forbore involving you in such a responsibility & drawing you into such a net. I took Wilson with me. I had courage to keep the secret to my sisters for their sakes—though I will tell you in strict confidence that it was known to them *potentially* .. that is, .. the attachment & engagement were known,—the necessity remaining, that, for stringent reasons affecting their own tranquillity, they sh^d be able to say at last ⟨...⟩ "we were not instructed in this & this." The dearest, fondest, most affectionate of sisters, they are to me—and if the sacrifice of a life .. or of all prospect of happiness, .. would have worked any lasting good to them, .. it should have been made even in the hour I left them. I knew *that*, by the anguish I suffered in it. But a sacrifice, without good to anyone ... I shrank from it! And also, it was the sacrifice of *two*. And *he*, as you say, had done everything for me— had loved me for reasons which had helped to weary me of myself .. loved me heart to heart, persistently .. in spite of my own will .. drawn me back to life & hope again when I had done with both. My life seemed to belong to him & to none other, at last, & I had no power to speak a word- Have faith in me, my dearest friend, till you can know him. The intellect is so little in comparison to all the rest .. to the womanly tenderness, the inexhaustible goodness, the high & noble aspiration of every hour. Temper, spirits, manners, .. there is not a flaw anywhere- I shut my eyes sometimes & fancy it all a dream of my guardian angel. Only if it had been a dream, the pain of some parts of it, would have awakened me before now: it is not a dream. I have borne all the emotion & fatigue miraculously well, though of course a good deal exhausted at times– We had intended to hurry on to the South at once, but at Paris we met M.rs Jameson, who opened her arms to us with the most literal affectionateness, *kissed us* BOTH, & took us by surprise by calling us "wise people .. wild poets or not". Moreover she fixed us in an apartment above her own, in the Hotel de la ville de Paris,[2] that I might rest for a week, .. & crowned the rest of her goodnesses by agreeing to accompany us to Pisa where she was about to travel with her young niece. Therefore we are five, travelling together––Wilson being with me! Oh yes!—Wilson came .. her attachment to me never shrank for a moment– And Flush came—and I assure you that nearly as much attention has been paid to Flush as to me from the beginning, so that he is perfectly reconciled, & would be happy, if the people at the railroads were not barbarians & immoveable in their evil designs of shutting him up in a box when we travel that way–

You understand now, ever dearest Miss Mitford, how the pause has come about writing. The week at Paris. Such a strange week, it was!—altogether like a vision. Whether in the body or out of the body I cannot tell scarcely.[3] Our Balzac sh.d be flattered beyond measure by my thinking of him at all– Which I did—but of *you*, more. I will write & tell you more about Paris. You should go there indeed. And to our hotel, .. if at all. Once we were at the Louvre——but we kept very still of course, & were satisfied with the *idea* of Paris. I could have borne to live on there—it was all so strange & full of contrast.

Now you will write—I feel my way on the paper to write this– Nothing is changed between us—nothing can ever interfere with sacred confidences, remember I do not show letters .. you need not fear my turning traitress. Do tell me all of yourself– You shall hear, on your side. We go down the Rhone from Lyons .. & give a day to *Vaucluse*. M.rs Jameson is a kind, delightful travelling companion, & as she professes to be very much "in love" with Robert for her own part, we agree perfectly well—& her niece is a charming little girl just seventeen, & looking fifteen .. enjoying the sun & the rain like a child. For ourselves we are altogether happy—he loves me a good deal more, he says, than when we first set out a fortnight ago—there is perfect knowledge & sympathy on each side, to begin & go on with. Pray for me, dearest friend, that the bitterness of old affections may not be too bitter with me—& that God may turn those salt waters sweet again[4]—pray for your grateful & loving

EBB

Is it really needful to say that he is ready to love you .. helping *me*? And we both thank you from our hearts, for his beginning. May God bless you, dearest Miss Mitford. Write to Pisa—Poste Restante. I am so tired—so tired!

Address: Angleterre / Miss Mitford / Three Mile Cross / near Reading.
Publication: EBB-MRM, III, 190–193.
Manuscript: Wellesley College.

    1. Year provided by postmark.
    2. On 19 September, the Brownings, Wilson, and Flush began their journey from England to Italy. From London they crossed to Le Havre and then on to Paris. Soon after their arrival RB called on Mrs. Jameson and her niece, Gerardine. According to the latter, "Mrs. Jameson lost no time in going to the hotel [Hotel Messageries] where her friends were staying, and induced them to come at once to the quiet *pension* [Hotel de la Ville de Paris] in the Rue Ville l'Eveque, where she herself was staying" (Gerardine Macpherson, *Memoirs of the Life of Anna Jameson*, 1878, p. 230).
    3. Cf. II Corinthians 12:2.
    4. Cf. Exodus 15:23–25.

2623. JOSEPH ARNOULD TO RB

18. Victoria Square. Pimlico
Oct. 16th 1846

My dear Browning. It is of no use at all trying to express with pen & paper the burst of congratulation surprise & delight with which we (for Maria[1] begs to be included) hailed the announcement of your marriage! No—it lies not in mortal ink—one warm grasp of the hand, & one quick glance of the eye might do it—all else were tedious, and ineffectual: so do you and Mrs. Browning both take the friendliest of greetings & the sincerest of good wishes from two hearts, who having for six years beat together as one[,] know what a blessed thing "the marriage of true minds" is, & feel confident that your's will be "without impediment".[2]

Pisa being your first fixed point, I despat[c]h this thither trusting that you will have arrived there before it and that Mrs. Browning will have accomplished the journey as prosperously, as we hear from your Sister, she had commenced it.

And when will you be coming back amongst us? or rather is not that a most unfair question to put yet, when you have no right to tolerate the putting of any questions at all, and an undisputed claim to live wholly in the happiness of the present, without a thought about the future:—I asked the question because somehow it came spontaneously to the very tip of my pen—: in fact it is the mere expression in words, of what we are constantly asking ourselves: a sort of obstinate questioning which creates within us the only sort of drawback to the delight which the tidings of your marriage spread amongst us: we think in fact of certain dark intimations scattered by you to our secret dismay of intentions to remain some indefinite time in the Paradise of Exiles:[3] "years" we think we remember, but can only hope this will not

No. 2623 16 October 1846

be true & that our ears deceived us through the medium of our apprehensions. I hardly know though whether amid the autumnal fogs & cold rains of a London October, we ought ever to wish you back from that peaceful ci⟨ty⟩ between the mountains and the Sea where the ⟨in⟩habitancy of man seems least to have stained the clear beauty of Nature; where all is tranquil & harmonious alike in the sunny silence of the streets, and the shadowy solitude of the Campo Santo.[4] You, who at once find out every thing, and are fond of walking, will have explored & appreciated the beauty of that winding walk upon the great dike which stays the overflowings of the Arno and leads on through a fruitful wilderness of orchards & vineyards to the foot of the mountains which shut in the Eastern sky. It used to strike me that in all Italy, which is saying a strong thing[,] there is no more lovely walk. But I must not make myself miserable by letting my thoughts carry me out of London into Pisa. There are no news here which you care about or which you will not learn from those London papers which are as accessible in Pisa as in Pall-Mall: Chorley has not yet returned from his trip & is now at Paris. Dowson has I daresay written to you: do you remember that night! how thoroughly you mystified us, & I never dreaming of what was to be (how could I be so leaden!) fancied that as we were to meet at Wanstead[5]—I need not be guessing about Hatcham- Beast that I was—yea swinish in my stupidity- An affecting little incident occurred yesterday- Miss Browning sent me those cigars (delicious!) that you spoke of. I received them as the solemn legacy of your bachelorhood—"sooty retainers,'['] "fine negroes"[6] for whose maladroit services you had no more need. As their fragrant fumes rise round me, I need not say that the generous "testator" is vividly recalled and my eyes glisten through the smoke as I fancy myself grasping your hand in a paroxysm of congratulation which I feel too painfully how imperfectly I have conveyed to you in words[.] Maria unites with me in kindest regards to you and all the kindest expressions of good will which usage will allow us to proffer or Mrs Browning to receive[.]

Ever your sincere friend
J. Arnould

Address, on integral page: Robert Browning Esq[re] / Poste Restante / Pisa / Italy / via France.
Publicaton: Smalley, pp. 94–95.
Manuscript: Pierpont Morgan Library, Gordon N. Ray Bequest.

1. Maria (1821?–59), eldest daughter of H.G. Ridgeway, of Walworth, married Joseph Arnould in 1841.
2. Cf. Shakespeare, "Sonnet 116" (1609), lines 1–2. In this and subsequent Shakespearean quotations, the line numbers correspond to those used in *The Riverside Shakespeare* (Boston, 1974).
3. Shelley, *Julian and Maddalo* (1824), line 57.
4. An historic burial site next to the cathedral in Pisa, famous for its 14th and 15th century frescoes. This cemetery was founded in the 12th century by Archbishop Ubaldo,

who deposited earth from Mt. Calvary which he had brought back from the Holy Land, hence the name "Campo Santo."

5. The younger members of the Dowson family had a summer cottage at Woodford, near Wanstead, in the years 1837–44 (Maynard, p. 411).

6. Charles Lamb, "A Farewell to Tobacco" (1818), lines 17–18.

2624. EBB TO ARABELLA MOULTON-BARRETT

Pisa– Hotel Peverada
Tre Donzilla[1]
[16–19 October 1846][2]

Ever my beloved Arabel–

It is your turn, I think, to be written to, but I owe the best gratitude I have to give, to both of you .. to my dearest Henrietta as to yourself, .. for the happiness of hearing from you on the second day of our arrival at our great journey's end. Oh, if you think that ever I cease to think of you for one hour of the whole twenty four (except when I am fairly asleep you know, without dreaming) you mistake me altogether, as others have done from whom I might have hoped a truer comprehension. But surely you know & feel that I think of you, yes, & miss you, yes, & long for you & love you & pray for you my very dearest ones, & thank you from my heart for every thought of kindness you give me now that I am away from you thus. The letters made me happy last night .. made both of us happy—though you are not to fancy, by *that*, that I shall "show" anything secret; so write as openly as possible. Between R. & myself there is the fullest confidence & liberty too .. the liberty being a part of the confidence. But last night's happiness in the letters belonged to us both I thought,—particularly as he was looking into my eyes as anxiously as ever they could look, for the news from you– My own dear dearest Arabel .. I am glad you are at Little Bookham & that the country is pretty & I do hope that you make sketches & allow the time to pass pleasantly. The worst of all my thoughts is that of having given you all pain, & it is present too often notwithstanding my absolute contentment with my own choice & lot altogether. R. is more than ever I believed him to be, when the belief was at fullest before we married. I can only wonder increasingly at the fact of his selecting *me* out of the world of women—. Without the least affectation, it is the wonder of my life. Also, the repentence does not seem to come, nor to threaten to come. He loves me better every minute, he says, on the contrary– There is no honeymoon for us any longer, .. but the stars keep us in light. The goodness & tenderness of every moment is the "thing to dream of & not to tell".[3] At Genoa (where we disembarked, slept, & spent a day), he positively refused (quite "unreasonably," as Mrs Jameson agreed with me) to leave my side for the sake of the cathedral[,] the pictures, or any of the great sights, just because I was tired & could not go to see them. "He w.^{d} come with me to see them some future time .. but now .. no, .. it would not be the least pleasure to him if I were not there"– And so, notwithstanding all entreaties, there he sate .. & M^{rs} J & Gerardine went alone to see the glories of Genoa. One little walk however (it was that which tired me) he & I had together, & we wandered through close alleys of palaces looking all strange & noble, into a gorgeous church where mass was going on—altar pressing by altar, every one of a shining marble encrusted with gold– Great columns of twisted porphyry letting out the inner light of some picture: the frescoed angels glancing from the roof– Glory upon glory it was, as far as art went—and on the marble pavement, knelt monks with the brown serge & cord .. nuns of various orders—& Genoese ladies dropping their fans from their fingers, as they prayed covered with the national veil .. the head is covered, (not the face) & the white drapery is crossed over the breast in the most graceful manner imaginable. We met in the streets several ladies apparently of distinction, gliding along in these same white veils, & with large painted fans– And no woman takes a man's arm unless she is his wife or engaged to him. Beautiful Genoa—what a vision it is!—& our first sight of Italy beside. I am going backward in my story of our adventures & it ought to be forwards instead– So to begin properly. After our week at Paris we began our journey as I hope you heard from my Orleans letter, & a long time indeed we have been about it since then, .. far longer than either of us had contemplated. We took the water only from Lyons to Avignon, & the rest of the way went by diligence & vet[t]urino, in order to give Mrs Jameson the opportunity she required of seeing certain cathedrals. The one at Bourges is glorious & worthy of dear Mr Kenyon seeking the sight of by mesmeric trance,—it looks as if all the sunsets of time had stained the wonderful painted windows of which the secret is lost.[4] By two nights we had some travelling, resting during the days after—& often I felt desperately tired but always had the strength back again—renewed like the eagle's–[5] The change of air appeared to act on me like a charm, & then we had delightful weather & learnt to calculate on the sun by day as on the candle by night. Mrs Jameson declares that I look like altogether a different person from what I was—especially at our first meeting in Paris when the agitation & fatigue made me look like a ghost. Now, the ghost has its body back, with a little colour into its cheeks. No wonder that you wonder at me. I wonder at myself– Yet continual change of air with a climate growing warmer & warmer, were good for me even humanly speaking .. & though dear Papa said that I ought not to speak of Providence, God[']s mercies always seem too close to me for my unworthiness. One disappointment we had—for our only rainy day was the day we especially wished to keep bright .. the day of the *Rhone* .. from Lyons to Avignon– The wild, striking scenery .. the fantastic rocks & ruined castles we could only see by painful glimpses through the loophole windows of the miserable cabin—was'nt it unfortunate? At Avignon however, there was consolation. We stayed there three or four days, & made a pilgrimage to Vaucluse as became poets, & my spirits rose & the enjoyment of the hour spent at the sacred fountain was complete. It stands deep & still & green against a majestic wall of rock, & then falls, boils, breaks[,] foams over the stones, down into the channel of the little river winding away greenly, greenly—the great, green desolate precipices guarding it out of sight- A few little cypresses, & olive trees—no other tree in sight- All desolate & grand. R. said "Ba, are you losing your senses?"—because without a word I made my way over the boiling water to a still rock in the middle of it .. but he followed me & helped me, & we both sate in the spray, till M.rs Jameson was provoked to make a sketch of us-[6] Also Flush proved his love of me by leaping (at the cost of wetting his feet & my gown) after me to the slippery stone, & was repulsed three times by R. (poor Flushie!) till he moaned on the dry ground to see me in such a position of danger as perhaps it seemed to him .. poor Flushie! .. & he not suffered to share it with me.

From Avignon we took a voiturier, or rather a voiturier took us, on to Marseilles, .. sleeping at Aix, the city of troubadours[7] .. & embarking in a French steamer, of which we were the only first class passengers- M.rs J, Gerardine, Wilson & I had the ladies' cabin to ourselves, & every comfort & cleanliness (write down that the French are *not dirty*, .. & *not delicate* certainly—there was not a woman for any use—the 'garçons' did all the duty, .. & very pleasant, as you may think, *that* was) & at five oclock on one burning, glaring afternoon we sailed from glittering, roaring Marseilles .. *coloured* even down into its puddles- The heat was intense. I felt sick with it. And when we got to sea, everybody else was sick in quite another way & from another cause .. for we were cool enough then, the wind getting up boisterously. Such a rolling night it was, .. & when in the morning, I got up the cabin stairs toward the deck, I left behind me prostrate everyone of my companions- Robert, too, was very miserable—only when he heard my voice he would go with me upon deck .. & there we leaned, wrapt up in all come-atable cloaks, along the stern of the vessel, watching the magnificent coast along which a thousand mountains & their rocks leapt up against the morning-sun, & counted the little Italian towns one after another. I never saw scenery of such a character,—& it was lamentable to think that we had passed Nice & so much beside in the night, missing the glories of it. The ship was near enough to shore for us to see the green blinds to the windows of the houses,—& if it had not been for the roughness, we should have coasted still nearer. And the scenery .. the scenery!- In one place, I counted six mountains (such mountains!) one behind another, colour behind colour, from black, or the most gorgeous purple, to that spectral white which the crowding of the olives gives. And sometimes a great cloud seemed to cut off the top of a mountain from its foundations .. & sometimes fragments of cloud hung on the rocks, shining as if the sun himself had broken it. It was all glorious, & past speaking of. We were in Genoa by nightfall, .. slept under the frescoed roof of what had been a palace, .. & as the next night closed in, returned to our steamer for the Leghorn voyage & another night. Poor Wilson—how she suffered!- And M:rs Jameson too!—and she & Gerardine very much alarmed beside at the stormy weather, & because the engine stopped for two hours, & the waves dashed over the vessel. Perhaps *I* should have been, once—but through a strange re-action, I seem to be perfectly indifferent (as far as myself am concerned) to that sort of danger now. Not that really there was danger—I dare say not! So we landed at Leghorn, looking as miserable as possible—*everybody ill except me* .. observe that! & poor Wilson more dead than alive—but getting to the hotel & having breakfast & feeling ourselves close to Pisa soon produced a general revival. (M:rs Jameson had fainted, several times before we came to *that*.) And now this is Pisa—beautiful Pisa! A little city of great palaces, & the rolling, turbid Arno, striking its golden path betwixt them underneath the marble bridge- All tranquil & grand—it is the very place for being tranquil in,—& I am delighted with the whole aspect of it. Because we brought letters of introduction from Baron Rothschild, M:rs J's economy took fright, & she would not go to the same hotel—but the end is not precisely answered, I imagine. We have done *more* cheaply in fact, notwithstanding the horrific protection, than she has. For three days we were at the Tre Donzelle, taking merely bedrooms & dining at the table d'hôte .. where I sate next to M:r Surtees,[8] secure in the incognito of my new name. Wilson was warned not to betray me to the ladies' maid—such a fear I was in! And such a man he seems to be—talking of cauliflours & wine, & being an Englishman "*abroad*" in all possible senses. Also it was a detestable table d'hôte altogether, not like those we had been used to & which I did not object to in the least, but a regular dining-out party at it, everybody talking to everybody, on the strength of all being English. Then we met there the same people whom we had met in the French diligence, & in the Rhone steamer, & Robert with his perfect goodness & benevolence, cannot help talking kindly to people .. who are enchanted accordingly & unwilling to lose his acquaintance—. But we do mean to keep clear of the whole world, let it be hard or not. There was one lady travelling with her consumptive husband, who offered on his part & hers to take appartments in common with us!—horrible to imagine! By the way he could scarcely *walk* when he left England—would only creep along between his stick & his wife's arm .. & was given up by two physicians, .. having completely lost a lung .. and now after this long, fatiguing journey, & entirely in consequence of the change of air, he is wonderfully better & able to walk & talk & looking like another man.

Well—we stayed at this hotel of the Tre Donzelle till we could suit ourselves with an appartment, .. & since I began this letter we have had great difficulties. The prices of houses are higher than we imagined, & poor Robert has had ever so much uncongenial trouble going from house to house, & divided between his wish of putting me in a good situation, & our common fear of falling into undue expenses- He went & came, .. coming to insist on carrying me up stairs to see something that might be *possible*- At last the success came & the "very thing"—& now I write to you from our home, lying on the sofa thereof, & perfectly contented with the solution of the problem. Now I will tell you. We are in the very "most eligible situation in Pisa," as accidentally we heard proclaimed at the table d'hôte by the most intelligent physician in the place, Dr Nankivell[9]—close to the cathedral & leaning tower, as we see every moment from the windows & in an apartment consisting of one sitting room & three excellent bedrooms, with entrance rooms or hall .. & with attendance & cooking, & the use of silver, china, glass, linen (& the washing thereof)— .. all inclusive, for .. what do you think? .. £1 .. [s]6 .. [d]9 English money, a week. Hot water *á discrezione*. Is it not tolerably cheap? Moreover the house is a palazzo of the largest, & we inhabit the only let-apartments in it, & it has a grand name *Collegio di Ferdinando*,[10] & a grand marble entrance, marble steps & pillars & a bust over all of Ferdinand primo. Built too by Vasari. You would certainly smile to see how we set about housekeeping. R. brought home white sugar in his pocket—so good he is, & so little inclined to leave all the trouble "to the women" as nearly all men else would do! On the contrary his way is to do everything for me even to the pouring out of coffee, .. & our general councils with Wilson .. "What *is* a pound? what *is* an ounce?" .. would amuse you if you could hear them. Yesterday when dinnertime came (that was our first day 'at home' you must observe) we discovered that there was nothing to eat, .. an ominous beginning- So we set out to the "*trattoria*," the traiteur, & dined excellently for *sixteen pence, we two* (8[d] each), ... & sent a dinner apart home to Wilson—& were well pleased enough with our own proceedings, to make an arrangement that the said traiteur should send our repasts to us everyday at two oclock—& we are to try that plan, .. going ourselves there when we are inclined .. —& if it answers, we shall be freed from other domestic cares than of the coffee & milk & bread. Wilson is as an oracle—very useful too & very kind. She was delighted with your remembrance- Poor thing, the mosquitoes have singled her out for a special vengeance. They torment *me* in a measure, but she is tormented by them out of measure. And then, it is unfortunate, just when she had succeeded so well in French as to be able to ask for various things, to have to merge all the new knowledge in the Italian "which seems to her harder still"- But patience & a mosquito-net![11] Flush is much thinner, because he barks so violently at every beard that we do not dare to let him appear at tables d'hote,—but otherwise he is well, & fonder of me than ever, because he has not *you*. Oh, Arabel! I am almost glad after all that you did not get my letter from Havre .. the note, I mean, written to dearest Trippy .. for I was sad at heart when I wrote it & perhaps it would have made you sadder. How wrong Henrietta was, in fancying me too happy to write! Too happy! I loved R. enough to leave you for him, but not for that did I love any of you less than ever, & the anguish of quitting you *so* was not less felt. May God bless you my own dearest dearest Arabel. I love you.

My thoughts cling to you. Believe it, with the fullest knowledge however, otherwise, that I am absolutely happy in the one to whom I have given myself, & that he rises on my admiration, and is better & dearer to my affections every day & hour. *Ought* I not to be happy, with such love from such a man? And we have been together a whole month now, & he professes to love me "infinitely more", instead of the dreadful "less" which was to have been expected. He keeps saying that never he was so happy in his life—which is more magical than music in my ears, while I listen to him. Then such a delightful companion he is, .. with what Mrs Jameson calls "his inexhaustible wit, & learning & good humour." She said the other day "My dear Browning, I have admired your genius for many years, but now I feel it to be still better to love yourself." So I can repeat such things, you see, without the "blushing." And as for you, Arabel, you must love him, if you love me .. for all the tenderness which one human being can give to another, he gives to me every moment of my life. Love him for my sake & do not call him Mr Browning. How you would love him for his own sake if you knew him .. knew him thoroughly, that is .. in the soul & in the life!

Since I was writing two lines backward I have been reading Papa's letter at Orleans which then frightened me so with a glimpse, that I scarcely dared to read it, but put it by to read at leisurely courage.

⟨...⟩[12]

May God bless him, my dear Papa— As R. says, "Our Father who is [in] Heaven will judge us more gently"—yet I did not show it to R.—he only read it in my face. May God bless you all— If somebody sends to ask you if you have a parcel for Italy, send me my black cord, .. my mittens .. (out of the bag) your portrait (which I set aside for more care & forgot it) a locket surrounded by a serpent .. (also set aside) a little Virgil, sent to be bound .. can I think of anything else? I left on my table some letters & an Italian poem bound in pink paper, addressed to Robert .. (not by me) & his manuscript of a play—take care of these things, do.

Tell Surtees Cook that I cordially thank him for his kind wishes—tell him too that the little green book is of use & beauty every day. How long do you stay at Little Bookham? Do let me hear everything. *Has Papa forbidden you to write?*—answer that question. If he has not, I am gratefully bound to him still. I have written directions to George about the money, & those debts I mentioned to you— Minny's, dear Minny's, especially. Is Minny with you? & how are her legs? and who waits on you & H.? I want to know. To Mrs Martin, with a grateful sense of her goodness, I mean to write. I wrote from Marseilles to Bummy— I write to Papa by this post, as humbly as I can *with truth*. Let me hear every little thing. Poor Leonard, indeed!—[13]

Does Mr Stratten[14] blame me much? Oh—in any position except my own peculiar one, I would have *asked* .. of course .. But in my state of nervous weakness, I had not fortitude for the dreadful scenes & the resolute courage— I could not have held out, I am certain— It was bad enough as it was– I hope George gave my name to Blackwood as Elizabeth *Barrett* Browning––because I do not like to drop my old name which is my own name still. Also, do write to request that the immature translation of Prometheus be not brought before the public ⟨by any specific mention⟩.[15] If I had been in London, I would not have sent it to Edinburgh at all. It was enough to say that it was an early, immature translation, now out of print.[16]

We are going to be busy—we are full of literary plans.

But have I not written enough? May God bless you, my own, own Arabel! I trust Henrietta had my letter from Orleans. I love you all deeply & tenderly– Tell Stormie that I do love him & that he must think gently of me if he can.

$\qquad\qquad\qquad\qquad$ Your very ever most affec.^{te}
$\qquad\qquad\qquad\qquad\qquad$ Ba–

Dearest Trippy—does she love me still? Ask her not to forget me—& say if she is staying with you as she ought to be.

A leaf from an olive tree at Vaucluse[.]

You had better tell Mr Greville[17] to leave out the stanzas in question. Of the double letters, open & read, & send abstracts of the important parts.

Publication: None traced.
Manuscript: Berg Collection.

1. According to Murray's *Hand-Book for Travellers in Northern Italy* (1847), this hotel had previously been called Le tre Donzelle, but was now called the Hôtel Peverada (p. 440). Murray's *Hand-Book* notes that Sig. Peverada "speaks English well, is agent to Messrs. Coutts and Co., and carries on his banking business, both here and at the Baths of Lucca" (p. 441).

2. The Brownings arrived at Pisa on 14 October 1846. At the beginning of this letter EBB mentions hearing from her sisters "on the second day of our arrival," which would have been the 15th, and she then refers to that date as "last night." Thus, she would have started her letter on the 16th. The Brownings took their rooms in the Collegio Ferdinando on the 18th—a day which, near the end of her letter, EBB mentions as "yesterday." The Collegio Ferdinando is located in the Via Santa Maria, very near the Cathedral of Pisa.

3. Cf. Coleridge, *Christabel* (1816), I, 253.

4. In the description of the cathedral at Bourges, Murray's *Hand-Book for Travellers in France* (1847) notes that "one of the chief boasts of this cathedral is the quantity, excellence, and good preservation of the *painted glass* of the windows of the choir and chapels. They include specimens of the art from the 13th down to the 17th century" (p. 357).

5. Psalm 103:5.

6. Mrs. Jameson's sketch has not survived; however, her niece, Gerardine, recalled this occasion thirty years later: "We rested for a couple of days at Avignon, the route to Italy being then much less direct and expeditious, though I think much more delightful, than now, and while there we made a little expedition, a poetical pilgrimage, to Vaucluse. There, at the very source of the 'chiare, fresche e dolci acque,' Mr. Browning took his wife up in his arms, and, carrying her across through the shallow curling waters, seated her on a rock that rose throne-like in the middle of the stream. Thus love and poetry took a new possession of the spot immortalised by Petrarch's loving fancy" (Gerardine Macpherson, *Memoirs of The Life of Anna Jameson*, 1878, pp.231–232).

7. Murray's describes Aix as "the resort of the troubadours, the home of poetry, gallantry, and politeness" (p. 496).

8. Robert Surtees of Redworth, a distant relation of EBB's cousin, William Surtees Cook (see letter 2499, note 3). Robert Surtees and his wife, Elizabeth, together with their daughter, Margaret Caroline Surtees (1816–69), were travelling in Italy.

9. Murray's *Hand-Book for Travellers in Northern Italy* (1847) confirms that "Dr. Cook and Dr. Nankivell, English physicians, practise at Pisa" (p. 441). The archives of the Inter-Continental Church Society (London) indicate that Dr. Charles Benjamin Nankivell was sometimes secretary of "The Pisa Book Society."

10. The Collegio Ferdinando was first opened as a college in 1595, taking its name from its benefactor Ferdinando I (1549–1609). Although a contemporary Italian guidebook ascribes the design of the building to Vasari (*Nuova Guida di Pisa*, 1843, p. 202), a later work explains that Vasari was responsible for renovating the building that was formerly the home of the Familiati family (Giovanni Grazzini, *Le Condizioni di Pisa alla fine de xvi e sul principio del xvii secolo sotto il granducato di Ferdinando I de'Medici*, 1898, pp. 17–18). The Brownings resided here from 18 October 1846 until 20 April 1847.

11. Cf. Cervantes, *The Ingenious Gentleman Don Quixote of La Mancha*, pt. II, ch. 23.

12. Nearly four lines, containing comments about EBB's father's reaction to her marriage, were obliterated here by someone other than EBB.

13. EBB's cousin Leonard Edmund Graham-Clarke had married another cousin, Isabella Horatia Butler, in November 1843; she died on 26 September 1846, a few weeks before this letter was written (see letter 2485, note 4).

14. For details of Stratten's association with the Barretts, see the biographical sketch, pp. 357–360.

15. Bracketed passage is interpolated above the line.

16. In March 1845, after EBB had completed her revised translation of *Prometheus Bound*, she sent the manuscript to John Kenyon for his appraisal—"And then, you shall advise me whether it would be worth while for me to write & ask Blackwood to take it in Bodily" (letter 1872). Her request, directed to *Blackwood's Edinburgh Magazine* that autumn, was not answered until late August 1846 (see letter 2554). Most likely EBB sent the new version to *Blackwood's* a few days before leaving for Italy, together with the seven poems which appeared in the October issue. If so, we conjecture that when submitting proof of the poems, *Blackwood's* requested a copy of the earlier work. In her absence, EBB's brother George responded, indicating his intention of sending the work in November (see SD1281). Due to Arabella's timely report of George's intention and EBB's comment in this letter, the earlier work was not sent (see letter 2655). The new translation first appeared in *Poems* (1850).

17. Robert Northmore Greville, editor of *The Poetic Prism* (see letter 2563, note 3), which contained several of EBB's poems; however, we are unable to clarify which stanzas were "in question."

2625. EBB TO JULIA MARTIN

Pisa. Collegio Ferdinando
Octob. 2[2 1846][1]

My dearest M:[rs] Martin, will you believe that I began a letter to you before I took this step to give you the whole story of the impulses towards it, .. feeling strongly that I owed what I considered my justification to such dear friends as yourself & M:[r] Martin that you might not hastily conclude that you had thrown away upon one who was quite unworthy, the regard of years. I had begun such a letter——when by the plan of going to Little Bookham, my plans were all hurried forward .. changed .. driven prematurely into action .. & the last hours of agitation & deep anguish .. for it was the deepest of its kind, to leave Wimpole Street & those whom I tenderly loved, .. *so* .. would not admit of my writing or thinking—only I was able to think that my beloved sisters would send you some account of me when I was gone. And now I hear from them that your generosity has not waited for a letter from me to do its best for me, & that instead of being vexed, as you might well be, at my leaving England without a word sent to you, you have used kind offices in my behalf .. you have been more than the generous & affectionate friend I always considered you. So my first words must be that I am deeply grateful to you my very dear friend, & that to the last moment of my life I shall remember the claim you have on my gratitude. Generous people are inclined to acquit generously—but it has been very painful to me to observe that with all my mere friends I have found more sympathy & *trust*, than in those who are of my own household & who have been daily witnesses of my life. I do not say this for Papa .. who is peculiar & in a peculiar position—but it pained me that George who *knew* .. all that passed, last year for instance, about Pisa .. who knew that the alternative of making a simple effort to secure my health during the winter was the ⟨"⟩severe displeasure" I have incurred now—& that the fruit of yielding myself a prisoner was the sense of being of no use nor comfort to any soul .. Papa having given up coming to see me except for five minutes a day .. George who said to me with his own lips "He does not love you—do not think it" .. (said & repeated it two months ago ..) that George should now turn round & reproach me for my want of affection towards my family, for not letting myself drop like a dead weight into the abyss, .. a sacrifice without an object & expiation .. this did surprise me & pain me—pained me more than all Papa's dreadful words!—— But the personal feeling is nearer with most of us than the tenderest feeling for another—& my family had been so accustomed to the idea of my living on & on in that room, that while my heart was eating itself, their love for me was consoled, & at last the evil grew scarcely perceptible. It was no want of love in them, & quite natural in itself: we all get used to the thought of a tomb,—& I was buried—that was the whole. It was a little thing even for myself a short time ago .. & really it would be a pneumatological curiosity if I could describe & let you see how perfectly for years together after what broke my heart at Torquay, I lived on the outside of my own life, blindly & darkly from day to day, as completely dead to hope of any kind, as if I had my face against a grave, .. never feeling a personal instinct .. taking trains of thought to carry out as an occupation .. absolutely indifferent to the *me* which is in every human being. Nobody quite understood this of me, because I am not morally a coward, & have a hatred of all the forms of audible groaning. But God knows what is within & how utterly I had abdicated myself & thought it not worth while to put out my finger to touch my share of life. Even my poetry .. which suddenly grew an interest .. was a thing on the outside of me, a thing to be done .. & then, done! What people said of it did not touch *me*—a thoroughly morbid & desolate state it was, which I look back now to with the sort of horror with which one would look to one's graveclothes, if one had been clothed in them by mistake during a trance.

And now I will tell you— It is nearly two years ago since I have known M! Browning. M! Kenyon wished to bring him to see me five years ago, as one of the lions of London who roared the gentlest & was best worth my beholding—but I refused then, in my blind dislike to seeing strangers. Immediately, however, after the publication of my last volumes, he wrote to me, & we had a correspondence which ended in my agreeing to receive him as I never had received any other man— I did not know why, but it was utterly impossible for me to refuse to receive him though I consented against my will. He writes the most exquisite letters possible & has a way of putting things which I have not a way of putting aside .. so he came. He came—& with our personal acquaintance began his attachment for me .. a sort of *infatuation*, call it, which resisted the various denials which were my plain duty at the beginning, & has persisted past them all. I began with a grave assurance that I was in an exceptional position, &, saw him just in consequence of it, & that if ever he recurred to that subject again I never would see him again while I lived—& he believed me & was silent. To my mind indeed, it was a bare impulse— A generous man of quick sympathies taking up a sudden interest with both hands! So I thought; but in the meantime the letters & the visits rained down more & more, & in every one there was something which was too slight to analyze & notice, but too decided not to be understood,—so that at last when the 'profound respect' of the silence gave way, it was rather less dangerous. For then I showed him how he was throwing into the ashes his best affections .. how the common gifts of youth & cheerfulness were behind me .. how I had not strength .. even of *heart* .. for the ordinary duties of life—everything I told him & showed him—"Look at this—& this—& this," throwing down all my disadvantages. To which he did not answer by a single compliment .. but simply that he had not then to choose, & that I might be right or he might be right—he was not there to decide .. but that he loved me & should to his last hour. He said that the freshness of youth had passed with him also, & that he had studied the world out of books & seen many women, yet had never loved one until he had seen me. That he knew himself & knew that, if ever so repulsed, he should love me to his last hour—it should be first & last. At the same time, he would not teaze me—he would wait twenty years if I pleased, & then, if life lasted so long for both of us, then when it was ending perhaps, I might understand him & feel that I might have trusted him. For my health, he had believed, when he first spoke, that I was suffering from an incurable injury of the spine & that he never could hope to see me stand up before his face—& he appealed to my womanly sense of what a pure attachment should be, whether such a circumstance if it had been true, was inconsistent with it. He preferred, he said, ["]of free & deliberate choice, to be allowed to sit only an hour a day by my side, to the fulfilment of the brightest dream which should exclude me, in any possible world."

I tell you so much, my ever dear friend, that you may see the manner of man I have had to do with, & the sort of attachment which for nearly two years has been drawing & winning me. I know better than any in the world, indeed, what M! Kenyon once unconsciously said before me .. that "Robert Browning is great in everything." Then when you think how this element of an affection so pure & persistent cast into my dreary life, must have acted on it, .. how little by little I was drawn into the persuasion that something was left .. & that still I could do something to the happiness of another .. & he .. what he was! for I have deprived myself of the priviledge of praising him ... then, it seemed worth while to take up with that unusual energy (for me!) expended in vain last year, the advice of the physicians that I should go to a warm climate for the winter– Then came the Pisa-conflict of last year. For years I had looked with a sort of indifferent expectation towards Italy, knowing & feeling that I should escape there the annual relapse, .. yet with that "laisser aller"[2] manner which had become a habit to me, unable to form a definite wish about it. But last year when all this happened to me, & I was better than usual in the summer, I *wished* to make the experiment .. to live the experiment out, & see whether there was hope for me or not hope. Then came D! Chambers, with his encouraging opinion—"I wanted simply a warm climate & *air*, he said .. I might be well if I pleased." Followed what you know .. or do not precisely know—the pain of it was acutely felt by me. For I never had doubted but that Papa w!! catch at any human chance of restoring my health– I was under the delusion always that the difficulty of making such trials lay in *me* & not in *him*. His manner of acting towards me last summer was one of the most painful griefs of my life, because it involved a disappointment in the affections. My dear father is a very peculiar person——he is naturally stern, & has exaggerated notions of authority—but these things go with high & noble qualities .. and as, for feeling, the water is under the rock, & I had faith. Yes, & have it. I admire such qualities as he has——fortitude, integrity: I loved him for his courage in adverse circumstances which were yet felt by him more bitterly than I could feel them .. always he has had the greatest power over my heart, because I am of those weak women who reverence strong men: by a word he might have bound me to him hand & foot. Never has he spoken a gentle word to me or looked a kind look which has not made in me large results of gratitude,—& throughout my illness, the sound of his step on the stairs has had the power of quickening my pulse–[3] I have loved him so, & love him. Now if he had said last summer, that he was reluctant for me to leave him, .. if he had even allowed me to think *by mistake* that his affection for me was the motive of such reluctance, .. I was ready to give up Pisa in a moment—& I told him as much. Whatever my new impulses towards life were, my love for him (taken so) would have resisted all—I loved him so dearly. But his course was otherwise, quite otherwise—& I was wounded to the bottom of my heart .. cast off when I was ready to cling to him. In the meanwhile, at my side was another—— I was driven & I was drawn. Then at last I said .. "If you like to let this winter decide it, you may. I will allow of no promises nor engagement- I cannot go to Italy, &—I know as nearly as a human creature can know any fact, that I shall be ill again through the influence of this English winter. If I am, you will see plainer the foolishness of this persistence:—if I am not, I will do what you please"—. And his answer was "if you are ill & keep your resolution of not marrying me under those circumstances, I will keep mine & love you till God shall take us both." This was in last autumn & the winter came with its miraculous mildness, as you know—& I was saved as I dared not hope—my word therefore was claimed in the spring. Now do you understand, & will you feel for me? An application to my father was certainly the obvious course, if it had not been for his peculiar nature & my peculiar position:—but there is no speculation in the case, .. it is a matter *of knowledge* .. that if Robert had applied to him in the first instance he would have been forbidden the house without a moment's scruple,—& if in the last, (as my sisters thought best as a respectful *form*,) I should have been incapacitated from any after-exertion, by the horrible scenes to which as a thing of course, I should have been exposed. Papa will not bear some subjects .. it is a thing *known*: his peculiarity takes that ground to the largest. Not one of his children will ever marry without a breach,[4] .. which we all know, though he probably does not .. deceiving himself in a setting up of *obstacles* whereas the real obstacle is in his own mind. In my case there was, or would have been, a great deal of apparent reason to hold by—my health would have been motive enough .. ostensible motive .. I see that precisely as others may see it. Indeed if I were charged now with want of generosity for casting myself so, a dead burden, on the man I love, nothing of the sort could surprise me. It was what occurred to myself, that thought was,—& what occasioned a long struggle & months of agitation,—& which nothing could have overcome but the very uncommon affection of a very uncommon person .. reasoning out to me the great fact of love making its own level. As to vanity & selfishness blinding me ... certainly I may have made a mistake, & the future may prove it, .. but still more certainly I was not blinded *so*. On the contrary never have I been more humbled, & never less in danger of considering any personal pitiful advantage, than throughout this affair. You who are generous & a woman, will believe this of me, even if you do not comprehend the *habit* I had fallen into, of casting aside the consideration of possible happiness of my own. But I was speaking of

Papa—— Obvious it was, that the application to him was a mere form. I knew the result of it, .. I had made up my mind to act upon my full right of taking my own way– I had long believed such an act (the most strictly personal act of one's life) to be within the rights of every person of mature age, man or woman,—& I had resolved to exercise that right in my own case, by a resolution, which had slowly ripened. All the other doors of life were shut to me, & shut me in as in a prison .. & only before this door, stood one whom I loved best & who loved me best, & who invited me out through it for the good's sake which he thought I could do him. Now if, for the sake of the mere form I had applied to my father, & if, as he w^d have done directly, he had set up his "curse" against the step I proposed to take, .. would it have been doing otherwise than placing a knife in his hand? A few years ago, merely through the reverberation of what he said to another on a subject like this, I fell on the floor in a fainting fit & was almost delirious afterwards.[5] I cannot bear some words—I would much rather have blows without them. In my actual state of nerves & physical weakness, it would have been the sacrifice of my whole life .. of my convictions, of my affections, .. & above all, of what the person dearest to me persisted in calling *his* life & the good of it if I had observed that "form". Therefore, wrong or right, I determined not to observe it,—& wrong or right, I did & do consider that in not doing so, I sinned against no duty. That I was *constrained* to act clandestinely & did not *choose* to do so, God is witness,—& will set it down as my heavy misfortune & not my fault. Also, up to the very last act, we stood in the light of day for the whole world, if it pleased, to judge us. I never saw him out of the Wimpole Street house—he came twice a week to see me, or rather, three times in the fortnight, openly in the sight of all, .. & this for nearly two years & neither more nor less. Some jests used to be passed upon this by my brothers, & I allowed them without a word—but it would have been infamous in me to have taken any into my confidence, who would have suffered, as a direct consequence, a blighting of his own prospects. My secrecy towards them all, was my simple duty towards them all; & what they call want of affection, was an affectionate consideration for them. My sisters did indeed know the truth to a certain point—they knew of the attachment & engagement .. I could not help that: but the whole of the event I kept from them with a strength & resolution which really I did not know to be in me, & of which nothing but a sense of the injury to be done to them by a fuller confidence, & my tender gratitude & attachment to them for all their love & goodness, could have rendered me capable. Their faith in me & undeviating affection for me, I shall be grateful for to the end of my existence & to the extent of my power of feeling gratitude: my dearest sisters! especially, let me say, my own beloved Arabel, .. who with no consolation except the exercise of a most generous tenderness, has looked only to what she considered my good .. never doubting me, never swerving for one instant in her love for me. May God reward her as I cannot. Dearest Henrietta loves me too—but loses less in me, & has reasons for not misjudging me. But both my sisters have been faultless in their bearing towards me, & never did I love them so tenderly as I love them now.

The only time I met RB clandestinely, was in the parish church, where we were married before two witnesses—it was the first & only time. I looked, he says, more dead than alive, .. & can well believe it for I all but fainted on the way, & had to stop for sal volatile at a chymist's shop. The support through it all, was *my trust in him*—for no woman who ever committed a like act of trust, has had stronger motives to hold by. Now may I not tell you .. that his genius & all but miraculous attainments, are the least things in him—the moral nature being of the very noblest, as all who ever knew him admit. Then he has had that wide experience of men, which ends by throwing the mind back on itself & God—there is nothing incomplete in him, except as all humanity is incompleteness. The only wonder is how such a man, whom any woman could have loved, should have loved *me*,—but men of genius, you know, are apt to love with their imagination. Then there is something in the sympathy .. the strange, straight sympathy, which unites us on all subjects. If it were not that I look up to him, we should be too alike to be together perhaps—but I know my place better than he does, who is too humble. Oh, you cannot think how well we get on after six weeks of menage! If I suffer again, it will not be through *him*. Some day, dearest M!s Martin, I will show you & dear M! Martin how his *prophecy was fulfilled*[6] .. saving some picturesque particulars. I did not know before that Saul was among the prophets.[7]

My poor husband suffered very much from the constraint imposed on him by my position, & did for the first time in his life for my sake do that in secret which he could not speak upon the housetops. 'Mea culpa' all of it! If one of us two is to be blamed, it is I .. at whose representation of circumstances, he submitted to do violence to his own selfrespect. I would not suffer him to tell even our dear common friend M! Kenyon. I felt that it would be throwing on dear M! Kenyon, a painful responsibility, or involve him in the blame ready to fall. And dear, dear M! Kenyon, like the noble, generous friend, I love so deservedly, comprehends all at a word! sends us *not* his forgiveness, but his sympathy, his affections, the kindest words which can be written! I cannot tell you all his inexpressible kindness to us both. He justifies as to the uttermost .. &, in that, all the grateful attachment we had, each on our side, so long professed towards him. Indeed, in a note I had from him yesterday, he uses this strong expression, after gladly speaking of our successful journey ... "I considered that you had *perilled your life* upon this undertaking; & reflecting upon your late position, I thought that *you had done well.*" But my life was not perilled in the journey. The agitation & fatigue were evils, to be sure .. & M!ˢ Jameson who met us in Paris by a happy accident, thought me "looking horribly ill" at first .. & persuaded us to rest there for a week, on the promise of accompanying us herself to Pisa, to help Robert to take care of me. He who was in a fit of terror about me, agreed at once—& so, she came with us .. she & her young niece .. & her kindness leaves us both very grateful. So kind she was & is .. for still she is in Pisa, .. opening her arms to us & calling us "children of light"[8] instead of ugly names .. & declaring that she should have been 'proud' to have had anything to do with our marriage. Indeed we hear everyday kind speeches & messages from people .. such as M! Chorley of the Athenæum who "has tears in his eyes" .. Mon[c]kton Milnes, Barry Cornwall & other friends of my husband's .. but who only know *me* by my books .. & I want the love & sympathy of those who love me & whom I love. I was talking of the influence of the journey. The change of air has done me wonderful good, notwithstanding the fatigue, & I am renewed to the point of being able to throw off most of my invalid habits, & of walking quite like a woman. M!ˢ Jameson said the other day .. "You are not *improved*: you are *transformed*." We have most comfortable rooms here at Pisa, & have taken them for six months—in the best situation for health, & close to the Duomo & Leaning tower. It is a beautiful, solemn city—& we have made acquaintance with Professor Ferucci[9] who is about to admit us to ⟨access⟩ of the ⟨University lib⟩rary. We shall certainly ⟨spend⟩ next summer in Italy *somewhere*, & ⟨talk⟩ of Rome for the next winter—but of course this is all in air. Let me hear from you dearest M!ˢ Martin, .. & direct M. Browning, *Poste Restante*, Pisa—it is best- Just before we left Paris, I wrote to my aunt Jane, & from Marseilles to Bummy—but from neither have I heard, yet.

With best love to dearest M! Martin, ever both my dear kind friends
your affectionate & grateful
Ba

Address, in RB's hand: Angleterre viâ France. / Mrs Martin, / Colwall, / near Malvern, / Worcestershire.
Publication: LEBB, I, 286–297 (as [?20] October [1846]).
Manuscript: Wellesley College.

1. This letter is postmarked 22 October 1846. Evidently, EBB neglected to write the second "2" of "22." The Brownings did not take up residence in the Collegio Ferdinando until 18 October.
2. "Indifferent."
3. Cf. "Confessions," line 56; see also Alethea Hayter, *Mrs Browning: A Poet's Work and its Setting*, 1962, p. 119.
4. This statement proved to be true. When her sister Henrietta married William Surtees Cook in 1850 and her brother Alfred married a cousin, Lizzie Barrett, in 1855, they were disinherited.
5. For EBB's account of this incident to RB, see letter 2176.
6. Perhaps an allusion to RB's suggestion in letter 1983, in which he told EBB: "surely I might dare say you may if you please get well thro' God's goodness—with persevering

patience, surely—and this next winter abroad—which you must get ready for now, every sunny day, will you not?"
7. Cf. I Samuel 10:11-12, 19:24.
8. John 12:36.
9. Michele Ferrucci (1801-81) was a professor of history, literature, and archæology. He taught at the Academy in Geneva from 1836 until 1844, and at this time he held the chair of Latin and Greek Letters in the University of Pisa. His liberal ideas brought him into conflict with the papal government.

2626. EBB TO MARY RUSSELL MITFORD

Collegio Ferdinando. Pisa.
November 5 & 8– [1846]¹

I have your letter ever dearest Miss Mitford, & it is welcome even more than your letters have been used to be to me—the last charm was to come, you see, by this distance. For all your affection & solicitude, may you trust my gratitude!—if you love me a little, I love you indeed & never shall cease- The only difference shall be that *two* may love you where one did—and for my part I will answer for it that if you could love the poor one, you will not refuse any love to the other when you come to know him.- I never could bear to speak to you of *him* since quite the beginning, or rather I never could dare. But when you know him & understand how the mental gifts are scarcely *half* of him, you will not wonder at your friend—& indeed two years of stedfast affection from such a man would have overcome *any* woman's heart .. I have been neither much wiser nor much foolisher than all the Shes in the world, .. only much happier—the difference is in the happiness. Certainly I am not likely to repent of having given myself to him- I cannot, for all the pain received from another quarter, the comfort for which is that my conscience is pure of the sense of having broken the least known duty, & that the same consequences would follow any marriage of any member of my family with any possible man or woman.² I look to time, & reason, & natural love & pity, & to the justification of the events acting through all, .. I look on so & hope: & in the meanwhile it has been a great comfort to have had not merely the indulgence but the approbation & sympathy of most of my old personal friends—oh, such kind letters- For instance, yesterday one came from dear M.rs Martin who has known me[,] she & her husband, since the very beginning of my womanhood, & both of them are acute, thinking people, with heads as strong as their hearts. I, in my haste, left England without a word to them, for which they might naturally have reproached me— instead of which, they write to say that never *for a moment* have they doubted my having acted for the best & happiest, & to assure me that having sympathized with me in every sorrow & trial, they delightedly feel with me in the new joy—nothing could be more cordially kind. See how I write to you as if I could speak .. all these little things which are great things when seen in the light. Also R & I are not in the least tired of one another notwithstanding the very perpetual tête à tête into which we have fallen & which (past the first fortnight) w.^{d} be rather a trial in many cases. Then our housekeeping may end perhaps in being a proverb among the nations,[3] for at the beginning it makes Mrs Jameson laugh heartily—it disappoints her theories, she admits, in finding that, albeit poets, we abstain from burning candles at both ends at once, just as if we did statistics & historical abstracts by nature, instead. And do not think that the trouble falls on me– Even the pouring out of the coffee is a divided labour—& the ordering of the dinner is quite out of my hands. As for me, when I am so good as to let myself be carried upstairs, & so angelical as to sit still on the sofa, & so considerate moreover as *not* to put my foot into a puddle, why *my* duty is considered done to a perfection which is worthy of all adoration—: it really is not very hard work to please this taskmaster– For Pisa we both like it extremely. The city is full of beauty & repose—& the purple mountains, gloriously seem to beckon us on deeper into the vineland .. We have rooms close to the Duomo & Leaning Tower, in the great Collegio built by Vasari![4] .. three excellent bedrooms & a sitting room, matted & carpeted .. looking comfortable even for England. For the last fortnight except the very last few sunny days, we have had rain—but the climate is as mild as possible, .. no cold, with all the damp. Delightful weather we had for the travelling– Ah, you, with your terrors of travelling—how you amuse me! Why the constant change of air in the continued fine weather, made me better & better instead of worse! It did me infinite good! M.^{rs}– Jameson says, she "wont call me *improved*, but *transformed* rather."[5] I like the new sights & the movement, .. my spirits rise: I live—I can adapt myself. If you really tried it & got as far as Paris, you would be drawn on, I fancy, & on .. on to the East perhaps with H Martineau,[6] or at least as near it as we are here. By the way, or out of the way, it struck me as unfortunate that my poems sh.^{d} have been printed *just now* in Blackwood–[7] I wish it had been otherwise. Then I had a letter from one of my Leeds readers the other day,[8] to expostulate about the *inappropriateness* of certain of them!!!– The fact is, that I sent a heap of verses swept from my desk & belonging to old feelings & impressions, & not imagining that they were to be used in that quick way. There cant be very much to like I fear, apart from your goodness for what calls itself mine. Love me, dearest dear Miss Mitford, my dear kind friend, love me I beg of you still & ever—only ceasing when I cease to think of you .. I will allow of that clause. Mrs Jameson & Gerardine are staying at the Hotel here in Pisa still, & we manage to see them everyday, .. so good & true & affectionate she is, & so much we shall miss her when she goes—which will be in a day or two now. She goes to Florence, to Sienna, to Rome, to complete her work upon Art, which is the object of her Italian journey.[9] I read your vivid & glowing description of the picture to

No. 2626 5–8 November [1846] 39

her—or rather, I showed your picture to her, .. & she quite believes with you that it is most probably *a Velasquez*.[10] Much to be congratulated the owner must be. I mean to know something about pictures some day. Robert does, & I shall get him to open my eyes for me with a little instruction. You know that in this place are to be seen the first steps of art,—& it will be interesting to trace them from it as we go further ourselves. Our present residence we have taken for six months—but we have dreams, dreams!—& we discuss them like soothsayers over the evening's roasted chesnuts & grapes. Flush highly approves of Pisa (loving the roasted chesnuts)—because here he goes out everyday & speaks Italian to the little dogs. Oh, M! Chorley! such a kind, feeling note he wrote to Robert from Germany, when he read of our marriage in Galignani![11] we were both touched by it!- And Mon[c]kton Milnes & others!—very kind all. But in a particular manner I remember the kindness of my valued friend M! Horne .. who never failed to me nor c^d fail. Will you explain to him, or rather ask him to understand why I did not answer his last note?-[12] I forget even Balzac here—tell me what he writes. And help me to love that dear, generous M! Kenyon, whom I can love without help—— And let me love you! And you love me ... as
your ever affectionate & grateful
EBB.
Poste Restante Pisa

Since I began this note Mrs Jameson has left us much to our regret. Her kindness has been past forgetting indeed. How are you in health? Tell me dearest friend. Everybody writes kind letters.

Address, on integral page: Miss Mitford / Three Mile Cross / near Reading.
Publication: EBB-MRM, III, 193–196 (as [5 November 1846]).
Manuscript: Wellesley College.

1. Year determined from the Brownings' residence in Pisa in November 1846.
2. See note 3 in the preceding letter.
3. Cf. Deuteronomy 28:37.
4. See letter 2624, note 10.
5. For Mrs. Jameson's account of EBB's health on the journey, see pp. 362–368.
6. Harriet Martineau left England in October 1846 and travelled for the next eight months with Richard Vaughan Yates and his wife on a tour of Egypt and the Holy Land. She described her journeys in *Eastern Life, Present and Past* (1848).
7. Seven poems by EBB were published in the October 1846 issue of *Blackwood's Edinburgh Magazine*. They were "A Woman's Shortcomings," "A Man's Requirements," "Maud's Spinning," "A Dead Rose," "Change on Change," "A Reed," and "Hector in the Garden." In the following letter to Mrs. Martin, EBB reiterated her vexation at the "unfortunate" timing of the printing of these poems; and to Miss Mitford in letter 2642, she voiced her regret that anyone would associate the meaning of the poems with the recent events in her life. As she indicates at the end of letter 2627, her main concern was that her father might have interpreted the publication of the poems as a lack of regard for him. For her query to RB about publishing the poems and his reply, see letters 2554 and 2556.
8. Probably Ellen Heaton (1816–94), a wealthy lady from Leeds who had corresponded with and visited EBB in London. She became associated with the Brownings later in Italy.

9. See letter 2620, note 6.

10. In a letter to Emily Jephson, dated [ca. March 1847], Miss Mitford described "a magnificent portrait of Charles the First when Prince Charles, taken during his romantic expedition into Spain [1623], and supposed to be the last picture which Velasquez painted" (L'Estrange (2), III, 204–205, as Spring 1846). Miss Mitford had been shown the painting by the owner, John Snare, a Reading merchant. In early 1847, he took the picture to London where it was exhibited at a gallery in Bond Street. At the same time, he published *The History and Pedigree of the Portrait of Prince Charles, (Afterwards Charles I.) painted by Velasquez* (Reading, 1847), in which he acknowledged Miss Mitford's assistance in verifying the authenticity of the picture: "I was about this time much delighted by the approval of Miss Mitford, who came to see the Portrait, accompanied by Henry Richard Dearsly, Esq. The accomplished authoress of 'Our Village,' having scrutinized the Picture, and permitted me to state the facts I had ascertained, thought well of my ultimate success in establishing the authenticity of the Painting. Approval from a lady, for whose learning, taste, and genius, I have always entertained the most profound veneration, emboldened me to declare what I believe to be the truth" (p. 66). Despite Snare's conviction and Miss Mitford's "approval," the authenticity of the painting was disputed, and the painting has since disappeared. Some sources suggest the painting was taken to America; however, we have found no evidence to support this claim.

11. Chorley had left for the continent at the end of August (see letter 2570). He had seen a notice of the Brownings' marriage that appeared in the 28 September 1846 issue of *Galignani's Messenger*, an English-language newspaper started in Paris by Giovanni Galignani (1757–1821) and his English wife in 1814. The notice read: "R. Browning, Jun., Esq., of Hatcham, to Elizabeth Barrett, daughter of E.M. Barrett, Esq., of Wimpole Street." This daily paper was much relied upon by English residents and visitors on the continent.

12. Horne had written to EBB in early August to say he was returning to England and hoped to call on her, which she called a "vexation" and wanted to avoid (see letter 2523). RB had been concerned that if Horne saw her, he would then announce that she was either still a hopeless invalid, or that she had made a miraculous recovery, either way making marriage and a journey to Italy seem untimely (see letters 2527 and 2529).

2627. EBB TO JULIA MARTIN

[Pisa]
November 5. [1846][1]

It was pleasant to me my dearest friend, to think while I was reading your letter yesterday, that almost by that time, you had received mine, & could not even seem to doubt a moment longer whether I admitted your claim of hearing & of speaking to the uttermost. I recognized you too entirely as my friend. Because you had put faith in me, so much the more reason there was that I should justify it as far as I could, & with as much frankness (which was a part of my gratitude to you) as was possible from a woman to a woman. Always I have felt that you have believed in me & loved me,—&, for the sake of the past & of the present, your affection & your esteem are more to me than I could afford to lose, even in these changed, & happy circumstances. So I thank you once more my dear kind friends, I thank you both— I never shall forget your goodness. I feel it of course the more deeply in proportion to the painful disappointment in other quarters—. For instance, I tell you at once that Mrs Hedley's manner of speech & of *silence* (she does not notice my letter sent to her as we left Paris) both disappoints & makes me feel angry. As to dear Bummy .. it is different: when people act according to their own nature & foregone conclusions, I never could blame them for my part. I mean, *not for the act*. But when I consider all that has passed between the Hedleys & myself .. how they knew what my position was, & entered into it with such apparent feeling, & moreover certainly encouraged & advised me to go to Italy at whatever cost .. when I remember all the conversation & professions I do feel angry & as people are apt to feel at any ungenerous looking inconsequence. I feel that a good deal of *cowardice* enters into it .. a desire of avoiding the unpopular side. Ah well!—there may be inconsistency perhaps unconsciously to the inconsistent .. though I do wonder & marvel how my aunt Hedley can reason out to herself the line of conduct she seems to have adopted. But just see what is called *love* in this world!- how it *acts*, when set against a mere convention!- You should have pitied your bird through the bars of the cage, & left it there to die .. & so, the sensibility & the safety might have gone together. Or you might have said, "Fly over the tops of the trees, you bird," fastening carefully the cage-door. Am I bitter? The feeling however passes while I write it out, & my own affection for everybody will wait patiently to be "forgiven" in the proper form, when everybody shall be at leisure properly. Assuredly, in the meanwhile however, my case is not to be classed with other cases—what happened to me could not have happened perhaps with any other family in England— & no one knows this more entirely than Mrs Hedley does. I hate & loathe everything too which is clandestine—we *both* do, Robert & I—& the manner the whole business was carried on in, might have instructed the least acute of the bystanders. The flowers standing perpetually on my table for the last two years, were brought there by only one hand as everybody knew,— & really it would have argued an excess of benevolence in an unmarried man, with quite enough resources in London, to pay the continued visits he paid to me, without some strong motive indeed. Was it his fault that he did not associate with everybody in the house as well as with me? He desired it—but no .. that was not to be. The endurance of the pain of the position was not the least proof of his attachment to me. How I thank you for believing in him .. how grateful it makes me. He will justify to the uttermost that faith. We have been married two months & every hour has bound me to him more & more—if the beginning was well, still better it is now—that is what he says to me & I say back again, day by day. Then it is an "advantage," to have an inexhaustible companion who talks wisdom of all things in heaven & earth, & shows besides as perpetual a good humour & gayety as if he were a .. fool! .. shall I say—or a considerable quantity more perhaps. As to our domestic affairs, it is *not* to *my* honour & glory that the bills are made up every week & paid more regularly "than bard beseems"[2]—while dear Mrs Jameson laughs outright at our miraculous prudence & œconomy & declares that it is past belief & precedent that we sh^d not burn the candles at both ends, & the next moment will have it that we remind her of the children in a poem of Heine's who set up housekeeping in a tub, & enquired gravely the price of coffee.[3] Ah, but she has left Pisa at last—left it yesterday .. it was a painful parting to everybody- Seven weeks spent in such close neighbourhood .. a month of it under the same roofs & in the same carriages, will fasten people together—& then travelling *shakes* them together. A more affectionate generous woman never lived than Mrs Jameson .. & it is pleasant to be sure that she loves us both from her heart—& not only 'du bout des lèvres.'[4] Think of her making Robert promise (as he has told me since) that in the case of my being unwell, he w^d write to her instantly, & she would come at once, if anywhere in Italy. So kind, so like her!- She spends the winter in Rome, but an intermediate month at Florence—& we are to keep tryst with her somewhere in the spring .. perhaps at Venice. If not, she says that she will come back here, for that certainly she will see us. She would have stayed altogether perhaps, if it had not been for her book upon art which she is engaged to bring out next year, & the materials for which are to be *sought*. As to Pisa, she liked it just as we like it. Oh, it is so beautiful, & so full of repose, yet not *desolate*: it is rather the repose of sleep than of death. Then after the first ten days of rain, which seemed to refer us fatally to Alfieri's 'piova e ripiova,'[5] came as perpetual a divine sunshine, such cloudless, exquisite weather that we ask whether it may not be June instead of November. Everyday I am out walking while the golden oranges look at me over the walls, .. & when I am tired R. & I sit down on a stone to watch the lizards. We have been to your seashore, too, & seen your island—only he insists on it (Robert does) that it is not Corsica but Gorgona, & that Corsica is not in sight.[6] *Beautiful* & blue the island was, however, in any case. It might have been Prospero's instead of either. Also we have driven up to the foot of mountains, & seen them reflected down in the little pure lake of Asciano—& we have seen the pine woods, & met the camels laden with faggots, all in a line.[7] So now ask me again if I enjoy my liberty as you expect. My head goes round sometimes—that is all. I never was happy before in my life-

Ah—but of course the painful thoughts recur! There are some whom I love too tenderly to be easy under their displeasure .. or even under their injustice- Only it seems to me, that with time & patience, my poor dearest Papa will be melted into opening his arms to us—will be melted into a clearer understanding of motives & intentions—I cannot believe that he will forget me as he says he will, & go on thinking me to be dead rather than alive & happy. So I manage to hope for the best—& all that remains .. all my life here .. IS best already .. could not be better or happier. And willingly tell dear M.̲ Martin .. I would take him & you for witnesses of it—& in the meanwhile, he is not to send me tantalizing messages, no, indeed!– Unless you really, really, should let yourselves be wafted our way– And could you do so much better at Pau? Particularly if Fanny Hanford[8] sh.ᵈ come here—— Will she really? The climate is described by the inhabitants as a "pleasant spring throughout the winter" .. & if you were to see Robert & me treading our path along the shady side everywhere, to avoid the "excessive heat of the sun" in this November(!) ... it would appear a good beginning. We are not in the warm, orthodox position by the Arno, because we heard with our ears, one of the best physicians of the place advise against it– "Better" he said "to have cool rooms to live in, & warm walks to go out along." The rooms we have, are rather over-cool perhaps—we are obliged to have a little fire in the sitting room in the mornings & evenings, that is: but I do not fear for the winter—there is too much difference to my feelings between this november & any English november I ever knew. We have our dinners from the Trattoria at two oclock, & can dine our favorite way on thrushes & Chianti with a miraculous cheapness—& no trouble, no cook, no kitchen, .. the prophet Elijah ⟨or the lilies of the field⟩[9] took as little thought for their dining--which exactly suits us– It is a continental fashion, which we never cease commending. Then at six we have coffee & rolls of milk--made of milk, I mean: & at nine, our supper (call it supper, if you please) of roast chesnuts & grapes– So you see how primitive we are, & how I forget to praise the eggs at breakfast. The worst of Pisa is, or would be to some persons, that, socially speaking it has its dulnesses .. it is not lively like Florence .. not in that way– But we do not want society—we shun it rather. We like the Duomo & the Campo Santo instead. Then we know a little of Professor Ferucci who gives us access to the University library, & we subscribe to a modern one—& we have plenty of writing to do of our own– If we can do anything for Fanny Hanford, let us know– It w.ᵈ be too happy, I suppose, to have to do it for yourselves– Think .. however!—— I am quite well, quite well. I can thank God too, for being alive & well!– Make dear M.̲ Martin keep well, & not forget himself in the Herefordshire cold—draw him into the sun somewhere. Now write, & tell me everything of your plans & of you both, dearest friends!—— My husband bids me say that he desires to have my friends for his own friends, & that he is grateful to you for not crossing that feeling. Let him send his regards to you. And let me be through all changes,

      your ever faithful & most affectionate
     Ba

Do thank everybody who has been kind to me—among the first, I am *sure* .. the Peytons. Also I have a particular motive for thanking Rosa,[10] who had a kindness to send me a *shoe-embaliner* (is that word fine enough for its pretty red ribbons?) received by me the very morning of my leaving

Wimpole Street. I could not answer her note, therefore. But do thank her, & say that her present has been accounted both useful & kind.

I am expecting everyday to hear from my dearest sisters– Write to them & love them for me.

This letter has been kept for several days from different causes. Will you enclose the little note to Miss Mitford? I do not hear from home & am uneasy– May God bless you!——

Nov.r 9.

I am so vexed about those poems appearing just now in Blackwood!– Papa must think it *impudent* of me– It is unfortunate.

Address, on cover sheet: Angleterre– viâ France. / M.rs Martin / Colwall / Malvern / Worcestershire.
Publication: LEBB, I, 300–304 (in part).
Manuscript: Wellesley College.

1. Year provided by postmark.
2. James Thomson, *The Castle of Indolence* (1748), bk. 1, st. lxviii.
3. Cf. Heinrich Heine, *Reisebilder* (1826), "Die Heimkehr" ("The Homecoming"), XXXVIII.
4. Literally, "from the tip of the lips"; here the meaning seems to be "in a forced manner," or "paying lip service."
5. "Rain and more rain" (cf. Vittorio Alfieri, "Sonneto CXXXIV" (1789), lines 1–4).
6. According to Murray's *Hand-Book for Travellers in Northern Italy* (1847), water for Pisa was provided by a "watercourse ... from the *Valle d'Asciano*" (p. 441). Murray's *Hand-Book* also points out that "the island of Gorgona in the far horizon, and, in fine weather, even the island of Capraia" are visible from the top of the Campanile (p. 446).
7. In a description of the Cascine near Pisa, Murray's *Hand-Book* notes that "upwards of 1500 cows are kept here; but the camels are the principal curiosities. There are about 200 of these useful beasts, who do not here do much work; and the keeping of them is merely a whim" (p. 477).
8. Frances Hanford (1823–75) and her brother Compton John Hanford (1819–60), en route to Rome from England, called on the Brownings on 28 November 1846 (see SD1299). On their return from Rome they visited the Brownings in Florence in May 1847, and while they were there he witnessed the Brownings' marriage settlement, which they took back to England (see the end of letter 2678). Their mother, Elizabeth Hanford (1783–1844), was James Martin's sister. The Hanford family seat was Woollas Hall, Worcestershire, located approximately sixteen miles from Hope End.
9. Bracketed passage is interpolated above the line. Cf. I Kings 17:1–16 and Matthew 6:28.
10. Elizabeth Rosetta ("Rosa") Peyton (1825–74).

2628. EBB TO HUGH STUART BOYD

Pisa.
Nov.r 19 [1846][1]

My dearest M.r Boyd I do not know whether you have expected to hear from me, but certainly I expected to write to you long before this. Silent or speaking however, I have borne with me a constant remembrance of & gratitude for your sympathy & goodness to me,—and in looking back through all these thick vapours of dreamland to the friends whom I best love in England, your name stands among the very first. Indeed I seem to be living in a dream— life is so different to me from what it ever was. Can it be possible, I think to myself, that creatures on this side the grave, can be so happy? I am very happy, very strangely happy, in every possible respect except in the anger left behind where I do not like to think of it—but *here*, the constant companionship & tenderness of the best & most gifted of human beings, has transfigured life to me. No woman was happier in her choice—no woman. And after above two months of uninterrupted intercourse, there is still more & more cause for thankfulness, .. & more & more affection on his side. He loves me better everyday, he says .. & indeed I believe. Thank God for me that He should let me be so happy, .. & "according to Lowth's version" "*smile a little*, before I go hence to be no more seen."[2] If the world ended for me at this moment, I may now say the grace of life with satisfied lips, having tasted so much of its sweetness. It was worth the endurance & even the *survival* of all my trials, to have lived these last two months—so much do I thank God for them. My health improves still, too.

We saw Nôtre Dame in Paris, & the wonderful cathedral at Bourges, where the painted glass windows (of which the secret is lost) tortures the sun into giving out solemn & glorious oracles. We had a delightful journey through Provence, in the very steps of the Troubadours, to Marseilles—and made a pilgrimage from Avignon, to the fountain of Vaucluse where Petrarch *lives still*, through the strong memory of the great scholar & poet. The fountain, shut up in everlasting walls of rock, is full of beauty .. the little river flashing from it like a green singing-bird,—& we sate upon stones, in the middle of the water till Flush dashed through it to look for me. As to Pisa, it is a majestic, silent city, built of marble & backed by the purple mountains. We like it very much, & have rooms in an ancient college built by Vasari, & close to the gorgeous Duomo, the Campo Santo, & Leaning Tower. I am able to walk out every day through the mildness of the climate, & to sit in the sun to watch the lizards—and the other morning Robert caught me a gigantic gras[s]hopper, exactly like Anacreon's.[3] For the rest, we see nobody, but read & write & talk & never are tired of those three things. Sometimes too, we talk of you, and I teach my husband my affection for you, which cannot be a difficult lesson– Do think of us together as of two persons who have reason to love you gratefully. For me, the last sympathy you gave me, did not touch me least, of all you have given me in the course of my life– May god bless you my dearest friend– Shall I have a word from you sometimes? Say how you are. I am

your grateful & most affectionate
Elibet–

Will you have the enclosed put into an envelope & send it to Arabel? I hope you will see much of my dearest Arabel– How I miss her, for all the happiness!

Address, on cover sheet: H S Boyd Esq.re / 24 (a) Grove End Road / St John's Wood.
Publication: EBB-HSB, pp. 280–282.
Manuscript: Wellesley College.

1. Year determined from the Brownings' residence in Pisa in November 1846.
2. Cf. Psalm 39:13. EBB seems to be referring to *Select Psalms in Verse* (1811) by Robert Lowth (1710–87), Bishop of St. David's, of Oxford, and of London, successively; however, Psalm 39 does not appear in "Lowth's version."
3. An allusion to Anacreon's ode "Ad Cicadam," or "To the Cricket."

2629. EBB TO ANNA BROWNELL JAMESON

Collegio Ferdinando
Saturday– [21 November 1846][1]

We were delighted to have your note, dearest aunt Nina, & I answer it with my feet on your stool .. so that my feet are full of you even if my head is not, always. Now I shall not go a sentence farther without thanking you for that comfort—you scarcely guessed perhaps what a comfort it would be, .. that stool of yours. I am even apt to sit on it for hours together, leaning against the sofa, till I get to be scolded for putting myself so into the fire, & prophecied of in respect to the probability of a "general conflagration" of stools & Bas,—on which the prophet is to leap from the Leaning Tower, & Flush to be left to make the funeral oration of the establishment. In the meantime it really is quite a comfort that our housekeeping should be your "example" at Florence, & we have edifying countenances whenever we think of it– And Robert will not by any means believe that you have passed us on our own ground, though the eleven pauls a week for breakfast, & my humility, seemed to suggest something of the sort. I am so glad, we are both so glad, that you are enjoying yourself at the fullest & highest among the wonders of art, & cannot be chilled in the soul by any of those fatal winds you speak of! For me, I am certainly better here at Pisa, though the penalty is to see Frate Angelico's picture,[2] with the remembrance of you rather than the presence. Here, indeed, we have had a little too much cold for two days— there was a feeling of frost in the air & a most undeniable east wind which prevented my going out & made me feel less comfortable than usual at home. But after all, one felt ashamed to call it *cold*, & Robert found the heat on the Arno insupportable,—which set us both mourning over our "situation" at the Collegio, where one of us could not get out on such days, without a blow on the chest from the "wind at the corner." Well—experience teaches, & we shall be taught—&—the cost of it, is not so very much after all .. we have seen your professor once since you left us—(oh, the leaving!) or *spoken* to him once, I should say, when he came in one evening & caught us reading, sighing, yawning over Nicoló de' Lapi, a romance by the son in law of Manzoni. Before we could speak, he called it "excellent, trés beau,"[3] one of their very best romances .. upon which, of course dear Robert could not bear to offend his literary & national susceptibilities by a doubt even. *I*, not being so humane, thought that any suffering reader would be justified (under the rack-wheel) in crying out against such a book, as the dullest, heaviest, stupidest, lengthiest. Did you ever read it? If not, *dont*. When a father in law imitates Scott, & a son in law imitates his father in law, think of the consequences!–! Robert in his zeal for Italy & against Eugene Sue, tried to persuade me at first (this was before the scene with your professor) that "really Ba, it was'nt so bad" .. "really you are too hard to be pleased" .. & so on .. but after two or three chapters, the dulness grew too strong, for even his benevolence, & the yawning catastrophe (supposed to be peculiar to the "Guida") overthrew him as completely as it ever did me, though we both resolved to hold on by the stirrup to the end of the two volumes. The catalogue of the library (for observe that we subscribe now—the object is attained!) offers a most melancholy insight into the actual literature of Italy. Translations, translations, translations .. from third & fourth & fifth rate French & English writers .. chiefly French .. the roots of thought, here in Italy, seem dead in the ground– It is well that they have great memories: .. nothing else lives.

We have had the kindest of letters from dear noble M.ʳ Kenyon,—who by the way speaks of you as we like to hear him– Dickens is going to Paris for the winter, & M.ʳˢ Butler (he adds) is expected in London.[4] Dear M.ʳ Kenyon calls me "crotchetty," but Robert "an incarnation of the good & the true," .. so that I have everything to thank him for– There are noble people who take the world's side & make it seem "for the nonce" almost respectable—but he gives up all the talk & fine schemes about money-making, & allows us to wait to see whether we want it or not .. the money, I mean.

It is monday & I am only finishing this note. In the midst came letters from my sisters, making me feel so glad that I could not write. Everybody is well & happy, .. & dear Papa, *in high spirits & having people to dine with him everyday*--so that I have not really done anyone harm in doing myself all this good– It does not indeed bring us a step nearer to the forgiveness— but to hear of his being in good spirits makes me inclined to jump .. with Gerardine. Dear Geddie! How pleased I am to hear of her being happy .. particularly (perhaps) as she is not too happy to forget *me*. Is all that glory of art making her very ambitious to work & enter into the court of the Temple?

I fancy that M.? Martineau might have extended his subject, for that all moral as well as all religious mistakes whatever, must arise from partial conceptions of the nature of God.⁵ Now do let me hear from you soon, dear friend[,] & from Geddie too—dear Geddie!– Robert's love to you both. We often talk of our prospect of meeting you again– And for the *past*, dearest aunt Nina, believe of me that I feel to you more gratefully than ever I can say,—& remain, while I live,

your faithful & affectionate
Ba

Wilson is much pleased by y.? kind remembrance of her. The weather is delightful today.

Address: À Madame / Madame Jameson / Poste Restante / Firenze.
Publication: LEBB, I, 308–310 (in part, as 23 November 1846).
Manuscript: Wellesley College.

1. This letter is postmarked 23 November 1846, a Monday, from Pisa. The previous Saturday was the 21st, and EBB mentions finishing this letter on Monday.
2. From the context it appears that EBB is referring to a picture that Mrs. Jameson described in a previous letter. Mrs. Jameson refers to several works by Fra Angelico in *Sacred and Legendary Art* (1848), but it is impossible to know which, if any, of those she might have written about to EBB.
3. "Excellent, very fine." *Niccolò de' Lapi* (Paris, 1841) by Marchese Massimo Tapparelli D'Azeglio (1798–1866) is an historical novel set in early 15th-century Florence. "Although D'Azeglio's skill at blending historical themes with the private lives of his fictional characters is admirable, his novels fell far short of the literary achievements of Manzoni or Sir Walter Scott" (*The Macmillan Dictionary of Italian Literature*, 1979). D'Azeglio married Giulia Manzoni (1808–34) on 21 May 1831; however, the marriage was cut short by her death three years later. D'Azeglio's active role in the struggle for Italian independence and unity won him a place at the top of EBB's list of Italian heroes. He called on her in Rome in the spring of 1859, and before that had read lines from *Casa Guidi Windows* before the Piedmontese Assembly.
4. Frances Anne ("Fanny") Butler (*née* Kemble, 1809–93) was travelling in Italy with her sister and brother-in-law, Adelaide and Edward Sartoris. They returned to England in December 1846, shortly after which Fanny Butler published an account of her travels in a book entitled *A Year of Consolation* (1847).
5. Presumably a reference to James Martineau (1805–1900); however, we are unable to clarify EBB's comment.

2630. EBB TO ARABELLA & HENRIETTA MOULTON-BARRETT

[Pisa]
Nov.? [21–] 24 [1846]¹

My ever dearest Henrietta's letter which I should have received twenty days ago, no, not quite that .. but certainly ten .. arrived *with* Arabel's!– Which will account to her for my swearing at her & you so very intemperately in my last notes. Now the swearing goes to the post & the post-regulators ... only it was impossible to do anything but thank God & be glad when I held in my hands both your dear letters, my dearest kindest sisters, after a good deal of anxiety. In the future, remember to write over the address "*viâ France*" as that precaution secures the speed– I knew by the sound of Robert's step in the passage that he had letters for me from you, & held out two open palms to take them– Such ideas I had had about you, though I put them away as fast as I could .. but Papa's sending my letter back made an impression.[2] Oh but how happy, happy, happy, three times happy I am to hear of his being in spirits & in a mood to have people to dinner & to talk to them! I do thank God & you for sending me such good news! Let him be angry now with me & send back my letters unopened; I will bear it all patiently. What I could not have borne without deep pain would have been the thought of having thrown a shadow over his life–––which, observe, I did not anticipate the probability of– ⟨He⟩[3] lost in me nothing, just nothing—circumstances had bound me up past being of use to him:—then, whatever he may say, he cannot really think (nor can any of my family) that I have disgraced him or them by conducting myself as I have. Throwing all considerations of literature & genius into the fire, I have married a gentleman in every sense of the word, & a man of high principles & delightful manners—the whole world, with its code of artificial morality in its hands, can say nothing against *him*— & therefore I do consider that in consulting my own happiness I have committed an injury against no one .. unless indeed it is a painful thing to hear of my being happy & free, & the circumstances where I am able to recover my health & strength in the best way. Also it must be something to such as have ever loved me, to know me united legally to one to whom I am bound in the closest sympathies besides, as to the highest things or the lowest– When the first anger has past, these considerations must recur—& it will be better for Papa to have them than to have me shut up in a prison with a sense of responsibility on himself which he could not well cast off. On this account I think Surtees quite right in his opinion– Give him my kind regards & wishes that he ⟨may be as happy as I, which no mere worldly prosperity could secure alone.⟩ As for you, my ever dearest Henrietta, be wiser than I am & happier *so far,* that you may not (if it be possible) give offence where we all owe affection & reverence– God grant that it be found possible–

In the meantime, dont be too angry with poor George on my account– I know his heart– I have more faith in him than he has had in me– He wrote to me affectionately & as if he had loved me .. only treating the whole case, I must say, precisely as if I had run away without being married at all in "leaving the weight of sorrow & shame to be borne by my family." (The quotation is genuine–) How could he have said more in the other case? Still what vexed me most was something about "Mr Browning," & of course I showed none of the letter to *him*. I left the vexation of it to myself. But I know George's heart, & that he is good & kind & upright at the bottom, & will do everybody, & *especially himself,* justice in the end—I love him dearly, & if he would accept from me a scold & a kiss, at once, he should be welcome to both, one as the other—or the kiss ⟨I⟩ hope might come first- So let you & Arabel calm your perturbed spirits & forgive George for my sake- I always take his part, remember, & *shall*. Besides I am in a particularly good humour just now, because dearest Storm was going to write to me—was going—wont he? And who constituted the "all" who sent their love to me? Ah, if you think that I love anyone of them less because of late circumstances ... but *you dont*!- You perfectly understand. It is delightful to think that Storm meant to write to me, even if he meant it for only a minute- Robert says to me sometimes that though my brothers wrong him it is not so much HIM as the false idea they have of such a man & that had they known him personally, they would have done him probably more justice—& that had they known him entirely .. in his motives, desires & affections, .. the justice would have been *entire* too. His wish, often expressed, is to be as a friend & brother to them all—and as to *you* he loves you dearly & gratefully, & again & again says so to me,—& longs that it were possible to have you two alternately, to stay with us for six months together. He is about to write to you under this envelope, & has come to consult me on the audacity of calling you Henrietta & Arabel in a letter. "And why not, if they call *you* Robert?" "Ah, but that is different—they are women, you know, & they might think it overbold of me." I will answer for it that he loves you—& we talk of you so much that almost he has learnt his lesson of everything about you & all the reasons for love. Then I read to him things from your letters that he might catch the droppings of my happiness in them. This morning when we were at breakfast, sitting half into the fire & close together, & having our coffee & eggs & toasted rolls, he said suddenly in the midst of some laughing & talking, "Now I do wish your sisters could see us through some peephole of the world!" "Yes," said I, .. "as long as they did not HEAR us through the peephole! .. for indeed the foolishness of this conversation would—" ... On which he laughed & began, "Abstract ideas &c." *That* was for you to hear, you understand, to save the reputation of our wisdom. Certainly we are apt to talk nonsense with ever so many inflections & varieties .. & sitting here tête à tête, are at times quite merry- He amuses me & makes me laugh, till I refuse to laugh any more—such spirits he has & power of jesting & amusing .. alternating with the serious feeling & thinking, .. & never of a sort to incline him to leave ⟨this⟩ room for what is called "gaieties." Our gaieties are between the chesnuts & the fire .. the pine-fire "from the Grand Duke's woods." When Mrs Peyton fancied us about to be "very gay"—in the sense she meant, nothing c^d be more different from the fact. We have been no where but into the churches, & have exchanged no word with a creature, except on two occasions with Professor Ferucci who certainly threatens to bring his wife[4] to see me, but who is too much occupied at the university to spend time on any person. We have permission to go to the university library, but have not done *that*, even—being contented so far with subscribing 8ᵈ a month to a circulating bookshop, & yawning over the dreary state of Italian fiction– Robert says sometimes, in one of those desperate fits of philanthropy to which he is subject, "Really Ba, you are too severe!" (yawning) "really this is not so very heav … y!" (conclusive yawns!)– We wish, in time, to associate with a few Italians, for the advantage of knowing the people & speaking the language. (Professor Ferucci & his wife speak French as by a point of honour)—but for the present it is not possible to lead a more secluded life– I saw many more people in my room in Wimpole Street– And we both delight in the quietness & give no sign of being tired of one another .. which is the principal thing– For my part, I am happier now than at first—(not so extraordinary perhaps!)– But it is strange for *him* to love me *with increase, in this way*: it is not the common way of men. Wilson may well say what she does—yet Wilson does not know, of course– I assure you, I have far more extravagances & "voluntary humilities" to put away from me, than ever I had in the Wimpole Street days of adoration,—& now I begin to wonder naturally whether I may not be some sort of a real angel after all. It is not so bad a thing, be sure, for a woman to be loved by a man of imagination– He loves her through a lustrous atmosphere, which not only keeps back the faults, but produces a continual novelty, through its own changes– Always he will have it, that our attachment was "predestinated from the beginning,": & that no two persons could have one soul between them so much as we—which I tell you, but mind you do not tell it to … even dear Mʳ Kenyon, to whom every confidence is due & open, except .. such a letter as this for instance– You must not show him my letters– In other respects you were entirely right—⟨so ri⟩ght in my opinion, that I had written to the same effect to him, & I earnestly hope that the necessary communications, about money, may be made by letter & without personal intercourse between George & himself. He has a very strong opinion on the whole case, I can assure you,—& might be as warm as the other party. His generous & quick comprehension of myself & my motives, I shall be grateful for to the end of my life—& in his letter the other day, he calls Robert "an incarnation of the good & the true," which is the truest truth, of my husband, & draws from me a deeper gratitude still. It is nothing after that, that he desired us—desired *me* .. in the case of any accidental *hitch* as to funds .. to consider him as our banker .. appealing to me as "his Ba & very dear cousin" to look for no nearer friend under any circumstances– Though we did not require that kindness, it proved what his spirit was towards us—yet was less in its degree (to our feeling) than his sympathy so generously given. I love dear Mʳ Kenyon better than ever I did– I am bound to him for ever.

In answer to Arabel's question, I have not had one line from the Hedleys—though I wrote a long letter to them before leaving Paris. I am sorry for Jane's sake. Either she is wanting in consistency or in courage- I will not say which--but, considering all that passed between the Hedleys & myself, all they knew of my position, .. all they approved & thought desirable as to my prospects about Italy, the difference between our views must really be so small—that they ought to have written kindly to me, throwing into the scale the uncertainty about my health & power of resisting certain unkindnesses- Almost I feel sorry for having spoken my heart to them as I did- Still I am sorry for their sake .. for aunt Jane's ... much more than mine. (Where did you hear of the Bevans-) As to poor Bummy .. I smile too! But I never could quarrel with people for acting consistently with their nature or their conventional character which is sometimes stronger than nature. I wrote to her from Marseilles at great length. Give my love to dear Arlette if you write to her again- In answer to your question, I am happier than ever I was in my life .. except that now I know the uncertainty of all life, & that the horizon is not so broad. Childhood has infinite hopes for life—mine are beyond life!- While here the satisfaction is complete, with the exception of the displeasure of my poor dear Papa, whom I seem to love more dearly than when I was with him- But I tell you the simple truth—I never, in my earliest dreams, dreamed of meeting a nobler heart & soul, & a deeper affection—and remember, if you please, that I have been married nearly three months, though the first week (as I remind Robert) "went for nothing." (Remind dear Minny of what I said to her once about angels—*I have found my angel*-) I have a full satisfaction for earth, & a hope for over the grave. I mean the *infinite hope*—since for some finite ones ⟨there⟩ seems room still upon earth. And I remember always, how in our dreary marriage at Marylebone C⟨hu⟩rch, he pressed my hand which lay in his, declaring to me forever the union bound oath .. we have ⟨the⟩ hope in that which is infinite. Therefore, taking all in all, I am beyond comparison happier now than ever in my life I was. Who would have prophesied that to me six years ago? As to the liberty & the spoiling, both are complete- I am free for all things except a ⟨he⟩adache or any sort of ache .. which seems whenever it occurs, to be about to overturn the world- It is dreadful to be of such importance, I can tell you, Henrietta! Seriously I wish & pray for you & for my adored Arabel, some happiness to emerge, & that it may not be found offensive to others whom we all dearly love.

So now do write & tell me everything about Wimpole Street, what the workmen have done & undone & how Papa receives you. Provoking that they should *mar* my room for Arabel. I feel quite provoked myself. The necklace, I forgot to leave out, dearest Henrietta, & you must wait till we can come to England with the keys, I fear—only it is yours in the meantime, &

you shall have it certainly.⁵ I dont know why I sh̲ᵈ have taken the diamonds which would have been more useful to you—& I would far rather have had Arabel's picture, & the locket surrounded by the serpent .. both left to the last that I might have them nearer to me, .. & forgotten in the haste & agitation- I wonder I did not leave my senses behind me at the same time. In the locket, among other most precious hair, is yours, Henrietta. Arabel's I wear constantly since it was in the ring which Robert had as a pattern for the wedding ring, & which he restored to me on our journey. I wear it day & night. Tell Arabel too that I am quite ashamed whenever I think of the picture. I mean *mine*, which I meant to replace by the Daguerotype, & never did. One day she shall have it—it is my debt to her——— M̲ᵣ Stratten could not well disapprove if he knew none of the circumstances—ask her how he could—but it is kind that he & M̲ʳˢ Stratten should speak of me with interest. Tell me the name of your maid, *Bonser*⁶ .. do you say? Wilson is resigned to losing the place for her sister,⁷ but would be grateful by your enquiring for a situation for her- Will you? Oh, of course she c̲ᵈ not go to you under the circumstances- Why do you not make your new maid attend a little to poor Minny, which she might well do with the reduced occupation. Ask Arabel to tell dear M̲ᵣ Boyd that I answered Nelly Bordman's letter who had written me one & sent me a prescription from M̲ᵣ Jago, relying upon *his* hearing everything of me from herself .. viz. Arabel .. & wishing to defer my own letter till I was at the end of my journey & agitations, when my hand should shake less & write more legibly for Jane's perusal.⁸ I wrote to him two days ago & shall write to him again soon.- Let Arabel assure him of my grateful & affectionate thoughts in the meanwhile, & remind him that I trusted to his hearing of me through her- And did I not send a message? Yesterday came a letter from one of my American pilgrims .. a M̲ʳˢ Rebecca Spring⁹ .. who went to Wimpole S̲ᵗ with peas in her shoes & found the shrine deserted, & heard of me afterwards she said, by dining at Carlyle's. Her letter begins "Dear Elizabeth Barrett," & she gives me an account of her "delicate state of *health since the birth of a child nine years of age*"—which Robert declared must mean that the child was born at nine years of age, or else that there c̲ᵈ be no peculiarity in the circumstances worth relating- She said further, however, that at this dinner at Carlyle's where she had heard of our marriage, Carlyle had declared that "he had more hopes of Robert Browning than of any other writer in England,"¹⁰ which pleased me of course, though she talked besides of *coming to Italy*. May the gods keep us from all Springs or Springes!¹¹ While I write all this, .. a card comes in .. & Wilson asks if M̲ᵣ Browning w̲ᵈ see the proprietor thereof- I run into my bedroom, and Robert receives .. *M̲ᵣIrving*¹² who calls himself Papa's next door neighbour in Jamaica, & comes to enquire about me & to offer his services & his wife's to both of us- Robert says that he looks past sixty considerably, &

that he talks of having lived here four years, & of having saved by that means, a son in the last stage of consumption. Is it the father of your Mr Irving of the mortal memory? Mind you tell me. I am vexed to have to exchange visits with these people—though of course it must be done- Robert says that he seemed to have heard all about my illness, & discoursed accordingly of the climate. How kind of dearest dear Trippy to speak so kindly of *us*. Tell her that we speak of *her*, & that Robert has a whole bundle of love ready for her—dear Trippy- I am so glad she was with you at Little Bookham- The cold would have put an end to me, as you describe it, for even here I have felt what we call the cold .. which is a mere passing wind & an overpowering sun. We c.^d not bear fires in the bedrooms (indeed there are no fireplaces) & I have only one blanket & leave open the door for air- The climate is exquisite. Robert has (I rebelled against the decree in vain) insisted on having an armchair for me, so that, with the sofa, I am at my ease. Oh no, we did not put on mourning! Where was the use? Never having seen Isabel,[13] and knowing nobody here: but tell me how Leonard is—poor Leonard. I am full of pity for that pitiable Mrs English-[14] How did her husband die & how is she? If Arabel sees Flush in her dreams, he must disturb them—so impudent he has grown & noisy. It's his way of talking Italian. Best love to all—all. Do, do write .. & let me be your most attached Ba, & may God bless you constantly.

Tell me of Crow.

Robert & I have had a regular war about his letter- He wont let me see one word of it he says—not even the beginning, nor the end, nor the middle- And he has been telling you all my faults .. which is abominable. Let Arabel direct Mr Westwood's note for me .. if she has his address.

How amused I am about "poor Mr Chapman."[15] I wonder tho' that he sh.^d like it. Tell me anything. What is this appointment at Taunton[?] Surtees is very kind to speak kindly of me & sensibly I feel. Say how Henry is—*do*.

Address, on integral page: Angleterre viâ France / To the care of Miss Trepsack / Miss Barrett / 5. Upper Montagu Place / Montagu Square / London.
Publication: Huxley, pp. 3–8 (in part).[16]
Source: Transcript in editors' file.

1. Year provided by postmark. EBB originally wrote "Novr 21," the day she began the letter; she then changed the "21" to "24."

2. In October, near the conclusion of letter 2621, EBB expressed her intention of writing to her father. We conclude that she did so, and it is this second letter, not the one she left for him in London, that he has returned. This caused EBB to leave off writing to her father for a while, but she eventually resumed doing so and was encouraged by the fact that her letters were not returned. In mid-September 1851, when the Brownings were again in England, she wrote to her father "to say that I was *here* .. to beseech my father at least to kiss my child—and my husband wrote a letter which I fondly thought, would be irresistible. There was a violent reply to Robert, together with two packets enclosing *all* the letters I had written in the course of five years, *seals unbroken* .. several of them written on black edged paper, suggesting the death of my child, perhaps. The doubt had

No. 2630   [21–] 24 November [1846]   55

not moved my father to break a seal. They all came back to me. So now, I cannot write again" (EBB to Miss Mitford, 24 September [1851], *EBB-MRM*, III, 328). EBB's letters to her father surfaced in Florence in 1912 upon the death of the Brownings' son. Because of their personal nature, the letters were not offered in the 1913 Browning sale, but were retained by members of EBB's family. The last reference to the letters occurred on 20 February 1924, when her nephew, Colonel Harry Peyton Moulton-Barrett, acknowledged taking receipt of them from Henry Surtees, the family solicitor, in whose vault they had been kept for the previous ten years. In the same letter Colonel Moulton-Barrett went on to say that "the letters have been burned by me in the presence of a witness" (MS at Eton).

3. Reconstruction here and elsewhere in this letter is due to the fact that it was written on thin stationery that has frayed in a number of places.

4. Caterina Francesca (*née* Franceschi, 1803–87), a poet and writer.

5. "This necklace, which was a very valuable one, had belonged to their mother" (Surtees Cook, with a transcript of this letter, MS with Altham). A string of pearls, it was misplaced but was later recovered in 1855, when EBB insisted that Henrietta should take it.

6. Betsy Bonser was christened 18 May 1828, daughter of John Bonser and his wife Fanny of Holme Pierrepont, Nottinghamshire. Her name appears as Elizabeth Bonser in the 30 March 1851 census of 50 Wimpole Street, listed as a servant, aged 22. She had been engaged to replace Wilson as lady's maid to EBB's sisters, Henrietta and Arabel. In a letter to her sister Henrietta in October 1857, EBB said she "liked Bonser's lively manner." Bonser remained a member of the 50 Wimpole Street household until the death of Edward Moulton-Barrett in 1857.

7. Frances ("Fanny") Wilson (b. 1822), who had evidently hoped to take a position in the Wimpole Street household, but for obvious reasons was not hired.

8. i.e., Jane Miller, Boyd's maid.

9. Rebecca Spring (*née* Buffum, 1811–1911) was the daughter of one of the founders of the Anti-Slavery Society. In 1836 she married Marcus Spring (1810–74), son of Adolphus and Lydia Taft Spring of Northbridge, Massachusetts. Marcus Spring was a successful dry goods merchant who later became a prominent reformer. Margaret Fuller became a close friend of the Springs, and they invited her to accompany them to Europe in 1846. They arrived in Liverpool in August 1846, visiting Edinburgh and Birmingham before proceeding to London, where they arrived on 1 October, only a few days after the Brownings had left for Italy. Pilgrims traditionally put peas or pebbles in their shoes as an act of penance.

10. We have been unable to verify this statement attributed to Carlyle by Rebecca Spring.

11. i.e., traps. Cf. *Aurora Leigh*, II, 1095.

12. James Irving (1792–1855) and his wife Judith (*née* Nasmyth). Irving's grandfather, also called James Irving (b. 1713), traded his estate in South Carolina for Richard Dunn Lawrence's Ironshore, which was situated between Montego Bay and the Goodin estate of Spring. His father, yet another James Irving (1749–98), was Custos of Trelawney.

13. See letter 2624, note 13.

14. Jemima Georgiana English (*née* Carden) of Park Road, Regent's Park, whose husband Commander Charles English, R.N., had died 10 October 1846, aged 54 (*Gentleman's Magazine*, 26 November 1846, p. 553). His death certificate lists a combination of factors as the cause of death, including gout, gastric poisoning, and cerebral effusions. Mrs. English was a friend of Harriet (*née* Mallory), wife of Osman Ricardo, of Bromesburrow Place, near Ledbury, and was apparently related to EBB's early physician Dr. John Carden of Worcester.

15. Palmer Chapman had been one of Henrietta's suitors (see letter 2185, note 7).

16. See Appendix IV, pp. 405–407.

2631. RB TO ARABELLA & HENRIETTA MOULTON-BARRETT

Pisa,
Nov. 24, 1846.

Ba directs me to address this letter to "my sisters,"—or, even more familiarly,—to ["]Henrietta & Arabella"!- If I could make up my mind to obey her, the liberty would be in some measure justified, perhaps, by the unaffected sincerity of the brotherly feeling with which I must ever regard them both—nor have I any right to doubt that they will kindly accept an assurance which their own letters drew forth. For I will say, my dear sisters, that I had not to wait for those letters to know what your conduct has always been to Ba,—and whoever loves her as you do, must take my own love too, whether it be worth taking or not. But when I find that in addition to that constant love, continued under many trying circumstances, you further can afford to myself that generous sympathy which I never had the good fortune to be able to claim thro' a personal acquaintance,—what shall I say? Believe me thro' life, in all affectionate truth, your brother, as you have already proved yourselves the dearest of sisters—for which may God bless and reward you. I am the better enabled to bear what is at least as much a surprize to me as a matter of concern,—tho' it *does* concern me deeply—I mean, the light in which other members of your family, I am informed, look upon a step which your good sense must see to have been altogether unavoidable. There is no need that I should reiterate what was, no doubt, sufficiently stated at the beginning, and, so far as I can find, is not disputed now. I will only say that if, on a consideration of all the facts, your brothers can honestly come to the opinion that, by any of the ordinary methods applicable to any other case, I could have effected the same result,—that any amount of exertion on my part, any extent of sacrifice, would have availed to render extreme measures unnecessary,—*then*, I will express all the sorrow they can desire—tho' at the same time I shall expect some forgiveness for a very involuntary error—assuring them, as I do, that I believed,—and believe,—that their sister's life depended upon my acting as I acted. Nor can I think that, if they saw her, as I have the happiness to see her, so changed as to be hardly recognizable, and with a fair prospect of life and enjoyment for many years to come .. they could *not* be very angry I am sure! I can too easily understand the disappointment anyone must feel who has been accustomed to her society and is now deprived of it—but if I were convinced that her welfare was to be most effectually gained by her leaving me, she should leave me. This is a subject, as you feel, in which my tongue is tied- I could not help saying this much however- Now, let me speak of her. There are very few to whom I can be at liberty so to speak—but you will understand, and forgive what may seem superfluous,—knowing her as you do- I, however, thought I knew her, while every day and hour reveals more and more to me the divine goodness and infinite tenderness of her heart,—while that wonderful mind of hers, with its inexhaustible affluence and power,—continues increasingly to impress me. I shall not attempt to tell you what she is to me. Her entire sweetness of temper makes it a delight to breathe the same air with her—and I cannot imagine any condition of life, however full of hardship which her presence would not render not merely supportable but delicious. It is nothing to say that my whole life shall be devoted to such a woman,—its only happiness will consist in such a devotion.

How I wish you could see us in our strange home here! We inhabit a huge pile, (.. that is, some rooms in one corner of it—) on the front of which I counted about forty[-]seven doors and windows the other day- We sit there alone on mornings and evenings, seeing nobody in this strange silent old city. The weather continues very fine,—tho' the natives assure us the cold is portentously premature, and that January has got into November's place—accordingly they go about muffled up in vast cloaks, with little earthenware pots full of live embers to warm their fingers, besides. Our letters from England describe the cold there as something considerably more terrible,—so that Ba is better here—where at five oclock (*now* striking) I am writing at an open window whence I see not a few trees as green as in summer. In the middle of the day the sunshine is overpowering—but we have had one grievance in the east wind which has persisted for the last week. Or, perhaps, one may give a better notion of the general mildness of the season by telling you that the gnats continue to molest Ba (having always had the good taste to spare *me*). Still our woodfire will look very pleasant & cheerful when I go in presently, and Ba will sit at the table by it and make coffee with due ceremony. Could you not ever come and see all this for yourselves? I heartily wish you could, nor do I see why it needs be impossible. At all events some day or other we hope to return to England—and then I shall not despair of your giving that completeness to Ba's comfort which will be impossible *before*.

And now, may I ask you a favour? It is, that if any thing should strike you with respect to Ba's well-being .. any suggestion that you may think of for her comfort,—you will write of it to *me*—not to *her*, with her unselfish, generous disregard of what she fancies (most erroneously) to relate exclusively to herself– In all probability I should never hear of it—but for a hint, a word to *me*, directly, I shall be very grateful.

And now, my dear sisters—once more, God bless you for all your love and goodness. I thank you from my heart and shall never forget it—being ever most affectionately,

yours
RB.

Publication: TTUL, pp. 12–16.
Source: Transcript in editors' file.

2632. EBB TO THOMAS WESTWOOD

Pisa.
Nov.! 24– [1846][1]

Not dead & forgotten, dear M! Westwood .. no indeed! why can you think so of your friends, who lose your direction, & then look east & west in vain for you? If it had not been for *that*, you should have had some of my old notes from me, even if they struck an uncertain sound, through the agitation of causes which you may well deduce from my new name. In the meanwhile my sister sends your kind word of remembrance to Pisa to me, where I am very well & very happy, & very glad to remember you. More glad I should be if you had told me something of yourself & what you were doing & writing—?[2] In haste I slip this paper into my answer to my sister's letter, begging her if she has your address which she did not send me, (she copied your note written on overthick paper, & let me have no address with it.) to forward to you what is written here.

Most truly I remain
your friend
Elizabeth Barrett Browning

Address, on integral page: T Westwood Esq.!"
Publication: None traced.
Manuscript: British Library.

1. Enclosed in EBB's letter to her sisters, of the same date.
2. See letter 2638, note 5.

2633. RB TO ANNA BROWNELL JAMESON

Pisa,
November 30, 1846.

Dear good Aunt Nina, your note properly ushered in the sunny day, this morning. I fully meant to have written to you, but this is better fortune, to get an answer *first* (Hibernicè[1]); so on the strength of the continued gladnesses of the weather and the letter, we have just been driving for *due orette*[2] round the city and suburbs, and Ba comes in with an appetite for dinner—*she* says, and I am not so inclined to doubt as usually. Did she tell you that I discovered the famous walk "on the dyke," and that it really is worth its fame, being very pretty and characteristic, and extending quite to the foot of the mountain? We got out of our carriage just now, and climbed on to it—but were too far from a curious old church and tower I wanted to reach. Well, you seem to be enjoying Florence, which is quite right—we and everybody shall have our share of whatever you get there; but if we are the more happy that you remember us in the midst of your especial good, we are not at all surprised, I beg you to know, for we have long since made up our minds about the nature of your attachment to us, and having taken up Ba and me on account of so little (*I* go with her, observe, as a serious make-weight) we feel sure you will not let us go, now, after these travels and trials—no, not for ever so much; but even if you tried to do so, you would find it a hard job, so tightly we will cling![3]

The day before yesterday we got the kindest of notes from Mr. Kenyon, in which he speaks with great satisfaction and delight of the letter he received from you. He was, at the time of writing, engaged in all sorts of good offices on our account. I also was favored with a letter from Procter. We have been found out here by one or two people, but by Providence's help they don't much disturb us; one of them informed us that Pisa had never been so void of strangers as at the present time, at least within his recollection, while the two last seasons were "prosperous of English" beyond example; hence the additional numbers of apartments to let, and the increased price of them. It is very soothing on a rainy day, when one happens to suffer from bile, to see every blessed board about *appigionarsi*,[4] etc., etc., still dangling in the wind. Here we go on very well, certainly very quietly, although Wilson makes from time to time a discovery that sets one's hair on end— about ways of living and sleeping, *e sopra tutto*[5] cooking; all very new and dreadful. M. Verrucci[6] called once and means to call again. These are our events! or no! for another event is the opening of the completed railway to Lucca from this place, so that one may go without any trouble whatever, and had the weather been less outrageous on Monday or Saturday, now I think of it, we meant to go and assist at the exposition of the "*volto santo.*"[7] Next week perhaps we may manage a trip there. Meantime, we shall wait your letters with a modified impatience (don't you know that a professor in the quadrant issued prospectuses engaging to teach people, at so much per head, "dancing, deportment, and a modified gallantry to the fair sex"?). Seemingly the list you promise will be of the greatest service to us, and pray let me know when you mean to leave Florence for Rome, as you must do, must! I spoke at the post-office about your letters (one was forwarded to you a week ago or a little more), and shall continue to speak.

Dear Geddie is the best, most affectionate girl in the world. Ba tells me to say she thanks and loves her heartily, and I put my love into the parcel whether she notices or no. Have I told you in all these words, directly and not by implication, that Ba is admirably well, and more and more inclined to sleep after dinner? She desires me to give, first, her whole love, and, next, the good news that your strap is found in Wilson's baggage. I am sure I shall not object to such an article being got quietly out of the house, for there are certain uses to which Ba might turn a strap; but I need not tell you she shall not see this letter. God bless you and your dear Geddie, on account of Ba and your ever affectionate

R.B.

Text: The Nation, 23 March 1899, pp. 220-221.

   1. In an Irish manner.
   2. "Two hours."
   3. Up to this point, the editors have collated the published text with printed extracts in Bertram Dobell's *Browning Memorials,* London, 1913, item 598.
   4. "To let" or "to hire."
   5. "And above all."
   6. A mistranscription of Ferrucci (see letter 2625, note 9).
   7. The "Volto Santo di Lucca" is described in Murray's *Hand-Book for Travellers in Northern Italy* (1847) as "an ancient crucifix carved in cedar wood, and supposed to have been made by Nicodemus. According to an ancient tradition it was miraculously brought to Lucca in 782. ... It is only exposed three times in the year, when the head is adorned with a silver-gilt crown and the breast with a large trinket" (pp. 410-411).

2634. EBB TO HUGH STUART BOYD

[Pisa]
3 December 1846

Offered for sale in Sotheby's Catalogue, 10 March 1908, lot 285. 4 pp., 12mo. EBB writes: "You have again and again too generously praised me—beyond my desert and far beyond my expectation. It w^d be hard upon you if I insisted that you sh^d always praise me. Oh no! I am not spoilt so far."

2635. RB TO RICHARD HENGIST HORNE

Pisa,
Dec. 4 [1846][1]

Dear Horne,

Your good, kind, loyal letter gave me all the pleasure you meant it should. I mean to "answer" it ere long, but as my wife wants to send a letter by an enclosure I am now getting ready for this evening,[2] I could not help shaking your hand, through the long interval of Italian air, and saying, if only in a line, that I know your friendliness and honour your genius as much as ever. One of these days we shall meet again, never fear—and then you shall see my wife, your old friend, and hear from her what I have often heard from her, and what, perhaps, the note tells you. She has long been wanting to send it. She is getting better every day,—stronger, better wonderfully, and beyond all our hopes. It is pleasant living here. Why do you not come and try? This street we live in terminates with the Palace in which your Cosmo killed his son.³

Ever yours faithfully, as of old,
R. Browning.

Text: *EBB-RHH*, II, 182-183.

    1. Year provided by postmark on EBB's accompanying letter (2636).
    2. Packets of letters for the Brownings' English correspondents were often sent to RB's sister Sarianna, who then mailed them on to their final destinations, thus alleviating the need for the recipient to pay postage. RB was here referring to such a packet. The address on EBB's letter is in Sarianna's hand.
    3. RB alludes to the disputed story of the murder of Cosimo I's two sons, Giovanni and Garcia. One account has them both die from malaria, but another has it that while hunting together, they disputed over who had killed a deer, and a struggle ensued in which the younger Garcia struck a fatal blow to Giovanni, Cosimo's favourite, and the Duke, in a furious rage, killed his younger son with his own hands. Horne's drama, *Cosmo de' Medici* (1837), is based on the latter account, and, despite most historical sources locating these events in or near Pisa, the directions for Horne's play clearly states that "the scene of the Tragedy is in the City of Florence, and its environs."

2636. EBB to Richard Hengist Horne

Pisa. Collegio Ferdinando–
[4] Dec. [1846]¹

At last you see, my dear M! Horne, I am writing to you .. and if I could but (while I write) with a breath 'dispel' all my misdeeds against you, I should be glad, believe me. But the truth has made itself apparent to you– I hope .. that my silence & backwardnesses of late, have been all parts of .. anything but an unkind feeling to you--of a difficult position of my own indeed, which it was scarcely possible to move in without the risk of falling from it. If I had seen you for instance, in the course of the last two years, you would have seen what I wished you not to see .. not through distrust, of *you*, as you may suppose– I have been tied & bound– I could not help myself– Then, in not answering your last Dublin note, I knew I should be away when you returned, & I could not say so—& I did not choose to leave our Chaucer & send you a "double" letter .. for another end than the postage. You had deserved better from me, & I had it in my head to write to you to another effect just before my marriage—which I did not do .. precisely because the head whirled & whirled– Our plans were made up at the last in the utmost haste & agitation—precipitated beyond all intention. Now you will forgive me, & try to think of me as I have never ceased to be .. as your friend in the truest sense. I have a good deal surprised you, I am certain, though you have written to my husband so very kind a note, for which we both gratefully thank you—& perhaps it has struck you that a woman might act more generously than to repay a generous attachment with such a questionable gift & possible burthen as that of uncertain health & broken spirits. To which I can only say that I have been overcome in generosity as in all else, though not without a long struggle in this specific case- Also there was the experience that all my maladies came from *without*, & the hope that if unprovoked by English winters, they would cease to come at all. The mildness of the last exceptional winter had left me a different creature, & the physicians helped me to hope everything from Italy. So you see how it all ended!- I have been gaining strength every week since we left England, & Mrs Jameson who met us in Paris & travelled to Pisa with us, called me at the end of six weeks notwithstanding all the emotion & fatigue, "rather transformed than improved". She has now gone to Florence, & we are left to ourselves in a house built by Vasari, & within sight of the Leaning tower & the Duomo, to enjoy a most absolute seclusion & plan the work fit for it- I am very happy & very well. Pisa was recommended to me for its climate, & besides is a good beginning of Italy both for language & art. We have heard a mass, a musical mass for the Dead, in the Campo Santo—and achieved the due pilgrimage to the Lanfranchi Palace to walk in the footsteps of Byron .. & Shelley .. & also of Leigh Hunt.[2] He inhabited, I think, the ground-floor. Then, a statue of your Cosmo[3] looks down from one of the great piazzas we often pass through, on purpose to remind us of you- This city is very beautiful & full of repose—"asleep in the sun"[4]—as Dickens said for the best word of his Letters from Italy- What are you doing, & where going? Shall we hear? Whenever there shall be means of seeing you again, be sure that I shall not talk of *hearing* rather. Except the guitar should tempt!!-

Think of me, dear Mr Horne, as always

Most truly & gratefully your friend
Elizabeth Barrett Browning

Address, in hand of Sarianna Browning: R.H. Horne Esq. / Miss Gillies, / Hill Side, / Fitzroy Park. / Highgate.
Publication: EBB-RHH, II, 183–188.
Manuscript: Pierpont Morgan Library.

1. Dated by RB's reference to this letter in the preceding letter. Year provided by postmark.

2. The Brownings' "pilgrimage" took place on 25 October (see *Reconstruction*, H587). Two days later, Mrs. Jameson wrote Lady Byron: "We went to see the Lanfranchi Palace which he inhabited when here—it is now the property of a rich & noble family, the Toscanelli & retains nothing to recall his memory except the Garden in which he walked & studied—as it is said- I had my own thoughts—more with you than there—it was all sad to me, tho' you do your best to put that feeling out of my mind–" (SD1291). The task of finding a suitable residence in Pisa for Byron and his circle had been taken up by Shelley, and it was he who made the arrangements and signed the contract for the Casa Lanfranchi on Byron's behalf in late 1821. Leigh Hunt and his family occupied "the ground-floor of his lordship's house, the Casa Lanfranchi" (*The Autobiography of Leigh*

Hunt, 1850, III, 12). Byron's biographer, Peter Quennell, describes a less than congenial domestic arrangement: "Byron drank heavily and wrote late: Hunt retired early and rose irritable" (*Byron*, 1974, p. 421). By the time the Brownings were in Pisa, it was known as the Palazzo Toscanelli.

3. A work by Francavilla in the Piazza dei Cavalieri, which is described by Murray's *Hand-Book for Travellers in Northern Italy* (1847), as a "fine statue of Cosimo I. as grand master of the order [i.e., of St. Stephen's, of which he was the founder]" (p. 462).

4. In his description of Piacenza, Dickens wrote: "What a strange, half-sorrowful and half-delicious doze it is, to ramble through these places gone to sleep and basking in the sun" (*Pictures from Italy*, 1846, p. 89). As indicated in letter 2373, RB read this work, and evidently he shared it with EBB.

2637. JOSEPH & MARIA ARNOULD TO RB

[In Joseph Arnould's hand]   18 Victoria Square, Pimlico.
Dec.! 6th 1846

My dear Browning. I ought to have thanked you before this for the most delightful letter I ever received in my life; both from the warm expressions of regard which it contained for myself (would that I were worthy of them): and from the gratifying tidings of the restoration of Mrs. Browning's health &, (though this we knew beforehand) your very perfect happiness at Pisa. Indeed, my dear friend, with love, marriage, & delightful literary occupation you have given me a picture of an existence which would be perfect anywhere, and hardly wanted the graceful solitude of Pisa to lend it an additional charm.– Before receiving this you will have heard that I have (provisionally on your & Mrs Browning's approbation) accepted the office of Trustee to your Mar[r]iage settlement, at the request of your Sister & Mr Kenyon: need I say that I did so with a feeling of high gratification & a sense of great honour in acting *for* such friends. (May I venture on the plural already—as I *feel* it, pardon my *writing* it): & with such a *magnificent* co trustee as Mr. Kenyon. Of course, my dear friend, I have now heard *all*— were I with you in the body I should convey the impression the narrative made upon me with one warm grasp of the hand: let me, as I can only communicate my thoughts on paper do so by a silence which I feel will be at once more expressive and becoming than words—which would either be totally inadequate to convey the feelings of which my heart is full, or, if less measured, might renew in yours the sorrow & the anger to which your noble nature will I know never allow you to give utterance. I feel that I should be insulting both you & myself—by attempting to express in writing how completely I sympathize with & admire your whole conduct.

Owing to Maria's continued indisposition from influenza we have not been able to go down to Hatcham as much as we could have wished, and as we mean to do, now that she is better: we had however a most delightful evening there last Saturday: one of the old evenings, in which we should have indeed missed you irreparably had we not made up for it by talking incessantly about you:- I was very glad to see Mrs. Browning looking, for her, decidedly well: quite cheerful & free from pain: your Sister I had not seen looking so well for a very long time- I have written to Domett, as I thought you would wish me to, fully & confidentially about the whole business- You know what a fine fellow he is & how entirely this will fill his large heart with joy. Yesterday evening at Chorley's I had the high gratification of meeting for the first time—that noble minded man, Mr. Kenyon. Need I say that I was as delighted as all else who meet him must be by the frank, cordial & unaffected goodness of his whole manner, transparent dress of a noble, genial nature; having so pleasant a common topic as yourself we speedily became very friendly & I shall not be surprised if I have to thank you for another most agreeable addition to my list of acquaintances.

All success to the revision of Paracelsus & the Bells & Pomegranates:[1] I can fancy no pleasanter occupation for the six weeks of Italian winter: we ⟨shall⟩ all be eager here to see the results: of course as one of the pit audience in the great literary theatre I say run the risk of all things for the sake of being clear; sacrifice the private boxes to the gallery, the coteries to the multitude, as far as is practicably consistent with the plan of revision; but, of course don't let us miss one of the characteristic features or well known hues which have long since settled so deeply into all our hearts:—in fact I know you will not do this.

I fully enter into your utter distaste for London news: I you know live within the bills of mortality,[2] but not in London, in the ordinary sense of the word—& therefore know nothing which would bear pos⟨ting;⟩ besides I know you have many friends who will keep you constantly supplied with all literary news—and indeed my dear Browning I feel very unaffectedly how little more a letter of mine can convey to you except a mere evidence of the truth & sincerity with which I am & ever shall be your faithful friend. I hope Mrs. Browning will allow me to offer her my very kind regards & you believe me to be

as ever your true friend
Joseph Arnould

[Continued by Maria Arnould]

My dear Mr Browning. I hope you thoroughly understood when my husband wrote last time, that nothing but the blindness from which I was just then suffering could have prevented me sending with my own hand my WARMEST *congratulations* to you and Mrs Browning, for believe me none of your friends could have felt more TRULY and DEEPLY *rejoiced* at your happiness, than I did, & *do*. I am so delighted that you love Pisa. You have found out one old walk, (the grassy bank by the side of the Arno), is it not lovely? We resided there two month[s] so I have many grateful memories of it. I spent a long & happy day with Mrs Browning & Sarianna about a week back, and they were so good as to wish me to go down again before Xmas which I intend to do. We missed you very much, but we rejoiced in the *cause* of your absence. It would be folly in me to attempt to give you any news for you know my quiet life and Joe will have told you all I know, so I will only beg you to present my sincerest regards to Mrs Browning (I would if I could, express how *proud* I feel at the prospect of making her acquaintance) and with kindest regards to yourself & every sincere wish for your happiness in all things

Believe me always
Your very sincere friend
Maria Arnould

On Saturday we had the pleasure of meeting at Mr Chorley[']s that dear good *noble* man—Mr Kenyon.

Address, in Maria Arnould's hand, on integral page: Mr. Browning Esqre / Poste Restante / Pisa / Italia.
Publication: Smalley, pp. 95-96.
Manuscript: Pierpont Morgan Library, Gordon N. Ray Bequest.

1. RB had evidently mentioned to Arnould that he was revising published works for his first collected edition. Published in 1849, this collection did not include *Sordello*, and marked the change in RB's publisher from Moxon to Chapman and Hall. RB had referred to the possibility of a new or "second edition" as early as February 1846; see letter 2209.

2. "Or weekly bill, a periodically published official return of the deaths (later, also the births) in a certain district; such a return began to be published weekly by the London Company of Parish Clerks in 1592 for 109 parishes in and around London; hence this district (the precise limits of which were often modified) became known as 'within the bills of mortality' " *(OED).*

2638. THOMAS WESTWOOD TO EBB

7 Denmark St
Camberwell
10th Decr 1846.

My dear Mrs Browning,

It was all ill temper—it is of no use disguising it—that shut me up in brevities in that note of mine- I was a little--disappointed at your long dreary silence—you know how talkative such silences are, & what uncomfortable things they are apt to say—but I tried to believe that you were still in Italy, till, on a sudden, some indifferent person told me that you had returned to England, & with recovered health, & were married, & had gone away again— whither, he knew not—and all this without one word to a poor friend who would have rejoiced as much as any other at these changes, & the blessings that were in them. So when I wrote to congratulate you, I did it in that infinitesimal sort of fashion, holding in my natural utterance with a light rein, & not letting one half the pleasure, that I felt at heart, peep out in my greeting—there you have all my peevishness, in a frank confession—it is lucky for me that you are in the land of absolutions.

Do you know that I cannot believe you really *are* in Pisa. I cannot separate you from Wimpole St—my faith cleaves to the old associations—all the rest is a dream. I honour the new name, as you know, but it is hard to realize its being yours. With me the case stands thus—to day, I part with you ill, & in England—to morrow, I find you well, & at Pisa, and with this new name—for the interval was a blank to me as you are aware, & without any connecting links. So that when the news reached me first it seemed too much like magic to be true—& even now, if I send my thoughts over sea to find you, just as I fancy that they've reached their journey's end—it's not Italy after all, but Wimpole St once again.

In the mean time, I have your assurance to strengthen my faith, & that you are "well & happy" is quite sufficient to reconcile me to any sundering of old associations, or to any changes that speak out with so pleasant an utterance.

My own story, I will not deny you,—it is so very short- That I have left green quiet Enfield, you know, & I believe you know too, that in so leaving I exchanged my former vocation for a mercantile one.[1] Since then, I have been learning,—somewhat clumsily I fear,—to walk over this new ground, which is not smooth ground by any manner of means, but rather rough on the contrary & provocative of all sorts of tumblings & stumblings, which I have had enough to do to avoid. I have no aversion, however[,] to my present craft, & it has at any rate one bright face (a three-quarters one) & that is the permanence- I am at least not eaten up by those thousand & one minute anxieties that swarmed about me, like angry ants, at Enfield.

My mother and myself (there are no more of us *now*—I have lost my sister since you heard from me last)[2] are residing in a little house about 3 miles from Town, just on the outer verge of the city fogs, & where a cloudy sunshine hovers now & then. I look back, almost remorsefully sometimes to the old faces, & the old home, but I am happier on the whole, and—contented—& this is 'finis' to my personal history--almost. Flossy[3] has become a city dog too, & is sitting on the rug there, with a most wise ledger-like visage, as if he were deep in the mysteries of 'debtor & creditor'--& a little confused withal. He is very fat—invincibly happy, &——presumes that when Flush comes back from his travels, he will be far too conceited to acknowledge an old acquaintance who has never been far from the sound of Bow-bell.[4] *Is* Flush with you? Tell me about *him*, if you should ever write to me again.

As for *my* writing—it goes on in driblets, just as it used to do—dropping, perhaps, a little faster than heretofore, but by no means wearing its way into the stony heart of my public. What I have written has been chiefly for the Athenæum, & one or two of the magazines.[5] I have got enough to make another book, but I have little courage to enter on the task—surely there are "small poets" enough—& then, the "shelves"—carpenters' work, you know, is not so strong as it used to be. No—I shall leave my lyrics to evaporate in the usual way—& find comfort in others folk's eternities[.]

Are you as Briarean[6] in your grasp of news as you used to be? Do you remember how I would send you now & then what I conceived to be a very bran-new novelty, & how you would gently intimate to me in return, that with you, it was a week old at least--the "Raven" for example- I have not much heart to touch on news, I can assure you. I have an internal consciousness that this morning's Times is lying at your elbow, & that you are cutting open some new English book that *we* shall not catch sight of here till—the day after tomorrow—so that it seems like a jest to ask you whether you have seen the last number but one of the 'Eclectic'—but as there is just a fraction of a chance of its having escaped you, I will venture to hint that it contains a review of yourself, very favourable and written in a kindly tone that it pleased me especially.[7] I see also that Mr. Marston has been lecturing in Edinburgh & that his last lecture contains an "estimate of the genius of Elizabeth Barrett, & the author of Festus."[8] Stone by stone, my dear Mrs. Browning, you are building up your fame. For the new books, Mary Howitt promises a volume of Ballads—old ones, I trust, for she has not been just to herself of late—& Mrs Norton has a book of ballads too—child ballads.[9] Ralph Waldo Emerson advertizes "[']Poems' in a few days". Bulwer's 'Lucretia' has been out some time—and is characterized by the Athenæum as "a bad book of a bad Class["][10]—rather too summary a judgment, & yet right in the main, I think, .. the book has some good features, & powerful passages, but it is very melodramatic in its effects, & is less artistic in its treatment, as it seems to me, than Bulwer's books usually are. Tennyson—I hear sad, sad things of Tennyson- I fear he will keep his promise & write no more poems. Mr Horne is quite dumb—in the advertisements, and—was it *you* who said 'this far & no farther' to the 'Bells & Pomegranates'? That eighth & LAST was a spiteful thing to say in running away from us-

How Mariana-like you will feel, when you have waded thus far through my platitudes. I can fancy you jingling the refrain, with a slight twist of the text into "I would that *he* were dead!"[11] One word more, notwithstanding- Now that you have given me so many pleasant things to think of concerning you, & have assured me that you have, now & then, just once in six months or so, a faint recollection of an old correspondent, I can content myself with those thoughts & that assurance, without being unduly selfish by asking you to write, so dreaming that you *may* write, I will dream that perhaps, when you come back to England—& have an idle half hour to bestow. Till then, & always—believe me, dear M:[rs] Browning.

Very faithfully yours
T. Westwood.

It will sadden you to hear that poor M:[rs] *Hood* is dead.[12] She died last Friday of an illness brought on, her physicians say by the trial she has undergone- I saw her a few weeks since, when she appeared quite well- The children are both young—Fanny Hood is only fifteen—but so old, so old in heart! so unchildlike. She has taken the management of everything—& has evidently nerved herself up the firm endurance of her affliction. Did I tell you, that she is considered to have even more than her father's poetical genius- Her friends are exerting themselves to get the pension which was settled on M:[rs] Hood transferred to the children—& I do not anticipate any difficulty in this. They intend to memorialize the government, & second the memorial with private letters to such parties, Lord John Russell, Maucaulay, & others, who, as men of letters, may be induced to move in the matter.

Again, good bye-

Address, on integral page: M:[rs] Robert Browning / Collegio di Ferdinando / Pisa / Italia / viâ France.
Publication: None traced.
Manuscript: Michael Meredith.

1. It was about this time that Westwood became employed with an Anglo-Belgian railway. He eventually left England for Brussels, where he became director (see letter 1881, note 5).
2. We have been unable to identify Westwood's sister. His mother, Mary Westwood, moved with her son to Brussels, where she died on 13 March 1888, aged 72.
3. In a letter to Alwyne Compton, dated 9 April 1870, Westwood explained that "Mrs. Browning and myself were both possessors of Mitford dogs (hers, Flush—mine Floss) and between these two many tender messages were continually exchanged" (*A Literary Friendship*, 1914, p. 20).
4. Cf. the last couplet of the well-known verses that are meant to imitate the bells of the old churches of London. It is said that every true Cockney is born within hearing distance of the legendary bells of St. Mary-le-Bow, Cheapside.
5. Several of Westwood's poems appeared in *The Athenæum* in 1846, including: "The Burden of the Bell" (5 September, no. 984, p. 908); "Earth" (17 October, no. 990, p. 1068); "The Maiden's Secret" (7 November, no. 993, p. 1141); and "A Song of Wassail" (5 December, no. 997, p. 1244). Three others had been published in the September, October, and November issues of *Douglas Jerrold's Shilling Magazine*. They were "Love Her Still" (vol. 4, no. 21, pp. 266-267); "The Poet's Flower-Gathering" (vol. 4, no. 22, pp. 300-305); and "A Vision of Old Fames" (vol. 4, no. 23, pp. 413-416).
6. i.e., far-reaching, from the hundred-handed monster of Greek Mythology, Briareus.
7. A review of EBB's *Poems* (1844) appeared in *The Eclectic Review* for November 1846; for the complete text, see pp. 375-380.
8. The *DNB* states that "after his marriage [1840] Marston lived entirely in London, except for ... short lecturing tours in Scotland and Lancashire"; however, we have been unable to trace further details of his lectures.

9. *Aunt Carry's Ballads for Children* (1847).

10. *Lucretia: or the Children of Night* by Edward George Bulwer-Lytton was reviewed in *The Athenæum* for 5 December 1846, which called the novel "a bad book of a bad school" (no. 997, p. 1240). The marked file of *The Athenæum*, now at City University (London), identifies H.F. Chorley as the author of this review. Emerson's *Poems* was published in Boston in 1847.

11. Cf. Tennyson, "Mariana" (1830), line 12 ("I would that I were dead"); this line recurs at the end of each of the first six stanzas.

12. Jane Hood (*née* Reynolds, 1795-1846) died on 4 December. She and Thomas Hood had married in 1825, and had two children. Their daughter Frances ("Fanny") Freeling Hood (afterwards Broderip, 1830-78) was the author of a number of children's books, many of which were illustrated by her brother Thomas (1835-74), known as Tom Hood. In addition to Tom Hood's talents as an artist, he was also a novelist and a poet. His *Rules of Rhyme, a Guide to English Versification* (1869) was reissued twice. Together, but principally the work of his sister, they issued the *Memorials of Thomas Hood* in 1860. A footnote on the penultimate page answers the query about the pension: "... we must not pass unnoticed the generous subscripton entered into shortly after our father's death for the support of his widow and orphan children. Nor would it seem gracious to omit mention that in 1847, after our mother's death, the pension, originally granted to her by Sir Robert Peel, was revived in our favour by the kindness of Lord John Russell, as soon as it was suggested to him by some considerate friends. For both these instances of the generosity and kindly feeling we have had extended to us for our father's sake, we return our earnest thanks" (II, 278).

2639. EBB TO SARIANNA BROWNING

[Pisa]
Dec. 12. [1846][1]

Robert says that he thinks I may write a few words to you without overboldness,[2] and as I have often silently wished to do so, the courage comes through what he says—just as, through what he has said of you, the affection has come long ago. Let me write to you then, not as to a stranger, but as a dear sister & friend, whom I love & would be loved by, for his sake & for her own .. for I have known you by your kind feeling towards me, if I have not by your face & voice .. & your gift to me, with the words written on it, lies on the table to represent this. Think how I must value it. And believe of me that whatever shall represent or express any degree of sisterly affection from you to myself I shall value while I live .. as I do the first mark of it: I need not say any more.

Of your & his father & mother, it is harder to say even so little. From the beginning I have felt ashamed before you all, of being the occasion of a sort of difficulty, perplexity & anxiety, to the person dearest to you & to me, which he was born superior to, & has incurred through an excess of generous attachment, which you well might blame though I could not, owing to it as I do & have done, the whole happiness of my life. That his father & his mother have not been severe upon it nor upon me, .. that, on the contrary, they have been gentle & kind to me .. (& one of the earliest comforts I had was an affectionate message from your father) .. has left me so deeply grateful to them both, that I leave my future life to speak what these words cannot, .. with the dutiful affection which they never shall find wanting in me. I shall not cease to remember their goodness—will you tell them so, that they may hear it in the voice of a *real daughter*? Such, I will be to them, whenever I can, to the extent that I may,—& of course, my best & only way of being so *now*, is .. by making their son happy .... but I stop suddenly in that fine phrase, which sounds to my ears both unnatural & arrogant: the happiness always seems to come so necessarily FROM HIM *to me*!—— Yet, again, nothing makes one happy, so much as making another happy!– So my phrase may stand. For my own part, I hope to be spared the pain of giving him pain on account of my health, which improves steadily & is not likely to fail while we have such unwintry weather as this Italy gives us: and for the rest, I can understand & love him as well as if I were worthier of him, I beg you all to believe.

He calls himself better far, than he was in England, & is in very good spirits. I wish we could hear as satisfactory news of your mother's improvement. We talk of you all every day, & I learn my easy daily lessons of the reasons for loving you more. Flush opens his eyes wide to hear of Mother Puss– He has taken to bark on every occasion, in emulation of the Italian language—pure Tuscan he thinks!

So here at last I shall end. Will you think of me as *one of you* .. because I have the heart of one .. and understand that instead of wishing to deprive you of any dear affection, I would add mine, .. and remain always, dear Sarianna's (if really I may call her so) affectionate sister

Ba

Address, on integral page: Miss Browning.
Publication: None traced.
Manuscript: Lilly Library.

1. Year determined from EBB's correspondence to Sarianna occurring regularly in 1847 and later.
2. With this letter is a separate slip bearing Sarianna's notation, "her first letter to me."

2640. EBB TO ARABELLA MOULTON-BARRETT

[Pisa]
Dec 14– [1846][1]

Now I am certain it is Henrietta's turn to be written to—but this is only a note, and chiefly on business. The next long letter shall be hers– My own dearest Arabel, I have asked M! Kenyon to send you *seventy pounds* in his good time, ... out of which you will have the goodness *with as little talking as possible*, to pay dear Minny, Bell's bill of £16..4..0, & the trifles owing to Ma^{dme} Alajnier, & Mrs Blizzard .. & Mr Jago ... a bare few shillings, I think.[2] And I believe that nothing beside is owing. When this is done, I shall breathe a little .. It would have been pleasant to me, if my own family had settled all this as a previous arrangement, before Mr Kenyon had taken up the affair .. but Papa's resolution threw me off this possibility, & now there is no other way- Mr Chorley has accepted the trusteeship, & also Mr Arnould I fancy—& the "settlement" is to be of the strictest—tying up into a knot a hundred a year's separate allowance on me! When I cry out against it, Robert says, "*Pray* dont be pedantic" .. and I am silent,—through the extremity of the absurdity!- Only, I do hope, people will open their eyes & observe that this is my husband's own doing, & that he would not precisely have done it if he had calculated his "advantages" after the fashion of the world or counted like Judas the "forty pieces of silver."[3]

Two days ago I had two letters .. from Bummy & from Jane—the first a regular thunderstorm .. the scold coming & rolling & crashing! oh, such a letter- My conduct is to be a "drawback to my happiness through life," & perfectly gratuitous wickedness, inasmuch as if I had but consulted Papa he would have approved & blessed Robert & me as Jacob blessed Esaw [*sic*]-[4] Well, that is all very convincing & satisfactory, is'nt it? She says that the world blames me dreadfully (which being a reprobate, I dont believe) & that perhaps I may hold her "in enmity" because she writes me all this truth .. which as certainly I shant do. Poor dear Bummy—the foolishness of it strikes me more than anything else! but she means no more. Then she says, after all the rest, "I hear that Capt C[ook]. is constantly in W St, & that Henrietta *is preparing her trousseau*. Surely she will not plunge herself into poverty & disappoint her father's expectations." Jane's letter is quite of a different character .. as cordial & affectionate as possible- If I fancied that her silence came from coldness & disapproval, (which certainly I did) I never was more mistaken! Directly she got my letter, she drove to our hotel in Paris, & heard with dismay that we had been gone two days!- Then she did not know where to direct!- Then, her hand was weaker than usual! So, time went. She is delighted to think of me as free & happy in Italy, instead of that gloomy chamber! She has the greatest affection for me, thinks I had every right to do as I please, & takes my part stedfastly. Still, she will be frank & say that it was a pity & wrong not to have declared my intention to Papa by letter previously to marrying. To have asked his consent, w^d have been, she thought, a sort of mockery—but I ought to have declared my intention, & so have removed the sting of having deceived him, of which he complains. Uncle Hedley sends the kindest messages—& Arabella & Mr Bevan "would have assisted me in my escapade" they desire Jane to tell me—which she comments on as "very wrong." You see the kind of letter. Oh, nothing could be more affectionate .. if it had but come a little earlier. The contrast between her's & Bummy's is curious. At last however she says .. "Bell tells me that Capt C. is constantly in W St,—& that Henrietta is preparing her trousseau & to follow your example– Is this true". And there is a duplicate of 'Reports' about Henrietta's trousseau. Is she hemming a new pocket handkerchief (as I imagine) or what?

Mr Bevan is praised, & Arabella called a 'lucky girl'—who is still "idolised". Glad I am, that they are so happy. They are staying with the Hedleys, & in the spring, go to England "to settle"-

Yesterday & today have been the only cold days we have felt in Italy .. & yesterday, was a sleet falling for half an hour, so like snow as to be awful .. I keep close, close to the fire .. but the house is very bearable– We have entered on our fourth month of matrimony, & what do you think Robert said the other day—"The great charm of marriage I feel to be the *stability*" .. I told him it was the best word he could say on the subject .. the most welcome, I mean, to *me*. I am happy as any one ever was in the world, as far as he is concerned, the only thing is that he loves me too much .. so much that I feel humiliated, as some one crushed with gifts. If ever we quarrel, you may expect it to snow stars.—

Think of poor Flush, the other day– He is as insolent to all the strange dogs in the streets as possible, & the consequence the other day was, that a great black Beelzebub of a dog, siezed him by the nose, & bit him & nearly killed him, rolling him over & over. Robert interposed just in time—and Flush yelled piteously all the way home, looking up into his face as much as to say "Why did not you *prevent* it?" For two or three mornings after, he w^d only go out with Wilson--which was ungrateful & undiscerning of him I must say– I often talk to him of you, and he always makes his eyes *dim*, as he does when sorrowful. Most impatient & ⟨ab⟩solute he has grown—barking violently if Robert loiters in preparing to go out, or if I dont give him my toast directly he asks for it. He barks at the doors too, when he wants to get in. Twice as violent he is, & impatient, as ever you knew him. Pray when am I to hear from you, my very dearest Arabel & Henrietta? Every day I expect a letter—& if you mean your last inch-square notes to be sufficient for my necessities, you are altogether mistaken, I do assure you. Do, do write regularly & at large– At little, too, when you have the opportunity. Say how dearest Trippy is– While I write, my head *swims* with Chianti– And if you think *that* a mystical dew of the Muses, you are not right– How are dear Minny's legs? Do keep her in bed– And get George or Alfred to place her money well for her, when Mr Kenyon gives it to you–

May God bless you, my own dear dearest! I am your Ba-
always & always–

No. 2641 19 December [1846] 73

Best love to all—if all love me or not—.

I cant write this over again .. so forgive & try to read– Robert's love to you & Henrietta—& (he has the impertinence to say) *kisses besides.*

Address, on integral page: Miss Arabel Barrett / 50 Wimpole Street.
Publication: None traced.
Manuscript: Berg Collection.

1. Year determined from EBB's references to the "settlement" and to initial letters from her aunts, Arabella Graham-Clarke and Jane Hedley, following EBB's marriage.
2. Due to the hasty and secret nature of the Brownings' departure from England, EBB had left certain debts unpaid. In late February (see letter 2656) EBB reminded Arabella that Mr. Kenyon needed to pay Minny £55. Mary ("Minny") Robinson (1785-1864) was the housekeeper at 50 Wimpole Street. EBB also owed money to the chemist, Robert Bell, 34 York Street, to Dr. Jago, one of her physicians, and to other tradespeople.
3. Cf. Matthew 26:15.
4. Genesis 33:11.

2641. EBB TO HENRIETTA MOULTON-BARRETT

Collegio Ferdinando
Dec. 19– [1846][1]

My own dearest Henrietta has reproached me perhaps for not paying my debts to her– I am certain I would have written before now if the "turns" had been properly considered. Still it is the same thing—and, for instance, I write at this moment to her, with Arabel's letter just read & it scarcely out of my hands. In which, was a note from you to Robert though .. & who sh^d thank the writer of *that*, except myself? It pleased him, & it pleased me .. you are too affectionate to me, but cant be to him– Not that I mean you can LOVE me too much—oh! but you understand! You can understand & my darling Arabel can understand a great many things by the way through what George calls your "sexual sympathies" ... by which, if he means that no one can be generous except a woman, he goes rather too far, however upon a right road. I love dear George, but at last he will wring my patience from me– Those insinuations about money & "Mr Browning," being reiterated, are really "de trop"[2] altogether. I refer to what Arabel told me about my request to him, & how he said that his principles were stronger than his feelings &c—which is right of course .. for principles to be stronger than feelings--only when the feelings *permit* such insinuations about a man who has given up the whole world for his sister's sake & is devoting every hour & moment of life to her happiness .. the triumph of the said principles is not quite so great or apparent– Money, money, money .. nothing but money—— My brothers are all of them considerably younger than my husband or have seen less of the world, but that he is infinitely less worldly than any of them, taking no thought of this filthy money, money, .. is as *true* as that he w.^d be no husband of mine if it were otherwise. I wish with all my heart that my sense of duty (with this uncertain future as concerns my health & other things) w.^d allow me to go to him & say, "Now, let us do as you have wished——let us throw this money back to my family, & trust to ourselves for the rest. Accept such a situation—& let us be clean of the imputations of which now for the first time I will tell you." Good Heavens,—how little they know *him* .. and how ungenerous men can be in their guesses at the unknown. Would George himself act so, for instance—if he married a woman under informal circumstances, so that her money became his without bond or drawback ... would *he* object to the payment of the debts incurred by her previous to becoming his wife & would he consider it an insult or not if her brother *supposed*— that he might object?- Ungenerous supposition—call it by the lightest name!—— Also, he must do me a greater injustice by imagining that I could owe debts under these circumstances, without informing my husband of them. I must be worthy indeed of his, or anybody's esteem if I could act so .. just as Robert w.^d be of my affection, if he could THINK so. Let my brothers learn, if they do not, by their own hearts, guess it .. by their own hearts & sense of honour, .. that precisely *in consequence* of the informality of our marriage, & of my money falling therefore into the unrestricted possession of my husband, .. he shrinks from touching it, & forces me to consider & determine the manner of spending it, until I come to reproach him .. yes, *I*,[3] *too*!- Only, that nothing, & least of all, matters of such vile interest, could ever produce a division between *us*- And now I have done with my indignation 'for the nonce.' Tell Arabel that a few days before her letter came I had written to Mr Kenyon to ask him to send to her £70—but she must be patient, as I do not know from what fund he will take it, having left the decision to him. I wanted Minny's debt settled, before the trustees busied themselves about the lawpapers, & therefore wrote to Mr Kenyon at once. We have had the very kindest letters from Mr Arnould & Mr Chorley accepting the trusteeships, .. both being proud & happy so to express their high esteem for Robert. Mr Kenyon himself is the third trustee, & it was at his suggestion that the other two were selected- I who began by being so vexed about this settlement-business am now satisfied that it is necessary—that it is necessary, I mean, that *I should not oppose it* ⟨in justice to Robert⟩[4] .. *George convinces me*, for instance!- If the world talks Chinese, one must talk back Chinese to it or not be understood- I wonder they do not say in Wimpole Street, that he married me in order to murder me at leisure—there really w.^d be more sense & consistency & probability in *that*, considering what Robert is. Now I am angry, you see ..!—— ......——— And to be sure, when one considers besides what a great marriage he has made in marrying me, one may be at liberty to impute such things- There is the rank, in the first place—and for the riches .. when there is money enough barely to live by in a tête à tête, with future contingencies of sickness & the like, in my case, to lighten the prospect. A fair exchange for a man's freedom, and a brilliant life in London, as he had opportunities of leading it. Your friend Mr Bell[5] will do somewhat better with his heiress, I imagine, .. though with women in general .. of rather inferior influence perhaps, than Robert Browning was. There now!——I have done.

Give my love to George & all the rest, to make up for my savageness— What makes me savage today is the weather .. set it down to that .. for after the divinest summer temperature, suddenly the air has taken to itself frost, and Pisa has had actual *snow* "the first time for five years" say the inhabitants. For more than a week I have not stirred from these two rooms .. sittingroom & bedroom .. dressing & undressing by the fire here, as there is none where I sleep. I feel languid & the old uneasiness in the throat, but am well otherwise, & have the hope & certainty that this is an exceptional state of things & that a few hours may set us right at any time. The last time I was out I could not bear my shawl,—and now, even, the sun is so hot that women are seen walking out with *furs and parasols together*. The snow is on the Duomo, interposing between the yellow marble & blue sky .. & the mountains are powdered with snow--yet the sun burns, burns .. Robert says to the degree of making him feel sick when he walks in it .. we heap up the pinewood .. that is, he does—he is so afraid of my suffering: indeed I am afraid too .. for if I were to be ill after all, I feel I should deserve to be *stoned* for having married– But I shall not be ill ... the cold will go off in a day or two,—and even as it is, it is different from English cold– In the bedroom, for instance, where there is no fire, .. not a sign is there of frost on the window, .. and the air is not sharp & metallic like that which cuts away the breath .. it is a different air altogether. I sleep well, & all day sit half in & half out of the fire, so that I shall do well, I dare say. To give me 'dressing room,' Robert goes into the cold, at morning & evening, like the kindest person in the world which he is—it makes me ashamed. I wrote to dear Jane yesterday .. but delay my letter to Bummy, though she is very mistaken in fancying that I am cherishing a mortal enmity to her on account of it. She did us the honour of saying that she hears Robert's *talents* recognized in various quarters! This is encouraging: poor dear Bummy! after all she means kindly & affectionately to us all—but the world is growing enlightened on certain subjects, & the exercise of the rights of men & even women, rather better understood– Did Jane tell you that the Bevans are as happy as people can be? Very glad I am to hear it– They are staying in the house with her .. which Arabella may not perhaps like so well– It is sad to think of this new malady of the Tic– Always there is something the matter, notwithstanding their perpetual clientship to medical men. Tell Arabel that I have not left off my draughts—oh no!– I have not been "charmed" up to that point—though gradually I am diminishing it. Indeed, Nelly Bordman (my physician in ordinary) will tell her how I was not at all well soon after I came to Pisa, & frightened poor Robert out of his propriety .. & only at the end of a few days set him at ease by tracing up the whole indisposition to a freak of the chemist here who "thought the morphine must be ordered in such large quantities by a mistake" and therefore modified the whole *at discretion*. I am forced to take it still, & can leave it off only by degrees, without risking my health in a dangerous manner. Patience & security go together, you see— and by the summer, we may do much– By the way, what does my dearest Arabel mean by making herself uneasy about summers & such things? I began directly by scolding Robert ... "Where was the use of your talking wildly in that way about Venice?" To which he answered very humbly .. "He did not know .. he was not aware of having done it .. it must have been some allusion to some possibility .. he was certain he said no more than that." — Well .. he ought'nt to have done it, I said—& in an hour after taking up the letter, I perceived with shame & confusion of face, that it was *I* who had spoken of Venice, & he, of coming to England "*one day*"– So of course I had to apologize .. for I remembered then what I had said of Venice .. and I turned round, observing graciously, "Whenever I blame you, I find myself in fault afterwards." To which he answered with the greatest quietness .. (of course I *expected* him to say "My Darling, when you find fault with yourself, you are most in fault of all," or something pretty of that kind) but he just answered .. "It is a satisfaction at any rate, that you should admit it"– So I admired his infinite "modesty," which had quite taken me by surprise, I assured him .. & then Wilson brought in the chesnuts .. which were hard & bad enough to avenge me. But now, let my dear dearest Arabel be uneasy about anything except Venice. Why M.rs Jameson is going to Venice too; and she *must* be in Paris in the early summer, & in London in the autumn. Our plans are all mist just now—mere vapour in the wind. We think & talk, & then talk & think—and dont *you* think, both of you, that it is an inducement to go home directly,—this painting out of one's footsteps in the old room, & this generous interpretation put on one's actual & possible deeds, by my brothers? If I had committed a murder & forgery, I dont see *how* Papa could have shown his sense of it, otherwise than he has done. To have thrown the books out into the street, would have produced a crowd & some inconvenience to himself.—but the act w.d not have been more significant than what he has done.[6] When I hear of such things & *feel them*, Robert says to me "you have come to a greater love than you have left—of that, you may be sure. If you were to wrong me as a man is most wronged, leaving me who am your husband for another, .. (imagining for a moment such a possibility) .. yet for the sake of the last few months' happiness by means of you, I never would seek to wound you,—never send back your letters if you wrote to me, Ba .. never." Which is true, I know: he comprehends better the nature of love!

It appears to us both (to shift the side of the subject) that to let those boxes remain at Tilbury,—will mean for us the most unnecessary expense. If M!. Kenyon should be able conveniently to make room for them, I know he will not spare the kindness- *Ask him from me* .. write a note & ask him, telling him how it is: but in the case of its being an inconvenience, which depends entirely upon his house & not himself, or I should not doubt about it (say this for me) let him speak the truth frankly, & we must have them sent to New Cross instead. Tilbury is out of the question. Oh—how unkind it all is!- Set my fault at the largest .. call it fault or crime, if you choose,— and the unkindness covers & overpasses the whole. I could not have had the heart to act so to anyone I had ever loved, had that person wronged me more than I ever wronged .. an enemy!- It is hard & cruel, I think, & is moreover my *predilection* to the uttermost- I will not say any more. What particularly vexes me is the conduct permitted towards you both, especially to Arabel in the matter of the chapel & the room- To turn her out of that room! Such an inconvenience too—if she does not care as she says, I at least do care—my dear dearest Arabel!- I do hope, darling Henrietta, you have a fire *everyday & all day* up stairs- If you have it lighted early in the morning, there will be no smoke discernible in the drawingroom and it is really necessary for Arabel who is used to it, and good for you both- That room is very cold. Now, for the love of me, do not neglect this precaution, I beseech you. Tell me if you go to chapel every morning in your usual devout manner .. and if your walks are as long & as agreeable as ever- Give my love to Susan & Surtees—the only people who sent their love to me, by the way, in Arabel's letter- Oh, that last day at dearest Trippy's .. my dinner there .. my thoughts![7] How the scene has come back to me again & again, like something half dreamed, half lived- Whenever I see Robert in the unmentionable Scotch plaids, it comes back so vividly! Surtees's costume, & Trippy's excommunication of the same. Do you remember? When I dine with her next, I hope to feel happier & calmer than I was that day!—and it will not be long before I dine with her I dare say. We do not give up England, I assure you, only we keep to our plans of wandering up & down—it is necessary for my health, and convenient to our means .. and we like, both of us, this way of living, free from domestic cares & the ordering & cooking of dinners. Will you take us in some day, Henrietta, & "include the cooking & housekeeping"? & see us "properly *done for*"? Robert & I are just alike in every fancy about those kind of things—he turns away from beef & mutton, & loathes the idea of a Saturday hash! A little chicken & plenty of cayenne, and above all things *pudding*, will satisfy us both when most we are satisfied--and to order just what is wanted, from the "traiteur," apart from economical consideration of what "is in the house" & sh^d be eaten, is our "ideal" in this way. My appetite is certainly improved– I finish my egg for instance in the morning. Then at dinner we have Chianti which is an excellent kind of claret—and fancy me (and Wilson) drinking claret out of tumblers– Ask Arabel if she wishes Robert to make me *drunk* (I write the broad word that she may have room to consider it) as well as .. *replete with fish* .. to try,—by a reaction, the more delicate phraseology. He aspires to make me take more of this claret than he w^d take himself .. pouring it into the glass when I am looking another way .. & entreating me by ever so much invocation when I look & refuse .. and then *I*, never being famous for resisting his invocations, am at the end of the dinner too giddy to see his face & am laid down at full length in the armchair, & told to go to sleep & profit by the whole. What is curious, is, that this process never gives me the headache, as two spoonfuls of your port used to do & never makes me feverish– It is a light wine, you know, & not heating .. the famous Chianti. A few days ago, our lady of the house sent me a gift of an enormous dish of oranges .. for the "Signora" .. great oranges just gathered from her own garden .. two hanging on a stalk .. & the green leaves glittering round them—twelve or thirteen great oranges, they were, & excellent oranges– We have one everyday after dinner: & the sight of the green crowding orangeleaves is very pretty, & keeps us from thinking too much of the cold– We have taken these rooms to the 17th of April, & are sorry for it. Four months w^d have been better than six, for Pisa .. and the Italian spring beginning in February, we might just as well have spent it in Florence for instance, as here– Not that we do not like Pisa—but there is little to see in it, and the country, as far as walkers usually penetrate, is very monotonous .. and when I drive Robert out for his hour's solitary exercise, he goes "along the flats" ever & ever in the same scenery, the forest is three miles off .. the first *hem* of it .. & the mountains, five, .. & he does not touch either. Then he has an extravagant fancy (oh .. can *I* call it unreasonable) that, except this walk for his health, he will go no where without me .. "cannot enjoy it" .. and thus, he quite lives by my chair.– What I *cannot* do, he *will* not! Now, when we are in places where there will be more to see within reach, it will be better for him—though he declares that it is not dull by any means & that he never was so happy in his life, for his own part. As to 'faults,' Henrietta, you & Arabel, may laugh as you please at my blindness-- Of course he is quite capable of doing & thinking wrongly, & he will tell me things of himself, of which I say at once "*That* was wrong .. very wrong—" how much more wrongness must there be in God's eyes? But for defects of character, for deficiencies in the heart & moral being .. for such faults as make themselves habitually felt in persons .. & in most persons, I will say, & it is honestly speaking, I never perceived one sign of such things in him, and do

No. 2641 19 December [1846]

not perceive them now more than the first day- Faults towards *me* he never committed, & I believe will never commit—and by faults towards me, I *simply* mean an ungentle or impatient word, a cold look, an exception to the usual tone of tenderness- He says (said it just when I was observing the exact contrary) that it has been the greatest *advantage* to us to be shut up in this seclusion without any distractions .. that we have *learnt one another* better by it, than we should have done if we had taken the usual course of newly married people who live so for three weeks or a month, & then proceed to other amusements. I had been calling it "rather a trial"—*he* said, that it could only be so in cases of unreal & fanciful attachments. So I *leave* you this philosophy to make the best use of in your own experience—& do earnestly hope & trust for both my beloved sisters, that they may be as happy, or even *nearly* as happy as I am--& *without the drawbacks in England.* What is this which "Lord Teynham said"?[8] I never heard, though Arabel thought she told me. The clergyman has not appeared,—and tell her that certainly if we live we shall pray with her one day at M.ʳ Stratton's, whether Papa may or may not see right to do so. I want to know more of M.ʳ Stratton, by the way- Has M.ʳ Hunter returned? When he is in a good humour, Arabel may give him my love in a branch of olive. I have not a genius for quarrelling with people I ever liked & loved; & if I had, should find it hard to exercise just now. As Robert said when he threw the bad chesnuts into the fire "to have a blaze at any rate" .. "Really these 'grave years that bring the philosophic mind'[9] only seem to bring me an excess of imbecile good humour. It is quite dreadful to be a *family man* & feel gayer than ever." Not that I apply all *that* to myself, nor the idea of bad chesnuts to my friends .. but I mean just so much, as that *I* too, being happy, cannot be bitter & cross at the same time .. not at least for five minutes together- I feel to love them all at home more perhaps than ever I did, & certainly I can bear more from them forgivingly. *Suggest*, now that it is Christmas time, that they & ourselves here should hold out our hands to one another, & forgive & forget every fault & crossness on each side- Will they? Will Storm begin? I love them all dearly & tenderly—I never disproved that love, I think, for a moment—for if I married, it is an act which the very tenderest sisters have been allowed to perform without a reproach—and if I did not previously consult & apprize them, it was, as God knows, ⟨for their⟩ sakes & that I should not involve them in any manner of evil. How easily I might have trusted my secret *to the honour of any one of them*—& how impossible, under that bond, they would have found it to speak a word or take a step in hindrance of any project of mine. But if I had done so, they w.ᵈ *have suffered*—— Why, they must see this surely. I propose, then, a general new compact of affection for this christmas time—a general amnesty—they shall try to love my husband for my sake, before they have knowledge to love him for his own- Ah—

they turn away their heads I dare say! They will follow Papa's flag for the present. If they do or not may they have bright days this winter, & take up their christmas pies in no unseasonable spirit.

Nobody tells me the colour of the drawing-room carpet & paper & curtains to help my imagination. I do hope & trust you have indeed, persuaded, *forced* dear Minny to go to bed, & see out her Christmas *so*! I grieve to hear of her looking unwell– I tell Wilson all the messages, & she is ever so much flattered by it. Cant Bonser[10] (what a name!) help Minny .. make herself useful to her, now that she has only *two* to dress .. remember– My love to my dear Minny .. & particular entreaty that she will go to bed!—and mind you give my love to Crow– No wonder that she could not guess who was married!—— How many people thought me mad, I dare say. Yet I was not mad, most noble Festus![11]—not mad, by any means– More & more I am persuaded of the wisdom of my choice & resolution– Now let me hear every detail of everything. Not a word of Lady Bolingbroke?[12] Did that succeed? Tell me all– We have returned cards to M!̣ Irving.[13] M!̣ Surtees called two days ago when we were at dinner & Robert studies his dinner hour to return the call. M!̣ˢ Turner met him out walking today– "Notwithstanding your very intelligible hints, I mean to call on M!̣ˢ Browning". "She will be happy to see you" he replied .. "but I tell you honestly *I never return any visits*". That is civility! He declares that he said so, word for word!—— And now he says to me .. "Ba, if *I* leave off writing, will *you*?" .. which I must reply to by a "Yes, agreed"—shutting up my letter.

My beloved Henrietta's ever attached
Ba–

Write directly & mention Papa—& *dear Treppy*!-
Robert's best love to you both. Do you go out much this winter?

Address, on integral page: Miss Barrett, / 50, Wimpole Street, / London.
Publication: Huxley, pp. 8–13 (in part).
Source: Transcript in editors' file.

1. Year determined from the Brownings' residence in Collegio Ferdinando in December 1846.
2. "Too much."
3. Underscored twice.
4. Bracketed passage is interpolated above the line.
5. Matthew Bell was one of Henrietta's former suitors, who had earlier left the field open for Surtees Cook and Palmer Chapman, to whom he referred, respectively, as "Perseverance" and "Despair." "His heiress" was soon given up; see letter 2185, note 7, and letter 2647.
6. EBB's father had her possessions placed in storage with Edward Tilbury & Co., 35–49 High Street, Marylebone, after she left 50 Wimpole Street.
7. EBB dined with Miss Trepsack on 14 September 1846, two days after her marriage; see letter 2599.
8. The Hon. and Rev. George Henry Roper-Curzon, 16th Baron Teynham (1798–1889) was a Baptist minister and friend from Herefordshire days. Apparently he had mentioned that a fellow clergyman might be visiting in Italy.
9. Cf. Wordsworth, "Ode: Intimations of Immortality" (1807), line 186.

10. See letter 2630, note 6.
11. Cf. Acts 26:25.
12. She was a family friend (see letter 2560, note 3). It appears that Henrietta was seeking her help in trying to find a suitable position for Surtees so that they could more easily marry.
13. See letter 2630, note 12. For Mr. Surtees see letter 2499, note 3. We have been unable to identify Mrs. Turner mentioned here.

2642. EBB TO MARY RUSSELL MITFORD

Pisa.
Dec 19—— [1846]¹

Ever dearest Miss Mitford, your kindest letter is three times welcome as usual. On the day you wrote it in the frost, I was sitting out of doors, just in my summer mantilla & complaining "of the heat this December"! But woe comes to the discontented. Within these three or four days, we too have had frost, yes, & a little snow .. for the first time, say the Pisans, during five years. Robert says that the mountains are powdered toward Lucca, & I who cannot see the mountains, can see the cathedral .. the Duomo .. how it glitters whitely at the summit between the blue sky & its own walls of yellow marble. Of course I do not stir an inch from the fire, .. yet have to struggle a little against my old languor .. only, you see, this cant last! it is exceptional weather, & up to the last few days, has been divine. And then, after all we talk of frost, my bedroom which has no fire-place shows not one English sign on the window, .. & the air is not *metallic* as in England. The sun, too, is so hot, that the women are seen walking with fur capes & parasols .. a curious combination.

I hope you had your visit from Mr Chorley, & that you both had the usual pleasure from it. Indeed I *am* touched by what you tell me—& *was* touched by his note to my husband, written in the first surprise—& because Robert has the greatest regard for him, besides my own personal reasons, I do count him in the forward rank of our friends. You will hear that he has obliged us by accepting a trusteeship to a settlement, .. forced upon me in spite of certain professions & indispositions of mine—but as my husband's gift, I had no right it appeared, by refusing it to place him in a false position for the sake of what dear Mr Kenyon calls my 'crotchets.' Oh, .. dear Mr Kenyon!- His kindness & goodness to us have been past speaking of, past thanking for .. we can only fall into silence. He has thrust his hand into the fire for us by writing to Papa himself, by taking up the management of my small money-matters when nearer hands let them drop, ... by justifying us with the whole weight of his personal influence—all this in the very face of his own habits & susceptibilities. He has vowed resolved that I shall not miss the offices of father, brother, friend, .. nor the tenderness & sympathy of them all. And this man is called a mere man of the world!—and would be called so rightly if the world were a place of angels!- I shall love him dearly & gratefully to my last breath—we both shall!-

Ah—so you have K with you again, & her child .. now that I am too far away to scold you!- And yet I should not have courage for it perhaps—or I should be content to say as usual "You are *too* good, *too* kind, too forgivingly imprudent"- So tell me—is it true that *bonâ fide* she is your servant again?[2] But in any case, dear, dearest Miss Mitford, you will not lean your trust too heavily where the ice has once failed you. Now, *do not*!- I fear for your generous confidence, & the results in new pain to yourself. As to the poor, poor little child, why there can be no feeling for it but pity & sympathy—the poor little child. Tell me more of it—and of *you especially* .. I miss the report of your health. And tell me if K is really settled with you, & if you are happier & in greater comfort since her return——which will reconcile me, after all, to very questionable processes- Besides .. if you believe in love, for my sake, what should not I believe in for yours. And pray (talking of *that*) receive further into evidence that though Robert & I are deep in the fourth month of wedlock, there has not been a shadow between us, nor a *word*, (and I have observed that all married people confess to "*words*") and that the only change I can lay my finger on in him, is simply & clearly an increase of affection. Now I need not say it, if I did not please—and I should not please, you know, to tell a story. The truth is, that I who always did certainly believe in Love, yet was as great a sceptic as you about the Evidences thereof .. & having held twenty times that Jacob's serving fourteen years for Rachel[3] was not too long by fourteen days, I was not a likely person (with my loathing dread of marriage as a loveless state, & absolute contentment with single life as the alternative to the great majority of marriages) I was not likely to accept a feeling not genuine .. though from the hands of Apollo himself, crowned with his various godships-[4] Especially too, in my position,——I could not, would not, should not have done it. Then, genuine feelings are genuine feelings, & do not pass like a cloud- We are as happy as people can be, I do believe, yet are living in a way to *try* this new relationship of ours .. in the utmost seclusion & perpetual tête á tête .. no amusement nor distraction from without, except some of the very dullest Italian romances which throw us back on the memory of Balzac with reiterated groans. The Italians seem to hang on translations from the French .. as we find from the library .. not merely of Balzac, but Dumas, your Dumas, .. & reaching lower .. long past De Kock .. to the third & fourth rate novelists. What is purely Italian is as far as we have read, purely dull & conventional-There is no breath nor pulse in the Italian genius. M[rs] Jameson writes to us from Florence that in politics & philosophy the people are getting alive—which may be for aught we know to the contrary—the poetry & imagination leave them room enough by immense vacancies.

Yet we delight in Italy, & dream of "pleasures new" for the summer .. *pastures* new,[5] .. I sh^d have said—but it comes to the same thing. The "padrone" in this house, sent us in as a gift (in gracious recognition perhaps of our lawful paying of bills) an immense dish of oranges .. two hanging on a stalk with the green leaves still moist with the morning's dew .. every great orange of twelve or thirteen with its own stalk & leaves. Such a pretty sight! And better oranges, I beg to say, never were eaten, when we are barbarous enough to eat them day by day after our two oclock dinner, softening with the vision of them the winter which has just shown itself. Almost I have been as pleased with these oranges, as I was at Avignon by the *pomegranates* given to me much in the same way. Think of my being singled out of all our caravan of travellers .. Mrs Jameson, & Gerardine Jameson[6] both there .. for that significant gift of the pomegranates! I had never seen one before—& of course proceeded instantly to cut one "deep down the middle"[7]—accepting the omen! Yet in shame & confusion of face I confess to not being able to appreciate it properly. Olives & pomegranates I set on the same shelf .. to be just looked at & called by their names, but by no means eaten bodily.

But you mistake me, dearest friend, about the Blackwood verses. I never thought of ⟨wr⟩iting *applicative poems*—the Heavens forefend!- Only that just *then*, ⟨in⟩ the midst of all the talk, *any* verses of mine sh^d come into print .. & some of them to *that particular effect* .. looked unlucky. I dare say poor Papa (for instance) thought me turned suddenly to brass itself. Well—it is perhaps more my fancy than anything else, & was only an impression, even there. Mr Chorley will tell you of a play of his,[8] which I hope will make its way .. though I do wonder how people can bear to write for the theatres in the present state of things. Robert is busy preparing a new edition of his collected poems[9] which are to be so clear that everyone who has understood them hitherto will lose all distinction. We both mean to be as little idle as possible. Your plan (by Bentley) I do not perfectly measure the length of. Translations are they to be? And if merely issues, are they likely to answer, competing as they must with the Belgic books?[10] The 'Mystères' & the 'Juifs', I have seen translated & *illustrated*, each in one volume. 'Notre Dame' too, has had a *course* in England already. Probably you mean *purified French editions* .. is *that* it? And if so, you will have hard work, I think, & satisfactorily *resultive* work only in a few cases, with the very best books—with the 'Mystères' certainly not. You might select easily though from George Sand—there is the "Maîtres Mosaistes," to begin with- With Eugene Sue .. yes, Jean Cavalier-[11] But you w^d have to read with such a different mind & aim, to read everything over again- I, for one, do not pretend to remember what 'la prude Angleterre'[12] would think "moral", and in spite of what you say of Leghorn,[13] I have not seen a French book since I came here, though translations enough are down in our catalogue.

We do not even see a newspaper .. a Galignani .. which everybody else sees. I wish I c̹ do something for you, &, for myself, see Balzac's 'last'– And after all, to see *you*, would be best of all. Write to me often, & tell me of you in every detail. We have heard that report of Moore contradicted.[14] If true, how strange that another poet should go drivelling to the eternal silence. Then, poor M.̹ Darley![15] May God bless you, beloved friend! We shall meet one day in joy, I do hope—& then you will love my husband for his own sake, as for mine, you do not hate him now–

Your ever affectionate
EBB—as ever.

Address, on integral page: Miss Mitford, / Three Mile Cross, / near Reading.
Publication: EBB-MRM, III, 197–201.
Manuscript: Wellesley College.

1. Year determined from the Brownings' residence in Pisa in December 1846.
2. Miss Mitford had difficulty trying to replace her former maid Kerenhappuch (generally referred to as "K"), who had been dismissed in 1844 when she had an illegitimate child. When "K" married in 1851, it was not Ben Kirby, the father of her children, but Sam Sweetman, the gardener/handyman who replaced Kirby, with whom she had another child. "K" and her husband remained in Miss Mitford's service until her death in 1855.
3. Cf. Genesis 29: 18–30.
4. Apollo, the representation of perfect young manhood, was the god of the sun, of poetry, of music, of art, and of the healing arts.
5. Milton, "Lycidas" (1638), line 193.
6. Mrs. Jameson's niece Gerardine Bate (afterwards Macpherson) was often introduced by Mrs. Jameson as Gerardine Jameson.
7. "Lady Geraldine's Courtship," line 165.
8. Presumably his tragedy *Duchess Eleanour*, which he had been working on during his autumn holiday abroad. The play was somewhat inspired by Chorley's impressions of Charlotte Cushman's performances in London in 1846, and "the part of his heroine was designed with express accommodation to her *rôle*" (*Henry Fothergill Chorley: Autobiography, Memoir, and Letters,* comp. H.G. Hewlett, 1873, II, 129). Nevertheless, *Duchess Eleanour* was not produced until 1854, when Charlotte Cushman was again performing in England.
9. See letter 2637, note 1.
10. It is unclear what Miss Mitford was proposing. From the context it seems likely that she hoped to produce a selection of French writers similar to her volume of Dumas; however, there is no evidence that her plans were ever realized.
11. A translation of Eugene Sue's *Jean Cavalier* (1840) would not be published until 1849, in three volumes. Translations of his *Les Mystères de Paris* (1844) had appeared in 1844 and 1846, both in single-volume editions and with illustrations, and a translation of *Le Juif errant* (1845) was also published in 1846. At least four different translations of Hugo's *Notre Dame de Paris* (1831) had been published by this time, and George Sand's *Les Maîtres mosaïstes* (1838) had been translated by Elizabeth A. Ashurst in 1844.
12. An allusion to the morality of "prudish England," of which EBB approved, as opposed to her disdain for the "intellectual narrowness" of a single English prude (see letter 1764, note 6).
13. Miss Mitford had evidently suggested the possibility of Leghorn as a source of French books for the Brownings, but EBB explains the difficulty of such a plan in letter 2654.
14. See letter 2513, note 5.
15. George Darley, Irish poet, died on 23 November 1846. He had corresponded with Miss Mitford, and she described his death as "even more lonely than his life," referring to his brother's death in Ireland at the same time as his own (Mitford, p. 509).

No. 2643   21 December [1846]   85

2643. EBB TO HUGH STUART BOYD

[Pisa]
Dec. 21. [1846][1]

You must let me tell you my dearest M.[r] Boyd, that I dreamed of you last night & that you were looking very well in my dream, & that you told me to break a crust from a loaf of bread which lay by you on the table .. which I accept on recollection as a sacramental sign between us, of peace & affection. Was'nt it strange that I should dream so of you? Yet no!—thinking awake of you the sleeping thoughts come naturally. Believe of me this Christmas-time as indeed at everytime, that I do not forget you, & that all the distance & change of country can make no difference. Understand too (for *that* will give pleasure to your goodness) that I am very happy, & not unwell,—though it is almost christmas. It is a little cold just now .. but, until these few days, I have been walking out every morning, & sitting out of doors in the sun, and I hope not to lose much strength by the temporary change of weather— Even now, the sun shines so hotly, as to inconvenience the walkers in it,—and I thankfully admit that the climate, upon the whole, is more qualified to do me good, than I had been led to hope.

Does Arabel go to see you properly, .. that is, frequently? It is a grief to me that she should be treated coldly on my account; and the injustice is *rampant*, as she knew nothing, you know, of the marriage. For myself, I am wounded, .. yet feel myself *justified*, both by the hardness *there*, & the tenderness *here*. Completely spoilt & happy, I may write myself down. Now, everything I ever said to you of my husband, seems cold & inadequate. He is my compensation for the bitterness of life, as God knows & *knew*.

Dearest friend—are you well & in good spirits? Think of me over the Cyprus, between the cup & the lip .. though bad things are said to fall out so. We have, instead of Cyprus, *Montepulciano*, the famous "King of wine," crowned King, you remember, by the grace of a poet![2] Your Cyprus, however, keeps supremecy over me, & will not abdicate the divine right of being associated with you. I speak of wine—but we live here the most secluded, quiet life possible,—reading & writing & talking of all things in Heaven & earth & a little besides, .. & sometimes even laughing as if we had twenty people to laugh with us—or rather .. *had'nt*. We know not a creature, I am happy to say, .. except an Italian professor (of the university here) who called on us the other evening & praised aloud the scholars of England. "English Latin was best" he said, "and English Greek foremost." Do you clap your hands?

The new pope[3] is more liberal than popes in general, and people write odes to him in consequence.

Robert is going to bring out a new edition of his collected poems, and you are not to read any more, if you please, till this is done. I heard of Carlyle's saying the other day "that he hoped more from Robert Browning, for the people of England, than from any living English writer"[4]——which pleased me of course. I am just sending off an anti-slavery poem[5] for America .. too ferocious, perhaps, for the Americans to publish: but they asked for a poem & shall have it.

If I ask for a letter, shall I have it, I wonder? Remember me & love me a little—& pray for me, dearest friend, and believe how gratefully & ever affectionately

I am your Elibet–

.. Though Robert always calls me *Ba*, & thinks it the prettiest name in the world!!! Which is a proof, you will say, not only of blind love but of deaf love– I hope Jane is well—& your Toby besides. Flush has grown insolent, & barks when he wants a door opened. Do you see Nelly Bordman? She has been very affectionate to me.

Address, on integral page: H S Boyd Esq.re / 24 (a) Grove End Road / St John's Wood.
Publication: EBB-HSB, pp. 282–283.
Manuscript: Wellesley College.

1. Year determined from the Brownings' residence in Pisa in December 1846.
2. Francesco Redi, *Bacco in Toscana* (1685), line 972.
3. Giovanni Maria Mastai-Ferretti, Pius IX (1792–1878), known as "Pio Nono," ascended the papal throne shortly after the death of Gregory XVI in June 1846. He began his papacy by granting a general political amnesty and called for a spiritual revival in the various religious orders. These early liberal acts identified him as a reformer, and EBB joined those who hoped that he would offer moral leadership for the national movement, but he was unable to meet demands quickly or broadly enough. EBB's early optimism for his attempts at progress soon gave way to disenchantment and disappointment.
4. See letter 2630, note 10.
5. See note 1 in the following letter.

2644. EBB TO JAMES RUSSELL LOWELL

[Pisa]
[Postmark: 23 December 1846]

Cover sheet only.[1]

Address, on cover sheet: J R Lowell Esq.re / Cambridge, / Massachusetts, / United States. / Amérique.
Publication: None traced.
Manuscript: Armstrong Browning Library.

1. EBB enclosed her poem "The Runaway Slave at Pilgrim's Point" which remains with the cover sheet. In a three-page covering letter (since lost, but described by Goodspeed's, catalogue date unknown), EBB mentions Lowell's *Conversations on Some*

No. 2645 [24–25] December [1846] 87

of the Old Poets. She also expresses concern that he "perhaps will think [her contribution is written] too bitterly and passionately for publication in your country." EBB had mentioned her intention to write this poem in December 1845; see letter 2122, note 4. It is of interest to note that Thomas Wentworth Higginson quoted from memory a passage that may have appeared in this letter, when he indicated EBB said she had come to "life and light and Italy and more happiness than a woman ought, perhaps, to speak of, except when she thanks God" ("A Great Poet in her Prime," *Book News*, March 1906, p. 457).

2645. EBB TO ARABELLA MOULTON-BARRETT

Pisa–
[24–25] Dec– [1846][1]

My beloved Arabel, your letter .. your letters .. for Mr Boyd's envelope counts .. are three times welcome. In the first place, pray believe that I do not keep a "separate account" for all manner of maladies, & that I tell you honestly the precise truth about myself .. for better or worse. I dont tell you that I am ill, because, I *am not ill*—there's the satisfactory reason. As to all that story of the morphine, I told it to Nelly Bordman, in consequence of her sapient interest in drugs—it was a passing inconvenience, just proving that I could'nt do without the medecine, with all my arrogance of health,—& not otherwise regarded even by Robert, who if my foot goes to sleep, gets the headache with the fright of it, & who certainly, before the cause was ascertained of that sudden change in me, was seriously uneasy. The right quantity of morphine being restored, I was as well as possible again, & have had no more reason to complain of Italian pharmacy. Oh—do not think, Arabel, of sending any medecines from Bell or elsewhere. I should have asked you if it had been necessary, but it is, in fact, most unnecessary. Our Italian explained afterward, with a multitude of apologies, that the English preparation of morphine being nearly always of an inferior strength to what they are able to procure here, he conscientiously thought it right to make allowances for that difference—! Which was wrong, of course! In every case he sh^d have explained the matter to Robert! I doubt the motive a little. Still, it has been right ever since, & Dr Cook[2] observed to Mrs Jameson that the people here were in general distinguished for the excellence of their drugs & the fidelity of their attention to prescriptions, & that in his opinion, the man was startled at the quantity in my case.– This quantity I am diminishing gradually—a little interrupted by the late cold, .. when I took more of course to stop the evil symptoms– While there was frost, I did not leave these two rooms, the bedroom opening on the sittingroom, & wore the red chinese crape shawl crossed over my chest, undressing & dressing by the fire here. A little languid & uncomfortable in the throat & chest, I felt during that time, .. but it did not last long, .. & now I am revived & enjoying the thaw—and you will believe that I am well when I tell you that I am going out tonight at eleven to the cathedral to witness the great ceremonies of the season .. It is so warm that Wilson with whom the casting vote was left (Robert did not dare to take the responsibility. Oh, you would laugh to see how he goes to consult Wilson on every occasion about me,—she is the Delphic oracle!) Wilson decided that I could'nt be hurt by this warm air, particularly as the cathedral is so near, & I could wear my respirator- He wants to carry me under his cloak .. he is sure he could carry me perfectly well!- Which I decline with ever so much gratitude, for myself & him- And think of my going out to walk at eleven oclock at night—Christmas eve too- I am sitting on a stool (while writing this) a stool which M[rs] Jameson made for me .. between the tail of Robert's coat and the fire, as he sits at the table preparing the new edition of his poems- After tea, it is, with us, & before supper .. & here we shall sit till eleven oclock .. which is quite contrary to our usual habits- The fire is nearly on a level with the floor .. my knees being higher .. Now fancy us- My thoughts went to you & I was forced to write, to draw you closer to us & wish the right Christmas wishes! What are you doing, I wonder, at this moment? At dinner, you are, perhaps— taking wine with M[r] Bell! My poor darling Arabel!- I *know* you miss me,— for with all I have gained here, (which seems to me everyday a greater gain) *I* miss *you*, & bear the thought of you close to my deepest affections, never to be cast out while I have life & reason. How perfect & generous you have been to me—how true & tender!- Yes, let me always be in your prayers- Perhaps it is to them, that I owe all this joy & satisfaction- You are doing me good as usual, even at this distance!- May God bless you!—and my dearest Henrietta whom I love so, .. and all of you whom I must continue to love. I hope, Arabel, that you are right in your assurance, & that there is exaggeration in M[r] Boyd's statement-

⟨...⟩[3]

We have just had such a kind letter from M[rs] Jameson, who having been snowed up at Florence, is just about to set off to Rome. She says that she reckons among her best blessings of the year, having won the friendship & intimacy of "two such Hearts"--think of my reciting compliments to you like a paternoster!—only she loves us both, I know, & I like you to understand it. Her eyes were full of tears when she took leave of me, & Robert, who took her to the railroad was cordially *kissed*, at parting, both by herself & Gerardine! I assure you he was .. She says that Lady Byron says that she (Lady B) has had a letter from Joanna Baillie, "full of interest" about us—& Lady Byron herself (I told you) has taken us up with both hands. Think of M[r] Forster (of the Examiner) writing to Robert at *Vaucluse*!- So the letter has of course been waiting there these three months- I laughed so when I heard it .. could not help laughing— If you knew what a place Vaucluse is! A chasm between two black rocks with a black face of another rock shutting it up, out of which rushes, rushes, & roars the immortal fountain! There are a few caves here & there, to be sure, .. and a little inn at the outer end, like the smallest village-alehouse you ever saw in your life. Now think of a man's understanding that we had taken up our abode at Vaucluse! One supposition is that we being perfectly & most poetically mad, to his mind, he fancied we had gone *tout de bon*[4] to live in a cave. We have sent to Avignon for the letter. Dear M? Kenyon says that "a new pleasure awaits me in England .. the finding in how strong an affection & a no less strong respect, my husband is held by his many friends." But I need scarcely go to England for it—such proofs of it come to us day by day. When I go to England it will rather be to talk to you & see your faces, you who love me, & whom I love continually,—and we shall accept dearest Trippy's invitation some day, tell her with a kiss from me. Is she with you? Why do you not mention her— M? Kenyon says too .. "How you will love your sister in law when you know her!"– He speaks warmly of all Robert's family. Also he talks of coming to see us before very long—not this winter exactly .. say nothing about it!— and of M? Chorley's coming with him. Is it not too late in the year for the Martins to travel so far, by the way, as this Italy? They always set out too late. We shall be very pleased if we do see them, appreciating them as they deserve .. *I*, most affectionately,—and Robert, delighted with the letter M? Martin wrote to me. *So* characteristic, *that* was!—they have been true, stedfast friends to me! I have not written to Bummy yet. I shall write in time, & there is time enough. Did I tell you that Miss Bayley said of us in a note she sent to M? Kenyon, that "surely our marriage was made in Heaven.'[']!—which I believe too, in the sense of its being a providential grace & gift .. to *me*, at least!—& when I hear Robert speak of his "unutterable happiness", & *feel* that instead of decreasing, his attachment to me deepens day by day, I take courage to believe that so, it is, to us both. If ever I wish for you & Henrietta (and I do persist in wishing it for you, notwithstanding your being an infidel on some points & laughing when you sh:d look grave) if ever I wish for you both an equal happiness .. I am stopped by the persuasion that there never was nor can be such another husband as mine, giving up his whole life & soul & tenderness– Why, where are such men in the world? M? Boyd says rightly that I owe everything to him—a debt of inexpressible gratitude. When I write of it all, I give you but faint ideas .. as I had myself before I married. I knew then, though loving him enough to act as I did, only *something* of what he was, & of the happy atmosphere into which I was raising myself. Thank God for me always, beloved Arabel—my own thanks seem too cold .. too weak.

Christmas Day– Well! we went last night to the Duomo (the cathedral) & did not come home till nearly one in the morning– Now I am tired, very tired .. but have caught no cold, which indeed was impossible with all the precautions taken. When Robert found that he *was'nt* allowed to carry me, he wanted me to put his cloak over my head & wear it—& tried the effect of it, making me look "just like a little monk"– But the cloak was too heavy for me to carry .. I begged to eschew it—so we settled at last that he sh^d wear his own cloak & make room for me under it—which was perfectly effectual. Fancy me, respirator-bound, shawled & furred, & then covered with the cloak from head to foot .. face & all. I could not see a ray of light— only he made me a crevice just as we got to the Leaning Tower, that I might see it by moonlight—for the rest .... "here's a step .. a second .. three .. four," .. I was as blind as THAT! Yet the air was perfectly mild: with a good deal of soft west-wind though!– The Duomo was very striking as we entered it, illuminated from end to end .. Galileo's great lamp[5] glittering with a starry splendour .. then the choir & the organ!– I was impressed for the first ten minutes! Afterwards it grew all weariness of the flesh & no edification of the spirit, certainly. I sate on that hard oaken seat under one of the columns, till my back & head ached one against another,—Robert whispering at intervals "Are you tired, Ba? oh, so am I!" We were both following humbly in the steps of the Pisan martyr San Torpé.[6] We did not manage ourselves as well as two signoras on their knees beside us, who were laughing & talking to one another with all their might. Nothing does strike me so much in these Catholic churches, as the want of all reverence & decency ever in the people. Call them congregation—call them rather promenaders. In the cathedral last night .. it was a grand religious festival, observe, & everybody in Pisa who c^d go, I suppose, thought it a religious duty to go. Well—the people walked up & down & talked loud while the service proceeded—loud enough for me to hear three yards off—or else they stood in groups & talked. The people who did'nt talk, stared. Here & there, somebody was kneeling down .. and the chance was that the kneeler was talking too, .. as in the case of our neighbours—but really scarcely anybody knelt anywhere. They just walked, & walked, & talked & talked. A dog that sate in the midst with his eyes gravely fixed on the altar, Robert pointed out as the most reverent member of the congregation .. "That's a new picture" .. "C'è un nuovo quadro," .. "put up today" .. I heard said several times—& then, the criticisms!—just as if it were a picture put up in a dining room– The service in the meantime was carried on at the altar with the usual hoarse chanting of old priests, & curtsies & gestures of various sorts—all magnificent & feeble .. saying nothing to the senses even,—which mine c^d be impressed by. If they would have let the organ & the choir sound & sing on, & the incense burn .. I liked that cloud of incense floating about the brazen crucifix .. we might have felt an effect—but the priests dispossessed us of our own imaginations even!- At the moment of the uplifting of the host, .. for that one *moment* .. there was attention & silence, & everyone knelt or stood still. That one moment of devotion was the only one for the *people*, observe- I have looked everywhere to see more than this & cannot see it. In the French churches it did not surprise me, but here it does—and how English protestants can come here, & ever be English Puseyites afterwards I cannot understand or hope to understand. Wilson went with us last night as she wished it, & Flush was shut up in my room (poor Flush,—I c^d hear him begin to cry) because we feared a crowd .. but in the great cathedral there was no crowd—oh, plenty of room to walk about! If Stormie saw these things as I see them, he w^d be surprised I think. We have tried again & again to hear a sermon preached—but it seems the most difficult thing possible, to hear a sermon. The giving of religious instruction in that form, seems shrunk from- Only once, Robert entered some church by accident, as he was taking his walk, and came on a monk, who was preaching- Did I tell you that? and how the people hissed at the end, some of them, & some clapped their hands? I am not apt, you know, to be narrow, & attach undue importance to unessential doctrines .. much less to forms—but the state of things in this Italy does seem to me most melancholy,—melancholy beyond all my expectations. They have the sun, & no light. Oh, such a day we have today, for Christmas Day! So *hot* it is—the air so soft, the sunshine so bright!- But I am too tired with last night's great deed, to go out this morning- I must forego my walk. Robert has returned Mr Surtees's card .. just the card- Mr Surtees showed no sort of *empressement*,[7] about coming to see us, so we may do as we please I suppose- Mr Irving had a card too .. but meant for a visit, that was, .. & he was not at home. How detestable it w^d be if we were to be drawn out at everyone's ⟨★★★⟩

Publication: None traced.
Manuscript: Berg Collection.

    1. Dated by EBB's references to Christmas Eve and Christmas Day. Year is determined from the Brownings' residence in Pisa in December 1846.
    2. Francis Cook (1810?-1903) took his qualifications from the University of Edinburgh in 1836, and was the author of *A Practical Treatise on Pulmonary Consumption, Its Pathology, Diagnosis, and Treatment* (1842), as referred to by RB in letter 2655. He returned to England and conducted a successful practice at Cheltenham from 1849 until his retirement.
    3. Someone other than EBB has marked out eleven and one-half lines of the letter at the bottom of the second page and the top of the third.
    4. "Really," or "for good and all."
    5. "The bronze lamp suspended in the nave, and of fine workmanship, is said by some to be by *Tacca*; by others, by Vicenzo Possanti. According to the well-known story, this lamp suggested to Galileo the theory of the application of the pendulum" (Murray's *Hand-Book for Travellers in Northern Italy*, 1847, pp. 445-446).
    6. San Torpes was a 1st-century Christian martyr under Nero and is one of the patrons of the Republic of Pisa.

7. "Eagerness," "enthusiasm," or "urgency."

2646. EBB TO ANNE THOMSON

Pisa, Collegio Ferdinando
Decr 26– [1846][1]

My dear Miss Thomson

Your kindness in writing to me on the occasion of my marriage, added much to the pleasant & grateful sense of the sympathy you have given me on other subjects & so long. I have been on the very point several times, of saying this to you, but once or twice have been prevented, & thus drawn into the procrastination, which does all manner of evil certainly, but does *not* mean thanklessness from me to you .. cannot. I never was thankless to you for the kind feelings you gave me, & least I could be so now, when my dear friend Miss Bayley's kindness to me, makes my heart overflow upon you who are the nearest to her– If not for your own sake yet for hers .. but for your own sake too—let me say that I thank you warmly.

You will care to hear that I continue to be well and very happy .. happier than I ever dreamed of being .. as far back as when I had lived a little in the world, & was able to dream still. We like our seclusion here at Pisa, though rather extreme perhaps, for people who want to see Italy & the Italians .. for I might as well almost (for the world-seeing) be shut up in my old room—so very, very quiet we are .. knowing not a creature. We have modern Italian books from the library & are at liberty to abuse them righteously, .. & can look out of the window at the Duomo & Leaning Tower, .. and on mild days (which are in the majority) I am able to walk out, & watch the lizards in the walls, & see the ceremonies in the churches .. the lizards being the more rational of the two .. lizards & ecclesiastics. All is delightful to me .. and the quietness, to us both—but in the spring, we mean to learn something from the *faces* of these Italians, from living Italy, & see the country better,—& we have plans of visiting Florence & Venice & Rome .. what names!– Dear Mrs Jameson, whom we love with good reason, wrote to me from Florence two days ago, & was then snowed up fairly, & prevented from beginning her journey to Rome. We have had snow here even .. but it did not last long, .. and on this Christmas night when I write to you the air is like June's—. What a climate! My health is much improved, & I escaped suffering from the week's cold weather we had, by some simple precautions & by the strength I brought to meet it– Perhaps I could not walk so far now as before that interval of cold .. but otherwise I am well.

And you? and your book?[2] If you have the goodness to write to me ever, I hope you will tell me all about yourself. Shall you be in London this year?

Dearest M! Kenyon, that prince of friends, has been more than himself to me on the late occasion, & dearly & gratefully & more than ever I love him.

And now my dear Miss Thomson, as you have heard my husband speak of *me*, will you hear *me* speak of *him*, & offer you his regards, with most affectionate thoughts & wishes

from your friend
Elizabeth Barrett Browning.

Address, on integral page: Miss Thomson / Primrose.
Publication: Manuscripta, October 1960, pp. 164-166.
Manuscript: Biblioteca Apostolica Vaticana.

1. Year determined by the Brownings' residence in Collegio Ferdinando in December 1846.
2. A reference to Miss Thomson's "Classical Album," for which EBB had provided translations (see Appendix IV in vol. 10); however, this projected work was never completed.

2647. EBB TO HENRIETTA MOULTON-BARRETT

Collegio Ferdinando
Jan? 7– [1847][1]

My dear dearest Henrietta, Praise me as the best letter writer in the world of frosts– If I had been with you, I should have been frozen white .. thrown out of use, as the pipes of the Shower bath .. Such accounts as the newspapers give of the cold in England![2]—for we see the newspapers now—so much the more credit to *me*! I have teased & entreated Robert for two things ever since we have been here—to have a piano, and to subscribe to a better library than the purely Italian one, .. somewhere where we could have French books & newspapers– The last point is gained at last—through my perseverance, & through the persistent dulness of these modern Italian writers who have'nt a soul among them all– If it were not for the Bible & Shakespeare, we might say seriously that we had not seen a real book since our arrival in Pisa, until my great victory a few days ago, of the new subscription– And now Robert is as pleased as I am, after all his jokes against "his little Ba-lamb" (one of my names!) "Who in spite of her innocense, could'nt live without wicked books by Eugene Sue." Now, we have every evening at five oclock, just as we sit down to coffee, a french newspaper .. the Siècle—and besides, Robert when he goes to the post, may have a glance, if he feels inclined, at the English & German newspapers—& then he brings home both in his pocket. We never see a creature, & to talk for four & twenty hours together, would be rather exhausting—& one is not always in a humour for writing prose or rhyme. As to the piano, I begin to despair. I was foolish enough to say that I did not play—and the idea of even *seeming to have anything for himself,* ...

(though I have talked myself hoarse about my love of music & so on) is quite enough to make Robert turn back determinedly. He calls it a foolish expense, & wont listen to it– Such pleasure it would be to me to hear him– M.rs Jameson told me that his playing was "full of science & feeling," which I can easily believe, for he could not do a thing moderately well. By the way we heard from her, two days ago, from Florence, on the verge of setting out for Rome—the most disconsolate letter, possible!- She had suffered herself to be drawn into the English society in Florence, & had lost time & patience, & gained nothing .. except the acquaintance of two interesting foreigners whom she considered unfit for Gerardine to associate with– She is, of course, particular about Gerardine—or she herself would have enjoyed it– The English seem to have made a most *tedious* & dull impression– "Miss Garrow spoke of" me "with enthusiasm"—and M.rs Stisted[3] meant to come to Pisa on purpose to have the sight of US—you ought to have seen Robert's & my consternation. Wilson has received "instructions" accordingly. When we go to Florence, .. & early in April we turn our faces that way, .. it will be in the most royal state of incognito– We mean to cut everybody we ever knew, so that nobody need be offended. Robert works himself up into a fine frenzy in talking of the horrors of mixed society, & sometimes exhorts me just as if I wanted exhortation– "Those people will spoil all our happiness, if we once let them in, you will see! If you speak of your health & save yourself on that plea, they will sieze upon *me*—oh, dont I know them?" He walks up & down the room, thoroughly worked up!- "But, dearest," say I, with my remarkable placidity, .. "*I* am not going to let anybody in! If one of us lets them in, it will be Wilson, most probably—! but we need not suffer it—I desire it quite as little as you." —"There is that coarse, vulgar M.rs Trollope– I do hope, Ba, if you dont wish to give me the greatest pain, that you wont receive that vulgar, pushing, woman who is not fit to speak to you." —"Well .. now we are at M.rs Trollope! You will have your headache in a minute— now do sit down, & let us talk of something else, & be quite sure that if we get into such scrapes, it wont be my fault." —I assure you I dont exaggerate his visionary fears of 'the world', & 'society'- What makes *him* perfectly happy is to draw his chair next mine & to let the time slip away. We should like to know one or two Italians, to have an opportunity of speaking the language, .. but that is the whole of the ambition, as to things of that sort. The weather is mild, but too damp underfoot for me to walk, & I keep by the fire, feeling very contented & very well. Surely it must strike some of those who are angry with me, that by staying in England through this severe winter, I should have probably been put an end to .. & *certainly* have lost all the advantages & strength which the summer & mild season before it, had allowed me to receive– Only that is no argument to those who wish me dead!-

Dearest Henrietta, I could not hold out against poor Bummy when the old year ended, so on the first day of the new I wrote to her not an unaffectionate letter certainly– At the same time I told her the truth as I understood the truth– I was as sincere as possible. With regard to you I just said that you were not in the least a likely person "to follow in my footsteps",[4] & that whatever you did or did not do, every usual form of respect & affection would be strictly observed by you– When I had done my letter I thought that I w^d enter on the subject a little more, & wrote on a paper my opinion specifically upon persons & rights .. which, when written, I took fright & burnt .. I did not dare send it, lest I might do some harm in an intention of doing good. I thought to myself, "Why Bummy will not take up my view of this question for anything I can say—she has lived too long in a different mould: but she may make some mischief perhaps, with as good an intention as mine, & therefore" ... So I burnt what I had written. I cant think who can send her such accounts of you .. *all* that absurdity about 'trousseaus' & the rest– Louisa cannot, you know. It is also a complete mystery to me how Anne Gent had the information about me, which assuredly she had .. since Minny was not the informant. Could Arlette have said anything to Patten?[5] but that is improbable too– Bummy talks decidedly of coming to Italy, & all on account of *Arlette's singing*. Also Jane talks of it .. of either Nice or Florence for the winter, & probably Florence. Do write to me soon, & let me hear how you have lived lately & whether my darling Arabel has her room yet, & whether Papa is kinder to her. I want to know too of other things ... but I dare not hope that my brothers will accept the peace offering I sent them. I suppose they mean to salute me with the point of the sword for the rest of my life. As to making friends with *me*, with an "avaunt" to *mine*, they have better taste than to dream of such an impossible thing. Does Alfred get on in the railroad?[6] Has Occy made any good drawings lately? Did George go to Cambridge? How is the Law, too, with both him & Sette– And tell me of Henry. As to dear Stormie, I do trust that he has other plans than for that dreadful Jamaica[.] I love them all very dearly .. better than any of them loved me ever, or we should not be thus. We were talking this morning at breakfast of O'Connell & the Irish, & I was describing Stormie's enthusiasm for both–[7] "Indeed" said I, "he is so generous & tenderhearted, that he naturally takes the part of every party or person attacked by others– He defends *everyone* who is *accused*." —"Everyone, except YOU" ... observed Robert gravely. I could not speak a word; my heart was full. The observation was too true a one, indeed. From Stormie, the pain has been more disappointing than from some others, for I could not have expected this from *him* .. but rather quite, *quite*, an opposite course.

How is Minny? Do you take as much care of her as you can, & make her rest– I think it is unkind, tell her, that she should refuse to lie down properly. The new maid, I have taken into my head, is not a pleasant person. Why do you keep her, in that case? Give my love to dear Minny. I am very glad that she took my carpet. Remember to tell me the colour of the drawingroom curtains & paper &c, that I may conjure you up properly. Has Papa made it up with Alfred? is it a settled thing? Question after question, I could ask you. So Matilda Bell[8] is going to be married to a man with a *purse*. So much the better if she likes it, but the transferred heart .. the family inheritance .. I wonder she *should* like. Wilson fancied, too, that she was *inclined* to another quarter, herself. Tell me of the Barretts—I heard that Maria had a sixth child–[9] Poor children, poor mother! He ought to get something to do on the foreign railroads, which w:d not be difficult. M:r Bell gives up his heiress then, & is not thinner for it, I dare say. Has dearest Trippy been with you during the Christmas? My love to her & ten kisses—and tell me how she looks & whether she has given another festival since the one you told me of .. & how the lodgers on the lower floor go on, & whether she still likes her house. So you go to church to hear matins, just as much as ever. I agree that there is no harm in going to church. Otherwise, *we* are strongly against every pretence or pretext of Puseyism—Robert *so* strongly, that I wish sometimes to "pit" him against M:r Bevan—only .. *poor M:r Bevan*! He understands the scriptures thoroughly & learnedly, & begins by denying that there is any Priesthood but Christ's, or any christianity apart from the doctrine of justification by faith as taught by the first reformers .. then wishes for more Martin Luthers, & disdains all saints like San Ranieri & San Torpé![10] —thanks God that he is likely to die a dissenter .. then admits that, as a body, the dissenters have quite as many faults as any other class of christian men. What he likes *alone* among all the catholic forms, is the carrying of the crucifix before the corpse, in the many ghastly funerals which pass our windows. He thinks it significant & touching that the sign of faith should precede the dumb Dead, & "would rather like it" to be done in his own case. The funerals throng past our windows– The monks, sometimes all in black,— & sometimes all in white (according to the order) chant in a train, carrying torches .. & on the bier, comes the corpse .. open faced .. except just a veil. At first, we both used to rush to see the sight—but the horror (my old horror, tell Arabel) grew too strong for me soon: & he feels it too, & attends to me often when I say, "Oh, *dont* go to the window." But sometimes he cries out .. "I cant help it, Ba—it *draws* me". Such horrible, hoarse chanting, it is– Like the croaking of death itself.

Give my love to Susan & Surtees Cook—they always remember me– Does he go again to Taunton this spring? does he dine with you often? Tell me everything– Have you heard from Lady Bolingbroke & is it good news? Be wiser than I have been if you can, & give no occasion for conversation. My thoughts are with you at the tenderest & faithfullest! when they are prayers. I pray for you & my dearest Arabel, that you may be as happy as I am (or nearly!) as far as personal position goes, & happier in other respects. I say "nearly", because I do not in my conscience believe that there can be

No. 2647   7 January [1847]   97

another husband like mine—it is such a perpetual & unexceptional tenderness. Indeed all women might not like *the excess* .. I do not know. If you ever thought I was likely to *be afraid*, that is a mistake at any rate .. there is on each side, the most absolute confidence– How God has blessed me infinitely, after all the trial!—— I look at myself in wonder.

Always I pour out the coffee now .. it is my only "active duty" I think— that, & to keep Flush in sight, to prevent his barking.

Dearest Henrietta .. or dearest Arabel .. if you will send Mrs Jameson's mittens .. having found them .. (those she gave me) together with Arabel's picture, & the *Serpent locket* .. left somewhere on my table .. under cover (making a small parcel of them) to Sarianna Browning, she will let us have them together with a book of Robert's which he requires for his new edition. She sends the book, understand, .. & will enclose the other things from you– Do not delay– Miss Browning, New Cross, Hatcham, Surrey. The full direction– There is a M·S. book too of mine .. left behind—but I am afraid I cant describe it– It has some translations from Petrarch.[11] Never mind, if you cant find it. Why is there no letter today? Write, write, & at large, & in detail. Believe that I am with you both in my heart– Dont grow thin again, dearest Henrietta– Also, keep up the fire! Tell Arabel (in sympathy) that *I*, too, sleep in the most uncomfortable of beds .. stuffed with orange tree shavings—but I sleep well notwithstanding, & have a regular siesta after dinner. Mind! Arabel *did'nt tell me that her bed was uncomfortable.* You may send me a yard or two of elastic (black) for sandals—but I dont care much– May God bless you, dearest & best .. both of you! Robert's "dearest love" (his own words) to you both.

                            Your ever & ever attached
                                   Ba–

Love to Lizzie—dear Lizzie! tell her, my "portrait".[12]
     I am glad of the good news of Crow.[13] *Say whether I may safely direct to you in Wimpole Street.*

Address, on integral sheet: Miss Barrett / 50 Wimpole Street.
Publication: TTUL, pp. 16–26.
Source: Transcript in editors' file.

     1. Year determined by the Brownings' residence in Collegio Ferdinando in January 1847.
     2. *The Times* for 16 December 1846 reported that "the frost continues with increasing severity."
     3. Clotilde Elizabeth Stisted (1790?–1868) was the author of *Letters from the Bye-Ways of Italy* (1845), illustrated by her husband Colonel Henry Stisted (1786?–1859), and published by subscription in support of an English Chapel at Bagni di Lucca. The Stisteds lived in the Villa Brodrick at Bagni di Lucca. She had met EBB some twenty years earlier, probably at Malvern through Lady Knowles, a mutual friend. Mrs. Stisted also knew EBB's aunt Jane Hedley.
     4. i.e., to marry without her father's permission.

5. Martha Patten (b. 1804) and Anne Gent, both originally from Northumberland, were lady's maids to EBB's aunt "Bummy" and cousin Arlette.

6. Alfred had taken a position with the Great Western Railway in late 1845. A sketchbook containing drawings of his fellow workers has survived; see *Reconstruction*, H101.

7. Charles John's ("Storm") admiration of O'Connell is noted in letters 1124 and 1292, and his kind and generous spirit is mentioned in letters 1105, 1113, and 2179. He left for Jamaica in early 1847 where he remained until after his father's death in 1857.

8. Matilda Jane Bell (b. 1808) married John Moore on 12 January 1847 at Long Houghton, Northumberland. Matilda Bell was the sister of Susanna Maria Bell referred to in the following note.

9. Dulcibella Barrett (1846–79), the third daughter and sixth child of Samuel Goodin Barrett (1812–76) and Susanna Maria Barrett (*née* Bell, 1816–1904), was born on 11 November 1846.

10. For San Torpes, see letter 2645, note 6. San Ranieri of Pisa (1117–61) was the well-educated son of a wealthy Pisan merchant. After a pilgrimage to the Holy Land, Ranieri returned to Pisa where his successful healings and conversions resulted in his eventual canonization, probably by Alexander III. Ranieri became the patron saint of Pisa in the 13th century, and according to Murray's *Hand-Book for Travellers in Northern Italy* (1847), "there is a triennial *fête* in honour of him called the *Illuminaria*, early in June, when the whole of the Lung'Arno is illuminated. It is a beautiful sight" (p. 452). Murray's *Hand-Book* also notes that the transept in the cathedral is "called the *Crociera di San Ranieri*," (p. 444), and there are various representations of his life and works by Simone Memmi in the Campo Santo (p. 452).

11. A notebook containing numerous manuscripts by EBB, including translations from Petrarch sold as part of lot 111 in *Browning Collections* (see *Reconstruction*, D1422, D1247–1248, and D1252–1253).

12. EBB's cousin, Georgiana Elizabeth ("Lizzie") Barrett, was the subject of EBB's poem "A Portrait," which appeared in *Poems* (1844).

13. Perhaps news of a pregnancy.

2648. EBB TO CORNELIUS MATHEWS

Pisa– Collegio Ferdinando.
[mid-January 1847][1]

Now once for all, and I say once for all, not so much because my hope is desperate of being forgiven, as because, when forgiven, I really mean to leave off sinning—I stand before you in sackcloth, praying for absolution. Hope is not desperate altogether; for I do think that by the time you have considered the "extenuating circumstances" of my being actually married, and of the very imaginable conditions and anxieties which are apt to precede such an event in every woman's life when she feels at all, and especially when, as in my marriage, the event involves other change—as from the long seclusion in one room, to liberty and Italy's sunshine in these two kinds'—when, for a resigned life, I take up a happy one, and reel under it with my head and heart, why you will understand it to be pardonable, I do think, that I should too have forgotten some obvious social duties, such as writing letters, even to such true and tried friends as yourself. Shall I tell

No. 2648 [mid-January 1847] 99

you, I find in my writing case an unfinished note to you, began before I left England, which I did immediately on my marriage—a fragment of a note, begun to inform you briefly of the position in which I stood, and of the meaning of my "extraordinary conduct" to you. Now, have not you called it "extraordinary" twenty times? But the course of events was too strong and full for me, and I was carried off my feet before I could have strength to speak my speech audibly. So forgive, forgive me. I shall behave better you will find for the future, and more gratefully, and I begin some four months after the greatest event of my life, by telling you that I am well and happy, and meaning to get as strong in the body by the help of this divine climate as I am in the spirit—*the spirits*! so much has God granted me compensation. Do you not see already that it was not altogether the sight of the free sky which made me fail to you before. So forgive me for all, all at once, forgive for all. My husband's name will prove to you that I have not left my vocation to the rhyming art, in order to marry: on the contrary, we mean, both of us, to do a great deal of work, besides surprising the world by the spectacle of two poets coming together without quarrelling, wrangling, and calling names in lyrical measures. He is preparing a new edition of his collected poems, in which he pays peculiar attention to the objections made against certain obscurities. As for me, the last thing I did was to send to Mr. Lowell, who wrote to me a year ago on behalf of the American Anti-Slavery Society, (Mrs. Chapman doing the same thing,) the poem which they asked for.[2] My conscience has been restless about it ever since, (whenever I thought that way,) but neither head nor heart were at liberty sufficiently to do anything. What I have sent at last, my belief is, will never be printed in America, or will, if it should be, bring the writer into a scrape of disfavor. But I did only write conscientiously, you know, in writing at all; and my "Cry of the Children," was not less written against my own country. Your "Man in the Republic" should have had the article "Slave." And now let me thank you for the pretty minute copy of the last edition, which you had the goodness to send me.[3] I was glad to receive it on every account, and not least as an evidence of the success of your work. My husband desires me to thank you on his own part, for gifts of this sort which you have sent to him, and which he did not know how to return his acknowledgements for until the present time, when he is able to do so, with your permission, as to my friend and his friend together. Talking of friends, Miss Fuller[4] was too late for me; I have not seen the track of her footsteps, otherwise I should have gladly received a woman who had brought the sign of your friendship with her, apart from other merits. We live here in the most secluded manner, eschewing English visitors and reading Vasari, and dreaming dreams of seeing Venice in the summer. Until the middle of April, we are tied to this perch of Pisa, as the climate is recommended for the weakness of my chest, and the repose and calmness of the place are by no means unpleasant to those who, like ourselves, do not lack for distractions and amusements in order to be very happy. Afterwards we go anywhere but to England—we shall not leave Italy at present. If I get quite strong, I may cross the desert on a camel yet, and see Jerusalem. There's a dream for you—nothing is too high or too low for my dreams just now. In the meanwhile you rage at me for my impertinency as to business, and common sense. I do believe that I sent no answer to the proposition of printing a selection from my poems,[5] and perhaps by this hour of the day, both booksellers and public have forgotten me perfectly. If they care a jot for the said proposition, let me know; for I should like to have a voice in the selection of the poems. As to the prose volume I can't do it here, I am afraid—perhaps nobody cares for that. Tell me what you are doing, writing, thinking, because I care for all three. Mr. Poe sent me his book, and I had grace enough to send him my thanks—though you would not think it of me!!![6] Ashes I cast upon my head for all my misdeeds[7]—now do, do forgive me for all!—I have Flush with me here, and he adapts himself to the sunshine as to the shadow, and when he hears me laugh lightly, begins not to think it too strange. As to news, you will not expect news from me now—until the last few days, we had not for months even seen a newspaper, and human faces divine, are quite "rococo" with me, as the French would say. Mrs. Jameson however travelled with us from Paris, and we all went together to do pilgrimage at Vaucluse, where the living water gushes up into the face of the everlasting rock, and there is no green thing except Petrarch's memory. Yes, there is the water itself—that is brightly green—and there are one or two little cypresses. Now she has gone on to Rome, where Mrs. Butler and her sister are residing.[8] Dickens is in Paris—Tennyson, when I heard of him last, was in Switzerland, and "disappointed with the mountains." I wonder how anybody can be disappointed with anything—with nature, I mean. She always seems to me (or generally) to leap up to the level of the heart. Miss Martineau is gone to Egypt it appears—all the world is abroad. And all England is freezing—such accounts we hear of the cold—and then the dreadful details from Ireland—oh, when I write against slavery, it is not as one free from the curse—"the curse of Cromwell,"[9] falls upon us also! "Poor, poor Ireland." But nations, like individuals must be "perfected by suffering."[10] In time we shall slough off our leprosy of the pride of money and of rank, and be clean, and just, and righteous. Can you read a word I have written? Good pens are in civilized life, and this shadowy paper we glide through the foreign post office with.

Now shall I hear from you? My address is, A Madame Browning, Poste Restante, Pisa, Italy. Only remember that we shall not be here after the middle of April—not at Pisa. A letter might be forwarded, to be sure. We understand from our dear friend Mr. Kenyon, that Dickens' Christmas story has had a great success—nineteen thousand copies in two days.[11] It is criticised

No. 2648 [mid-January 1847] 101

however by critical people. Since we came here we have been to the Lanfranchi Palace, Lord Byron's. The marks of his feet are painted, plastered and gilded out, and another Italian family has given it a name, no longer Lanfranchi.[12] We could only pass where the poet had been in the garden, where the Guiccioli used to shake the golden ringlets. I brought away some orange leaves.[13] My husband offers you his regards,—and believe of me, that I am not less your friend, as

Elizabeth Barrett Browning.

Text: Powell, pp. 150-152.

1. Dating is approximate, based on EBB's reference to this being "some four months after the greatest event of my life," i.e., her marriage on 12 September 1846.

2. "The Runaway Slave at Pilgrim's Point," which was published in 1848 in *The Liberty Bell*. She mentioned writing this poem in letter 2122 (see note 4). Maria Weston Chapman (1806-85) was the editor of *The Liberty Bell* from 1839-46. She had been active in the abolitionist movement since 1834, and was the leading figure in the Boston Female Anti-Slavery Society. James Russell Lowell had taken up the Anti-Slavery cause under the influence of his wife, and in 1848 he became the "corresponding editor" of *The National Anti-Slavery Standard*. The American Anti-Slavery Society was formed in 1833.

3. A copy of *Man in the Republic* (New York, 1846), published in 32mo, and inscribed by Mathews: "Elizabeth B Barrett with the Respects of the Author, N.Y. Dec. 1845." is now at Wellesley (see *Reconstruction*, A1570). Mathews had presented EBB a copy of the earlier edition, published in 1843; see letter 1389.

4. Although Margaret Fuller had arrived in England in mid August 1846, she did not reach London until late September, after the Brownings had left for Italy. Mathews had provided a letter of introduction for Margaret Fuller; see letter 2538, note 3, as well as SD1292 and SD1321.

5. This is probably related to the "proposition about prose miscellanies" discussed in letter 2128. Presumably there had been a mention of a selection of poetry as well.

6. For EBB's acknowledgement to Poe, see letter 2284.

7. Cf. II Samuel 13:19.

8. The last line of Fanny Kemble Butler's account of her travels with her sister and brother-in-law in Italy—*A Year of Consolation*, 1847—states that "on Thursday, the 8th of December [1846], I left Rome" (p. 325). This two-volume diary was published in April 1847.

9. An allusion to Cromwell's campaign against Ireland from 1649 to 1650, in which he employed harsh and cruel policies to subdue the Irish people.

10. Cf. Hebrews 2:10.

11. *The Battle of Life* was published on 18 December 1846, with an initial print run of 24,000 copies; by 26 December another 1,500 had been printed, and of the total all but 668 sold by the middle of 1847. In a letter to his wife, dated 19 December 1846, Dickens reported "23,000 copies already gone" (*Dickens*, IV, 681, and V, 11).

12. Murray's *Hand-Book for Travellers in Northern Italy* (1847) explains that the palazzo was now called "Toscanelli" (p. 459); see letter 2555, note 6.

13. This leaf has been preserved (see *Reconstruction*, H587). Mrs. Jameson saw Teresa Guiccioli (*née* Gamba, 1801?-73) shortly after leaving the Brownings in Pisa. She wrote to Lady Byron from Florence on 12 November 1846: "When we first arrived here, I went for a day to the Hotel d'York, where the table d'hote is celebrated for the company & the viands—opposite to me was a lady who immediately fixed my attention—first by the extraordinary beauty & abundance of her hair & then by the strange contrast between this beautiful hair & her face which was oldish & with no pleasing expression—it was the Countess Guiccioli" (SD1296).

2649. EBB to Septimus Moulton-Barrett

[Pisa]
[mid-January 1847][1]

My dearest Sette, I must thank you for the affection which still you seem to feel for me, as I find it expressed, however expressed in your letter. At the same time you must understand that I am not *alone* here .. which you felt indeed all the while .. let the cover of the feeling be what it may—and it is a dishonor to me to suppose that my hand can be clasped by any of you, without the hand of another. You would not desire for your sister, I am certain, that she should stand apart from her husband before the face of any one— *this* should not be, even if he were a criminal .. how much less when whatever degree of fault has been committed (about which, I will not contend) is more my fault than his, or at least mine equally with his?—how much less when his goodness & tenderness to me, touch me to the quick of the heart every day?- I appeal to you as from one human being to another- Can I consider that you love me while you do not stretch out your hand to *him*? You say that you have never said harsh words, any of you. George wrote to me precisely in the terms he w^d have used; if *I had left England without being married* .. (committing a forgery on the road, to boot!—) Moreover, I have heard from different quarters (exclusive of my sisters, mind! for *they* have represented these reports to be "exaggerated") that not merely harshnesses but "calumnies" against me & mine, have been traced up to my "brothers.."!

Alas, in the matter of these legal papers, dear Mr Kenyon's kindness cannot prevent my being thrown upon strangers for the complement of trusteeships, which has rendered the explanation of certain circumstances to uninterested persons, a matter of bare necessity—i .. e .. rendered it necessary for *him* to explain them, Robert & myself having said nothing whatever. In all this, I certainly have felt wounded, & I cannot take a light tone in speaking of even a supposed failure in any of you, whom I never loved better than now when I am away from you.

For the rest, .. my dearest Sette, I have neither "the strongest nor the weakest head in England"—I have an average quantity of common sense & conscientiousness, .. and if I do not deal much in worldly-wisdom it is because I have come to the conclusion that it is the most foolish thing in the world,—& by no unreasonable process. Such as I am, nobody can properly treat me like a weak woman who falls in love (or fancies it) & breaks in the fall, any rational & conscientious consideration. My intellect & conscience as well as my heart, assented to the connection I formed ... which, if it could have been formed another way, would not have been formed *so*. I never can regret having formed that connection .. & I certainly did not resolve to form it in a hurry & without thought. Two persons never married who knew more of one another previously, than I & my husband did, & who had fuller sympathies on every subject: no woman ever married, with a completer evidence of attachment from the man who professed to love her, than I had: no man, moreover, acted to the woman he loved, a franker & nobler part, from first to last, than Robert has done to *me*. Why even if I were an idiot & a child, *he* is not a man who would have *borne* to persuade anyone to an act contrary to her convictions—he is not such a man. He never did attempt to persuade me .. except of his love for me—that was all. At the very last his words to me were .. "You are free from all engagement toward me. I do not pretend to instruct you in your duty to God & your father—judge, yourself .. I will love you for ever, to whatever decision you come". Now you tell me that you believe me to be "TRUTHFUL". Should I be so, if I withheld or distorted the truth on this subject? Can you believe me to be so, if you continue to act as if it were no truth? What he knows of my family, came simply from my representations—& if it had not been for those, there would have been no secresy from the beginning—& never was there a man to whom anything secret & underhand is more repugnant & odious than to this man. I told him that if he spoke to my father, we sh^d probably never meet again—that if he spoke to my brothers, the confidence w^d injure their prospects without helping us. Which facts being obvious, there was one alternative to our parting at once. You blame us for adopting that course—but it was natural I think, & wronged nobody, & was the exercise of a right on my part, which few persons would deny to be a right. At any rate, the fault, such as it is, is *my* fault, *as* much as another's—it is *our* fault, .. and I will not accept an exemption from hard imputations, which I am to have, *alone*. I appeal to you all whether it w^d be worthy of me to do so, .. worthy of any woman .. or just in itself– For my part, I never anticipated certainly the view you have taken .. I believed that you w^d have all been in haste with kindness, to me & mine. I supposed that Robert w^d not have been blamed heavily by those who loved *me*, for loving me too well– What has he gained in me, but the priviledge of living the quietest of all lives side by side with me,—exchanging for *that*, the liberty & amusement which he had in London? If you could see how he lives with me, though we live very, very happily, you would not take it for the 'ideal' of a man's life .. apart from the affection which consecrates such things. I cannot induce him, though with ever so many entreaties, even *to take a ride*, .. because it is a pleasure I cannot share with him– And you w^d have me stand apart from HIM, to receive the assurance of your remembering me still?– No, *that*, I cannot do.

    I could understand if you blamed *me* most, & especially on the point of being ungenerous to him in allowing him to bear the burden of my shattered health & spirits, .. & to run the risk of its being a perpetual burden. There was a great deal to say & think on this point .. & I myself said & thought it all: my conscience struggled with me on this one point. It was a point however for the exclusive consideration of *himself & me*, as to the practical conclusion from it: and if he preferred & determined to run certain risks, he was the master--& there were probabilities on the other hand, from the influence of a mild climate, to which I could not shut my eyes. These last have all been realized up to the present time .. & you w^d be surprised perhaps, as others are, to see how much better I look & am .. how much stronger & revived in every way .. though of course it w^d be imprudent of me to go out on the days when the air is cold. I am obliged to take care. The sun is so hot on our coldest days, that the women use parasols– Mr Jago, who is kind in continuing his medical directions to me, bids me beware of the treacherous sun when the air is at all sharp. Where did you hear that we had *back* rooms? They face, on the contrary, the best street in Pisa, with a view of the Duomo & Leaning Tower, which are both within a stone's throw. As for society, we should like to know a few Italians, and shall get letters of introduction perhaps, when we go to Florence in April,——but for the 'English abroad', I am sure you never heard me say that I desired to have anything to do with them– The Irvings & Surteess have called on us .. & we have returned cards, in a significant enough way, as to our wishes of seeing them– In the first place, (& last) I cannot pay visits in the winter to any good effect. An Italian professor (Sig^r Ferucci) comes to see us sometimes—but he is not an interesting person, & speaks French instead of Italian .. which we do not like. He has lived at Geneva & got into the practice of it. Robert w^d get letters from Mazzini, but has been afraid for my sake, lest getting involved with the republicans, we sh^d fall into some scrape, & be ordered out of Italy in haste,—Mazzini's friends being marked men, of course. But I say that I dont care .. should'nt care, in the least, .. for any scrape of that sort– Mazzini offered him letters. I wish I could think you right about Arabel & Papa——*it is so unjust*, if he is cold to her on my account. When I come back, will you all be kind to me & mine? Otherwise I had better stay here, I think. My love to dearest Storm. And do you, dearest Sette, continue to love me, & to believe that my wishes & prayers follow you in every step in life.

Your most affec^{te}
Ba

Address, on integral page: S. James Barrett Esqre
Publication: None traced.
Manuscript: Gordon E. Moulton-Barrett.

1. Conjectural dating based on EBB's references in letters 2650 and 2652 to having written this letter.

2650. EBB TO HENRIETTA MOULTON-BARRETT

[Pisa]
[23 January 1847][1]

My own dearest Henrietta must, to begin, forgive me all untoward & objectionable words, however & whenever let fall, about "Puseyites" "Newmanites" "Tractarians" or whomever so called or miscalled. I cant remember what I wrote, but I am sure that if it was written in an ungentle spirit, I am sorry for it, & agree it was wrong, without a word more.[2] Dont you know that I hate a controversial & bitter tone in religion, above every error or whatever may so seem to me, in the same? Only standing here upon the shore where all those waves of certain ideas & trains of thought naturally tend & break, I spoke upon impulse, just as I should have done if face to face with you,—& you must forgive me as you should have forgiven me then– Even at that moment I did not mean the least reproach by the word "Puseyites" .. one *must* use words you know, or the meaning one has, lies in the dark. I meant simply the holders of the opinions revived by D: Pusey, & about which there has been so much contention. If I had said "members of the church of England", I might have referred to persons as absolutely opposed to those I spoke of, as possible—low churchmen for instance! And, High churchmen, even, would by no means have expressed the precise thing, for there are high churchmen & high churchmen. Now forgive me for saying awkwardly & harshly whatever I may have said so. Of course there are Christians in every body of men who call on Christ, .. while the purest Christianity may probably be on the outside of all– I went into the church here with the desire of praying with the people, &, with all my disappointment of distraction & quenching of the imagination, I hope I did it a little—the worst was that they did not appear to pray themselves very much. By the way, some things I cant make out– Will Storm reveal to me, for instance, why it is that the fasting is done in Italy on saturday, & not on friday? On friday they eat magnificently. On saturday they come to the eggs, & the beans .. beans pounded into the likeness of *peas-pudding*—we had some the other night for supper, from our people of the house, who sent it in to us with an "aviso al publico," that to enjoy it to perfection we should add some white sugar & plenty of oil! Perhaps it was the ideal perfection which disturbed my positive pleasure, but really & altogether it was beyond me. Peas-pudding "adapted to the capacity" of horses, may rather be like it in the state we saw:—with the oil, it would be brought down to the pigs, I should fancy. So I swore by the celebrated pork of Epicurus,[3] never to touch it again. Robert always says that I have dreadful prejudices, & he is so ambitious of surmounting his & talks so learnedly of the instincts of nations in relation to the food they select, that you would take for granted (to hear him) that he lived here upon oil & garlic .. whereas, most happily for both of us, he never touches either—"the signora's fault," as he explains to the Trattoria people, when they open their eyes at the barbarism of our taste. Not to like oil!!– The fact is that he hates it just as much as the signora, only with remorse!!– i.e. wishing that he did'nt: while I avow my frailty as shamelessly as I should eschew (rather than chew) the acorns of our English ancestors–

Jany 27.th) Dearest Henrietta, This letter was begun last saturday, & now it is wednesday night, .. but really I have not had the heart to go on writing. I will tell you why—Wilson has been ill .. not very ill, & not in the least dangerously, & now she is a good deal better, .. doing as well as possible in fact—still, the feelings of responsibility, & also of sympathy with a person for whom I have so much regard & with so much good reason, have kept me uneasy of course– In England, it would have been a lighter thing—but to bring her here & to see her ill at such a distance from her friends—you will understand how I could not have the heart to write– Last week she complained of a pain in her left side .. just where Arabel used to have hers .. & we both fancied that it was obstruction or indigestion—and she confided to me (I making exclamations!) that she had bought & partly taken *eight shillings worth* of English pills for bilious disorders & that they did not seem strong enough. So at her request, I made Robert bring home from the English Dispensary, three grains of calomel & so much rhubarb– Taken on friday night. On Saturday morning, she appealed from the rhubarb to certain cream of Tartar & herb water employed by the people of the house & strenuously recommended—entreating me not to tell Robert. This seemed to relieve her, she said, .. but the pain returned .. burning up into the breast. I could'nt help telling Robert because I was frightened—& we both wished her much to go to Dr Cook .. which indeed I had pressed on her before .. Robert declaring that she w^d kill herself at last with taking such redundancy of medecine. She w^d go, she said, if she did not feel better—& once she put on her boots with the intention of going, & fancied herself better .. she would'nt go– Which went on till Saturday night while I was putting my feet into hot water by the fire here, all undressed .. here in the sitting room. All at once she sank down on the sofa, shivering all over, & cried out that she was about to be very ill, & that she would go to Dr Cook at once, .. asking me to ask the Signorina of the house to accompany her. I asked—(frightened out of my wits) & the girl was afraid to go with Wilson who "w^d certainly faint in the street", .. & though I proposed having a carriage for both, she drew back .. & with very good reason as grew plain to me & to poor Wilson too. So, recovering my senses by degrees, I dried my feet, & ran away with the basin, & put on a dressing gown & sent Wilson to bed, while I went to ask Robert to dress himself & set off himself for Dr Cook .. which he did at the quickest. It was past ten, & he had to go to the other side of the Arno & a good way beside,—"And what am I to do if D.ʳ Cook wont come? if I cant get in?." "Oh, get somebody to come—" "My love, how can I get somebody at this time of night? I will do what I can .. but if I *cant*"? "Oh, you *must* get somebody." I was so afraid that as people in a fright generally are, I could'nt be reasonable. But he ran out, eager to do the impossible—& I ran in to Wilson, poor thing, who was in bed, with her pulse beating very fast, but a good deal from nervousness, I have been certain, since. Still there was fever enough, & for the rest it was quite natural for her to think of her friends as I did for her—and she told me that ever since the sea voyage (or, for four months) the whole stomach had been swelled .. distended—not a word of which, I had even heard before– But D.ʳ Cook came, & I rushed away—& presently Robert followed to tell me that there was nothing to be uneasy about .. nothing whatever .. but that there *would* have been something, with a very little more provocation of 'remedies'. In fact, it is said to be a slight inflammation of the mucus membrane of the stomach, arising primarily from the sea sickness when in a state of indigestion, & further irritated by those English pills, which might have been good in England, but in *Italy* are too *hot*. If the symptoms had gone on, it would have ended in a gastric fever, which is crowding the hospitals at this instant, from the combination of hot sunshine & moisture common to the climate—even here in the winter. She was desired to lie in bed & to have five leeches on her side, & D.ʳ Cook comes every morning, & today & yesterday she has been up for half an hour, & appears very satisfactorily relieved. I asked him this morning if there was the least cause for apprehension—"Not the slightest[']' was the answer, "she will be quite herself in a day or two." I asked too (being fearful) whether she could bear without risk the hot weather of Italy .. whether it was safe for her to remain. "*Quite* safe", he said, "only she must be careful of her diet, & live in the simplest way". He forbids *coffee altogether* .. also wine. He says that she was not well when she left England, .. that the biliary system & organs of digestion were out of order, .. but that everything is coming right quite fast. If the inflammation had extended to the bowels, it w.ᵈ, of course, have been more serious. Poor dear Wilson! My fright that night, I shall not easily forget .. & to complete the whole, when the rest was over, Robert gave me a tremendous scold for having run to Wilson's room without any stockings. "I wanted to kill him .. I played with his life &c &c". Poor me! nobody catches cold, in such a fright as I was! There, now!—I have told my whole history. She is very much better tonight, & in quite good spirits .. & is sure that she was near the same sort of thing in Wimpole Street, but the *sea* evidently did the great harm. Tell Arabel about the coffee—coffee is considered *very bad* for weakness of the stomach & digestion– *Tea* is ordered to be substituted. All this time, I have been perfectly well & active to a miracle– Think of me, dressing myself all these days, doing my hair, attending to everything. Robert being the kindest of possible persons, brings me the tea kettle of hot water, at nights & mornings .. but other assistance I have none—the Signorina has enough to do in waiting on Wilson & preparing our breakfast. The people here have been very kind indeed, & one could not take advantage of it. Of course we would send Wilson home at once if she desired it, but I believe it w^d be a disappointment to her, & Dr Cook, who is a very intelligent man in his profession, assures us of the safety of her being here in the warm weather. She has little to do, with us, & is never fatigued, & takes exercise regularly out of doors—& really what has been striking me all this time, is her improved appearance .. looking so much fatter & more rosy. Fallacious signs, I fear!- (Friday morning) Dr Cook has just been here—she is much better & he is not coming again for a day or two. With a little attention to diet, & a good deal of exercise, she is likely to be well for the future. Thank God for all things—and now I may write on.

Thank my own Arabel for the long dear letter which made me so glad some days ago, & enclosed a note from you, dearest Henrietta, to make me gladder still. About the same time I had a most kind one from Mr Martin, from Paris—he is a kind, earnest friend .. & so is dear Mrs Martin! I shall not forget among other things, that at the very first & without waiting to have a word of explanation from me, they wrote to me in the spirit of the fullest faith & esteem. Robert always says that he w^d do anything for either of them, .. & indeed we should have been both happy to have seen them here, let Arabel smile as she may! I should like them to KNOW *him thoroughly*, .. so as to have the evidence of their senses (besides other evidences) that I have done the wisest thing in the world. And now, as to the rest, ... Mr Martin's note pleased me much, by the account he gave of all in Wimpole Street- Oh, let Arabel be sure that I am not irritated against any one of them, & that my whole heart has been open to them from the beginning, to the end, to hold & to love them as ever. Sette's letter was affectionate, & affectionately responded to by my inner feelings .. only he & they all must understand & feel that it would ill become me in my position, to accept as a personal kindness to me, what refused so emphatically to extend itself to the person nearest to me. If they knew him whom they misknow, how different it would be indeed! a reflection which always arrests me when I am inclined to be vexed for a moment. Let them reflect for their own part .. Why not let the past be past, & forbear on each side every sort of recrimination? They may think on to themselves, or even say out frankly .. "You two have both acted foolishly & rashly, & we do not approve of it on any ground: but inasmuch as the thing is done, & we love our sister & desire to love the man who loves her, here is our hand for you both"—something to that effect might be said without inconsistency & without sacrifice, I fancy—even something *more might* be said, considering whom I have married, & what an absolute happiness (as far as he is concerned) I have received from him. Give my love to them all, at any rate. It is painful to me, to have been the means of painfulness to any of them—— I did not think that they w.^d have taken it so. Still they ought to be able to see what every other person of sense, saw in an instant, that to have *given them my confidence* & have destroyed their prospects in the same breath, would have been an act of the most atrocious selfishness on my part, & impossible to one who loved them as I did & do.

Two things in Arabel's letter made me uneasy—she refers incidentally to George's speaking of Storm's going to Jamaica .. which I hope refers to something long ago .. & not that there is talk now of his going to Jamaica. Oh—if dearest Storm w.^d but turn his eyes another way .. any other way in the world. Why not come our way, in the Statira? if the Statira proceeds to the Mediterranean this year? Why not image out some new plan of farming, or .. or .. I should not mind what– Now listen .. cant he & George & Sette & Occy go up the Rhine this summer & meet us in the Euganean mountains? By the way, assure Arabel that we have not taken root in Italy for life– Dont let her have such fancies. Seriously, though, we talk sometimes of going to Jerusalem, & we are both to be marked on the arm as pilgrims, whenever we do, that you may not doubt too much our "complete narrative" .. but we shall see you before we see Jerusalem. — The other thing which makes me un⟨easy⟩ is her account of Mr Boyd. How is he "more infirm"? Has he ⟨had⟩ medical assistance? & did the cold affect him much? Let me ⟨know.⟩

The Martins saw a great deal in Paris of the Hedleys, & M.^r M⟨artin⟩ observes that dear uncle Hedley "won their hearts", by the warm affection & interest with which he spoke of me & "Mr Browning", taking our parts in a strenuous manner. Arabel too is mentioned .. but without a word of her illness. They desire me to write to them at Pau. It was so delightful to hear of my dearest Henrietta & Arabel from their sincere testimony, though I could not help envying a little the beholders of their faces– My own dearest sisters, how I love you & thank you & bless you for all you have been to me! May the hour come when I may be able to give you back a little of the good— the love only, can go to you now. While I am writing, comes an awful interruption, in the shape of *Mrs Cook*![4] She is an unpretty likeness, .. though rather a pretty woman even so, .. of Susan Cook .. but very vapid in expression, & weak & commonplace in conversation .. I mean to say, *very*. She told me however of her intimacy with the Garrows, & how she had had a letter from Miss Fisher[5] two days since. To my astonished ears moreover she revealed, that Pisa was very "gay" just now .. a weekly "reception" at the Governor's, besides the Baroness .... When Robert came in, I divulged in my turn, where he might go if he pleased, to which he irreverently replied that the Governor & the governed might be hanged first. I have not even returned M?ˢ Turner's courtesy in coming here to witness our papers—though I have been once out in the carriage since I wrote to Arabel- We drove down through the pine forest to the sea side, & met the camels & enjoyed it all exceedingly.[6] The carriages are delightful- Wilson & Flush were on the outside. The weather is fine, & if we were on the Arno I might walk out everyday: but as it is the wisdom seems to be on the side of shunning the cold air which waits at our front door. D? Cook says that even if I did not go out during the winter (which you know I have done) the advantage of being *here* is incontestable. He himself is in Italy on account of weakness of the chest, many of his family having died of consumption.[7] He says that he could not *breathe* while he was in England a month ago- Certainly I am very well indeed—better than I could hope to be in the winter. Robert's love to you & Arabel, whose note quite touched & pleased him, & he shall write to you next time. Love to dear Trippy & to Lizzie, dear child--

            Your own attached
              Ba

Love to Minny. *Speak of Papa always.*
Does dear Occy get on with the drawings? Tell me.

Address, on integral sheet: Angleterre .. via France / To the care of Miss Trepsack / Miss Barrett / 5- Upper Montagu Street / Montagu Square / London.
Publication: TTUL, pp. 26–39.
Source: Transcript in editors' file.

 1. Dating based on notation "Jany 27" (a Wednesday) at the beginning of second paragraph. At that point EBB said that the she had started the letter "last Saturday," which was the 23rd, and further along she wrote "Friday morning," which was the 29th. Year provided by postmark.
 2. Perhaps Henrietta had reacted to EBB's comment about Puseyism in the third paragraph of letter 2647.
 3. Cf. Horace, *Epistles*, I, iv, 16.
 4. The wife of Dr. Francis Cook.
 5. Harriet Fisher (d. 1850) was the half-sister of Theodosia Garrow, who later married Thomas Trollope.
 6. See letter 2627, note 7.
 7. He lived to be 93 years of age.

2651. RB TO HENRY FOTHERGILL CHORLEY

                  [Pisa]
              [ca. February 1847][1]

⟨★★★⟩ Tell me of your success in your own negotiations, which I confidently expect, and beforehand rejoice in. . . . I do feel that you are safe in the hands of those truthful-looking Cushmans; and being very glad you have got *them*,

No. 2652   1 February 1847   111

shall be yet gladder when the world gets *you*, and helps to realise the good wishes of such as myself, with only wishes at their disposal, for a most conscientious artist, honest critic, and loyal friend. ⟨✻✻✻⟩

Text: *Henry Fothergill Chorley: Autobiography, Memoir, and Letters*, comp. Henry G. Hewlett, 1873, II, 129–130.

1. Approximate dating based on RB's references to Charlotte and Susan Cushman, as well as EBB's comment in letter 2653 "that Miss Cushman means to be imperious about Mr. Chorley's tragedy .. the 'Duchess Eleanor.'" See also letter 2642, note 8.

2652. EBB TO JAMES & JULIA MARTIN

Collegio Ferdinando.
Feb. 1. 1847.

I should have written before to thank you both, my very dear friends, for your letter & all the kindness & comfort in it, .. but for the last ten days I have had a new uneasiness, in Wilson's illness .. my maid whom we brought from England—& of course the responsibility made itself felt painfully. The English physician has however left off his daily visits now, & she is out of bed for a few hours everyday,—& we have assurances that, with care, she will do well for the future. It was *very near* being a "gastric fever", .. arising from the neglected effect of our stormy passage from Marseilles & her severe sickness, four months ago. She said nothing to me till she could not help it, & then, would not see a physician, till I was frightened out of my wits one night by her sinking down on the sofa while she was undressing me. So this has finished reversing the world for me, & I have been learning all these days what it is possible to do for oneself in the matter of one's own hair & other people's medecines—only the anxiety was so much the worse, that it took away the thought of the fatigue altogether, .. & Robert was as anxious as I, or more perhaps, being anxious for *me* besides– It has been his department to see to the fire & carry the teakettle here & there … I bid him observe what he has come to!—— Still, it is all over now (or as nearly as possible) thank God .. and, throughout it, I have been quite well, & am entirely so at this moment, with the advantage of having learnt a little more of "constitutional independence," in my own experience. And now let me thank you, my dear Mr Martin, my dear friend, for your goodness in everyway .. believe me I never shall forget it. I had a letter from Sette, before I had yours, written in a light way, which half pleased me (that he should write at all in a kind tone) & half vexed me for the manner. I will explain exactly what vexed me .. I would not have you think that I cannot make allowances, or that I am "stiff", & expect impossible concessions. But when they write to me, as Sette did, as to somebody who had done a foolish thing without meaning the least harm, through being overpersuaded by somebody else who was the real criminal .. when that is insinuated, & expressed by interlineations & the rest, ... I appeal to you if it becomes me to accept any such kindness. So I answered Sette (all this before your note came!) affectionately but frankly, to the effect that whatever had been done (whether ill or well, we need not now discuss) had been done by *me* willingly & by choice & with both my eyes open, & that therefore I would not submit to be set on one side, when blame was to be given .. that moreover, I was here with my husband, & that if they still loved me enough to mean me any kindness, they must extend it to him at the same time. Was it wrong, dearest M.rs Martin, to say this? was it wrong, my dear friends? I would concede anything but the one point they wish to wring from me——in their blind ignorance (the excess of which consoles me almost) of the man with whom it is their honour to have any connection. As to my not having given them my confidence, .. if I had not loved them too tenderly for it, they might not have had that reason for complaint. But I love them tenderly now, & will be patient, & take your advice & not be too exacting– George has not written—poor George!- I will let him say again that I have "sacrificed all delicacy & honour", if he will graciously forgive me at last, & vouchsafe the tips of his fingers to Robert. Really it makes me half laugh & half cry when I think of some of these absurdities, the reason for which, is passed even in this absurd world!- So, .. instead, .. let me ask how you find yourselves at Pau & whether you feel nearer the sun. The weather here is mild & wet. I have been out only once or twice in January, .. this from simple precaution, for I am very well, & we are full of schemes .. of seeing Venice for instance, in the summer. Then we are reading (much at the latest) Custine's Russia,[1] & it has been proposed that *when we go to the East*, we may return by Odessa to Moscow & Petersburg, .. observing to do so by sunlight of course!- So you may guess what our schemes are. Tell me in return how you both are, which is the single kindness your last letter forgot. Dear uncle Hedley! he is always good to me. M.rs Hedley too wrote to me very kindly when she did write. Does Fanny Hanford delight in Rome? & will she return without seeing Venice? That w.d be a shame. Our Pope is winning golden opinions on all sides, for a liberal Pope that is. Do you get books at Pau? Have you read Jules Janin's graceful book upon Italy?[2] written a few years since. May God bless you both. Do write. Robert's regards to his & my dear friends–

         Your grateful & affectionate
         Ba.

Address, on integral page: À Madame / Madame Martin / Poste Restante / Pau / Basses Pyrenées / France.
Publication: None traced.
Manuscript: Wellesley College

1. *La Russie en 1839* by Astolphe, Marquis de Custine, was published in 1843, and an English translation appeared the following year. In a letter written in November 1844, EBB asked Julia Martin if she knew about this book; see letter 1761, note 7.
2. *Voyage en'Italie* (1839).

2653. EBB & RB TO ANNA BROWNELL JAMESON

[In EBB's hand]   Collegio Ferdinando.
Feb. 4. [1847][1]

We were very glad to have news of you at last, my very dear friend, & that it should be better news, at least more cheerful, than any which came to us from Florence. You seemed *done for* by your hospitable acquaintances there, & you cant think how we painted a mural over that last letter which sounded like a last gasp of exhaustion, .. to the effect that when ourselves went to Florence we should keep out of the mud of the English by all possible means. The sort of thing is bad anywhere, .. but here in Italy, just when one's personality is tuned up to the highest, to have it meet the confusion of ever so many rough fists, is enough to break the instrument— So I am glad you are away in Rome & the mediæval ages, & with friends round you to help the charm with their sympathy. Had Mad.me de Goëthe *too much* pleasure in seeing dear Gerardine?[2] You do not tell us,—& what you told me before, interested me into wishing to hear the end. You did not find M.rs Butler,[3] we learnt by the papers, .. for observe, we see the papers now,—or did I tell you that before? Also, M.r Hemans's Roman journal[4] had apprized us of the safe arrival in Rome of a "celebrated authoress" & our dear friend, who put off writing to tell us of herself, a great deal too long. Otherwise, you might have been supposed to be '*lost* in admiration' before the productions of that eminent artist of Sienna,[5] who makes such a point of being known by the whole world, as Signor Ferucci laboriously impressed upon me. I was innocent enough to take into my head at the moment, by the way, that you would not get much out of such a man, & the fact proves so— Three days at Sienna! Would, that we might have met you there! But it was out of the question. I have been out of the house *just once* since Christmas, though not in the least inclined to be otherwise than contented with Pisa & the climate & the weather, on that account: *precaution* explains everything. Indeed if we had been on the Arno, I should have had much more liberty— But you know how the wind waits to devour one just at our door; & even with a very sufficient mildness of temperature, it seemed unwise to run the risk of meeting it, particularly when I was so well in this room. I have been & am very well, & we burn the Grand Duke's pinewood & talk & get on delightfully, & I wont have Pisa abused, let Robert come in from his dreary hour's walk on

Lung'Arno (when it is wet he can go no where else) in ever such an imprecative humour on the soul-less faces he meets there. After all, he is in excellent spirits, & we make amends for being shut up a little for the present, by various sublime schemes of going to Jerusalem, & Moscow, besides *Volterra*[6] *& Sienna*. And then, by the grace of M. Ferucci, we have Vasari from the library, & are ploughing through it .... will you let me say *ploughing*? Really I do venture to think it a dull book. Perhaps when we reach his contemporaries, we may find more flesh & blood. And Robert is *very* busy with his new edition, & has been throwing so much golden light into "Pippa," that everybody shall see her "pass" properly .. yes, & *sur*pass.[7] Now, let me tell you of our adversity– A fortnight ago poor Wilson was taken ill, & for several days was confined to her bed, & indeed is only at present beginning to be able to resume her occupations. We had Dr Cook here constantly—and at first I was frightened out of my wits, .. sending Robert out to fetch him at ten oclock at night. It was inflammation of the mucus membrane of the stomach, arising (said Dr C.) from the *sea sickness*, which had produced swelling & irritation increased by improper remedies. A little longer, & a dangerous gastric fever w^d have been the result. We like Dr Cook, who has shown a great deal of prompt intelligence .. & she is recovering her strength in a satisfactory manner .. poor Wilson!– And think how I missed her, & had to learn (besides) what a quantity of things I could really manage to do for myself when I tried!! It has been a lesson in moral & practical philosophy, & finished reversing the world for me. Robert in the meanwhile, carried the teakettle; saw to the fire .. I bade him observe what he had come to at last— but the goodness & affectionateness were strong enough for all things. I wonder at the strength & depth of them more & more.— Do write—& thank Gerardine for me for her letter, & tell me how long she & dearest Aunt Nina are likely to stay at Rome. Shall we not hear without such a long pause? Letters from England bring me the best accounts of my father's spirits & the most affectionate words from my sisters. I heard yesterday from Miss Mitford, .. but no news, I think, except that Miss Cushman means to be imperious about Mr Chorley's tragedy .. the 'Duchess Eleanor' .. & to insist on its being acted.[8] Are you well *now*, dear friend? Give my love to Gerardine, & tell her I am delighted that she is an enchanted 'philosopher' now she is in Rome! Do believe me,

your ever affec^{te}
Ba.

[Continued by RB]

    Ba evidently thinks me the "minute Philosopher"! See what a little space she allows me to say so much in—but next time .. I will write, and leave her the precincts of the sealing wax. Dear Aunt Nina, kind, dearest friend, keep on making us happy by such letters, with good news of yourself. We are

No. 2654   8 February [1847]   115

quite well—but Ba will have told you—all things go well with us—but will go still better when we see you—don't forget that! We *think* .. with all the rational hesitation, and refusals to determine .. that we shall spend *next* winter at Florence,—*next* to *that*, at Rome—there is only one thing *quite* settled,—what you may term, settled—that is, that we return to England viâ Moscow—(we have been reading Custine's not very wise book)[.][9] Good, *best*, bye, dear Aunt, and dear Geddie-

RB.

Address, in RB's hand, on integral page: Mrs Jameson, / Dama Inglese, / Uffizio delle Poste, / Roma.
Publication: None traced.
Manuscript: Wellesley College.

1. Year provided by postmark.
2. Ottilie von Goethe (1796-1872), Goethe's daughter-in-law, and Mrs. Jameson had been friends and correspondents since the early 1830's. In a letter to her sister in March 1847, Mrs. Jameson wrote: "Mme. Goethe is occupied with her sick son; she has given Gerardine a beautiful scarf" (*Memoirs of the Life of Anna Jameson*, 1878, by her niece Gerardine Macpherson, p. 239).
3. See letter 2648, note 8.
4. Charles Isidore Hemans (1817-76) founded *The Roman Advertiser* in October 1846 as the first English-language newspaper in Rome. The issue for 16 January 1847 carried the following announcement: "On the 15th arrived Mrs. Jameson, one of the first female writers of England, whose works display refined justness of taste, powers of thought and analysis, in a high degree."
5. We take this to be a reference to Duccio di Buoninsegna (*fl.* 1278-1318).
6. Volterra is some 55 miles southwest of Florence, via Empoli and Pontedera. It is noted for its Etruscan architecture as it was one of the twelve cities in the Etruscan confederation.
7. A reference to EBB's initial incomprehension of *Pippa Passes*; see letter 827. For RB's revisions of Pippa Passes for the 1849 edition, see *The Poems of Browning*, ed. John Woolford and Daniel Karlin (1991-), 2, 7, and *The Poetical Works of Robert Browning*, ed. Ian Jack and Rowena Fowler (Oxford, 1983-), 3, 15.
8. See letter 2642, note 8, as well as letter 2715, note 5.
9. See note 1 in the preceding letter. For more information about RB's thoughts on Russia, see Patrick Waddington, "Browning and Russia," *Baylor Browning Interest Series*, no. 28 (October 1985).

2654. EBB TO MARY RUSSELL MITFORD

[Pisa]
Feb. 8- [1847][1]

But my dearest Miss Mitford, your scheme about Leghorn is drawn out in the clouds-[2] Now just see how impossible!- Leghorn is fifteen miles off, & though there is a railroad there is no liberty for French books to wander backwards & forwards without inspection & siezure— .. why, do remember that we are in Italy after all! Nevertheless I will tell you what we have done .. transplanted our subscription from the Italian library which was wearing us away into a misanthropy or at least despair of the wits of all southerns, into a library which has a tolerable supply of French books, & gives us the priviledge besides of having a French newspaper, the Siècle, left with us every evening. Also, this library admits (is allowed to admit on certain conditions) some books forbidden generally by the censureship, which is of the strictest—and though Balzac appears very imperfectly, I am delighted to find him at all, & shall dun the bookseller for the "Instruction Criminelle" which I hope discharges your Lucien as a *"forçat"*[3] .. the only destiny due to him. You know I have no patience with that "femmelette" .. neither man nor woman, .. & true poet, least of all. I see by the 'Siecle' that Balzac's works are coming out in a complete edition arranged by himself under the title of "Comedie Humaine," and, with the idea, that this arrangement may be of use to you in various ways I send you a copy of it as printed at large in the French paper.[4] Observe that 'Esther' is separated from the series of Illusions Perdues .. I do not understand why,—& so is the "Instruction Criminelle". It seems to me that you might publish a charming *selection* from the shorter tales, & that it would be well to begin so. 'L'Absolu' for instance!–[5] These would be more likely to prepare the way in England for the longer works & for the appreciation of the writer than such a book as Cæsar Birotteau.[6] At the same time M.͞r Bentley, having to contend with those cheap Belgian editions, should look to his prices, or the whole scheme will surely fail, I fear. Do tell me all you decide. I am afraid of trusting to my recollection– Bentley sh.͞d send you down the 'Comedie Humaine' as a whole .. to look over & decide upon .. for, in that way, you will get at the *order* as well as other things. Tell him to let you have it. The 'Siècle' has for a feuilleton a new romance of Soulié's called "Saturnin Fichet,"[7] which is really not good .. & tiresome to boot. Robert & I began by each of us reading it, but after a little while he left me alone being certain that no good could come of such a work: so, of course, ever since, I have been exclaiming & exclaiming as to the wonderful improvement & increasing beauty & glory of it, .. just to justify myself, & to make him sorry for not having persevered! The truth is however that, but for obstinacy, I should give up too. Deplorably dull, the story is, .. & there is a crowd of people each more indifferent than each, to you .. the pith of the plot being (very characteristically) that the hero has somebody exactly like him. To the reader, it's *all one* in every sense ... who's who, & what's what. Robert is a warm admirer of Balzac & has read most of his books, but certainly .. oh certainly .. he does not in a general way appreciate our French people quite with our warmth .. he takes too high a standard, I tell him, & wont listen to a story for a story's sake. I can bear to be amused, you know, without a strong pull on my admiration. So we have great wars sometimes, & I put up Dumas's flag or Soulié's or Eugene Sue's (yet he was properly possessed by the Mystères de Paris) & carry it till my arms ache. The plays & vaudevilles, he knows far more of than I do, & always maintains they are the happiest growth of the French school .. setting aside the *masters*, observe—for Balzac & George Sand hold all their honours:

and before your letter came, he had told me about the 'Kean'[8] & the other dramas. Then we read together the other day the "Rouge et Noir", that powerful book of Stendhal's (Bayle)[9] & he thought it very striking, & observed, .. what I had thought from the first & again & again, .. that it was exactly like Balzac *in the raw* .. in the material, .. & undevelopped conception. What a book it is really, only so full of pain & bitterness, & the gall of iniquity! The new Dumas I shall see in time, perhaps—& it is curious that Robert had just been telling me the very story, you speak of in your letter, from the Causes Celebres–[10] I never read it, .. the more shame. Dearest friend, .. all this talk of French books, & no talk about you! .. the *most* shame! You dont tell me enough of yourself, & I want to hear, because (besides the usual course of reasons) M.r Chorley spoke of you as if you were not as cheerful as usual—do tell me. Ah—if you fancy that I do not love you as near, through being so far, you are unjust to me as you never were before.——

For myself, the brightness round me has had a cloud on it lately by an illness of poor Wilson's, who for ten days was confined to her bed by inflammation of the mucus membrane of the stomach, said to be the consequence of the violent seasickness in our stormy passage from Marseilles four months ago, irritated by improper remedies. She would not go to D.r Cook, till I was terrified one night while she was undressing me, by her sinking down on the sofa in a shivering fit—oh, so frightened I was!—and Robert ran out for a physician—& I could have shivered too, with the fright. But she is convalescent now, thank God—and in the meanwhile I have acquired a heap of practical philosophy & have learnt how it is possible (in certain conditions of the human frame) to comb out & twist up one's own hair, & lace one's very own stays, & cause hooks & eyes to meet behind one's very own back, besides making toast & water for Wilson, .. which last miracle, it is only just to say, was considerably assisted by Robert's counsels "not quite to set fire to the bread" while one was toasting it. He was the best & kindest all that time, as even *he* could be, & carried the kettle when it was too heavy for me, & helped me with heart & head—M.r Chorley could not have praised him too much, be very sure. I, who always rather appreciated him, do set down the thoughts I had, as merely unjust things .. he exceeds them all, indeed. Yes, M.r Chorley has been very kind to us—I had a kind note myself from him a few days since—& do you know, that we have a sort of hope of seeing him in Italy this year, with dearest M.r Kenyon who has the goodness to crown his goodness by a "dream" of coming to see us? We leave Pisa in April (did I tell you *that*) & pass through Florence towards the north of Italy .. to *Venice*, for instance. In the way of writing, I have not done much yet .. just finished my rough sketch of an antislavery ballad & sent it off to America, where nobody will print it, I am certain, because I could not help making it bitter.[11] If they *do* print it, I shall think them more boldly in earnest, than I fancy now. Tell me of Mary Howitt's new collection of Ballads:[12]—are they

good? I warmly wish that Mr Chorley may succeed with his play—but how can Miss Cushman promise a hundred nights for an untried work?[13] Mrs Butler seems to be wise neither for herself nor for others—& I do not understand a love of Art which measures itself out to the weight of so many ducats, .. any more than I can the love of love, in a man, like Mr Butler, with whom she had not an idea in common.[14] What a discovery this seems to be of the sulphuric æther![15] Why it replaces magnetism at the usefullest. By the way I am curious to hear of Harriet Martineau's meeting with the Ægyptian magi & soothsayers—who will say soothest?—— Oh yes, do go & see my dearest sisters—they are dearest & best, & tenderest to me!—& think of me cheerfully when you see them, as still with you in heart & affection,—as unchanged except in being happy. My poor dear Papa is said to be in the highest spirits—which saves me from the possible pang. May God keep them all, dear things- So I was *out* in the matter of K ..! but it is your fault .. you have taught me to seek & expect every sort of extravagance in your generous affectionateness—truffles grow, they say, at the foot of the oak; & if ever *I* say "the swine sh^d not go so near," it is because I know the reason. Not that poor K. in her penitence (if really she is penitent) sh^d be classed with swine! indeed no! May she & her little boy be pure & happy, both of them.[16] How is good Mr Lovejoy's child?[17] We hear that the Howitts have "shown up" the poets, in rather an offensive way. For instance it was hard on LEL's poor family to make the probability of her suicide so sure a thing, as the anecdote of her having shown a bottle of prussic acid to her friend, under the pressure of former circumstances, must render it-[18] Perhaps you may find the two last numbers of the Bells & Pomegranates less obscure—it seems so to me.[19] Flush has grown an absolute monarch & barks one distracted, when he wants a door opened. Robert spoils him I think. Do think of me as
        your ever affectionate & grateful
          EBB--Ba

[*Enclosure:*]
     La Comédie Humaine

Scenes de la Vie Privée	Une Fille d'Eve
La maison du Chat-qui-pelote	La Femme abandonnée
Le bal de Sceaux	La Grenadiere
La Bourse	Le menage
La Vendetta	Gobseck
Ma^{dme} Firmiani	La Femme de trente ans
Une double Famille	Le contrat de mariage
La Paix du ménage	Béatrix
La Fausse Maîtresse	La Grande Breteche
Etude de Femme	Modeste Mignon
Albert Savarus	Honorine
Mémoires de deux mariées	Un Début dans la vie

Scenes de la Vie de Province
  Uranie Mirouet
  Eugenie Grandet
  <u>Les Celibataires</u>

  Pierette
  Le Curé de Tours
  Un menage de garçon
  <u>Les Parisiens en Province</u>

  L'Illustre Gaudissart
  La Muse du Departement
  <u>Les Rivalités</u>

  La V[i]eille Fille
  Le cabinet des Antiques
  Le Lys dans la Vallée
  <u>Illusions Perdues</u>

  Les Deux Poëtes
  Un Grand Homme de province à Paris
  Eve et David

Scenes de la Vie Parisienne
  <u>Histoire des Treize</u>

    Ferragus, chef des Devorans
    La Duchesse de Langeais
    La fille aux yeux d'or
    Le Pere Goriot
    Le Colonel Chabert
    Facino Cane
    La Messe de l'Athée
    Sarrassie
    L'Interdiction
    Cæsar Birotteau
    La Maison Nucingen
    Pierre Grassou
    La Princesse de Cadignan
    Les Employés
    <u>Splendeurs & miseres des courtisanes</u>

  Esther Heureuse
  À combien l'amour revient aux v[i]eillards

Instruction Criminelle
Un Prince de la Bohême
Esquisse d'Homme d'affaire
Gaudissart II
Les Comédiens sans le savoir

Scenes de la Vie Politique
  Un Episode de la Terreur
  Une tenebreuse affaire
  Z. Marcas
  <u>La femme de soixante ans</u>

Scenes de la Vie Militaire
  Les Chouans
  Une passion dans le Désert

Scenes de la Vie de Campagne
  Le medecin de campagne
  Le cure de campagne

Etudes Philosophiques
  Le Peau de chagrin
  Jesu Christ en Flandre
  Melmoth réconcilié
  Le Chef d'œuvre inconnu
  La Recherche de l'Absolu
  Massimila Doni
  Gambara
  L'enfant maudit
  Les Marana
  Adieu
  Le Requisitionnaire
  El Verdugo
  Un Drame au bord de la mer
  L'Auberge Rouge
  L'Elixir de longue Vie
  Maitre Cornélius
  <u>Sur Catherine de Medecis</u>

  Le Martyr Calviniste
  Confidence des Ruggieri
  Les Deux Réves
  Les Proscrits
  Louis Lambert
  Seraphita
  Philosophie du mariage.

Observe that I have copied this exactly, & that the double interlineations simply represent capital letters. Then he may have changed the names of several of the works, or he may .. nay, must .. have added new works—I miss 'La Derniere fée' & others, I think. There is a double name to the "Instruction criminelle" … "*ou menent les mauvais chemins,*"—& also to "La femme de soixante ans" … "*l'envers de l'histoire contemporaine*"- Both are new works of course.[20]

Have you seen "Agnes de Meranie" the new play by the author of Lucretia?[21] A witty feuilletoniste says of it, that, besides all the unities of Aristotle, it comprises, from beginning to end, *unity of* SITUATION- Not bad!— is it? Ma[dme] Ancelot has just succeeded with a comedy, called "Une année à Paris".[22] By the way, *shall you go to Paris this spring?*

Address, on integral page: Miss Mitford / Three Mile Cross / near Reading.
Publication: EBB-MRM, III, 201-208.
Manuscript: Wellesley College.

1. Year provided by postmark.
2. As indicated in letter 2642 (see note 13), Miss Mitford had evidently suggested the possibility of the Brownings obtaining French books in Leghorn.
3. "Convict" or "condemned criminal." Lucien Chardon, or Lucien de Rubempré, first appears as a character in *Illusions perdues* (1837), and EBB's lasting impression of him was that of a "femmelette," or weakling (see letter 1794). In that letter EBB foresees his "ruin," which is realized in *Une Instruction Criminelle* (1846), when Lucien commits suicide in his prison cell.
4. EBB has copied out and enclosed an advertisement from the 9 January 1847 issue of *Le Siècle* for a "nouvelle edition" of *La Comédie Humaine* in sixteen volumes. This is the only known instance in which EBB refers to the title that Balzac gave to the composite grouping of his works, published by Furne, et. al., from 1842 until 1846. Similar advertisements appeared in other French newspapers, for example, *La Presse.*
5. In letter 2219, EBB called *La Recherche de l'absolu* (1833-34) "Balzac's beautiful story."
6. Balzac's *César Birotteau* was published in 1837.
7. *Les Aventures de Saturnin Fichet ou la Conspiration de la Rouarie* appeared as a feuilleton in *Le Siècle* from 16 December 1846 to 8 May 1847. Referring to this work and another historical novel written the preceding year, *Les Quatres Napolitaines,* Soulié's biographer says that "in neither is there much pretense of documentation or of accurate local color" (Harold March, *Frédéric Soulié: Novelist and Dramatist of the Romantic Period,* 1931, p. 230).
8. Dumas's 1836 drama was sub-titled *Désordre et génie*; it was one of his 67 dramatic works.
9. Stendhal was the pseudonym for Marie Henri Beyle (1783-1842), whose *Le Rouge et le noir* was published in 1831. EBB had recommended this book to Miss Mitford in letter 1885.
10. *Crimes Célèbres* (1839-40), a seven-volume series of stories about infamous criminals or victims. The preface to the English translation published by Chapman and Hall in 1843 states that "several of the histories in this collection are founded chiefly on the *Causes Célèbres* [1734-45] of Gayot de Pithoval."
11. See letter 2644, note 1.
12. *Ballads and Other Poems* (1847). An American reviewer said that "the prominent faults in this volume will be found to be a lack of originality in the style of treating subjects in themselves interesting; a certain homeliness, occasionally observable, where elegance would have done just as well, as it will not always; and an irregularity of metre, which implies hurry or indolence, such as putting in a line a foot or two too long where it would have cost some trouble to make it shorter" (*The Literary World,* 13 February 1847, p. 32).
13. See letter 2642, note 8.

14. After a year of travelling in Italy, Fanny Kemble Butler had only recently returned to England where she was about to take up her career as an actress. She asked Alfred Bunn for £100 a night, and he responded with an offer of £50. Alternatively, she accepted Knowles's offer of £40 a night in Manchester, which was the start of her tour of the provinces (*The Terrific Kemble*, ed. Eleanor Ransome, 1978, pp. 196-197). An account of her travels in Italy appeared in early 1847 under the title *A Year of Consolation*.

15. William Thomas Green Morton (1819-68), a dentist from Massachusetts, was the first person to publicly demonstrate the use of sulphuric ether as an anæsthesia on 16 October 1846; the first demonstration in England occurred on 21 December 1846 at University College Hospital in an amputation performed by Robert Liston. Cf. *Casa Guidi Windows*, I, 695.

16. See letter 2642, note 2.

17. EBB often asked about Patty Lovejoy (1836-56) the consumptive daughter of Reading bookseller George Lovejoy.

18. In *Homes and Haunts of the Most Eminent British Poets* (1847), William Howitt asserts that there is "no rational doubt that she [Letitia Landon] died by it [prussic acid], and by her own hand," but that it was "by mistake" (II, 140).

19. *Dramatic Romances and Lyrics*, the seventh in the *Bells and Pomegranates* series, was published 6 November 1845, and the eighth, *Luria, and A Soul's Tragedy*, was published in April 1846. Miss Mitford's opinion of RB's poetry was not favourable (see letter 2198, note 1).

20. *La femme de soixante ans* was a "provisional title" for *L'Envers de l'histoire contemporaine*; see Herbert J. Hunt, *Balzac's Comédie Humaine* (1959), p. 492. The first part had been completed by this time, but the second part was not published until 1848 (Hunt, p. 409). According to Hunt, *Une Instruction criminelle* was finally entitled *Où mènet les mauvais chemins* and constituted Part III of "the Esther cycle" (p. 358). *La dernière Fée, ou La nouvelle Lampe merveilleuse* had been published in 1823.

21. François Ponsard (1814-67) was the author of *Lucrèce* (1843), a classical tragedy that had premiered at the Second Théâtre Français in April 1843 with Rachel in the title role. *Agnès de Méranie* was presented at the same theatre on 22 December 1846. Ponsard's popular success was largely due to the public reaction against the romantic style of Hugo and others in the 1830's. In *Lucrèce*, Ponsard returned to a closer adherence to the Aristotelian unities of time, place, and action.

22. *Une Année à Paris* premiered at the Odeon on 15 January 1847; the author, Marguerite Louise Virginie (*née* Chardon, 1792-1854), was the wife of dramatist Jacques Arsène Ancelot.

2655. EBB & RB TO ARABELLA & HENRIETTA MOULTON-BARRETT

[In EBB's hand] [Pisa]
Feb. 8– [1847][1]

My own dearest Arabel, this will not perhaps be a long letter, but I can send you satisfactory news of Wilson, thank God– She is reinstated in her various offices, & has taken leave of D: Cook though still weak & restricted as to diet. Coffee she is commanded to take leave of for ever .. mark that, Arabel! Where the stomach is feeble & irritable, it is very bad– And no eggs, no butter, .. poor Wilson!–& no wine,–& no potatoes .. I wonder how she gets on. There is still swelling in the side, but it is going away gradually, & she looks very well, & is likely to be really well, I hope & trust, & she is not at all afraid of Italy—& she takes rice & milk & tea & chicken & the light rolls we have here, & presently promises to add a great deal of exercise– As to what she has to do for us, it is light work as you may suppose, & we have, both of us, every reason for feeling a regard for her & attending to her comfort .. poor Wilson! A most excellent & amiable girl she is,—& I never shall forget what she has done for me.

And now my dear dearest Arabel, do tell me why you dont write to me, .. neither you nor Henrietta?- Unfortunate me, if you have sent a letter in the little parcel; because Sarianna Browning finds no means of sending it until March—and I may wait till April for a word from you, at that rate- The steamers from England dont begin to come until March—so provoking. But as to the letter, it was my fault if you sent one so, seeing that I ought to have explained how a parcel comes to Italy on four feet, & a letter flies on wings. Arabel! do write directly! Henrietta, I entreat you to write- And Arabel, beware of *ever* thinking of returning that watch to *me*- It is your own—& I shall be dreadfully offended by a word against my resolute word on the subject long ago. If you like, you know, to change it for a watch of a more useful size, it will be the same thing, & I shall have my *share* in the gift & in the thoughts—— There, now!- This is the third time of answering- Let me remember while I can, to say that I am very well, .. even if only to change the subject- Write, write!-

I dreamed of you last night—always I am dreaming of you, & when you dont write, I dream blackly & wide awake. The weather does not admit yet of my going out .. but as soon as we have a few fine settled days we are certainly going to Volterra & Siena for one excursion, & to Lucca & the Baths of Lucca afterwards, for another, .. & both must be in the course of the next two months as we leave Pisa then. We can go to Lucca & return in one day by the railroad, but the Baths being eight miles farther & exquisitely situated in the Apennines,[2] I was saying yesterday to Robert, that I should like to sleep there & have time to enjoy it, to which he replied that we could spend a week there if I preferred it .. but we shall see—it depends on the weather & the chesnut trees, to say nothing of our caprices- I have a fancy rather for those Baths of Lucca: for being IN the mountains—think of it, Arabel! So often I wish & long for you!- So often Robert says "I wish your sisters were with you", .. knowing what my thoughts are- Still, the hour of meeting will come, & in the meanwhile we love one another heart to heart as always- May God bless us all to the best ends of love- Now what am I to tell you? One of our days is like another,—& the only 'news' is, that we have both had excellent reports from Moxon as to poetry,—the *proceeds* this year being seventy pounds! There's riches for you--all expenses paid!- Moxon desires however, .. as some copies remain of some of Robert's works, that the issue of the new edition sh^d be delayed till our return to England, in order to secure, as he says, "an immediate success". Altogether we are sufficiently pleased, I assure you, by this report--& are turning our faces to a new book on Italy which is to move the world– Not that we shall spend money in printing anything—oh no!—you shall see presently .. only not immediately, if you please!- I must know rather more of Italy in the first place, before I can do my part– Talking of worldly prosperity, however, I shall tell you that I proposed to Robert the other day to put into the Pisan lottery ... there's immorality for you! but Jules Janin, the French critic, hazarded once five shillings & won a palace with orange groves & marble balustrades & the ghosts of the Medici know what,[3] .. & I suggested the risking of only five shillings. It would be as well, I thought, to have a palace too,—where was the objection? Oh, but Robert would'nt hear of it, & looked rather shocked at me for my want of principle in the matter. He said quite coolly that he had no doubt of being successful, if he considered it a justifiable experiment & so made up his mind to try it,—but that he would rather get a palace by any other means .. some honest means—he should only be ashamed of it, after he had won it so,—he seriously hoped that I was only in jest in proposing such a thing. I declared that I was perfectly in earnest, but laughed outright at his gravity while he cut his pencil & put away his palace, just as if they both were in his hand together—he always believes that he has only to wish for a thing, to have it—he believes it as I do that the sun will rise tomorrow– There is a tradition in his family that "a Browning can fail in nothing"—& in his own ex⟨per⟩ience, is proved by ever so many miracles, that he has only to wish for ⟨...⟩ for that impossible thing,—to find it close to him the next moment– So, this ⟨...⟩, he wont have a palace by any manner of means—more's the pity, *I* think! Jules Janin, besides his orange groves, had plate & linen & furniture, .. all in a glorious situation in the Baths of Lucca. The lottery is very popular in Italy--a lottery carried on by small sums– The people want amusement & excitement:—if they did not, they would be freer perhaps: as it is, the intellectual & moral degradation is striking. The national newspapers sound like theme-writing by boys of twelve years old,—the literature reminds one of the "World of Fashion" or "Belle Assemblée":[4] there seem to be no *men* here. France & England are centuries before these Italians—to judge from the *writings*! (observe!) Of the living humanity, we shall know more presently. We heard from dear M! Kenyon (oh, so kind he is!) two days ago—and Mr. Panizzi (of the British Museum) & M! Babbage[5] have given us letters of introduction to two or three more professors here– I argue ill of professors, though, since our Signor Ferucci, who, as Robert says, is just "the husk of a man",—full of platitudes & commonplaces. Oh thank you, Arabel, for sparing us "the Groemes".[6] Most curiously, just before your letter mentioned them, Robert who had been down to Peverada[7] upon business (he keeps the Hotel sacred to the English in Pisa) had been making me laugh by a story about the miraculous stupidity of some M! Groeme (your very Groeme!) whom Peverada could not instruct in the necessity of being subject to the custom house officers. It is too long to tell but it made me laugh at the moment .. & induced Peverada to exclaim with a long drawn sigh .. "See what I have to endure"—for his office is to explain everything to everybody ... who can understand anything. He speaks excellent English & is a person in great request of course.- Mr Kenyon says that George is in the country, & Mrs Martin told me that I was to hear from him– Tell me about him, & *Storm*, & all of them .. & dont let dear Sette think that I was ungrateful for his letter.- So Leonard Clarke is by no means inconsolable—it makes one laugh & sigh at the same time—but she never was much his companion—⟨tha⟩t makes a difference: still it is not decent conduct, considering how, af⟨ter all⟩ she was his wife & the mother of his child–[8] Bummy does not wri⟨te ... ⟩—she told me that aunt Fanny had been ill—did you hear of it? Do let me hear every detail of how you get on & whom you see & where you go—& do go among your friends a little more, my own Arabel? Does Mary Hunter continue better?—mention her- And tell me too of Mr Hunter, & if there should be room with him for my love, give it to him! & instruct me concerning his visit to Paris—let me lose no detail. Surely he must be in a kinder mood by this time. I shall write to Blackwood & send him some old sonnets,[9]—& take the opportunity of enquiring about my Prometheus & explaining why the other was not sent.[10] Dear Henry must be wholesomely disgusted of his Austrians, I should think by this time, considering the Cracow business.[11] Neither have my French much distinguished themselves as to integrity & righteousness in the matter of the Spanish marriages—I say my French .. because I have been taking Guizot's part against Robert,[12] evening after evening—reading the despatches & arguing on each of them .. (such discussions we have had!) till at the last revelations I was forced to give in——though it was wrong of me to blame "my French" .. when simply it was my Guizot who failed. In fact the French people are highly indignant .. I like & love the French: & Guizot only stands up to face the charge of defective honour & truth, such as appear too undeniable.- Tell me of Occy's drawings—I love him dearly, dear Occy .. tell him so- I love them all, dear things, with all my heart. Mind you speak of dearest Papa- Are Minny's legs better? My best love to her- Mention dear Trippy, & say how she is & if she is with you much—I never forget her, tell her- And thank Lizzie for her welcome little letter—she is a darling. Does Surtees Cook get his appointment .. & Susan, does she return from the country—the more you instruct me in, the better. So you are of opinion that Robert & I sh^d quarrel rather, to break up the monotony? How we sh^d ever quarrel, is impossible for me to conceive of—though I have had my pardon begged several times for mysterious offences beyond my apprehension. Seriously, how sh^d we quarrel, when I am always in the right, & *he knows it*? He loves me more every day, he says & I believe—yes, sure I am, that he loves me, ..

these five months being e⟨...⟩—more than when we married .. inexpressibly more- Yet his ⟨...⟩ dogma is, "that I do not know & never shall know, how much he loves me—and, as to loving him in a like proportion ... why, it is foolishness of me to pretend to such a thing—it cannot be-" If all married people lived as happily as we do, how many good jokes it would spoil! against marriage & so on!—only the world w^d be too happy for the graves in it—far too happy.

When Lent begins we hear that one of the first preachers in Italy is to deliver a discourse in the cathedral, four days of the week—& we mean to go, if the weather sh^d anywise admit of it- I shall like it much on every account-

How is Arabella Gosset? & Miss Russell?[13] I thought of HER, when I heard of the sulphuric æther experiments: & how wonderful *they* are!—and what a merciful remission of the pangs of humanity! I write in the greatest, greatest haste, & can read over nothing. Mrs Martin made me glad at heart by the assurance that you & Henrietta looked well—you are very idle though, as to writing- Oh now, do, do write. Wont the new debtors act enable uncle Richard & the poor Barretts to come to England?[14] Indeed the account of the latter is very melancholy,—but I never can comprehend how a man like him, in the prime of life, & with a sufficiency of intelligence & energy I suppose, should not at once exert himself to get occupation either in England or France- The French railroads are as feasible as the English- Occupation is not only his resource, but his duty!- I grieve for poor Maria & her six children- And is it not his fault & his reproach, that those debts in Jamaica are unpaid at this day?

Observe, Arabel, that the cathedral is close by, .. as near to us in this house, as Devonshire Place .. the beginning of Devonshire Place—is to you— so that the distance was not great enough for a car⟨riage, w⟩hile the great cloak covered me into the very depths of prud⟨ence—therefore⟩, there was no danger! Then the cathedral is not like cathed⟨rals in⟩ England—I felt no cold at all. Three days ago we had a letter from Mrs Jameson, who is enjoying herself in Rome & wishing for us, she has the goodness to say, most fervently. I heard too from dear Miss Mitford who spoke of receiving a kind message from you & of intending to visit you when she shall be in London this summer.

Now I shall write no more- May God bless you, my dearest own Arabel, my dearest Henrietta—may God bless you always- Give my love to those whom I love, & who will have it- I write like a race horse "scouring the plain"[15] .. or as an Italian writer *quotes* from the "Gintilman's Magasine", .. "like a *scouring race horse*"- May God bless you- Pray for me as I do for you-

Understand that I can write better than this really, when I try: but the haste drives the words before one!

Your own ever attached
Ba-

Flush has grown, from being simply insolent, a complete tyrant now— another Nicholas– He barks one distracted, the first moment he takes it into his head to want anything– I was saying to Robert (who spoils him) the other day, that soon we sh.d have to engage a page for his sole use—or brown livery turned up with white.

Yes, I think he *does* mean it for Italian—*pure Tuscan*, you know.

N.B—mind, nobody makes me melancholy by writing about my birthday–[16] (Speak in time!) How I think of you all!

[Continued by RB]

Pisa,
Feb. 8 '47.

I have to thank you, my dearest sisters, for two of the kindest notes in the world. It is an unspeakable delight to me to find that I can sympathize with Ba in every thing, and love most dearly the two whom she loves most dearly– I know, and nobody so well, what you have lost in her—that is, lost for a time—yet your generosity pardons me that loss, while your *woman's* tact and quickness of feeling does justice to the conduct which occasioned it— for both of which, I am, and always shall be most truly and gratefully your debtor– You tell me that the way to pay such debts is to love Ba—but I cannot obey you there—she takes all my love for her own sake—just as you,—whom I was prepared and eager to love for her sake,—you make me love you on your own account. You wish to know how Ba is—from me, as well as from her. I assure you that thro' God's goodness she appears quite well; *weak*, certainly, as compared to persons in ordinary health, but with no other ailment perceptible. A few days ago, she seemed to have caught a slight cold—(thro' her kind care of Wilson, who has been ill as I am sure Ba will have told you)—but yesterday & today the few symptoms of aching &c have disappeared. Dr Cook, the physician we called in to Wilson, who had seen Ba just on his arrival, expressed his surprize & delight at the manifest improvement in her appearance—and he observed to Wilson, "this comes of a visit to Pisa *in time*"—(he is learned in pulmonary disease and has written a book about it[17]—he has just returned, moreover, from England—"where the cold was intense" he said[)]. Here, also, the cold has been considerable, and we are too indebted to the good already produced by the climate, to peril it by going out rashly at this (as we hope) the winter's end: but I trust and believe that, with the stock of strength *preserved* thro' the winter we shall so profit by the coming fine weather, as to need fear no relapse. Ba sleeps admirably—and is steadily diminishing the doses of morphine, quite as much as is prudent. I daresay she explained to you the cause of the

No. 2655 8 February [1847] 127

Apothecary's mistake about the prescription, at the beginning—he really believed *his* morphine to be so superior to what we could get in England that he felt himself bound to diminish the quantity—ever since, his performances have been unexceptionable—indeed, he is said to be one of the best Chymists in Italy. What, I think, you would be most struck with in Ba, is the strengthened voice- Wilson hears it, she says, thro' her door and ours. I cannot tell you of other qualities that are "strengthened," however—no words can convey the entire sweetness, unselfishness of that dear nature! Yet I have been used to the kindest of natures, and am by no means likely to err from excess of indulgence to any one.

You found fault, I am told, with our midnight attendance at Mass on Christmas eve—but we took great precautions and the Cathedral is but a few paces from our house. When the weather permits (and not before) we hope to make an excursion to Sienna, Colle, and Volterra,—fine old Etruscan cities, one & all. In the meantime, we are in Carnival season, and I saw full half a dozen masqueradors yesterday,—a more effective sermon on the vanity of human pleasure you would not wish to hear! It may grow better by and bye. There is to be a grand affair in August, a service to a particular picture of the Virgin "Sotto gli Organi"[18] which, they say, saved this city from the earthquakes last year—but we shall be away. I believe I have filled my envelope without telling you very much, but another time I shall succeed better. Know me for your most affectionate

RB-

Address, in EBB's hand, on integral page: (To the care of Miss Trepsack) / Miss Arabel Barrett / 5- Upper Montagu Street / Montagu Square.
Publication: NL, pp. 40–42 (in part).
Manuscript: Berg Collection.

1. Year provided by postmark and the dated continuation in RB's hand.
2. According to Murray's *Hand-Book for Travellers in Northern Italy* (1847), Bagni di Lucca is "about 15 miles from Lucca" (p. 415).
3. In *Voyages en Italie* (1839), Jules Janin gives an account of his lottery success in a chapter entitled "La Palazzina Lazzarini," the name of the house he won near Lucca.
4. A reference to *La Belle Assemblée, or Court and Fashionable Magazine* and to *The World of Fashion and Continental Feuilletons*, both of which would have fit EBB's implication here of a publication comprised of writing in the style of the blue-stocking school.
5. Charles Babbage (1792-1871) was a mathematician and inventor of an elaborate calculating machine. Antonio Panizzi (1797-1879) had become assistant librarian of the British Museum in 1831, and keeper of printed books shortly afterwards in 1837. Acquisition of the Grenville library in 1846 was mostly due to his efforts, and he was largely responsible for the design of the reading room.
6. Unidentified.
7. See letter 2624, note 1.
8. Mary Frances Graham-Clarke (afterwards Wilmer, b. 1845) was the only child of Isabella and Leonard Graham-Clarke. EBB's allusion to his conduct is unclear, but it might refer to his subsequent marriage to Lavinia Horsford.
9. EBB sent *Blackwood's Edinburgh Magazine* eight sonnets. Four of them appeared in the May 1847 issue: "Life," "Love," "Heaven and Earth. 1845," and "The Prospect.

1845." Four more appeared in the June 1847 issue: "Two Sketches" (depicting her sisters Henrietta and Arabella), "Mountaineer and Poet," and "The Poet."

10. See letter 2624, note 16.

11. The Republic of Cracow had been an independent state since the Congress of Vienna in 1815, but the Austrian government sent troops to Cracow in March 1846, and in November 1846 it was incorporated into the Austrian empire. Despite the protests of other countries, especially England and France, it remained under Austrian rule until 1918, when it was returned to Poland.

12. On 10 October 1846, Queen Isabella II of Spain and her sister Luisa Fernanda, the Infanta, married the Duke of Cadiz and the Duke of Montpensier, respectively. Despite agreements previously made between the French and English governments, the marriage of the Infanta to Montpensier was not to have taken place until after the Queen's marriage. For this reason, Guizot, Louis Philippe's minister, was accused of deceit in the affair. Although he was under strong pressure from his sovereign, he also saw the advantage of the triumph as a political victory for his party, as well as feeling a sense of personal pride because of his dislike for Palmerston. Despite initial success, these events led to the fall of Guizot and the Orleans monarchy the following year.

13. Mary Anne Russell (1816?-70); she was a sister of Sir William Russell (see letter 2165) and of Emma and Jane Munro. EBB's cousin, Arabella Sarah Butler, had married Allen Ralph Gosset in 1835.

14. EBB's uncle by marriage, Richard Butler, and her cousin Samuel Goodin Barrett (with his wife Maria and their family), were residing outside England to avoid their creditors and imprisonment. EBB is apparently referring to the "Act to abolish the Court of Review on Bankruptcy, and to make alterations in the Jurisdiction of the Courts of Bankruptcy and Court for Relief of Insolvent Debtors" a new act which was being debated by Parliament. It became law in July 1847, but it would not have affected EBB's family members since its advantage was to creditors who could recover small debts without great cost. Imprisonment for debt was not abolished until 1869.

15. Cf. Pope, *An Essay on Criticism*, line 372.

16. RB did not learn the day and month of EBB's birth, 6 March, until 1885 (see *Reconstruction*, A232, now at Eton). RB was informed of the year, 1806, by her brother George in 1887 (*Harper's Monthly Magazine*, March 1916, p. 530).

17. *A Practical Treatise on Pulmonary Consumption, Its Pathology, Diagnosis, and Treatment* (1842) by Francis Cook; see letter 2645, note 2.

18. The "*Madonna dell'Organo*, the object of Catholic devotion ... is a Greek painting venerated at Pisa before 1224, and may possibly be as old as the first foundation of the present building" (Murray's *Hand-Book*, p. 445). Another guide-book to Pisa calls it the "Madonna di sotto gli Organi" and says it has been attributed to Francesco Curradi (*Nuova Guida di Pisa*, Pisa, 1843, p. 93).

2656. EBB TO ARABELLA MOULTON-BARRETT

[Pisa]
Feb. 24– 1847.

My most dear Arabel, here am I waiting, waiting for letters!– There may be one today perhaps, & while Robert prepares to go out to the post & Flush adjusts himself for an interrogative bark ("am I to go too"?) I begin an answer to what *may* arrive .. I do hope so. Something will be said in it of my dear Stormie, .. of the manner of his going, & whether his joy lasted to the end. It is certainly a comfort to think that his choice was in the matter, .. & also (what George tells me) that he goes for a short time only & may travel in another direction afterwards. I dont find fault with people for wanting to travel .. it seems as natural as wishing to read– It is only the *climate*, which frightens me—ah well, but Retreat[1] is cool, I suppose, & he will take care, he promises .. and God is over all. I have heard from George, you see– Not an unkind letter, if considered by itself, & considering me by myself .. but unkind, I must think, after all I have said, & in relation to the circumstances in which I am– Good Heavens, how little they know of me, if they imagine it to be possible to thrust me into the position, the possibility of which they assume! There is one person in the world who might do it .. *Papa might*. If he said "I will write to you .. I will see you .. your husband's name never being named between us", .. I should think it my duty to accept under any condition any alms of kindness from him– He is my father .. I would kiss his hands & feet at any moment– Also he has peculiarities which I deeply pity the tendencies of, & which, where it is possible, should be dealt with tenderly. But to my brothers .. in fact to another human being except my father, .. *this does not apply*– I have used my last word on the state of the question as relates to *them*—they must choose their alternative,—& if they do not love me enough to accept *mine* with *me*, why they must cast me off at their pleasure– I cannot help it. I say it in sorrow more than in any anger– I should not have acted to them as they have acted to me. Here have six months passed since my marriage, & I hold that the merest natural affection calls loudly for a different line of conduct– I do not however invite them to it .. they are judges of what becomes them best– Only I, for my part, will not be so base & ungrateful as to admit the formula of a kindness which insultingly excludes the one who has given up his life to me with the very perfection of tenderness! He who from first to last, never for a moment failed to me, .. I am to stand aside from *him* as if he *had* failed! No!– As my *husband* he has claims on the respect of those who love me—but as Robert Browning, he has stronger claims on *me* than even the word 'husband' suggests, .. even as his goodness & persistent affection have exceeded far & far the common kindness of kind husbands & the expectations of reasonable women. If I sinned against him *so*, I should scorn myself—there is an end!– Tell dear George that I dearly love him .. better than he ever loved me, .. but that I do not answer his letter for these reasons– It is better not to answer it .. we cannot hold a false position .. false on his side, .. most unworthy on mine. Oh, when Robert saw me ruffled about that letter the other day, he begged me not to care for it .. to let it pass .. "It is enough for me, darling, that *you* understand me .. that *you* know my heart & my motives". But I appealed to him whether if *his* family agreed to blot me out of the world after that fashion, he could bear it—"*He! his* family! to me!"– So then he was bade to observe that it was my affair, & concerned my own feelings, & that he had no right to interfere– And in fact it is simply my affair. My brothers confer no honour on my husband by their notice, nor inflict any injury by their neglect– The injury is *mine* .. to my feelings .. my affections! the blow falls *there*. This is all, I think, that is necessary to say.

Wilson is getting strong by degrees, I am glad to say, & last night put me to bed for the first time since a month—it has been a long illness—that is, the weakness hung round her long: and it seemed best that she should rest & not sit up after seven. But last night she rebelled, & w.d have it that such early hours kept her from sleeping, and our vigils at the latest, are not apt to be exhausting. With all the improvement she cannot touch butter .. and has only taken chicken two days with impunity—she suffered so, she had to leave it off. Rice milk & tea & roll are the whole of her sustenance, .. & of course she must be weak. She goes out twice in the day to walk, & looks by no means ill—oh, she will be strong, I hope & trust, in a little while– D.r Cook seemed to have no fears– She & I agree sometimes (by way of comfort) that if she had gone to Jamaica with the Barretts, it would have killed her outright, & that (our way) she has been only half killed, poor thing. I never saw anyone suffer so from sickness—& then the mucus membrane of the stomach was previously in an irritable state—and the 'remedies' upon *that*!– The weather is turned to spring– Every day last week I was able to walk out ... Robert, as delighted to have me with him as a child when the flowers take to blowing in the garden! Moreover we heard three sermons last week at the Duomo, besides one (by far the worst) in the English church[2] ... Arabel, we *could* not go often to hear such trash .. it amounted to imbecillity, .. M.r Green's trash, you are to understand that I mean. The catholic discourses delivered four times a week during Lent, I had much more satisfaction in listening to, though fluency & great earnestness & an adroitness in the arrangement of commonplaces, made the chief merit of those. There was not a word of controversial matter .. of peculiar doctrine .. except when the preacher desired from each of the congregation at the end, an *ave maria* "in *sua* ritenzione",[3] .. for his particular benefit– But the voice, the articulation, the vibrative earnestness of the tones of the preacher .. a friar in a brown vesture & a rope round his waist .. legs & feet as bare as nature left them .. his striking gestures as he stood in the chair of the great cathedral .. above all, the crowds of listeners .. men .. thronging, standing leaning against the columns with uplifted dark Italian faces, .. such a crowded & breathless congregation .. all made a grand sight; & the coloured sunshine streaming through the windows, was scarcely wanted to complete the effect– Just see how this people give their attention & reverence when they *understand*– It makes all the difference, the understanding. The chanted, muttered Latin mass leaves them as I told you, a congregation of promenaders—but the words of their own language, appealing to their sympathies & experience, draw them, fasten them, impress them .. the silence in the great crowd seemed to take away your breath. We had chairs under the pulpit, but the majority stood the whole time, .. *an hour* .. most of them, men. Some appeared very much moved. The last subject, the text delivered in Latin "Be not deceived, God is not mocked",[4] had rather more doctrine than the preceding ones, & scarcely anything to object to, I think, & some good things without the least trace of original thinking. But oh, M! Green, I would rather listen to our friar than to you! The imbecillity & inconsequence of the English preacher is something past describing, .. & in order to *afficher*[5] it in the strongest way, he preaches extempore, & says like an orator that "gratified ambition gratifies," & profundities of that kind– It is a shame that the church of England should not place here some man of faculty & instruction, where both among visitors & residents there must be such noble opportunities. We found it disagreeable altogether to go to that room .. a mere room .. into a selection of pink & blue bonnets, everybody looking at everybody—"*a shilling each for entrance*" like a religious academy. I do wish the Scotch church at Leghorn were here[6] .. but soon we shall go away, & hope to do better perhaps—& in the meanwhile we mean to hear all the Lent sermons in the cathedral. Our present plan is (the way we make our plans up & down, w!! quite amuse you) to go to Florence for a month & then to the north of Italy— there are cool Baths near Vicenza[7] said to be the coolest place in this country, .. & there, we are close to Venice, observe!– We shall travel slowly, & through Bologna, of course, where by means of letters of introduction, we shall visit Rossini, tell Henrietta, who resides there.[8] How M!! Jameson meets us, is not decided yet. She leaves Rome early in April, & we shall find it hard to give up our month at Florence .. but we must contrive somehow. Such affectionate letters she writes to us, first to one then to another, then to both together—& I love her the better that I think she loves Robert the best of us two– Over & over I have heard her say .. "No, I never did see before such a combination in mortal man .. such intellect with such moral excellence—it is really *not fair*". As we landed at Genoa, & he who had been as ill as he well could, began in his old way to keep up everybody's spirits forgetting himself altogether, she whispered to me, "My dear, that inexhaustible sweetness of disposition of *his* is worth to you just ten thousand a year .. or a good deal more perhaps". Which is my own opinion .. upon still fuller evidence. You cannot know what he is to me & how deeply I believe that there is not his like among men now alive. All these months we have passed together in this little room, ... every hour of time has drawn us nearer .. & when he tells me that he loves me more than ever, why I *see that* before he speaks—& I feel it by my own feelings too. There is no restraint .. no reserve & at the beginning, when people love one another at best even, there is apt to be a touch of either– As to *fear* .. why the day before we married he said to me, "Ba, if ever I thought it possible that you should be afraid of me, I should have strength to give up everything at this moment—I could bear anything from you but THAT" ... so now I say sometimes, "If I am very impertinent to you, it is'nt *my* fault, remember .. it was *in the bond*."⁹ And really I am very impertinent not infrequently, & we have great arguments about the Spanish marriages & M. Guizot, & Balzac & Rousseau, & subjects not to be counted .. & he, who mounts an argument just like a battery, growing warmer & warmer, till he gets quite into extravagances, (that's a tendency of his) makes me feel warm too .. & then I take up a book & observe in a provoking way .. "I wont dispute a moment longer—you say things that you dont mean or that you ought'nt to mean. Only, I protest against all you have been saying .. & there's my last word". The other day, there was a silence after this, of at least ten minutes, & I confess, I thought to myself .. "now he is angry with me at last". Seriously, I was plotting how to be forgiven, & how to put my impertinent book down with sufficient dignity .. when lo, a voice said .. "Ba, do you know one of the reasons why I love you?"- "Hard to guess", I answered, in a resumption of goodhumour .. "you know very well that your reasons for loving me, I have always ranked among the mysteries". "Then I will tell you one of the many reasons. When I get into a petulant irritable humour ... " (*he*!!) "& have the headache as I have now, & say unreasonable & improper things, which my own reason would recoil at another time, you do not give up to me, & attempt to soothe me by agreeing with me or letting it pass, as so many good tempered women do to the eternal injury of foolish men, .. but you always tell me the truth plainly, Ba". .... ⟨"The reason is, that I have too much *respect* for you not to tell you the truth, when I apprehend the truth myself, .. or at least what I take to be truth—"⟩¹⁰—— But the goodness & tenderness of this return quite moved me of course- Think what an adorable disposition, what candour, what an unmasculine freedom from pride, it expresses—! I tell you just as it comes into my head, because you have not had opportunities of knowing him, & I want you to know him—but this only is one of the thousand traits which I might make the same use of. He is too good—he puts me to shame, sometimes. May God make me at least grateful, if I cannot be worthier.--

The weather has seemed suddenly to burst into summer, though today there is a cold wind & it is safer to keep at home. Robert brought me heaps of violets the other day which he had gathered himself beyond the walls of the city, & soon we shall think of our excursion to Volterra & Siena. When we leave this place, we shall be *housed* more cheaply .. (that our hosts have perfectly "taken us in & done for us" here is indisputable) but in other respects, there cannot, I think, be an improvement- Our dinner yesterday, for instance, .. consisting of soup for two .. roast chicken, browned potatoes, a pudding, & a bottle of the best wine .. our Chianti .. cost two shillings & a halfpenny—this for three people .. at least Wilson had some of the chicken. Now, you see, there is no pitiful œconomy in all this—we *require* nothing more, in the way of luxury even– Viva la trattoria, I say. It is cheap & direct, & saves unlearned people like Robert & me from the dreadful pass of "keeping house." What w^d become of me, I am sure, I cant imagine, if I had to manage & manage! And then to have to eat cold mutton & other delicacies of small establishments, w^d be as difficult as the rest & neither Robert nor I have been used to it, & we have not the trained appetites for the sort of thing. If we lived in Paris, especially during the mild weather, we sh^d always go to the traiteur's[11] .. that's still better perhaps—but here, it is a dark place, a good deal thronged with men, & we find the advantage in having the dinner sent. The other day Mr Irving called on us again, & I saw him– Really an intelligent, *very* gentlemanly ⟨per⟩son—& with a benevolent countenance & smile. He gave us sundry pieces of advice, & praised Italy to the uttermost—"he wondered, for his part, how anyone could live out of it, who could live in it"—he could not bear the winters in England, & had his two sons in the university here at Pisa .. otherwise he should go to Venice, which he believed to be the best winter climate in the country .. better than Pisa itself. Tell me if this man is father to the celebrated person of the same name who used to visit you (& *other people*) in Wimpole Street? He is of Jamaica .. & has estates next Papa's[12] .. Also, think of our having an invitation in form from Mrs Cook to an evening party for thursday! I sate down to answer it in form, & not being "native to the manner",[13] tore up one manuscript before I could write another fit to send, Robert sitting opposite to me in admiration at my want of dexterity!! Tell Henrietta that I wished aloud for *her*. I w^d rather have written a sonnet, I thought. It was his fault, in some measure, because he kept on saying– "Mind, you dont put down that we are engaged .. *pray* be very decided .. *do* be as civil as possible" ... till at last I retorted .. "Dont talk to me .. dont look at me .. *pray* take up your book & read". I grew quite desperate– I wish darling Arabel, you would write a little note to Mr Kenyon & tell him from me that when he pays Minny's fifty five pounds (is'nt it fifty five) he would pay besides the half year's interest .. amounting to thirty shillings, .. as they will be due to her justly. Give my best love to dear Minny .. I shall write her a little note some day soon– Tell her that from me. Is Crow's youngest child likely to keep its dark hair & eyes?[14] Let me hear something about her & Lizzie. Tell me particularly too about Mr Boyd, (my love to him always, Arabel) & what you mean by his being more weak & whether it is the effect of the cold. George thought that we c^d not beat at Pisa your thermometer being at 50 one day out of doors. Why I was sitting out of doors last week in the shadow of the cathedral—the coldest situation in Pisa, & feeling it too warm—& when Wilson goes on the Arno she comes back exhausted. Do tell me everything—of dear Stormie especially. Any news of Bummy & the Hedleys. Yes, I love uncle Hedley, & I *believed* that he could not be otherwise than kind to me under all circumstances. Even Bummy, in the memorable scolding letter, sent a very kind message to Robert, keeping the stripes for my particular use—poor, dear Bummy. Do you hear of Leonard's child?[15] & of the Bevans? & of Arabella Gosset's health? Let me hear of all at home at full length though. I shall write to Blackwood, tell George, to arrange that matter. Dearest Trippy is the most hospitable & dear of hostesses, tell her with two great kisses .. & Robert sends his love to her too, mind. Oh, we shall go to drink tea with her, some of these evenings. Ask Lizzie, dear Liz, not to be too tall to look down & see me when I come back— My love to George & all of them, dear things. I love you my own Arabel. Bear me on your heart & in your prayers .. & Robert .. he says—

Your ever attached & grateful
Ba--

Speak of Papa.

Address, on integral page: (To the care of Miss Trepsack) / Miss Arabel Barrett / 5– Upper Montagu Street / Montagu Square.
Publication: None traced.
Manuscript: Berg Collection.

1. Retreat Penn, a Barrett estate, was located in the parish of St. James, Jamaica.
2. The Chapel of St. George the Martyr was situated near the Lungarno on a site that had been purchased in 1839 with money raised by subscriptions, and built to the design of Joseph Pardini. The building was completed in 1843. The Rev. Henry Greene (1808?–76) was Chaplain from 1846 until 1875 (Archives of the Inter-Continental Church Society, London).
3. "To keep in your memory," or "to keep in mind."
4. Galatians 6:7.
5. "Show."
6. In the entry for Leghorn, Murray's *Hand-Book for Travellers in Northern Italy* (1847) notes that "every species of religion is permitted to have its place of worship. The English chapel is regularly served by a resident chaplain" (p. 471), but it does not specifically mention a "Scotch Church" at Leghorn.
7. At Recoaro, which is "about 3½ posts from Vicenza to the north-west" (Murray's *Hand-Book* p. 293). Evidently they had discussed going to Recoaro with Mrs. Jameson; see letter 2666.
8. Rossini was in Bologna, off and on, from 1837 until 1848, when the revolutionary movements and his ill health caused him to leave Bologna for Florence, where the Brownings finally met him in 1849.
9. Cf. *Merchant of Venice*, IV, 1, 259.
10. The bracketed passage was originally written in narrative form and introduced by "I told him," but EBB later altered it, making it a direct statement from her to RB.
11. "Restaurateur" or "caterer."
12. See letter 2630, note 12.
13. Cf. *Hamlet*, I, 4, 14–15.
14. Ellen Treherne, second child and second daughter of William Treherne and his wife Elizabeth (*née* Crow), was born at Kentish Town, St. Pancras, on 29 June 1846.
15. See note 8 in the preceding letter.

2657. RB TO EDWARD MOXON

Pisa, Collegio Ferdinando.
Feb. 24. '47.

My dear Moxon,
    Many thanks for your note with its good news. I delayed answering it in the expectation of a note from Procter, whom I had asked (as I told you) to lend me his eyes, for I don't trust mine implicitly when they look on home interests through this lazy Italian air. He does not write, however, so I must.

    I and my wife think your account a very satisfactory one, and we have commissioned Mr. Kenyon to receive what you promise us; that is to say, so much of the £75 and odd, as shall remain when you have deducted the proper sum for those advertisements you advise. I suppose £15 will be quite enough for them, so that we take £60 with the best will in the world. All your advertisements are in such good taste, that one needs say nothing about dropping "Esqs." and "Mr's." and "Mrs's." and putting simply R.Bs. and E.B.Bs.

    With respect to what you recommend to me in the matter of a new edition,[1] nothing can be more sensible—only, observe, I use the words people put into my mouth when they begin to advise me. They will have it that the form, the cheap way of publication, the double columns, &c., do me harm, keep reviewers from noticing what I write—retard the sale—and so on. For myself, I always liked the packed-up completeness and succinctness, and am not much disposed to care for the criticism that is refused because my books are not thick as well as heavy. But the point which decided me to wish to get printed over again was the real good I thought I could do to *Paracelsus*, *Pippa*, and some others; good, not obtained by cutting them up and reconstructing them, but by affording just the proper revision they ought to have had before they were printed at all. This, and no more, I fancy, is due to them. But you know infinitely best what our policy is; "ours," for if we keep together, there is not such a thing as your losing while I gain. When you speak of postponing this till my return to England you may be thinking of a speedier return than is probable. I shall certainly stay another year, if not longer, in Italy; but by Christmas, Providence helping, my wife and I want to print a book as well as our betters, after what we think a new and good plan—all which it would be premature to allude to at present. To return to the matter in hand, therefore, thank you heartily for your kind wishes, and prompt attention to my note. Surely, after all, the account is not unfavourable. If all these "devices" can sell, without a single notice except from the *Examiner*, things will mend some day, we may hope.

    I say nothing of my wife's poems and their sale. She is, there as in all else, as high above me as I would have her. She sends her best respects and regards to you—for I must leave off.

And do you, dear Moxon, believe me,
Ever with great sincerity,
Yours,
R. Browning.

I look out in the *Times* for your notices, and hope this novel of Knowles'[2] will profit you.

Text: *LVC*, 1st Ser., I, 15-18.

1. See letter 2655 for EBB's reference to Moxon's suggestion that the new edition of RB's works be delayed until the Brownings returned to England.
2. An advertisement in *The Times* of this date announced that James Sheridan Knowles's novel, *George Lovell*, was "just published." It was reviewed in *The Athenæum* for 27 February 1847 (no. 1009, pp. 223-224), which said that "it is written earnestly rather than eloquently." The marked file of *The Athenæum*, now at City University (London), identifies H.F. Chorley as the author of this review.

2658. EBB TO SARIANNA BROWNING

[Pisa]
[late February 1847][1]

I must begin by thanking dearest Sarianna again for her note, & by assuring her that the affectionate tone of it quite made me happy & grateful together .. that I am grateful to *all of you*! Do *feel* that I am– For the rest, when I see (afar off) Robert's minute manuscripts, a certain distrust steals over me of anything I can possibly tell you of our way of living, lest it should be the vainest of repetitions,[2] & by no means worth repeating, both at once. Such a quiet silent life it is,—going to hear the Friar preach in the Duomo, a grand event in it!—and the wind laying flat all our schemes about Volterra & Lucca! I have had to give up even the Friar for these three days past—there is nothing for me, when I have driven out Robert to take his necessary walk, but to sit & watch the pinewood blaze. He is grieved about the illness of his cousin[3]—only I do hope that your next letter will confirm the happy change which stops the further anxiety, & come soon for that purpose, besides others. Your letters never can come too often, remember, even when they have not to speak of illness——and I, for my part, must always have a thankful interest in your cousin, for the kind part he took in the happiest event of my life. You have to tell us too of your dear mother– Robert is so anxious about her always. How deeply—tenderly he loves her & all of you, never could have been more manifest than now when he is away from you & has to talk *of* you instead of *to* you. By the way (or rather out of the way) I quite took your view of the proposed ingratitude to poor Miss Haworth[4]—it would have been worse in him than the sins of Examiner & Athenæum. If authors wont feel for one another, there's an end of the world of writing! Oh—I think he proposed it in a moment of hardheartedness .. we all put on tortoise shell

now & then, & presently come out into the sun as sensitively as ever. Besides, Miss Haworth has written to us very kindly; & kindness does'nt spring up everywhere, like the violets in your gravel walks. See how I understand Hatcham!—— Do try to love me a little, dearest Sarianna—(with my grateful love always to your father & mother) let me be your affectionate sister,
Elizabeth Barrett Browning
or rather Ba.

Address, on integral page: Miss Browning.
Publication: LEBB, I, 321–322.
Manuscript: Lilly Library.

    1. EBB's reference to having "had to give up even the Friar for these three days past" seems to place this letter shortly after letter 2656, in which she mentions having "heard three sermons last week at the Duomo."
    2. Cf. Matthew 6:7
    3. RB's cousin James Silverthorne (1809–52), who witnessed the Brownings' marriage, suffered from inflammation of the lungs, eventually resulting in his death on 19 May 1852.
    4. Apparently RB was displeased that Fanny Haworth had included a poem about EBB in her volume, *St. Sylvester's Day, and Other Poems* ("To Miss Barrett, on Hearing of Her Secluded Life from Illness"), and from the context it seems that he had suggested writing to her to express his displeasure. He had responded positively to her request to include a sonnet about him (see letter 2449, note 2). The volume was published between 30 December 1846 and 14 January 1847 (*The Publisher's Circular,* 15 January 1847, p. 27). Evidently Sarianna was concerned that a review of Haworth's poems had not appeared. Subsequent to this letter it was mentioned in *The Athenæum* as "an ornament for the drawing-room table" (1 May 1847, no. 1018, p. 463), but we have found no review of Haworth's poems in *The Examiner.*

2659. EBB & RB TO ANNA BROWNELL JAMESON

[In RB's hand]   Pisa.
March 4. '47

Dearest Aunt Nina, How I hope you have thought it a long while to be waiting for news of us, and have heartily abused us, and forsworn us, and all that proves people really love each other! In fact our Pisa-life glides so equably by, with its days and weeks, that .. but I won't begin these bad, futile reasons for just as I know that the news of your shoe pinching you would interest us, so you would put up with the baldest chronicle of our no-doings. Ba is pretty well, spite of the bitter cold weather (at Florence they have fresh snow; here, the wind is the grievance)—I am perhaps ungrateful when I say only "pretty well" .. but she has been better, and, I hoped would grow "best": we keep the house, of course—but on, and just after, Ash Wednesday, the fit of spring which the weather took, let us go and hear the preaching at the Duomo,—a man with a vibrating voice and a great style of pointing out commonplaces: and there is another brother, every bit as voluble, at the

Cavalieri Church.[1] Now to business: we leave here on the 17.th April for Florence, where we hope to stay a month—thence we think of going gently thro' Bologna, to Verona or Vicenza for the Summer and as much of the Autumn as we can take liberties with—(there are some very cool Baths at eight miles distance from Vicenza,—probably we may stop there)[2]—and last of all, we go to Venice—where Mr Kenyon is to endeavour and meet us in October, possibly with Chorley: we should have tried hard to effect this meeting even had we been forced to return to Florence or farther South for winter-quarters, as we supposed would be the case: but to our great comfort Venice is recommended to us on high authority as an admirable situation for Ba: one of the best, indeed: so we trust to pass the cold time there. Now, dearest Friend, where will this plan co-incide with yours? We have a few unforseen expences in England, and must not go unnecessarily out of our way here— but surely you join us at Florence, (if you leave Rome in April as you propose,) or at Bologna, if your stay is prolonged: observe, I say nothing of, what I fancy, impossible meetings—at places where we could go, but you could not—thus, we mean to make a circuit to Sienna, Colle, and Volterra— and another to Lucca, Prato & Pistoja,—returning *from* one of these excursions to Pisa, (we don't yet know *which* one—) and making the other take us to Florence. Do try and concert for us, according to your better knowledge: we need be more economical this year than next, in all probability. But *see* you we must. So—contrive, dear Aunt Nina! And let dear Geddie help with her counsel!

– Have you not had a horrible catastrophe on the 2.^{d} Feb. in your vicinity? I will just say, I knew the wretched man (Angelo Cerutti) very well— who was my Sister's Master—his Italian Grammar is one of, or rather, *the* best grammar I know: I saw the account yesterday in "Galignani"—will you endeavour to find out what this "Autobiography" is about?[3] It is in choice Tuscan, I warrant you, for the poor man was most zealous on that head— telling me that he wished Alfieri had never written, since his style was no freer from Gallicisms!

I have just rec'd a note from Mr Kenyon in which he speaks of his pleasure at having recently heard of you, if not from you. Now I shall hand the corner of this over to Ba, for her contribution– God bless you, dearest friend and dear Geddie who is a part of you—come laden with heaps of news of Rome to yours ever most affectionately

R Browning.

[Continued by EBB]

Thanks upon thanks for your most kind & welcome letter, my very dear friend, dearest aunt Nina—we shall meet soon certainly .. shall we not? We have been building plan upon plan, & everything seems to come to the ground

No. 2260 [?5-] 9 March [1847] 139

except Venice *for the winter–* Does this sound to you very aerial, or watery rather? Are we likely to bring it to bear? and shall we bear it afterward, do you think? In any case we shall talk over "all things & a few beside" with yourself at Florence– You will be forced to pass through Florence & dear Geddie wont be sorry, I hope. You delight me by what you say of "our poet"—thank you, dearest friend!– He is as well as anyone can be without eating– Yesterday, he & Flush & I had for dinner & supper one pigeon– Flush & I doing the honours of it. Wilson is convalescent & Dr Cook has left an impression on us of his ability & intelligence. Now do write & say how you are, & whether Geddie has recovered from the carnival. God bless you.

Your very affectionate Ba.

Address, in RB's hand, on integral page: Mrs Jameson, / Dama Inglese, / Piazza di Spagna, 53. / Roma.
Publication: None traced.
Manuscript: California State University, Hayward.

1. Located in the piazza of the same name, this church and palazzo which were allocated by Cosimo I when he instituted his Order of St. Stephen in the mid-16th century. The designs of the piazza and its buildings were executed by Vasari.
2. The Brownings left Pisa on 20 April 1847 and travelled directly to Florence. After that their plans changed, and except for an ill-fated five-day journey to Vallombrosa in July 1847, they remained in Florence until July 1848.
3. *Vita di Angelo Cerutti con Ragionamenti e Digressioni Morali e Filosofiche da lui scritta e pubblicata lui vivente* (Florence, 1846). Presumably the account in *Galignani's* was similar to the one in *The Athenæum* of 20 February 1847, which stated that "a Roman correspondent of a morning paper has communicated some curious particulars relating to the death in that capital of a man of letters, who formerly resided for some years both in London and Paris—where his name may be remembered, perhaps, by some of our readers. 'Two days ago, the Piazza di Spagna was the scene of a strange transaction. An author of several treatises on educational matters, Angelo Cerutti, after spending the last few months in composing his autobiography—which fills two octavo volumes—and having caused supplies of the work to be distributed for sale at the various booksellers' shops throughout the city, on the morning of the 2nd inst. ordered a number of bill-stickers to placard all Rome with the title of the said autobiography—"*scritta lui vivente:*" and while they were executing his job in all directions, he quietly, at noon, blew his brains out'" (no. 1008, p. 202).

2660. EBB TO ARABELLA MOULTON-BARRETT

[Pisa]
[?5-] Finished on the 9th of March. [1847][1]

My own dearest Arabel, I know that this letter is not in turn .. but it seems to me that we are entangled in our correspondence some way, & that I answer Henrietta's letters to you, & yours to her– Therefore I shall try to set the threads straight, & begin by thanking you for the kindness I had from you yesterday in these dear sheets– The next letter will be from her, & so we shall be all right again. Very anxiously I have been waiting to hear of dear

Stormie– As he was to go, he could not go better– May God bless him & us by keeping him well & bringing us all together happily. Oh, I know & understand that he has a tender heart .. & I believe that under different circumstances, the impulses of it would have acted quite differently. As it is, he wrote me a frank affectionate letter, for which I shall thank him .. dear Stormie!– How much better it would be if Papa had spoken before, openly, calmly, kindly, .. & not kept for the hours of parting, confidences which would have brightened & softened the years of actual association. I know by myself & ⟨...⟩[2] his influence over me, how one is powerless, .. how I should have dropped .. not the sense of a right, .. but the power of claiming a right, .. before a little frankness of affectionateness. As to prayer, I really do *not* understand the principle he goes upon—& of course it is one which, if carried out, would dissolve every congregation in the world. I love him & grieve for him—he cannot be happy, I think, in the depths of his heart, when he can give no sympathy, extend no pardon, make no allowances—it must be a continual wrestling against those natural feelings which he HAS, let him heap the stones over them ever so–[3] The whole Repose of Christ lies in one word .. *forgiveness* .. and if we cast it from us, what remains?– Is Alfred any nearer than he was to being shaken hands with as *Alfred*? I wish Stormie had taken courage & spoken for him before he went—and this for dear Papa's sake more than Alfred's own. You do not say whether he gets on or how—whether new offers have been made to him & what? If I were Surtees Cook I would sell my commission, & embark in some civil employment at once—military affairs will not prosper nowadays, though Ld Palmerston & M. Guizot quarrel ten times over.[4] He *may* get his appointment .. but it is a chance; & to my mind, other chances are better. Agencies upon properties he has not the necessary vocation & instruction for I imagine—a great deal of specific knowledge being necessary for the management of a property. Do you think I could undertake to manage a dairy? .. *par exemple*!– The cream w^d turn sour in the pans at the very prospect of it. If I were he, I sh^d try for a share in some business .. & *advertize*, for the first step—and that is, because so many employments appear to be infra dig .. for "a man in the army." Otherwise it w^d not be difficult, I sh^d think, to take occupation on the railroad, somewhere, at home or abroad—& as an *engineer*, observe, this *may* be done, certainly, as captain or major even. Where is Mr Hunter now? you do not say. Has his pupil left him? is he in London—Norwood? tell me. What his pretext can be for quarrelling now at least, is a question that moves my wonder. Did he mention my name when he was with you? Can anything be in more excerable [*sic*] taste than the whole bearing of him!—& yet have patience with him, & remember how he walks among the thorns– Last time I was at the Duomo, three chairs off from us sate a man so like him that he quite distracted my attention from the friar—only there was less intellect in the face, & more good humour .. & also he might have been a few years younger. But the eyes, nose, mouth, shape of the cheeks, manner of the hair .. oh, so like! I pushed Robert to make him look at him—it was a most striking likeness. Very glad I am to hear of dear Mary's position, because it is safe & happy for her- Otherwise she certainly might have forty or fifty pounds a year I sh.^{d} fancy, in a private family .. but then she w.^{d} not be with her friends. Give her my best love & say that often I think of her.

—As to Bummy .. dont mind, my darling Arabel!—dont be angry- She has ideas of a different "dispensation" from the one regnant in the world just now, when (to do the bad world justice) it has got to be more enlightened on certain social rights than it used to be. People have learnt now the possibility of being tolerably upright & pure out of buckram—and then, Bummy, ... why you know her so well that you c.^{d} not certainly be surprised at anything written either to you or to me. For my part, I dont feel in the least angry—& if you see her, you may give her a kiss for me without drawback of malice. Besides, she laid all the blame on *me* (which was just & right) & sent a very kind message to Robert—. Only I was a naughty child, & whipt, .. which I did'nt mind so very much!- So dont *you* mind- Consider, that she has to choose examples for Arlette .. & for you & Henrietta besides!- Jane's letter & her's received on the same day, made certainly a curious contrast. For my part, to friends & opponents, I wish nothing better nor worse (as far as concerns me) than for both to witness & see how perfectly happy I am in my new position—and as to Robert I will answer for it (let *that* sound ever so conceited!) that he has not repented yet for half a moment. We are not rich—but on the other hand, we neither of us wish to run into expenses—— Oh—by the way, Arabel, you ask about the proceeds from Moxon- The seventy five pounds this year represent both Robert's & my poems—and then you are to remember that he published last summer *three* "Bells & Pomegranates"[5] which made a certain expense, all safely covered & leaving an overplus. An hundred & eighty copies of my poems remain, together with copies of his—and nothing forbids .. indeed it seems a matter of course .. that next year, we sh.^{d} have at least as much. For several years now the expenses of publication have been so surely covered—his poems, that Moxon has sent him in no bill even .. but the overplus was a pleasant surprise- I assure you we shall make our way by poetry yet .. you will see. The ship money this year is not so well as George supposed[6] .. but it is of no consequence to grand people like us .. we always end by saying to one another "Oh, we shall do very well". As for me I dare say I sh.^{d} get into ever so many scrapes & debts if left to myself .. but he who hates a debt like a scorpion, (or rather far worse) not only has everything paid at the moment, but puts it down in a book, so that we may not unconsciously transgress the limit of the in-comings by the out-goings. His poems (having survived all the flat years of poems) are getting on now .. it will be all clear gain now, says Moxon .. & there will be a regular income, even apart from our great schemes—and before the year closes we hope to bring out a collection of poems on Italy, with our separate signatures.[7] Then there is his second edition, .. & presently, perhaps, mine .. in neither of which we shall risk anything– Send me a list of what did appear of mine in Blackwood,[8] because I have no copies & must enquire what they mean to do with the rest– Dearest Arabel, why send *any* MS book, if you could not the right one? It is of no consequence however– You are far far too kind & dear, in thinking to send me the mittens—but they will be most useful gifts to me. I am writing now in detestable leather ones—the shops here not being of the most various– Often I wish (in spite of my manifold extravagances in London) to have brought with me just twice as much as came. The green gown like yours, Robert likes so much that I wont wear it while we have fires– You cant guess what our pinewood fires are. They shoot one through & through (at least one's gowns) with red hot arrows. This black silk gown, I have on, is shot into fifty holes .. besides some lawful wearing out at the elbows—and Wilson says "Really you must make it last till the fire is done with." You see, there is no 'guard,' no 'fender' .. and splinters of the wood fly every moment. Flush looks up in horror & gets close to me for protection. But I was talking of the parcel– I shall write to thank dearest Trippy– As for your goodness, you *know how to please* me, Arabel– And Henrietta's slippers, how I shall like to have them!– My direction about the others (the antiques) will have come too late, I observe– Never mind! The teapot is a happy thought too, and I shall like to have it for dear Trippy's sake.[9] Such a kind affectionate little note she wrote to me—tell her that *two* people here love her for it .. besides all other reasons– Robert was quite touched by her way of speaking of him– But what is this about *her eyes*, Arabel? You never told me of this weakness in her eyes .. she says she has lost the sight of *one*. Why how is this? Do tell me– I hope she does not expose herself to the cold unnecessarily. It is cold here again .. indeed nearly as cold as ever, & we hear of snow at Florence. We thought that summer was come, a week ago .. but *pazienza*! Our hosts say "Cattiva Pisa"[10]—& Mr Irving's son,[11] I am sorry to say, is ill again. For my part, I dont run risks like rash people, but keep in these rooms which are very warm. Talk of the coldness of Italian houses!– Why the walls are as thick as an English house almost. We had a visit the other day from M.^r & Mrs Irving. Forced to see them!– She is a very young looking woman, & so glorious in silk & velvet as to astound one. Is she a *second* wife?[12] Surely she must be. Young enough she looks, to be her husband's daughter. The 'celebrated Mr Irving' cannot in any case be her son—the thing is impossible– Very cordial they both were, and I like *him*. The Surtees's have changed their house & come into our street—and I heard of

Miss Surtees professing to "feel quite well," in the warm weather a week ago—but now, he told Robert on meeting in the street, she was *in bed* as a matter of precaution. He called on us the second time, & we were again "at dinner"—"how unfortunate"!- Mr Irving said the other day that his son who is the invalid, was very much vexed not to be able to go out & see Robert— "he has a strong feeling about literary people, & is a great admirer of Mr Browning's poetry."——

Not a word yet of poor Wilson! By which you will conclude rightly that the convalescence continues. She is able now to take chicken & pudding everyday without suffering from it, .. and in other respects, seems quite strong. Being desired to take a great deal of exercise, she goes out generally twice a day & walks into the country with Flush. Still, the swelling in the left side is not quite gone .. but it is going off she says, & Dr Cook did not think it important .. & she feels very well when she does not transgress in point of diet. The least fragment of a potatoe, or of *butter*, she dares not touch- My darling Arabel, I dont beat the air as much as you seem to think, in talking about *coffee*. It may do your headaches good for the moment, for the occasion, .. as anything warm & stimulating would,—& yet it may be keeping up the cause of the headache, & preparing the next day's- Dr Cook explained to us how things, really injurious, appear to be *remedies*, while in effect they are doing harm. Wilson's complaint was just a *crisis*, of many of your symptoms- But for the violent sea-sickness she might not have been ill .. but the tendency to the irritation on the coats of the stomach was *there* .. & any weakness of that sort is increased & exasperated by coffee—it is a specific evil under some circumstances. Oh—I would not exhort you *never* to touch it!—only to be more moderate than I know you are inclined to be, & not have three great cups a day—as of old- And then the *no* exercise, .. the staying at home, you hint at!—now is it wise & right of you? Which reminds me (now that I have filled you up to the brim with ill humour .. as far as such a thing can be, that is!) of my own imputed offences about morphine. Always I forget to tell you that I gradually diminish .. to seventeen days for twenty two doses, .. which I used to take in eight days. Whether it is desirable to diminish still faster indeed, I have enquired of Mr Jago- So you may see if I am obstinate, & if I deserve a return-scold. 'I speak as to a wise woman—judge what I say.'[13] Robert is very anxious for me to be free of the morphine, & yet even he admits that I do what I can- The cold weather, of which we have had too much for Pisa, has been against great progresses, observe, in this particular respect,—for though it has been very different from England, & I have had much more liberty, .. yet during the whole of January & the beginning of February I was shut up fairly in these rooms, & to leave off morphine by teaspoonfulls at a time.-

March 8.th Dearest dear Arabel, I have not written in this letter for two or three days, & here come, inside M.r Kenyon's letter, your & Henrietta's most welcome little scraps—oh, how happy it makes me to see your writings!- You are both the best, kindest, dearest .. the words go, which should praise you aright!—so good you are to me. To hear from you is the greatest pleasure I can have .. remember it always! After which proper expression of gratitude, I ought really to scold you, because it is very unreasonable & wrong in you to think of buying gowns for me, & I should be perfectly angry, if anyway I could have the heart. When I say to you all sorts of stuff, it is just for the pleasure of talking stuff to you .. as if we could afford such words .. sitting together over the fire. I open my eyes with wonder at the idea of your making conclusions, & buying for me at Davis's[14] what I sh.d have bought for myself in Florence- Everything is to be bought at Florence, say the learned—& at the cheapest. So mind you never do such a thing again, you naughty dearest people .. it is at once too good & too bad of you—so good as to be bad!- Then for *you*, Arabel, to make me another pair of slippers!! What am I to say? If feet could blush mine would be red as the brick floors you refer to—but as it is they pray my cheeks to do it for them. By the way, it is only in travelling that we fall on the brick floors sometimes, & ours are very carefully covered with reed matting & carpets .. there is more *comfort*, in fact, than I expected. I must tell you however, now I think of it, (never surely were such rambling letters as mine, .. treating of Heaven, earth, & the kitchen, in paragraphs mixed together!) that dear Treppy's teapot will form an extraordinary contrast to the general aspect of our "plate & china." When D.r Cook attended Wilson, & came in to us to make his report, the preparation for our breakfast looked so remarkable, that, after a glance at Robert's face, I ran away with the teacups into the bedroom-- Do you know what a blue mug is .. a real blue mug, such as when I was a child, I drank my milk out of?- Such is our idea of a teacup in this land of Taste! The coffee pot & milk jug, .. if I call them pewter, you will add a false splendour—they look more like *lead* .. only I hope they are rather pewter under a cloud. You never saw such "utensils" in the course of your life, I am certain. Item .. two silver spoons, which have to put the sugar into the cups, then, stir the coffee., & then, help the eggs- If I forget to stir my coffee before I break my egg, I turn to supplicate Robert for the use of his spoon .. "just for a moment". And if both eggs have employed both spoons, & one of us requires another cup of coffee .. should it be Robert, .. I hold out the sugarbasin & graciously enquire if he will put in his own sugar with his own fingers. As to sugartongs I have never seen such a thing since I saw you——neither in France nor Italy. M.rs Jameson used to laugh at my 'scrupulousness' in our fine hotel in Paris even!- For the rest, I dare say we shall find more luxury in our next residence,—& indeed here we might have done better if we had made a fuss & not been so supernaturally contented with everything– Our hosts will certainly be in despair to lose us .. for we have paid double like angels, & never rustled our wings– The lady said to me the other day "I loro signori sono buonissimi,"[15]–& in spite of all modesty I did not so very much wonder– Think of having lodgers who pay by the clock, (& twice as much as they ought to pay,) & except on Christmas eve at the cathedral, have not once been "out" later than six in the evening. They must doubt whether Robert is saint or martyr, most. Never even the odour of a chance cigar!– Their garlic has it all its own way along the passages!– They enquired the other day of Wilson if "there were no hope of our staying a little longer" ... but for *that*, no. Five weeks more, & we are gone to Florence. In the meanwhile we have made a great discovery at the Trattoria, of the possibility of a pigeon pie even in Italy! Robert & I were so blasés on the eternal roast chicken, that we both felt inclined to leave off eating altogether, .. and as *he* began to carry the inclination into practice, I protested, & we resolved to change the dynasty– First we made a desperate irruption (not for the first time!) into what are called the "made dishes" (for good reasons) of Italian cooking! & there arrived, .. at the first glance upon which, what Robert calls my "prejudices" rose up rampant. "Really, Ba, you *are* so prejudiced! Now *this* seems as good as possible" ... (choosing the least questionable shape!) "Well, dear, I am delighted that you like it .. I only hope it wont poison you"– "Very good indeed!—only rather rich .. here, Flush, *you* shall have it."!– And Flush after a great deal of hesitation & meditation with the end of his nose, submitted to be the victim– Poor Flush!– You, Arabel, never could imagine the blacknesses or brownnesses & greynesses, all swimming in oil, which define themselves eatable substances here .. and I never can get over the oil to begin with .. having "prejudices." So we held a council & wondered whether these Italians who really excel in pastry, could not cover some pigeons with a pastry. Robert went to give his directions, & after a long speech .. "vedete"—said he .. "é una specia di pasticcio"[16]—"una specia di *pigeon pie*" was the quick answer .. oh, they understood perfectly! A pigeon pie had manifestly a continental reputation!– And never was a better pie than what they sent us .. an immense one too, large enough for two dinners for us three, & at the expense of 2^s– 2^d.. by which let Minny judge of the cheapness here of the means of life. By the way, Robert showed to me the other day that our *six months spending, inclusive* of our journey from London, & week at Paris, medecines & everything in the world, had amounted to *one hundred & fifty pounds* .. and *three* of us, remember!– Wilson having shared equally in all respects– Also there has been no painful & niggardly œconomy—we have had every comfort. So we are *more* than at ease as to our future prospects, & feel ourselves free to please ourselves about Venice .. or wherever our next fancy may turn itself. Such planners & dreamers we are—and having shifted plan & dream so very often, I for one, do not trust quite so much as I did to the present plan & dream– If it were not for "the fashion of England" we should yield to the spring-temptation perhaps of the mountain scenery & the chesnut forest, rocks & cataracts of the Baths of Lucca, which must by all description, be quite exquisite .. but the English fashionables, the pink mantillas & gaming houses keep us off—so we shall go there only for a day or two or three, in April perhaps & on the way to Florence. Mrs Jameson leaves Rome on the 10th of April & is very anxious for us to meet & travel with her– We w^d willingly do it, only there are difficulties .. we cant give up Florence for instance .. & we have written to ask her to give us tryst *there* at least.

Impertinent Arabel!—how you made me laugh about my chronological observations, & the more that I had a sort of recollection of having gone still deeper into the subject in my last letter which you had not received in writing this– Was I ever chronological in my life before, I wonder? Perhaps some of it, is Robert's fault, who began by keeping the 'anniversary' of our marriage once a week, & who now, three days in every month as I assure him, says "Another month is gone, Ba." He is fond of telling me that I have not "the least idea" of the depth of the love he feels for me, & that by the time we have been married "ten years" I may guess at it perhaps .. therefore he wants the weeks & months to go fast. For my part I am too well contented ⟨with⟩[17] everything as it is—I seem to "guess" quite well enough⟨.⟩ Otherw⟨ise I sh⟩ould be very obtuse .. because no human being could give to another ⟨better⟩ *proof* of attachment than he does to me every moment of ⟨...⟩. I am *certain* that he loves me far better than at the ⟨...⟩ says himself. Between you & me, Arabel, Mrs Jameson ⟨...⟩lly by her dreary jests about the passing nature ⟨...⟩tance at Genoa, when he chose to sit by me, instead ⟨...⟩ts, .. which really *was* foolish & vexed me ... ⟨...⟩," in one extreme or another. My dear Browning, you ⟨...⟩ but in a month or two, unfortunately, the reason ⟨...⟩ "*Ba* said so for nearly two years," he answered ⟨...⟩ (getting up impatiently!) He never w^d contest such points with ⟨...⟩– Only, afterwards, when with me alone, he declaimed against ⟨...⟩ & bad taste" .. (being fond of using strong words)—but the truth ⟨...⟩ Mrs Jameson has been unhappy in her own experience & in the experience ⟨...⟩ best friends– She has not been used to deal with such natures ⟨as Robe⟩rt's .. as who has, not dealing with himself? "The happiest marriages" ⟨she say⟩s, "end quickly in an affectionate friendship"—"just what one might feel for an old armchair,"! ... is his commentary aside to me– "Why if I thought such a thing possible, I never w^d have married you, Ba—never– If you live to be eighty & have hair as white as snow, I can only admit of the change of loving you *better*!! I know I shall love you better *then*."—— A great deal too frank I am, in telling you such things, Arabel .. but the position is peculiar & justifies or rather demands that I sh^d set your dear tender affectionateness at full rest

Collegio Ferdinando, Pisa

4222 (now 6) Via delle Belle Donne    Palazzo Guidi from Via Mazzetta

1881 (now 21) Via Maggio    1703 (now 8) Piazza Pitti

The Brownings' Florentine Residences

No. 2660 [?5–] 9 March [1847] 147

from a full evidence. Not being able to be frank enough *before*, I am led to be overfrank *now*– Oh, you understand *that*! Then I want you to know *him*, & what he is to me .. & to thank God for me, with "connaissance de cause."–[18] Write always & every detail– My best love to dearest George & all of them– To my very dear Henrietta, my next letter shall go, & make up, perhaps, for the lack of news in this. I do like to hear of "happy days"—their joy reaches me– How I love you all, .. sometimes I think ⟨...⟩ Be happy, *you*, my darling Arabel! Where is Emma Monro? Do ⟨...⟩ come & go? I am glad that Papa is relenting into some justice to ⟨...⟩ he might as well be angry with the angel Gabriel. Poor, unfortunate A⟨nnie Hayes, whether⟩ she thinks so or not![19]—for *degradation* is the worst misfortune, & ⟨it is degra⟩dation to live on with such a wretched man as *that*. Right or W⟨rong I would⟩ not do it– I could not. "Divorce" was another extreme: but I ⟨do not⟩ *live with him*. While I write, a M.rs Young[20] calling herself a friend of M.r Stratton's, ⟨whose daughter⟩ has married a Professor Matteucci (both settled in Italy) make their way in to me. ⟨They⟩ could not be resisted. Not very charming though!—sensible, & cold! We sh.d scar⟨cely lack for⟩ visitors if we were to stay here long– I am gl⟨ad for⟩ M.r Hunter. Should he first rise to the estate of yo⟨ur ...⟩ my love– Also to dear Mary. I c.d write on ⟨... Robert⟩ tells me to say that "he loves you & Henrietta with ⟨...⟩—& give it to Lizzie Barrett. Your very own Ba.

⟨...⟩ the same thing happened to another friend of yours on a certain solemn occasion. ⟨...⟩ face & negligent costume produced this natural effect.[21]

Address, on integral page: Angleterre, viâ France. / To the care of Miss Trepsack, / (Miss Arabel Barrett) / 5. Upper Montagu Street, / Montagu Square, / London.
Publication: None traced.
Manuscript: Berg Collection.

1. Dated by EBB's reference on 8 March to having "not written in this letter for two or three days." Year provided by postmark.
2. EBB has written and crossed out "the fear of".
3. Cf. Genesis 31:44–49.
4. An allusion to the dispute between England and France regarding the marriages of Isabella II of Spain and her sister Fernanda; see letter 2655, note 12.
5. Evidently EBB is confused about the number and dates of RB's *Bells and Pomegranates*. *Luria* and *A Soul's Tragedy* were published together as the eighth and last of the series in April 1846, which she is counting as two numbers. Prior to that, *Dramatic Romances and Lyrics* had been published in November 1845.
6. Part of EBB's income was an annual return from shares in a West Indies packet ship called the *David Lyon*. She also received dividends from a legacy of £4,000 left to her by her paternal grandmother.
7. This idea for a joint collection of poems on Italy was never realised.
8. Seven poems by EBB were published in the October 1846 issue of *Blackwood's Edinburgh Magazine* (pp. 488–495). For a complete list, see letter 2554, note 6.
9. See *Reconstruction*, H348.
10. "Nasty Pisa" or "Bad Pisa."
11. Mr. & Mrs. James Irving (see letter 2630, note 12) had two sons: James (1822–56) and Robert Nasmyth (1827–94). This is doubtless a reference to the elder son, who died aged thirty-three at Leghorn.

148   [?5–] 9 March [1847]

12. The Irvings married in 1819, and there is no evidence that he had been married before.

13. Cf. I Corinthians 10:15.

14. Unidentified; however, *The Post Office London Directory* for 1846 lists John Davis, a dyer, at 91 High Street Marylebone.

15. "You are (both) very good."

16. "You see," —said he "it's a kind of pie."

17. Final sheet of this letter is badly crumpled; at this point, a large torn area begins.

18. "Full knowledge" or "knowledge of the reason."

19. From the context, EBB is referring to Annie Hayes's marital difficulties, which finally resulted in divorce in 1854.

20. Mary Young (*née* Ancrum, d. 1867). Her husband, Robert Young, a minister in the Church of Scotland, died four years after they were married. After his death she adopted Robinia Elizabeth Young (1812?–97), daughter of his brother Samuel. Robinia married Carlo Matteucci (1811–68) at All Souls, Marylebone, on 7 September 1846. He was a Professor of Natural Philosophy in the University of Pisa. He later became an Italian senator, and was the source of political information for EBB in 1860 and 1861.

21. This passage appears as a marginal notation on the next-to-last page. Because of the damaged condition of this sheet, we are unable to determine its placement within the context of the letter.

2661. EBB TO THOMAS WESTWOOD

Pisa. Collegio Ferdinando.
March 10. [1847][1]

If really, my dear M! Westwood, it was "*ill temper*" in you, causing the brief note, it was a most flattering ill temper, and I thank you just as I have had reason to do for the goodnature which has caused you to bear with me so often & so long. You have been misled on some points– I did *not* go to Italy last year (or rather the year before last!)[2] .. I was disappointed & forced to stay in Wimpole Street after all: but the winter being so mild, so miraculously mild for England, you may remember, I was spared my winter-relapse & left liberty for new plans, such as I never used to think were in my destiny. Such a change it is to me .. such a strange happiness & freedom! You must not, in your kindness, wish me back again, but rather be contented like a friend as you are, to hear that I am very happy & very well & still doubtful whether all the brightness can be meant for *me*! It is just as if the sun rose again at seven oclock p.m. The strangeness seems as great– And, that long time, though I was very much absorbed in various ways, yet I should have written to you, be sure, if I had known your address– Sending to the old place, seemed quite vain, .. & I went on hoping that I should have a word from you some day to set me on your track again. As happened at last. But I did not think of its happening *so*.

Thank you, thank you, for all you tell me & what relates to yourself. I thank you most for telling me, of course. Accept my sympathy for the sadness

& the gladness, & believe that whatever circumstances I may be in, it will not fail you. May prosperity creep toward you more closely every year .. only not too closely to exclude *happiness* .. which by no means is the same thing. You always seem to me so good & rightminded that if either prosperity or happiness "went by deserts" which neither does, your friends need never fear for you—at any rate you may sit in one particular "centre & enjoy bright day",[3] let it be otherwise dark or light. Your health is good now, I trust, in spite of the severe English winter which we hear described– Mine has profitted wonderfully from the change of air & scene & climate .. though I was considerably better in the first instance, & suffering more from nervous debility than other causes. We met Mrs Jameson in Paris, who travelled south with us & did not leave us till she saw us safe at Pisa, when she continued her own route to Florence & Rome. We stay at Pisa during the winter on account of its being recommended to me for the warmth's sake. I am very well, when spared blows *from without* in the shape of frosts & piercing winds, .. & therefore while under shelter in this way, there is every reason both from experience & medical opinions, to believe that my health will gradually fortify itself. In England the misery was that the winters threw me back from my summer's climbing—it has been less disease with me than a morbid delicacy which diminishes when not exposed to disastrous irritation—& I am now very well, & so happy as *not to think much of it*, except for the sake of another–

And do you fancy how I feel, carried into the visions of nature from my gloomy room? Even now I walk as in a dream. We made a pilgrimage from Avignon to Vaucluse, in right poetical duty—& I & my husband sate upon two stones in the midst of the fountain which in its dark prison of rocks, flashes & roars & testifies to the memory of Petrarch. It was louder & fuller than usual when we were there, on account of the rains. And Flush, though by no means born to be a hero, considered my position so outrageous, that he dashed through the water to me, splashing me all over: so he is baptized in Petrarch's name. The scenery is full of grandeur—the rocks sheath themselves into the sky .. & nothing grows there except a little cypress here & there, & a straggling olive tree: & the fountain works out its soul in its stony prison, & runs away in a green rapid stream– Such a striking sight it is! I sate upon deck too in our passage from Marseilles to Genoa, & had a vision of mountains six or seven deep, one behind another. As to Pisa, call it a beautiful town, .. you cannot do less with its Arno & its Palaces .. & above all the wonderful Duomo & Campo Santo, & Leaning Tower & Baptistry, all of which are a stone's throw from our windows– We have rooms in a great college-house built by Vasari,[4] & fallen into desuetude from collegiate purposes & here we live the quietest & most tête à tête of lives, knowing nobody, hearing nothing, & for nearly three months together never catching a glimpse at a paper—oh, how wrong you were about the Times!- Now however we subscribe to a French & Italian library & have a French newspaper every evening,—the Siecle, .. &, so, look through "a loophole at the world".[5] Yet not too proud are we even now, for all the news you will please to send us in charity—"da obolum Belisario"![6] What do you mean about poor Tennyson? I heard of him last on his return from a visit to the Swiss mountains, which "disappointed him" he was *said to say*. Very wrong, either of mountains or poet![7] Tell me if you make acquaintance with Mrs Howitt's new ballads——and if Mrs Butler's book is a good new thing.[8] I heard from you with the greatest interest of Hood's daughter-[9] Yes, sorrow makes wise and old. The English government will remember her father's claims if it would not dishonor itself. Mrs Jameson is engaged on a work on art which will be very interesting I think, illustrative of the subjects of ancient Christian painters, sculptors, &c .. a fragment of it appeared in the Athenæum, you will remember, & the whole work is promised to the bookseller by the next autumn. She has been very busy at Rome, & desires to meet us .. perhaps at Florence, .. in order to travel together in Italy. Our plans are all afloat still, or rather *adream*. In the middle of April, however, we leave this Pisa for Florence, with a lingering-round through Volterra & Siena—stay at Florence a month, perhaps, & then slowly proceed by Bologna to Verona, .. pass the heats of the summer there, .. or escape them into the Tyrol .. and winter at Venice——a well-sounding plan .. is it not? For fear of its uncertainties, I will ask you, as you are so kind as to write to me, to address the letter (written on thin paper) under cover to my sister .. Miss Arabel Barrett, 50 Wimpole Street .. you do not forget the old direction. Flush's love to your Flossy. Flush has grown very overbearing in this Italy, I think because my husband spoils him, (if not for the glory of Vaucluse!) Flush barks when he wants a door opened, or another lump of sugar. Robert declares that the said Flush considers him, my husband, to be created for the especial purpose of doing him service—& really it looks rather like it!—— But you write sometimes?—you do not let the numbers overpower the numbers? I hope not. Never do I see the Athenæum now, but, before I left England, some pure gushes between the rocks, reminded me of you. Thank you for telling me of the lectures in Scotland, of which I had not heard- Tell me all you can—it will all be like rain upon dry ground. My husband bids me offer his regards to you .. if you will accept them: & that you may do it with your heart, I will assure you (aside) that his poetry is as the prose of his nature .. he himself is so much better & higher than his own works-

May God bless you, dear Mr Westwood! Bear in kindness
your friend
E Barrett Browning

Address, on integral page: T. Westwood Esqre / 7. Denmark Street / Camberwell.
Publication: LEBB, I, 323–325 (in part).

Manuscript: British Library.
1. Year provided by postmark.
2. Parenthetical passage is interpolated above the line.
3. Milton, *Comus* (1637), line 382.
4. See letter 2624, note 10.
5. Cf. Cowper, *The Task* (1785), IV, 88.
6. "Give Belisarius an obolus!" Belisarius (d. 565), the greatest of Justinian's generals, was accused of conspiracy and reduced to begging; according to legend, he put a sign over his dwelling which read: "Give an obolus to poor old Belisarius."
7. Tennyson had visited Switzerland with his publisher, Edward Moxon, in August 1846. Their holiday had not been a great success; Tennyson's disappointment was due partly to his memories of an earlier visit to the Pyrenees with Hallam in 1830, which had inspired them both. Tennyson's poor health in early 1847, caused by worry over *The Princess* and general nervousness, led him to take a water cure in May 1847.
8. Concluding a two-part review, with copious extracts, of *A Year of Consolation* (1847), *The Athenæum* reviewer stated: "We know no other tourist who has so lovingly and so picturesquely done justice to the natural beauty round about Rome:—and therefore have expatiated perhaps disproportionately on what may be called the peculiar and principal grace and beauty of the book" (8 May 1847, no. 1019, p. 493).
8. See letter 2638, note 12.

2662. JOSEPH ARNOULD TO RB

18. Victoria Square, Pimlico
March 24th [1847][1]

Your letter, my dear Browning, was a great delight to us filled as it was with so many evidences of your continuing happiness & M.rs Browning's increasing health & strength: no one can pay so graceful a compliment as yourself but I take what you say of my wedded happiness to be more than a compliment, first because I feel it in my inmost heart to be a truth in itself, & next because I know that in such a matter you would only speak in a language deeper & truer than that of mere compliment: yes for 6 years past I have been becoming more & more convinced day after day that for man's true happiness there is nothing equal to the loving companionship of one who halves all sorrows with you & doubles all joys: if I were to rack my brain for good wishes I could find none better than that you might be as happy in married life as I am & have been: need I say that this wish is one of that fortunate class in which the wisher feels sure of it's accomplishment. The only part of your letter which sounded at all like bad news, was that in which you talk of staying longer in Italy than you at one time contemplated: I think you will find all your English friends joining in a protest against this: but you know best, & above all I am sure need not be told how many true & sincere well-wishers you have here waiting & eager to welcome you. Would that I could indulge the hope of being able this long vacation to have a glimpse of you at Venice or Verona: but I must, for *this* year, give up all notion of the kind & content myself with making Pump Court, & Brick Court & Fig Tree Court additionally cheerful by the thought that while I am engrossing you are "swimming in a Gondola".² If any thing could make the prospect of such a trip additionally alluring it would be the knowledge that M! Kenyon may probably be there with you: what 'a piece of virtue'³ is that excellent man: was ever so clear an understanding joined to so good a heart, such a thorough knowledge of men & their ways, with such a fresh, unworn sympathy for all that is good & noble in human nature: all the instinctive impulses in their first blossom & all the acquired powers in their full maturity: among the very, very many things I have to thank you for[,] the pleasure of his acquaintance stands among the foremost: there is only one still higher claim on our gratitude that we are looking for at your hands and that is on some future day to be made personally known to Mrs Browning:—there is nothing of which we talk more frequently—Maria, I must tell you privately being very nervous on the subject until reassurëd by my constant repetition of my old creed, in which I have never yet found reason to disbelieve, that there is nothing so tolerant as genius, nor any people more indulgent to the shortcomings of others than those who are themselves highly gifted: so in this faith we both trust that Mrs Browning will one day admit us into the number of her friends.

To come to me for news, my dear Browning, would be something like going to Pisa in quest of gaiety, or to Mayfair, in the season for solitude: this letter too is enclosed in one from Chorley, who is perpetually in the side scenes of the great Theatre: & can tell you all about all the performers both before & behind the curtain, from the call-boy—to the prima donna—from the critic in the pit, to Her Grace in the private Box—few people I suppose know better the dress circle of this great London: I suspect you who read the English & French papers at Pisa, know more about all these matters than I can tell you, so I wont send you stale news in this cramped hand.

Domett, did I tell you?—has been nominated by the New Governor Captain Grey—to a place in the legislative council of New Zealand[4]—with a salary more than adequate to all his wants *at present* & with a prospect of course of rising, which I think *now* he will improve: such is the excellent arrangement of the Post in the Antipodes that I have no letter from him of later date than August last, when the appointment was only in prospect, but it is now fixed & he had been reported as having already taken his seat, & some part in the public discussion.

Dowson, I have not seen for some time, he is unluckily 7 miles on the other side of London[5]—which with all London to drag through & no Railway, makes him further from one in point of time than though he lived 60 miles away: we always talk a great deal about you when we meet. The day before yesterday I happened upon Captain Pritchett[6] in a coffee house hard by the Temple & I was very glad to see him looking so well: my wife &

myself have been sometime meditating a trip to Hatcham, on my first open day, for we have not been there since your sister was staying with us, which to our very great delight she was kind enough to do in the winter: the fact is that here, as with you, the inclemency of the season has been almost unparalleled, & Maria had been a good deal an inmate of the house: now however there is a promise of something more like spring & her first excursion will be to see M.rs Browning:- Today London is in mourning—shops shut—no omnibus's to be seen .. streets noiseless as churchyard walks—it is a general *fast* for the good of Irish Famine.[7] Fortunately, as the Papers will have told you—the English nation has taken more direct measures of relief, with a magnificence which has not often been surpassed: nevertheless, bating altogether the religious question, this solemn fast is a far more solemn thing than I could have fancied it would be, in this great, noisy Protestant city: by the bye 'spite of our Protestantism it is rumoured & I hope truly that we are to send an ambassador to the Pope; a man who seems to have the simple heroic greatness of another age; I am glad also to see, as you will if you look for it in the Times of yesterday (March 23.d) a recognition of the Pope & the King of Sardinia as the heads of Italian nationality;[8] and the expression of a strong disposition, I suppose on the part of Lord Palmerston, to lend the force of England both moral & if need be physical, to the noble work of Italian regeneration: with prudence & *one* master mind one fancies that the dream of the last 50 years[9] might at length be accomplished: meanwhile here in England Jesuitry or Priestcraft creeps on stealthily, but apace: doctrines of Church absolutism &c which would have made dinner tables "stare & gasp"[10] ten years back, are now admitted as fixed points in the religious world: & no one can help being struck with the change produced in this respect in the higher & middling classes; but after all the thing has no life in it: Wesley had not returned from his chaplaincy in Georgia 10 years before he numbered some 80,000 disciples:[11] Newman has been working either under, or above ground for double the time & his followers at most count by hundreds: to be sure there is this wide difference: Wesley acted on the masses: the other people have let alone the masses (except indeed in the Roman sense) and gained a hold upon the gentry, professional & trades'-men- Do you make out at all what notion the well informed Italians have of Puseyism?—— I only meant, my dear Browning, that should you chance to be making a long stay in Florence & happened some day to be taking a walk out of the city you could look in upon my sister en passant.[12] They live at Villa Cresci, on the Bologna road, about a mile & a half out of Florence—very near the *Villa Catalani*- He is a Pole turned artist- I don't think you will much like him— & pray don't think of going unless the whim happens to take you- I have merely mentioned to them quite casually that you would probably be passing through Florence & if so—might possibly call—— I have left no room except to desire the very kind regards of both Maria & myself to M:^rs Browning: your affectionate Friend

J Arnould

Address, on integral page: Robert Browning Esq:^re.
Publication: None traced.
Manuscript: Alexander Turnbull Library.

1. Year determined by the reference to the Brownings' residence in Pisa and their plans to travel to Florence.
2. Cf. *As You Like It*, IV, 1, 37–38. The courts mentioned here were near Middle Temple Lane; only Fig Tree Court has not survived.
3. *The Tempest*, I, 2, 56.
4. According to E.A. Horsman, in his introduction to *The Diary of Alfred Domett: 1872–1885* (1953), George Grey "visited Nelson in 1846 and offered Domett a seat in the Legislative Council. This he now felt able to accept. He took his seat at the opening of the next session on 5 October, though the copy of the minutes in the Public Records Office ... shows he did not attend the meetings of 1847" (pp. 21–22).
5. Apparently by this time Dowson had moved to Blackheath Terrace, Greenwich, where he died in September 1848, from his previous address at 3 Albion Terrace, Commercial Road, Limehouse, as recorded in RB's address book (see vol. 9, p. 390).
6. RB's friend Captain James Pritchard.
7. By order of a royal proclamation a general fast was appointed for the 24th of March 1847. *The Times* for 20 March explained that "by an order in council all the government offices ... will be closed to business," and *The Times* for the 24th noted that "this day has been set apart for solemn humiliation and prayer on account of the unparalleled calamity with which a portion of the empire has been visited."
8. The report in *The Times* for 23 March 1847 noted the tribute by Sir Robert Peel "on the character and policies of Pope Pius IX," and it included the following comment: "We trust that England will not allow an obsolete prejudice, shared by no other Protestant Power, to leave her without a representative at the Court of a Pontiff whose personal character she respects, and whose political independence she ought to uphold."
9. An allusion to the treaty of Campo Formio in 1797, which resulted in the formation of the Cisalpine Republic, afterwards named the Italian republic with Napoleon as president, and which abolished feudalism and offered the hope for universal suffrage.
10. Milton, "Sonnet XI," "On the Detraction Which Followed Upon my Writing Certain Treatises," (1645), line 11.
11. Arnould's statistic is somewhat exaggerated; at the Methodist Conference of 1769, some thirty years after John Wesley's return from America, the total number of Methodists in England, Scotland and Wales was just over 28,000.
12. We are unable to provide further details concerning Arnould's sister and her husband.

2663. EBB & RB TO ARABELLA & HENRIETTA MOULTON-BARRETT

[In EBB's hand] [Pisa]

[26 March 1847][1]

My ever dearest Henrietta .. Dont reproach me! spite of seeming sins. Though the last letter was out of turn, & unfollowed immediately by the due one, as I meant at first, .. & though when you read this you may be tempted to lay

No. 2663   26 March 1847   155

to my charge most unkind reserves, yet dont reproach me! I am not indeed *so* to blame– And now listen to what comes next—& remember that I *write it myself* & am doing as well as possible– I have been *stupid* beyond any stupidity of which I ever, that I know of, was thought capable, by me or others,—and the consequence has been a premature illness, a *miscarriage*, at four oclock last sunday morning, & *of five months date*, says Dr Cook, or nearly so … all the pain of it for just nothing, except this purchase of experience. Everything, I did wrong, .. & he attributes the result to the heat within & without .. sitting on the rug to bake myself if I felt the least uneasy … taking hot coffee to boil myself at other times .. choosing the worst positions possible, out of an instinct of contrariety … yes, and until the event, believing like a child or idiot that I had just "caught cold," & nothing else was the matter– Pray laugh at me– As for me, I could cry, out of the sheerest remorse– And dont think that ever I deceived you about my state, calling myself well when I was'nt—no, indeed– Until about six weeks or seven weeks ago I was perfectly well in all respects .. & then, for a week or two or three, became subject to sudden violent pains which came on in the night, relieved by friction & a few spoonfuls of brandy, & going off as suddenly as they came. Wilson told me at last that she *suspected my condition*, & that if it were so, the pains were "not right" & signified the possibility of miscarriage; & she had great fears about the influence of the *morphine* &c. Robert of course made a fuss besides & entreated me to call in Dr Cook—— I was frightened out of my wits by the suggestion about the morphine, & out of my *wit* by the entreaty about Dr Cook … & being wrought upon on all sides, I pacified Robert & my own apprehensions by agreeing to appeal to Mr Jago .. just to ask him whether *in such a case* the morphine w^d produce *such another case*. My letter was no sooner out of the house however than I repented sending it– You know it would seem so ridiculous, merely to *imagine* a case—& I had at best doubts! Oh, of course, I did doubt—I have always had such good general health that some symptoms made me doubt– But then, I thought, if when Wilson was ill, I unconsciously caught cold by going out into the passage, I might be affected so & so & so. As to Wilson, I fancied her determined to make a certain set of deductions from any sort of premises– If my finger ached, she w^d say "*This* means *that*". So I would not be convinced by her .. & when my poor dearest Robert besought me about Dr Cook, I put him off with ever so many impertinent speeches, yes, & obstinate ones— meâ culpâ!. I repent in dust & ashes. In fact, by the time the event took place I was perfectly convinced, would have died for it at the stake, that I had just caught cold! Most stupid, stupid!-

 The night pains quite went away, & I had only one return after writing to Nelly Bordman. But last Friday I felt unwell & submitted to see Dr Cook. He came .. declares that he found the room at seventy, a scandalous fire, a wrong posture, & my pulse very irritable—laid me down on the sofa—commanded cold tea .. & promised to come again on sunday. Though his opinion went with the majority, the minority of one remained obstinate .. mark that. Still I did what I was told, & on saturday morning felt rather better. Towards evening however regular pains came on, every five minutes .. & these lasted for above four & twenty hours, much as in an ordinary confinement– Oh, not so very violent! I have had worse pain, I assure you– It did not continue long enough at once to exhaust one! and when my eyes were open to the truth, I was as little frightened or agitated as at this moment, & bore it all so well (I mean with so much bodily vigour) as to surprise Wilson .. & D! Cook, too indeed–

⟨...⟩²

Robert was rather worse than I, I think, on sunday evening, when we had our tea together, Wilson shaking her head behind the curtain. In the first moment of his readmission into this room he threw himself down on the bed in a passion of tears, sobbing like a child, .. he who has not the eyes of a ready-weeper. He had better have scolded me well, I say, for bringing all this agitation on him—for D! Cook pronounces that if he had been called in six weeks ago, everything would have gone as right as possible ... he had only to lay me on the sofa for two months & to apply leeches to the back, keeping the temperature cool .. & he is said to be an experienced accoucheur. Well! A wilful woman who has her way, must have her punishment—or rather, let it be God's will, if my wilfulness. As Robert says .. "we are rebellious children, & He leads us where He can best teach us". In the meanwhile I am getting strength fast, & everything of this sort, D! Cook tells me, is *excellent* for my chest ... Indeed I have wondered lately where my chest had gone to, it seemed so entirely clear & right ... & it puzzled me rather to think how after all I could catch cold, & feel well in the chest. D! Cook is of opinion that I am likely to be wonderfully benefitted by what has happened– So, remember that you are to be glad upon the whole, however you may condole with me on my stupidity– For three days I kept quiet, .. & was *up* for an hour on the sofa on the fourth, & on the fifth, for two hours– Today this sixth day, I am to go to the sofa in the next room—& by the time you get this letter, the convalescence, should it please God, will be complete. D! Cook does not come "for a few days" .. So you see! Robert wrote to dear M! Kenyon on sunday night, but by my especial desire, begged him to keep the news from you until I could write it myself—& this, for the obvious probability's sake of your being most unnecessarily alarmed otherwise. If Robert had written to you, you w! have been frightened—now would'nt you? .. Not that we ever keep from you anything– I w! have told you long ago, had I *known* myself. Now I must not write anymore, because I am under a vow

No. 2663   26 March 1847   157

to Robert. He laid his commands on me not to write much (or *I could*, I assure you!) & just at present my mood inclines to be a more obedient wife than I have been.

Will my darling Arabel write for me to dear Nelly Bordman & say that her kind letter arrived just too late, & that I shall write very soon a full account of myself. Thank her most affectionately in the meanwhile, & our kind good friend M! Jago & say that I admire his sagacity (with the few data I gave him) as to the *time*—but it was farther off still .. beyond all calculation– Say too how well I am, & in excellent spirits notwithstanding disappointments. God's will be done—&, we are happy enough here. How can I tell you what Robert has been & is to me throughout this illness—so tender, past speaking of! Which reminds me, mind him more. May God bless you! my own dearest sisters–

Your Ba.

The morphine did *no* harm at all–

Wilson is much better, & a great comfort of course. Love to all & Trippy– I will write again very soon. Do write–

[Continued by RB]

Pisa,
March 26, '47.

My dearest sisters: You may *depend* upon the most satisfactory state of Ba, as, I make no doubt, she has described it to you in the enclosed letter. She will have told you that I wrote to Mr Kenyon on the 22^d, but,—being persuaded there was no danger,—could not help seeing the force of her arguments against informing you of the matter by any other hand than her own. She is at this moment on the sofa in our sitting-room, and wonderfully well and strong—beyond all reasonable hope, indeed. It is entirely thro' my begging & praying that you have so short a letter—but that will be remedied in a few days. I shall not try to tell you how perfectly good and patient she has been. Be sure, quite sure, that we will take every precaution. I have a very good opinion of our Physician, and we abide implicitly by his commands.

Let us congratulate each other on the safety of this dearest of creatures, and be thankful to God for his great goodness. God bless you.

RB.

Ba was delighted to receive your joint letter with Mr Boyd's—and I shall write my own answer to my own kindest of notes that came last week[.]

Address, in EBB's hand, on integral page: Miss Barrett / 50 Wimpole Street.
Publication: TTUL, pp. 39–46.
Source: Transcript in editors' file.

1. Dated by the continuation in RB's hand.
2. EBB has obliterated about one line, including an interpolation of several words.

2664. EBB TO HENRIETTA MOULTON-BARRETT

Pisa,
Tuesday & Wednesday. March 31 [1847][1]

Now I am going to give you the best account of myself possible, my ever dearest Henrietta. You shall have a second letter, you, to make up for the last short one, with bad news too in it! This is to be full of good news, with not a shadow across it to spoil the effect. D[r] Cook was here yesterday & gave leave to sit up, & even to stand up on my feet & walk a little—the reclining posture to be kept only as the general rule. Not a symptom, he said, was wrong .. everything as right as could be on the contrary—a glass of wine (claret) commanded for everyday .. and I am to be quite able to go to Florence next saturday fortnight according to the first arrangement- But our other plans of course are modified .. for instance we are not to travel northward & pass our summer at Verona- He has advised repose for me at the Baths of Lucca, & after a month or six weeks at Florence (just as the heat may decide) we shall settle for the season at the highest point of the mountain, so as to escape as much as may be from the "company" & the mosquitos, the two great evils to be guarded against- The scenery is said to be exquisite .. & we mean to ride our donkeys & mules (I am to have a donkey with a spanish saddle,) & explore the mountain paths, & clefts of the rocks, & darknesses of the chesnut forest—and we have a plan besides of sitting at the window & blowing soap-bubbles, which will tend to general edification, I think. D[r] Cook says that in that situation, there is a continual breeze & freshness, & we never shall feel the heat overpowering- Then, at the end of September, should all be well, there will be no hinderances to a slow northward journeying, a week at Bologna to visit Rossini & so on, till we arrive at Venice in time to *winter* there, keeping clear of the autumnal damps & malaria- We must see M[r] Kenyon, if possible .. that dearest, best friend to us!- When I talk of his being *kind*, the word seems to mock itself for being so miserably inadequate- A good deal lately, while I have been lying here, I have thought of him & of the noble generous goodness which he has exercised towards me & mine in a manner uncalled for, unsolicited, unexpected. Sympathy was all we asked him for, or thought of receiving— & he gave us head & heart & both warm hands, & thrust himself into most unpleasant positions for a man of his delicacy, rather than lose sight of an interest of mine by one moment's shrinking. Oh, I have been thinking it all over—And do you know, Henrietta, I did not even *encourage* his kindness when it showed itself in this form .. I hate so these money-questions .. and I abhorred so the very idea of Papa's being spoken to on such questions, though relating to my own income- But dear, admirable M[r] Kenyon was stopped by nothing- I cannot tell you, you cannot be aware, of the full extent of his goodness & excellence—but I measure it at its height & depth, & am sensible to it with an increasing gratitude. At the same time I thought the other day somewhat bitterly, that if I had died last sunday week, there remained not one member of my family, except himself (& he my relative scarcely more than by name!) to whom my husband could communicate such an end of all. Of course I speak of male relations .. for even an illness, you see, could not be communicated to my own beloved sisters, without running risks which should not be run– But just observe, that there was no one except Mr Kenyon to whom Robert could write in any event, or did write, as the thing happened … not one of all those whom I have tenderly loved & who have professed to love *me*– Well!– There shall be no word spoken more of it on my part: the choice of the position is not mine, nor ever was. I understand better what Love is .. its necessities & exigencies. But of this, enough– And pray dont think that I was in danger of dying on sunday week—it is only my imagination which suggests cases– Dr Cook assured Robert that there was no danger.– Still the period was so advanced that everybody wonders a little to see me recovering my strength now by handfuls, or heartfuls (a large measure!) & God's mercy is wonderful in my own eyes– I had no sort of fever .. perhaps some exhausting symptoms at the beginning, prevented the usual fever further on—and, observe, Dr Cook persists in thinking that I shall be infinitely the better on the whole for what has happened, though it might as well have happened four months hence .. Today I walked from the next room to this, all dressed & ringleted, .. & looking in the glass on the road, saw myself a little blanched, but otherwise … rather improved than not. Both yesterday & today, Robert & I had dinner together—& really it was time for me to come back, for he had given up eating 'tout de bon,'[2] & I expected him to turn into a shade– He was so dreadfully affected by my illness, as to be quite overset, overcome––only never *too* much so, to spend every moment he was allowed to spend, by my bedside .. rubbing me, talking to me, reading to me .. and all with such tenderness, such goodness!– Wilson says "I never saw a MAN like Mr Browning in my life"—and I hear that Dr Cook made a remark to the same effect. How am I to feel, do you suppose? What I always do, … that I am not worthy—only *that* feeling makes me more grateful than ever– I am bound to him indeed with all the cords of my heart. For several days .. (three ..) I kept one position in bed .. not suffered to move—& indeed I thought of you & wished for you .. I thought of poor dearest Papa, too .. but without taking any different view of what has been & is. Wilson's sleeping on the sofa in my room reminded me so & still reminds me so of my darling kindest Arabel, that my heart is full when I wake at nights & look that way. May God bless you all, as I love & think of you–

Wednesday

I am going to do my very best to leave off the morphine, but gradually—though it was by no means the cause of anything that happened—on the contrary—I sh.^{d} have done better by not diminishing it *when I did*- Only in the sunday crisis, Dr Cook did not dare let me have it all day—& would have been considerably embarrassed he has since told me, if the symptoms had not taken a turn precisely *then*, to know how to act in such a straight- It would have been highly dangerous either to give or not to give it- So he urges me to take care for the future. Also, the climate, he says, will allow me great facilities for leaving off the opiate, .. & "if he is not mistaken, my late illness will remove the need of it by diminishing the irritation about the chest." My appetite is good, & sleep, sound .. you have not the least cause for uneasiness, remember. Even Robert is in good spirits now, & we have gone back to our castle building- I was half afraid that I was to be kept "under Dr Cook's eye" for the rest of my life,—as Robert actually dropped something about our taking an appartment in the same house, at Lucca ....!! Oh, so delightful, *that* would be! San Ranieri forbid such a consummation! Now, it is not thought of, of course—& we are going to Florence to see the great sights, just as if one of us had'nt been frightened out of his wits- Dr Cook goes to the Baths of Lucca every summer, & most Pisans do the same. This place is untenable in the hot weather. Wilson is much better, thank God, & Lucca will be as good for her as for me. Just before my illness, she seemed unwell & out of spirits, & Robert & I agreed that we would send her home instantly, if she chose to go .. & for some little time I thought it all but a settled thing- Distressing to me of course, the idea of parting with her was—but for her to lose her health through staying, was more intolerable to think of—and also, you know good kind Wilson .. she is excellent, but timid—and I could not say to her as I should have done to my sister .. "Take courage, & look facts in the face bravely-" I did not dare, of course- So I could not say a word in favour of her remaining, though she begged me to decide for her. I told her that her health was the first consideration, & that it was her duty, both to her family & herself, to consider it- So she went to Dr Cook to lay everything before him, & take his final counsel, in expounding to him particularly her fears of the Italian summer. Dr Cook examined her scrupulously, & assured her, at last, that although no human being could be secured against illness in any situation, she was likely to do perfectly well here, if she would but take exercise & attend to her diet. He said that she was by no means a weak person .. that she was in perfect health in every respect but the irritability of the stomach & bilious tendencies .. that the attack she had had was the consequence, not of climate but of sea sickness .. & that her present symptoms were only a form of heartburn. In short, poor Wilson came back with a new prescription & the highest spirits, & decided at once that she w^d be delighted to stay– Think how pleased I was—and so was Robert! And ever since she has been growing better & better. Still not able, though, to touch butter or coffee—she is forced to be most abstemious every way, but she looks very well, I never saw her looking better in my life. Since the fatal fire, excommunicated by Dr Cook, we have had none at all. Nobody has a fire now indeed .. the weather is divine– When I am once able to get out in the carriage (& I dare say I shall, by the beginning of next week at any rate) there will be no bounds to the strength I shall gain,—and as it is, we have the window open– The air seems to float its balmy softness *into* you– Oh, & such air! Observe, that if I am weak again (I think I hear some one saying .. "There! Ba's weak again, you see") observe it's quite a different thing from the prostration arising from disease .. and by the time you get this letter, Ba probably will be strong again .. if God shall please .. the strength returns quite fast, hour by hour– Now do write & let me hear every detail. Tell me of visitors & residents. We have made great discoveries here on the arts of housekeeping & housetaking, & have had our eyes unsealed to the abominable impositions practised upon us. Cheating is systematized in Italy to the most frightful extent, & nobody sees any harm in what everybody does. Foreigners are considered the lawful prey of the natives and the *battu[e]s* are as frequent as in an English "preserve". You will be amused to learn that Robert & I are held to be "millionaires" in our neighbourhood, through the sublime indifference with which we have suffered ourselves to be taken in on all sides, .. & that all the letters of apartments have been grumbling around the boastful contentment of our "padrone". The owner of the house opposite in defence of his own dignity, was obliged to get up & swear that Mrs Browning (mark .. Mrs Browning) had offered *him* a fabulous price for *his* rooms if he w^d break a prior engagement with Major Loftus's wife[3] who thereupon being a woman of masculine understanding, (& superstructure besides) walked about Pisa, abusing Mrs Browning in good set terms for being unladylike & the saints know what. Robert was furious, & would write a note & present his compliments & deny the fact broadly. We did not even know that those rooms were to let, till our own were taken and occupied for a full month. It was just a lie of the lodging housekeeper, in order to prove that *he* might have taken us in, if he had pleased, .. precisely like his honorable friend– And of course *I* never did anything about taking houses .. as you may suppose. They have cheated us in weights & measures, besides the prices of every single thing,—& we have been paying twice as much as we sh^d have paid. We hear now that for two hundred & fifty pounds a year, we might & ought to live in excellent apartments, & keep our own carriage & two horses,—& a man servant to boot—and we see how this might be done easily. At Florence too the cheapness is wonderful—only one must understand a little. Wilson opens her eyes at the system of iniquity worked out in such detail, minute by minute. It was that kind M?^s Turner who set us right in these things, & took Wilson round with her to some shops & showed her how to do some small marketings—for as we were going away so soon we would not make a great revolution & fuss—only we take the liberty of buying our own coffee, tea & sugar, in despite of the black looks of our hosts—and when we go elsewhere, we shall take our experience with us–

Yesterday, a priest came in full canonicals to bless all the rooms of the house .. omitting ours on account of our being heretics .. Robert met him in the passage & taking off his hat, desired him not to turn from his usual course on our account, as nobody's blessing could do anybody any harm. But our hosts observed that it was better *so*, as the signora was ill! Of course they did not like to throw benedictions away on the prophane!

Do tell me how you get on while I throw you mine .. Oh, I understand so very very well .. though not exactly how Bummy makes up her mind to go to court & present Arlette!—— Why what a conclave of relations will be held in London!- Tell me of the Hedleys, & of ⟨Arabella⟩[4] Bevan. I have had no further sign of existence from anyone .. not even from Jane. One letter in six months. I really never thought it so easy as I observe it to be now, to let people down into oblivion .. and I shall lie flat & not stir a finger evermore, I do assure you. Ah, how good & perfect you have been to me, you .. my own beloved sisters .. heart & eyes overflow when I think of you! Tell my darling dear Arabel that when Robert said of her note "something in it will make your heart leap," & I read that M? Stratten advised her to come & see me, I fell into a muse! .. We should both hold out our arms, & four of them w? be enough to hold her fast. Oh, what a dream! But you must see, dearest Henrietta & Arabel, how foolish & imprudent it w? be for us to go to England this summer. There is the expense, for one thing, of going & returning—for you w? not like me to run the hazard of a winter in England: & then, there w? be bitterness on all sides .. bad enough as it is, but intolerable under nearer circumstances. I cannot *help* considering myself *wronged* .. that is my impression: and it could only deepen painfully by a return to England at the present time. Then there w? be no use, except for the glance at your beloved faces .. and we have seen & done nothing yet in Italy of all we have to see & do. Thank you for the dear welcome letters .. thank you both. The next will be from Arabel, & I shall answer it straightway- Tell her to thank M? Boyd for his kind one- M? Boyd's & the crossings, the dear crossings, came when I was ill & Robert read them to me- Not that he reads my letters so in general, mind, .. but that my head swam on that particular occasion & w? not let me read properly. Does Bummy talk of Florence for the winter? or do the Hedleys? Let me hear everything- May it all go smooth for you my dearest Henrietta. I am very glad indeed to hear of Alfred's success—he will do excellently. The worst of bank occupations is, that you have *to begin*, & that for persons with a made position to have *to begin* is unpleasant. Robert has two uncles .. (that is, two half uncles[5] .. some of his aunts & uncles are younger than himself[6] .. through his grandfather's having married late in life very much in order to disinherit his father[7]) who are .. one of them, Rothschild's chief man of business, & the other the head of the English firm at Madrid[8] .. but then, they began early & went through an immense drudgery .. also they are very good linguists—*German* is of great consequence. I am driven to end here, with heaps of things to say- Tell me if Surtees gets his appointment or has a *strong* hope of it. Mr Fox Maule[9] Robert knows nothing of. Give my love to Surtees & Susan too. Give my best love to dearest Trippy & ask her to understand that I will write to her as soon as I get a little stronger—& this letter does to take my love to her as well as to you, you know. Her dear, tender letter made me very grateful to her. I feel that she loves me—and I for my part, never shall forget her. Write .. write .. write .. Robert will write soon—but this suffices for today. Love to dear Minny always- Robert's love always to both of you-

Your own attached
Ba-

Direct Poste Restante, Firenze, Toscana .. *via France*

Address, on integral page: Miss Barrett / 50 Wimpole Street.
Directive, in RB's hand, on address panel: Enclose to Mr. Kenyon.
Publication: Huxley, pp. 13–18 (in part).
Source: Transcript in editors' file.

1. Year determined from the Brownings' residence in Pisa in March 1847.
2. "In earnest," or "for good," or "entirely."
3. Margaret Harriet (*née* Langrishe), the wife of William Francis Bentinck Loftus (1784–1852).
4. Conjectural reading, due to ink smudge.
5. Actually RB had three half-uncles: William Shergold Browning (1797–1874), Reuben Browning (1803–79), and Thomas Browning (1809–78). The last had left England in 1829 for Tasmania, and he later moved to Melbourne, Australia, where he died.
6. RB had one aunt, Margaret Morris Browning (1783–1858) and six half-aunts: Christina Browning (1799–1825), Jane Eliza Browning (1800–80), Mary Browning (1805–64), Louisa Browning (1807–87), Jemima Smith Browning (1809–78), and Sarah Browning (1814–1902); only the last was younger than Browning.
7. Five years after the death of his wife Margaret Tittle in 1789, RB's grandfather married Jane Smith (1771–1848).
8. This is doubtless William Shergold Browning, who had been with the House of Rothschild in Paris until 1846. Reuben Browning was associated with the Rothschilds in London for the whole of his career.
9. Fox Maule, 2nd Baron Panmure and 11th Earl of Dalhousie (1801–74), was "secretary at war under Lord John Russell in 1846–52" (*DNB*). Presumably Surtees was hoping for some assistance from him in finding a post.

2665. RB TO RICHARD MONCKTON MILNES

Pisa,
March 31, '47.

Dear Milnes, When I left England, I bade my Sister at Home open all letters sent to me, and only forward the *pith* of them: but a little note of your writing was *all* pith, so I got it in its entireness—and very pleasantly your voice sounded, in the few words of it, as I read them here under the grim Campanile—the top of which, when the earth next quakes in these parts, will just hit the roof of this huge old Collegio Ferdinando, "where Bartolo," of crabbed memory, "once taught"—as an inscription states—and where I now write—you patience, if your goodnature reads to the end.[1] Well—your good wishes for my sake have been wonderfully realised. My wife is quite well, and now that the weather permits, we begin our spring progress, Florence being the first stage, whence, when the heat obliges, we mean to go the round of Siena, Colle, Volterra, Lucca, Pescia, Prato, Pistoia—Bologna—and so get, at the year's end, to Venice for the winter. Next *winter* to *that*—(if one dares look forward so far)—finding us in Rome.

Now I want to speak to you—and your old kindness will understand, I am sure. A six month's residence in Pisa is favourable to a great deal of speculation and political study—and though last week's papers prove that a capital speech about Cracow may be as well studied in Pall Mall as on the spot—yet *here*—what shall I say?—here—one sees more clearly than elsewhere, that .. why, only that England must,—needs must not loiter behind the very Grand Turk in policy,[2] but send a minister, before the year ends, to this fine fellow, Pio Nono—as certain, that is, as that his name will be Lord Somebody—against which, the time is not yet come to complain.

But I should like to have to remember that I asked you, whose sympathy I am sure of, to mention in the proper quarter, should you see occasion, that I would be glad and proud to be the Secretary to such an Embassy, and to work like a horse in my vocation. You know I have studied Italian literature sedulously. Governments now-a-days give poets pensions—I believe one may dun them into that. Now I and my wife "keep our pen out of lenders' books, and defy the foul fiend"[3]—we are quite independent, thro' God's goodness, and trust to continue so. But, as I say, I should like to remember at a future day that I proposed—(and thro' the intervention of such a person as yourself, if you will lend it to me) to deserve well of my generation by doing, in this matter, what many circumstances embolden me to think few others could do so well. One gets excited .. at least here on the spot .. by this tiptoe straining expectation of poor dear Italy,—and yet, if I had not known you, I believe I should have looked on with the other byestanders. It is hateful to ask .. but I ask nothing; indeed—rather I concede a very sincere promise to go on bookmaking (as my wife shall) to the end of our natural life, and making the public & ⟨...⟩⁴ a present of our hard work, without a pretension to the pension list. Will you think of this and me? Whatever comes, I hope to remain in Italy for years—so let me shake your hand over the sea, and take that much by my motion.

Ever yours faithfully,
Robert Browning.

Address, on integral page: Angleterre, viâ France. / Richard M. Milnes Esq. M.P. / &c &c &c / Pall Mall / London.
Publication: None traced.
Manuscript: Trinity College, Cambridge.

    1. Bartolo da Sassoferrato (1314–57), a renowned professor of jurisprudence, whose teaching was enhanced by his own experience from working in the law. He taught at Pisa in the 1330's before going on to Perugia where he held the chair of law, and where he eventually died. The inscription reads: "Ferdinandus Medices / Magnu Dux Etruriæ III / Has Edes / Quas Olim Bartolus / Iuris Interpres Celeberr. Incoluit / Nunc Renovatas Et Instructas / Adulescentibus Qui Ad / Philosophorum Et Iuris-Consultorum / Scholas Missi / Publico Urbium Atque Oppidorum Suorum / Sumptu Separatim Alebantur / Tulit An. Salutis / MDLXXXXV" (Giovanni Grazzini, *Le Condizioni di Pisa alla fine de xvi e sul principio del xvii secolo sotto il granducato di Ferdinando I de'Medici*, Empoli, 1898, p. 18).
    2. In a report on the efforts of Pope Pius IX towards reforms in Italy, *The Times* for 23 March 1847 stated that "the time is come when the presence of ... a representation of this country at the Court of Rome is indispensable. Even Turkey has sent an ambassador to the Vatican." See letter 2662, note 8.
    3. *King Lear*, III, 4, 97–98.
    4. Word indecipherable, due to water damage.

2666. RB TO ANNA BROWNELL JAMESON

Pisa,
April 1, '47–

Dearest friend—let me lose no time in replying to your note, just received. Ba is next to quite well—dressed at this minute and lying on the sofa—and only affected by the weakness that is inevitable. No cold, no feverishness,—all one steady progress to perfect health, thank God, as I am sure I hope I do. This good, moreover, has been nature's doing, without strengthening-medicine of any kind. The fine spring weather is very favorable.

    And now for our travelling-projects—which go easily together, you shall see—for ours was only changed in order to meet what we took to be your convenience. We leave here on the 17.ᵗʰ inst. for Florence,—as we always meant to do—the *way* to Florence was the uncertain point. Had the weather permitted, we might have made the circle of Sienna, Colle & Volterra, and returned here, to leave again, by Prato & Pistoja, for Florence. In that case, we should have seen enough of Tuscany for the present, and be ready for Bologna and the north. But, Ba's illness changes the *ulterior* plans altogether—we cannot venture to do so much, I fear—and we now mean to return from Florence, when the heats oblige us, to the Baths of Lucca, as a *safe* place,—and as our road will lie viâ Pistoja, *then* will be the time for that visit, and *now*, (we thought) for Volterra & Sienna, as we go to Florence: we also thought this made no kind of difference to you, as, since you had arranged to see Bologna *before* Ravenna, thro' Florence you could not but pass,—and we intended to order our journey, as I said, so as to coincide with your arrival, making a three days' affair of it, or prolonging our stay at each city, just as that event should prescribe. But when your last letter mentioned your objection to even crossing Florence if it could be avoided,—I merely spoke of our being *able* to meet at Sienna or Volterra—for, of course, if you could reconcile yourself to Florence, we should prefer it. Now, you *decide* for "Florence on the 22"—do you not? If Ba had been well, and the original journey determined on, the interval of six days would have satisfied all our curiosity and punctually on the $22^{\underline{d}}$ should we meet: but yet another variation (the last, I do hope) fits our projects to yours most perfectly: it is this. To run no risk, and escape the possibility of the cold lingering on these high nests of Etruscan cities, we shall not see them till *after* our stay at Florence: it will evidently be better to go *at once there*, on the $17^{\underline{th}}$—get Ba well rested for a month or six weeks,—*then* return by the aforesaid Sienna & Volterra, to Lucca & the B⟨aths⟩ and thence, in early Autumn, go by the one picturesque way you mention, to Bologna and Venice. So we shall be arrived six days before you,—and the good *seventh*, blessed in all way, will bring you to us. There! And now a dear kiss by anticipation, if you please! Do you think we would let you leave Italy without seeing us?- And as for seeing anybody else, you *cannot* .. for our current of talk will hold out two mortal days and then be unexhausted, be sure! Meantime, I will make all enquiry about the books you ask for, and get them, if possible—with whatever else you may want. And you,—will you not write a word to say this last of all arrangements is also the best- Write soon—for who knows but we may coax yet another final letter out of you? Ba's love and thanks,—the extreme of both,—to you and Geddie—mine go with them too. Can you get us any precise information about those Recoaro Baths?[1] We would have gone there, could we have ventured, *and about the capabilities of Venice as a winter residence.*

Ever yours,
RB.

Address, on integral page: Mrs Jameson, / Dama Inglese, / Piazza di Spagna, / Roma.
Publication: LRB, pp. 15-16.
Manuscript: Yale University.

    1. See letter 2656, note 7.

No. 2667 [ca. 10 April 1847] 167

2667. EBB TO ANNA BROWNELL JAMESON

[Pisa]
[ca. 10 April 1847][1]

Dearest friend,[2] As Robert's letter of explanation seems to have missed its way to you, it shall be my turn to try to show what we wish & what we are likely to attain to, leaving to your goodness to judge, & see that if we break tryst with you it is not a matter of choice with us at least. Our first plan was to meet you at Florence or Bologna if you pleased, & go north with you at Verona .. to pass the summer there or at Recoaro, & to winter at Venice. Then came my illness .. & everything was changed. It was thought that I might get to Florence, & thence as the coolest place near at hand, retreat to the Baths of Lucca– D[r] Cook recommended repose, & poor dearest Robert caught at the very first suggestion, .. & thus all our fine plans were pulled down in the face of our wishes. As to Lucca (the Baths) the idea of the place or rather of the concomitants of the place, always was most detestable to us, & except as the absolutest 'pis aller'[3] we should not have recourse to it, be sure– Also, it is most probable that we *shall not*– People grow insolent as they grow better, you know, & since I have been better, we both have begun to plot so hard against Lucca, that if we can stay & recover the necessary strength at Florence we shall certainly push on our way northward .. perhaps to Recoaro .. or remain on the Fiesole hills, till the hour for Venice strikes. If Siena was mentioned, it was thus. We saw you averse to Florence, & having an idea of going round ourselves to Florence by Volterra & Siena .. creeping round & remaining a day or two at each of the towns .. Robert suggested what threw you so into confusion– But the plain fact appears now of the impossibility of my making any such round—. Indeed I am afraid .. afraid .. afraid that the shortest journey to Florence, the directest & easiest, will be beyond my strength so soon as the 17th D[r] Cook speaks of another week—and I who am hopeful, cannot hope for less than a few more days instead. If we set out on the twentieth for instance, it will by no means disappoint me– I am looking well & often feeling quite so, but to walk from one room to the other ⟨...⟩[4]

Publication: None traced.
Manuscript: Fitzwilliam Museum.

   1. Conjectural date based upon EBB's reference to the preceding letter from RB to Mrs. Jameson, which had apparently gone unanswered. EBB reiterates many of the same points of that letter.
   2. A comparison of this letter with RB's letter of 1 April to Mrs. Jameson identifies her as the intended recipient of this letter.
   3. "Last resort."
   4. EBB did not finish this letter, and it was never sent. Apparently, the Brownings heard from Mrs. Jameson, making this letter unnecessary.

2668. EBB TO ARABELLA MOULTON-BARRETT

Pisa—
Direct– Poste Restante, Firenze, Toscana, Italy.   April 12– [1847][1]

Now my own dearest Arabel it is your turn– I have expected to hear from you with or without a reason. Perhaps I am unreasonable. Certainly you are, when you persist in telling atrocious things about postage[2] ... oh Arabel— is it not too bad? Judge yourself! Would you, do you, can you calculate postages in your own case? As for ours, why Robert observes constantly that he would rather find a letter from some indifferent person at the office than none at all .. a stupid letter from an indifferent person. Think then, what it is to us to have letters from the dearest people, every word of which is full of interest. It is our *one* luxury—and you grudge it, you unkind naughty Arabel! All this about such an obvious matter! I drop the subject for ever, entreating you to put away the thought of it for as long. Only think that by writing to me you give me the greatest joy you can give me, & that the oftener you give it the more generous a giver of gifts you are! There's an end!—or here's a beginning, rather. The next thing to say is that though going on well, I have not done being an invalid yet--not quite. I look well, sleep well, eat well & am in good spirits—but still to lie on the sofa is a necessary inconvenience because of a persisting symptom which does not suffer one to be oneself altogether. D[r] Cook says that it is a "slow & sure" affair ... satisfactory in every respect except as to our Florentine schemes! There seems little hope of a journey to Florence as soon as the seventeenth, and very vexatious it is to be kept here .. "a week" says D[r] Cook, .. "a month" says Robert when he is out of spirits .. "a few days" say I when inclined to laugh doctors & prophets to scorn. M[rs] Jameson will be at Florence on the twenty second on purpose to meet us (by the way), and if we cant go on time we shall have no opportunity of apprizing her of the fact. And then these cheating signori of ours have ceased to be agreeable "padroni"—altogether it is vexatious. D[r] C. affirms that if anyone except myself were in question, he could set all to rights by a few doses of quinine, but that he is half afraid of giving it to me, .. awed by the nervous instability of which he read the signs .. & would rather trust to nature's own resources, taking a little more time. He assured me the other day that while he has attended me, he has seen nothing morbid about me *except the state of the nerves*—neither disease nor the tendency to disease—& that the lungs from first to last have been perfectly unembarrassed.

⟨...⟩[3]

—& there is no wonder that at the end of these weeks, a woman not originally strong, should be still weak—is there? Oh, I wish you could answer that question as quickly as it goes, to you! Robert's goodness & tenderness are past speaking of, even if you could answer me. He reads to me, talks & jests to make me laugh, tells me stories, improvises verses in all sorts of languages (did I ever tell you that he was an improvisatore? indeed he is, & a surprising one! What is there that he cannot do & know?) sings songs, explains the difference between Mendels[s]ohn & Spohr[4] by playing on the table, & when he has thoroughly amused me, accepts it as a triumph, a pleasure of his own .. the only pleasure he will have for himself. Of course I am spoilt to the uttermost! Who could escape? I think sometimes of your opinion on the demoralizing effects of "a long courtship" .. & then I admit that "the courtship," with me, was by no means the most dangerous thing. There has been a hundred times as much attention, tenderness, nay, *flattery* even, ever since—and is not this the close of the seventh month, Arabel? .. is'nt it? You will be disappointed if I dont continue my calculations .. you know you will. Our parcel has left London only ten days by a *sailing packet*, & I despair to calculate in that direction. Sarian[n]a Browning waited for the steamers in vain, & so the time passed. M:rs Browning's health is better, I am glad to say. Did I ever tell you that the Brownings were fierce & strong Puritans in the old years? Always, since I knew it I meant to tell you, feeling sure that you would care more for *that* than for our noble deeds at the battle of Harfleur, or even perhaps (who shall say?) than for the old poetical laurel of the first English poet, who was a *Robert Brunynge*,[5] yes, really- In the register of the Tower of London, is still to be seen the name of a Browning puritan who suffered imprisonment & death there in James the first's reign, & Robert says laughingly that perhaps it is the old Puritanism which brews in his blood against the very sign & symbol of any sort of gambling, inclusive of my lottery-phantasms of palazzinos in orange-groves. The Drama was a different thing—it conquered: but he never touched cards .. shrank from them by a sort of instinct, even in Russia where everybody plays his course through society. By the way, Arabel, or out of the way, we *never do "quarrel"* whatever you may imagine- Not one breath of unkindness or crossness has passed between us .. not one, for one moment. It is not *my* credit, & I do not mention it for that- I should be as savage as a tiger if I would get up a quarrel any way. Yet Henrietta is not right—there is no "hen-pecking" in the case either- I am satisfied with picking up my seed. I have too much reverence (seriously speaking) & he is too much above me, to admit of such a thought. But simply I am spoilt & petted, & the object is to watch for my least wish & turn it to a reality. If you saw how I have to beg & entreat & draw him out to take his walk everyday! Otherwise he would not leave me at all- We are very happy-

Do you remember my ending one of my letters with a visit from a M:rs Young who called herself a friend of M:r Stratton's & whose daughter had lately married Professor Mat[t]eucci of this university?[6] Now I will tell you a history. She & Madame (the daughter) had sate with me about half an hour when Robert came in. I had hoped that he w:d not come in, knowing how he hates indiscriminate visitors (worse than I, he is!) but he heard from Wilson in the passage as he returned from his walk, that M:r Stratton's name had been mentioned, & desired to show whatever respect he could to a friend of his– Well! but upon coming in & the ordinary conversation continuing, he was struck with a sudden dislike of both visitors (he never was deceived in his life, he says, about *physiognomy* .. it is his "one strong point" .. that's what he says of himself!) & all I could explain of my own view as to Madame's apparent stiffness being shyness & so on, went quite for nothing— they were detestable people .. not kind, not unaffected, not anything good. He & I argued the point half the day after. M:rs Young seemed to *me*, a rather sensible woman & meaning to be cordial .. & her daughter reserved, to an appearance of coldness—not much over-refinement .. but passable enough— so of course I argued the point. Well—the memory of these things had vanished almost, when a week ago Robert came to me in "considerable excitement" .. "Oh, that hateful woman! that wretched M:rs Young!– Tell me again, Ba, that I dont see through people at a glance—doubt my judgements again! but hear first about what that detestable woman has been saying of *you*!" "Of *me*!" I could not help laughing a little at the very idea of such a thing, & opening my eyes incredulously– And then it came out that M:rs Young who had called upon me with every intention of showing me civility ... of inviting me to her soireés, & various condescendences, professed herself to be absolutely astonished at the rudeness with which I had repulsed her advances,—never returning her visit, nor meaning to do so! The airs I gave myself were quite prodigious! I had even told her plainly face to face that I did not *intend* to return her visit! (Which was my *politeness*, you are to understand, Arabel, as far as the intention went—I thought I had explained ever so blandly, that if I did not call on her instantly, she was to be kind enough to remember that the causes were this & this .. telling her how I had to shun an exposure to cold winds &c.) M:rs Y. had delivered herself of the above declaration to kind M:rs Turner who was "sure there was a mistake somewhere,["] as from what she had seen of me—she thought me incapable of giving myself "airs"– "Incapable! after her conduct to M:rs Loftus!!"—— My female major aforesaid!—whose apartment I wanted to "take over her head" (a feat, considering that she is nearly six feet high!) & pay double or triple for—you remember– Also you may imagine how furious Robert was to hear all this from M:rs Turner who told him with the best motives, "as there must be a mistake & it ought to be cleared up"– He sate by me using his very strongest language & at last sprang from his chair .. "He should go & call on that M:rs Young instantly as she wanted a visit." I begged, for the sake of peace & me, that he would not do such a thing .. dreading a fuss & a scandal– "What nonsense! do let the foolish people talk out their foolishness"– But he insisted on going—["]he sh^d make no fuss .. he sh^d avoid of course being rude to a woman—whatever the woman might be .. but directness was the best thing in the world & he would *directly* make them all ashamed of themselves." Off he went to Mrs Young's– A splendid apartment—the lady & her daughter visible. Great politeness on all sides. Did me the honour of enquiring after me– Robert replied in measured language that I had been very ill, .. (He thought, he says, that under the circumstances he could not be too specific)– "And yet I understand" he continued, (after they had expressed some civil regret) "that, in the face of these circumstances, & of the other fact that Mrs Browning came to Pisa on account of the previous weakness of her health, there are persons here who have absolutely taken offence & made it a ground of complaint against her because she has not returned their visits–" (Obvious embarrassment & a glance exchanged from mother to daughter)—"But how could that be? People must surely be unreasonable if they could complain …." said Mrs Y. "Most unreasonable indeed," pursued Robert, .. "& not only so, but uncharitable, unsympathizing, & unkind"– Poor Mrs Young agreed with him *à l'outrance*,[7] looking painfully embarrassed– "And you will admit" he went on to say, ["]that such a want of consideration & good feeling is enough to produce, among persons who like ourselves are seeking in Italy just health & tranquility, a disinclination towards the society of our own country people—"– She *admitted it was quite enough*– (Such cowardice! says Robert to me!) And then, to clinch the argument, he narrated to her the Loftus affair as if he were talking to a sympathizing listener—explained how we were ignorant of the existence of Major Loftus's apartment .. & how the whole lie had probably originated. She listened .. & when he found that the impression was complete he let the conversation turn into other channels, & met with extraordinary cordiality at every turn of it– Italian newspapers were thrust into his hands, & he came home laden with messages & assurances to me– Three days after, the professor & his wife called here & a note came last night .. (to Robert himself, mind!) overflowing with interest about me, & suggesting that if I could get to their house for change of air &c &c– Oh, such affection—it grows like mustard & cress!– Moreover we have had a humble apology from the Major's minor, who for the future "never means to believe what she is told." Altogether, I am glad now that the truth was set in the light– Mrs Loftus had raged against me *even to Dr Cook*, he has admitted since, and declared that she intended to take the first opportunity of complaining *to Mr Browning of the unladylike conduct of his wife*– She had been uncomfortable in her apartment throughout the winter because of me & "had no idea of it"! .. There's Pisa gossip for you!—just observe how people can talk in Italy & .. not of

Michael Angelo!– M?ˢ Young went to M?ˢ Turner to reproach her with reporting her conversation—but M?ˢ Turner reminded her that she, M?ˢ T., had said at the time she should find out whether there was a mistake or not– So all is right now– I shall leave cards on everyone before quitting Pisa, should it be possible, & lose my bad character of "giving myself airs" as completely as I can. M?ˢ Young & Madame are said to give great soireés in Pisa & to "have everybody"– They receive the Religious, one night, to tea & serious conversation, .. and the irreligious, another, to the sound of music & dancing– There's gossip, you see, on my side! But this place is too English for us, in the social party-giving sense– We cant be left alone, observe. Venice will suit us best, .. & Florence better .. in the meanwhile.

My best darling Arabel, you go out to walk, I do trust & entreat– Do it for my sake & when you think most of me. The weather is exquisite, & D? Cook who has just been here, thinks that in a few days I may try the *carriage* ... which looks like Florence, does'nt it? He is going to give me *iron* .. I cant persuade him to attempt the quinine .. and I am to have a glass of port wine a day, besides French wine .. claret. Sette would call that "jolly", I think .. & my own opinion is that I shall be an irresponsible agent by eventide. But you will at once see how free I must be from fever & bad symptoms, to admit of this excess. Then I have two eggs a day, at breakfast & tea, besides animal food at dinner—seed cake for supper & luncheon– I am inclined to eat everytime, I assure you, & take the whole egg, the shell being once broken, so that *egg* stands for *egg* with me now– D? Cook thought me looking better, & said that no symptom except such as arose from weakness occurred. The iron, he hopes a good deal from. Pray take for granted that there is not a single thing to be uneasy about in my behalf ... except indeed the port wine!– I tell you everything, that you may understand, & not be uneasy. Write & give me all the news of all. Have you heard from my dear Stormie yet? I dream of you all often & cry in my sleep. Tell me of Papa. Has George returned from circuit & did he do well? Bid Henry take courage & look about for an occupation. There is hope in the world for him, bid him be sure with my love. I fear, for Sette, that the Law is not the best profession just now—but it gives a *position*, which is something. Occy & M? Barry must triumph in the House of Lords–[8] As to Alfred he triumphs *alone*, it appears. Good speed to them all. Tell me of Papa– Do you ever paint now, dear dearest Arabel! Speak of yourself. Henrietta takes long walks I know.– When is Susan Cook to be married? My love to her & Surtees. How does Annie Hayes get on with her husband? & how is her health, poor thing? My best love to my dearest Trippy, & *assure* her that I have a letter in my heart for her, yet unwritten. In the meanwhile, this will do as well, considering her kindness & that I am forbidden to write much. I want to write several

No. 2669   24 April [1847]   173

notes .. to dear M! Boyd (tell him so) & to others– Who has reached London, of the Expected? If Bummy has, & if she cares still for any of my love, you may give it to her. Also *to Arlette*. I want to write a little note to dear Minny, & it shall be written some day.

Wilson continues better. Robert tells me to give his love to you & dearest Henrietta, which I agree to– I am your own Ba in deepest affection–
Flush's love & a paw.

Address, on integral page: To the care of Miss Trepsack, / (Miss Arabel Barrett) / 5. Upper Montagu Street / Montagu Square / London.
Publication: None traced.
Manuscript: Berg Collection.

1. Year determined from the Brownings' residence in Pisa during the first half of April 1847.
2. Letters from England to Tuscany had to be paid by the sender through France; postage from the Italian border to the final destination was then paid by the receiver. Evidently, Arabella was primarily concerned with the Brownings having to pay the high rates of postage on receipt of her letters.
3. Two and a half lines have been obliterated by someone other than EBB.
4. Ludwig Spohr (1784–1859) and Felix Mendelssohn (1809–47). Spohr's compositions (now seldom performed) were romantic in style, whereas Mendelssohn adhered to a more classical tradition. Both enjoyed success in England during their careers.
5. Perhaps a reference to Robert Mannyng, or Robert of Brunne (fl. 1264–1340), author of *Handlyng Synne* and a *Chronicle of England*. We have been unable to identify any ancestor of the Barrett or Moulton families who fought with Henry V at the Battle of Harfleur in 1415, nor any Browning ancestor being a prisoner in the Tower.
6. See letter 2660, note 20.
7. "Beyond all measure."
8. Octavius Moulton-Barrett was studying with Charles Barry (1795–1860), the architect chosen to design the new Houses of Parliament. Drawings by Octavius made during this period are extant (see vol. 1, p. 296).

2669. EBB TO JULIA MARTIN

Florence–
April 24– [1847][1]

I received your letter my dearest friend by this days post, & wrote a little note directly to the office, as a trap for the feet of your travellers. If they escape us after all, therefore, they may praise their stars for it, rather than my intentions ... *our* intentions, I should say, for Robert will gladly do everything he can, in the way of expounding a text or two of the glories of Florence, & we both shall be much pleased & cordially pleased to learn more of Fanny & her brother than the glance, at Pisa, could teach us– As for me, she will let me have a little talking for my share—— I cant walk about or see anything .. I lie here flat on the sofa in order to be wise, .. I rest & take port wine by wineglasses; and a few more days of it will prepare me I hope & trust, for an interview with the Venus de' Medici.[2] Think of my having been in Florence since tuesday, this being saturday, and not a step taken into the galleries!—— It seems a disgrace .. a sort of involuntary disgraceful act, or rather no-act, .. which to complain of, relieves one to some degree! And how kind of you to wish to hear from me of myself! There is nothing really much the matter with me—I am just *weak*—sleeping & eating dreadfully well considering that Florence is'nt seen yet, .. & "looking well" too, says M.rs Jameson, who, with her niece, is our guest just now—. It would have been wise if I had rested longer at Pisa—but you see, there was a long engagement to meet M.rs Jameson here, & she expressed a very kind unwillingness to leave Italy without keeping it—also she had resolved to come out of her way on purpose for this, and as I had the consent of my physician, we determined to perform our part of the compact,—and in order to prepare for the longer journey, I went out in the carriage a little too soon perhaps & a little too long. At least, if I had kept quite still I should have been strong by this time!—not that I have done myself harm in the serious sense, observe—and now the affair is accomplished, I shall be wonderfully discreet & selfdenying, & resist Venuses & Apollos like someone wiser than the gods themselves. My chest is very well .. there has been no symptom of evil in that quarter—& D.r Cook thought that I should be the better for what has happened, in the result of all: it is only the *broken* sort of feeling, which means nothing—you are not to fancy me unwell otherwise than must of necessity be- We took the whole coupé of the diligence, (but regretted our first plan of the *vettura* nevertheless)—and now are settled in very comfortable rooms in the "Via delle Belle Donne" just out of the Piazza Santa Maria Novella .. very superior rooms to our apartment in Pisa, in which we were cheated to the uttermost with all the subtlety of Italy & to the full extent of our ignorance—think what *that* must have been!—— Our present apartment, with the hire of a grand piano & music, does not cost us so much, within ever so many francesconi!-³ Oh, and you dont frighten me though we are on the north side of the Arno! We have taken our rooms for two months & may be here longer; & the fear of the heat was stronger with me than the fear of the cold—or we might have been in the Pitti & "arrostiti"⁴ by this time. We expected dear M.rs Jameson on saturday,—but she came on friday evening, having suddenly remembered that it was Shakespeare's birthday, & bringing with her from Arezzo a bottle of wine to "drink to his memory with two other poets"—so there was a great deal of merriment as you may fancy, & ⟨Robert played Shakespeare's favorite air, the "Light of Love", and⟩⁵ everybody was delighted to meet everybody, & Roman news & Pisan dulness were properly discussed on every side. She saw a good deal of Cobden in Rome, & went with him to the Sistine chapel. He has no feeling for art, & being very true & earnest, could only do his best to *try* to admire Michael Angelo: but here & there where he understood, the pleasure was expressed

No. 2669   24 April [1847]

with a blunt characteristic simplicity– Standing before the statue of Demosthenes, he said .. "That man is persuaded himself of what he speaks & will therefore persuade others".[6] She liked him exceedingly. For my part I should join in more admiration if it were not for his having *accepted money*—but paid patriots are no heroes of mine—"Verily they have their reward".[7] O'Connell had arrived in Rome, & it was considered that he came only to die. Among the artists, Gibson & Wyatt are doing great things[8]— she wishes us to know Gibson particularly. As to the Pope he lives in an atmosphere of love & admiration—and "he is doing *what he can*," M.[rs] Jameson believes. Robert says .. "A dreadful situation after all, for a man of understanding & honesty! I pity him from my soul, .. for he can, at best, only temporize with truth". But Human Nature is doomed to pay a high price for its opportunities. Delighted I am to have your good account of dear M.[r] Martin, though you are naughty people to persist in going to England so soon. Do write to me & tell me all about both of you. I will do what I can, like the Pope—but what can I do? Yes indeed,—I mean to enjoy Art & Nature, too .. one shall not exclude the other– This Florence seems divine as we passed the bridges .. and my husband who knows everything, is to teach & show me all the great wonders, so that I am reasonably impatient to try my advantages. His kind regards to you both & my best love, dearest friends!– Dearest M.[rs] Martin, the Hedleys may be in Paris perhaps—but I told you my news, which fluctuates with the uncertainty of their plans– The great news now is that Arlette Butler is to be married directly to a Capt Reynolds.[9] Approved of by the authorities. Write to me, do, soon, & let it be to Poste Restante, Florence.

                          Your very affec.[te]
                          Ba.

Address, on integral page: À Madame / M.[dme] Martin, / Poste Restante, / Dieppe, / France.
Publication: LEBB, I, 325–328 (in part).
Manuscript: Wellesley College.

    1. Year provided by postmark and by the Brownings' removal from Pisa to Florence in April 1847.
    2. This famous statue, discovered at Hadrian's Villa about 1580, and attributed to Cleomenes, was taken to Florence during the reign of Cosimo III. It has been in the Uffizi since 1680.
    3. According to Murray's *Handbook for Travellers in Central Italy* (1843), "the Tuscan francescone [a silver coin], which is also a piece of 10 pauls, is equal to 10¼ Roman pauls, or 4*s*. 5½*d*. English" (p. 3).
    4. "Roasted."
    5. The bracketed portion has been squeezed in as an afterthought. The 16th-century melody, "Light o' Love," is said to have been Shakespeare's favourite tune. EBB's source for this tradition was Charles Knight's *The Pictorial Edition of the Works of Shakespeare* (1839–42), vol. 8, p. 142.
    6. In the entry for 22 February in the diary of his visit to the continent from 5 August 1846 until 11 October 1847, Cobden records that he "went with Mrs. Jameson to the Vatican ... the Braccio Nuovo contains a statue of Demosthenes in an attitude most earnest;

there is no appearance of effort or art in the figure, and yet it is endowed with earnest and sincere expression which an actor would seek to imitate. The countenance expresses a total forgetfulness of self and everything but the subject on which the mind of the orator is intent. ... the artist knew where the secret of oratory lies, and I can fancy that Demosthenes himself might have been the instructor of the sculptor on this point" (John Morley, *The Life of Richard Cobden*, 1881, I, 432-433). In a description of Mrs. Jameson's *salon* in Rome, her niece notes that "Mr. and Mrs. Cobden—English of the English in strong contrast to the brilliant and sentimental Germans—were very constant during their stay in Rome" (Gerardine Macpherson, *Memoirs of the Life of Anna Jameson*, 1878, p. 240).

7. Cf. Matthew 6:2. EBB's comments refer to Cobden's acceptance of a subscription of £80,000 which had been raised two years earlier when, according to the *DNB*, "his public labours had been disastrous to his private fortunes." The subscription "was collected in commemoration of his services to a great cause."

8. John Gibson (1790-1860) and Richard James Wyatt (1795-1850) were English sculptors. Gibson had studied with Flaxman and others, and they were fellow students of Canova in Rome.

9. EBB's cousin Charlotte Mary ("Arlette") Butler (1825-88) married army Captain Charles William Reynolds (1813-85) on 24 June 1847 at St. George's, Hanover Square.

2670. EBB to Henrietta Moulton-Barrett

via Delle Belle Donne 4222–
But direct Poste Restante– Firenze– *it is safer*
[?24–] [30] April [1847][1]

I begin to write in the expectation of having a letter to answer before I have done mine—but I must begin, my ever dearest Henrietta, & thank you for what you wrote last to me, & tell you that we are safely established here in this beautiful Florence in an excellent apartment & that I am gaining strength every day, & that M:rs Jameson & Gerardine are our *guests*, & that it will be a week before they leave us. We have taken a bedroom for them in our house .. (you know the *houses* in Italy would be palaces in England ..) & they spend their whole time with us of course—only I dont go out with them, being wise, & resolved on keeping virtuously to the sofa until the weakness is tired out of me—poor me, who in the meanwhile am within a stone's throw of the Raphaels & the Michael Angelos & can see nothing at all. But D.r Cook in giving consent for me to travel, exacted a profession of intending to be "very quiet indeed" for a little time after the arrival: and I find from experience that absolute rest does such infinite good, it is worth persisting in through every sort of temptation. And then Robert says "Dont be drawn into going out, Ba, I beseech you"—and it seems better to wait now in order to enjoy perfectly hereafter, & escape the risk of adding more painful anxiety to what he has already endured about me. He is so dreadfully nervous when I am in the least unwell, that not to be in the least so acquires an undue sort of consequence in my eyes, observe– Otherwise, & if I thought only of myself (and have I not to think of *you* besides of him?) I sh^d not mind being thrown back a week or two for the sake of a degree of delightful imprudence– As it is, the jurisprudence carries it. The *coupè* we took in the diligence, did very well, but was by no means equal to a coupè in a French diligence, & though I lay half the time or more across Robert's knees, the shaking made itself felt, & we regretted the private carriage which was nearly engaged when the Diligence people siezed on us. Still, it did very well, & the country with vine-festooned plains & breaks of valley & hill .. ridges of mountain & sweeps of river, .. was far more beautiful than I expected between Pisa & Florence– As to Florence I could see it only in our rapid passage to our hotel, across one of the bridges of our old dear yellow Arno— and when Robert had carried me into the Hotel du Nord[2] & laid me down on the sofa, I could only wait for coffee & dream of being in the city of the Medici– The next day he went out to hunt for apartments, & the day after, we were settled in our present one—of which I send you a plan .. the cross + expressing windows and the square ☐ doors— & for which we pay about four pounds a month, having 'engaged' it for two months. It is curious that Robert fluctuated between this apartment & one just left by the Garrows[3] & inhabited by them for eight months—but though we pay rather more for the one we decided for, it appeared to him worth the difference of price. I should have thought that the Garrows would have required more rooms– They are re-settled close by us, but are to leave Italy we hear, in May, altogether; & I hope to escape them in as complete a totality. As soon as we had fixed ourselves I persuaded Robert to get a piano—and we have a good one, a grand one[,] a German one, including the hire of music, for about ten shillings a month. Then with a trattoria, hard by, we have an agreement for dinner at three, at the rate of 2^s- 8^d a day, .. covering the whole, observe! and they send us soup & three dishes, besides vegetables & pudding or tart. Everything hot, & well cooked—& there are three of us. Wine, we have separately—and Robert pays three pence or four pence a bottle for what he drinks. My port, he never will touch, let me ask him ever so. Our payment for the apartment includes everything, linen, plate, china &c .. and this time, everything is in order—we have real cups instead of the famous mugs of Pisa, & a complement of spoons & knives & forks, nay, we have decanters & champagne glasses ... we have come to the remote extreme of civilization. As Wilson says succinctly, "*it is something like*". Moreover there is a spring sofa, the most delightful of possible sofas, and a spring chair, and I resume my habits of lolling, with extraordinary pleasure. At Pisa, Robert hired a chair for me, at five shillings a month; so that before we were done with it we had paid the full price– And this, besides the additional *one pound six* a month for the *rooms*—one pound six more than we pay here, where everything is infinitely superior—the drawingroom for instance so much better & more comfortably furnished, & of more than twice the size– Oh, we subscribe to the proverb "Pisani traditori",[4] though we left poor Pisa without any rupture with our 'padroni' of the Collegio– Deeply sorry they were to lose us, and hoped fondly to the last that I might have a relapse, so as not to be able to go. "The signora will be as ill as ever if she does not take care" said the chief matron to Wilson, when she saw me preparing for our journey by going out in the carriage— and if Wilson ever said that I was not so well, one of these affectionate friends looked unto another, with an expression of unmistakeable & most flattering pleasure. So of course we were altogether grateful, both for the honesty & the kind sympathy, though not "unconsoleable" perhaps for having got away. Robert declares that if we had staid on there much longer, we should have fallen fixed into barbaric habits, & that on returning to civilized life we should with difficulty have extricated ourselves & been apt to cry out unawares, "Lady Londonderry, shall I give you a mug of coffee?" or "Will your Ladyship be good enough to thump with your fist on that door"?—(Because at Pisa, there was not a bell in our rooms, & Wilson was summoned by a knock—it was our only way.)

—(April 31)[5] Well! we are alone again. Dear Mrs Jameson & Gerardine left us this morning, much to our regret—& both of them most affectionate .. & she (Mrs J.) a high minded, true, generous woman. Very much I like, yes, & love her. They went at seven & would not let me get up to breakfast, all I could say .. so I had to let them come into my room & give me a farewell-kiss between sleep & wake on my part. If you should see her, .. if she sh^d take courage & go to see you in London (but she wont be in England yet for some time,) mind you are kind to her, both of you, & make her feel that I have spoken gratefully of her. She deserves *that* of me .. & of you. The amusing part of it all is, that she has been charged on all sides with the arrangement of our marriage! You see the coincidence of her being in Paris & receiving us & travelling with us looked so wonderfully suspicious! She says, people write to her who never can be persuaded but that she managed the whole .. "Oh, it is discreet of you to *deny* it! Of course you would deny it! And yet you need not to *me*—you never would shake *my* conviction? And besides, where in the world is there anything to be ashamed of?" Her answer is, "I tell you the truth– If I had had the least thing to do with it, I sh^d have considered it a very great honour––but I knew nothing .. suspected nothing".

To which people shake their heads incredulously over writing paper of various sizes. She had fixed on last saturday as the day of her arrival at our door, but on friday evening as Robert was playing, to me prostrate on the sofa, Shakespeare's favorite air (as discovered by poetical antiquaries) a voice said "Upon my word .. here's domestic harmony!" and lo! Mrs Jameson stood in the room! Both of us leapt up, one from the piano & one from the sofa, & we had our arms round her in a moment, & were listening to all the news from Rome– And it appeared that she had come one day sooner because the thought had struck her of the friday's being, *Shakespeares birthday*—so she had brought a bottle of wine from Arezzo in order to do it the due honours in company with "two poets"—to compass which seemed worth an effort. So we had coffee & supper together for the travellers, & a very joyous evening on all sides .. and she cried out as usual "Oh, that inexhaustible man!" meaning Robert, .. to which I rejoined, "And think of the stream running just the same for these six months past, ever since we parted"! And she thought me looking very well considering everything .. and before she went away I looked well without any manner of consideration & allowance. I could not go to the galleries with her, which was a great disappointment, .. but it w.^{d} have been foolish, just for the sake of a temptation, to have risked a future prosperity. Now, at the end of the week's rest, I am quite another person, & move about without showing symptoms of dislocation, .. & the back is getting quite strong again– I am surprisingly well for the time .. for after that journey, I gave myself a fortnight to be fit to resume my activities. Wilson too is drawing health with every breath of this Florentine air. She was much better before, but certain symptoms remained such as the swelling to a degree, .. and an occasional sense of inward heat, & a general languor .. all which symptoms Dr Cook thought of no importance, but which incommoded her of course, poor thing, & made me uncomfortable to observe. From her arrival here however, there has been a complete change, & she feels quite another person, she says, & perceives herself to be better & better every hour. You see, the Pisan air is very soft & relaxing & heavy, and here the air is clear & brisk & bracing, let it be ever so hot—that is, bracing *for Italy*. Poor Wilson is quite in good spirits, & likes Florence, though her friends of the Creswell establishment are gone,[6] & she has had a great deal to do, with our visitors, of course. I am sure it is very kind in her to speak of the little I could do for her as if it were an obligation– I wish we could have saved her from the necessary suffering– Very painfully we both felt that for our sakes she had incurred it all, and a more honest, true & affectionate heart than Wilson's cannot be found. Dr Cook repeated to me at our last interview his conviction of the whole evil having proceeded from the sea sickness, & not in any way from climate, and she was quite willing to stay on with us. She was in no *sort of danger of life* at any time, so that her impression was wrong in that respect. Well! but I was talking of M.rs Jameson. Think of our "doing hospitality" for a week! Was'nt that rather magnificent of us! And the only thing in the world that Robert cant do well, is *to carve*—and my accomplishments are not very much beyond him even there. Yet we managed .. oh, we managed—& M.rs Jameson was goodnatured as she always is, & had an opportunity of completing her miracles of the saints by our *matrimonio miracoloso*,[7] with as much love at the end of nearly eight months as at the beginning thereof. I am sure she looked on in utter astonishment, while Robert siezed on the place next me on the sofa, just as if he saw me once in three months at the uttermost. She told me before she went away that every hour of her intercourse with him, from first to last, had raised him higher in her estimation & her affection—dear M.rs Jameson! In July or August she may be in England for the publication of her book of saints & painters, after which her intention is to return to Italy .. to Rome, for subsequent volumes on the Virgin & her painters.[8] Gerardine is a "sweet girl" .. just that .. accomplished & affectionate, but rather childish for her age, which has its attraction also. Now that they are gone, we go back to our old habits .. to the owl's nest in the hollow tree– Shall I tell you our dinner today .. our dinner for two shillings & eight pence? You like the report of dinners, Henrietta– Vermicelli soup—turkey .. (not a whole turkey but the third of one at least) .. Fish (sturgeon) .. (I should have mentioned the fish before, I think.) Stewed beef .. (done something like fricandeau)—mashed potatoes—cheese cakes. We dont *order* dinner here, which is delightful. They send us what they like, & everything cooked excellently & well served & *hot*—as superior as possible to Pisa! Wilson dines after us, & something is always left for supper. When M.rs Jameson was here, we gave about four & sixpence, & were served excellently—green peas, asparagus, everything. Observe the difference of the possibilities, of social life here & in England. No fuss, no need of management or money. When we go to see Arabel in her cottage & you in yours (a thousand thanks to all inviters!) we shall make you spend more I fear, even if you give us mutton chops only & port– And you will never give up the port, you unabstemious people, you! By the way, we expect the Hanfords day by day, as a kind letter from dear M.rs Martin assured us of their being about to approach Florence & that a note from me at Poste Restante w.d bring them to us. So I have written, & Robert will do what he can for them in the way of pictures & statues. Now do, both of you, write to me without fear of postage– If you knew what a comfort I draw from your letters, you would. And we shall soon hear from Stormie, surely. Tell me of everyone—oh do! & how George got on on circuit—& of Henry, & Sette & Alfred & Occy & of dearest Papa chiefly. I think of you, pray for you, love you. Does darling Arabel walk out as she ought for love of me? I talk of venturing to get out

No. 2670   [?24-] [30] April [1847]

on monday, being so much much better. Tell me of Arlette's marriage. When is Susan's?[9] Love to her & Surtees. Do you see Bevans, Butlers, Hedleys? My very best love to dearest Treppy & tell her that I have a letter begun to her .. but Robert hurries me about the post—bringing me your letter, darling things .. I cant read it before I seal this .. but in a few days you shall hear again, because we just have a notice of the arrival in Leghorn of the parcel & expect it every hour. So you shall hear directly- Mind, I *am well.* Robert will write.

Your very own
Ba

    Love to dear Minny-

Address, on integral page: (To the care of Miss Tripsack.) / Miss Barrett / 5. Upper Montagu Street / Montagu Square.
Publication: Huxley, pp. 19–23 (in part).
Source: Transcript in editors' file.

    1. Dated by EBB's reference to beginning the letter shortly after Mrs. Jameson's arrival on 23 April, and finishing on the day of her departure, 30 April, despite EBB's date of "April 31" within the letter.
    2. According to Murray's *Hand-Book for Travellers in Northern Italy* (1847), this hotel, located "in the handsome Palazzo Bartolini, and in the same Piazza, is a small clean hotel with a good table d'hôte at 5 pauls. It is now (May 1846) kept by a Frenchman, who was cook to Jerome Bonaparte" (p. 474).
    3. Joseph Garrow (1789–1857) and his wife, Theodosia (*née* Abrams, 1766–1849), were living in Via dei Malcontenti in Florence at this time with their two daughters: Theodosia (1825–65) and her elder half-sister Harriet Fisher (d. 1850). EBB had been acquainted with Theodosia and Harriet in England in the 1830's. Theodosia married Thomas Adolphus Trollope in 1848, and together with his mother Frances Trollope, they purchased a house in 1850 in Piazza Maria Antonia (now Piazza dell'Indipendenza), which became known as the "Villino Trollope," a popular meeting-place for the Anglo-Florentine community.
    4. "Treacherous Pisans." Cf. the proverbial "Fiorentini ciechi, Senesi matti, Pisani traditori, Lucchesi signori." ("Blind Florentines, mad Sienese, treacherous Pisans, pretentious Luccans.") EBB's source for this tradition was probably Murray's *Hand-Book for Travellers in Northern Italy* (1847): "It is said that when the Florentines (1117) assisted the Pisans by guarding their city during the expedition which achieved the conquest of Majorca, they were offered their choice between two of the trophies won in the island, certain bronze gates, or two splendid columns of porphyry. The latter being selected, they were duly transmitted to Florence, covered with scarlet cloth: but, when the drapery was removed, they had lost all their beauty, for the rival republicans had spitefully passed the gift through the fire, whence, as it is said, arose the proverb *Fiorentini ciechi, Pisani traditori*" (pp. 490–491).
    5. See note 1 above.
    6. We have been unable to trace any additional information or identification for the "Creswells". The Cresswells were and are (now Baker-Cresswell) an ancient Northumberland County family, and Wilson being from Rothbury might well have known some of the Cresswell servants.
    7. "Miraculous marriage." Doubtless an allusion to the mystical marriage of St. Catherine of Alexandria; see Anna Brownell Jameson's *Sacred and Legendary Art*, 1848, II, 95–98.
    8. Mrs. Jameson and her niece arrived back in England the following month, but *Sacred and Legendary Art* was not published until November 1848. *Legends of the Madonna*

was published in December 1852; it contained quotations from the poetry of both RB and EBB (p. xlvi and p. 273, respectively).

9. Susannah (Susan) Cook (1822?-61), sister of Surtees Cook; he eventually married EBB's sister Henrietta. From a letter to Henrietta in early July (see letter 2684, note 5), it seems likely that EBB was confusing Susan Cook with someone else. She married Thomas Bruce Stone (1820?-55) on 9 May 1855.

2671. EBB TO MARY RUSSELL MITFORD

[Florence]
April 31- [sic, for 30] [1847][1]

Have you thought me vanished from the world, my dearest friend, that I have yet made no sign in recognition of your last welcome letter? I hope so, rather than any thought of neglect or forgetfulness, .. which must always be amiss, remember, when attributed to *me* by *you*. The truth is very different indeed. Your letter found me unwell, & at the brink of a crisis from the effects of which I scarcely have recovered at this moment though we came to Florence nine days ago and I hope in two more days to be able to get into the galleries & see a little of the wonders of our beautiful city here. So ill I have been,—not from the old causes nor in the old way—(my chest indeed has made itself forgotten lately, the air of Italy agrees so well with its requirements) but from a *new* cause, & in a way you will guess when I tell you that I had treated myself improperly for a condition of which I was unaware & brought on a premature conclusion as might, I suppose, be expected. Then, as it was of *five months date*, of course the trial to the constitution was great; and the exhaustion has been very great, though I bore it all with more vigour than anyone w^d have thought possible in me, & rallied more quickly. Still it is nearly six weeks since the event, and the strength has not all come back yet—and Tantalus & I may lie together in a myth, I on a sofa, as thirsty as he,—within a stone's throw of the Venus & the Raphaels.[2] Having been very headstrong in the beginning (refusing to give ear to my husband's entreaties about seeing a physician in that good time which would have saved everything) I determined to make up for it by obedience & submission at last; & Dr Cook let me travel to Florence on condition of resting absolutely, afterward—so I rest, & resist all temptations of the devil & Michael Angelo. It is but fair to poor dearest Robert, whom I frightened out of his wits nearly, & quite overcame in his spirits—& who has been lavishing on me for these six weeks, even an *excess* of the ordinary overflowings of the deepest & tenderest nature in man- He has nursed me, comforted me, loved me—the words fail me, (as *he* never did) when I try to describe what he has been & is to me. If marriage was a little oftener what I have found it, how different the world would be, & how much happier, women! Well!—but I must hasten to tell you that we were in haste to leave Pisa for Florence because Mrs Jameson gave us tryst at the latter place, two days after our arrival. She was to come last saturday—but on friday night when Robert & I had just finished coffee, & he was at the piano playing to me, as I lay prostate on the sofa, Shakespeare's favorite air which the antiquaries turned up, a voice at the door said "Upon my word! here's domestic harmony!" & in walked Mrs Jameson & her niece, that moment arrived from Rome. They had come a day sooner, to keep Shakespeare's birthday with us (friday was Shakespeare's birthday) & with a bottle of wine from Arezzo to drink deathless memories withal—and we had a merry supper accordingly & welcomed our guests gladly, &, as our guests, they remained in this house for a full week, till seven oclock in the morning of this present writing, when it is friday again & we have lost them. For now they are gone towards Paris, towards England, through Ravenna & Venice & Milan—to remain a month at Paris, & return to London to publish the book which has been growing & growing with gradual accumulations of Art & criticism. A pleasant week we have had, & now Robert & I are alone again with many grateful memories of the agreeableness & affectionateness of dear, kind, generous Mrs Jameson, whom you must try to like better, seeing that indeed & indeed she deserves it. For Gerardine she is a sweet creature, & full of the sort of accomplishment which gives grace to countenance & manner—I love them both & so does Robert—and Mrs Jameson stands high with us when we count our friends. She has been kind & true. For Pisa, we confess that never was deeper dulness & nowhere a completer system of cheating .., that we were cheated in house & board, as perfectly as Italians can cheat .. "Pisani traditori"[3] says the proverb: but we were happy, happy, happy at Pisa & grew quite pathetic on having to leave it. And I never went to the top of the Leaning Tower, & left most of the churches unseen .. because so much was put off to the last & at last I was ill—it was very provoking. Here I have just had a moment's vision of this beautiful Florence as in entering it we passed the bridges & glanced up & ⟨down the⟩ dear yellow Arno, shot between the double range of marble pala⟨ces. We⟩ are settled in an excellent apartment, & mean to be well & strong, ⟨if⟩ God will let us, & enjoy everything to the heart of it. In the meanwhile I will pray you to write to me & tell me that you have lost your rheumatism (do tell me *that*) & are in good spirits! Tell me all you choose to tell me—for no little detail, though it only relate to your shoestrings, will find me indifferent. At Pisa, Robert read to me while I was ill, & partly by being read to & partly by reading I got through a good deal of amusing French book-work, & among the rest, two volumes of Bernard's new ["]Gentilhomme Campagnard."[4] Rather dull I thought it, but clever of course—dull for Bernard. Then we read "Le Speronare" by Dumas—a delightful book of travels.[5] Even Robert who took your view of the trial[6] & swore he never would read a book of Dumas' again, was charmed with the Speronare (being beguiled into a glance at a page of it,)[7] admiring the vividness & vivacity, & the *bonhommie* besides the grace of style. But Robert & I had ⟨tre⟩mendous combats about the trial—and I am not tired .. I will take up your gauntlet in turn .. I dont see things as you & he do, about poor Dumas, and I will confess to you, dearest Miss Mitford, that I read with a certain admiration & sympathy of a man's brains being actually torn out & pulled for & tugged for & struggled for by a pack of newspaper hounds. There was something to me almost grand in that charge of having written only twelve volumes in three months—only forty eight volumes in eight months—of having folded his arms & written only forty eight volumes besides translating Shakespeare![8]—almost sublime in those attending certificates of medical advisers & friends, "Vous allez crever mon cher ami"[9]—if you dont take breath a little on the coast of Africa or at some royal marriage.[10] Nay, I forgive him that folding of the drapery, about his marquisates, it is so French & Dumastic. He wanted to prove that as he could write a multitude of books, so he could double his identity. The "moi, Alexandre Dumas, Marquis de P_____"[11] .... well, I for my part, could only laugh outright & forgive him with all my heart. I am certain he only meant to produce an effect .. a sensation, .. just as in the 'Reine Margot'[12] & elsewhere, a thousand times & in a thousand places. As to the challenge he put forward the Marquisate there not improperly to catch the sword. He had been insulted by an 'aristocrat' who called him a man & an individual & an author in the most contemptuous way possible—to which he answered "Marquisate to Marquisate, come & fight me".[13] If he was to send a challenge at all, I dont object to this form of it, nor believe that he meant anywise to be ashamed of the people & his old republicanism. He threw aside "his cloth"—that was all. Oh, I take Dumas' part. People in Paris are jealous of him & deny (perjuring themselves) that ever he was in a "speronare".[14] He is a wonder in his way .. not the best nor the highest way certainly .. but still wonderful, & worth what he requires .. a good clapping of hands from the galleries– So I clap.—

OConnell arrived in Rome as Mrs Jameson left it, & was supposed to be dying slowly. Cobden she saw & was pleased with—but he could only try to be delighted with the Sistine paintings—being eminently true & simple. Think of my eating & sleeping in this Florence & not having seen a thing yet! It is shameful. May God bless you. Write to me & speak of yourself to

your ever affec^{te}
EBB.

Do take care of yourself dearest friend—do– George Sand has just gone to Rouen, to marry her daughter.[15] I have delightful letters from my dearest

No. 2671 [30] April [1847] 185

sisters—& all are well at home. One of my brothers is gone to Jamaica.[16] Did I tell you?

Address, on integral page: Miss Mitford / Three Mile Cross / near Reading.
Publication: EBB-MRM, III, 209–213.
Manuscript: Wellesley College.

1. Dated by EBB's reference to writing on the day of Mrs. Jameson's departure, 30 April, despite EBB's date of "April 31." Year provided by postmark.
2. The Brownings were temporarily living in an apartment at 4222 (now 6) Via delle Belle Donne, near the Piazza Santa Maria Novella, and only a short distance from the Uffizi Palace. EBB's allusion to Tantalus refers to her inability to enjoy the temptations of artistic Florence around her as a result of her recent miscarriage; see letter 2663.
3. See note 4 in the preceding letter.
4. Charles de Bernard's *Le Gentilhomme campagnard* was published in six volumes in 1847.
5. *Le Speronare* (1842) chronicles Dumas' travels in Italy and Sicily.
6. In early 1847, Dumas was tried for violation of contract by *La Presse, La Constitutionnel,* and several other periodicals for not providing feuilletons he had agreed to write. The judgement eventually went against him, but it was greatly reduced from what the prosecution had hoped to receive.
7. Parenthetical passage is interpolated above the line.
8. During the trial Dumas gave detailed accounts of his literary output in his own defence. Dumas and Paul Meurice had collaborated on a revised version of *Hamlet,* which was first performed at the Theatre of Saint-Germain-en-Laye in September 1846.
9. "You are going to work yourself to death, my dear friend." Dumas also used this as part of his defence.
10. In 1846 the Minister of Public Instruction had asked Dumas to visit Algiers, and to write an account of his journey as a means of promoting colonization. When the Duc de Montpensier heard of this, he suggested that Dumas travel via Spain and attend his wedding which took place on 12 October 1846. Dumas witnessed the marriage contract between the Duc and the Infanta. Two volumes resulted from these travels: *De Paris à Cadix* (1848) and *La Véloce* (1851), the latter from the name of the government vessel in which Dumas made his Algerian journey.
11. Dumas was the grandson of the Marquis de la Pailleterie. In pleading on his own behalf, Dumas pointed out to the court that he had been invited to the royal wedding, and that he had received the Grand Cordon of Charles III, not as a man of letters, but as Alexandre Dumas Davy, Marquis de la Pailleterie. At least one newspaper account added parenthetically that this declaration was made while the speaker pounded his chest (*La Presse,* 30 January 1847), and that this was met with outbursts of laughter in the courtroom.
12. *La Reine Margot* (1845) is an historical romance dealing with the reigns of Charles IX and Henri III. It was reworked as a drama and presented at the opening of the Théâtre Historique in September 1846. The performance lasted from three o'clock in the evening until three o'clock the following morning. Several reports state that at 3:00 a.m. there were more people outside the theatre than inside.
13. Perhaps EBB is referring to Dumas's declaration that the trial was a kind of duel of honour (*La Presse,* 30 January 1847).
14. A small sailing vessel that can be rowed if necessary.
15. George Sand's daughter, Solange Dudevant (1828–99), married Jean Baptiste Auguste Clésinger on 19 May 1847 in the chapel at Nohant, George Sand's country estate. The couple met only a few months before the rather hurried marriage between the great woman's daughter and the disreputable sculptor took place.
16. Charles John (Stormie) had gone out to manage the family's estates earlier in 1847.

2672. EBB TO ARABELLA MOULTON-BARRETT

Florence
May 6– [1847][1]

Thank you, thank you, my beloved Arabel! thank you my ever dearest Henrietta! thank you for these slippers which make the soles of my feet pink with shame, .. to say nothing of the gown & the soul of my body strictly speaking! It was an extravagance in you to send me the gown, as I explained to you before .. but nothing could be prettier or more after my particular taste, than the colour & texture of this gown. Robert too likes the colour .. it is a favorite colour with both of us: and if you had sent me instead of it, a scarlet garment turned up with yellow, it would still seem to me best, beautifullest, welcomest, with the touch of your affection so warm upon it, dearest Both of you! Now I need not, I think, buy a summer costume—I think not. And also I can wear nothing which will not remind me of you .. the green plaid which is Robert's favorite & which I just begin to wear every day, brings Arabel before me bodily in a great vision between the hooks & eyes: the silk shot, will bring Henrietta; this blue barége, both of you. How hard it will be to keep from thinking of you! Even my shoes will not help me into a distraction .. for here are these prettiest of possible slippers, which Henrietta has made for me! & these other pretty ones .. yes, pretty ones, .. with the dear stitches in the soles, which would perish, they swear, if I dared to use them for washing slippers, till they are worn out for higher purposes. They are very pretty & will look well with the blue gown– As to Henrietta's, Wilson & I are lost in admiration, tracing the intricacy of the silken embroidery! And both pairs fit perfectly, perfectly– Then comes the crimson notebook, like a rose leaf. Robert says that it w[d] be better to keep it for addresses, which we are always in a maze about, .. so that it may lie on the table & be free from such blots & erasures as come with the composition of "great works." Thank you dear darling Arabel! how too good to me you are! and then, your goodness about Wilson's gown! She desires me to thank you much for it: she was very much pleased. As to the purse, .. though the one concerned will write his own feeling about it, I must press in with a word of gratitude, & in the spirit, kiss your dear fingers which constructed it, .. because they could not (dear fingers) give me more pleasure than *so*– His eyes shone with pleasure, for his part, at receiving such a mark of kindness from you– Thank you for him & for me. We had other presents by this box, besides Trippy's & yours: for with our cards, which Robert left behind him in the hurry, M[rs] Browning sent me (among other things) a carved cardcase, something like the one Arlette gave to Arabella Bevan on her marriage, only with more carving .. & prettier altogether;—and Sarianna, a little gold pencil case set round with turquoises .. far too pretty. Do you remember my pencil case, with the little *Ba* seal– Well! one day as I walked out at Pisa, the ring broke & the pencil case was lost of course. Very sorry I was—and Robert in his kindness, without saying a word to me tried every shop in Pisa, to replace it, all in vain. The Pisan barbarians (you have no idea how barbarous those Pisans are, Arabel!) could not conceive of pencil cases except of thick silver ones four inches long, and seals the size of a small fist .. therefore, still without a word to me, he wrote to ask his sister to buy what he wanted, .. which *she* sends as a gift of her own, & as I describe it, worth six of the one I had lost. Such a pleasure it was to me to have the box! So impatient I was about it's coming that Robert was quite amused at me! I longed to see slippers & purses .. all the marks of your dear fingers:—and the dear old teapot, out of which we had such excellent coffee last night & this morning. Strange it seemed indeed! It is just large enough for Robert & me, with some superfluity for Flush. Darling Arabel, I had yours & dearest Henrietta's joint letter a few days ago, as I was about to seal mine to you– Dear, dear, dear you are—both of you! But be perfectly at ease about me for the future– I am honest & frank to you & *will be so*, and I do assure you that I am as well as you could wish me to be, if not yet quite as strong, & that the strength is coming in long strides. The journey to Florence was undertaken by medical permission, remember; & I have fulfilled the condition of keeping six weeks to the sofa, .. now this fortnight, without stirring out of doors— and I shall lie down a good deal for a long while, by the purest discretion, although meaning to get out in the carriage & to the galleries in a day or two. The journey retarded the recovery a little—I wont say that it did not: but then it was only a little, & the change of air & the increase of comforts here, were in my favour—& I have steadily been growing stronger & stronger ever since our settlement. Two days before Mrs Jameson left us, there was suddenly a great improvement (like a leap) and after she had gone, .. from that time to this, .. I have recovered & *something over* .. for certainly I have not looked so well for years & years as I do now. Robert drew me into the light yesterday, &, after a due period of contemplation, exclaimed, "No, your sisters would not recognize you! Seriously I say that they would not recognize you." Which I flatter myself is *rather* an error, in despite of *his* flattery—but the truth is that I have grown fatter & look different to my own eyes in the glass– I can *see* how much better I look. There now! I do hope you are satisfied! On the other side of the question, the walking is less agile than usual & stooping is still rather painful– Of course! So I shall lie down still a good deal & make myself *perfect* .. if God's will permit it. In the meantime it is dreadful not to see the Venus de' Medici! but I shall see her now in a day or two, & without indiscretion,—and what I already behold is better blessing to the eyes than any marble goddess in the world .. *videlicet* ARABEL'S PICTURE. Thank you my dearest dear Arabel, thank you again &

again for the delight of having this picture! it seems like a renewal of the first gift of it, with more than the first joy!. Oh, so like! so *yourself*! Only the eyes are drawn up with a sun's ray transfixing them—& the blotting shadows are too strong! As Robert says, it is you at the greatest disadvantage! But what full joy to have you to look at & kiss, through the cold glass or any way. And dont think that it does'nt remind me of my *debt* to you– I owe you a likeness of myself, & you shall have it, be sure– Otherwise I should be a traitor & a highwayman—oh, I understand all that perfectly– You have me fast by the collar of my conscience.——

To go to other subjects then, you cant think, Arabel, how much & increasingly I like these rooms of ours, & how we enjoy the accession of comfort on all sides. The Pisa apartment did very well at the time– We were quite contented, except in the cheating which spoilt something of the *prestige*. But now we look back on poor Pisa, at least on our accommodations there, with absolute scorn, & wonder how we could bear this thing & the other—see how ungrateful a little prosperity makes one! The hard chairs & sofas, the stony beds .. the linen of sackcloth—the teaspoons & teacups of immortal memory! Here we have every luxury really—& I never sh^d desire to live in better rooms (& these are carpeted all over) nor with completer comfort. And the cheapness is something miraculous .. frightful almost .. I open my eyes wider & wider every day as our dinner comes! Observe, that according to our present arrangement, *nobody orders the dinner*– The restaurant agrees to send us a certain number of dishes every day, on the payment of so much a week .. about nineteen shillings. Now is'nt it delightful to take no thought of what we shall eat, & without so much as rubbing a lamp like Aladdin, to see the table covered, with a dinner cooked [&] served hot in the flash of a miracle, precisely at three oclock?! I told Henrietta some particulars in my last letter, but really I must tell her some more,—because the genies of housekeeping never did nor can do as much for her, nor for dear Minny, as the Genii of us ignorant people for ourselves .. see if it can. Yesterday's dinner for instance—now observe! Soup à la macaroni– A shoulder of lamb, roasted– A chicken, boiled, served with peas. Risolles of veal– Fried potatoes & spinage[–] A rice pudding– I could not help saying, "I do wish my sisters were here! There is dinner enough for four besides Wilson; & it's really a pity that my sisters are not here." To which Robert answered, .. "How glad I should be if they were! it w^d give me the greatest, greatest pleasure". And we are as loud in our wishes at coffee times, because the coffee being peculiarly good & aromatic (& at 6^{d1}⁄$_2$ a pound, tell Minny! but there are only ten ounces in an Italian pound, & I heard the other day that you count twelve in England) it drives me to wish for you, my own Arabel– Oh, for a good & happy talk over the Mocha! "Give us a wind, if you are kind"[2] Mr Stratten, & send her out to us! You should have bread & butter too, both excellent, & the latter stamped with the arms of the Medici—all I have seen of the Medici, by the way, since I came to Florence- But tell me if people of small incomes are not justified in leaving their own country of *dear* England, on the mere ground of the cheapness of this Italy? I did not imagine the difference to be so great. Which reminds me of my surprise in hearing of the new plans of Tours, adopted by the Hedleys. Do you imagine that uncle Hedley has lost money in the late French railroad panic? because *I*³ *do*! I cant otherwise explain his leaving Paris to settle for three years in such a place as Tours. I heard it with astonishment. Tours is cheap, & affords facilities for education, I believe, cheaply—but to settle down in that close provincial atmosphere, *asphyxié* by the worst kind of English wateringplace society, is a position which for myself I should not choose by any means, & which I should have supposed undesirable to the Hedleys for various reasons- And for three years! I fancied that they fluctuated between Nice & Florence for next winter—and how anyone in the world could prefer Tours to Florence, is incomprehensible, even from motives of pecuniary prudence. Perhaps they want to be within reach of Pau, & think of the expense of travelling. Expense has something to do with it, be sure- When does Arabella Bevan arrive? & how is she? And tell me everything of Mr Bevan, & whether the turning Roman Catholic be true or not- If true, I am sorry on some accounts—but you know my opinion that as far as a man is personally concerned, on all essential points, he might as well be a Catholic by profession, as what he was when he talked in my room. A man with a conscience put in irons by other men under the name of "Church" & "Tradition", .. a man who cannot think or love, or breathe, in fact, intellectually, but under the biting pressure of such iron, is a Roman Catholic already, & *worse* than many Roman Catholics, who being born in their creed instead of choosing it, often hold to it more loosely than a convert can by possibility do- I felt sure that Mr Bevan would not stop where he stood—I told Jane so quite openly. Not that persons may not stand there & stop—hundreds of persons stand there & stop: but then they stand there because pushed there by the shoulders, & they stop there because *not* pushed away by the shoulders. But when a man has walked there of himself, or even partly of himself .. there's no reason why he shd not walk away of himself—do you understand? if he has thought for himself (very falsely as *I* think) to A, he is likely to think for himself to B .. that is, if there is any logic in the man, .. for everything depends on *that*. And Mr Bevan's views were not hastily taken up without examination. He had examined, he was in earnest—it was'nt a mere matter of either feeling or fashion, remember. I felt very sure of the conclusion in his case, just as I feel very sorry for the Hedleys- Uncle Hedley will be distressed, I think. Will Arabella settle in England really? or does *she* go to Tours? & is *that* the object? Mind you tell me the whole history of Capt.

Reynolds. Henrietta says that she likes what she hears of him. Wont it be a long while to wait for his Majority? and in the meanwhile *will* it be pleasant to live near Canterbury, under cover of a regiment? Will Arlette like it? Above all things dont let dear Bummy (if the persuasion of all of you can do anything) bury herself in the country in a cottage, unless she can press near some other cottage with a loving friend in it. Little she knows the effect of such a life on her– In no way, is it a healthy, wise life, for one of her temperament—advise her against it earnestly. And yet it is difficult to know what to substitute .. it is difficult to advise: but certainly I would not advise *that*– Anything but *that*, I think. I do wish she had a friend to live with or travel with—change of scene w^d be good for her spirits & health, but she w^d not have courage to travel alone, like our friend Mrs Jameson, & other female friends of hers. Perhaps she will go back to Ireland with the Butlers– Poor dear Bummy– Give her my love, if she holds it worth having. Papa's refusal to receive her, accounts sufficiently I think, for her silence lately towards you—it was strange in Papa!—but he probably thought awfully of the gallant Captain & the matrimonial plague-spot. I wish he had spared poor Bummy the expense of taking lodgings, so considerable at this time of year in London. Tell me all about Bummy, .. & Arlette too—& tell me how Arlette behaves under the approximated shadow of orange-blossom & if she is very much in love indeed; & where she goes after the marriage.

By the way, we are amused at *my* 'settlements' just arriving! They came in the box, you know, which was'nt the reason of my being so anxious about it's safety, I do assure you, Arabel. Eight months after my marriage, it will be a most satisfactory settlement indeed, & Robert will "tie himself up" after his good pleasure rather than mine, against the temptation of ... what w^d the temptation be? .. of ruining me & letting me have no more coffee! Oh, the wisdom of this world, how foolish it is!– I do laugh it all to scorn from the deepest of my soul, knowing what HE is, & what *I*[4] am even, & what the world is that would guard one of us from the other!– These settlements make such a packet, I could not hold it in one hand– Very good settlements, I have no doubt at all. There they are, thrown into the cabinet for the present, because, being just too late for Mrs Jameson, we want another witness to the signatures. Perhaps the Hanfords, when they come, will afford us one .. or two– Afterwards I am to make my will, says Mr Kenyon .. & Robert is to make another will in addition to the one or two made already—oh, there cant be too many wills & precautions. It is only a pity rather that we have not each of us fifty thousand a year to make it all worth while. Now pray dont be anxious about Venice– IF we spend the winter there, we shall hear & give good reasons for it—we dont bind ourselves to Mr Irving's theory, although founded on the experience of an invalid who had tried other places. I know it is the fashion to cry out against poor Venice; & very likely the fashion may be able to justify itself—we shall enquire further & not be rash, though of course wishing to be at Venice & to keep tryst with dear M! Kenyon who proposes to meet us there late in October– Now October is *too late*, unless we c? winter in Venice—only I dare say we might draw him further on to the south, were it needful. *We dont go to the Baths of Lucca.* We said we would, when I was ill & Robert was frightened, but now in this smooth water we say nothing of the sort—I would'nt go there for the world if I could draw breath anywhere else in Italy. The scenery is beautiful, .. but the society .. the ways & means of the place .. nothing can be more detestable! "divided between Gambling & Church of Englandism", say our informants— meaning no disrespect to the church of England, observe, but simply that the schismatic & controvertial spirit is keen & bitter there. Then there are races, & promenades, & soirees east & west; & people live so close together in the small mountain hive, that one could'nt escape the buzzing & stinging. No—our plan is to remain at Florence as long as the heat will let us:—(and I cant fancy these rooms being hot, let the sun do its best! ..) & then ... why, then, we must fix on some one plan of the hundred. We want to take the round through Sienna & Volterra & Pisa again—& Prato & Pistoia—we want them for our book. I have seen nothing yet to write of. Depend on our shunning the heat, & the cold– Robert would think for me if I did not for myself. I assure you quite enough fuss is made about my taking a step on the floor– Mrs Jameson said, "Now my dear Browning, dont force Ba to eat anymore than she really *can*[.]" The fuss made about me is something extraordinary. Moreover I heard the other day, in consequence of being so much better, that "for the rest of my life" I was to drink every day so many glasses of port wine—a libation poured out of gratitude, I suppose, for want of another reason. Naples is the most uncertain of climates, tell Mrs Orme[5]—hot sun, cold winds. Pisa & Rome are considered equable & mild beyond other places– Wilson has revived since she came here, as by a miracle. She feels, she says, quite herself, quite well—I am so glad. It is a pure, clear air, & the weather has been lovely, & she likes & admires this beautiful city .. with the exception of the statues in the piazzas & gardens, which appear to her quite scandalous. She confesses to me in confidence that she would'nt "walk with a gentleman" in the piazza Gran Duca,[6] "on any account." Today Wilson has bought a very pretty watch for herself .. silver .. but very small & flat & elegantly made, & has given for it only £2—4.^{s} If the works are really good, it is surprisingly cheap .. but I sh? be afraid.– Sorrento (I just think of Sorrento) is such a way off, remember! Tell Henrietta THAT![7] I wonder poor Mrs English sh? return to Torquay– Such things surprise me always. If Wilson's sister sh? go to the 〈...〉[8] I *shall be sorry* .. & this "*pour cause*".[9] Cant you get her some *milder* situation .. talking of climates, & begging my dearest Henrietta's pardon for some of her friends. You cant think what pleasure it is to me to have this piano for Robert's playing– He plays well, & has a great deal of science, & we have a constant succession of new music. The library too is excellent—& Flush approves of the sofa. Did you hear that Heraud had been lecturing somewhere (at Manchester I think) on the poems of Robert & Elizabeth Barrett Browning "now joined together in the bonds of holy matrimony".[10] Just that form, as it was repeated to us! How exquisitely absurd, to be sure! I tell you all sorts of things huddled up together but not "joined together" by any means or order– Now do you sit down & write me a delightful, delightful letter, as so often you do, & never often enough. When I write next, which will be to my dear, dear Henrietta, I shall be able to say perhaps a little about the Venus. Robert went today to reconnoitre the staircase, & there are five flights! But he can carry me up he says, though half it frightens me lest all this carrying sh^d injure *him*—only it w^d not be right for me just now to walk upstairs, .. & if it were right, .. cospetto di Bacco![11] .. why my conscientious convictions w^d avail nothing. I might as well talk to Fiesole in the distance as try to persuade him. Since my marriage I have scarcely walked up any sort of stairs above three times, even when as able to walk up stairs as you: its a thing not permitted ... "Pray what did I marry you for but to carry you up stairs". I am going out to drive tomorrow by the way .. its settled at last .. & Wilson thinks, can only do me good– We shall engage a carriage for a month, so as to have an hour's drive every day—just engaged, understand, for that hour or hour & a half: & the expense will be a daily fifteen pence: & already it is so hot that we are to go "in the cool of the evening" at about six. I who have not been out, cant fancy its being hot .. these rooms are so very cool—and if it were not for Robert's & Wilson's *affidavits* to its being "burning, out of doors", & to possible walks between hedges of scarlet roses in full bloom, I should laugh at the idea of taking such precautions. No warmth, except the most temperate has penetrated to me yet. We are on the north of the Arno, you see— & are *perforated* with doors & windows & protected from the sun both by walls of marble, & Venetian blinds. I do hope we shall be able to remain here some time. We shall have letters of introduction to Powers[12] & some other artist. Mrs Trollope is said to have settled herself in Florence *by purchase*,[13] but she is absent, & our terrors have "for the nonce" subsided– Till now I have put off mentioning the books George sent to me,[14] because I wanted to look into them a little first. Tell him with my best love that I thank him affectionately for his kindness & sh^d still more thank him if he had written something rather, RATHER kinder than that "Mrs Browning" on the fly leaf,—but I have corrected it in my own hand and put "To Ba from her ever dear George", so it is all right now. Emerson has fine thoughts but seems to want the artistic faculty wholly. Sir L Bulwer is justified to the utmost, I think, & is a gentleman in his justification. The Eclectic Review is on the excess side of flattery.

No. 2672   6 May [1847]   193

How curious, the quotation from Landor's poem on Robert, is on the last page! quite unconsciously done too of course! Give my best love & thanks to my dearest George. And mind you congratulate dear Sette for me. And speak of Henry & Alfred & Occy. Why cant George speak to Papa of Henry's wish to accept M.ʳ Margary's offer?[15] It really does at this distance, appear to me a quite *monstrous* state of things, that he sh.ᵈ be hindered in the legitimate & honorable desire of taking a step out into life for himself. Best love to him & all of them.

Robert has just received such an affectionate letter from M.ʳ Forster of the Examiner that my heart has melted like wax .. beginning "my very dear Browning" & ending "yours & *M.ʳˢ Browning's* much attached friend["]! you know he had written to us at Vaucluse, & Petrarch's ghost absorbed the letter– And he is going to write a third time next week he says—there never was such affection, I assure you– He tells Robert that "the first place in English poetry" is waiting for him,—& as for me, I am caught up into the cloud too–[16] He wants to hasten Robert's second edition. Then he tells us of having spent three weeks in Paris with Dickens, in the course of which he breakfasted with Châteaubriand & dined with Victor Hugo—& of Tennyson's new poem which is "full of sweet & noble grandeur" & "certainly the best thing he has done yet."[17] Very glad I am for Tennyson & the world. Do you see M.ʳ Hunter often? Tell me of him, & how Mary is– Any prospect of settlement? What bazaar are you working for? Do walk out Arabel, if ever you think of me. Do you see M.ʳ Boyd? My love to him: I shall write soon. You sh.ᵈ be very flattered by the extraordinary confidence reposed in you by your friends. Tell me more & more. Why does'nt Susan *have* bridesmaids instead of enacting them?[18] I thought .. I thought! ... My love to her & Surtees too. Is the successful man at Taunton likely to move soon? Mention your headaches & love me as I love you. To dearest Henrietta I shall write next. Shall I dare to put my feet into these too beautiful slippers of hers? And what fairy gloves you send me! Dear & kind, both of you! Remember now that I am well .. eat, sleep, look .. but I cant describe myself. God bless you dear, darling Arabel! How I love you!

your Ba–

Best love to dear Minny, whom always I mean to write to & shall soon. Do remember me when you hear of dear Storm.

Address, on integral page: Miss Arabel Barrett / 50 Wimpole Street.
Publication: None traced.
Manuscript: Gordon E. Moulton-Barrett.

1. Year determined from EBB's reference to the Brownings' removal from Pisa to Florence in April 1847.
2. Cf. *Macbeth*, I, 3, 11–12.
3. Underscored twice.
4. Underscored twice.

5. Evidently Mrs. Orme was considering a visit to Italy for her health after her unfortunate experience with the cold water cure the previous year (see letter 2165).
6. Now called the Piazza della Signoria.
7. Underscored three times.
8. The name of the family to whom Wilson's sister may go into service has been obliterated by someone other than EBB. It is unclear as to which of Wilson's five sisters EBB is referring; they are identified in volume 13, p. 381.
9. "With good reason."
10. John Abraham Heraud (1799–1887), poet, dramatist, and journalist, was at this time the editor of *The Christian's Monthly Magazine*. Although Heraud reviewed RB's works, for example *Dramatic Romances and Lyrics* in *The Critic* for 27 December 1845 (see vol. 11, pp. 366–367), we have been unable to verify EBB's reference to him "lecturing."
11. Literally, "by the face of Bacchus!", used as an exclamatory expression to mean "good heavens!"
12. Hiram Powers (1805–73) was an American sculptor from Vermont. He and his family had been living in Florence for ten years, and they were to become some of the Brownings' closest friends in Florence. The "other artist" might be Horatio Greenough (1805–52), another American sculptor living in Florence at this time. John Kenyon wrote a letter of introduction to Powers for the Brownings in April (see SD1316), as did George Duyckinck on 10 May (see SD1319).
13. The Casa Olivieri rather than the Villino Trollope; the latter did not become the Trollope family residence in Florence until 1850 (see letter 2670, note 3).
14. George sent a copy of *The Eclectic Review* (*Reconstruction*, A846) along with books by Ralph Waldo Emerson and Edward Bulwer-Lytton. A review of EBB's *Poems* (1844) appeared in the November 1846 issue of *The Eclectic Review*; for the complete text, see pp. 375–380. Westwood had mentioned this review to her in a letter in December 1846 (see letter 2638, note 7), but he seemingly failed to make the connection of the closing lines of the review as those from Landor's "To Robert Browning." The work by Emerson which George sent was doubtless Emerson's *Poems* (1847). Describing the poems in general, a review in *The Athenæum* for 6 February 1847 parallels EBB's criticism, suggesting that "a wild, low music, indeed, accompanies these artless strains; an indistinct, uncertain melody" (no. 1006, p. 145). *A Word to the Public* (Leipzig, 1847) by Edward George Earle Bulwer-Lytton, sent by George, sold as lot 529 in *Browning Collections* (see *Reconstruction*, A526; present whereabouts unknown). George inscribed the volume "Mrs. R. Browning," and EBB added "From dear George to Ba, Florence, 1847."
15. It is unclear what position Peter John Margary had offered to Henry. Margary married Emma Monro (*née* Russell) in July 1847 (see letter 2697, note 9). Her first husband had died in 1843.
16. Cf. I Thessalonians 4:17.
17. Tennyson's poem *The Princess* was published in December 1847. EBB had referred to the poem in January 1846; see letter 2191, note 5.
18. See letters 2670, note 9, and 2684, note 5.

2673. RB TO ARABELLA & HENRIETTA MOULTON-BARRETT

Florence,
May 6, '47.

My two dear sisters' notes have been left for too long without acknowledgment—but I know Ba could not have written those long letters wherein I see her put her very heart & soul, without saying something of my gratitude and delight—indeed, she always promises me to do so—but when I watch the little rapid fingers working, I can never flatter myself so far as to say—"now she is delivering *my* message"! So, this time, there shall be a word from myself—a word of sincerest thanks for all your kindness, from those first days which Henrietta reminds me of so charmingly and unnecessarily, down to that last letter of hers which came to Pisa, and this very pretty purse of Arabel's which arrived two days ago. How perfectly good of you both! You do, indeed, deserve Ba for a sister—and she also, deserves you,—if the truest, warmest affection can deserve anything. And do you not conceive what a happiness it is to me that I can so entirely sympathize with Ba in this bestowal of her love, and feel that instead of losing by it, I gain infinitely? Henrietta speaks of the early discoveries which you both made—but neither of you has yet to discover, I hope, that all that delicacy and considerateness was quite understood and appreciated then and now—altho' I could not, certainly, know the *full* value of your behaviour at the time. I earnestly trust you may yourselves find such friends as you have been to me—such admirable, perfect friends!

Let me say no more of this now, when I can please you more certainly by speaking of Ba– She will have told you about our arrangements at Florence—how happy we are, and hope to continue. She is fast recovering health and strength, and, I doubt not, will be in a few weeks better than ever. Henrietta asks me to say candidly if she is "always obedient"; this Ba, who is my wife;—very *dis*obedient she is—for all my commanding, and imploring to boot, will not make her eat a little more at dinner, or supper—nor fancy something she would like me to get her from this gay Florence—nor otherwise occupy her thoughts with herself for one moment. The serious truth is, that I no more believe her to be capable of one selfish feeling than of— .. but the comparison breaks down altogether,—or, rather, I can find nothing to compare with her entire generosity and elevation of character—and when I solemnly affirm that I have never been able to detect the slightest fault, failing or shadow of short-coming in her,—recollect that we have lived constantly together for eight months: I certainly never believed such a creature to be possible, and am full of thankfulness to God for blessing me with such a priceless gift. I can hardly talk after this fashion to all the world, you will easily conceive—but it is my privilege to be able to make such confidences to you—quite inadequate as they are!

I delight myself by thinking that one day you will see Ba again, and hear all the things never to be written—I cannot help thinking, also, that your eyes would detect many particularities in which we go wrong, like beginners as we are—(or rather, as I am—for Ba never sets me right—I can only guess what tends to her good—and therefore to mine)- But whether we meet sooner or later, be very sure of one thing—that I am now and shall ever be attached to you by every feeling of gratitude and affection. This is just a line for the present—but I will soon write at greater length, when we fairly settle. God bless you—dearest Sisters, as you are to your

RB.

Address, on integral page: Miss Barrett.
Publication: TTUL, pp. 46–48.
Source: Transcript in editors' file.

2674. EBB TO SARIANNA BROWNING

[Florence]
[7 May 1847][1]

How am I to thank you, dearest Sarianna, for all your goodness & kindness to me, & your dear mother's which touches me so deeply? Believe of me that your affection is precious, & that every sign of it has a price to me beyond itself– And these signs .. these gifts .. make me ashamed. I scarcely know how to thank you both, for what seems to me too much & too pretty in this prettiest of possible cardcases & pencilcases. Will you thank for me your dear mother? And *you*, who send me back my lost goods transfigured into something ten times prettier than what I lost, will you let me thank yourself, dear Sarianna? And for having spent time on me in worsted work boots, & cap & muffetees, (are they not called muffetees?) which Robert & I turn round & round in wonder & admiration as some new miracle of San Ranieri's ..!—thank you, thank you– I like to remember gratefully that while these miraculous stitches were being taken one after another, you had kind thoughts in your head which were of still more price to me than the work of your fingers!– Then your father's sketches which we spent half an evening in admiring .. (what expression & character they have) .. here are true thanks for them too. I may well be out of breath with thanking you all—you are good, kind, & dear to me. Have I not a note of yours, or two notes, full of your own & your dear mother's goodness to me? It is well that it is so much easier to be grateful than deserving, and it is happy when one feels satisfied with that knowledge, as I do every day. My strength is very much recovered since we arrived in Florence, being determined to atone for a most exceptional course of stupidity & wilfulness, by the utmost prudence & submission in the way of lying flat on the sofa instead of doing after the desires of my own heart. Really I eat & sleep, & look scandalously well, considering that I have'nt seen the Raffaeles & Michael Angelos yet & have been a fortnight within half a mile of them. I should despise myself if it were not for the glory of the selfdenial, which always makes people proud, you know, in this virtuous world of ours. 'En revanche'[2] I was humbled enough in Pisa ..

so much, that I wont talk of it any more. Only I should not certainly have imagined it possible for me to be so stupid. I did everything wrong, tell your dear mother, *except* "walking up stairs" .. we had no stairs to walk up unless in entering from the street; & as Robert has always maintained since our marriage that he married me *principally* in order to carry me up stairs, I never was allowed to set foot upon stair from the beginning to the end:—it's the only kind of tyranny he ever has used against me. Yesterday for the first time we went out in the carriage & drove through Florence—it was like a vision—& the air & the light of it like paradise itself. The hills round the city are so wonderfully beautiful, through the variety of form & the number & the colour– Such clustering hills, doubling every light with a shadow! I wish you were here,—to walk with Robert. May God bless you my dearest Sarianna! Give my grateful love to your mother & father– She is better still, I do hope. Think of me always as

your affectionate sister
Ba

May 8–

Your picture, Robert came suddenly & made me break off my note without speaking of. And yet how eagerly I looked for it & at it, in the hope of knowing you 'face to face' after some imperfect fashion at least. After all he wont let me flatter myself .. he declares that it is'nt in the least like you .. except the hair. A very pretty sketch, in any case, & it is something to be able to call it by your name.

Address, on integral page: Miss Browning.
Publication: None traced.
Manuscript: Lilly Library.

1. Probable date suggested by the postscript "May 8," which suggests that the letter was written the previous day; year determined by EBB's references to the move from Pisa to Florence.
2. "In return."

2675. EBB TO GEORGE L. DUYCKINCK

4222. Via Delle Belle Donne. 2.d piano
Monday morning– [10 May 1847][1]

M.rs Browning presents her compliments to M.r Duyckinck[2] & thanks him much for his kindness in sending her the new American Journal,[3] which in spirit & ability makes no common promises & suggestions. It gives her pleasure to hear in Italy of her American friends .. especially of M.r Mathews to whom she wrote some months ago from Pisa, & is still hoping to be written to in turn. The name *Duyckinck* was pleasantly associated in M.rs Browning's recollection through what M.r Mathews told her, (it is only grateful to say) before she received from M.^r G L Duyckinck the courtesy she now thanks him for.

Address: George L. Duyckinck Esqre / 4272. Via della Scala, 3.^d piano.
Publication: None traced.
Manuscript: Manuscript Division, New York Public Library.

    1. In the following letter, dated 12 May [1847], EBB refers to a visit from an American, and the new periodical which he sent. SD1319 indicates that Duyckinck was the American. 10 May 1847 was the previous Monday.
    2. George Long Duyckinck (1823–63), American editor. He and his brother Evert Augustus Duyckinck (1816–78), together with their brother-in-law John Albert Panton, were travelling together in Italy at this time.
    3. The "new American Journal" has not been identified, but may be the same one EBB describes in the following letter quite differently as "a new literary periodical of the old world." See note 5 in the following letter.

2676. EBB TO ANNA BROWNELL JAMESON

Florence.
May 12– [1847][1]

I was afraid, we both were afraid for you, dearest friend, when we saw the clouds gather & heard the rain fall as it did that day at Florence. It seemed impossible that you should be beyond this evil influence, should you have travelled ever so fast—but, after all, a storm in the Appenines, like many a moral storm, will be better perhaps than a calm, to look back upon. We talked of you & thought of you, & missed you at coffeetime, & regretted that so pleasant a week (for us!) should have gone so fast—as fast as a dull week, or rather a good deal faster. Dearest friend, do believe that we *felt* your goodness in coming to us .. in making us an object, before you left Italy! it fills up the measure of goodness & kindness for which we shall thank & love you all our lives– Never fancy that we can forget you or be less touched by the memory of what you have been to us in affection & sympathy .. never! And dont *you* lose sight of *us*—do write often, and do, *do* make haste & come back to Italy, & then make use of us in any & every possible way as housetakers or housemates, for we are ready to accept the lowest place or the highest. The week you gave us would be altogether bright & glad, if it had not been for the depression & anxiety on your part—. May God turn it all to gain & satisfaction, in some unlooked for way. To be a *roadmaker* is weary work, even across the Appenines of life. We have not science enough for it, if we have strength, which we have'nt either– Do you remember how Sindbad shut his eyes & let himself be carried over the hills by an eagle?[2] *That* was better, than to set about breaking stones—. Also, what you could do you have done, .. you have finished your part; & the sense of a fulfilled duty is in itself satisfying .. is & must be– My sympathies go with you entirely, while I wish your dear Gerardine to be happy .. I wish it from my heart. Do let me hear the decision at Milan– If you elevate *two* instead of *one*, it will be better still, will it not? *Your* Ravenna does not look as well however as *ours*, of our dreams. There is only the pine forest & Dante's tomb to fall back upon, I think. Tell us if it seems to you a place for a few weeks loitering in, & dont forget to say whether the osteria is *cheap* & comfortable. Tell us too particularly about Venice––about the climate in winter, .. the best situations .. cheapness &c &c. We hear bad accounts of the winter there, & as Robert says, are "nearly *bullied* out of" our first plans. My sisters write to me in consternation, much as if we were about to make a villeggiatura[3] on the Maremma. "What! Venice for the winter"!– So do give us a little information out of charity. Just after you left us arrived our box, with the precious deeds, which are thrown into the cabinet for want of witnesses! And then Robert has had a letter from M.r Forster, with the date of *Shakespeare's birthday*,[4] & overflowing with kindness really both to himsel⟨f &⟩ me. It quite touched me, that letter. Also we have had a visitation from an American ... but on the point of leaving Florence & very tame & inoffensive, & we bore it very well considering. He sent us a new literary periodical of the old world, in which among other interesting matter I had the pleasure of reading an account of my own "blindness," taken from a French paper (the *Presse*)[5] & mentioned with humane regret. Well!—& what more news is there to tell you? I have been out once, only once, & only for an inglorious glorious drive round the Piazza Gran Duca, past the Duomo, outside the walls & in again at the Cascine. It was like the trail of a vision in the evening sun. I saw the Perseus in a sort of flash.[6] The Duomo is more after the likeness of a Duomo than Pisa can show:—I like those *masses* in ecclesiastical architecture. Now we are plotting how to engage a carriage for a month's service without ruining ourselves, .. for we *must* see, & I *cant* walk & see .. though much stronger than when we parted & looking much better, as Robert & the looking glass both do testify. I have seemed at last "to leap to a conclusion" of convalescence. But the heat—oh, so hot it is! If it is half as hot with you, you must be calling on the name of St Lawrence[7] by this time & require no "turning". I sh.d not like to travel under such a sun. It w.d be too like playing at snapdragon.[8] Yes—"brightly happy."! Women generally *lose* by marriage—but I have gained the world by mine. If it were not for some griefs which are & must be griefs, I should be too happy perhaps .. which is good for nobody. May God bless you my dear dearest friend! Robert must be content with sending his love today & shall write another day. We both love you everyday. My love & a kiss to dearest Gerardine who is to remember to write to me.

Your ever affectionate
Ba–

Direct *Poste Restante*.

Address, on integral page: À Madame / Madame Jameson / Poste Restante / Milano.
Redirected, in an unidentified hand: Verona.
Publication: LEBB, I, 328-330 (in part).
Manuscript: Wellesley College.

    1. Year provided by postmark.
    2. A reference to "The Story of Sinbad the Voyager" in *The Arabian Nights*, trans. Jonathan Scott, 1811, 2, 20-22.
    3. "Holiday." The Maremma, a marshy area south of Pisa on the Tuscan coast, was at the time considered unhealthy and malarial.
    4. Mrs. Jameson had been expected to arrive on the 24th of April, but surprised the Brownings when she arrived a day early, which she did when she remembered it was Shakespeare's birthday (see letter 2669)—hence EBB's emphasis here.
    5. The American visitor is George L. Duyckinck; see the preceding letter and SD1319. We have been unable to identify the "periodical" to which EBB refers, nor have we been able to trace the "account" in *La Presse*.
    6. "Perseus and Medusa," in bronze, by Benvenuto Cellini (1500-71) in the Loggia dei Lanzi.
    7. An allusion to the martyrdom of Lawrence of Rome, a deacon of Rome who, according to tradition, was martyred in 258 by being roasted on a gridiron.
    8. A traditional Christmas time activity which involves soaking raisins in brandy, setting the brandy alight, and plucking the raisins from the flames with one's fingers.

2677. RB TO THOMAS CARLYLE

Florence,
May 14, '47.

My dear Mr Carlyle—

Mr Kenyon writes to me, that, in a letter which ought to have arrived a month ago, he mentioned your kindness in keeping me in mind and wishing to hear news of me: when I read this second letter with my wife yesterday morning, we took it as the best of omens in favour of one of our greatest schemes, which had been discussed by us in its length and breadth only the evening before, and then, not for the first time. We determined that whenever I wrote to you, as I meant to do for the last six or seven months, it would be wiser to leave unsaid, unattempted to be said, my feelings of love and gratitude for the intercourse you permitted since a good many years now—but go on and tell you what an easy thing it would be for you to come to Italy,—now, at this time of times, for its own sake and the world's,—and let us have the happiness,—the entire happiness of remembering that we got ready the prophet's-chamber in the wall, with bed and candlestick, according to scripture precedent.[1] In this country, the wheels of one's life run smoothly—a very simple calculation finds what kind of a carriage, with more or less commodious fittings-up, is within your means,—and once fairly started in it, you may look out of the windows or ponder the journey's end without further cares about lynchpins or grease-money—(in Germany you must know, you are taxed every post for "schmier-gelt"[2] &c)- One man finds you house and furniture for so long—another contrives you dinner—for so many—you pay what you mean or can, and there is an end of it. Then in this land of solid vast honest houses, built to last,—a few rooms cost more than many,— or not less—seven or five, nine or seven, it is little matter. You see all I mean, I am sure; and it would not become me to speak more. Only, if ever you are disposed[3] to pass a winter here, we will go to any part you decide for, and be ready for you at any time. I hope it is not wholly for ourselves (for my wife and myself) that I say this—I heard you once allude to Jesuitism[4]—to an intention you had of writing about it: and when I look over the extracts from books on that and similar subjects, as I find them in Newspapers here, I ejaculate (like I don't know what virtuoso, in some great gallery of pretentious painting), *"Raphael, ubi es?"*—[5]

But in Italy, or in England, I shall ever keep it my first of affectionate prides—something beyond affection and far better than pride—that you have been and are what you are to me—not a "friend," neither. I dare believe, on the whole, that there is no better nor sincerer relation than that in which you stand to me. One might fancy I did not profit as I might have done by the facilities you gave me for seeing and communicating with you in England; but I always hoped to be better qualified to profit one day. I don't apologize for writing in this way, and of these things. Here in Italy, it seems useless and foolish to put into a little note any other matter than what comes uppermost (and yet lies undermost).

When I was about to leave England I should have been glad to talk over my intentions with you, respecting my marriage, and all the strange and involved circumstances that led to it. I did not do so, however, not from any fear of your waiving the responsibility of giving counsel, but because, in this affair which so intimately concerned me, I had been forced to ascertain and see a hundred determining points, as nobody else could see them, in the nature of things. And I was nearly as convinced then, as by all that has happened subsequently, that I had the plainest of duties to perform; and there was no use in asking for an opinion which I might know as certainly as I know anything—without giving us both much pain and many words. Through God's providence, all has gone with us better than my best hopes. My wife, in all probability, will become quite well and strong. She only feels weakness, indeed, and may be considered well, except for that. I believe—from the accounts from England, and from the nature of the place in the country to which she was to have been removed a day or two after that on which we determined to leave England[6]—that this winter would have ended the seven years' confinement without my intervention. You will let me say that it could be nobody's true interest that this should be, with an entirely good, unselfish, affectionate creature, in whom during these eight months that I have been by her always, I have never seen an indication of anything but goodness and unselfishness. When I first knew her more than two years ago, we soon found out a common point of sympathy in her love and reverence for you—she told me how you had written to her, given her advice.[7] So that there was one way left for me to love you the more. She is sitting opposite now, and answers (when I ask her, this minute, what I am to say for her), "But you *know* my feelings"! And I do know them.

Much of what I have written will go to Mrs. Carlyle likewise—I never can dissociate you in my thoughts: if we, or *when* we go to England again, I shall try and live near you—as much nearer you as I can. Will you give my truest regards to her? I trust you are both well. You would not suffer by the cold weather I think. It is very hot here just now, but has been cold beyond example.

I see Lely's picture of your Cromwell, in the Pitti Palace here.[8] I make no doubt you do not want any news now about the reported *cast* of the head; but I will inquire and let you know, on the chance of your wishing it.

Mr. Kenyon mentions a note you have given Miss Fuller—and which she will probably bring when she comes here; it is a delight to expect. Let me say, that should you want a *person* to find me, the address is *Via delle Belle Donne*, 4222—but for a *letter* the best direction is to R.B., *Poste Restante, Firenze, Toscana*, simply, as I get such a note duly when I go to the Post Office, and not when it pleases the man to call.—All my space is covered, except to reassure you

I am ever yours,
R. Browning.

Text: The Cornhill Magazine, May 1915, pp. 645–647.

1. Cf. II Kings 4:10.
2. "Bribe."
3. Up to this point, the editors have collated the published text with a facsimile page in Sotheby's Catalogue of 14 June 1932, lot 144.
4. The eighth, and final, of the series entitled *Latter-Day Pamphlets*, called "Jesuitism," was published in August 1850.
5. "Raphael, where art thou."
6. See letter 2621, note 2.
7. EBB sent Carlyle a copy of *Poems* (1844), which led to a brief correspondence between them. In letter 1704, EBB reported that Carlyle had told her "that a person of my 'insight & veracity' ought to use 'speech' rather than 'song' in these days of crisis."
8. Murray's *Hand-Book for Travellers in Northern Italy* (1847) describes Peter Lely's portrait of Cromwell as "one of the few authentic portraits of the Protector; it was painted expressly as a present to the Grand Duke of Tuscany, and sent by the Protector in his lifetime; it is perhaps the truest likeness that now exists of that great man" (pp. 563–564).

2678. EBB TO HENRIETTA MOULTON-BARRETT

[Florence]
May 16 [1847][1]

My ever dearest Henrietta. I shall begin my letter & let it go on till it is ready to go by the post. Arabel's & your note which it chaperoned, reached & made me happy three days since & I seem not able to bear the load of thoughts & feelings which accumulate hour by hour after such reading is done. So let me "draw off" gently– I thank her, I thank you .. for I have had a regular letter too from yourself since I wrote to you, and I have to thank you besides for a pair of slippers, Cinderella's being nothing to them as to beauty, and half a gown, which I have on at this moment & which struck Robert backward with sudden admiration when he saw me sitting in it at the breakfast table. These thanks were sent to you before, but I fall into vain repetitions[2] with a sublime unconsciousness, in writing to you directly– Forgive them.– You & Arabel deserve to be thanked to death, that is bored to death by thanks, for your dear foolishness, & extravagance of kindness, so you need'nt complain much. As to the gown, it is prettier made up than in its original element. Wilson has made it beautifully, & the colour is Robert's favorite & mine—he likes all the dark colours (which is my fancy you remember, besides) & not those fainting-away blues & pinks & lilacs & greens. Talking of such things I have just been ordering a drawn white crape bonnet, which is to cost 13^s– 6^d .. like one which did not fit me but was pretty otherwise. He objects to the *fancy* straw (.. Tuscan ..) worn a good deal here—and the plain Tuscan & Leghorn are said to be heavy in the heat. Oh, so hot it is. The thermometer at seventy seven & eight. And this to begin with .. in May .. & after every possible precaution—doors open crossways for the encouragement of thorough draughts—windows thrown also open, (& French windows they all are opening like doors) .. green blinds shut carefully against every ray of sun. Yet there the thermometer stands unabashed. We give up our hope of being able to stay in Florence longer than the one additional month for which our apartment is taken. It will be impossible. Not that I have not felt it far more *oppressively* hot in London; but then it is only *May*, we consider, and if this is the beginning what will the end be? Otherwise we have *air*. At six oclock the muslin curtains seem to sigh themselves out—blowing to & fro. After our three oclock dinner, Robert wheels the great chair into his dressing room, which just then has the deepest shadow in it, & makes me sit in the chair, & pours eau de cologne into my hands & on my forehead, and fans me with a fan till my eyes shut of themselves for that is the hour of the *siesta*. Scarcely a day passes that I have not a regularly sound sleep after dinner. And understand, if you please, that since the heat set in we have reformed our hours, & get up in time to breakfast at half past eight or nine. Is'nt it wonderful? & I wont tell you what an excess of radical reform, for really I should be a little ashamed– Then we sit up, now, sometimes, almost to half past ten: it is enough altogether to justify a siesta of considerable length, I think. Robert does'nt go to sleep though:—he leaves the sleep & the port wine to me. But we both make plans how & where to go on the 22^d of June when we must leave Florence, for a cool place. I say sometimes, "Oh, I wish we were in the Tyrol."—to which the reply always is, "Well, dear, you shall go if you like it." Only we ought to consider the distance & expense & everything disagreeable on the other side. If we could spend the winter in Venice indeed ...! But you wont let us. Robert declares that you have "half *bullied* him out of it"– There's a thing to do! We mean to *appeal* however to somebody who will take a different view from yours & Mrs Ricardo's & Mrs English's, & swear perhaps that the sun shines on the Lagunes all night long without winking. Naples is an immense way off, and if we travel south it will be to Rome rather. The Baths of Lucca we wont hear of, and Pisa, have had enough of! "perplexed in the extreme"[3] we are–

Meanwhile I am getting strong, & have had two real walks, to my own surprise. The first was impromptu—nobody thought of my walking out. Robert came in at six yesterday & found me sighing up against the green blinds for the possibility of a breath of air. "Now, Ba, do you want to be cool?" "Yes, very particularly." "Then take my arm & come down stairs! there's quite a bath of cool air at the bottom of the house". "Oh—and for you to carry me up again! no, no, it is'nt worth while." "But it *is* worth while, and I shall like to carry you– Now come, dear! take courage & come"– So he drew me along while I kept on grumbling about its being nonsense— but found to my pleasant surprise that I was infinitely stronger in getting down stairs, which together with the coolness, excited me into an adventurous humour. "How delightful! Shall we walk along the street a little? Need I care about my bonnet?" Just then, Wilson came .. on *her* return from walking—so we sent for bonnet & gloves by her, and in a minute were on our way to Piazza Santa Maria Novella, leaving our "street of pretty women"[4] for what Robert calls "Trot the jackass street" (*Trotto del asino*) & enjoying it ... oh, I did enjoy it so much, the liberty of it, & the sweet fresh air which blew gently along the ground; and as for him he said he should be too happy if always I could walk out with him in that way. Last night we went out again & got as far as the Baptistery where we sate down in the half dark & talked of Dante. I seem to have grown strong quite suddenly at last. You see it was bad for me to walk when I was weak, so that I did not try continually .. and indeed the effort was quite painful. Now Richard is himself again, & need'nt call for "a horse,"[5] seeing that he has feet of his own for action. We have had no carriage you will be surprised to hear, & have entered no gallery yet. The truth is, just as we were about to make our compact, it appeared that there was some previous engagement unconcluded, & were desired to wait a week– Then I said .. "it may be better for *us* to wait perhaps—I shall be stronger"—it seemed better to wait until now when we are on the point of making our own terms. In the meanwhile every glimpse I catch of Florence makes me more eager to see all. Oh, this cathedral!! So grand it is, with its pile of tessalated domes,—the massiveness glorified with various marbles—the porphory [*sic*] crossed with the dim green serpentine .. the white & black heightening & deepening one another. Think of a mountainous marble Dome, veined with inlaid marbles .. marble running through marble: like a mountain for size, like a mosaic for curious art .. rivers of colour inter-flowing, but all dimly. But you hate descriptions of travellers, & I shall keep mine for the printing press & yawning readers .. "my great work" as Arabel says encouragingly. Now I am going to tell you things unattempted yet in prose or rhyme.[6] I went a week ago into Wilson's room & stood by the table in my lazy careless way, turning over the leaves of an old book which lay there. "Why, Wilson! you have another Italian grammar–" "Yes, I could'nt understand a word of the other,—and the man of the house lent me this"– I turned to the title page—written in a large distinct hand .... *James Johnstone Bevan, Milano*...!![7] Wilson thought me mad I cried out so loudly, & rushed so vehemently out of the room to show it to Robert in the drawing room– And upon enquiry, the whole wonder of the coincidence developped itself– The book was M.r Bevan's book, the landlord was M.r Bevan's landlord;[8] & in a house of the said landlord (not this house but another) had M.r Bevan & two of his friends lived for a whole winter. Moreover, this landlord had travelled with M.r Bevan & his friends as *courier*, from Florence to Rome & Naples, (because they did not speak much Italian) he said, and from Naples to London, because M.r Bevan had been a good deal affected & shaken by the death of his friend at Naples, (and did'nt speak much French)– Two years ago therefore, this landlord was staying in Devonshire Place with M.r Bevan's family. Of himself, he speaks in the highest possible terms, & heard with deep interest of his having married the "fairest of the fair" of Paris, which Robert instructed him in duly. Is'nt this curious as a coincidence? And "a most amiable, excellent young man," Arabella's husband was called .. (such *issimos*[9] I assure you!—) "with a leaning to the *santissima* Roman Catholic religion, & a great deal of talent." By the way as you say nothing more of Louisa's[10] report about the conversion, I hope there is no truth in it—a little fancy. Tell me if Arabella is in good spirits & well– I understand *underlines*, tell *my* Arabel– May the other not be "turned back" like some of her friends who sigh still to think of it– Will she take a house of her own in *October*? Bummy wrote to me—I had her letter of announcement in reference to Arlette's marriage: and most earnestly I do trust that this Cap.t

Reynolds is worthy of the trust reposed in him– The fact of such things being *said* of a man, I do not like—especially as the man is not so rashly young– I do not like the class of men to which he seems to belong, those racing, hunting, billiarding, betting men, who are not tired of such amusements as they grew tired of playing at leap frog, by the simple consequence of growing older—but he may have good points & be qualified to make dear Arlette happy perhaps, & the worst things said of him are not true, I hope & trust. Robert says, "and even if they are, he may mean to reform altogether—" .. but it w.d be dreadful to lean her happiness on such a bending bough as that possibility– Gaming is less a fault than a *passion*—and love itself is not equally absorbing– And then, love .. love! How does such a man love: what does he mean by it? after dancing two quadrilles, as he would take an ice!– It makes my blood run cold to think of a woman trusting such a man, by the experience of three weeks– Send me a better account if you can– A sweet, amiable, pure-hearted creature like Arlette too, with all her life before her to 'risk'!– Does she care much for him, do you think, and does he seem to care for her? tell me whatever you can– The fear in my mind is, that her happiness at home was not great enough to induce sufficient consideration of the subject—for if Bummy's report of the turning conversation was correct, there did not appear to be much illusion– Think of a woman selecting a man (for instance) on the ground of his being "gentlemanly" ... viz *after the likeness of other gentlemen*– Still it w.d be dreadful to annul everything now, and I wish earnestly that uncle John[11] & all doubters may be wrong in their doubts– Give my love to Arlette & say how much happiness I wish her too. She was feeling & kind to me always, I do not forget– How are Bummy's spirits? If you & Arabel did'nt laugh, tell her, *I*[12] did, at the account of your introductory interview. The Indian gifts made me smile a little besides. The chaste memorial of Dyce Sombre's mother, is a strange thing to invoke before one's nuptials.[13] I HAVE seen more graceful gifts of betrothment– *Have'nt* YOU? Does he call himself Cap.t Reynolds, having sold out? Is it to be Cap.t in perpetuity? And do they come abroad directly on their marriage? and shall we not be sure to see them in that case? Ah, "*to be as happy as I*[14] *am,*" may indeed be wished by the Kindest to the Dearest when wished to be the happiest—so I wish it for *you*, my dearest Henrietta, and I wish it for my dearest Arabel, but can't believe in the possibility of a Reynolds making any woman half .. half as happy as I! For *half as happy* would be *very very happy*, do you understand. *Quite as happy* w.d be *frightfully happy .. heureuse à faire fremir,*[15]—considering life & the conditions of life to human beings.

Now I am going to write some more gossip. I dare say Arabel remembers my talking of the famous "Father Prout" (M.r Mahoney)[16] & how Robert told me about a year ago that always he was meeting that Lion in strange out of the way places roaring wildly– Father Prout had even seen Robert without salutation, the reverend father had said, "in various parts of Europe"—and certainly Robert had seen *him* whenever the sight was least expected- Well—while we travelled across France, my fellow traveller laughed a little as he told me that in crossing Poland Street with our passport, just at that crisis, he met .. Father Prout- "Oh, of course, he met him just then!" It was a moment worthy of being so signalized. Robert told me this, & I said, "Curious", & the conversation changed. On our landing at Leghorn, at nine oclock in the morning, our boat which was rowed from the steamer to the shore, passed close to a bare jutting piece of rock on which stood a man wrapt in a cloak, he also having just landed from an English vessel bound from Southampton. FATHER PROUT!! Was'nt it an extraordinary "dramatic effect?" Robert had no idea of his meaning to come to Italy, nor had he of Robert's coming. Robert cried out, "Good Heavens, there he is again! there's Father Prout!" We went to the inn & breakfasted, & after breakfast the reverend Lion came into the room, & I had the honours of introduction—not of examination though, for, as he told Mrs Jameson afterwards when he met her in Rome, he could'nt see my face through my black veil. Nor could I much better see *him*. I kept on the other side of the room, feeling both shy & tired. Mrs Jameson says he is the bitterest of clever talkers, and that Robert is nearly the only man in the world whom he speaks well of- He is a Jesuit, &, it is supposed, an active organ of the body- Dont imagine that he is a friend of Robert's—I assure you, *no*—and now I have told my story.

(May 19-) We have been out in our carriage—for the first time this evening, having engaged it for a month, two hours a day, two shillings & eight pence. Dearer than at Pisa: but it is a very easy & most comfortable German barouche (I think you call it a German barouche—four seats, you understand, two of them shutting up at will) & looking as well as any private carriage—a pair of horses, & a coachman to match—with something in the likeness of a livery! Robert wishes me to drive out a few times—to improve my strength before we go to the galleries,—and so today at five oclock we went to the *Cascine*[17] which is the drive *par excellence*, the place of meeting for all lawful carriages, from the grand Duke's to ours- Really I have seldom enjoyed anything of the kind more. I expected very little,— nobody praised these Cascine as they ought to be praised- And suddenly I found myself swept through avenue after avenue of limes & blossoming acacias meeting overhead to roof out the sky, while beyond the line of trees on each side, deep green woodlands draw your soul into their recesses .. and here the Arno runs to the pace of the carriage-horses .. & here a garden red with roses is made clear of the trees .. & there they grow again wildly till you think yourself in a forest—. So beautiful, so vernal—with breaks of the Appennine between the evergreen oaks & cypresses, & those floods of deciduous foliage more tenderly green than such leaves as never fall. It was a surprise of beauty & freshness to me, & I enjoyed it past description— So did Robert who had not been there before. The coolness was delicious, and we talked & were silent just as the inclination came—and agreed that some other day we should stop the carriage and explore all those little dark-green pathways which wind & stoop under the trees. Also through having gone out too early, we had everything to ourselves, for the people only began to come as we began to leave the place. I assure you its an improvement on the London Parks, let who will say to the contrary. While we sate at tea yesterday evening, in walked Mr Powers the sculptor, (he of the Greek slave and Fisher boy,)[18] and had coffee with us & stayed more than an hour. Like most men of true genius, he is as simple as a child, quiet & gentle, calling himself "a beginner in art," which is the best way of making a great end. I took one of my fancies to the man, and might well do so as he was very kind to me & begged me to go to see his studio— Robert & he had a great deal of talk, and I did myself the honour of pouring out his coffee; and as when he went away he said it had been an evening both of pleasure & profit to him, I, of course understood that he referred to my coffee with the due appreciation.

In the letter of Mr Kenyon's which was lost, Mr Landor sent a note of introduction for me to Miss Garrow—and hearing this makes me doubt a little whether I ought'nt to call on her—. I w.^{d} rather not: it makes me rather uncomfortable— I have had the kindest letters from Miss Bayley & Miss Thomson, both mentioning you & Arabel & that you were going to have tea with them—Arabel w.^{d} like them for the head & the heart if she knew them, I know, notwithstanding the notion of dyspathy which also I know.[19] The Martins must by this time be in London, and mind you see them & talk to them—you cannot too openly—I agree with that intention altogether— I hold them in high esteem & very grateful regard, & for the best reasons— Tell me how Mr Martin looks. They comprehend life wisely just because they do not coldly—they touch the warmth of it with a genial finger & understand. I would rather accept their opinion on most practical subjects, than that of most other experienced persons— What does dear Henry think of doing? Pray persuade him not to suffer Mr Margary's proposition to fall to the ground. Let George speak to Papa. Henry w.^{d} be infinitely happier if he had a place for his foot, an occupation which w.^{d} be an independency—and surely the thing is to be achieved on the railroads in England or elsewhere; even if Mr Margary does less than I desire— I wish I could do anything *in this way*—but often people whom Robert knows are precisely those who in Art & Politics would help to give opportunity to any specific Faculty, but are useless as finders of mere occupation with their merely lucrative consequences. There is indeed the Bank-business, but from what I hear, men sh.^{d} be boys to do much in it at all pleasantly, & also there is the need of languages. The Queen's messenger loses his breath .. is in fear of his life .. understand. Tell me if

Surtees is really likely (if he has reasons for his hope, that is—) to get the military post at Taunton. Does he ever think of advertising the gift of the first quarter's income to any one who would get him a situation. It might quicken somebody's goodnature perhaps. Miss Thomson's father is a great manufactor & learned in the art of money-making–[20] You dont say when Susan is to be married– Emma Monroe's engagement surprised me—no, *did* it surprise me? I rather believe now that I was'nt surprised. It was so certain to me that she w:d: marry one day. Only M:r: Margary having been rejected ... Well, but he *loved* her. A man who loved her all those years with all that constancy against all those obstacles, is worthy of being loved. A proved, tried love is always worthy. And then it always (besides what it is in itself,) involves some strength of nature, some nobleness & excellence, .. I *like* a man who can love against the tide. When you see what men are on all sides ... why, just see what they are!– I dare say she will be very happy, & I dont think it quite so much "an experiment". Tell Arabel, as I said if *she* were going to marry somebody "without being in love" ... because, because .. Emma was happy with poor Theodore & I have my own opinion about her degree of attachment for him as it was in the beginning. If M:r: Margary is kind & tender to her, she will love him & be happy—now see if she will not .. with that sweet frank face of hers!– A single life did not suit her, .. could not .. never could. He will care for the child for her sake I dare say. Robert exclaimed at the idea of marrying a widow—"it's what he never c:d: have done." And I laugh & shake my head, because he's not a man to calculate the thousands if he loved any one, the last unit even. If a woman whom he loved in that least degree, had had six husbands & killed them all, he w:d: put his head under her feet & think it much to his advantage– No human being ever comprehended human love so divinely, which *I* say who know what he is. But is there not in respect to M:r: Margary, some conflicts on the ground of religion? Tell Arabel to tell me. Poor dear Flushie has been very ill, and I was quite unhappy for two days, and Robert declared that I gave up loving him & thought of nothing but Flush. It began with what we supposed to be spasms—he had fits of screaming. And then he crept under the sofa & beds, & would not touch water; and, if drawn out kept in one place for half an hour together, staring wildly as if he knew nobody. Robert made me promise not to pat him, & we all thought of hydrophobia—the heat you see, had been so intense. At last, Robert went out twice in one day & brought home each time, & administered, a copious dose of castor oil, and poor Flush had a rope tied round his neck and a mat was provided in the kitchen. This in order to take all due precaution. When the oil was administered I ran away & shut myself in the farthest room (was'nt that like my wisdom?) but Flush did not even struggle, they say—he knew it was something done to relieve him– Poor little Flush. The next morning he was much better, and expressed it by moaning piteously directly he saw me– To Robert & Wilson he simply wagged his tail, but he looked up in my face & moaned .. moaned .. as if to say "Do see how ill I am! So very ill"! I said "Poor Flushie" and then he moaned again .. put up his head & moaned. "Will you have a lump of sugar, Flush?" A decided affirmative with the tail—so I called for sugar and he moved himself on the mat to sieze on it. How glad I was to see him do that! and Wilson held the water to him & he drank it. An hour afterward he was convalescent and is now quite well & insolent as ever. The castor oil did the good, we think. He calls me "Miss Barrett" still, & has all his old ways, and behaves better than at Pisa. Do write to me– Dear dearest Henrietta & Arabel how I thank you for your letters, both of you! I envy Robert sometimes for hearing oftener from home than I do! .. and then he envies *me* for having such long long letters, full of details. There cant be too many *little* things .. or "too much gossip" tell Arabel– Ah, if you knew the worth of those least little things at a distance! Because *I* know it, I tell you what pudding we have for dinner sometimes. Dont I now? Tell me everything. Always mention dearest Papa. I love him & pray for him. Do, *you*, be in good spirits my best dearest Henrietta, and take courage & hope for all things. Make Arabel go out for my sake– Kindest love to dear Trippy & all at home .. how I love them all!– Interrupted!– It is May 21st The Hanfords have been here: just one day—& I like them both much– They went with us to the *gallery*, and then dined with us .. & Robert wd give them champagne! I am giddy still more with the Raffaels though. No room for a word. Love me always as

your most affectionate
Ba.

The Hanfords witnessed the signature of the great "*Settlement*"[21] & take it to England to Mr Kenyon. Neither Robert nor I read it—we only signed. It was enough for me & my particular satisfaction to see, by a glance, that provision was made for a countless progeny! & all "future husbands!!"

Robert's best love——

Address, on integral page: Angleterre .. viâ France / (To the care of Miss Tripsack) / Miss Barrett / 5– Upper Montagu Street / Montagu Square / London.
Publication: Huxley, pp. 24–31 (in part).
Source: Transcript in editors' file.

1. Although started on 16 May, EBB's notation near the end indicates that this letter was continued over the next five days, and not finished until 21 May. Year provided by the postmark.
2. Matthew 6:7.
3. *Othello*, V, 2, 346. Mrs. Ricardo is doubtless EBB's acquaintance from Hope End days: Harriet (*née* Mallory), wife of Osman Ricardo, of Bromesberrow Place, 5 miles from Ledbury. For Mrs. English, see letter 2630, note 14.
4. i.e., the "Via delle Belle Donne," the name of the street on which the Brownings' lived. We have been unable to identify a street called Trotto del asino; perhaps this was RB's playful name for the Viale del Trotto in the Cascine.

5. Cf. *Richard III*, V, 4, 7.
6. *Paradise Lost*, I, 16.
7. Bevan had married EBB's cousin Arabella Hedley the previous August (see letter 2390, note 4).
8. Francesco Centofanti, as identified by EBB in letter 2680. The Brownings later engaged Centofanti as their agent for letting Casa Guidi while they were away; however, the association came to an abrupt end when they discovered that he had been less than completely honest in his dealings with them.
9. The superlative ending in Italian. "Most holy" Roman Catholic religion.
10. We take this to refer to EBB's cousin Louisa Charlotte Carmichael (*née* Butler, 1817–99).
11. EBB's uncle, John Altham Graham-Clarke, was apparently dubious about the match between "Arlette" Butler and her fiancé Captain Reynolds.
12. Underscored twice.
13. David Ochterlony Dyce-Sombre (1808–51), son of George Alexander Dyce and Juliana Dyce (*née* LeFevre). He inherited a vast fortune from his grandmother, the Begum Samrum, and in 1838 left India for England, where his arrival was the main event of the season. The *DNB* mentions a book by him called *The Memoir*, but it gives no other details, and neither the catalogue of the British Library nor that of the Library of Congress lists a copy; we speculate that this is the work to which EBB is referring.
14. Underscored twice.
15. "Happy enough to make one shudder."
16. Francis Sylvester Mahony (1804–66) wrote mainly for newspapers and journals, using the pseudonym Father Prout. He was at this time the Rome correspondent for *The Daily News*. His association with the Jesuits had ended in 1830. For RB's earlier reference to him see letter 2202, note 8. Mahony later settled in Paris, where he died.
17. Murray's *Hand-Book for Travellers in Northern Italy* (1847), describes the Cascine as "the Hyde Park of Florence, for displaying fashionable carriages or exhibiting horsemanship" (p. 576).
18. The "Fisher Boy," begun in 1841, had been completed in 1844. "The Greek Slave," a nude female figure, was completed in 1843. The latter work caused controversy in America, where the morality of its nudeness was a focusing issue. The work was first exhibited in London in 1845, and again at the Great Exhibition in 1851. It was the subject of a sonnet by EBB, published in *Poems* (1850). See letter 2680, note 7.
19. Evidently Sarah Bayley had rather unorthodox views on religion, for example a disbelief in life after death (see vol. 10, p. 326), which would not have met well with Arabella's more fundamentalist opinions.
20. James Thomson (1778?–1850) was a calico printer in Lancashire. He was also a Fellow of the Royal Society, Vice-President of the Manchester School of Design, and Member of Council of the Government School at Somerset House.
21. The Brownings' marriage settlement is no longer extant. For Fanny Hanford's record of her visit with the Brownings see SD1320.

2679. EBB TO HUGH STUART BOYD

Florence.
May 26 [1847][1]

I should have answered your letter, my dearest friend, more quickly, but when it came I was ill, as you may have heard, and afterwards I wished to wait till I could send you information about the Leaning Tower and the bells—. The book you required, about the cathedral, Robert has tried in vain to procure for you. Plenty of such books, but *not in English.* In London such things are to be found, I should think, without difficulty,—for instance "Murray's Handbook to Northern Italy", though rather dear (12^s) would give you sufficiently full information upon the ecclesiastical glories both of Pisa and of this beautiful Florence from whence I write to you. He says of the Leaning Tower .. "On the summit are seven bells, so arranged that the heavier metal is on the side where the weight counteracts the slope of the building. These bells, of which the largest weighs upwards of twelve thousand pounds, are remarkably sonorous & harmonious. The best toned is the fourth, called the Pasquareccia: it was this bell which was tolled when criminals were taken to execution. It was cast in 1262, & has many ornaments, a figure of the virgin, & the devices of Pisa. The Bell-founders of this city enjoyed great reputation."–[2] So far Murray! I will answer for the harmony of the bells, as we lived within a stone's throw of them, and they began at four oclock every morning and rang my dreams apart. The Pasquarrecia (the fourth's) especially has a profound note in it, which may well have thrilled horror to the criminal's heart. It was ghastly in its effects,—dropt into the deep of night like a thought of death. Often I have said "Oh, how ghastly", and then turned on my pillow & dreamed a bad dream. But if the Bell-founders at Pisa have a merited reputation, let no one say as much for the Bell-ringers– The manner in which all the bells of all the churches in the city are shaken together sometimes, w^d certainly make you groan in despair of your ears. The discord is fortunately indescribable– Well—but here we are at Florence, the most beautiful of the cities devised by man! I was too weak when I came, to see anything, & had to lie on the sofa & grow strong, while the Venus of Medici stood two or three streets off—think how tantalizing!—but my poor dearest Robert had suffered great anxiety about me, and it was only just to him to run no risks– Now I am well and beginning to go out & see all the glories. I am really quite well & look better than I have done for years, and we have ever so many wild schemes– Here is one! We talk of spending the heat of the summer in Vallambrosa with the monks[3]—yes, indeed, we almost have settled it– We shall enjoy so infinitely the sublime solitude of the mountains, rocks, cascades, and chesnut forests. There is not a carriage road .. so much the happier! Oxen will drag us in baskets up the precipitous mountain-side– Then we shall sit out in the forests & write poetry which you shall read, and the poems will be as wild as the poets– One difficulty we apprehend, from my sex, as the monks have vowed "their holy sod shall ne'er by woman's foot be trod"[4] .. but if I promise to behave well & do nobody in the confraternity any manner of harm, it is supposed that the Archbishop of Florence[5] will let me go in with my husband. What do you think? Will it not be delightful? Flush wags his tail when we consult him on the subject, and seems to draw a rapid conclusion that liberty & coolness in the woods, will be clear gain after this intense Florentine heat, of eighty four degrees of Fahrenheit. Always it is cool at Vallambrosa- Oh, the cool, green, lonely, deep chesnut forests! How pleasant they will be to me & Flush!-

In the meanwhile I have seen the Venus—I have seen the divine Raphaels .. I have stood by Michal Angelo's tomb in Santa Croce .. I have looked at the wonderful Duomo!. This cathedral!! After all, the elaborate grace of the Pisan cathedral is one thing, and the massive grandeur of this of Florence is another and better thing—it struck me with a sense of the sublime in architecture. At Pisa we say "How beautiful", .. here, we say nothing .. it is enough if we can breathe- The mountainous marble masses, overcome us as we look up—we feel the weight of them on the soul- Tesselated marbles, .. (the green treading its elaborate pattern into the dim yellow which gives the general hue of the structure) .. climb against the sky, self-crowned with that prodigy of marble domes. It struck me as a wonder in architecture. I had neither seen nor imagined the like of it in any way. It seemed to carry its theology out with it: it signified more than a mere building. Tell me everything you want to know .. I shall like to answer a thousand questions. Florence is beautiful as I have said before, & must say again & again, most beautiful. The river rushes through the midst of its palaces like a crystal arrow; and it is hard to tell, when you see all by the clear sunset, whether those churches & houses & windows and bridges and people walking, .. in the water or out of the water, are the real walls & windows & bridges & people & churches. The only difference is that, down below, there is a double movement .. the movement of the stream besides the movement of life. For the rest, the distinctness to the eye is as great in one as in the other. My dearest friend, I was much pleased to have your account of yourself, as it was better than I had feared. Let me entreat you, now that the summer has come, to take the opportunity & the advice of the wise, & change the air—ah, if I dared say *for my sake*! A little exercise—consider how necessary it must be to your health. I hear on all sides that *you have it in your power* to recover habits of healthful activity & to prolong your life *with enjoyment*. Dearest M! Boyd, I excommunicate that chair of yours, .. I beseech you to take courage and to remember the duty of self preservation. Robert & I drank your health two evenings ago in wine of Cyprus- It is good wine, brought straight from Cyprus, at sixteen pence a bottle—but for some reason or other I thought it inferior to yours—yes, certainly it is inferior. Tell me whether drinking your health did you good. Do you see M!ˢ Smith?[6] Do you see my dearest Arabel? & Nelly Bordman? Remember me to such of my friends as remember me kindly when unreminded by me. I am very happy—happier & happier. My late indisposition had nothing to do with former illnesses, but it prevented, no less, my ascent to the top of the Leaning Tower—a disappointment, notwithstanding your exhortations. Is Jane [Miller] still a comfort to you? If so, thank her from *me!*—who never cease to be your grateful & most affectionate

Elibet.

Robert's best regards to you always.

Address, on integral page: H S Boyd Esq.ʳᵉ / 24(a) Grove End Road / St John's Wood / Regent's Park.
Publication: EBB-HSB, pp. 283–286.
Manuscript: Wellesley College.

1. Year provided by postmark.
2. EBB is quoting from Murray's *Hand-Book for Travellers in Northern Italy* (1847), p. 446.
3. Murray's *Hand-Book* explains that the monastery at Vallombrosa was "founded in 11th century by S. Giovanni Gualberto" (p. 583). According to the *Hand-Book*, carriages could pass as far as Pelago, where "the traveller must take to a saddle or walking" (p. 582).
4. Cf. Thomas Moore, "St. Senanus and the Lady," in *Irish Melodies* (1821), lines 5–6; see letter 2700, note 2.
5. Ferdinando Minucci (1782–1856) was consecrated Archbishop of Florence in 1828.
6. Adam Clarke's daughter (see letter 1590).

2680. EBB TO ARABELLA MOULTON-BARRETT

[Florence]
May 29– 30– [1847][1]

My own dearest Arabel here I am, writing to you again– Yesterday was Papa's birthday[2] & made me sorrowful with the recollections of which I had of course a whole heartfull– I could not drink his health though Robert proposed *that*. I only could pray for him, & think for myself & him that no one in the world has more tenderly loved him than one he has cast off– *Has* loved him? *does* still love him, as God knows well. There is no use in talking. To be so cast off is a lasting grief to me, notwithstanding all other sources of happiness: I cannot, as seems easy to some, forget in a moment the beloved of a whole life—and for Papa, my love for him has always been a peculiar thing, and if he had stooped to hold me by a thread, why the thread wᵈ have been strong enough. I would give my life for his .. even now, when my life has acquired a new value– Well—I am glad that yesterday is done with at any rate– And now I shall try to write to you of something else–

We are thinking, Arabel, of a wild, delightful way of spending the summer .. at least of spending *some* of the summer months .. or weeks even .. for we need not bind our inclinations: we are thinking of going to VALLOMBROSA. You know, Milton knew, everybody has a degree of knowledge about this place—has seen it between sleep & wake– There is a monastery like an eagle's nest, in the Apennine, .. in the midst of mountains, rocks, precipices, waterfalls, drifts of snow, and magnificent chesnut forests–

> "Thick as autumnal leaves that strew the brooks
> Of Vallombrosa."[3] All from chesnut trees!

The solitude is complete .. a few cottages, & some house of refuge .. no carriage-road within five miles of it. You go in a kind of basket-sledge drawn by oxen, if you cant ride on mules, and in order to any sort of residence, you must have a "permission" from the Archbishop of Florence. The monks w^d admit you, upon this, to their interior; but Wilson & I being women, we sh^d be the ruin of the confraternity of course, & so we must stay outside in the house assigned to meet fair perditions, .. being supplied with food from the monastery– Now what do you think, Arabel? The plan is to me the most exquisite of the hundred we have made. The solitude, the wildness, the coolness—and then the nearness to Florence—for it is within twenty miles, though from the precipitous character of the road, thrown out of the usual casualties of 'neighbourhood.' Practically we shall be a hundred miles off, or more– Also, in the case of our being tired or unwell, forthwith we can tumble down the mountains back into Florence—no harm is done. But we shant be tired .. we shall sit & wander in the forests, & do a great deal of writing I hope, & get old books from the monks, & enjoy the change from this present luxurious way of living– I hope I shall have rather a soft sofa, & for other things I dont care a straw[4] now, being well enough to walk on my two feet– Arabel, you w^d be surprised to see how transformed I am since even I wrote last. There is a continual moaning & lamenting about the heat .. I cant help moaning .. I cant do a single thing in the way of coherency of ideas .. I read six sentences & fall fast asleep—the thermometer standing at eighty four you will imagine the effect on all breathing beings, Flush included!. But after all, & though going out in the morning to see any sight under the sun is out of the question, I am well & getting fatter & stronger day by day .. and when we drive to the Cascine at six which we do every evening for two hours, .. open carriage, parasol over one's eyes, .. & as little clothes as possible .. why at one certain little gate we leave our vehicle & walk into the hayfield, & walk & walk .. & watch the pheasants & hear them crow in the woods—Robert was in raptures at my walking as far as I did yesterday, without being in the least tired by it. I am surprised myself indeed– I sh^d have thought that nobody c^d get strong in such a temperature– A most unaccustomed heat say the Italians, for May, .. and they only hope that it does'nt threaten something prodigious—not an earthquake perhaps, but certainly a "*burrasca*".[5] In England such heat w^d be past supporting– Here the air is elastic, & there is always a breath of wind about six oclock in the evening, which comes to revive us. Earlier we sit with every door open, every window open, every green blind shut fast, in as deep a darkness as can be cultivated. I generally sit in a doorway .. in a confluence of distant doors– The worst is *at night*. Doors & windows stand wide open then just the same .. but Flush & I cant sleep, & are given to wandering from one room to another– I sleep half the day instead .. so nothing is lost .. as you w^d say indeed if you could see me. Nothing lost, except the great sights—but the galleries close at three, and you may conceive the impossibility of going out in the morning– At six, we begin our drive generally by entering some church .. by looking at Masaccio's frescos, or standing by Michael Angelo's tomb[6] .. & then proceed to the Cascine which we more & more enjoy– Robert says that the effect of that peculiar scenery, half woodland half suburban, is calming to the nerves—and I think the same. We fall into deep silences which turn to reveries of themselves. Some of the avenues remind me of Cheltenham—the trees take hands over your head & perfectly shut out the sky .. but then, there are depths of wood, & ravishing glimpses of hills, & sometimes the shining river. It is not of course very extensive– I speak more of the influence of the place, & of the impressions you take from it– I have been twice to the galleries .. once to the Pitti, & once to the Ufizzii [*sic*] .. which is nearly equal to not going at all, so impossible it was to gather in one sight of every thousand.

But the heat .. the heat!– Oh, one cant dare it or bear it– If the weather does not change a little, we must return from Vallambrosa in the autumn (which *is* our plan indeed) & catch up what we let fall now. The first day, the day of the Pitti, was cool enough—we went there with the Hanfords. Was'nt it curious that we sh^d go with the Hanfords? The carriage had been ordered the preceding day to be at the door at nine the next morning—& at eight oclock while we were at coffee, (eight in the evening) the Hanfords arrived—were to leave Florence by diligence the evening after, & would go with us to the Pitti gallery. So in the morning we called at their hotel for them, & we took them to the Pitti, & then to Powers's studio .. & he was kind & cordial & showed us his Greek Slave & Fisher boy, and the Eve yet unworked in the marble .. of which I liked the Eve best & the Fisher boy *least*, I think– Go to see the Fisher boy & tell me how you like it– Oh, it is beautiful of course .. but less satisfying to my imagination than either the Greek Slave (exhibited in London last year)[7] or the Eve .. though Robert admired it beyond my admiration– The Eve stands in divine unconsciousness of naked beauty—the apple, plucked, in her hand .. plucked but not *tasted* .. the sadness rather than the impurity of sin is in her face .. just one touch of sadness, .. the foreshadow of all loss– The serpent has his trail about her feet, loosely, not touching them, & looking into her eyes with his eyes of satisfied expectation, having no need to tempt any more, after the first failure. What she has plucked she will taste, he knows. It is very serenely, beautifully sad—the passion is behind a cloud, as it ought always to be in sculpture—& I admired it more for having just seen the Venus of Canova,[8] with her large ringletted head, huddling her drapery round her waist with some suggestion of indecency. But oh, Arabel, the Raffaels of the Gallery!- I shall not speak of them- I cant paint Raffael over again. Divine, divine they are- The Madonna della Seggiola[9]—and the Madonna del Gran Duca, *my* madonna, which stood on my chimneypiece in Wimpole Street- Oh, that divine child, that infantine majesty—that supernatural penetrating sweetness of the eyes & lips- Raffael understood better than all your theologians how God came in the flesh, "yet without sin."[10] *Divine* is the only word for these works- No engraving can give you an idea of them- Another day when we went to the other Gallery & saw the famous Venus,[11] I am almost ashamed to tell you that I was *disappointed in the Venus*- It produced (to tell you the bare truth) very little effect on me- My own fault I do not doubt—& Robert says that I shall feel differently in a little time: I do hope I shall- You see I was familiar, from drawings, with the attitude .. the turn of the head, the position of the arms .. (such great hands, Arabel!) .. & what was new to me in the whole did not suffice to produce an emotion,— except that I thought, "Here I am face to face with the Venus"—I would rather have that unfinished "Dead Christ & the three Marys"[12] which was the last work of Michael Angelo & struck me so in the cathedral, two days since—how infinitely rather. The work is unfinished .. the marble half awake—but the passionate suggestiveness of what is done there, in the midst of which the artist fell asleep, is to *me* worth a hundred of such elaborated shining things as that Venus—& I cant help telling you so, indeed.

As I told Henrietta, the Hanfords came to dinner with us after the gallery, & I was .. *we* were .. much pleased with them both .. especially with Fanny who talked more than her brother, & was very affectionate to me- Mind you see her when you have an opportunity- She would please you: she ought to please you. We siezed upon M.r Hanford as "a witness" to the great "Settlement", which had arrived a fortnight before & been cast into the cabinet unexamined. An English witness had been recommended: and by no means, let me assure you, was it agreeable to go about soliciting our compatriots in Florence to witness our marriage settlement nearly a year after our marriage--(nine months, Arabel!) There was not the least need of further gossip about *us*: and it is so delightful to gossip, that nobody would abandon the opportunity, if we let them have it .. of *that*, we were certain- M.r Hanford's goodnature made to the rescue, then, just in time- I did not mind *him*—of course he knew everything from the Martins, long before: & willingly, he said, he w.d do anything. So Robert & I when he & Fanny had left us on the first evening, pulled out the Deed from the cabinet (quite large enough to convey all the Rothschild funded properties to all possible generations) & began to look into it a little, because we were told to correct something—some trifle ... about a name. (The lawyers told us.) .. (Nothing in the world altogether could be more legal.) It was half past ten oclock, & Robert said .. "Now, Ba, do you lie down on the sofa, and I will read this to you"- "Oh," I exclaimed, throwing myself down in utter prostration of body & soul, .. "if you read a page of it to me, I shall be fast asleep! .. I give you warning. I feel half asleep already at the very idea of it- I dont *pretend* to listen—& CANT, I assure you. So I shall go to bed, if you please, and *you* may sit up all night, & read; & I wish you joy of it, & a very good night. I will find you asleep here in the morning, I dare say." "But my darling, you cant behave in that way ..." "But my dearest I can indeed .. It's *your* Deed, you will please to remember, yours & M! Kenyon's, & not mine by any manner of means. I do a great deal more than I ever meant to do, I can tell you, when I write my name to it as I shall, tomorrow, I suppose—" - Well & how do you think the discussion ended? *He would'nt read it either*—but "if I w^d just stay, we w^d draw the ends of our fingers down each page, to find the word we wanted",.. which I did .. I dont suppose that any legal instrument of the kind was ever signed unread, so, by the male principal? Women may do it—men scarcely ever perhaps- I should have insisted on his reading it, but he had put the business into M! Kenyon's hands & resolved to sign whatever might be written—therefore there was not much use in wearying one's soul with that detestable jargon .. was there? ⟨Then he knew the general purpose, of course.⟩[13] As for me while we were drawing our fingers down the parchment, oftener than once I had strong temptations to put the whole into the lamp—if it had been MY Deed, nothing could have saved it, I assure you- One might laugh at the sixteen children (oh,—a countless progeny rather!) but the "*future husbands*" were a little *strong* .. "un peu fort" .. as a legal provision in a marriage-document. Say nothing of all this to dear M! Kenyon- He has had a great deal of trouble & the best kindest & most generous intention in everything both to Robert & myself—only no possible argument could have induced me to consent to a document of this sort, when I was mistress of my own money & will & opinions- Moreover I think that any woman w^d have shrunk from it, if she had respected the man she was ⟨about to marry⟩[14] in the most vulgar sense. Robert is tied up in his hands & in his feet—but HIMSELF *has done it*—my single consolation.! And now I have to make a will, having the power "in virtue of my marriage-settlement", and M! Kenyon advises that I should nominate my husband as sole executor- I would rather make *no will* & leave it to Robert to fulfil my wishes which he knows already—but he insists on my openly expressing them, .. for generous, characteristic reasons which he gives me, .. & alas lest we sh^d both die on the same day which is a possible casualty. But after all these provisions, I am a little uneasy, & shall remain so, I fear– He has solemnly assured me that if he survived me he w.d instantly throw back the whole into the hands of my family, & upon that single point no word of mine could make the least impression on the resolve he had taken– Knowing him; I know he would do it– I see it as a fixed resolution. And now he refuses to discuss the subject any more– (Say nothing when you write.) Of course I refer only to his *lifetime*, .. for perfectly I agree with him that the ultimate disposition of money received from my family, should (in the failure of directer heirs) regard my family exclusively– There is a clear justice in *that* .. which is better than Law– But anything is better you will say, than a dull letter– I think the "public notary" who has been here to witness a "power of attorney" has "infected" me with his odour of parchment– And then the heat .. *oh*, the heat– You never felt such heat, Arabel! I dont dare to go to church through it—for the church of England has a "pied de terre"[15] here also .. & makes everybody pay sixteen pence .. every individual .. for every service—is'nt it quite shameful? Murray promises the discontinuance of this blot on the Establishment, in his book; but they discontinue nothing, not they! I had hoped to find here some "branch company" of the Scotch church at Leghorn[16] .. hoped in vain: & from what we hear, the Church of England is as ill represented in this Florence as we found it at Pisa! It is a drawback to Italy, you will say, to lose sight of the means of open communion among Protestant Christians—but we must try to open our hearts instead, & enlarge the circle of Christian communion which God sees, larger than we are apt to try to see. In the meanwhile, if dear M.r Stratten were here himself, I could'nt go out to his preaching .. unless he did it "in the cool of the evening,"[17] .. and *you* couldnt, even .. unless you aspired to St Laurence's martyrdom on the gridiron–[18] Poor O'Connell! Robert has this moment been saying, "After his troubled, stormy life, just a finger is held up, and the quiet comes".! I wish they had let him die in England, & not agitated his last hours by the fatigues of quarelling—yet there was a last vote, I suppose, to satisfy: and all was done for the best– Poor O[']Connell![19] To go out with the extinction of his people, is a melancholy end– I have felt more for him lately than ever I did, .. more *with* him– Dearest Stormie will be in despair– By the way we shall have a letter soon, I do trust, to set a crown on the head of the other good news of the safe arrival–

Now while I think of it, let me answer your enquiry into the size of our drawing room—it is twenty four feet by eighteen, and high more than in proportion, with two very large windows– The dining room is smaller, .. & with only one window, .. eighteen feet by twelve .. we use it only for dining. We have been forced to have all the carpets taken up .. there was no bearing the heat of a carpet: so that the rooms are less pretty to an English eye than when we took them first. 'En revanche'[20] we keep totally free from *fleas*, .. next to mosquitos, the pest of the country. The mosquitos have not begun their regular persecutions yet, but there were a few .. & it is a matter of struggle & doubt whether to run the risk of a nocturnal pillage that way, .. or of a nightly suffocation under the mosquito net– My horror of them is fair game for Robert, whom they never bite at all– If our Stormie suffers more heat than we do, it must be ill with him—& I do hope you entreat him in all your letters, as I shall, to take precautions .. to drink only cooling things. It was wrong to arrive in Jamaica just as the great heats were setting in– I am expecting Henrietta's letter day by day .. I have just heard from Sarianna Browning, .. enclosed in a letter to Robert .. but I wanted one from my very own sisters besides. Not that I mean to reproach you, you Dearests—you are always kind—and I am always impatient, as well you know– You never *can* (only) write too often. When we are at Vallambrosa our letters will be forwarded to us, so go on directing to Florence, Poste Restante—and understand, O considerate calculator of postages, that we pay less for our letters here than we did at Pisa where the people charged us more or less precisely as they wanted pauls. "Pisani traditori":[21] I stand by the proverb– We get our letters here about as soon, I think .. but they go through Pisa, always– I have written to Bummy to her lodgings, and hope to hear that she bears up cheerfully under the parting from Arlette, and that she has some more cheerful plan for the summer than a visit to Kinnersley– She hinted to me about their wishing her to join them in the Tours colony .. and *that* sounds to me feasible & pleasant– But how *could* the Hedleys take a house for three years at Tours? Nobody sends me the riddle– Ends of œconomy might be compassed equally I should think at a less sacrifice in other ways– Italy cannot be exceeded anywhere for cheapness, be certain– Our "*donna di faccenda*"[22] (we have a donna who comes for a few hours everyday to make the beds, clean the rooms, brush Robert's clothes, wash up the cups & saucers &c &c, & give her about six shillings a month for it) our donna was complaining of the price of meat the other day, the best being three pence a pound– It is dearer than usual just now– Then fruit on which the poor live so much, is to be had almost for the asking– We had a dish of excellent cherries the other day for a penny—and presently cherries are to be more than half as cheap again, they say– Figs & grapes are most wholesome nourishment– Think of these advantages for the *poor*! *I* think sometimes of our *poor*, Poor of England, & sigh for them– Robert, in his fits of abstinence, has *dined* sometimes on three halfpence worth of macaroni— the cooking & serving up & cheese being included. The accounts from England are melancholy indeed, as to the poor! How I have wandered (I observe) from the Hedleys & Tours & the hypothetical œconomy, & now I come back just to prophecy that they never will live out the three years there .. never. Dont forget to tell Mr Bevan of my adventure with his Italian grammar, and of our 'padrone' Signor Centofanti .. Francesco Centofanti,— who enquires of him continually, & whom I should like to be able to tell that his favorite master remembers him.[23] We like Centofanti very much, & if we return here from Vallombrosa to see Florence in the autumnal coolness, should like to be in a house of his if we could manage it—besides he is curious in all sorts of spring sofas & chairs & soft cushions .. wherever I sit I sink—and this touches me sensibly. Certainly I think we shall be in Florence in the autumn .. unless we go to Venice .. unless you will let us: and dear M.r Kenyon says that a hundred miles or so should make no difference to him in his journey to see us- Oh, how I wish Papa would send you down the Rhine this year—we w.d compass anything to meet you- Go to the Tyrol .. even go into Switzerland, I am sure- George at any rate, had better come & see us in his vacations & "make it up" for once & all, & make me very happy besides- Tell me of Henry—& indeed of them all- How is dear Trippy? Give her my best love always; & say how her landlord goes on. Mention her hands & eyes- We like Florence so much that if we found it possible by the selection of a warm situation, to winter here, we should like *that*—the beauty on all sides is past speaking of, & the resources most various- Oh, there is no harm of M.rs Young—she *mistook*—that was all- We were excellent friends at parties.[24] The amusing part was that I was under the delusion that Robert had displeased her and I had reproached him a little for talking of George Sand & abusing Italian literature- But by no means—, he was in the odour of sanctity with her.-[25] Last night (I finish this on the 30.th,) we went to the Center of Florence to take ices, everybody being there. It was Florence in an undress, I assure you. Women with short sleeves—& who c.d wonder? This at eight oclock after our dinner. Then we came home to coffee- Wilson is much better in spite of the heat, & likes Florence exceedingly- Tell me of M.r Hunter & Mary- Do you ever hear of Eliza Giles—*ever*?[26] You will wonder how she came into my head—but I want to know if she took any notice of my marriage. May God bless you my dear beloved Arabel- Think & pray for me- Love me—as I love you- Robert's best love to you & Henrietta- Do write, write!- Has Lizzie come back? Do you see the Cooks? Love all ways- I am

your ever most attached
Ba.

Of course you will write the moment you have a letter from dearest Stormie- I mean to write to him soon—& to think of him in the meanwhile, every day, very anxiously.

Always mention Papa particularly—will you? I wish Emma Monro had been about to marry some one settled in London for your sake—but will she reside *always* in Devonshire?[27] There may be an alternative settlement I sh.d fancy-

God bless you dearest Arabel! how I love you!–
Love to dear Minny– I am sorry about Mr Boyd.

Address, on integral page: Angleterre—viâ France / To the care of Miss Tripsack / (Miss Arabel Barrett) / 5– Upper Montagu Street / Montagu Square / London.
Publication: None traced.
Manuscript: Berg Collection.

    1. Year provided by postmark.
    2. His 62nd.
    3. Milton, *Paradise Lost*, I, 302–303. These lines are quoted in Murray's *Hand-Book for Travellers in Northern Italy* (1847), p. 583, and EBB's description of Vallombrosa clearly echoes Murray's (pp. 582–584).
    4. Cf. "ego non flocci pendere" (Terence, *Eunuchus*, 411, trans. John Sargeaunt).
    5. "Storm."
    6. In the church of Santa Croce. The frescoes of the life of St. Peter by Tomasso Masaccio (1401–28) are in Brancacci Chapel in the church of Santa Maria del Carmine.
    7. "The Greek Slave" had been exhibited in London in May 1845, and *The Athenæum* for 24 May 1845, said "the figure in question is certainly a very remarkable work,—and might be thought still more so as the work of an American, were it not remembered that the sculptor has been for ten or a dozen years past resident in Florence" (no. 917, p. 522). The reviewer also commented at length on the nudity of the figure (see letter 2678, note 18). "Eve Tempted" had only been completed in plaster; the marble would not be finished until 1849.
    8. In the Pitti Palace; Murray's *Hand-Book* describes it as standing in the centre of the "Hall of Flora ... upon a pivot, and can thus be turned round by the custode. Her head, owing to the hair being curled and arranged, seems to be too large for her body. When the Venus de' Medici was carried off to Paris, this statue replaced her in the tribune" (p. 564).
    9. Murray's *Hand-Book* describes this as "the sweetest of all his Madonnas, if not the grandest" (p. 560), and the Madonna del Gran' Duca as "a very singular and beautiful picture. It consists simply of the Virgin and Child upon a dark background, almost without any accessories" (p. 563). It had previously been in the possession of Grand Duke Ferdinand III, "who was so pleased with it, that whenever he travelled he took it with him on his journey" (p. 563). Evidently, EBB's father had owned a copy or print of this famous painting; however, it does not appear in the Christie's catalogue of the sale of his effects (see *Reconstruction*, pp. 593–606), nor in a list of paintings made by EBB's brother Alfred in 1853.
    10. Hebrews 4:15.
    11. The Venus de Medici; see letter 2669, note 2.
    12. Murray's *Hand-Book* explains that "behind the high altar is a group of Joseph of Arimathea, the Virgin and another Mary, entombing the body of our Lord, left unfinished, by *Michael Angelo* ... It is said that he worked at this group during the later years of his life, intending to have it placed upon his tomb" (p. 487).
    13. Bracketed sentence is interpolated above the line.
    14. EBB has written the phrase in angle brackets above the word "married," which she has crossed out.
    15. According to Murray's *Hand-Book*, "Divine service is performed every Sunday at 11 in the morning, and 3 in the afternoon, in a new church situated nel Maglio, at the back of S. Marco. It was built by subscription, and opened in Nov. 1844. A debt is charged on this church which it is hoped the liberality of travellers will soon discharge. Persons wishing to engage seats for any period, should apply at the church every Saturday from one till three o'clock. The price of admission is 3 pauls. This charge was made at the doors, but was about to be discontinued, and the contributions left to the generosity of those frequenting the church, and who had not taken sittings for a fixed period" (p. 477).

16. See letter 2656, note 6. There was no Presbyterian Church in Florence at this time; however, one was eventually established, and the service was "performed on Sundays, in the morning in French, and in the evening in English, at the Swiss Church, next the Casa Schneiderf, on the Lungo" (Francis Coghlan, *Handbook for Travellers in Northern Italy*, 1856, p. 169).
17. Cf. Genesis 3:8.
18. See letter 2676, note 7.
19. The Irish politician Daniel O'Connell (1775-1847) had left England on 22 March 1847 for Italy, as opposition within his own ranks weakened his already failing health. He reached Genoa on 6 May where he died nine days later. Although his heart was embalmed and carried to Rome, where it is entombed in the Church of St. Agatha according to his wishes, his body was returned to Ireland and buried in Dublin.
20. "In return," or "on the other hand."
21. See letter 2670, note 4.
22. "Housekeeper."
23. See letter 2678, note 8.
24. See letter 2660, note 20.
25. i.e., all is well. EBB is referring to an old tradition that the bodies of saints, or saintly people, give off a pleasant odour at the time of death.
26. Eliza Wilhelmina Giles (*née* Cliffe, 1810-48) was EBB's neighbour and correspondent from Hope End days. In her *Diary* entry for 16 November 1831, EBB recorded that "Eliza had stated that I would not marry an angel from Heaven" (p. 180).
27. See letter 2672, note 15.

2681. EBB TO ARABELLA MOULTON-BARRETT

Florence
June 22-23-24-25. [1847][1]

My own dearest Arabel I am writing what I hope may reach you on a day when I shall think much & tenderly of you[2] .. more than I do everyday, & that is saying a great deal- You will know, whether it reach you or not, that I most think of you .. that no absence could make you less present to me—perhaps you will guess that I shall love you more than ever. May God bless you dearest dearest Arabel, & make you happy according to your choice & His will, recompensing you for all the good & gracious affections which is the debt I owe you forever- To see you & hear you would be the greatest of joy to me—believe it while you believe me- May God bring us together before long .. yet how close to you I feel while I write this—close in heart & in love-

Robert declares to me that I am writing to you now for the *third* time- To which I answer that I must at any rate, write to you now, for especial reasons, but that assuredly my last letter but one went to dearest Henrietta- *Did'nt it*? Do tell me. I meant to preserve the perfect symmetry of my correspondence—only there are necessary exceptions as on the present occasion- And I have just had your letter .. went to the post office for it myself. How far can I walk?—farther than Hodgson's do you ask? Yes, certainly farther than Hodgsons. The post office is in the Piazza Gran Duca, where the Palazzo Vecchio is & the gallery of the Uffizzi. Well, when I got your letter I was on my way to the Gallery .. walked to the doors .. perhaps about as far as to Cavendish Square .. or say, Oxford Street .. then, up stairs, (stairs as high as to my Wimpole Street room,—positively refusing to be carried) & through & through the gallery, sitting down of course at intervals—then, returning by carriage– I was tired, but not too tired for our drive in the evening, and altogether I call it miraculous– If you had but seen me when we came here first! It is only a month, recollect, since I began to go out even in the carriage—and now I am stronger than before the Pisa illness .. oh, infinitely stronger– The air of this Florence vivifies, I think, & yet is not too stimulating: it agrees with all three of us, Robert,—Wilson & myself, and we might perhaps do a foolisher thing than settle here, for next winter & autumn, after our escapade to Vallambrosa– Yet we *shant*[.] Robert is afraid of the winds for me, and he is cherishing a rather romantic speculation about my being able to escape all shutting up next winter if we go to a warmer place– But even at Pisa you see, there were two months imprisonment for me—only I admit that that winter was unusually cold for Italy, & that we were in a wrong situation—still, a perfectly free winter seems too high an aspiration– Everywhere there will be occasional cold winds and there is a habit of irritability, I suppose, about my throat & chest .. which however are well now to all intents & purposes– I walked up quite a hill in the Boboli Gardens last Thursday & felt no inconvenience—no gasping for breath .. the very place in respect to which M[rs] Jameson said to me six weeks ago, "ah Ba, you will never be able to go there– I have no hope for you! You must give it up." Robert said that she made much more fuss & sighing in the walking there, than I did– Only it is to be admitted that the carriage took me to the gate of the gardens– So beautiful they are. High overarched embower all sorts of trees. You look down green galleries of shade—not a stripe of blue sky visible. Some of these bowery alleys are as long as you can see: you just see a little light at the end. We did not explore the gardens, of course; it w[d] have been too much; but we saw enough to understand the character & feel the beauty. The cypresses & acacias in this Italy are very beautiful, and so are the evergreen oaks, .. & they strike our English eyes wherever we look. The stone pines too are characteristic—but I like the cypresses. One thing I observe .. the extraordinary luxuriance of the *ivy*, which enwraps & hangs in festoons on nearly every tree of the Cascine, without appearing to do the harm which ivy in England w[d] certainly do. The effect is beautiful. Still more beautiful however are the vines, trained everywhere in Tuscany upon trees. The manner in which the tendrils climb & climb, & then throw down floods of leaves, even to the ground, is a thing to see once in a life & never forget afterwards– Ah, people may talk about *hops*– There's no comparison

I assure you. They might as well talk about peas. People who, having seen both, prefer hops to vines, I am prepared to think very small beer of– I am writing now on the 23^d but I thought yesterday of Arlette's marriage & of poor Bummy, who seems as usual to have embittered to herself this event, as much as possible. Really it is a misfortune to be *ridden* so by one's temper .. so kind & affectionate as she is under it all, & so sure to be loved less perhaps than she w^d have been if less heart-kind & more gentle of manners– I hope however that Mr Reynolds will remember the *fact* of her having tried to take the mother's part towards Arlette—it ought not to be forgotten. Extraordinary, that you sh^d not be asked to be bridesmaids. So much the better for you of course, but it is not altogether *kind*, I must be allowed to think, & I wonder how they could make up their minds to venture on the *appearance* of such a slight– Do tell me all about the ceremony– Poor Arlette .. I do hope she has chosen wisely! That you sh^d like him better is a better sign– So the mustachios linger, Henrietta says! Talking of mustachios, I cut off Robert's with my own hand before we left Pisa; it was my last wish on the last night .. and Mrs Jameson reproached me for it, & so did Gerardine, when they arrived, having been used to nothing but mustachios & beards at Rome. But I was right I know. Robert let it be as I liked, & I accepted the full responsibility. He looks much better so– Not that I have changed my mind about beards– I am as little a misopogonist[3] as ever– Only what gives character to common faces, is a detriment to his, I think– The mouth was quite materialized by the mustachio– So I cut it off with a pair of scissors & my own right hand .. "myself I did it" .. & I dont repent the least in the world. Otherwise, everywhere you see superfluities of hair; nothing is less singular than a beard of three or four inches, & very picturesque these beards are, black, brown, & white I assure you– The majority of English gentlemen even, has the moustache; so perhaps Mr Reynolds's looks towards Italy. How I laughed, & so did Robert, at Bummy[']s successful readings from my letter– So she just made out that I was going to retire with "some artist to Vallambrosa". Well!–

⟨...⟩[4]

No wonder that she is a little shy of the subject of me. Pray explain that when we do go to Vallambrosa, there will only be fortyfive monks within reach, & not an artist among them .. but we are not gone yet, you see .. & we are entering on our third Florentine month after the greatest uncertainties. Being able to do just what one likes, is not always the smoothest & easiest thing in the world, I observe. Robert quite vexed me last week with his exhortations every half hour, "Now, you MUST decide, Ba". At last I said, half in a jest & half in a pet, "Then I WONT decide," ... & ran out of the room. The truth is that it was'nt so easy. I wanted to go and I wanted to stay, & what could one *do* under such difficult circumstances? Then the weather grew suddenly cold & rainy, & people said on everyside "If you go to Vallambrosa so early in the summer, you will be blocked up with snow." Altogether we talked & talked, & hesitated & hesitated, & the days passed & found us here still: yet we may not stay to quite the 22ᵈ of July: if the heat shᵈ be intense, we shall probably persuade M. Centofanti into letting us go & return in the cool of the year to serve out our time. Meanwhile, here is the grand festa of San Giovanni, the patron saint of Florence, the grandest festa of the year[5]—and there are to be chariot races in the piazza close to us, & horse races (without riders) somewhere else—games in the manner of the ancients—also fireworks at night- We had intended to have hidden our sublime faces from these things—but after all, I suppose we shall not—it seems foolish not to see what is so characteristic of the people when we have only to open our eyes—so we have ordered the carriage as usual at six, & I will tell you the result. The fireworks I certainly shall like to see: for I like fireworks, & Robert says that Italy is famous for them. Altogether it will cost us a few pauls & two headaches, perhaps. Now you will never guess where I was, last night .... Drinking tea with the ex consul of Venice & his family, Mʳ & Mʳˢ Hoppner[6] .. the Hoppners mentioned & written to in Lord Byron's letters & I think Shelley's. Mʳ Kenyon sent us a letter of introduction to Mʳ Hoppner; & on Robert's returning his visit, so much was said so kindly about our going there in the evening to hear all about Venice & Rome, that I could see Robert wished me to go, .. & went accordingly at half past eight & returned at ten. I was dreadfully nervous, but got over it all pretty well- Everybody in morning gowns up to the throat, & everything to "sans façon"[7] as was promised to Robert in the first place—only a Mʳˢ Collyer who is a friend of Miss Dowglass's & lives at Rome, and a Mʳˢ Freeman, an artist, and a Frenchman who spoke in an undervoice, & Mʳˢ Hoppner's daughter & niece-[8] She (the mother) is French herself, & speaks her very fluent English with an accent, but is one of the frankest & most pleasing women I ever saw .. full of vivacity & intelligence- I remember that Lord Byron praises her in one of his letters. He, Mʳ Hoppner, appears full of refinement & shrewd sense .. but I like his wife .. she was very cordial to me, & I shᵈ have liked her, I think, even without that. The daughter is rather pretty & very cultivated—and the niece is pretty too, as Robert makes affidavits- There was a table cloth on a table, & tea & bread & butter just as if we were on English ground again, and a good deal of talk about poor Shelley & his wife, & how they passed three weeks, with the Hoppners once at Venice, & how on their arrival they ate nothing except water gruel & boiled cabbages & cherries, because it was a principle of Shelley's not to touch animal food, & how Mʳˢ Hoppner did, as she said, "seduce" him into taking roast beef & puddings ..

"Dear M! Shelley, you are so thin["]. (Fancy all this said with a pretty foreign accent.) "Now if you w? take my advice, you would have a very little slice of beef today- You are an Englishman & you ought to like beef- A very little slice of this beef, dear M! Shelley"- And so, she said, by degrees, he took a little beef & immediately confessed that "he did feel a great deal better"—"Why of course he did. He was so thin". The news of Venice were anything but as satisfactory. Venice is said to be cold & damp in the winter, & they left it simply on account of the climate- And so, there's an end of poor Venice!- Yes indeed, what you said of your fears made a great impression on Robert- He said that even if there were no risk but of making you uneasy, it w? be enough to deter him from wishing to go—but M! Hoppner's opinion is final for the present; and now our uncertainty is between Florence & *Rome*—but we shall at any rate stay at Florence until November, to give us a chance of seeing dear M! Kenyon—who frightens us by threatening not to come at all. Dont misunderstand- We dont mean to stay at Florence from this time to November- We shall go for the summer to Vallambrosa or elsewhere perhaps, & return here for the autumn months. November is excellent travelling time in Italy, & even better than earlier- Or we may stay altogether at Florence—who knows? .. viz—*after* November. In the meanwhile we must get to Vallambrosa—if we can. We tremble a little, because we have not yet absolutely received a permission, & because M! Hoppner prophecies that we shall not .. declares that some friend of his was lately refused an entrance there: it appears that there's a new prior who is an austere man & fears the approximation of unclean beasts- It will be a serious disappointment if we are rejected applicants at last—& the decision will probably reach us tomorrow- Why, notwithstanding your conjecture, even Wilson will be disappointed- She seems to think it an excellent jest to be shut up with fortyfive monks between precipices, and the Centofantes are getting up a laugh about it, she says: "there is not a woman within miles & miles, & we shall have to send five miles to have our washing done- "Oh they w? not let us in on any other pretext but that of *bad health*"—but *as invalids*, the chemist is sanguine as to a probability of our being admitted- My darling Arabel, I knew you would like to come with us—I knew it was just the thing for you. And as to the "musty books" dont suppose that we shall have any part or lot in them, except when perfectly tired of the rest— we shall make the most of the grand, wild nature we expect to see. "Like Switzerland", they say it is. M!ˢ Collyer last night told me to my surprise, that Miss Dowglas[s] was at the *Baths of Lucca* .. Think of that! She will however return to Rome. Her health is wonderfully better & she is very fond of the very young wife lately married by her cousin D! Pollock[9]—married last year, & only eighteen .. "just taken from the nursery", said M!ˢ Collyer, "but very intelligent & affectionate." Rome is said to be not dear, except as to apartments. Dont tell M！ Kenyon anything of our thoughts of Rome, & assure him that we shall be here in October & early in November, even if we dont winter at Florence: because if he fancies that we are going to Rome, he is capable of not coming to see us for fear of keeping us from the journey. Interrupted by M！ˢ Hoppner—by a visit from her. Charming she really is, from the heart & goodness in her face & manner, and as vivacious as if she were fifteen—and she is not young, as you may suppose of a friend of Lord Byron's. I am captivated with her & so is Robert .. It is pure *sweetness* .. that's the word! but not vapid sweetness– Wine of Cyprus as M！ Boyd has it– She came to tell us that we had very little chance of Vallambrosa, & therefore, but for the *charm*, we sh！ have taken her for the most disagreeable woman on earth– "She has enquired this morning; & the opinion is that *strangers* like us, have no manner of chance of getting the permission, since the only way of processing it is through a monk & on personal grounds." Still, when we told her of our chemist and of our plea of ill health & of our hold on the physician of the monastery, she thought there was still hope for us, & we hope on. By tomorrow, it will probably be settled.——

Now I am going to tell you of the chariot races & of much beside– I am out of breath with news. We went (Wilson with us––she took it into her head to be very shy at first & refused to go, because M. Centofanti had assured her that she w！ be the only *femme de chambre*[10] in a carriage, so,—but it was quite right that she sh！ see it all, it w！ have been a shame otherwise) we went to the piazza Santa Maria Novella close to us here, & one of the larger piazzas in Florence though scarcely as large as Montagu Square perhaps: It is not like a square—but open, in the manner of your Trafalgar. On all sides up against the houses, up against the great church, up against the convent walls, seats were raised, one over one, and the people crowded everywhere close as bees, only shining like butterflies, with their pretty dresses & glittering fans– Every seat, every window looked alive. The monks stood at the monastery windows, & we laughed to observe that there was room for just two at each, they were so holely fat. A recess hung with crimson drapes, held the Grand Ducal court & the ambassadors, all in full dress .. the duchesses & princesses with bare shoulders & arms, looking as royal as possible. For the rest, nothing could be more childishly innocent than these "races", I do assure you. There were bursts of laughter & the waving of fans—but no betting, no gambling, no drinking—the most peac[e]able good humour on every side. The spectacle was brilliant—the houses letting down silken drapperies from window to window, seemed to catch life from the enthusiasm of the people– We drove round the piazza twice or thrice, & then were deposited on seats, up against the church, up high. All this occupied an hour— & straightway the races began after the long, gorgeous preparation & filled just *three minutes*—that was all. There were four chariots, precisely of the

No. 2681   22-25 June [1847]   229

ancient form & device gilt all over .. the charioteer standing upright in a flowing robe, with bare arms. (My horses are just like dogs I observe, but you must help them with your imagination)– Round the piazza they gallopped about three times, & the people shouted & clapped their hands at the winner— .. & then we looked at one another & laughed to think it possible that *that* could be all– I did not believe it for some time– While it lasted my attention was dreadfully distracted by two dogs, who w^d persist in running in the course of the chariots & whom I expected to see crushed by the wheels every moment. It made me quite sick. Well—but nobody was hurt, not even a dog. The crowd flowed off—in little rivulets, & we got quietly to our carriage about half past eight. The driver drove to the Lung'Arno to take possession of the window at an hotel, provided for us by Mr Centofanti very goodnaturedly, in order to see the fireworks– My reflection as it went, was, that never was a more childish people, amused more innocently– In England we sh^d at any rate take advantage of the occasion & do something wicked to prove ourselves of mature age– I felt quite tenderly towards a people capable of making so much fuss, from their Grand Duke downwards, about that game of the chariots .. for they have been at work putting up seats in the piazza for weeks & weeks, really. The ambassadors must find it hard work to keep their countenances. Throughout the whole, the spectators were the true spectacle—the whole population was there, .. the very poorest of the peasants in their great uncut Leghorn bonnets nodding over their eyes, and the very richest of the nobles in dresses suitable to their degree. Half a religious ceremony, you see, it is– There are three days of the Feast of St John the Baptist, & yesterday was the vigil–

But, now I am going to tell you of the fireworks. We had a window in a little bedroom all to ourselves, in the great hotel opposite to the house in which Alfieri lived & died[11] & it w^d have been perfect, we agreed, if we had remembered to bring a bottle of Champagne .. only we did'nt. You know the Arno cleaves the city in two, and the houses (palaces) on each side, press forward into the water– They were illuminated up to their last window .. and the spire of the Campanile behind was drawn out in light against the sky as black as ink. (I was dreadfully afraid of its beginning to rain & spoiling the fireworks .. nota bene!) Do you see how the river runs between the houses through my scratch? The three bridges were equally drawn out in light, and little boats with coloured lamps, floated up & down. On the bottom bridge, the fire works were exhibited at about nine oclock & lasted for half an hour without intermission .. and I do say that it was worth while coming to Italy only for that sight– I could'nt help screaming out for pleasure, and surprise– I never had seen any good fireworks, but Robert, who had, declared that nothing ever met his eyes to compare with these .. and then the whole scene, the river, the people, the gardens & characteristic houses[,] contrived to throw one into a fit of ec[s]tasy—it was my turn to be a child, after all my fine reflection of the hour before. Beyond description beautiful, these fireworks were. Great temples, living in light up in the sky, .. fantastic palaces, burning there & going out, fading away, leaving rains of glory, .. fountains of flame rising upward as if to find the stars, & then falling, falling into the river, .. dripping in a regular noiseless splendour which took away your breath! and then entire globes which leapt above the houses, & there broke into a rain of fire or of living fiery serpents which seemed tensing & curling when you looked at them! I cannot describe to you how marvellously beautiful it was– At last there was a great explosion of Light—& down on both sides of the river & up into our faces & over all the bridges at once broke the trailing fire .. oh, glorious it was! Only, the smoke & smell & noise were rather overcoming! I coughed, & so did Robert– As to Wilson she was in a rapture. Coming home we bought three pence worth of San Giovanni-cakes on the bridge, & poor Flush who had been shut up in the house, was consoled in good time. This was last night & neither of us c^{d} sleep much after it—⟨though we did'nt go to the ball indeed! .. nor even to the concert!⟩[12] Robert took out with him one of his worst headaches, which was not of course improved by the smell of gass & gunpowder– It is said that Dante drew some of his ideas of hell from this annual exhibition, some five hundred years ago– How the world goes, yet stands still! This morning we walked to the Duomo, as the air was cool, & saw & heard what impressed me very much .. & Robert was struck too I think. It was the music which was so grand, & the sight of the crowding people, in that dim cathedral—the crucified Christ hanging, with its bent deathly head of marble in the midst of the choir, & a hundred burning candles, three times the height of a man, sending up their smoke about its feet– I felt quite overcome for a few minutes & could not keep from tears– There! now I have told you the whole, I think– We shant go out to see the lottery & the riderless horses—it is quite enough as it is– Yes, & we met our friend the chemist who cant he says get us a decision from Vallambrosa before two or three days; & therefore I shant be able to mention it in this letter– My dearest beloved Arabel, I am the most ungrateful of women not to have acknowledged the arrival of what you wrote, enclosing Nelly Bordman's letter– Certainly I received it. I thank you for that, & also for the last dear packet .. oh, how glad it made me. The news of dearest Stormie were worth a thousand thanks, of themselves .. and yet I was a little, little vexed at his talking so of *postage*, just as if he did'nt mean to write to me. Really I *can* pay still for letters & my daily bread—& if I carried œconomy out further, it w![d] be because I was not hungry & did'nt love anybody at a distance. As it is I dont understand this calculating of postages– Well! At any rate Storm might send a note to me *through you*, & then we might correspond without any postage at all. It will be too hard, now that the others wont write to me, that he sh![d] take up such a motive of another sort. Thank dear Minny for her kind note & tell her that Robert was quite pleased with some of the words—he *knows her* though he has not seen her yet. I shall write to her on some other day. Give her my love & say so. Nobody tells me if Crow's youngest child is pretty.[13] And nobody tells me (though I ask & ask) if M![r] Bevan is a professed Roman Catholic. I heard lately of a major in the English army taking "office" .. serving .. under the Duke of Tuscany. Ask Surtees the meaning of that, with my love, & whether the change admits of pecuniary advantage. Not that I particularly like this, serving in foreign troops, of an Englishman, .. only these Tuscans here are comparatively enlightened & liberal—they are not altogether like the Austrians .. whisper to Henry. I dont speak of serving in Tuscany for *him*, by the way: & there w![d] be no adequate pay for a beginner. It might be otherwise for *officers* in the army perhaps .. but I know nothing, nor have means of knowing, & only because the thing came into my head, spoke of it. The Pope is perfectly idolized in Italy, & we heard of a riot in ⟨...⟩ the other day because eight hundred people "conspired" .... to cry 'viva Pio nono'. Of such innoxious childish stuff are Italian conspiracies generally made! People talk or cry aloud like children, & there an end. And when other people get up amusements for them .. gilt chariot races & the like, .. why everything gets right again & smooth. I have just been entreating Robert to go out & be about– Half I am inclined to be out of humour. Exercise is necessary for him & he knows it, yet positively he will only walk as far as I do-- except just to the post in the morning– Now this morning because I was with him at the cathedral & confess to feeling tired, he refuses to leave this house any more—yet it is a lovely morning & the whole city being in a state of festa, there is plenty everywhere to see & hear– No, he wont stir. We have been standing up at the window & watching the people go by, & feeling the cool air. Wilson, I think, has gone with Madame Centofanti to see the riderless horses– We stood at the window till I could'nt stand anymore— it is a sight, to see the people. Every human being looks something like a countess or her cousin .. I mean of beings female. Where all the poverty of the world has gone, you would take for a problem– Elegant bonnets & sweeping muslins, & bare throats strung with Roman pearls & gold chains, catch your eye wherever you look. If it were not for the men, who generally forget *their gloves*—, there w^d be no end of the wonder .. & altogether it w^d be very pretty, ... except for the women's faces– You smile at my exception .. but Robert & I, having given the deepest investigation to the subject, are really of opinion that the faces are not pretty at all. Robert says that the ugliness indeed is wonderful—and I will answer for it that a like number of Englishmen would give a very different deduction. As to delicate youthful beauty, such a thing is not to be seen. Plenty of red hair & colourless skins instead. Otherwise, great black eyes, & brows rather stern. The quite old women are hags, & all the uglier for their habit of never covering their heads—oh, you would see many a half bald head I assure you, in opposition to your theory, the white lanky hair hanging on each side the bareness.

—Today we had a letter from Mr Chorley—a very affectionate letter— Robert had it, but he spoke of "dear Mrs Browning". Only, Mr Forster's letters are the most tender of all—you w^d think that he adored us. I cant think where Mrs Jameson is .. she does not write. I did not understand till you told me that Mr Powers's *Eve* was in London– Mrs Powers called on me the other day.[14] Not quite Eve! though by no means an ill-looking woman .. we agreed that she looked & talked like a woman who had been battered about among the open ways of the world: ever so many children she has, & her voice has had to keep silence only by crying louder than the loudest, & scolding the maid perhaps– Also she is'nt by any means refined in manner & accent & language—& what, in the man of genius, struck us as a charming simplicity, was another thing in his wife. But I dare say she is an estimable woman, & one ought'nt to be critical on such. Flush is quite well, but very thin, & I dont understand why. I am putting him on a milk diet (besides the meat) to try to fatten him a little like poor Shelley[.] Exercise he has more than ever in his life yet not too much exercise. The other day when we had put him & Wilson out of the carriage at the Cascine, & she had finished holding him (we being out of sight) he set off suddenly & ran like a hare & came up with us panting & gasping & with his eyes stuck out– So delighted he was to be taken into the carriage again– He is in great spirits & as full of caprices as ever .. only thin. Why sh^d he be thin, I wonder. Wilson thinks it is the change of climate. She is well & liking Italy much better than in the Pisa days. I could not help telling her what Minny says of her so truly– You are imag⟨...⟩[15] .. and to trival. But it really ⟨...⟩ have happy results in many ways; but ⟨...⟩ observances I sh^d want if I I were she,—⟨...⟩bulation. Unless she can put away the sense of ⟨...⟩ DUTY to have a full liberty—not a ⟨...⟩. I wonder at a man's expecting to respect ⟨...⟩ her now to suppose that he w^d interfere with ⟨...⟩ matter. For my part in it ⟨...⟩ single ⟨...⟩ you blame of such interference. ⟨He⟩ would not ⟨ha⟩ve it. Oh yes, Arabel! you do right in considering our marriage as *exceptionally* happy. I tell you openly & truly that if I had expected such a measure of happiness, my own thoughts would have seemed to myself romantic & unreasonable. I did not expect it. Love, trust & sympathy, I expected, because I knew what *he* was from whom I looked for them; I knew in a degree .. but I had schooled myself from all the traditions of married life, from the experience of life in general, to be satisfied with a modest proportion of even these things, and not to stretch out my hands to the impossible– Yet, you see, the Impossible, or what I took for the impossible, came to me, of itself .. or rather of God's great mercy—& I never could wish to the dearest, a happier life than mine .. as far as depends on my husband– Never was a more united life led, than this of ours .. never! People say that the married get tired of one another if they live too much together … but when people say this loudest, they must admit the perfection of happiness to be the living together always—& never being tired, *if the thing is feasible*– Well!– it is feasible to *us*—& *that* is saying all– I am certain that we are happier now than at first .. & that he loves me better– I am certain of it—and yet we are constantly in the same room, at the same books, in the same thoughts even .. there is every opportunity of being tired. Thank God for me always dear, dearest Arabel!

You do not tell me a word before of Eliza Giles. Ah, my own Arabel! ⟨…⟩[16] I think that it w^d be wrong in you to give up Mr Stratton's from the cause in question, & also I believe that if you did so it w^d not draw back Papa to a position he has quitted long enough to form a habit. The scene of the toast made me wonder & smile a little. His heart is soft in strange corners– Poor dearest Papa! It is a great blessing to hear of his being well & in good spirits in any case. Your dreadful headaches!– how are they, do you think, on the whole? How is dearest Trippy? You speak of her dining in Wimpole Street which is a good sign, but I want to hear all about her, dear thing– Does she ever go with you to the schools? Tell me of her, & tell her that I love her always .. signed & sealed with a large kiss– I could not believe that anything but a consideration of œconomy w^d fasten down the Hedleys at Tours—it was my way of complaining of their taste, observe– As to Bummy's settling at Leamington, why ⟨…⟩[17] doubt there is a good deal to say on either side of the subject– If I were she I would go to Tours I think .. to the Hedleys– No wonder that she took Sarianna's writing for yours—yet your writing is more rapid & flowing & characteristic: but the likeness is extraordinary otherwise. Tell me any little detail about yourself my beloved Arabel. As an example, I have had my new gowns made up with quite *plain bodies*, notwithstanding my vow against it .. but it was to please Robert who liked Fanny Hanford's. By the way you shant see the Hanfords I fancy– They were to pass too quickly through London—only if it were possible, Fanny meant to try to see you. Arabel, I wish you had gone to Miss Bayley's .. not for my sake but yours– You visit the poor & not the rich as dear Minny says. Now I want to know why you sh.d draw a line between rich & poor– Does God, do you think? Because I have a piece of gold in my purse, am I shut out from your sympathies? *Poor me, then.!*— Do consider this– I want you to have mental intercourse, which you cant well have with the uneducated– Certain I am that it is wrong & disastrous for you to refuse all equal society .. looking both to the fact & its consequences– My love to George & all of them– My next letter is to dearest Henrietta of whom I think very much. Love me as always, both of you, & let me be known for my own Arabel's most affected & grateful Ba–

Robert's best love of course– He was ⟨deligh⟩ted with H's note. Ah .. I find from the almanack that the 4.th of July is Sunda⟨y—⟩& that you cant get this till monday– May God bless you. My regards to the ⟨Stra⟩ttens– Love to Lizzie. Count that I remember anyone who remembers me, as Henrietta suggested, tell her.

Wilson has made us some knead cakes![18] R. will be delighted to accept any hospitality of which knead cakes are constituent elements, he likes them so much. Arabella, when you begin "gypseying," we claim you, remember!–

Our letters will be sent after us to Vallambrosa– The monks get theirs, & medecines &c from Florence—send for them.

Think of M.r Giles[19] & M.r Browning! There's a combination!- By the way, I call him M.r Browning sometimes, that is, whenever he is impertinent & calls me Miss Barrett.

Love to M.r Boyd. I am very glad about M.r Hunter– Do write, both of you– Here's an example of a letter!– Does M.rs Orme really go to Naples[?] Dearest Arabel, how dear you are to me!—— May God bless you always.

Oh, you need not keep a secret against dear M.r Kenyon. You may tell him if you have the opportunity that we think of Rome—only you must add that we shall not think of going south until *November*, whether he comes or not.

Address, on integral page: (To the care of Miss Tr⟨ipsack⟩ / Miss Ara⟨bel⟩ Barrett / ⟨5– Montagu Street / Montagu Square / London⟩.
Publication: None traced.
Manuscript: Berg Collection.

1. Year determined from EBB's references to residence in Florence after the move from Pisa.
2. i.e., her birthday, 4 July; her 34th.
3. "Beard-hater," from the title of the 4th-century satire *Misopogon* by the Emperor Flavius Claudius Julianus.
4. A little more than a line has been obliterated by someone other than EBB.
5. The feast of St. John the Baptist is celebrated on the 24th of June. EBB's description is similar to Murray's *Hand-Book for Travellers in Northern Italy* (1847): "*Midsummer-day*, or the feast of St. John the Baptist, the ancient protector of Florence, is solemnised

by the races of the *Cocchi*, in the Piazza of Santa Maria Novella. These *Cocchi* are imitations of Roman cars, but have four wheels, and were invented by Cosmo I ... On the vigil of the Saint's day there are fireworks on the Ponte alla Carraja, and an illumination on the Lungarno. On the morning of the festival the Court attends high mass in the cathedral, and afterwards the races in the Piazza di S.M. Novella" (p. 571). The *Hand-Book* does not elaborate on the "riderless horses" referred to here and below.

6. Richard Belgrave Hoppner (1786–1872), the son of the artist John Hoppner, married Marie Isabelle May in 1814 at Brussels. He was the British Consulate-General at Venice from 1814–25, the time Byron was there, and was described by the poet as "a good listener" and "a thoroughly good man" (*Conversations of Lord Byron with the Countess of Blessington*, 1834, p. 153). Shelley called Hoppner and his Swiss wife "the most amiable people I ever knew" (*Essays, Letters from Abroad*, 1840, II, 136).

7. "Simple," or "without ceremony."

8. Mrs. Hoppner's daughter and niece have not been identified, nor has the "Frenchman," or Mrs. Collyer (EBB later spells the name "Colyar" in see letters 2696 and 2702). Mrs. Freeman was Augusta (*née* Latilla, b. 1826), an Anglo-Italian sculptress, who married James Edwards Freeman (1808–84), an American artist, in 1845.

9. James Edward Pollock (1819–1910) who practiced medicine in Rome from 1842 to 1849; he became Physician Extraordinary to the Queen in 1899. His marriage to Marianne Malvars on 2 September 1846 at West Derby, near Liverpool, was witnessed by his cousin Frances Dowglass.

10. "Lady's maid."

11. Vittorio Alfieri (1749–1803) was a poet and author of nineteen tragedies, of which *Saul* (1782) is considered the finest. He spent the last ten years of his life in Florence. In his autobiographical *Memoirs of the Life and Writings of Victor Alfieri* (1810), he wrote: "Towards the end of that year [1793], we found out near the end of the bridge of Santa Trinita a house, which, though small, was admirably adapted for our accommodation, situated on the Arno, and facing south. We took possession of it in November, since which I have uniformly occupied it. I shall here probably close my earthly career, should fate cease to persecute me" (II, 249).

12. Bracketed passage is interpolated above the line.

13. See letter 2656, note 14.

14. Elizabeth Powers (*née* Gibson, 1810?–94) was the eldest of five daughters of James Gibson (d. 1862) and Anna Reilly (d. 1854) originally of Philadelphia and later Cincinnati, where Powers met her and where they were married on 1 May 1832. At the time of this letter, five of their nine children had been born; however, the eldest child, James, had died in March 1838, only a few months after the Powers family had arrived in Florence.

15. A large portion of the final leaf of the manuscript is missing, causing loss of text from here to the end of the paragraph.

16. Almost one line has been obliterated here, by someone other than EBB.

17. A few words are missing due to loss of manuscript.

18. "These knead cakes have been famous things in the family for many generations, especially do they come forth to conduce to the glories of *festa*-days—Christmas mornings—birthday-breakfasts &c. The custom comes from Northumberland, we believe. These cakes, flat as pancakes are made of flour and milk, with, or without dried currants, and are baked on a fire, on an iron plate, or pan called a girdle—hence they are sometimes called *girdle*-cakes in the north" (Surtees Cook, in an editorial note with his transcript of EBB's letters to his wife, Henrietta; MS with Altham).

19. George Giles, husband of Eliza Giles (*née* Cliffe); see note 26 in the preceding letter.

2682. THOMAS CARLYLE TO RB

Chelsea, London,
23 june, 1847—

Dear Browning,

Many thanks for your Italian Letter;[1] which dropped in, by the Penny Post, with right good welcome, like a friendly neighbour, some week or two ago. I am right glad to hear of your welfare; your's and your fair Partner's. No marriage has taken place, within my circle, these many years, in which I could so heartily rejoice. You I had known, and judged of; her too, conclusively enough, if less directly; and certainly if ever there was a union indicated by the finger of Heaven itself, and sanctioned and prescribed by the Eternal Laws under which poor transitory Sons of Adam live, it seemed to me, from all I could hear or know of it, to be this! Courage, therefore; follow piously the Heavenly Omens, and fear not. He that can follow these, he, in the loneliest desert, in the densest jostle and sordid whirlpool of London Fog, will find his haven: "*Se tu segui tua stella!*"–[2] Perpetually serene weather is not to be looked for by anybody; least of all by the like of you two,—in whom precisely as more is given, more also in the same proportion is required:[3] but unless I altogether mistake, here is a Life-partnership which, in all kinds of weather, has in it a capacity of being blessed to the Parties. May it indeed prove so. May the weather, on the whole, be moderate;—and if joy be ever absent for a season, may nobleness never! That is the best I can wish. The *sun* cannot shine always; but the places of the *stars*, these ought to be known always, and these can.

What you say of visiting Italy is infinitely tempting to one's love of travel, to what small remnants of it one still has. I was in young years the most ardent of travellers; and executed immense journeyings, and worshippings at foreign shrines; all in idea, since it could not be otherwise: neither yet has the passion quite left me; tho' a set of nerves, in the highest degree unfit for locomotion under any terms, has taught me many times "the duty of staying at home." In fact there are moments, this very season, when I do scheme out a Winter in Italy as no unsuitable practical resource for me. There is, in many ways, a kind of pause in my existence this year. Ever since I got the Cromwell lumber shaken fairly off me,[4] I am idle; idle not for want of work, but rather in sight of a whole universe of work, which I have to despair of accomplishing, which in my sulky humour I could feel a disgust at attempting. My value for human ways of working in this time, for almost all human ways, including what they call "Literature" among the rest, has not risen of late! We seem to me a People so enthralled, and buried under bondage to the Hearsays and the Cants and the Grimaces, as no People ever were before. Literally so. From the top of our Metropolitan Cathedral to the

No. 2682   23 June 1847

sill of our lowest Cobler's shop, it is to me, too often, like one general *somnambulism*, most strange, most miserable,—most damnable! Surely, I say, men called "of genius,"—if genius be anything but a paltry toybox fit for Bartholomew Fair,[5]—are commissioned, and commanded under pain of eternal death, to throw their whole "genius," however great or small it be, into the remedy of this; into the hopeful or the desperate battle against this! And they spend their time in traditional rope-dancings, and mere *Vauxhall* gymnastics;[6] and talk about "Art," and "High Art," and I know not what; and show proudly their week's salary, of gold or of copper, of sweet voices and of long-eared brayings, and say comfortably, "*Anch' io!*"[7] Surely such a function, gas-light it as we may, is essentially that of a *slave*. Surely I am against all that, from the very foundations of my being;—and the length to which it goes, and the depth and height of it, and the fruit it bears (to Irish Sanspotatoes visibly, and to nobler men less visibly but still *more* fatally) has become frightfully apparent to me. A mighty harvest indeed; and the labourers few or none. O for a thousand sharp sickles in as many strong right hands! And I, poor devil, have but one rough sickle, and a hand that will soon be weary!— And, in fact, I stand here in a *solitude* (among so many millions of my fellow-creatures) which is sometimes almost sublime, which is always altogether frightful and painful,—if one could help it well. God mend us all! In short, I believe it would do me real good to get into some new, concrete scene for a while: and if I *could* travel, Italy might be the place rather than another. Or perhaps to get into dialogue with the crags and brooks again,—that might be the best? That is the likeliest: for I am called to Scotland, where my good old Mother still is,[8] by a kind of errand; and elsewhither there is none precise enough. I will think farther. Italy is not quite *impossible*; but I guess it to be too improbable. After all, the true remedy comes of itself, so soon as one is miserable *enough*: work, some farther attempt at work,—even by the pen!

We have no news here worth spending ink upon. Miss Martineau has been to Jerusalem, and is back; called here yesterday: brown as a berry; full of life, loquacity, dogmatism, and various "gospels of the east-wind."[9] Dickens writes a *Dombey & Son*, Thackeray a *Vanity Fair*;[10] not *reapers* they, either of them! In fact the business of rope-dancing goes to a great height; and d'Israeli's *Tancred*[11] (readable to the end of the first volume), a kind of transcendent spiritual Houndsditch, marks an epoch in the history of this poor country.—— ——

When do you think of coming home? Is not Chelsea an eligible side of London? My Wife salutes you both, with many true regards. Adieu, dear Browning, and dear Mrs. Browning.

                                                      Yours ever truly
                                                      T. Carlyle

Margaret Fuller is the name of the American Lady:[12] I think she has no writing of mine to your Address: but she knows you, both of you, well; and will really prove worthy (when once you get into her dialect) of being known to you.

Address, on integral page: Robert Browning, Esqr. / Poste Restante / Firenze, (Toscana, / Italy).
Docket, above address, in RB's hand: June 23. '47.
Publication: Carlyle, 21, 239-241.
Manuscript: Berg Collection.

1. Letter 2677.
2. "If thou follow thy star" (Dante, *Inferno*, xv, 55, trans. Laurence Binyon).
3. Cf. Luke 12:48.
4. Carlyle's edition of *Oliver Cromwell's Letters and Speeches* had been published in December 1845; Carlyle had enlisted RB's assistance (see letter 1612). A second edition was published in June 1846.
5. From the 12th century, a three-day cloth fair commencing on the eve of St. Bartholomew's Day (24 August); however, in later centuries the fair was the scene of tawdry entertainments and cheap merchandise. It was replaced by the Smithfield Market in 1866.
6. Vauxhall Gardens were located on the south side of the Thames, and were first laid out in the seventeenth century. The gardens were closed in 1859; however, "in 1816, Mme Saqui gave her first performances, ascending and descending a tightrope tied to a sixty foot mast amidst a cloud of fireworks" (*The London Encyclopædia*, ed. Ben Weinreb and Christopher Hibbert, 1983, p. 911).
7. "I too," (cf. "anch'io sono pittore!," "I, too, am a painter!," Correggio's legendary remark on seeing Raphael's "St. Cecilia" in Bologna).
8. Margaret Carlyle (*née* Aitken, 1771-1853). A week later on 30 June, Carlyle wrote to his sister, Jean Carlyle Aitken: "Our own movements lie utterly in the vague yet; never once turned over, or canvassed. I calculate loosely on a glimpse of Annandale and my dear old Mother again: but I am too bilious and melancholic to do much good there beyond a few days" (*Carlyle*, 21, 246).
9. Cf. Job 15:2.
10. These two works appeared almost simultaneously in monthly installments: *Dombey and Son* between October 1846 and April 1848, and *Vanity Fair* from January 1847 until July 1848. Despite Carlyle's dismissal of these novels, each marked important points in the authors' careers.
11. *Tancred: or, the New Crusade* (3 vols., 1847) was the last of Disraeli's trilogy that included *Coningsby* (1844) and *Sybil* (1845). Houndsditch is an area in the east end of London that was noted for its used clothes stalls, and popular for Jewish merchants of lesser quality goods.
12. Margaret Fuller (1810-50), American author and journalist, had reviewed the works of both Brownings in American publications; see letter 2538, note 3. Miss Fuller and the Brownings corresponded and eventually met in 1849.

2683. RB TO EUPHRASIA FANNY HAWORTH

Florence,
June 29 1847.

Dear Miss Haworth—
I have let a long time go by since your letter reached me at Pisa—one reason was, that the parcel containing your book[1] ought to have arrived directly, but did not—and the gap of time once grown big, widens so insensibly! I wonder if you are in London,—at all events, I will thank you, and very sincerely, for both book and letter- I don't know how the former may have "succeeded," as people say—but the striking things ought to strike most where they are least expected,—which means, that I, who have known you long and prophesied about you loudly, am prepared for a good deal whenever you seriously address yourself to write or draw. But is it in you to take the trouble?—there my prophesyings dwindle into a mutter, or perhaps it is only said to bore you—for words are no use, you will do as you please. And I—(if you care to have such an illustration)—, I should not altogether wonder if I do something notable one of these days, all through a desperate virtue which determines out of gratitude—(not to man and the reading public by any means!)—to do, what I *do not* please .. I could, with an unutterably easy heart never write another line while I have my being—which would surely be very wrong considering how the lines fall to poets in the places of this world generally- So I mean to do my best whatever comes of it—meantime, (not a stone's cast from the housetop under which I write) sleep, watch, and muse those surpassing statues of Michael Angelo,[2]—about the merits of which there are very various opinions, as you know—

What can I tell you about myself? I have been here some ten weeks,—gone like a day! The weather which threatened excessive heat, in May, has become quite cool and propitious, so that I hope to be able to stay even till the middle of July. My wife, who had an illness at Pisa, is quite well. We go about, sit on the bridge and see people pass, or take an ice inside Doney's, after the vulgarest fashion- We know next to nobody,—Powers the Sculptor, we see every now and then, and have made a pleasant acquaintance with the Hoppners, the old friends of Byron- But what do you think we are setting our hearts upon? —A permission to go and stay at Vallombrosa—a real month or two month's stay—but the Abbot-General is said to be savage on the subject, just now, and everything is to be feared- "Whether, if we wrote him a mollifying latin letter?" says my wife[.] "Rather a Greek one," say I, "and so *stifle* the old fellow at once"- We do not despair, but that is all.

To day, being St. Peter's feast, ends the time of feasts- We saw by a pure accident, on turning the edge of our street, the horse race,—but we took quite trouble enough to see the notable "Cocchi" or chariots, last

Wednesday[3]—and I can warrant you that a better spectacle waits you every day that a man calls a cab and four leave the stand to dispute his custom— but the fireworks in the evening, with the illumination of the Arno, were magnificent-

July 4. We have got a kind of recommendation tantamount to a permission to go and stay at Vallombrosa, and there we hope to pass a few cool weeks accordingly at this month's end: the weather is very bearable and we can easily stay till then— Whom do you know that I know in London? If you see Mrs Gibson you shall remember me to her.[4] How I thank you for the portrait of my sister—which may be more like the person you see in her, than my particular fancies—and yet it is not unlike even those—the features, understand, are clearly hers—only the expression strikes me as not the accustomed one. I have put it here, opposite me-

Good bye, dear Miss Haworth- I cannot write, out of the very fullness of matter—one day perhaps I sha⟨ll⟩ see you and talk it all over—as you propose—but in any case I shall always keep your kindness and sympathy in my mind and heart- Meantime, I am glad you know the Arnoulds—my very dear friends too- Also you are good to like Sarianna—who would be angry if I simply said that she "liked" you! What good people there are in the world, and at London, when one is away at Florence! Will you write to me, not in return for this notable piece of penmanship, but for your own friendship's sake?—which is, always of the old value, to yours ever faithfully

RB

My wife sends her truest regards—she continues very well.

Address, on integral page: Miss Haworth / London.
Publication: NL, pp. 42-45.
Manuscript: Yale University.

1. *St. Sylvester's Day, and Other Poems* (1847) contained "illustrative designs by the author," and RB's remarks here may be explained by some of Fanny Haworth's comments in the preface: "I send forth my little book into the world with such faint hope of what is called success, that I can scarcely be disappointed if it remain unknown and unnoticed by any but those few who are likely to be more partial than critical judges."
2. The tombs of Lorenzo and Giuliano de'Medici, grandson and son of Lorenzo the Magnificent, in the New Sacristy of the Church of San Lorenzo. Lorenzo, deep in meditation, and Giuliano, watchfully active, face each other across the sacristy. Reclining at their feet are symbolic representations of Night, Day, Dawn and Twilight. These six Michaelangelo statues were well known to RB and EBB; EBB describes them passionately in *Casa Guidi Windows*, I, 73-97, as waiting the new dawn of Italian liberty.
3. See letter 2681, note 5.
4. Doubtless Mrs. Thomas Milner Gibson, with whom RB was acquainted in London (see letter 2517, note 2). Her name appears in RB's address book (see vol. 9, p. 391).

2684. EBB TO HENRIETTA MOULTON-BARRETT

Florence–
July—9– [1847][1]

My ever dearest & sometimes most illused Henrietta .. can it be possible that Robert is right & I so very very wrong! I cant delay five minutes longer from throwing myself at your feet & confessing myself ... whatever you may be pleased (being displeased) to call me– So wrong & ungrateful of me! But I seemed to feel confident of writing in the right & just alternation, & I could scarcely listen patiently to Robert when he spoke out & rebuked me for my injustice– The *third* time was the birthday-necessity—it was the *previous* time which I sinned in– But you forgive me—I did not mean to be so unkind. I siezed on this paper directly on receiving your letter to express this remorse: and then Robert siezed on *me*, & declared that it was dinner time & that I sh^d sit by him on the sofa instead of writing at all– Observe, how I correct my own iniquities! I would'nt be held tight—I would'nt be persuaded & talked to—& I offended him & was called "the unkindest creature in the world" rather than abstain from washing my hands of remorse, for half an hour. So do *you* forgive me Henrietta, & understand how the fault arose from my *uncounting* spirit, of which you know something already. I never could count quite to ten, I think, without making a mistake. I forget days of the month, & the year of the century even, and if, as Arabel swears, I count right & right often the months of my being married, it is simply because Robert keeps the feast day of that event so very rigorously that there's no escape for my stupidity. Talking of marriages, what an amusing chronicle you have sent me of Arlette's! I was very much amused indeed, & thank you for the whole. Only, forgive me, I *cant* admire Mr Reynolds .. I know the man exactly .. I *see* him & hear him & could'nt admire the sort of man on any sort of pretext– That "Come along young damsel" finishes the full length as I perceive it– I do detest a want of refinement which shows itself *in sentiments*, I mean in positions of sentiment .. A coarse man even, will sometime *rise* at a touch of feeling!—but one capable of such a speech at such a moment–– .... Well! let me say no more of what you may blame, both of you. He may be a good and sociable man & attached to Arlette & that may be all required perhaps– She chose for herself. Of course the meaning of so much being *"settled on her"*, is in the event of her husband's death— the phrase is always worded so—but *six hundred* is not much if anything above the amount of her own fortune. Still it is a liberal provision I believe, as settlements go & the makers of them. Had she a carriage? you do not say. If we go to Rome this winter we shall see them, & I may come to another conclusion, as you bid me. What a calm marriage in all sides! Ah yes! it was rather different from mine indeed. Three times I tried to write my name &

could not form a letter, and some one said, I remember, "Let her wait a moment", and somebody else thrust in a glass of water .. What a wild, dreadful, floating vision it all looks like, to look back on it now! Only, to make amends, the service was read in a decided *abbreviation*--and almost I am certain by the same clergyman who married Annie Hayes:[2] he has done better work this time, I thank God- Henrietta, do you wonder much at Arlette's lack of tears & calm satisfaction? She does not leave a happy home & tender relatives, like Arabella, consider .. and the perpetual irritation to which she was subjected, had its effect of course .. its natural effect. Human beings do not *love* up against the pricks, whether they kick back or not.[3] Bummy is not her real mother, that she sh^d endure such things, "*quand même*":[4] she passes out to liberty in the way of her own choice, & naturally she does not look behind much. I do hope she may be very happy. Perhaps it was in *my* sleep rather than *yours*, that you seemed to tell me of Susan Cook's marriage,—but it did run in my head- Oh, and Mr Horne's—did you see Mr Horne's in the newspaper?[5] To a Miss Catherine Foggo! not the prettiest name, nor one to be changed for the worse at all. The poets are draining off into marriage very gradually, I think. By the way, I ought certainly to tell you of a delightful letter which Carlyle sent to Robert the other day,[6] which when I had read I kissed for gladness & gratitude, it gave me so much of both- He says that not for years had any marriage, occurring in his circle, given him an equal pleasure to our marriage- Here are his words as he goes on .. "*You*, I had known & judged of: *her* too, conclusively enough, if less directly; and certainly if ever there was a union indicated by the finger of Heaven itself, and sanctioned & prescribed by the Eternal Laws under which poor transitory sons of Adam live, it seemed to me, from all I could hear & know of it, to be this! Courage, therefore; follow piously the Heavenly omen, & fear not. He that can follow there, he, in the loneliest desert, in the densest jostle & whirlpool of London fog will find his haven-— Perpetually serene weather is not to be looked for by anybody; least of all by the like of you two, .. in whom precisely because more is given, more also in the same proportion is required: but unless I altogether mistake, there is a Life-partnership which, in all kinds of weather, has in it a capacity of being blessed to the parties. May it indeed prove so. May the weather on the whole be moderate,—and if joy be ever absent for a season, may nobleness never! That is the best I can wish. The *sun* cannot shine always; but the places of the *stars*, these ought to be known always and these can." Is'nt that full, full of kindness? We had had kind messages from him before, but it is the first letter .. and I have copied more than I could becomingly perhaps. If so, you will make allowances, knowing my reverence for Carlyle, & the natural pleasure which words like those from him must overflow me with. Overflow me with! What a delightful metaphor in the actual weather, when we are being burnt up, suffocated[,] exterminated .. here's the thermometer at eighty again, & Flush turning his head away from warm milk & his tail from soft cushions. Tell dear Minny that he w^d indeed be glad of his old place in her room, I will answer for him– Now he goes creeping under the sofas .. having the delusion that every sort of darkness must be coolest .. whereas the sofa-drapery scarcely helps him much, poor Flushie– I wish we *were* "overflowed", .. he & all of us.! I sh^d like a little Arno just now, in a ripple or a rush! The heat is intense, and the worst is that having taken & paid for our apartment up to the twenty second, it seems a reckless extravagance to leave it on the eighth– Because it was cooler, we thought we might engage for the month without danger; & here, we are, caught in a suntrap! If it were not for the saving little wind which gets up lazily towards evening, we sh^d be done for, put an end to– Robert in the meanwhile is perpetually tempting me with, "Now Ba, if you w^d like to go away, we will go tomorrow–"– "Now, my love, if you feel in the least overcome with the heat, we wont mind the money"– "Now, make up your mind & let us go"——and I .. in an agony of prudential considerations .. gasp for breath & an opinion. At last we have resolved to *bear it as long as we can*, & then go– A cloud is seen afar by the readers of almanachs! We have strong faith in our Italian almanach, & it prophecies for Monday, *rain* which "mitigherà l'eccessivo caldo".[7] If rain should'nt come on monday, we shall go, that's certain– At any rate we shall be gone in ten days, and to *Vallambrosa* after all—yes, to Vallambrosa! We have a permission at last after being held over the abyss to frighten us into a due reverence .. we have a letter to the Superior of the monastery, recommending us for various rare & valuable qualities as a most "stimabile famiglia"[8] on the whole, .. & requesting him out of the writer's dear love, to let us stay as long as the sanctity of the place will admit of– So *that* point is gained in the face of a hundred fears– .. I was quite in a pet about it at one time– Robert said "Never mind them, dear! dont mind the fanatics! Choose some other *place*—take out the map & choose for yourself; & we will go *there* without anybody's leave." "But I want to go to Vallambrosa. I dont want to go anywhere else." I went on crying for my moon, like a spoilt child in a pet. Nothing but my moon did for me– The prettiest morningstar in the world, what was it, compared to my moon?– So now we have it, and perhaps as I was saying this morning at breakfast, it will disappoint us in the having, .. by turning out something different or inferior to our imagination– But the scenery must be sublime—there are forty miles through the mountains of wild, roadless, rock & forest, the monasteries of Laverna & Camaldoli being further on, & all belonging to the same Rule or order. Vallambrosan monks are of noble families, the aristocracy of Italy.[9] One thing I am half prepared for– They will take Robert into the monastery, & leave Wilson & me on the outside with other unclean beasts. We shall not be let dine together, even, I dare say! Perhaps we may have coffee sometimes, or walk out—but otherwise there will be a divorce—oh, I expect it I assure you- So, as I tell him, it would be wise if we began to accustom one another a little to living separated for half an hour now & then-

Henrietta, you frighten us by what you say of M[r] Kenyon. He is going to Vienna to see his brother in any case, & certainly he had fears of some cousin of his coming from Jamaica to prevent his absence from England being long enough to admit of his further visit to us[10] .. particularly as we dont go to Venice to meet him. Still, he said, that Florence w[d] not make the difference of his coming or not coming to Italy, and I had felt sure in my mind that after all his doubts he w[d] come. Do, if you see him, tell him how anxious we are—and tell him from me that we shall be at Florence till November & only go to Vallambrosa for shadow & rest intermediately. The plan of plans w[d] be for him to join us here in October or November, & then that we sh[d] travel together to Rome for the winter, & so escape the cough he had last year. Would it not be wise & pleasant? Observe that the pleasantest things are always the wisest, .. except what *pleases* the moralists to say. Is nobody out of Wimpole Street going up the Rhine this year, pray? If George will spend his vacation so, we will house him & love him here at Florence .. tell him *that* from me, dear George! Tell him to come & see how I love him. He need be at no expense when once *with* us, and to us it could be pure pleasure & nothing less- I dont speak vain words now- Or if George wont, will anyone? Henry, Alfred[,] Sette, Occy? If Papa knows that they are on the Rhine, or at Milan, that will be enough: there need be no scrape with him. I long to see some of them; & such a proof of their still caring for me, w[d] go to my heart, where is the love of them. As for you & Arabel, is there a hope of your leaving London this summer? Oh, I hope, I hope—I do hope! You desire to go, I suppose .. do you, Henrietta? So, after all, you were bridesmaids to Arlette. Well, I did wonder how Bummy could escape asking you: and Arlette certainly would have liked to have you—that was clear to me—the doubt was of Bummy! Strange that Papa sh[d] not invite her to Wimpole Street! No, *you* could'nt, of course!—if you longed for her as I do for a little wind .. Hot, hot, it is!——

To hear of M[r] Hunter gives me the greatest pleasure; & ask Arabel to tell Mary that it does. It is quite a relief to the sad thoughts due to his late dreary position—poor M[r] Hunter- And Mary will be happy, I trust, in this return to a home, & release from anxiety for the future .. dear Mary. I am very glad- As to M[r] Boyd, I cant be glad. Jane holds him in a spell. I should have thought that he w[d] not have followed an angel into a crowd & a noise- Why how can he *bear* a noise, such as Arabel describes? My best love to him when she sees him next .. but I shall have his letter, I suppose, before then. Were the Bevans not at the marriage, that you dont mention them- I

No. 2684 9 July [1847] 245

never doubted his being an excellent, conscientious man——only my dearest Henrietta, he certainly does accept the teaching of men. What is a Church? You call it a *she*. But "she" is just a compound idea: to the compounding of which, go, Snokes (bishop of Jerusalem) Snooks (bishop of Rome) .. Sneaks (archbishop of Canterbury) .. if not D.ʳ Pusey of Oxford- I dont mean to make unseemly jests .. but the truth is that a church is made of *men*—and that to say "I follow the Church" and "I follow no man's teaching" is to say two contrary things. Ask if it is'nt so, the teacher you most respect. Nothing is so dangerous as to set up words—without analyzing them- A church *means* an assembly of men. Holy & venerable men perhaps ... but men *incapable of an error*? .. there, is the question, solved in different ways by churchmen, so called, & dissenters therefore dissenting. I forgot when speaking of Carlyle to tell you that he told us of Miss Martineau's having called on him the day before he wrote .. "As brown as a berry, full of life, vivacity, dogmatism, & all the gospels of the east wind". She has been to Jerusalem since last autumn. M.ʳ Westwood's letter at any time!—— There's no haste nor cause for it. Will Miss Mitford call on you, I wonder. Mind you see her, if you have the opportunity- I have not heard from her these three months, & am set wondering—but perhaps she wondered first at my silence, her previous letter having reached me when I was unequal to any sort of writing- Explain, when you see her.

Œconomical people you & Arabel are, to make Arabella Bevan's bridal bonnets do such double duty- My white crape one, bought the other day, is positively waxing dusty- The dust here is like the smoke in London: if we return presently to Florence, I must get Wilson to cover it, I almost fear. My little front-caps you asked about, she makes very prettily of net in the old fashion, but with a worsted edge, as slight as possible to be embroidered at all- You think they look heavy & hot? Not in the least—and so they are washable like a pocket handkerchief, & very pretty, at the expense of a few pennies—(Seven pence a cap!) I advise you to try the morning effect of one. Robert likes them so, that I scarcely wear anything else, & have them in various colours, blue, green, lilac, purple, with my hair done in the old Grecian plait behind, which Wilson sighs in the doing of, & unflatteringly (yet oh, so pleasantly!) refers to the old days when "Miss Arabel's looked beautiful, plaited *in* that way." There is no ribbon, except for the strings—he hates ribbon, & prefers everything as simple & quiet as possible, and we never quarrel about the more or less glory .. yes, I think my gloves were accused of a want of brightness one day .. charged with dirtiness & a hole—but even then we did'nt quarrel. I was calm & changed them-

Dont I improve in wisdom & drawing? Really it seems so to me! This half page could scarcely be exceeded perhaps on either ground,—and it must explain a little by the intense heat of the weather, in which one's brains melt away, & one's paper *perspires* in the manner of blotting paper, & for every hair-line you wish to make, you make a tail. Talking of hair, I was observing to Robert the other day, à propos to a little girl of about fourteen who was beginning to be quite bald at the forehead & temples, how curiously the Italians are defective in this respect of baldness .. as I told Arabel in opposition to her and that fancy- "Why," he said, "dont you know the meaning of that? They never comb their hair." He assured me it was simply so—& that at Naples the women plaited up their long tresses in silver & gold, & there an end .. sleeping, waking, eating, living, till the plait & the silver were apt to drop off together. The little girl—aforesaid, opened the gate to us when we went the other evening to see Galileo's villa, where Milton visited him, at the top of Bellosguardo one of the beautiful hills round Florence.[11] We drove there one evening, & had the honour of being jammed in, on the road, with the Grand Duke's carriage, who in return for our respectful salutation, took off his hat in the sun- We were on our way, for our parts, to see higher dignities .. the place of Milton's & Galileo's steps. The villa itself too, apart from association, was worth seeing—perched on a green eminence, a little terrace overlooking beautiful, beautiful Florence garlanded with olive yards & vineyards, & shining with her own marbles: and if the eye sweeps beyond .. mountains, mountains on all sides! We were struck with a sudden temptation (at least *I* was!) to take some rooms in the villa (which we might do) & be false to Vallambrosa—but no, after all it was not worth the monastery & the forest .. & besides Robert spoilt everything by suggesting .. "And the sightseers who come day by day .. what sh^d we do with the sightseers"? No, it would not have answered our purpose at all.-

Very sorry indeed we were for the poor Surteeses- Always I have forgotten to tell you that. Do tell us whatever you may hear further of them, & whether Miss Surtees[12] is likely to remain in England. He hated Italy & seemed as unhappy & out of place as possible, Robert said- Tell Arabel that Mr Powers's Eve is *not* in London—is not finished in fact.[13] He has exhibited only the Greek Slave, of last year or the year before, and the Boy listening to the shell, in the present- I wish in return that she w^d tell *me* the last artist to whom the new pictures in Wimpole Street are attributed. The great Christ over the fire .. to whom? The Holy Family to the left .. to whom?[14] Are there any other pictures bought? tell me. You would smile to see how interested I have grown in the Jamaica crops &c- Robert shows me the least of the news that way, & certainly it never interested me so before. But I think now of the pleasure it gives my poor dearest Papa- I like to think that he is in good spirits- As to dear dear Stormie, it is not for his sake so much- Crops are not wanted to make him rich—and a little liberty is, I know, a nearer object with him in leaving home than all the rest. Let me have every detail of him, .. and mind you get him to write to me. Sometimes I think & turn round in my thoughts in every light, the question of writing again to Papa- If there were a certainty even that he wᵈ put the letter *into the fire*, why I shᵈ have done it long ago—but it is dreadful to have one's letters sent back *so*¹⁵ .. you dont imagine what a shock it is—and it makes Robert angry .. makes him think Papa cruel & hard. God Himself might wonder to look down & see human beings thrusting aside the hearts that love them most,

⟨...⟩¹⁶

But no, not for ⟨my⟩self, will the beloved make an allowance, enlarge in sympathy, extend a pardon- I will not write any more of this. I have no pride, for ⟨my⟩ own part, only let me say .. & for having grieved & displeased any of them I am sorry .. & not least sorry when I enter least into their views—but whether I *have been right or wrong, they* ARE *wrong now* .. or there is ⟨no⟩ right in Love—neither right nor significance—&—they are wrong who stand aloof from me thus & thus----

Fanny Handford [sic] ⟨doubted⟩ that she could remain in London l⟨ong⟩ enough to see ⟨you. How⟩ unfortunate it was for Arabel to have ⟨missed⟩ her visit. She left a very pleasant ⟨...⟩ with us, & we too wᵈ have been glad if she cᵈ have stayed longer- While I think of it, Wilson (who is delighted by the way, with your remembrance of her) complains grievously of dear Minny's never writing- She begs me to say ⟨...⟩ I ask for a message, that she is disappointed by Minny's silence, Wilson ⟨is⟩ angry with her sister Fanny's ⟨...⟩.¹⁷ Her sister has not written since she ⟨ca⟩me to London. Exiles, like us, care for letters, as no one else in the world can .. except lovers- Remember *that*, all of you- Only my sisters are perfect—*almost* perfect .. for I waited too long for the last letter. Tell Arabel who does'nt like to hear it, that Robert hears from home just three times to my hearing!—not long letters though it's fair to say. We are the coolest people to his family, you can conceive of, sending always a heap of inclosures, and just an envelope the size of this paper. Oh, you may well exclaim! I have refused again & again to be a party to such a thing, (Robert might do it with his letters but for *me*, it seemed different) but Mʳˢ Browning was quite hurt—& insisted that we shᵈ both go on sinning & sinning ... What wᵈ you say if I enclosed to you six sealed letters, & wrote six lines on the envelope? We began by sending through the Rothschilds, but there was a delay which Mʳˢ Browning did not like- Well, I shall make Robert let me send this directly to Treppy's- While we were at breakfast this morning came a card & a note .. "Will Mʳ & Mʳˢ Browning permit a young American who has known them in his own home, to obtrude on their seclusion for a few moments by paying them his respects?" Only the second American since we have been to Florence,—& nobody c^d be angry .. so of c⟨ourse⟩ ⟨...⟩ A M.[r] Curtis,[18] says the card. I think I told you of the other visit, & of the American newspaper which was sent to our visitor,[19] containing an extract from a French paper which mentioned piteously that the English poetess EBB had *gone blind* as people say of horses. Wilson has at last (talking of eyes) ventured into the gallery: but she only went to the door of the Tribune, being struck back by the indecency of the Venus–[20] I laughed .. laughed, when she told me– She thinks she shall try again, & the troublesome modesty may subside .. who knows? but really the sight of that marble goddess .. & Titian's[21] (painted stark), just overhead, were too much at first– She is quite well, & so am I, in spite of the heat. Florence w^d agree, I think, with any one. Tell my dearest Treppy that my heart sprang up to meet her message. I do like so much to be still & ever her "precious child"– Tell her that I love her dearly, & that Robert & I, in having our coffee from her gift, talk of her often & often as if we both loved her.. as we do. May God bless you all! Darling Arabel will mind to write soon .. & then you—to your own affectionate

                                                                                    Ba–

Address, on integral page: Via France—Angleterre. / To the care of Miss Tripsack / (Miss Barrett) / 5– Upper Montagu Street / Montagu Square / London.
Publication: Huxley, pp. 33–39 (in part).
Source: Transcript in editors' file.

    1. Year provided by postmark.
    2. Annie Boyd and Henry William Hayes were married on 1 August 1837 in the St. Marylebone Church by the Rev. Edward Johnstone; the Brownings had been married by the Rev. Thomas Woods Goldhawk (see letter 2606, note 2).
    3. Cf. Acts 9:5.
    4. "Nevertheless," or "all the same."
    5. The announcement of Horne's marriage appeared in *The Times* of 26 June 1847, and read: "On the 17th inst., R.H. Horne, Esq., to Catherine, daughter of the late David Foggo, Esq." Horne's marriage to Catherine Clare St. George Foggo (1826–93) in St. Pancras Church was witnessed by Thomas Southwood Smith and Georgiana Harrington Barrie. For EBB's reference to Susan Cook, see letter 2670, note 9.
    6. Letter 2682.
    7. "Will mitigate the excessive heat."
    8. "Estimable family."
    9. According to Murray's *Hand-Book for Travellers to Northern Italy* (1847), on which EBB seems to be relying for her information, Guido Aretino was "among the remarkable men who have been monks of Vallombrosa" (p. 583), who follow the rule of St. Benedict. Murray's *Hand-Book* describes the journey from Florence to Vallombrosa as 18½ miles, and from Vallombrosa to Camaldoli and La Verna an additional 27 miles (pp. 582 and 584).
    10. John Kenyon's brother Edward (1786?–1856) lived with his Austrian wife Louisa in Vienna. We are unable to identify to which of their many Jamaican cousins EBB is referring.
    11. EBB is referring to the Villa Segni at Bellosguardo, which Galileo occupied from 1617 until 1631 (cf. *Casa Guidi Windows*, I, 1179–84); however, Galileo was living at the Villa Gioiello at Arcetri, near Poggio Imperiale, when Milton visited Florence in 1638;

see Murray's *Hand-Book*, p. 574. This visit between poet and astronomer was the subject of one of Landor's *Imaginary Conversations* (1846), which EBB would have presumably remembered.

12. Robert Surtees's wife, Elizabeth, had died on 8 May 1847. Their daughter, Margaret Caroline Surtees (1816-69) and her father were back in Pisa in October (see letter 2707). She married Theodore Bryett in England in 1862. See letter 2624, note 7.

13. See letter 2680, note 8.

14. Evidently new pictures had been acquired and hung after the cleaning and redecorating of 50 Wimpole Street the previous autumn. We are unable to identify the works referred to here; however, in the catalogue of the effects of EBB's father, sold after his death, there is listed a "Holy Family" by Bronzino, described as "a very grand composition," and a work by Alonzo Vazquez of "the three Maries, mourning over the dead Christ ... a most important work" (*Reconstruction*, p. 605). Another "Holy Family" by Domenico Ghirlandaio is among the list of pictures in Wimpole Street made by EBB's brother Alfred in 1853; see *Reconstruction*, L182.

15. See letter 2630, note 2.

16. The last part of this manuscript, written on the covering sheet, is extensively damaged, which evidently occurred in transit.

17. Frances Wilson (b. 1822). For an account of Wilson and her family, see vol. 13, Appendix I.

18. George William Curtis (1824-92), American author and journalist, was travelling in Europe with his brother Burrill, Christopher Cranch, and Cranch's wife Elizabeth. He had been in southern Italy and was on his way to France. Curtis published an account of his meeting with the poets in *Harper's New Monthly Magazine* for September 1861, which was later revised and reissued in the same publication for March 1890. For the text of these articles, see pp. 408-412.

19. See letter 2675, notes 2 and 3, and letter 2676, note 5.

20. i.e., the Venus de Medici.

21. The "Venus of Urbino" (1538) depicts the goddess nude and recumbent; it was brought to Florence in 1631 as part of the Della Rovere legacy.

2685. JOSEPH ARNOULD TO RB

18. Victoria Square, Pimlico
20 July. 1847.

My dear Browning

Silence is the sole extenuation of a fault that admits of no defence; I will not therefore even raise a hand against the sentence that I know must pass against me for my long silence. Something I could say about a long & dreary task now just brought to a close, a sorry law book which has not only kept body, but mind too, so strictly confined within a narrow range of place, & of thought, that neither the one nor the other have been even of their usual poor service to my friends: now however I am within sight of shore & though "no pomp or pæan glorious"[1] attends the return from such a cruise, yet I am content to take it as a sign of better times, that I find myself able to write to you. I heard from Domett (you always ask with such interest about him that I take him first in order) 3 days ago date of his letter 17 January last: at that time he had been for some months a member of the legislative council, &

was evidently (spite of his modesty one could see this) first friend & confident of Grey the clever & able governor;[2] whose policy hitherto has been merely putting into act, what Domett had previously advised on paper: since then, the present government have entirely identified themselves with the New Zealand land Company, have passed a bill conceding to the Company more than they even desired, or, to say the truth, deserved. I have not the remotest doubt from the high esteem in which our friend is held by them, that his future is quite made unless he takes more determined pains to mar it; than I think even he is likely to do.

Of poor Chris. Dowson of course you have heard: about 9 months back he broke a small blood vessel;[3] (either in the throat or chest—they do not it seems know which) in itself I believe the matter was a very trifle; but you know his highly sensitive & nervous temperament: well the thing has had the effect of so entirely prostrating his spirits, that he has been only the shadow, the very ghost of his former self (mentally I mean)—all his quips & cranks gone poor fellow, & in their place a low, fixed melancholy very painful to witness: at last his good little wife who has behaved to perfection in the whole matter got him to think that a voyage to S! Petersburgh & back would amuse him more than anything else—& so about three weeks back, leaving the children behind she started with him. I make no doubt that it shall do him great good & we are soon expecting to hear of his arrival. Chorley I know tells you, what he being in the centre of the great wheel of fashion—, perpetually standing whip in hand in the middle of the giddy merry-go-round of scandal, small talk & (God save the mark) *literature!*—can really tell you better than almost any body, viz how the world goes on where "reeking London's smoky caldron simmers"[4]—he has been working this year double tides—having had two operas going the whole season- Literature however, for this season, has given the critics a complete holiday—there having been I think not even a novel worth a nine days wonder.

We are just going to Election without a cry[5]—unless which the Lord forbid, they get up the old abomination of the Church in danger—No Popery—& No Education- How delightfully little the great nation & its great doings must seem to you in Vallombrosa—do the Etrurian shades, by the bye, really embower there high-overarched[6]—for your sake, in these heats, I hope so; for even here we have had a week of temperature ranging from 75 to 80 Fahrenheit & yours must be at least 10 degrees higher[.]

I am going to take this down with me to Hatcham to morrow & keep it open in order to tell you in one of the corners how they are all looking. — My wife desires her kindest regards to Mrs Browning & yourself, will you add mine & believe me my dear Browning

your affte friend
Joseph Arnould

No. 2685   20–21 July 1847   251

I dare not *say* write soon, after my last gap of silence—but I *mean* it.

Hatcham New Cross
July 21st

I brought this with me to Hatcham purposely to give you a genuine account how they are all looking[:] Impressive[.] Mrs Browning is apparently stronger & better than I have almost ever seen her—always cheerful & *really* in all respects looking far better than she did this time last year.

Your Sister I have done nothing but pay compliments to since I came in—if compliments those can be called which were the sincere expressions of my pleasure at seeing her in all respects so fully in possession of free elastic cheerful health.

Mr Browning, looks a little fagg'd as all we London working people do with the late heats which have indeed been as I think I told you intense– We all trust you will be back next spring– Mrs. Browning especially has that thought above & beyond all other thoughts uppermost in her mind: to her I am sure it would be new life. To think you were really resolved so to do! So I *do* trust you will– By the bye—we all executed the deeds—in due form last Tuesday week– I do so long to have a *trust dinner* honoured by the presence of the cestui que trusts[7]—there if that is not a lawyers anticipation I don't know what is! never mind it is none the less sincere– God bless you my dear friend– I wish you could feel the grasp of the hand I give you in mine.

Address, on integral page: Robert Browning Esqre / Poste Restante / Florence / Italy.
Publication: None traced.
Manuscript: Alexander Turnbull Library.

1. Cf. *Paracelsus*, IV, 471.
2. See letter 2662, note 4.
3. This led to Dowson's death in September 1848.
4. Byron, *Beppo* (1818), XLIII, 8.
5. A reference to the general election held the following week. The "Chronicle" of *The Annual Register* for 1847 explained that since "the old Parliament had been dissolved from consideration of the near efflux of the time limited by the constitution for the existence of any one Parliament, and not upon any political consideration, and as the great party questions had either been laid at rest or confounded with other circumstances, the present was probably the most quiet general election which has ever occurred" (p. 95).
6. An allusion to Milton, *Paradise Lost*, I, 303–304.
7. i.e., the persons who will benefit by the trust. Arnould is referring to his appointment as a trustee to the Brownings' marriage settlement.

2686. EBB TO ARABELLA MOULTON-BARRETT

Florence. Palazzo Guidi. Via Maggio.
July 26– [1847][1]

My own dearest Arabel,
I had said & promised myself to make up for the lightness of the scale on Henrietta's side, by writing this present letter to her, but since it must relate to your particular subject of Vallombrosa, where you agreed to go & live with us, you have a right to it I think, & I make over the two next times instead, to the beloved creditor– For we have been to Vallombrosa, Arabel—we have been .. seen & "came away conquered,"[2] excommunicated, thrust out ignominiously by the Father Abbot .. who being a holy man, "cant abide" anything impure & feminine to keep a stinking in his nostrils above three days– Now let me begin from the beginning– We left M. Centofanti's house on the wednesday of last week .. nearly a week before our time was up, just as we thought the heavens & earth of Florence were about to be dissolved downright, so excessive the heat was. Thermometer at eighty five, and my bedroom growing furnacelike by three in the morning, & the state of the atmosphere rendering the noises of that street (which always were the great evil of the position) scarcely endurable. So we fled before it all, drove round the city at eight or nine in the evening to say goodbye to M[r] Powers & the Hoppners, and at *four* the next morning were swallowing our last Florentine breakfast as it seemed to us, & in the carriage immediately afterwards– Even at that hour the heat was wonderful—we left Florence steeped in a hot vapour, and every mile seemed to throw off a blanket– At a less early hour there w[d] have been no travelling at all, though we soon were in the mountains & able to breathe– The carriage took us to Pelago,[3] a little mountain-village perched on the rocks where the road for wheels, (the *via rotabile*) stopped altogether; & so far it was a delightful drive & we were in great spirits, .. the scenery rejoicing our eyes with hill & valley, purple hills & vine-covered vallies, & the river rushing at our right hand as a companion of the road. As the carriage stopped at Pelago, before the door of the little inn, a voice said "M[rs] Browning"—and I started as well I might, at being called by my name in that wilderness by any mortal voice. It was M[r] Curtis, our American friend, who introduced himself to us by letter as I told you, & had taken coffee with us one evening in Florence, impressing us most agreeably by his refinement & cultivation—quite remarkable in so young a man, for he cant be more than five & twenty I sh[d] think– He is travelling with his brother & two or three

other American young men, and their plans had drawn some three of them to Vallombrosa where they meant to sleep, he said, & leave the place on the following day. We heard all about it in the little inn while our conveyances were being prepared– The Americans very considerately w.d not intrude on us, & went forwards on horseback. Robert too rode,—only keeping by me of course: and Wilson and I took our places as my illustration shows, in what they call a sledge or *treggia*, but which is nothing but a common wine-hamper, (you know those brown baskets) with two chairs tied into it by ropes, for us to sit on, and a little hay (disagreeably populous) strewn at the bottom– There is no wheel of any kind; & two white oxen dragged it as if they dragged a plough. A second sledge of the same fashion took our luggage,— and so we set off, with four wild looking men to drive the four white oxen & prevent accidents at the dangerous places—and really you w.d have opened your eyes if you could have seen at all the way we were bound for. A more romantic excursion, could scarcely be I think, and when I tell you that we were four hours in travelling five miles, you will have some notion perhaps of the difficulties of the road– Then, the scenery! Precipices striking down from under the feet of our oxen into the deep dark gullies, dark with shade,— rocks above, straining upwards as precipitiously,—& mountains, mountains everywhere, on all sides, as if they caught one from another an aspiration to the Infinite—often I thought of Malvern– Malvern was nearest of all that I had seen to what I saw– But then the wildest and the greatest of Malvern was but as the *seed* of this grand, developped nature– Where the Malvern hills throw out a single ridge, here are seven times seven of hills– You remember Walm's Well?[4] Take the remembrance, & multiply it fifty times, & you fall below the sight of what I saw– A sort of paved path, impossible indeed to wheels, threaded up & down the mountain ground—and how we descended without rolling, & ascended at all, is a little wonderful to me when I think of it coldly now– "As steep as a house" may be an exaggeration— but "as steep as the Leaning Tower" scarcely any– I was so frightened about Robert's horse! Only these horses receive a peculiar education, & w.d walk up & down stairs without blinking or stumbling– Well! five hours we spent in climbing, .. & our poor oxen were so fatigued that I moaned in the spirit through sympathy for them, & Wilson & Flush & I got out to let them breathe & sate in the chesnut forest– By the way Flush was very lazy & insisted on sitting in the sledge when rather he might as well have run by the side– The truth however was that Flush was distraught with fright– The whole time he was at Vallombrosa he never recovered his equanimity,—& nothing could be plainer both to Robert, Wilson & me than his manner of protesting against the whole scheme of going out into the wilderness, among the mountains & pines & waterfalls, away from civilization & little dogs. There was a black pine-forest close by the monastery which was his special horror: he would not leave the hem of my petticoat when we walked there– And when Wilson took him up the hills, why, there at the ridge of the steeper places, he used to sit & see her safe to the bottom, & look & pause & muse till he was called "cowardly Flush,".. with one foot out in the air– He likes fresh fields!.. as many of those as you please!—but for wild solitary nature, 'no, I thank you', says Flush .. 'there's neither pleasure nor safety in it'. He w^d as soon trust himself in a den of cats as near a convent of monks– But I was telling you of our ascent to them– Up from Pelago, .. straight up we went, along a thread of mountain-path which wrapt round & round & still up & up those savage eminences– The first mountains, skirted with grey olives & vineyards which seemed to creep upward painfully as far as they could & then let go– Beyond the mountains were mountains & presently we had to drop down into the gorge to the right & cross the torrent & pass into the chesnut forest & climbing[,] climb there more than ever– At the end of four hours, we had arrived– The monastery stood vast & blank before us, on a strip of tableland, flanked with pine woods– Arched with the mountains– To the left, was an open stretch of Prospect .. a great sea of Appenines .. I counted a fold of eight mountain ridges, all wild & purple. The nearest were clung to by the woods—beach woods, chesnut woods, pine woods– The monks may cut with a thousand axes, but those woods are too strong for them still– Now look at the monastery

Something like it,
only the mountains are higher, & I cant throw out the grey island of rock where the chapel stands with any expression. There is another rock-island opposite, on which is the hermitage– The "house of strangers"[5] where we were received, faces the tower of the monastery, & is after this fashion containing simply a few rooms on the ground floor. Here the women-guests go, and their husbands or fathers—otherwise all male strangers betake themselves to the monastery itself. The Americans dined with us, & we had dinner on our arrival– I was dreadfully tired as you may imagine, & the magnificent scenery could scarcely do more than make me feel that I had a soul somewhere, if I could but get at it. Then Father Egidio had come to assure Robert that we were most welcome for three days, but that no power in Heaven or earth, except the Pope's or Archbishop of Tuscany's could induce his Abbot to admit of our staying longer– What we had called .. a "permission," was merely a "recommendation", & inefficient in the case.

Robert poured floods of eloquent amiability against the iron of this resolve—
no, nothing would achieve anything– Afterwards he was half vexed & swore
that he never had been so "subservient" in his life before, & that he "only
did it for *me* & that I sh.d not be disappointed"—"those idiots of monks"!
(relieving himself from the pressure of his own compliments, in an aside!)
So provoking it was, after we had brought the whole of our possessions & a
dozen of port up to that eagle's nest in the clouds, .. to be pecked out by the
eagle! I was lying on the sofa perfectly exhausted, for my part, & failed in
power to protest even against Robert's desperate crisis of appeal in my behalf, as having written about & translated from the Greek Fathers! Yes, he
was driven to that, I assure you. "She is'nt frivolous like women in general,
though she looks young enough still .. as you, padre reverendissimo,[6] may
see". The reverend father smiled benignantly, but evidently thought that no
woman in the world young or old-looking could be called otherwise than
frivolous except by an heretical device– As to the Gregories & Chrysostoms,
he never had *heard* of them at all, I fancy, unless in some dim, indefinite
way, as more modern saints than St Joseph perhaps. He said that our American friends (very goodnatured of them) had spoken highly of us both, as
literary persons &c &c .. and when Robert assured him in conclusion, by
way of producing a final, thrilling effect, that we never ate anything nor
caused any sort of trouble, he could say beside only that he would do what
he could for us, & procure us two more days if possible,–– Beyond the *five*
days, was no possibility. So there we had to yield, the Lord divo[7] being obdurate. We stayed from wednesday to monday, & it was all. On thursday
morning I did not feel well & looked worse, and Robert fell into despair &
declared that he never saw such a difference in anyone, from three days before, ... until it was discovered that the confusion had caused Wilson & me
to forget my medecine both at night & in the morning;!! which, added to the
fatigue, had produced the evil of course. I set myself right in an hour, & was
very well indeed afterwards, *so* well, that we had a little talk about an extravagant project of plunging deeper into the mountains & extending our
pilgrimage to the more distant convents of Laverna & Camaldoli[8] .. only it
w.d have involved *thirty miles* of either riding on mule back or sledge-driv-
ing, and there might be imprudence, ... we thought, ... though we went
ever so slowly. Some day we may return & attempt it—oh, we dont give it
up for ever. Because there are intermediate villages––and if we travelled
only four miles a day in the glorious mountain-wilderness, it w.d be a peopling
of one's dreams for the whole of a life– For the rest, it was probably a less
evil than first appeared, that we sh.d have been restrained from our intended
two months retreat at Vallombrosa. With all drawbacks, I sh.d have liked it,
mind—still there were drawbacks. In the first place, we were there as mere
guests & dependents. What we paid (though our payment was more than

sufficient to cover our expenses) was to be considered as a pure *gift* to the convent;—& what we received, as the purest *hospitality* .. for which we were to return ever so much pure gratitude over & above. In this position, we could make no request for little matters necessary to our comfort– If waiting an hour for breakfast, (between the hot water & dry toast) & having the coffee altogether forgotten at night, struck us as an inconvenience, we had to look in one another's face & be "*contentissimi*", perfectly satisfied. We were never sure of strangers not being thrust into the midst of us, never– There was not a woman within reach of service, of course; & the beds were made by a young 'secular', who attended to other details of the same class– Then as for food, .. you know I profess to care for nothing, if I can have good bread & eggs .. & coffee for a luxury--and in going to Vallombrosa, Robert meant to live upon milk & cheese & fruit, & I on curds & whey, .. fixing on the simplest things. Now these were precisely the things, we could not attain to by any means– Plenty of beef & veal & fish, steeped in floods of oil, .. & the wine—excellent & copious supplies, we had—but we never saw fruit nor vegetables, nor cheese, nor whey .. and the milk was mere city-milk for wateryness, & such as it was, hard to procure—& the butter came & went once in two days like a very apparition .. and the hens of the convent thought it improper to lay more than one egg all the time we stayed. What they called *coffee*, I take to have been the emptyings of the holy water-vase at the monastery door, with the taste & colour of the crossing finger of every holy monk communicating by it some perpetual benediction. Worst of all, the bread was– To call it sour w^d be flattery– Neither was it only bitter: *Nasty* resumes everything. Robert swears that it had in it the "flavour of corruption"- But perhaps it was only made out of sawdust from the firs, & kept with the beef .. which combination will account for a good deal. These things I call drawbacks, and if we had stayed as we wished, certainly we sh^d have been thinner by force of them– Still .. we did wish to stay. The glorious scenery .. the black, breathless silence of pine-forests, .. the sweep of the infinite mountains, the sound of water breaking on & gurgling down among the rocks .. these were greater things than a mere care for bodily comforts could counterbalance. I thought, while Robert & I & Father Egidio were walking together in the forest of pines, how strange it was, & how I sh^d have started to have seen myself *so* in a vision, some three years since. I thought too of you, my own Arabel, & how strange it w^d seem to you & Henrietta if you caught a sudden glance at us from England– I walked out two or three times a day every day we spent there, & sate out of doors in the woods & enjoyed it as much as I could; but Robert & I falling into a sudden panic or prudence, I did not as we had planned, take a mule & ride out farther– We may go again, without the panic perhaps—we shall see. Father

No. 2686 26 July [1847] 257

Egidio led him to the more salient places & showed him all the sights hidden from my eyes .. for of course they would'nt permit an unclean beast like me to pass the threshold of monastery or chapel .. oh no!– Out of spite however, when nobody was looking, I put my foot through the gateway & stamped on the gravel of their courtyard—(see the gate in my drawing)– There, was profanation for them, poor men! The little Abbot will have had a visitation of Satan through it, by this time, after the manner of St Anthony.⁹ If it had'nt been for Robert who w^{dnt} let me, I should have run in & opened the way for a troop of devils, so provoked I was– These monks are Benedictines & said to be for the most part wholly noble & originally rich– They have each an apartment & food supplied, and from four to six pounds for a yearly income of pocket money[.] Father Egidio is the only one who had intercourse with us, it being his peculiar province to attend to the guests (he is likely to be Abbot some day!),—and a goodnatured, narrow-minded uneducated host we found him, .. gently insinuating at the close, that although he was forbidden by the Rule to receive *money*, his hands were free toward other gifts, & that several strangers had presented him with snuffboxes, coffee pots & the like– In reply to which, we really could'nt give him Trippy's coffee pot—and, having no snuffbox in either pocket, we had to delay our generosity to another occasion–¹⁰

—Well—so we passed the time till monday, .. reading the Life of San Gualberto¹¹ (who established the monastery) & learning from that only book within our reach, how spiritual holiness & benediction float in the air of the place & purge the waters thereof, & how no mortal soul can approach the mountain, without partaking the sanctifying advantage. Certainly we lost there the very memory almost of the heat of Florence– The change of temperature was extraordinary– Wilson & I had to put on our flannel petticoats as soon as we c^d unpack them, and even then we were rather too cool– Once or twice somebody talked of "shivering with cold"—& somebody else said "Do shut that window"– But on monday morning it all ended; & in order to escape the dreadful Heat which waited to catch us up again in the valley, it was agreed that we sh^d set off at four. At three, we were up, & having hoarded the dry toast of the previous evening (which was'nt *much* harder than a slice of fir tree) we soaked it in the glass of port wine Wilson had provided for me, & so she & Robert & I broke fast for the day, & then set out on our travels– Sledges as before—and the descent rather alarming, I assure you. But oh, how grand the mountains were, rending the clouds & feeling through them for the sun! Never shall I forget the glory of that morning's spectacle. We came down so much faster than we went up, that we reached Florence at nine oclock, and it was very much like going into the fire. But, Arabel, where could we go? There seemed no choice, no alternative. We had missed

Vallambrosa after considerable expense of both strength & money, & were not rich enough to begin a hunt after cool places—and all we had to do was to make the best of our disappointment & take Florence at its shadiest side.

⟨...⟩[12]

So back we came to Florence, & home to M. Centofanti's .. a day or two of our time remaining there. Annunziata,[13] the servant who had served us & was still in the house, rushed down stairs in an ecstasy, & after rapturously kissing both my hands threw herself into Wilson's arms. It was really a scene—and to tell you a secret to boot, Robert & I were the happiest of disappointed people when we found ourselves on the old sofa & the breakfast table drawn close to it– We laughed & talked exultingly over the coffee & bread & butter, & praised them up to the height of the Ideal of coffee & bread & butter, .. we never had seen coffee & bread & butter before, you w^d have thought certainly–!. Still, the coffee passed away & the heat remained .. a blind smothering heat. Night would come, & how was I to sleep in my bedroom? Fitter that room was, to bake rolls in– So after breakfast I lay stretched on the sofa & Robert went out (poor dearest Robert) to try to get cooler rooms, .. the coolest rooms he c^d get in Florence– Two or three times he came back in despair, looking *white* with exhaustion, .. but at last the grand success befel us .. at last .. the next day .. and we have been in our new apartment now these five or six days. Such fortunate people we are: it is extraordinary I think– We thought at Pisa that we did well in an apartment, .. but at M. Centofanti's we did so much better that we took to scorning Pisa altogether—and here is best, best of all—you w^d be rather surprised if you saw what an apartment we have in this Palazzo Guidi, a few steps from the Grand Duke's palace & in THE situation of Florence & close too to the Boboli Gardens to which we are to have daily access in right of our position, and on the first floor besides.[14] Of course, we could not achieve such rooms except now in the dead part of the season, but with every consideration, it is cheap & happy & I wonder to find myself here as successor to a Russian Prince, & suite with satin couches & arm chairs "à discretion"– And we pay precisely what we paid M. Centofanti .. a guinea a week .. with an additional nine shillings the month to the porter who is a necessary part of the grandeur it appears, & lights the staircase & brings water & so on– The rooms, that is the drawingroom diningroom & my bedroom are very large, very much larger than any room in Wimpole Street, & furnished & overfurnished as I told you, .. marble consoles, carved & gilt arm chairs, all in crimson & white satin, noble mirrors, & instead of the memorable Pisan spoons (or spoon, was it?) such splendours fit for the entertainment of the court of Tuscany, that we grow a little nervous for fear of being ruined to the end of our days by the chipping of a teacup.

No. 2686   26 July [1847]   259

There's the plan of the apartment! The eight windows which are very large, opening from ceiling to floor, open on a sort of balcony-terrace .. not quite a terrace, yet no ordinary balcony neither .. which is built out from the house, giving it an antique & picturesque appearance to the exterior– And you may suppose what a pleasure it is to have such a place to walk up & down in, when we are not inclined to go into the streets. Opposite is the grey wall of a church, San Felice,[15] and we walk on the balcony listening to the organ & choir– Nothing can be much more delightful after all—so let the monks keep their Vallombrosa– Robert was unwell with pain in his head, all the time we were there, the consequence *he* thought, of a slight smell of paint in the House of Strangers, but just as attributable to the food, perhaps .. whereas here at Florence we are all well, it agrees with us all three, let us burn through it ever so– As for coolness we are cooler than at M. Centofanti's considerably—at night particularly. I can sleep, & the oppression loses itself in these large rooms, where the sun never comes except for a side-glance. Still, every place in Florence must be hot, & you would be rather amused to see the costume I appear in day by day–

⟨...⟩[16]

You know I have my mantilla—and besides Robert insists on it that I look just as well without any, .. & seriously he proposed to me the other morning that I never sh.d put them on again. And the white gowns he particularly admires,--Oh, I assure you there never was a less critical husband in the world. As long as I eat enough, & have my hair in tolerable curl & wear clean gloves, all the rest pleases however it be—and the eating enough is the chief thing. We have taken our apartment for two months certain, & may have it perhaps for a third month—after which the world is all before us where to wander,[17] & I cant tell you what our plans are, they shift so, and are so dependent on circumstances independent of us– Also, we have agreed, seeing how an excess of scheming defeats itself, to leave the future alone a little .. God takes the best care of us and events fall into their places without our meddling over much– It is curious how Robert *gets his wishes*! Since we have been in Florence, walking carelessly past this palace & admiring the architecture, he has wished two or three times to live here ... just as you might in a fancy wish to live .. where shall I say? .. at Northumberland House or Chiswick! He did not suppose even that appartments were to be let here— ... yet here, lo! we are! The next thing may be that the Grand Duke may invite us to occupy the left wing of the Pitti .. I dont know what's to come next. What

nonsense I write to you, to be sure! We have taken Anunziata with us in our
⟨place⟩ of residence- Flush likes it much better, he ⟨...⟩ than he liked the
mountains- At about eight in the evening we walk in the comparative cool
.. stand on the bridge of Santa Trinita,[18] & go eat an ice at Dony's .. then
return to supper, & dont sit up three m⟨inutes⟩ afterwards- Think of our
taking a dozen of port wine up to Vallombrosa! That was Robert's insisting
for thought for *me* & he *will* make me hold to the port wine, though it is
quite unnecessary, so well I am--none the worse for the fatigue- Which
surprises me- We did not expect an opportunity of such bold adventure, and
in the midst of it, when it was too late to go back, I certainly feared that I
might suffer in some way—but you see——— Give my love to dear M.[r]
Boyd & thank him very much for his kind letter which I will answer soon-
It is delightful to me, tell him, to be remembered by him so affectionately ..
Always, dear Arabel, let me have the least detail which reaches you about
Stormie. Give him my love & pray him to write to me- My love to them all.
I had a letter from M.[rs] Martin while George was with her, & she talks of his
'*success*'——is it true? Such kindness too she writes to me of myself, & of
her "exulting" sympathy in my happiness- I imagine that the Hanfords have
spoken of us to her very kindly .. I mean, of us *both*- Indeed I could not
understand how anyone could see Robert for an hour, & not carry away a
pleasant impression—I say *that* as if in the capacity of the Goddess Justice
herself, carved in marble in the Piazza & holding the scales[19]—*far* on the
outside of all affection & intimate knowledge- What he is to *me*, only God
knows. We shall be here to keep our wedding day on the 12th of September,
& we mean to do it very jovially—very thankfully, I hope. Neither of us has
repented for one half moment what was done on that day—that fountain of
blessing for all other days—*repented* .. oh no! And yet there have been pain
& sorrow--only not from *him* to *me* .. nor .. I thank God .. even from *me* to
him. It has been for us, a perfect union of two lives & souls, .. happier than
anyone can understand from these words of mine, or any like them. Let me
hear of Emma .. no more Monro[20] .. do congratulate her from me- It seems
to me that the repetition of such a ceremony, must be *awkward*, to use no
sadder word. She must be glad that it's over. What do you mean about 'morals' in relation to Fiesole? I intended to suggest no moral, I am certain, &
do'nt remember what you refer to. Tell dearest Trippy that I love her & will
write soon to her. Perhaps the Reynoldses will be too charmed with their
house to leave it for Rome-

⟨...⟩[21]

Always mention him particularly .. poor dearest Papa! Ah, if he knew how I
love him through it all!! Kiss Lizzie for me .. Lizzie Barrett. My love to the
Cooks—does Surtees get an appointment? Remember me gratefully to M.[r]

No. 2686　　　　　　　　26 July [1847]　　　　　　　　261

& M.rs Stratten .. mind you do— I hope you had a pleasant day. My beloved Arabel take care of yourself for me & be wise, & *dont* choose a monastic life out of which no good comes— Be certain that no good comes of it ever— See the fruit of it at Vallombrosa! There, be "*morals*" for you! so be quick & gather them up. How is the school? Tell me everything—as I shall tell you, .. when I have anything to tell. Oh, to compare Vauxhall[22] to Florence! Tell Alfred he is a barbarian. Robert has seen Vauxhall, & Wilson the Surrey Gardens, but the sight here—was the wonder of wonders— Write, write— I love you, both of you .. *all* of you, .. & am my own Arabel's

　　　　　　　　　　　　　　　　　　most attached
　　　　　　　　　　　　　　　　　　Ba.

Love to dear Minny— Tell me of Crow—
Robert's best love to you & dearest Henrietta.

Address, on integral page: (To the care of Miss Tripsack) / Miss Arabel Barrett / 5. Upper Montagu Street / Montagu Square / London.
Publication: None traced.
Manuscript: Berg Collection.

　1. Year determined from EBB's reference to the recent trip to Vallombrosa.
　2. Cf. "I came, I saw, I conquered," ("veni, vidi, vici," Plutarch, *Lives: Caesar*, 50).
　3. A small village about 14 miles from Florence on the road to Vallombrosa; see *Aurora Leigh*, I, 111.
　4. A spring on the side of a hill near Hope End; see *Diary*, p.88.
　5. Murray's *Hand-Book for Travellers in Northern Italy* (1847) identifies "a building called the *Forestiera* for the reception of strangers, upon whom it is the duty of one of the monks to attend" (p. 584), presumably, in this case, the Father Egidio mentioned below.
　6. "Most reverend father."
　7. "Divine," i.e., the Abbot.
　8. See letter 2684, note 9.
　9. St. Anthony (ca. 251–356) whose life of solitude in the desert was beset by temptations, artistic representations of which have taken the form of ugly demons, fantastic creatures, or naked women.
　10. Murray's *Hand-Book* explains that "Gentlemen are provided with comfortable beds in the convent; but ladies, who are not allowed to enter the convent, have apartments assigned to them in this building [i.e., the Forestiera]. No charge for board or lodging is made upon the traveller: the usual mode of payment, therefore, is, to give the monk who attends upon strangers a sum of money requesting him to distribute it among the servants" (p. 584).
　11. Giovanni Gualberto (d. 1073) was canonized in 1193. He joined the monastery of San Miniato in 1013, but when a simoniacal abbot was elected, he chose to remove to the monks of Calmaldoli, and from there he retreated to a severer rule of monastic life at Vallombrosa, and eventually formed his order according to the rule of St. Benedict. The order was approved in 1070 by Pope Alexander II. EBB recalls this visit to Vallombrosa and San Gualberto in *Casa Guidi Windows*, I, 1129-64. There are several accounts of his life in verse, as well as the *Historia di San Giovangualberto* (Firenze, 1640) by Diego de Franchi.
　12. Nearly three lines have been obliterated by someone other than EBB.
　13. She was the first of two domestics of this name employed by the Brownings in Florence.

14. The Brownings moved to Palazzo Guidi on 20 July 1847, and, except for the six-and-a-half month period of 19 October 1847 until 9 May 1848, it was their principal residence until EBB's death in June 1861. Soon after the birth of their son in 1849 the Brownings began calling their apartment Casa Guidi, by which name it is known.
15. This ancient church was largely rebuilt in the 14th and 15th centuries. EBB refers to it in the opening lines of *Casa Guidi Windows* (I, 1-2).
16. Three lines have been obliterated, by someone other than EBB.
17. Cf. *Paradise Lost*, XII, 646.
18. According to Murray's *Hand-Book*, "this bridge is a favourite evening walk" (p. 481). Murray's *Hand-Book* also notes "The café Doney, in the Piazza Sta. Trinita is the most frequented in Florence. Doney is the Gunter of Florence as regards ices, confectionary, &c." (p. 474).
19. In the Piazza di Santa Trinità. The porphyry statue by Ferrucci is mounted on a granite column brought from Rome by Cosimo I and erected in 1554 (Murray's *Hand-Book*, p. 528).
20. See letter 2672, note 15.
21. A little more than a line has been obliterated, by someone other than EBB.
22. See letter 2682, note 6.

2687. EBB & RB TO ANNA BROWNELL JAMESON

[In EBB's hand]   Florence. Palazzo Guidi– Via Maggio
but direct as usual Poste Restante
July 29. [1847][1]

You will be surprised perhaps, or perhaps not, dearest friend, to find that we are still at Florence. Florence "holds us with a glittering eye"[2]—there's a charm cast round us, & we cant get away. In the first place your news of Recoaro[3] came so late, that, as you said yourself, we ought to have been there before your letter reached us. Nobody would encourage us to go north on any grounds indeed—and if anybody speaks a word now in favour of Venice, straight comes somebody else speaking the direct contrary. Altogether, we took to making a plan of our own .. a great, wild, delightful plan, of plunging into the mountains & spending two or three months at the monastery of Vallombrosa, until the heat was passed & dear Mr. Kenyon decided, & we could either settle for the winter at Florence or pass on to Rome. Could anything look more delightful than that? Well! We got a letter of recommendation to the Abbot, & left our apartment, via delle belle donne, a week before our three months were done, thoroughly burned out by the sun .. set out at four in the morning, reached Pelago, & from thence travelled five miles along a "via non rotabile"[4] through the most romantic scenery .. oh, such mountains .. as if the whole world were alive with mountains!—such ravines .. black in spite of flashing waters in them! .. such woods & rocks! .. travelled in basket-sledges drawn by four white oxen, .. Wilson & I and the luggage, .. and Robert riding step by step. We were four hours doing the five miles, so you may fancy what rough work it was– Whether I was most tired or charmed was a *tug* between body & soul. The worst was, that there being a new abbot at the monastery, an austere man jealous of his sanctity & the approach of women, our letter & Robert's eloquence to boot, did nothing for us .. & we were ingloriously & ignomin[i]ously expelled at the end of five days. For three days we were welcome .. for two more we kept our ground .. but after *that*, out we were thrust, with baggage & expectations. Nothing could be much more provoking— And yet we came back very merrily for disappointed people to Florence, getting up at three in the morning, & rolling or sliding (as it might happen) down the precipitous path, & seeing round us a morning-glory of mountains, clouds, & rising sun, such as we never can forget—back to Florence & our old lodgings, and an eatable breakfast of coffee & bread, and a confession one to another that if we had won the day instead of losing it & spent our summer with the monks, we should have grown considerably *thinner* by the victory. They make their bread, I rather imagine, with the sawdust of their fir trees——and except oil & wine, yes, & plenty of beef (of *flesch*,[5] as your Germans say, of all kinds, indeed!) which is'nt precisely the fare to suit us, we were thrown for nourishment on the great sights around. Oh, but, so beautiful were mountains & forests & waterfalls, that I could have kept my ground happily for the two months—even though the only book I saw there was the chronicle of their San Gualberto– Is he not among your saints?[6] Being routed fairly & having breakfasted fully at our old apartment, Robert went out to find cool rooms, if possible, & make the best of our position—and now we are settled magnificently in this palazzo Guidi on a first floor, in an apartment which *looks* quite beyond our means & *would be* except in the dead part of the season .. a suite of spacious rooms opening on a little terrace & furnished elegantly .. rather to suit our predecessor the Russian prince, than ourselves .. but cool & in a delightful situation, .. six paces from the piazza Pitti, & with right of daily admission to the Boboli gardens. We pay what we paid in the Via Belle Donne– Is'nt this prosperous? You would be surprised to see *me*, I think, I am so very well (& look so) .. dispensed from being carried up stairs, & inclined to take a run, for a walk, every now & then. I scarcely recognize myself or my ways, or my own spirits, all is so different– Now let me talk of *you*, my dear friend, to whom I never shall change, I hope & believe. With the most earnest sympathy I read what you wrote of dear Gerardine & yourself; & understanding your feeling in writing it, in all its painfulness & tenderness, I understand besides that she COULD NOT *choose as you would choose for her* (—the thing is not possible—) and that she has a *right* to choose, if it is once granted that she is old enough to marry– Therefore & whatever your regret & grief may be, there is not room for blame—it seems to be a natural result of causes out of reach. You have played the best & tenderest part,—& if she is happy or not happy, she must in after life be g⟨rateful⟩ to you, if grateful to any in the world. I certainly wish that she had waited, seen more men, & had time to take measure of her own nature & the needs of it .. but this is as vain a wish as any other: and if the man she has accepted now, loves her faithfully enough to make her his object for one year, it is an argument in his favour, seeing what men are– If he is worth just nothing, why absence & time will rot the straw-rope .. dont you think so? I hope in the meanwhile that dear Gerardine will be thrown into society as much as possible, & thoroughly amused & excited from other quarters. My cruelty to her would consist in distracting her into inconstancy– If she holds fast .. good .. it is in her favour & his– Remember there is a whole year—& that a year at Gerardine's age is a long time. Give my love to her. Thank you for your notes on Venice, but you said nothing of the healthfulness in winter, which was what we wanted to know. You forget about Pisa. It was not through œconomy that we made our mistake in choosing too cold a situation– The mistake was D[r] Nankevill's, with D[r] Cook to help him a little.[7] Wilson is quite well here, as are we all. We have made the acquaintance of M[r] Powers, who is delightful .. of a most charming simplicity .. with those great burning eyes of his– Tell me what you think of his boy listening to the shell– Oh, your Raphaels! how divine! And M. Angelo's sculptures! His pictures I leap up to in vain, & fall back regularly. Write of your book & yourself & write soon .. ⟨let⟩ me be always

your affectionate
Ba—

We are here two months certain, & perhaps long⟨er⟩– Do write.

[Continued by RB]

Dear Aunt Nina– Ba has said something for me, I hope– In any case, my love goes with hers– I trust you are well and happy as we are, and as we would make you if we could. Love to Geddie.

Ever yours
RB

Address, in EBB's hand, on integral page: Angleterre via France / M[rs] Jameson / Ealing / near London.
Publication: LEBB, I, 332–334 (in part, as 7 August 1847).
Manuscript: Wellesley College.

   1. Year provided by postmark.
   2. Cf. Coleridge, *The Rime of the Ancient Mariner* (1798), line 17.
   3. The baths near Vicenza to which RB refers in letter 2666.
   4. "A road impassable for wheeled traffic."
   5. "Meat."
   6. In *Legends of the Monastic Orders* (1850), Mrs. Jameson devoted a section to "the Order of Vallombrosa," in which she referred to the "Legend of San Gualberto."
   7. See letter 2624, note 9.

No. 2688

2688. EBB & RB TO RICHARD HENGIST HORNE

[In RB's hand]   Florence,
                                                     Aug. 1. '47.

Dear Horne, I wish you joy with all my heart—and for all its old-fashionedness, I seem to invent the phrase while I write it- You wished me joy, in better words, and all you wished has come true, so true that I shall hope to be as lucky an augur in my turn. Was it not strange?—I carried my wife's letter to you, with an added word from myself, to the post one morning, and then went duly to the News-room,—and the first glance at the "Times"[1] informed me of your altered way of life—it was too late to get the letter back, but you will have collected so much from its contents, no doubt. Dear Horne, I put you among the very few workers we have—your genius you did not give yourself—but you use it, turn it to account, as some men turn mere talent—though not with their reward, I am sure. I hope and will believe you have got a reward of your own kind now, and that only in this apparently indirect way, do "Orions" and "Cosmos" pay their pains- The effect of being away from England and in Florence is curious—the loose literature in one's head *settles* fast, nothing *stays* that should not—but I often find, just when I want it, some grand, weighty line of yours—not to speak of general conceptions which also make themselves felt for true and complete- Now, don't you let marrying spoil you any more than, God willing, it shall me- I shall never write without thinking you are across the sea to read and judge me—and do you always know there is one of your truest admirers .. not very far from another truest admirer—seeing that here is my wife waiting for her little space in this little letter-

And will you let me begin acquaintance with Mrs Horne on this auspicious ground and not another—of my admiration and friendship for her husband? She will let me tell her .. No, the absurdity! She has divined all I could tell her- God bless her and you, my dear Horne,—is the very truthful aspiration of

                                          Ever Yours
                                          R Browning.

[Continued by EBB]

My very warmest wishes & kindest thoughts, will you accept my dear friend, with those of another?- It was with true pleasure that I learnt from the newspaper, the fulfilment of the oracle you sent me last year, & which I scarcely dared (with all my inward comprehension) read aloud as I understood it when I wrote to you last. May you indeed be very, very happy, on the road where I^2 first learnt the meaning of the word *happiness*—in a complete sympathy

& confidence– And will Mrs Horne be kindly prepared to acknowledge me one day as the true friend of both of you–?

Elizabeth Barrett Browning

Address, in EBB's hand, on integral page: R. H. Horne Esqre
Publication: None traced.
Manuscript: Michael Meredith.

1. See letter 2684, note 5.
2. Underscored twice.

2689. EBB TO HENRIETTA MOULTON-BARRETT

Florence
August 2 [1847]¹

This is the first of the two letters due to you my ever dearest Henrietta, and it will be shorter than usual, seeing that Robert is suddenly going to send home & offers to make room for me if I make haste. The condition must be kept therefore– Thanks many & warm, for my dearest Arabel's letter yesterday & your note inside—— How I thank you both! how dear you are & kind! What sh^d I do without you, even with Robert here? Your letters seem to draw us all close together, & to take away the sting of thoughts which else w^d be insupportable– I love & thank you from the bottom of my heart my dearest kindest sisters– May God bless you beyond my love & thanks!

Why in the world, now, was Arabel uneasy about me? Oh, do put down such fancies, you dear Things. I am as well as possible .. and really the chief reason for anxiety for me is, that, being supernaturally happy, the miracle may'nt be expected to go on in this mortal atmosphere. It *could'nt*, I suppose, .. if there were not a leaven to leaven it all, in dear Papa's anger against me & in the separation from him & others, & in not seeing Arabel & you– But as you bid me I *hope* even for that .. and for the rest, *nothing* could be changed except by losing something, .. and I at the end almost of our first year of marriage!– Tell Arabel she is impertinent—we began by keeping "The Day" once a week .. but since the weeks have multiplied themselves so often by four, it's celebrated only once a month– Oh, *I* ² should'nt remember– I never can think of the day of the month you know. But Robert reminds me without once failing. "Do you recollect what tomorrow will be?" & "what today is?" I tell him that he keeps it two or three times in the month, instead of once—at any rate the echo is very long. Ah yes– Do think of us on the twelfth of September– We have not made up our minds how to celebrate it, but the celebration is to be august anywise .. and we talk of claiming that idea! "*Flitch*",³ promised to people a year married who never have quarrelled. Only, as I say to Robert, it will scarcely be a fairly devised

recompense, because he will have the bacon to himself, & I the beans, ..
and that wont be fair, will it? It's bad enough that he has the figs every day,
and I sit by never touching them—for I do *not* like figs- I never did, you
know, .. & having tried again with all my might, I cant like them .. not even
the look of them .. though these Florentine figs are considered peculiarly
good, .. and are *great*, I will answer for it- We have a large dish of the finest
for a penny, and always I think of Papa, when they are brought to table- In a
week, the grapes begin,—and in the meanwhile we have immense melons, a
penny each- Consider how the poor must rejoice in all this fruit .. heaps &
heaps of fruit that might have ripened in Paradise! and they make fruit a
large proportion of their diet, here, and it is very wholesome on account of
the climate. Why how hot you must have been in England!- We were at *86*
by the thermometer, but that was the highest, .. and Wilson & I agree that
the meaning of heat in Italy is a different thing from what it is in England—
the air is so much lighter & more elastic with us than with you- Then the
little wind which regularly rises at six oclock & blows the curtains in &
out!- And then, the construction of the houses .. the great windows!-
Throughout this summer I have lived in the open air, I may say correctly.
We never shut the windows .. only the green blinds .. Venetian blinds .. by
day or night: and as they open from ceiling to floor, it is precisely as if one
lived out of doors, you see- There's no fog .. no falling of dew, .. none you
could detect: and I have not had the slightest cold since I left home. Of course,
so much of the outward air is strengthening & reviving, where it does not
injure, and accounts for my progress in health & change of appearance. We
more & more like our new apartment. When I am tired of the sofa I get *into*
the window in one of the deep spring-chairs .. as soft as if it were made of a
cloud: and after our coffee at half past seven, we regularly go out to walk on
our terrace, where there is just room for two to walk .. walk backward &
forward till the moon rises! it's so easy when one is tired, to step in at the
window & drop into a chair. And the moon rises beautifully, & drops down
the grey wall of San Felice, and it's altogether delightful to walk there without one's bonnet and talk of going to Rome or of loving you, or .. even of
keeping the twelfth of September. The weather is cooler rather than it was,
at least this apartment is much cooler, and the thermometer was under eighty
all yesterday- Indeed we have not once repented of our resolve to stay in
Florence through the hot months—we have suffered by it in no degree. Yet
it was very vexatious to hear yesterday from dear Mr Kenyon that he is not
coming to us—no, he is not coming; though he means to cross the Alps perhaps as far as the northern lakes .. being involved in a plan which excludes
us, with Mr Bezzi & Mr Chorley- They cant afford the time, it appears, &
Mr Kenyon's own time is short- He does not even see his brother, in Vienna- So we might as well have gone to Perugia or elsewhere- Never mind!-

Nobody regrets time spent at Florence, and we have been especially happy here. What good delightful news of dearest Stormie! And I dare say Papa is pleased! and after all, Jamaica appears cooler than Italy this summer. Tell Stormie that he is not to let the humming of the bees be too loud for thoughts of me–

Good news too of dear George!– When he begins to get *on*, he will run fast very soon. Is Alfred succeeding to his mind? And what of Henry? Does Henry hear of a chance of occupation? Talking of occupations, my dearest Henrietta, a merely passive position of listening & waiting will do nothing, or often will do nothing—but an energetic seeking & turning over all the little stones, .. that's the right thing & will always (giving time) secure a result! Did I not say so to Alfred? And where is Alfred? Sir Robert Price[4] sh^d not, I think, be applied to again– Terrible, the account of the Barretts is– I grieve for poor Maria– Now, *ought* Sam Barrett to wait to breathe even, before he gives himself an occupation? To *choose* an occupation takes time, .. but work of some kind, he might get surely .. & work in the *ditches*, w^d, to my idea, be more honorable, than rest under such circumstances–[5] It is dreadful indeed– There's the consequence of a "little imprudence" in the beginning, as he might have called it!—*not* the consequence of a narrow income, mind, but of an imperfect system of morals. I laugh insolently sometimes at Robert & his accounts, and his way of calculating for the days & the weeks—but always he is right & I wrong .. he is greatly right, & high up above laughter. His horror is of having to apply ever to any human being for pecuniary help .. of approaching the verge even of the least difficulty as to money—and these feelings of fear are crossed by others lest *I* sh^d ever need anything which he c^d not provide. These are his fears .. just these. And if you were to see how in obedience to them, our expenses are clearly arranged & set down .. if you were to see his little book, with our whole income accounted for to the uttermost farthing, week by week, and an overplus (yes, an overplus!) provided for casualties, & [']'lest Ba sh^d be ill", you would smile as I do, or be touched, as I often am besides– I am sure I could not manage after any such fashion .. and then when I think that he does it for *me*, & that all this care for money is contrary to his nature, he who is so generous & given to despise money .. I cannot help being touched .. how could I? For the rest we live most comfortably .. I never in my life lived more comfortably .. as the world accounts comfort. We have, however, given up our carriage for the present .. it was too great an expense to continue of course: but whenever we want a carriage, why we can have it, and now I am able to walk .. and here is our terrace which really I like as well, if not better. Robert was afraid that I sh^d miss the carriage .. but I do not indeed— and we paid more for it than for our house itself, cheap as for a carriage, it was– Did I tell you (while we are on such subjects) that what dear Mr Kenyon

No. 2689 2 August [1847]

called my "*profligate debts*" were paid out of our year's income, & without the "*selling out*" after all? Robert particularly wished it to be so from the beginning– He did not like the idea that any of my family who thought it worth while to enquire, should hear of any "selling out" from any motive whatever—and so it was managed, and the money in the Bank is intact– Well! you expect me to admire M! Reynolds, who went back, after his own marriage, to see somebody's else!! That completes the idea of them to my mind!—— A man certainly to cultivate a fire with, during the dog days, lest one sh^d freeze!—— Good Heavens, what men there are in the world—— I choose M! Bevan, oh without the least comparison .. M! Bevan is another stuff of men. Yet .. now tell me if you consider it right in him to send away his wife's maid for having a conscience of her own? On no principle could it be right or pardonable. Does Arabel hear from Emma Margary? & is she happy, so far? Does M!^s Orme really come to Italy .. & where? & when? I have just had the kindest letter from Miss Dowglass to invite us in the most affectionate & considerate way possible, to spend a fortnight with her at the Baths of Lucca .. myself & "the husband of my choice", promising us liberty, retirement, everything we could *not* ask for– So very, very kind!– But it will be impossible to go, though I never shall forget the kindness– The other day we had a visit from M! & M!^s Greenhough[6] .. he another American sculptor, but inferior every way[.] They are friends of M! Kenyon[']s. We continue to live in the quietest fashion possibly– Love to everyone who remembers me—to Susan & Surtees Cook always—to dear little Lizzie Barrett– How I love you. Soon you shall have a second letter better worth receiving, I do trust– I am with you every hour of the day in thought & love–

Your own Ba
in the utmost haste

Address, on integral page: (To the care of Miss Trepsack) / Miss Barrett / 5. Upper Montagu Street / Montagu Square / London.
Publication: Huxley, pp. 40–42 (in part).
Source: Transcript in editors' file.

1. Year provided by postmark.
2. Underscored twice.
3. According to the *OED*, a side of bacon "presented yearly at Dunmow, in Essex, to any couple who could prove that they had lived in conjugal harmony for a year and a day."
4. Sir Robert Price (1786–1857), Member of Parliament, was the son of Sir Uvedale Price, EBB's correspondent from Hope End days.
5. See letter 2655, note 14.
6. Horatio Greenough had married Louisa Ingersoll Gore (1813–91) in Florence in 1837, where they lived until 1851, when they returned to the States.

2690. RB TO ARABELLA & HENRIETTA MOULTON-BARRETT

[Florence]
Aug 2. '47

My dearest sisters– Every thing I hear of you from Ba, and every word you write to her, make me love you the more—you have this in common with her, that the more one knows of you the more dear you become– The increase to Ba's happiness and mine that arises from this constant affection of yours to her, and sympathy with me, is incalculable: and I comfort myself by thinking that she deserves it, at all events. It will be a perfect delight to see you face to face and not thro' these letters merely, plain as your kindness shines thro' them—and let us hope that this will be at no very distant day. Your Ba is looking very well, nor suffering so much from the weather as you would apprehend– Some very seasonable showers with a little thunder have reduced the temperature to .. at this minute .. 76–Fahrenheit—tho' we are at halfpast twelve– She will have told you about our doings in this new house, our evening walks on our terrace, and our other pleasant ways– Only I could not help slipping in this little word, poor return as it is for so many warmhearted greetings, every one of which goes to my soul– God bless you both for Ba's sake and that of

your affectionate
R Browning.

Address, on integral page: Miss Arabel Barrett.
Publication: None traced.
Manuscript: Armstrong Browning Library.

2691. EBB TO FANNY DOWGLASS

Palazzo Guidi– near the Pitti
but direct Poste Restante .. it is safer.
August 2. [1847][1]

I hasten to thank you my dearest kindest friend, with all my heart, for your goodness to me & mine. This must be the *first* word,—but the next presses in to set myself a little right with you in the matter of what may have struck you probably as most unfriendly & unaffectionate reserve & silence– Do pardon me for all things which have seemed unkind. Your name has again & again been present to my thought, though I could come & stay so long in your Italy without a word or sign .. yes, and leave England nearly at the same time with you & not say distinctly that I was going & how. Oh .. among many painful feelings this was one .. that you must be displeased with me!— and then I had no courage to write, & preferred to wait & see you face to

No. 2691   2 August [1847]

face in Rome & show you my heart at the same time. Was it not *pricked*, do you imagine, when M.''s'' Young found me out at Pisa & told me that you had bade a friend of yours enquire about me? Yes, indeed. Still I did not write .. I would wait, I thought– And I waited till on the only evening I have spent in society since my marriage (& for how many years before?) I met your friend M.''rs'' Collyer & heard of your being at the Baths of Lucca, & was promised your address which she sent to me a few half hours before we proceeded to scale the heights of Vallombrosa & persuade the monks to take us in for two months– Obdurate monks, who would'nt hear of it, and sent us back, rolling at the heels of the white oxen, at the end of five days,—because they have a new abbot who being a holy man puts away from before his face as fast as possible, all manner of unclean beasts, .. & women of course. It is a malign satisfaction to me that I put my foot over their threshold & stamped thrice on the ground, profaning it for ever—the only vengeance left to me!—— So I was to write to you, I thought, (for having your address I *was* resolved to write to you) from Florence instead of Vallombrosa—and since settling ourselves in the coolest apartment procurable, every morning I have said to myself "Shall I write, now, today"–? And in the midst comes your dear kindest letter, to take away all disquietudes & show me your faithful affection as if it showed me your face. Dearest friend, how I thank you for the good you have done me! I thank you warmly & gratefully—and so does my husband, he bids me say, both for himself & for me. We cannot go to you dear, dear friend, though it is a great temptation. We are *bound* here for the present:—which would be harder than it is, if I did not look forward to Rome & to seeing you in the winter certainly. You go back to Rome in the winter, .. do you not? Do let me hear from you & tell me of your plan in this respect, & of your health more particularly. M.''rs'' Collyer delighted me by saying that you were able to take daily exercise—— Is it true? So good of you it is to wish to have us .. one of us a stranger too!—to be received in faith .. and "who might be" as my husband says naïvely; "so *very* disagreeable".! One day I shall be happy & proud to make him known to you indeed, .. and in the meanwhile, do believe of us both, that we are affectionately grateful to you .. that is .. *gladly* grateful, glad to be grateful to you. We have heard much of the beauty of the Baths of Lucca & were as near as possible to going there for the summer—only the traditions of the place frightened us, as to "promenades" and "soirées" & various horrible rumours of the same class. With *you*, I should not be afraid of such things—but now we are bound here—perhaps in two months or less, to pass on through Perugia, Rome-wards. Our chief cause for hesitation about Rome is the *prices*, some of these Florentines assuring us that they quadruple the prices here, and as we are not rich it is a thing to consider of course. We have been paying nineteen scudi a month for an apartment including plate

& linen– Will you tell me (see how I make an unscrupulous use of you, dearest friend) whether any cheapness of the sort is attainable at Rome? We require some four or five rooms– I have my English maid with me & no other servant. For situations, we are not particular, except on the point of healthfulness, and rather eschew than seek after "English quarters" & fashionable neighbourhoods. We have thought of the Via Gregoriana[2]—. Once you said something to me of an apartment in Rome, .. but my head was going round so fast at that time that I recollect nothing, & have mislaid your note. To Pisa we shall not return certainly—and Florence is overcold in the winter—as it is overhot now! yet oh, this beautiful Florence, how we have delighted in it these three months past & more! It is scarcely fair perhaps to other countries that I should see Italy when I am happiest, .. it makes it look too beautiful. Also health & strength have come back in a sudden spring– God has been very good to me, & compensated for all the sadness of my past life in an unlooked for way & degree. Thank Him for me, if you love me! My marriage was my only "wilful" act through life, & cost me great pain in the doing .. but not more than it deserved & has justified—though there are still bitternesses behind. Some of my wisest friends have called me "wise" for it .. but I call myself only *happy* ... for really I chose & sought scarcely anything .. the blessing was thrust on me openly. I have married a man, for the rest, who is superior to me in all things, yet not too high for the completest sympathy, and who had loved me faithfully for two years, not only in spite of my adversity in body & spirit, but perhaps because of it—. Otherwise it might have struck you that it was not generous of me to allow one I loved, to bear the risk & danger of my uncertain health .. at best uncertain– But he convinced me that, even if Italy failed & I was thrown back into confirmed illness, he should be happier with me than without me .. even *so*—. He overcame me in generosity. What was I, to refuse to believe? Then I had the encouragement of medical opinions, justified by this result– My nervous system was shattered for want of air & from past mental suffering—and the lungs were rather delicate than diseased—. Since I reached Italy I have had no inconvenience in the chest, .. and week by week since an accidental illness at Pisa last winter, I have been growing stronger & stronger. We live in great retirement & very happily & cheerfully none the less— with books & the piano, and my dog .. who came with us from England .. and with frequent letters from my dearest sisters who are perfect to me in goodness & tenderness: and I am able to walk out every evening, .. and cant believe in my own identity with what I was three years ago, .. my face against a tombstone, & the ends of life hanging loosely in my hands! Even my spirits, which I thought broken for ever, are putting out green leaves. I ought to thank God indeed—and *much* the more, that I believe none to have suffered loss through my gain .. it w? have been miserable gain at such a cost. I have displeased some whom it was painful to me to displease .. but have *wronged none* .. as far as I know & believe .. for I tried to do my best for them before I did it for myself. Nearly a year it is now since my marriage .. a year in September .. and I have known only since then how happy it is possible to be "beneath the sun",[3] in being regularly petted & spoiled one day more than another .. (never was so tender a Heart as the one I lean on, through God's gift to me. Now, do write to me, & send me egotism for egotism. The more *Is* & *mes* the better—and certainly I have given you an example.) How you are, tell me fully .. & when you return to Rome. And let me be to you as ever, or more than ever, no Mrs Browning (oh no) but

your affectionate & grateful Ba–[4]

Address, on integral page: A Mademoiselle / Mademoiselle Dowglass / Casa Mansi / Alla Villa / Bagni di Lucca.
Publication: Taplin, p. 199 (in part, in facsimile).
Manuscript: Berg Collection.

1. Year provided by postmark.
2. According to Murray's *Handbook for Travellers in Central Italy*, (1843), "the Strada Gregoriana and the Via Sistina, at the Trinità de' Monti, and several streets near the Fontana Trevi, have also good lodging-houses" (p. 249); see letter 2702, note 4.
3. Byron, *The Corsair* (1814), I, ii, 54.
4. EBB has written the last line on the exterior of the folded sheet that makes up the envelope, just above her seal that reads "Ba," for added emphasis.

2692. EBB TO JULIA MARTIN

Florence.
August 7. 1847.

My dearest Mrs Martin how I have been longing to get this letter which comes at last, & justifies the longing by the pleasure it gives!– Ever since Fanny Hanford & her brother left Florence, I have wished too to write to you as well as to be written to by you, to tell you that we were quite pleased & more than pleased by what we saw of both of them, & full of regret that it should be *so* little. Such a pity it seemed .. such a shame almost, .. that we should have them only for a day here in Florence, where they had not seen everything where *I* for my part had seen nothing, & where we might have agreed so pleasantly in going about together to look at sights & learn to know one another in the same breath. I am sure I should love her warmly– I did not fancy that she would be so affectionate to me as I found her, .. & then the intelligence & quickness & freshness of mind struck both Robert & me as delightful– He liked her exceedingly .. & her brother besides: and we cant believe, (do tell her with my love) that we shall not soon meet again to catch up the drawbacks & supply the omissions of that short day's intercourse, which it was very good of her to mention kindly when she wrote to you– Quære .. if you & dear Mr Martin could do anything better for next winter than to bring her out with you to Rome, & let us all enjoy it thoroughly &

together?– There's a dream. I have a goose which lays a new golden egg of a Dream every morning,[1] .. and not so much of a goose either! Some swans are less wise perhaps!– What do you say .. or dream .. in return? Now I beg you to consider seriously this proposition, & to remember that when people once begin to travel, it is as easy to touch Rome as Pau, .. the difference is not worth an argument. Then, consider the Pope, & that such a Pope deserves to be looked at and supported. Pray think of it .. I appeal to dear M! Martin– Also, I want to look at *you* & to thank you both for all your warm sympathy better than can be done at this distance– How kind, how affectionate you are to me, .. and how strong your claim is that I should thrust on you in defiance of good taste & conventions, every evidence & assurance of my happiness, so as to justify your *faith* to yourselves & others. Indeed, indeed, dearest M!ˢ Martin, you may "exult" for me—and this, though it sh!ᵈ all end here & now. The uncertainties of life & death seem nothing to me– A year (nearly) is saved from the darkness: and if that one year has compensated for those that preceded it, which it has abundantly, why let it for those that shall follow, if it so please God– Come what may, I feel as if I never could have a right to murmur– I have been happy enough. Brought about too, it was indeed, by a sort of miracle, which to this moment, when I look back, bewilders me to think of .. and if you knew the details, .. counted the little steps .. & could compare my moral position three years & a half ago with THIS, you w!ᵈ come to despise San Gualberto's miraculous tree at Vallombrosa, which being dead, gave out green leaves in recognition of his approach, as testified by the inscription .. do you remember?[2] But you cant stop today to read mine—so rather I shall tell you of our exploit in the mountains ... only one thing I must say first, one thing which you must forgive me for the vanity of resolving to say at last, having had it in my head very often. There's a detestable engraving,[3] which if you have the ill luck to see, (and you *may*, because horrible to relate, it is in the shop windows) will you have the kindness, for my sake, not to fancy *like Robert*? it being, as he says himself, the very image of "*a young man at Waterloo House,*[4] in a moment of inspiration .. 'A lovely blue, Ma'am!'" It is as like Robert as Flush–

And now I am going to tell you of Vallombrosa– You heard how we meant to stay two months there, & you are to imagine how we got up at three in the morning to escape the heat (imagine me!) and with all our possessions & a "dozen of port" (which my husband doses me with twice a day because once it was necessary) proceeded to Pelago by vettura & from thence in two sledges drawn each by two white bullocks up to the top of the holy mountain. (Robert was on horseback.) Precisely it must be as you left it– Who can make a road up a house? We were four hours going five miles, and I with all my goodwill was dreadfully tired, & scarcely in appetite for the beef & oil with which we were entertained at the House of Strangers. We are simple people about diet, & had said over & over that we would live on eggs & milk & bread & butter during these two months .. we might as well have said that we w^d live on manna from heaven. The things we had fixed on, were just the impossible things– Oh .. that bread, with the fetid smell, which stuck in the throat like Macbeth's amen![5] I am not surprised you recollect it! The hens had "got them to a nunnery"[6] & objected to lay eggs— and the milk & the holy water stood confounded. But of course we spread the tablecloth just as you did, over all drawbacks of the sort—and the beef & oil, as I said, and the wine too, were liberal & excellent, & we made our gratitude apparent in Robert's best Tuscan—in spite of which we were turned out ignominiously at the end of five days, having been permitted to overstay the usual three days by only two. No, nothing could move the lord Abbot— He is a new abbot & given to sanctity, & has set his face against women. "While he is abbot" he said to our mediating monk, "he *will* be abbot". So he is abbot, & we had to come back to Florence. As I read in the Life of San Gualberto, laid on the table for the edification of strangers, the Brothers attain to sanctification, among other means, by cleaning out pigstyes with their bare hands, without spade or shovel .. but *that* is uncleanliness enough— they w^{dnt} touch the little finger of a woman! Angry I was, I do assure you— I sh^d have liked to stay there, in spite of the bread. We sh^d have been only a little thinner at the end. And the scenery .. oh, how magnificent! how we enjoyed that great, silent, ink-black pine-wood!—and do you remember the sea of mountains to the left? how grand it is– We were up at three in the morning again to return to Florence, and the glory of that morning-sun breaking the clouds to pieces among the hills, is something ineffaceable, from my remembrance. We came back ignominiously to our old rooms, but found it impossible to stay on account of the suffocating heat .. yet we scarcely could go far from Florence, because of Mr Kenyon & our hope of seeing him here— (since, lost–) A perplexity, ended, by Robert's discovery of our present apartment, in the Pitti side of the river (indeed close to the Grand Duke's palace) consisting of a suite of spacious & delightful rooms, which come within our means, only from the deadness of the summer season, .. comparatively quite cool and with a terrace which I enjoy to the uttermost through being able to walk there without a bonnet, by just stepping out of the window. The church of San Felice is opposite, .. so we have'nt a neighbour to look through the sunlight or moonlight & take observations. Is'nt that pleasant altogether? We ordered back the piano & the book-subscription, &, settled for two months .. & forgave the Vallombrosan monks for the wrong they did us, like secular Christians. What is to come after, I cant tell you– But probably we shall creep slowly along toward Rome, & spend some hot time of it at Perugia which is said to be cool enough. I think more of other things, wishing that my dearest kindest sisters had a present as bright as mine, .. to think nothing at all of the future. Dearest Henrietta's position has long made me uneasy—& since she frees me into confidence by her confidence to you, I will tell you so. Most undesirable it is that this sh^d be continued .. and yet where is there a door open to escape? I cannot see: at least I cannot for *her*, .. as she seems to make a larger income than seems within reach, a condition of any step forward. Captain Cook is very much attached to her .. very much, I think: his attachment has stood for years through a knowledge of every obstacle on the part of her family and through even coldness on her own side. There was long a struggle between him & another person for the first place in her affections, and I consider that she decided wisely at last. Surtees Cook is very faithfully therefore attached to her .. and you & I, as women, know how to appreciate such a claim. Then he is amiable & well-principled .. not above her in any way as to intellect, but sufficiently quick for the ends of life .. and as she is fond of saying of him, "a gentleman in all ways." Very popular he was in his regiment, & by no unworthy means. Altogether I do not doubt of her being happy with him, and moreover, happy or not, I am of opinion that after all which has passed, she could not in honour withdraw .. nor does she desire to withdraw—he has won her affections fairly. But now for the end ... What to do under these circumstances? He has been received in Wimpole Street as a guest *sans consequence*[7] for years, and everyone in the house *except the master of it* who, strange to say, never sees anything visible (though for things invisible he keeps a sword drawn) has been perfectly aware of the fact—perfectly .. but do not say a word to George who has been perfectly rude besides, & may do something rash in his horror of your knowing it .. of the subject's being made serious *so*. But I know that they know of it, .. because never was a courtship more public in this world .. poor Surtees's sobs, in the hour of his adversity, being heard all over the house, & discussed in my room in full conclave, by all my brothers, .. though now they say nothing, or satisfy themselves by some expressive rudeness to the successful candidate .. which much I regret .. very much! My dear brothers have the illusion that nobody sh^d marry on less than two thousand a year ..!- Good Heavens, how preposterous it does seem to me! *We* scarcely spend three hundred—and I have every luxury I ever had, & which it would be so easy to give up, at need—and Robert would'nt sleep, I think, if an unpaid bill dragged itself by any chance into another week. He says that when people get into "pecuniary difficulties," his "sympathies always go with the butchers & bakers–" So we keep out of scrapes—yet, you see!- Now Surtees Cook has at this moment nearly three hundred a year .. within a few pounds—and I tell YOU *what I would'nt on any account tell him or Henrietta*, that if I were *they*, I would marry directly on it, & *then* exert myself to increase the income .. which, in time, opportunities will occur, of doing. I would not tell them so .. because the responsibility is too heavy .. and the conviction should originate with themselves. They say that it must be four hundred a year to begin with .. Henrietta says that she c^d not "conscientiously" agree to marry on less. To this, I have nothing to answer—

only with ME[8] it w.d be very different, I can assure you, and I have now had some experience. What I (in my own mind) chiefly desire their increase of income for, is, that they might have a better case for Papa, when they lay it before his eyes. Two thousand a year would be unavailing in the way of procuring a *consent*—that I am certain of:—but it is desirable that there sh.d be something like "a case". Surtees Cook has activity & application—& if there were an opening anywhere, he would get on, I do not in the least doubt: and an additional hundred a year would make a clear road for them. He is ready even to sell his commission if there were a desirable channel for the money—. But this frittering away of life .. this ravelling of the golden threads in the daily walks and talks which make the gossip of Wimpole Street .. the continuance of this, I do deprecate & am sorry for on every account—and I dont wonder that my poor dearest Henrietta's spirits sh.d be a little worn by the uncertainty & delay.

Thank you for your dear & kind consideration in all things- Aunt Bell did write to me to announce Arlette's marriage. As to George, he is *too proud*! I assure you I have tried many sorts of affectionate humility with him, (everything except giving up my husband) and tickled his lips with the end of many an olive-bough .. but it is in vain .. they wont smile at me. So glad I am of the good news of dearest M.r Martin- Tell me that you both continue well. And do write .. & let me be as ever

your grateful & most affectionate Ba-

We have had the most delightful letter from Carlyle .. who has the goodness to say that not for years had a marriage occurred in his private circle, in which he so heartily rejoiced as in ours. He is a personal friend of Robert[']s .. so that I have reason to be very proud & glad.

Robert's best regards to you both always—& he is no believer in magnetism—(only *I* am!). Do mention M.r C Hanford's health- How strange that he sh.d come to witness my marriage settlement! Did you hear?[9]

Address, on integral page: Angleterre viâ France / M.rs Martin / Colwall / Malvern / Worcestershire / England.
Publication: LEBB, I, 335–338 (in part).
Manuscript: Wellesley College.

1. Cf. Æsop's second fable.
2. The Martins were in Italy in the winter of 1832–33, and they might have seen the famous tree that San Gualberto's followers accepted as a sign of God's special favour. "The tree which grew beside his hut, anticipating the ordinary season, put forth its leaves long before all the others; shaded it during the summer with its abundant foliage; and was the last, when winter came, to shed its leaves on the ground. This was repeated year after year, and was considered a miracle, so that a wall was built about the tree, and it was consecrated and held in highest reverence. The tree was in the year 1008 full-grown; and in 1640, when Diego de Franchi wrote his 'Life of San Giovanni Gualberto,' it was still flourishing, and a print of it is engraved in his biography, surrounded by a wall, and with an inscription. What is supposed to be the same tree, surrounded by a wall corresponding in appearance to the old print, is still living and flourishing after these many centuries" (W.W. Story, *Vallombrosa,* 1881, pp. 30–31).

3. We have been unable to identify this engraving of RB, but presumably it is similar to the one Horne used in *A New Spirit of the Age* (see our vol. 8, facing p. 271).
4. Waterloo House was located at Cockspur Street and Pall Mall East, and was occupied by the fashionable mercers and drapers establishment of Halling, Pearce and Stone.
5. An allusion to *Macbeth*, II, 2, 28–30.
6. Cf. *Hamlet*, III, 1, 120.
7. "Without consequence," or "significance."
8. Underscored three times.
9. See the end of letter 2678.

2693. RB TO GEORGE W. CURTIS

Casa Guidi, via Maggio. Florence,
Aug. 9, '47.

Many very hearty thanks, my dear Mr. Curtis, for your welcome letter, which reached me yesterday,—no earlier, through the direction to *Via della Scala*– The people of the house there told us honestly on the morning of your departure, that they could only receive us for a single month, at the expiration of which were to begin certain whitewashings and repaintings—we continued our quest therefore, and at last found out this cool, airy apartment we shall occupy for another month or six weeks, whatever be our subsequent plans—for Rome, or for the Venice you describe so graphically and pleasantly– I spent a month of entire delight there, some eight years ago—and tho' nothing I have since seen has effaced the impressions of my visit, yet your fresher feelings *bring out* whatever looks faint or dubious in them,—as a gentle sponging might revive the gone glory of some old picture—(you must know, I have seen an exquisite copy of a Giorgione, the original of which,—so I was told—grows only visible and intelligible while thus wetted)– I am glad the railroad and gas-lighting do Venice no more wrong, and that you find all the old strange quietness and .. ought I to be glad of this too? .. depopulation—for of late years we have heard a great deal of the returning life and prosperity of the place, and Mr. Valery, I observe, retracts his earlier bodements of a speedy extinction of what little glimmer of light he still saw[1]–– As for me, I remember that the accounts of the depreciation of the value of houses, coupled with the indifference of the inhabitants of them, were enough to set one dreaming (in one's gondola!) of getting to be rich as Rothschild, buying all Venice, turning out everybody, and ensconcing oneself in the Doges' Palace, among the dropping gold ornaments and flakes of what was lustrous colour in Titian's or Tintoret's time, waiting for the proper consummation of all things, and the sea's advent!

But do you really find the air so light and pure in this by-night mephitic time of August, with its close *calles*,[2] pestilential lagunes &c &c and all that our informants here frighten us with? Should a winter in Venice prove no more formidable in its way than, it seems, a summer does—why we may

No. 2694 20 August [1847]

have cause to regret our determination to give up our original plans. I am sure your kindness will tell us, should it be enabled, any good news of the winter and spring climate—if weak lungs may brave it with impunity—such information would greatly oblige us—and, dear Mr. Curtis, you have already obliged us so much in so unfortunately short a time!—of which, in any case we shall ever keep a most pleasant memory: I hope and expect we are yet to meet again, and a letter from you will always be a glad event to me and to my wife—who, having been gratified as I have been, desires her kindest regards, as I do, to yourself and to your brother—and our united best remembrances to the rest of your party. All good auspices attend it, prays, Dear Mr. Curtis,

                       Yours ever faithfully,
                       Robert Browning.

Publication: Harper's New Monthly Magazine, March 1890, p. 638 (in part).
Source: Typescript at Armstrong Browning Library.

   1. In *Italy and Its Comforts: The Manual of Tourists* (1841) by Valery (pseud. Claude Antoine Pasquin), the author states that "the population, which diminished rapidly, amounts at the present moment to 110,000 and increases every day: with sincere pleasure I retract the woeful prophecies pronounced in my *Voyages* against this charming city, then apparently but too probable" (p. 55).
   2. "Narrow streets," a term used particularly in Venice.

2694. EBB TO MARY RUSSELL MITFORD

                               Florence–
                            August 20- [1847][1]

I have received your letter at last my ever dearest Miss Mitford; not the missing letter, but the one which comes to make up for it and to catch up my thoughts which were grumbling at high tide I do assure you. No, I never had the letter you speak of .. the answer to mine—and if I had not heard now, I should have written, so uncomfortable did the long dismal unusual silence make me. Unlucky woman that I am, to have missed that letter .. yet lucky to have this!—and scarcely ever does it happen that I lose a letter, scarcely ever. I hear from & write to my sisters once in every ten days .. sometimes oftener; and neither they nor I have had to complain of a lost letter between us. But yours certainly is lost, and I am glad almost now to think that it is. Better lose a letter than a remembrance of yours! so much better. Dearest friend, let me begin by talking of your rheumatism- What! you have rheumatism after all the heat in England this summer, of which we hear!- I hoped that it w^d have been the merest history by this summer-time!—and it is terrible to listen to accounts of your being lame to such an extent, & so restrained in your healthy exercise. I do not like to advise you; but if I were you, as advisers say, I would turn to the water cure straightway. It is a legitimate case for the water cure, and if I were you I would try it. Where is M！ May? Can he do nothing? I sh![d] grieve if the HABIT of rheumatism were established in your constitution. That you sh![d] have rheumatism and friendship go to you together, is scarcely the least consolation to me ... *especially as I am not one of the friends*.[2] For the rest, they were very happy I am certain, & you seem to have been glad too, and to have received full compensation for not visiting London: and in the matter of K., why, dearest Miss Mitford, your being pleased & satisfied, makes *me* both in a measure, believe me. If ever I spoke bluntly on that question, it was chiefly to spare you what, from my own idiosyncrasy, I concluded to be a painful position .. it being to me so very painful not to trust those who are about me, that no advantage could counterbalance the pain.[3] But of course you know best, & can judge best of what is happiest for yourself; and having the assurance of her repentance & reformation, perhaps it is reasonable in you as well as generous & kind, to act as if the past were a blank and no treason had ever approached you from that side. Also *I believe & hold* that kindness is a compelling & purifying Thing, and that the hot coals[4] of a forgiveness like yours, would, to a nature not wholly corrupt, cleanse & whiten better than Justice. Is the child in the house with you? and is it a pretty child, and winning?——

Do tell me every little thing about yourself. I long so to hear. Do you ever hear of Ben? Perhaps they may marry, after all, and so end all. As you observed last year (not without reason) these are the days of marrying & giving in marriage[5] .. M！ Horne, you see!- No, I have nothing to tell you in the way of "memoires à servir"[6] .. M！ Horne wrote to me in the winter & called himself "happy with the best motives for happiness," which of course meant marriage or sudden death. He bade me "guess" and I concluded instead. The other day I wrote to him; & Robert who took my letter to the post, read in a newspaper before he came home, his marriage to Miss Foggo.[7] We have written our congratulations. From another quarter we heard that the lady was a "very nice person", young .. half his age .. and undowered altogether .. so he is generous, observe, after all- I am glad he has not married an heiress:[8] and fairly he may set his poetry against a prosaic youthfulness. With all my heart I hope he may be very happy. Men risk a good deal in marriage, though not as much as women do: and, on the other hand, the single-life of a man, when his youth is over, is a sadder thing than the saddest which an unmarried woman can suffer. Nearly all my friends of both sexes have been draining off into marriage these two years—scarcely one will be left in the sieve—and I may end by saying that I have happiness enough for my own share to be divided among them all & leave everyone contented. For me I take it for pure magic, this life of mine. Surely nobody was ever so happy before. I shall wake some morning, with my hair all dripping out of the enchanted bucket. Or if not, we shall both claim the "Flitch"[9] next september, if you can find one for us in the land of Cockaigne, drying in expectancy of the revolution in Tennyson's Commonwealth.[10] Well! I dont agree with M[r] Harness in admiring the lady of Locksley Hall.[11] I MUST either pity or despise a woman who could have married Tennyson, & chose a common man. If happy in her choice, I despise her. That's matter of opinion, of course. You may call it matter of foolishness, when I add, that I, personally, would rather be teazed a little & smoked over a good deal by a man whom I c[d] look up to & be proud of, than have my feet kissed all day by a M[r] Smith in boots & a waistcoat, & thereby chiefly distinguished. Neither I nor another, perhaps, had quite a right to expect a *combination* of qualities .. such as meet, though, in my husband, who is as faultless & pure in his private life as any M[r] Smith of them all .. who would not owe five shillings .. who lives like a woman in abstemiousness, on a pennyworth of wine a day, never touching a cigar even. But now for poor Tennyson, of whom you are not the first .. alas! .. to tell me these sad stories——is it sure of Tennyson that if he had been happy, if for instance that very woman of Locksley Hall had not embittered his life & cast him out into solitude, the bad habits in question w[d] have taken root & grown? There, is a doubt sufficient to condemn her out & out before the world, God & her soul. *I*[12] think so, at least. Do you hear, as we do from M[r] Forster, that his new poem is his best work? As soon as you read it, let me have your opinion. ⟨The subject seems almost identical with one of Chaucer's- Is it not *so*?⟩

We have spent here the most delightful of summers, notwithstanding the heat .. and I begin to comprehend the possibility of St Laurence's ecstasies on the gridiron.[13] Very hot, it certainly has been & is .. yet there have been cool intermissions,—and as we have spacious & airy rooms, & as Robert lets me sit all day in my white dressing gown without a single masculine criticism, & as we can step out of the window on a sort of balcony-terrace which is quite private & swims over with moonlight in the evenings, and as we live upon water melons and iced water & figs & all manner of fruit, we bear the heat with an angelic patience & felicity which really are edifying. We tried to make the monks of Vallombrosa let us stay with them for two months—but their new abbot said or implied that Wilson & I stank in his nostrils,[14] being women .. and San Gualberto the establisher of their order had enjoined on them only the mortification of cleaning out pigsties without fork or shovel. To have a couple of women besides, was (as Dickens's American said) "a piling it up rayther too mountainious".[15] So we were sent away at the end of five days- *So* provoking! Such scenery, such hills, such a sea of hills looking alive among the clouds. *Which* rolled, it was difficult to discern. Such pine woods, supernaturally silent, with the ground black as ink .. such chesnut & beech forests hanging fr⟨om⟩ the mountains!—such rocks & torrents, such chasms & ravines! There were eagles there too ⟨and⟩ there was *no road*. Robert went on horseback, and Flush[,] Wilson & I were drawn in a sledge .. (i.e. an old hamper .. a basket wine-hamper, without a wheel) by two white bullocks, up the precipitous mountains. Think of my travelling in that fashion in those wild places at four oclock in the morning! .. a little frightened, dreadfully tired, but in an ecstasy of admiration above all! It was a sight to see before one died & went away to another world– Well, but being expelled ignominiously at the end of five days, we had to come back to Florence, & find a new apartment,[16] cooler than the old, & wait for dear Mr Kenyon– And dear Mr Kenyon does not come,[17] (not this autumn, but he may perhaps at the first dawn of spring) and on the twentieth of September we take up our knapsacks & turn our faces toward Rome I think .. creeping slowly along, with a pause at Arezzo, and a longer pause at Perugia, & another, perhaps, at Terni. Then, we plan to take an apartment we have heard of, over the Tarpeian rock,[18] & enjoy Rome as we have enjoyed Florence. *More* can scarcely be. This Florence is unspeakably beautiful, by grace both of nature & art,—and the wheels of life slide on upon the grass (according to Continental ways) with little trouble & less expense. Dinner, "unordered", comes through the streets & spreads itself on our table, as hot as if we had smelt cutlets hours before. The science of material life is understood here & in France. Now tell me, .. what right has England to be the dearest country in the world?– But I love dearly dear England, and we hope to spend many a green summer in her yet. The winters you will excuse us .. will you not? People who are like us, neither rich nor strong, claim such excuses—. I am wonderfully well, and far better & stronger than before what you call the Pisan "crisis"– Robert declares that nobody would know me, I *look* so much better. And you heard from dearest Henrietta? Ah, both of my dearest sisters have been perfect to me– No words can express my feelings towards their goodness. Otherwise, I have good accounts from home of my father[']s excellent health & spirits .. which is better even than to hear of his loving & missing me. I had a few kind lines yesterday from Miss Martineau who invites us from Florence to Westmoreland–[19] She wants to talk to me, she says, of "her beloved Jordan". She is looking forward to a winter of work by the Lakes, & to a summer of gardening– The kindest of letters, Robert has had from Carlyle—who makes me very happy by what he says of our marriage. Shakespeare's favorite air of the "Light of Love", with the full evidence of its being Shakespeare's favorite air, is given in Charles Knight's edition.[20] Seek for it there. Now do write to me & at length, & tell me everything of yourself. Flush hated Vallombrosa & was frightened out of his wits by the pine forests. Flush likes civilized Life, & the society of little dogs with turned up tails, such as Florence abounds with. Unhappily it abounds also with *fleas*, which afflict poor Flush to the verge sometimes of despair. Fancy Robert & me down on our knees combing him, with a basin of water on one side!—— He suffers to such a degree from fleas that I cannot bear to witness it. He tears off his pretty curls, through the irritation. Do you know of a remedy? Direct to me Poste Restante, Florence .. Put *via France* .. Let me hear .. do! & everything of yourself .. mind! Is M.ʳˢ Partridge in better spirits?[21] Do you read any new French books? Dearest friend, let me offer you my husband's cordial regards, with the love of your ever affectionate

EBB—*Ba*

Address, on integral page: Miss Mitford / Three Mile Cross / near Reading.
Publication: EBB-MRM, III, 213–218.
Manuscript: British Library.

1. Year provided by postmark.
2. In a letter to Charles Boner dated 2 July 1847, Miss Mitford wrote: "I need not tell you how glad I shall be to see you, but you will be sorry to find me exceedingly lame— lame ever since my rheumatism four months ago. I now take three hours for walking the distance that I used to accomplish in one" (*Mary Russell Mitford: Correspondence with Charles Boner and John Ruskin*, ed. Elizabeth Lee, 1914, p. 72). Then on the 9th of following month, she wrote to Boner that "Mr. Harness and Mr. Dyce have been spending a day here" (p. 76). Boner was a frequent visitor during the summer of 1847.
3. EBB mentioned Miss Mitford having taken K back in letter 2642 (see note 2); see also letter 2654.
4. Cf. Romans 12:20
5. Cf. Matthew 24:38.
6. "Useful information."
7. See letter 2684, note 5.
8. EBB had often defended Horne against Miss Mitford's suggestions that money was his prime motivation for courting several heiresses (see, for example, letter 1369, in which EBB called Horne "generous, & high-hearted").
9. See letter 2689, note 3.
10. See letter 2672, note 17.
11. In a letter to Charles Boner, dated 9 August 1847, Miss Mitford wrote that "William Harness told me he met one day, at dinner, the Heroine of Locksley Hall and her husband, and he thought the lady had chosen wisely" (*Mary Russell Mitford: Correspondence with Charles Boner and John Ruskin*, ed. Elizabeth Lee, 1914, p. 75). Rosa Baring, who married Robert Duncombe Shafto in 1838, has been suggested as the inspiration for Amy in "Locksley Hall." For a discussion of the characters in Tennyson's poem, see *The Poems of Tennyson*, ed. Christopher Ricks, 1969, pp. 688–689.
12. Underscored twice.
13. See letter 2676, note 7.
14. Cf. Amos 4:10.
15. *American Notes for General Circulation* (1842), vol. I, chap. 2, p. 59.
16. See letter 2686, note 14.
17. In letter 2689, EBB explained to her sister Henrietta that Kenyon had written to say he was not coming to Italy.
18. Described by Murray's *Handbook for Travellers in Central Italy* (1843) as being "on the southern summit of the Capitoline, which faces the Tiber" (p. 321). This precipice takes its name from Tarpeia, daughter of Spurius Tarpeius. She accepted the Sabines' bribe of the ornaments on their arms in exchange for opening the gates of the citadel. When they crushed her with their shields—decorated with ornaments—she died, and thereafter traitors were executed by being thrown head-first down the face of the cliff.

19. In June 1847 Harriet Martineau returned to England from her tour of Egypt and the Holy Land; see letter 2626, note 6. She visited friends and family until October when she returned to Ambleside, Westmorland.
20. Evidently Miss Mitford had queried EBB's statement about this tune in letter 2671. See letter 2669, note 5.
21. Miss Mitford's friend Lucy Anderdon had been depressed and unhappy since shortly after her marriage to Rev. Partridge in 1842; see letter 1404, note 4.

2695. EBB TO SARIANNA BROWNING

[Florence]
August 21- [1847][1]

My dearest Sarianna it seems to me a shame that so many letters should go to Hatcham without a little note from me, who owe you thanks for yours, besides the other gratitude. And then I do want to beg you & your dear mother, never more to be "miserable" in consequence of what Robert may write to you in a moment of impulse & impatience. Surely you must know him, .. and that he is given to hear Lions roar round corners, and to see shadows of crocodiles dilated to the whole height & depth of his imagination. You know that it is his way to calculate how if such a thing does happen, & such a thing does'nt happen, & such another thing happens imperfectly, why so the world is to come to an end & not a raven be left to feed anybody.[2] The worst is that I am in disrepute as an upsetter of calculations & soother of fears,— my fault of *insouciance* in matters of this sort, having thrown me out altogether .. I am not worth listening to as an oracle. He says that I would never think of the means of life until I grew very hungry indeed, .. and that THEN, instead of setting myself to get some bread, I would snatch up a French novel to forget the hunger in. Which is rather *like me*, I do admit. I have rather a leaning toward shutting my eyes & opening my mouth, like the children. I believe in ravens & manna from Heaven. And after all, is'nt it better not to starve many times before one's starvation, I do humbly submit to Robert? Now he is unhappy because of having made you unhappy .. and now I come to beg you never to be unhappy again for any such reason,—& to forgive us both (will your dear mother?) for having suggested the least uneasiness & anxiety to her & your thoughts of us. The money was ready sooner than it was wanted—there is the fact! and if it had been for himself only, he would not have feared for it, with all his imagination for fears.

We are very much disappointed not to have a chance any more of seeing dear M! Kenyon this autumn,—having stayed in Florence on purpose as you know, & only to hear that he crosses the Alps in vain for us- So provoking it is! It was vexation enough, we thought, to be cast out ignobly from the monastery of Vallombrosa, .. rolled down the mountain-side at the heels of our four white bullocks! In time perhaps, we shall learn that the world is not made for us--

"The world for me," exclaimed a pampered goose! .. I have been so happy of late, that really I do rather open my eyes when the least thing goes or seems to go wrong, .. and this, after my long, long dreary apprenticeship to the sorrowfulness of life which is said to make one wiser. To be wise at all, one must have better Teachers than either Sorrow or Joy of itself can be. But make us joyful, if you can, by saying that your mother is not suffering– Robert thinks much & tenderly of her & of you all, and we talk together of the day when I shall see you, and not *love you*, for the first time. Meanwhile we are turning our faces toward Rome, & dream of setting off on this new journey in another month & of taking up our residence on the Tarpeian rock and of opening the lid of more wonders. Let us have your affection with us always, that we may go on to be happy, here or there .. and do remember us especially on the *twelfth of September*: I seem to feel as if the sun rose for me first on that day. With grateful love to your father & mother, I am, for every day, dearest Sarianna's

affectionate sister
Ba–

Address, on integral page: Miss Browning.
Publication: None traced.
Manuscript: Lilly Library.

1. Year determined from EBB's reference to visiting Vallombrosa.
2. EBB alludes to the ravens feeding Elijah by the brook Cherith (I Kings 17:3-6).

2696. EBB TO FANNY DOWGLASS

Florence–
August. 25. [1847][1]

Thank you again & again, dearest friend, for all your goodness to me. I must make haste to say so, not lest the grateful thought should get cold (of which there is no danger) but lest you should fancy so ever & for a moment. It is a great temptation, your Lucca & you, .. but we *cant* go to you—we must wait for the Rome-meeting: we cant even be unreasonable & take advantage of your great kindness (oh, how kind!) of proposing to go round by Florence to Rome,—inasmuch as we set out Rome-wards ourselves on the twentieth of September and shall be there nearly as soon as you. We mean to creep on gently, though– It is a long journey; & an object with us it is, to avoid unnecessary fatigue, besides the pleasantness of a pause or two on the road ..

at Arezzo, which has not changed, they say, since Dante's time, at Perugia, & at Terni- Thank you, thank you, for your advice & suggestions about Rome. You have set us on tiptoe of expectation towards the Tarpeian Rock, and every word you say of it, seems to set us higher. We dont want the English quarter—we dont care for any manner of glory in the way of furniture & champagne-glasses. We live in the quietest way imaginable & see nobody & go nowhere & require very little comparatively of what passes as accommodation. A comfortable chair & a comfortable sofa, and a complement of legs to the table, would satisfy us perfectly; and we are ready to take our apartment for six months & do everything else reasonable. The vision you hold out of ancient Rome, would compensate for all—and then we like your suggestion about the Lutheran chapel close by—it sounds perfect, altogether. I have been a little shy about writing to Mrs Colyar—but our common friends M^{r} & Mrs Hoppner half promised to bring us into communication. As to the Jesuitism, we are so entirely the other way, that I dont think (if to say so is not too audacious) any Jesuit in the world could manage to come near enough (in opinion) to either of us to do much harm—which does not prove us the safer you know, even in establishing *one* kind of safety. Talking of Jesuitism & Jesuits, my husband knows Mr Mahoney, the famous Father Prout, now at Rome, .. "a very dangerous person" as everybody knows .. and the first whom we caught sight of in landing at Leghorn- He drifts from land to land like a phantom.

Dear dearest friend, how delighted I am to hear of your riding, & of enjoying the influences of God in nature as I never hoped you would any more. It made me glad at heart to read what you wrote about it. And we shall meet under the sun after all—and you have not forgotten to love me a little!- Good, good of you it is, to care to keep me from the supposed risk of passing a winter in Florence. Well! Florence has its temptations, there's no denying—and to break the spell & leave it behind is difficult—the spell of beauty and of association with happy days .. to say nothing of the facilities of life .. the cheapness, the conveniences, the luxuries on every side within reach. Then, on one side of the Arno, the sun is said always to shine—and I am not like birds used to liberty .. I should be contented with a short string out of the sweep of the winds & the chill of the shadows. But content without seeing Rome, one cant be quite! and we shall go as certainly as any human project can be certain. Of Venice we had thought first—and I gave up my visionary gondola with a pang for which you must help to console me by the sight of your face & sound of your voice, dear dear Fanny!- You tell me so kindly that I am not to talk of trouble, that I will ask you to let me know whatever further you may learn from your cousin when he arrives.[2] My husband knows Rome & remembers the very house on the Tarpeian Rock,

No. 2696 25 August [1847] 287

and longs, just as I do, for the possibility of getting there. He says that I shall have walking room enough at the foot of Marcus Aurelius's equestrian statue.[3] Oh, indeed I am taken care of more than I am worth, and although the excursion to Vallombrosa sounded mad enough & confounded my sisters when they heard of it, we did not expect quite so much fatigue in setting out, & suffered no harm through all the fatigue—and even the heat of Florence does not seem to disagree with me, we have such large & sunless rooms, and it is so pleasant to sit in one's dressing gown with one's feet up, & eat ⟨ice⟩d water-melons, & wander in & out of the window to the moonshiney balcony. As to walking, properly speaking, it is impossible .. and the carriage seems nearly as difficult. You have the advantage over us of course .. and you will think perhaps that I have come to perfection in the Italian "Dolce far niente"[4] in a wonderfully short time.

When you write, say how you are—and .. oh no, .. *dont* send compliments to Robert .. who sends his regards to you (if you will have them) claiming, as he does, to love all who love me. What a Pope we have .. for a Pope! .. to reconcile us with the high places & even the seven hills of the world!—— As to your Duke[5] I fear there is nothing to be said for him, except by M.rs Stisted.[6] As to your Dog, I honour her!

May God bless you– Love your

                        Most affectionate Ba

I think we should not mind much about the *stoves*. I used to set myself on *fire* regularly everyday at Pisa last winter with the flying pine-wood—& *that* was'nt the worst harm I did myself, ... sitting on a low stool on a level with the flame for two months together. So it w.d be rather an advantage perhaps to have a stove, & another set of evils, in change.

Publication: None traced.
Manuscript: Huntington Library.

   1. Year determined from EBB's reference to the Vallombrosa visit.
   2. Dr. Pollock; see letter 2681, note 9.
   3. Completed ca. 176, this famous monument in the only equestrian statue known to have survived from antiquity. It was moved in the 16th century from in front of the Lateran to the Piazza del Campidoglio, which Michaelangelo designed specifically for it.
   4. "Pleasant idleness," or "pleasantly doing nothing."
   5. Charles Louis de Bourbon (1799–1883), Duke of Lucca (1824–47), and afterwards Duke of Parma (1847–49).
   6. See letter 2647, note 3.

2697. EBB TO ARABELLA MOULTON-BARRETT

[Florence]
August 29– [1847][1]

This very day I had my dearest Henrietta's letter and I lose no time in beginning to write back again—and now it must be to you my best own Arabel .. although it always seems to me more natural to answer the speaker, than to speak triangularly, in the fashion we generally do. Quoth Henrietta to Ba "so & so": quoth Ba to Arabel "so & so". Still as we say to encourage each other .. "it's the same thing when a letter comes who is written to" .. and it IS much the same thing: and also, have I not your little note to answer? let me remember all my duties. As Henrietta observes too, it was a little note filled up to the brim & worthy of especial thoughtfulness– As to the great letter today, directed to the Palazzo Guidi, it came to me while Robert was at the post looking for letters addressed to Poste Restante, and scarcely I could believe my own eyes when I saw it– He came back presently— "Where's my letter, pray?" (I had calculated that there must perforce be a letter for me that morning.) "Why, Dear– I am sorry to say that there are no letters–" "Yes, but my particular letter from Henrietta: there must be a letter for me." "Indeed there is not. I looked through all the letters myself and I can answer positively" .. "And I feel positive too– I feel as certain, .. as certain as can be .. that there's a letter from Henrietta for me by this morning's post. I think that for once, you have made a mistake". —He laughed .. laughed .. and said that nothing was more amusing than my positiveness ... "Why Ba, what have you got in your head". Whereat I answered triumphantly, "Say, rather, what have I got in my pocket" .. and pulled out my document & held it close to his eyes. But for the future tell Henrietta & yourself to direct as usual "Poste Restante" because it is safer on several accounts, one being that the accomplished postman cant read .. has stopped Robert twice in the street to beg him to interpret this & that direction written as plainly as the campanile against the sky—and as he goes to the post office every morning, it is best to let him have the letters there– By the way, mind you write oftener. On the twentieth of September we go—and shall have to wait till we get to Rome—after that date. So before it do be generous & let me hear. I do delight so in these letters—ah, if you ever think that I could be happy without them under the most sunshiney circumstances God could plant me in, you are three times wrong– It is a great mistake to fancy that being married can undo the past & make those you once loved less loved than ever .. oh no. I seem to love you all more dearly than ever on the contrary. So write oftener before the twentieth—there's my moral!—— I dont know exactly what we shall do on the twelfth. Have knead cakes perhaps? or a larger water-melon than usual .. or we shall think of something better, I dare say.

Being sunday, it's difficult—and saturday, Arabel, is *not* by any means the same thing. Before the year which that day brought in, I could not have believed to any one's swearing that a married life was so happy a thing .. so purely happy. We must take care to behave discreetly before ⟨the Reynoldses⟩[2] at Rome, & appear to hate one another with a due decency—oh, & we shall, of course. For my part, I always did, you know, hate & detest, those public expressions of affectionateness, and Robert hates them too——only it is my humble opinion, nevertheless, that before a cousin & intimate friend like Arlette, Mr Bevan might have been allowed to call his wife "Darling" without an observation. It was not highly improper, even in the presence of a stranger– Why how can you ask me to like ⟨Mr Reynolds⟩ after all this? What does he allow Arlette to call him, I wonder, without "turning her out of doors?" Ah, well—too much tenderness cannot be as a fault, I think, in a compact of the nature of marriage: nobody ever complained of being too tenderly treated in that relation, at least. It is not a relation for mere civilities & cordialities of next-door neighbours—it is something nearer than that, or worth nothing– Be sure that Arabella's lot is brighter a thousand times than Arlette's, though she does without the Brougham & phaeton. Robert said today, "I wish the Bevans were going to Rome instead of the ⟨Reynoldses⟩. I am sure I should like Mr Bevan." So we dont discharge him for discharging his servant, bid Henrietta know, though altogether that act of his seemed & seems to us wrong & illiberal, notwithstanding her apology. How good & kind he must be to Arabella—how he has justified his professions before marriage! how it does one's heart good to hear of such goodness!– Give my love to them both. May their anxieties be soon happily over! Perhaps the unusual heat may have helped to increase her indisposition—is it supposed to? To have her mother with her will be great comfort & happiness, of course. Tell me of the dear Hedleys when they come– Tell dear Henrietta that it is not at all on the ground of its being an act expressive of "ill-will" that I ventured to blame Mr Bevan for discharging his servant; I do not doubt that he meant it in all goodwill & benevolence, on the contrary .. that is .. that he meant well by the person discharged .. I blamed him on other grounds & on these .. namely, .. that we have no right to exact unity & agreement in matters of religion among the members of our household, & especially on what she calls herself "minor points." If God leaves his people at liberty to differ on such points, by what right do they refuse one another such liberty? Supposing that I sent Wilson away for not agreeing with me on this or that point of conscience, would dear Henrietta blame me or not? She ought, in any case, to blame me, I think. All persecution arises from such exactions, and if you admit the principle, it carries you to the Inquisition.

By the way, see what a Pope we have, & how bravely he is doing his work! The other evening there was a great shouting & crowd which drew us to the balcony—and we heard that the whole populace were gathered in the piazza Pitti opposite the palace to entreat the Grand Duke to grant them a civic guard as the Pope had granted at Rome. This is the way the popular feeling is expressed, here in Italy. It is said that the Grand Duke will grant it.[3] He means well but is timid. Did I tell you how our carriage-wheel was almost locked in his, some weeks ago, and we had the honour of a great stare, & salutation– Hat taken off most absolutely. He has a good frank face, much care-worn, & looks greyer than his years, being scarcely fifty yet. The new royal baby[4] has given occasion to various festivities, and Wilson met the wet nurse the other morning driven out gently to exercise like a milch-cow. A word which reminds me of grass & freshness, so I will tell you that we have had rain & are suddenly in the cool; and I have condescended to dress myself & signify to Robert that I was ready to walk out with him wherever he liked– If you were to see how pleased he is when I can walk out with him! nothing seems to delight him so:—and he was to choose the walk for himself—and he chose the Boboli gardens & took me to see a part of them I had not seen, the great fountain, surrounded with the famous nudities which overwhelmed Wilson at her first arrival at Florence .. and then we went into the arbour-walks, with lattices cut out of the deep green, showing glimpses of the Appenines, of Fiesole, of olive grounds grey against the hills: altogether it was delightful. The wind was as fresh as a night English wind, only softer; and the sun rather shone than scorched. Also in those shadowy walks, there was no need of a parasol. Robert carried mine, and then we sate down on the marble benches & talked of everything in Heaven & earth & Wimpole Street especially. The worst was that Flush could not come with us. The barbarians of the Boboli gardens do not admit dogs. Here in Italy they are civilized enough to let dogs into their churches, .. but into their gardens, no I thank you. Robert & I have various controversies on the church-question, because, notwithstanding permission & custom, he hates to take Flush into a church, whereas I, you know, like to take him everywhere– The fact is, that Flush *has*, it must be confessed, a way of walking straight up to the High Altar & performing his devotions thereat, which is scarcely orthodox, & might be objectionable to the faithful—Robert declares that he is in an agony the whole time ... "My darling, you dont see other dogs behave so".— (Ah yes!—*my darling*! Just so! You see what personal reasons I have for protesting against the Reynolds-theory, .. seeing that just that word is his very favorite .. or sometimes it is "*my* LITTLE *darling*", which of course w^d be considered twice as disgusting.) Flush is a sort of Luther, & "protests" more vigorously than gracefully– I must tell you what an illusion he fell into however, on the subject of water-melon. He saw one cut into slices, which being very red, he took it into his head could only represent slices of underdone beef; and dashed up against my knee, entreating with eyes coming out from under his ears, that I w.d give him some instantly! I acceded & he swallowed down a great piece without a moment's consideration—dreadful to be so deceived! slowly & mournfully he retreated with his tail between his legs & nothing more to be said– He never has asked for another slice. Talk of water-melon, & here it comes! Wilson brings me in a "small one" for our home consumption, a yard (except two inches) round, & price five pence halfpenny, .. which will last us five days (for dinner & supper) though Robert is a frightful consumer of it, eating it on so large a scale that only by experience I am satisfied that the excess will not hurt him ... he who scarcely eats anything else! We keep it in ice, & it is not like other melons .. it is not indigestible, I should think, and is much the more agreeable fruit besides. This which Wilson brought me in, I tried in vain to carry. I could just with all my strength lift it up. She is better, poor Wilson!– The lump is not to be felt now, & so it could only have been flatulency .. but there is a tendency to obstruction in the side, & exercise & diet are not sufficient to obviate the need for strong medecines. Sir Charles Herbert[5] says that her eyes and nails are of a better colour, & that he will soon set her to rights– If it had been *myself* I would not have gone to him .. I w.d have kept to the old prescriptions .. & walked more & eaten still less .. but I advised her to go to him of course, for she gets nervous .. and so do I, shrinking from the responsibility– The swelling she had at Pisa is gone, and she has looked as well as any one could look throughout our residence at Florence until quite lately, and in my own mind I do attribute the whole return of evil to that detestable bread at Vallombrosa which was enough to upset any delicate digestion. How well it was that we were kept from staying there, after all! Our disappointment was a "blessing in disguise" as usual & only that. Did I, when I mentioned Carlyle's letter, tell you that he suggested our going to live at Chelsea near him, when we went to England? At the same time he said, that he felt inclined towards Italy himself .. towards coming out here, as Robert had suggested. I have heard from Miss Martineau & she wrote one side of M.r Kenyon's sheet, & invited us in the kindest words to visit her at the Lakes. Now did I tell you that before? The other day Robert met in the street M.r Irving.[6] He had just come from Pisa & was going back for a day or two but "on his return would call directly on us". M.r Powers we see sometimes & like better & better. Never was a simpler man of genius in a better sense. He is meditating a statue of Franklin with uplifted hand plucking down the lightning .. and Robert in the flash of a moment gave him a motto, in a Latin line by a Frenchman, which he translated so "He snatched the bolt from Heaven, the badge from Kings."[7] M.r Powers, quite delighted, said he would engrave both Latin & English on the base of his statue.

August 31. Wilson is much better, I am happy to say, since I began this letter- In the former part of it I begged you, Arabel, to write often while we were at Florence, and now on calculation it appears that you have time to send me only one more letter—the more vexatious for *me*! .. & that to reach me it must be posted on the *next day* to the day on which you read what I write- I beseech you to let me have therefore, the one letter I can receive- Write instantly- Also, let the first letter which you write to Rome be written on a single sheet of paper, without envelope. To my horror & consternation Robert brings up before my eyes an idea which I struggle against receiving, about the postage-regulations in Rome on this head- He fancies, in fact he has seen in a newspaper, that enclosures are not permitted in the Roman post—a fact, which IF a fact, draws, to my mind, a permanent mist over the Seven Hills. He says that you must write oftener to us .. that is all! Yes! but nothing makes amends for my delightful thick packets, and the inconvenience on every account is great- I dont believe his newspaper authority, .. and indeed he & I had a regular quarrel about it last night, at the end of which we begged each other's pardon. He declared that never in his life, had he seen me so angry—and "was it HIS fault if the Roman postoffice was different from this at Florence?" Why certainly it was'nt his fault, and if really I was angry, the more foolish *I*..! but I dont think I was angry, exactly, with *him*—and I agreed at last to tell you; and if it is a mistake (which I cant help still hoping) I will tell you again the contrary. In the meantime, let the first Roman letter be written on as large a sheet as you can find- I hate, too, writing on those great sheets. Robert says that I dont believe it, just because I dont like it- Well, we shall see. I shall send you another Florentine letter before we leave Florence and he will enquire in the interim, so that perhaps I may be able to tell you something prior even to the Roman experience; but, if not, hold yourselves warned. We talk confidently of living on the top of the Tarpeian Rock, precisely as if we had taken the apartment already- A capital place for blowing soap bubbles!—and we have'nt yet blown ours. Florence is too public, rather. It will be grand & philosophical to send bubble after bubble over the ruins of old Rome—wont it?- We shall go on the twentieth of September, if everything goes smoothly besides—if I am well & prepared to travel .. for it would be easy to delay the journey for a month in case of its seeming better on any ground to do so- I am very well now .. only being made of doubtful stuff speculative people & cautious people take occasion from me for doubting this or that .. I only know that I am very well indeed. Also, we mean to travel very quietly & slowly, & eschew every sort of fatigue. The day after the Boboli gardens excursion, we went to the Museum close by,[8] to see the famous waxen preparations of plants .. the most beautiful & curious in the world—also the waxen representation of the plague, .. which I hesitated rather to see & sickened in the seeing .. it is so ghastly

& dreadful!—only, being on a minute scale, the horror is idealized away to a safe distance. The anatomical exhibition, also in wax, Robert would not let me see—nor did I desire it, for various reasons—though women are admitted indiscriminately, & the Italians come in crowds. I meant to write to M.̲ Boyd today- Give him my love if you see him before I send his letter. Think of Miss Mitford having taken back K___!! She says that she never has had a happy day since she parted with her, & now is entirely satisfied, & hopes that I shall forgive her for being so. Of course it is matter of feeling- For my part, it w.ᵈ be most painful to me to have close to me a person in whom I could not reasonably place the least confidence or faith. As to repentance & reformation, I hope the grounds for believing in them are good grounds—but I remember too vividly how after floods of tears, the woman sinned & sinned .. I cannot think that dear Miss Mitford has done well or wisely. It was such a flagrant case .. such a compound iniquity!- But the thing is done, & though I have let her see that I could not sympathize in any way in the doing, there was no use in making reproaches & I have not made them. She has been suffering from rheumatism, poor Miss Mitford, and on that account, changed her London-plan, & has been seeing her friends at dinner in the country instead, & enjoying herself, she says, a good deal. How glad I am that ⟨Emma Margary⟩[9] appears happy. Ah, Arabel!—yes!- You know my thought about a "first husband"- There was a grateful sort of affectionateness in that case, but as little *love proper* as might be- I do not doubt that she may not easily be happier in the new position than in the old. Give her my affectionate congratulations. M.̲ ⟨Margary⟩ is probably a stronger[-]headed man than ⟨M.̲ Monro⟩ was, and if a warm heart enters into the composition, why there is more stuff to hold by,—for an impulsive, vivacious woman like ⟨Emma⟩- I dare say they wont live very long at a distance from London. Does Alfred complain & fear for the Great Western in the general panic about railroads as constaté[10] in the newspapers. Hearing of it I fear a little for him- Tell me if he considers his prospects as good as ever- Something too is said of drought in the West Indies? I trust dear Storm is not thirsting for the watercourses. Are his bees the makers of golden honey for him? Never forget to mention anything relating to Stormie. It is delightful to hear of George looking well after his labours in the country. As to Henry, bid him be of good courage & look out steadily for occupation: he will get it in time, be sure- Occy .. and Sette the barrister at law .. whose marriage, *did* we see or not the other day announced, ..? S. Barrett Esq.ʳᵉ, barrister at law- Tell me of dearest Papa always- I wonder if really & in his heart, he does *not* love me now—while I love him so unchangeably- If he does not, .. God judges betwixt us two, which of us has loved the other best!-——— But it makes me giddy to look back & speak of the past, & of the present in reference to it. Tell my dear Henrietta that I took it into my head she wrote her last letter, being out of spirits, & that THAT, I really cannot permit—there is no reason for being out of courage & spirits, and to be unreasonable is to be very, very naughty– I wish Papa would send you all out of town as he did last year– She does not seem to care much for it, but it would do you all good, I think .. lift you up & turn your faces round into the light & sunshine– At any rate, do make Tripp, (dearest Trippy, give her my love) do make Trippy go. It is *necessary* for Trippy to have change of air. Do persuade her to go somewhere. You, my dear, dear Arabel, are going to Tunbridge to the Strattens, did you not say something of it? and you mean to have a pic nic in some quarter of the world, according to your announcement– Florence is a city & so is London; but Florence is not like London, I can assure you– If you were to see the moonlight dripping down the wall of our grey San Felice—and how presently we stand knee-deep in it; on our own terrace. Such moonlight—such a divine, still air!—— The worst of Florence is the noise. I do believe that the people never sleep at night except by the merest accident– The whole of the night they are walking & talking under my windows, and laughing & singing ... what Flush may call singing & music perhaps, for aught I know– Robert says that at Rome it will be very different, to which I answer that I hope it will be as different as possible– London-noise is nothing in comparison– The streets here, observe, are all narrow—and paved all over with flat ⟨★★★⟩

Publication: None traced.
Manuscript: Berg Collection.

 1. Year determined by EBB's references to the Brownings' plans to travel to Rome for the winter.

 2. The name has been obliterated here, and in two places below, by someone other than EBB.

 3. Leopold II (1797–1870), Grand Duke of Tuscany (1824–59), granted a civic guard on 4 September 1847, and the public celebration that followed occurred on 12 September, the first anniversary of the Brownings' marriage. For EBB's description and account of the occasion, see letters 2701 and 2703.

 4. Ludwig (1847–1915) was the ninth child of Leopold II and his second wife Maria Antonia (1814–98).

 5. Charles Lyon Herbert (1784?–1855) was one of the "excellent English physicians" practicing in Florence at this time (Murray's *Hand-Book for Travellers in Northern Italy*, 1847, p. 476).

 6. See letter 2630, note 12.

 7. "Eripuit cœlo fulmen, mox sceptra tyrannis"—cf. "eripuitque Iovi fulmen viresque tonandi et sonitum ventis concessit," Manilius, *Astronomica*, I, 104, which has been attributed to the French statesman and economist Anne Robert Jacques Turgot. The line was used as an inscription on the statue of Franklin by Houdon in 1778. Powers had accepted a commission for a statue of Franklin in 1843, for which he used a copy of a cast by Flaxman of the Houdon bust of Franklin. This and other study materials were sent to Powers some time in 1847 by his friend Richard Henry Wilde. Wilde was unsuccessful in raising the necessary subscription for the statue, and it was not until 1858, when Wilde received a commission from the United States government, that he completed the model. There are two marbles of this statue: one in the Senate wing of the United States capitol

building, and another in the Benjamin Franklin Senior High School in New Orleans (Richard P. Wunder, *Hiram Powers: Vermont Sculptor, 1805-1873*, 1991, II, 150-152). Neither of these, nor any of the busts of Franklin completed by Powers after Flaxman's cast in 1848 and 1849, bears the inscription suggested by RB.

8. The Museo di Storia Naturale, where, according to Murray's *Hand-Book*, "the models in wax are interesting. The more ancient by *Zummo*, a Sicilian, who executed them for Cosmo III, principally represent corpses in various stages of decomposition. The others are, more strictly speaking, anatomical, and display every portion of the human body with wonderful accuracy" (p. 565).

9. Emma Monro (*née* Russell), widowed the year following her marriage to Theodore Monro, had recently married Peter John Margary (see letter 2672, note 15).

10. "Observed."

2698. EBB TO FANNY DOWGLASS

Palazzo Guidi.
Monday. Sept. 6- [1847][1]

Now I dare say I shall make you smile a little, dearest friend, by this note & question to come .. but the truth is that we two have *laughed* in the agony of our doubtfulness about the lady,[2] whom, you intimate, we should recognize at first glance as "sister" & intimate, & whom with open eyes & utter consternation we cant either of us remember ever to have ...!! She writes so kindly to us that we would fain know what ought to be known at any rate. Oh, *will* you have the very great goodness to tell me what I ought to know? I seem to have heard the name. Has she written something, & what? Do tell me & let me breathe. Robert does not doubt (observe) that he has had the honour of an introduction to her .. only introductions pass so in London society, .. one mask follows another in such a slippery fashion, .. that with the best of memories & intentions it is impossible, I suppose, to keep one's recollections in order. He has seen a good deal of the world, .. always hating it, as he says, & yearning for the "garden of cucumbers"[3] to which he has come now .. though the best & brightest minds in England, which help to constitute London Literary society, are the flower of the world, perhaps, after all. Miss Boyle kindly wrote to invite us to Lorenzo's villa. I do not go out much just now, & have not been in the carriage since our return from Vallombrosa, on account of certain precautions which may or may not be wise ones; meaning to keep quiet until the time for the great journey comes on the twentieth. But, I shall write & tell her that we shall be happy to receive her here whenever she may think it worth while to bestow on us a few moments of a visit to Florence- Meanwhile, it would be pleasant to know how wide one should open one's arms for a first embrace-We stand confounded, at this writing, in a "grand peutêtre"-[4]

So you will let me hear again, dear dear friend, .. so I am to have a real letter from you presently! Glad I am of the prospect & the promise. Yet I wish that you had mentioned in the last little sheet, how you were, & if you had triumphed over the nettle-rash– Mind you speak of yourself when you write next. What delightful coolness & freshness! what rains, as if the Heavens were coming down in all their Grace!– I have walked up & down in the balcony & enjoyed .. enjoyed so much!– Thank God sometimes for your friend!– The people here are in great triumph & joy in the grant of the civic guard; and the *Te Deum* in the Duomo, which Robert went to hear yesterday, was a fine thing, he said– Nothing, however, disappoints me more than the *poetical effect* (if I may use the expression) than the *impressiveness* of the R Catholic ceremonies– There seems a want of reality & earnestness— there is something little & *mesquin* .. where I expected to be shaken & prostrated, I sit calmly & coldly still. We agree sometimes that there is more *poetry* in the best sense, in the poorest wildest methodist congregation, where the people lift up with their hearts the rugged rhymes of the old psalm, than in what we see & hear in Italy. But God looks through tinsel as through rags—the ONE finds the Unity where we count the divisions, we with our bisecting eyes!

I am writing hastily or could say so much more– Love your ever affectionate Ba–

Direct *Poste Restante*—it is safer.

Publication: None traced.
Manuscript: Huntington Library.

    1. Year determined from EBB's reference to the recent return from Vallombrosa.
    2. Mary Louisa Boyle (1810–90) youngest of five children of Courtenay Boyle (1770–1844) and Carolina Amelia (*née* Poyntz, d. 1851). Mary's sister Carolina Boyle (1803–83) was, for many years, Maid of Honour to Queen Adelaide, and her uncle was Edmund (1767–1856), 8th Earl of Cork. Mary Boyle wrote *The Forester* (1839) and *The Bridal of Melcha* (1844). Shortly after arriving in Florence in the summer of 1847, she, her mother, and her brother Charles John (1806–85) took up residence in the Medici Villa Careggi, which was owned by Henry Edward Fox, 4th Baron Holland (1802–59), who had been appointed envoy extraordinary and minister plenipotentiary to the court of Tuscany in 1839. See *Mary Boyle: Her Book*, edited by Sir Courtenay Boyle (1901), p. 201.
    3. Isaiah 1:8.
    4. "Great perhaps." Cf. "Je m'en vais chercher un grand peut-être," "I go to seek a great perhaps." (Attributed to Rabelais on his death-bed.)

No. 2700 11 September [1847] 297

2699. EBB TO MARY LOUISA BOYLE

Palazzo Guidi
[7 September 1847][1]

I thank you, dear Miss Boyle, for the kind feeling which induced your kind note to me, and for the desire to see us at Lorenzo's Villa which it would have been so natural & pleasant to have answered in person yesterday– But I have not been lately quite as strong as usual, .. at least it has been thought wisest for me not to exert myself as much as usual, as matter of precaution & preparation for our journey toward Rome on the twentieth: and the fact is, that I have not been in a carriage for several weeks on this account– On this, too, I must give up for the present your villa & Lorenzo—but why, therefore, must we give up *you*? Rather, if you ever come into Florence, (which of course you do), and if, having come, you ever have an unenchanted half-hour, (which is more doubtful) and if you think it worth while, in the spirit of your note, to bestow it on us, .. come & see us at any hour except from three to five, and believe of my husband & myself that we shall be happy to receive you as no stranger. ⟨...⟩

Publication: None traced.
Source: The Kenneth W. Rendell Gallery Catalogue 246 [December 1995], p. 11.

1. Dating is provided in the Rendell Gallery Catalogue without explanation. EBB's reference in letter 2701 to answering Miss Dowglass and then Miss Boyle indicates placement after 2698.

2700. EBB TO THOMAS WESTWOOD

Florence
Sept. 11– [1847][1]

Yes, indeed, my dear M! Westwood, I have seen "friars". We have been on a pilgrimage to Vallombrosa, & while my husband rode up & down the precipitous mountain-paths, I and my maid & Flush were dragged, in a hamper by two white bullocks, .. and such scenery!—such hilly peaks, .. such black ravines & gurgling waters & rocks and forests above & below!—and at last such a monastery & such friars who would'nt let us stay with them beyond five days for fear of corrupting the fraternity. Two women, .. why how could they be suffered upon holy ground? The monks had a new abbot, a St Sejanus[2] of a holy man, and a petticoat stank in his nostrils, said he, .. and all the beseeching which we could offer him with joined hands was classed with the temptations of St Anthony.[3] So we had to come away as we went, & get the better as we could of our disappointment; and really it was a disappointment not to be able to stay our two months out in the wilderness as we had planned it, to say nothing of the heat of Florence to which at the moment it was not pleasant to return. But we got new lodgings in the shade & comforted ourselves as well as we could- Comforted! there's a word for Florence!—— That ingratitude was a slip of the pen, believe me. Only we had set our hearts upon a two months seclusion in the deep of the pine-forests (which have such a strange dialect in the silence they speak with) and the mountains were divine, and it was provoking to be crossed in our ambitions by that little holy abbot with the red face & to be driven out of Eden even to Florence. It is said, observe, that Milton took his description of Paradise from Vallombrosa, .. so driven out of Eden we were literally. To Florence though!—and what Florence is the tongue of man or poet may easily fail to describe. The most beautiful of cities, with the golden Arno shot through the breast of her, like an arrow .. and "non dolet,"[4] all the same- For what helps to charm here, is the innocent gaiety of the people, who, for ever at feast-day & holiday celebration, come & go along the streets, the women in elegant dresses & with glittering fans, shining away every thought of northern cares & taxes, such as make people grave in England. No little orphan on a house-step, but seems to inherit naturally his slice of water-melon & bunch of purple grapes: and the rich fraternize with the poor as we are unaccustomed to see them, listening to the same music & walking in the same gardens & looking at the same Raffaels even! Also, we are glad to be here just now, when there is new animation & energy given to Italy, by this new wonderful Pope who is a great man & doing greatly. I hope you give him your sympathies. Think how seldom the liberation of a people begins from the throne, *à fortiori* from a papal throne which is so high & straight! And the spark spreads—here is even our Grand Duke, conceding the civic guard, & forgetting his Austrian prejudices- The world learns, it is pleasant to observe. I am glad that in your Belgic tour you have seen another side of it. *I* too, should like to see Belgium. After Italy though!—after Rome!,—where we shall probably be in a month from hence, with the intention of staying the winter- *Am I writing*? Do you talk to my conscience, pray. One may see & hear, muse, dream, & enjoy, & all *that*, you know, may justify itself in writing at last. My husband is busy still with the preparation for his second edition- Your tale of the Howitts is dreadful or worse .. hateful- As to Tennyson, hope for him—for M! Forster of the Examiner wrote to tell us some time ago that the new poem on a 'Commonwealth of Women' surpassed anything hitherto produced by the writer—and therefore we must pardon the pipe which is not pastoral, and the gin & water which .. is not bearable after all. One excuse for him is that he is of a morbidly irritable nature .. his nerves are so .. and he turns for relief, I suppose, to the first resource. I had a letter from Miss Martineau very lately, on her return to England, & she speaks in it of her "beloved Jordan" as if she had brought

such vivid impressions full of pleasure. Oh yes—we shall go back to you all one day– I have left full security in Wimpole St for my re-appearance, be sure– In the meanwhile you may have the "joint volume" you kindly desire[5] .. I wont swear against it. So well I am, dear M.[r] Westwood, and so happy after a year's trial of this stuff of marriage .. happier than ever, perhaps! .. & the revolution is so complete that one has to learn to stand up straight & steadily (like a landsman in a sailing ship) before one can do any work with one's hands & brain. Flush thanks you as his mistress does for the remembrance you give him. Flush hated Vallombrosa & the black pine-forests & the wild mountain-side, and rejoiced visibly in our return to civilized life and to little Florentine dogs. How is Flossie? Tell me of yourself & that you are going on well & being happy– We have had a delightful letter from Carlyle who loves my husband, I am proud to say– How good you are about the newspaper– Here we might have received one, but we are going from hence, & I am ignorant of the regulations at Rome– Let me have a letter from you in any case, and a letter, believe me, is better than any newspaper in the world– We knew of the People's Journal & the notice there–[6] Now farewell! With my husband[']s regards, I am ever most faithfully yours
EBB.

Direct care of Mess.[rs] Torlonia, *Rome.*[7]

Address, on integral page: T Westwood Esq.[re] / 1 or 7 Denmark Street / Camberwell.
Publication: LEBB, I, 342–344 (in part).
Manuscript: British Library.

1. The year is provided by EBB's reference to the recent visit to Vallombrosa.
2. EBB is referring to the Irish bishop Senanus (or Senan, 488?–560), who built a monastery on Scattery Island, to which women were forbidden. In fact, when St. Cannera arrived requesting to be buried there, St. Senanus turned her away. Thomas Moore put the legend into verse in "St. Senanus and the Lady" (1821). See letter 2679, note 4.
3. See letter 2686, note 9.
4. "It doesn't hurt" (cf. Barker, *Parriana,* II, 296–297).
5. From EBB's comment in letter 2660 (see note 7) and RB's comment near the end of letter 2657, it appears that the Brownings had discussed the possibility of producing a book together. Whether Westwood heard the possibility discussed, or proposed it on his own is not clear.
6. Either Westwood thought the poets had not seen the review of RB's *Colombe's Birthday* in the August 1846 issue of *The People's Journal* (for the complete text of this review, see vol. 13, pp. 402–404); or perhaps he had mentioned a review of Margaret Fuller's *Papers on Literature* (a collection of her critical essays previously published in *The New-York Daily Tribune*) in the February 1847 edition of *The People's Journal.* That review extracted a paragraph from her essay on RB's *Paracelsus*; for the complete text of her review of RB's works, see vol. 12, pp. 377–384.
7. Bankers in the Via Condotti at Rome (Murray's *Handbook for Travellers in Central Italy,* 1843, p. 251).

2701. EBB to Arabella & Henrietta Moulton-Barrett

Florence–
[13 September 1847][1]

Love to love my dearest both of you! How else should I thank you adequately for your kindest of letters, which happily came on the wrong day, saturday, inasmuch as if it had come on the twelfth we should have missed it till monday, it being impossible to force one's way to the postoffice through the crowded streets.[2] Robert expected a letter from home & had to give it up—the thing was impossible. The fact was, that our Italians had resolved to keep our day for us on a most magnificent scale; an intention which we, on our parts, not only graciously appropriated, but permitted in return to perfect the glory by keeping at the same time the establishment of the civic guard & prospect of the liberty of Italy through union– Ah, you should have seen our day! Forty thousand strangers were in Florence .. I mean, inhabitants of the different Tuscan states, deputations and companies of various kinds; and for above three hours the infinite procession filed under our windows with all their various flags & symbols, into the Piazza Pitti where the Duke & his family stood in tears at the window to receive the thanks of his people. Never in the world was a more affecting sight .. nor a grander, if you took it in its full significance– The magistracy came first .. with their flag, & then the priesthood (such as chose) .. and I saw some brown monks there, with the rope girdle, I assure you--and then & then .. class after class .. troops of peasants & nobles, and of soldiers fraternizing with the people .. Then too, came the foreigners, there was a place for them—& there are so many foreign residents here that it was by no means unimportant to admit their sympathy—French, English, Swiss, Greeks (such a noble band of Greeks!) all with their national flags– Meanwhile there was no lack of spectators. The windows dropping down their glittering draperies, seemed to grow larger with the multitude of pretty heads, & of hands which threw out flowers & waved white handkerchiefs– There was not an inch of wall, not alive, if the eye might judge– Clouds of flowers & laurel leaves came fluttering down on the advancing procession—and the clapping of hands, & the frenetic shouting, and the music which came in gushes, & then seemed to go out with too much joy, and the exulting faces, and the kisses given for very exultation between man & man, and the mixing of elegantly dressed women in all that crowd & turbulence with the sort of smile which proved how little cause there was for fear .. all these features of the scene made it peculiar, & memorable & most beautiful to look at & to look back upon. We went to a window in our palazzo which had a full view, and I had a throne of cushions piled up on a chair, but was dreadfully tired before it was all over, in spite of them, as you may suppose from the excitement of such a scene. And then Robert & I waved our handkerchiefs till my wrist ached, I will answer for mine. At night there was an illumination, & we walked just to the Arno to have a sight of it, .. and *then*, the streets were as crowded as a full route in London might be, only with less pushing probably, & with the soft starry air in change for a stiffling atmosphere— And even *then*, the people were *embracing* for joy. It was a state of phrenzy or rapture, extending to the children of two years old, several of whom I heard lisping .. "*Vivas*," with their little fat arms clasping their mothers['] necks. So was'nt our day kept well for us? Yes, and without a single discord to mar the harmony— You never see drunkenness nor brutality in any form in the gladness of these Tuscans. You never see fighting with fists, nor hear blasphemous language. It is the sort of gladness in which women may mingle and be glad too— Our poor English want educating into gladness—they want refining, not in the fire but in the sunshine. How different a thing a crowd is here to an English crowd, you must come here to learn—yet whose is the fault, I wonder? And why should it be so, with all our advantages of a more scriptural instruction and larger constitutional rights? One reason is that our religious teachers in England do not sanctify the relaxations of the people. The narrowness which cuts down literature & refuses to accept Art into the uses of the Christian Life, is more rife with injury & desecration than you see at a first glance— Of this I am more & more sure the more I see & live. It is a worse mistake than marrying on Litany wednesdays, and dining on fast-fridays, .. and we should repent it in the ashes of ash-wednesdays, if people repent deepest really in such ashes. You will say that it was'nt a very perfect keeping of sunday yesterday even though it did perfectly for our anniversary. The whole company of which the procession consisted, went in the first place to the cathedral, observe, the great Duomo, (where nobody unconnected with the ceremony was admitted, for the plain reason that there was no room) & there the banners were *blessed*, and the 'Veni Creator' & Te Deum sung in choral magnificence[3]—and I could not for my part take it for desecration when the next movement brought them to thank their sovereign, & fraternize in hope with one another. Besides their view of the meaning of the "Lord's Day" is different you know from the general view of it in England, .. whether nearer or farther from the true one, being another question— And now, pray dont take it into your dear imaginations that Italy is in arms, & that I am on the eve of being massacred—you & dearest Trippy may set your hearts at ease, on the contrary, for the safety of my head– The excitement here which certainly exists, & is at its height perhaps in Tuscany just now, is all joyous & good & innocent & *preventive* of evil. If Italians join hands, Austria may throw in vain her poisoned arrows, .. and the noise we hear is only the clash of the gauntlets as friend meets friend– Every Austrian in Florence was desired to keep the house yesterday, by an order of the police,—& this because it had been discovered that here as lately in Rome, *paid Austrians* were in league to produce disturbance in the streets, in order to justify the interference of the Austrian government. Is it not hateful & loathsome? Met[t]ernich puts out these fangs, .. trembling in his hole, poor reptile, for his power in Italy.[4] Which may God shiver into dust– Our grand Duke has behaved well– Think!—it was a hard position for him! himself an Austrian, & his family & associations leaning to absolutism naturally. But he sacrifices everything, & does it well & nobly, as if his heart helped him. After all, however, the Pope is the liberator– He is a great man .. I call him *great*. It is wonderful how a man in such a position, should have his soul free & pure for such a course of action. Liberty seldom originates for a people from the throne, .. and when you consider that it is a Pope's throne, the wonder grows most wonderful– I think I must go to see him when we go to Rome to express by that act what a man I hold him to be. And it is expected that after the court of the sanctuary, he means to wash the sanctuary itself,—to reform the priesthood (which requires it, as some of the laity know) and to cleanse various practises of the church.[5] A most devout man, he is said to be, and brave and gentle at once—and as the people in Rome adore him, he may attempt very nearly what he pleases without fear of being accused of heresy. He rides about the streets on a mule, they say, & dreams by night & day, of doing good *humbly*. Think of such a Pope!-

And of such a letter too!—you will be tired of it & of me long & long before this, I am certain, .. you who dont want to hear about Popes & crowds– So let me go on & tell you of our day. The worst of it was that Robert was not well—he had caught cold & felt unwell for several days, & yesterday he was as languid, as languid .. and looked so pale .. and of course it spoiled our good spirits rather, though he made me very happy by saying again & again such things as cant be repeated nor forgotten, besides, that never in his life, from his joyous childhood upwards, had he enjoyed such happiness as he has known with me—— *Too* happy it makes me to hear such things! Indeed if the perfectest love & sympathy can give any happiness, we both enjoy it– There has not been a cloud, nor a breath. The only difference is from happy to happier, and from being loved to being loved more– When he says he loves me more, I see that it is just so– Every word I say is something right & bright, let it be ever so dull: and if I say nothing, why then, I am sure to be looking right, or pouring out coffee right, or listening divinely to something said to me—so that mine is not a difficult part by any manner of means. We have gone over all our days last year in rather a pleasanter way than we did the original days, which were wretched, to say the best of them——oh, that dreadful day at Hampstead! If you knew how I suffered while I talked word upon word- My darling Arabel was grave, & you looked suspicious, and the life of us all seemed to hang on the suspicion being put away. But in talking lately of these things, I could not help laughing a little, & catching a glimpse of the ridiculous side as they turned into the passing year. Always it *does* make us laugh, for instance, to think of the official's (the man with the wand in the church) attitude & gesture of astonishment, as he stood at the churchdoor & saw bride & bridegroom part on the best terms possible & go off in separate flies. Robert was very generous & threw about his gold to clerk, pew openers &c &c in a way to convict us of being in a condition of incognito .. and this particular man with a wand, had hazarded, between two bursts of gratitude, a philosophic sentiment about "marriage being a very serious event in one's mortal life", .. this as we left the church- And there he stood in the doorway, his speech scarcely ended on his lips, .. mouth wide open in mute surprise! "Never had he seen anything more remarkable than *that*, in the whole course of his practice!"—— On our day we gave Wilson a turquoise broach as a memorial of it having chosen it on the jewellers bridge[6] the day before-. If it had not been for Wilson, on the real day, it w^d have been worse with me than it was. I assure you she only knew the *night before*, and, I am sure, had her own share of suffering, .. she who is so timid & easily daunted. She was more glad to make us knead cakes yesterday: & we had them for tea at seven oclock. But now I am going to tell you how a cloud came. Robert, as I said, was not well, & did not take his walk as usual with Flush for company—& therefore, because we hold it necessary for Flush to have daily exercise, we sent him down stairs with Annunciata just for one run- Well- Not only did he run, but he ran away. A little dog passed at the moment, & after the dog he went, & upstairs without him came Annunciata. 'Oh' said she .. ["]è niente! Tornerà presto, presto,"[7]— and really I thought he might be back soon .. but hours passed, & no Flush. Was'nt it too bad of him to spoil our wedding day so? As it grew darker & darker the tears could scarcely be kept out of my eyes, .. for Flush has a new collar & I feared that he might be stolen by one of the forty thousand visitors, and so farewell to poor Flush. And so passed the night- The porter left open the gates till twelve oclock .. but not a sign of Flush—and when Wilson came to dress me in the morning no Flush, no Flush! (Robert had gone round to Piazza Pitti in vain, I forgot to say .. but then who could see a dog in that crowd). Well, while I was dressing, in the morning and sighing over all these vicissitudes in the most melancholy of moods, a dash was made against the door of the room which either betokened Flush or the devil .. and of the two you may suppose that it was Flush– Yes! he had come back & laid down at the entrance of our appartment, & a charitable person had let him in—and very guilty he looked & tired, as if he had been roaming about all night. "Quite disgraceful for a respectable dog like him," as Robert said reproachfully. But I dont doubt that the great crowd & confusion & illumination of the night before had frightened & confounded him, & that he had lost himself completely– In the calm of the morning he had recovered his head a little—poor Flush—and in this way the evil was remedied. Ah, you dearest kindest best Henrietta & Arabel, how I thank you from my heart of hearts for your dear letters & tender words. First I read your letters always to myself, & then Robert sits down by me to hear everything that is not too secret. Well—I read your letter so, to him, yesterday, Henrietta, .. and then I began Arabel's, without the precaution this time, of reading it to myself first. I managed it all very well until I came to that part where she spoke of praying for me in the place where we used to pray together, and there, I could not get on but burst out crying in the most unforseen way possible, .. which was unfortunate, .. for he hates to see me cry & began to look a little unhappy himself just for company. Yet it grew better by degrees, and at last nothing was left but the brightness of knowing how you both love me who love you back again from the soul of my soul—dearest Things! May we look on one another's face before long—I long to see you!

We have had a great fair here, and the cheapness of everything has been miraculous. I have bought neck ribbons, five or six or seven of them, very pretty, at three pence a yard—such as you w^d give a shilling or fifteen pence for in England. Also a winter's gown, .. a sort of Orleans cloth, (more like *that* than anything else) with a silk stripe in it, .. really pretty & fine .. of an invisible green colour .. and I gave for the whole dress 5^s-6^d It was five pence halfpenny a yard– So much it pleased me that I wanted another in black, (which blackness is convenient at Rome, women being excluded from some of the ceremonies if unclothed in it .. and I have worn out my black silk gown) but it rained the last day of the fair and Wilson missed her opportunity of getting it for me. If I buy at the shops a black French merino, it will be a guinea—and to give a guinea for a dress in this land of cheapness, seems to me rather an extravagance. Yet you would give rather more in England .. would'nt you? Wilson paid three halfpence a yard for the lining of the green gown– Think of that! Such prices only, account for the elegance of the women of all classes, which strikes foreigners so much on the frequent festa-day. Otherwise it w^d be a problem to solve. Our baker's wife is an Englishwoman married to a German,[8] and she said to Wilson .. "Ah, you may talk of England—everybody does that! but when you go back you will cry your eyes out for Italy, just as I did when I thought I would return, and then longed to get out of it all again. England is not the place for the poor. They are treated like dogs there, and never enjoy anything like other human beings— The rich on one side, the poor on another, .. that's the way in England— Here we are all men & women & can reach to the same pleasures." Which has a great deal of truth in it— I am jealous for poor England .. Why should not her people be as happy? Why should I pay here only three pence for *two* large soft spunges, for which in London I sh^d pay some ten shillings? Wilson has this instant brought them in to my utter astonishment. She says that though the fair is done, she can get things even cheaper, and has brought some more neck-ribbons, three halfpence a yard. We are providing ourselves with everything at Florence, because Rome has a reputation of being dearer & more difficult— And now I am about to tell you of a new visitor we have had. I found a letter on the table from a Miss Boyle, enclosing a note of introduction from Miss Dowglass .. who said by the way, that she knew nothing scarcely of Miss Boyle except that she was in deep anxiety to find us out, having been already introduced to Mr Browning!! &c &c. & intimated that we both sh^d know in the flash of a thought all about the said Miss Boyle, she being a notorious personage. Well! Robert & I looked into one another's faces in blank confusion—how could he remember an introduction in London, one of the many? & as for me I had never heard of her, I thought. So I wrote back to Miss Dowglass, beseeching her to send us a key—and I wrote to Miss Boyle, who had invited us to the Carreggi villa (the villa of Lorenzo the Magnificent) in her mother's name, that I had not been much out lately but would gladly receive her in Florence if she thought it worth while to call on us. 1st Answered Miss Dowglass from the Baths of Lucca .. that Miss Boyle was the daughter of Lady Boyle, sister of the Queen Dowager's maid of honour, niece to the Earl of Cork, and authoress of certain poems, .. that she had met Robert, whom she excessively admired, at Lady Morgan's,[9] & had just begun a conversation with him in the hollow of a window when the lady of the house spoilt it all .. that knowing Miss Dowglass slightly she had caught sight of my books on the table & had begun to enquire eagerly "where M^r & Mrs Browning were, whom she had hunted for in vain through Pisa & Florence" .... she had heard of their having gone into Switzerland".[10] 2^d Answered Miss Boyle that she would come .. and she came straightway, at a most unfortunate moment, .. Wilson & Annunciata being both out, & Robert opening the door of our apartment, without the prestige of the cravat .. unanealed, uncravatted![11]— .. in the merest, wildest state of dishabile. He has the art however of making the best of a situation, & managed to laugh us back into respectability, and to be so cordial to the visitor that she condescended to say "Oh, you ought to see me & my sister in the morning".— As for me I had been lying prostrate on the sofa & leapt up in horror,—and if really, as he assured me afterward, my hair & appurtenances were 'quite perfect,' it was a miracle of the uncommonest. "Here's Miss Boyle, Ba, come to see you," did confound me utterly, I must admit– But she seemed after all, good natured, & was clever in conversation & made herself a good place at last. "A little lively aristocrat," as Robert describes her well .. and somewhat better under and over. He remembered about her in a moment as soon ⟨as⟩ Lady Morgan's name was mentioned, and says she is the 'crême de la crême' in London society, with certain literary pretensions to boot Almacks.[12] Clever ⟨&⟩ original she certainly seemed in her talk, and she sate an hour with us & "hoped to come again." Lord Holland had lent Lady Boyle the villa Carreggi & they had been there for months without suspecting that we were not in Switzerland, when a chance took Miss Boyle to Lucca Baths & threw her in with Miss Dowglass. Tell Arabel in regard to the latter, that in writing to me she is very reserved about religion, seeming to avoid the subject as much as possible. I *imagine*, that she unites with the church of England, .. with differences perhaps. She rides out a good deal in "gallops" .. it is her favorite exercise. How much better she must be to admit of this!– As to Mrs Cook,[13] I quite quite agree with you that Bummy sh^d be defendant rather than plaintiff– The case is obvious. Give my love to Surtees & Susan– How sorry I am about poor dearest Minny! Oh, Holloways pills![14] What could she be thinking of to be so rash– Keep her in bed as long as you can & mention her particularly– I am sorry too about Crow[15]—mention her when you write– Wilson is better again– You are not to fancy it another *illness*– It was only a return of unpleasant symptoms– Wisely, as I think, she has thrown away Sir Ch. Herbert's last medicine– Simple castor oil seems to do more good– It is a case in which diet & exercise are more active & necessary remedial agents than any drug– As to the heat, I do not, nor does she, think that it did the harm– We are all very sorry to leave Florence,—and I assure you Wilson has been invited to go to England for a husband & return with him to settle here. It does'nt seem so bad a plan to her, I fancy, as it would at one time. We are each of us "taken" in a different charm. Yet we go, & go on monday the twentieth—having doubted to the last,—but the winter prices (just double in these rooms) coming in to turn the scale. Also it is better perhaps on all accounts to travel now– We shall be ten days on the road which is usually travelled in five—but probably you shall hear again before we set out. I am perfectly well, only annoyed by a little occasional distress— & the change of air will do me good, I dare say. Dont be afraid of the Austrians, nor Italians either. Tell Arabel it would be impossible to get a passport at this time for Palermo, Naples & Calabria being in actual revolt. The Reynolds's wont go to Naples we prophesy. In other parts of Italy, where the government gives signs of sympathy with the people, there is no reason to fear for the tranquillity & safety of anyone– Tell my dear dear Treppy that her note shall be answered to herself & that meanwhile I love & kiss her through the air for it. Robert was so gratified, & both of us grateful. Is it

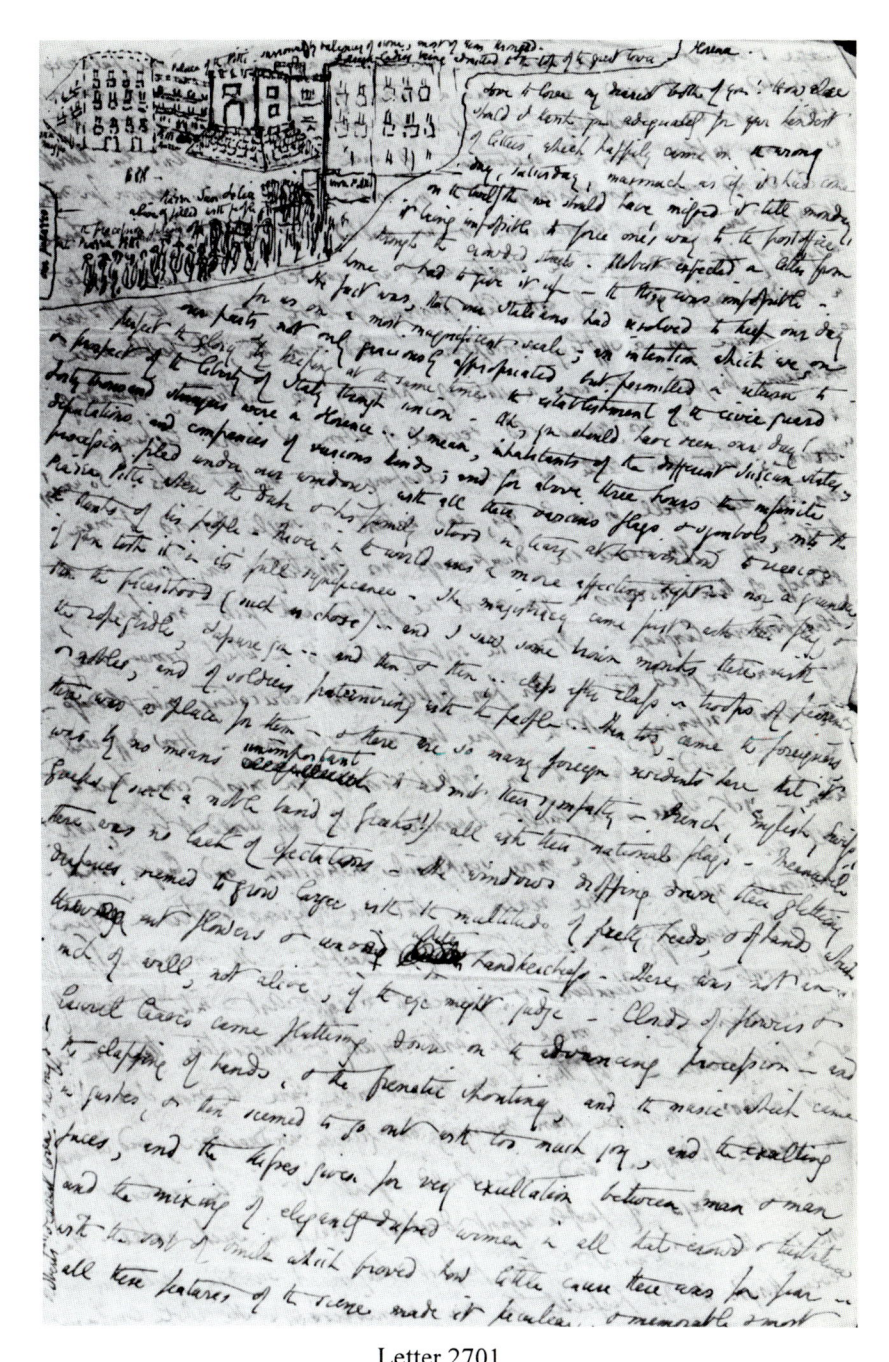

Letter 2701

Palazzo Guidi from Piazza San Felice

No. 2701 [13 September 1847] 307

possible that Henry will write to me! How happy that will make me— I love him & all of them from the roots of my heart—but it is difficult to believe that they love me as you say, when for my sake they refuse to give up a little of this .. what is it to be called? determination, any wise— Could I have stood aside from one I loved a whole year as they have done from me? Love to them is the uppermost feeling with me after all— Tell them all so— If I and mine have wronged them, why not forgive us legally? And so little thought as there was of wronging *them*! God bless you—

Your own
Ba—

Robert's *"dearest love,"* he says—

Address, on integral page: To the care of Miss Trepsack / (Miss Barrett) / 5— Montagu Street / Montagu Square / London.
Publication: Huxley, pp. 43–51 (in part).
Source: Transcript in editors' file.

    1. Dated by EBB's reference to the celebrations on the day of the Brownings' first wedding anniversary, and by her reference to their anniversary as "yesterday."
    2. Not easily seen on her sketch, EBB has identified or written the following: "Our palazzo"; "via maggio"; "Pitti Piazza"; "Palace of the Pitti—surrounded by balconies of stone, most of them thronged"; "Foreign ladies being admitted to the top of the great tower"; "The procession ending up at Piazza Pitti"; "Piazza San Felice alive & filled with people"; "Viva P. IX." EBB's illustration and description here is echoed in *Casa Guidi Windows*, I, 446–576.
    3. "Te Deum Laudamus" ("We praise Thee, O God") and "Veni, Creator Spiritus" ("Come, Creator God") are the opening words of two ancient hymns of praise and thanksgiving.
    4. Prince Clemens von Metternich (1773–1859) dominated European diplomacy during his term as Chancellor of Austria (1809–48). In July 1847 he had ordered Austrian troops to occupy the entire city of Ferrara, which was under papal sovereignty, thus violating international law. Pius IX was outraged, and lodged a formal complaint, but his revenge came a few months later when Metternich requested permission for Austrian troops to march across the Papal States to suppress uprisings in the Kingdom of Naples: the pope refused. Metternich's term as Chancellor ended the following March. EBB refers to him in *Casa Guidi Windows*, I, 662.
    5. Amongst other acts early in his papacy, Pius IX had called for a revival in the religious orders, urging bishops and other clergy to lead the way by example (see letter 2643, note 3); he was himself respected as a model of pastoral leadership.
    6. i.e., the Ponte Vecchio; according to Murray's *Hand-Book for Travellers in Northern Italy* (1847), "like the Rialto, it is a street of shops, appropriated with few exceptions to jewellers, goldsmiths, and other workers in metal" (p. 481). The Ponte Vecchio is still known for its many jewellery shops.
    7. "It's nothing! He will come back very, very soon."
    8. EBB provides "Miller" as the baker's name in a letter to Sarianna Browning dated [2 December 1854] (MS at Lilly Library).
    9. Lady Morgan (*née* Sydney Owenson, 1776–1859) was an Irish novelist and author of *The Wild Irish Girl* (1806) and *Florence Macarthy* (1818). For Miss Boyle, see letter 2698, note 2.
    10. Placement of quotation marks is EBB's.
    11. Cf. *Hamlet*, I, 5, 77.
    12. EBB is referring to the Almacks Assembly Rooms in King Street, St. James's, which had been opened in 1765 by William Almack, a Scotsman. Almacks soon became

a mecca for London society ladies, and was ruled by the patronesses, who alone distributed tickets of admission. Their power to offer or to deny entry made them the undisputed arbiters of fashion and manners.

13. Elizabeth Cook (1783-1862), the mother of Surtees and Susan Cook.
14. One of the "secret remedies" marketed by Thomas Holloway (1800-83), whose ointments and pills were widely advertised. In 1845 he spent £10,000 on advertising (*DNB*). Holloway was later founder and benefactor of Holloway College.
15. Based on EBB's comment at the end of letter 2647, we take this to refer to a failed pregnancy.

2702. EBB TO FANNY DOWGLASS

Florence.
Sept. 17. 1847.

I thought not to teaze you any more, dearest friend, till face to face I should do it,—but from a combination of reasons & temptations we have resolved on remaining where we are, for *one month more*, and I must tell you of it, lest you should pass through Florence & not catch sight of us in passing. Also there is need to tell you that Lady Morgan's name revived the whole remembrance you referred to, .. my husband remembered perfectly everything in the flash of a moment, .. & so he & I were prepared by your letter to receive our visitor that very morning, with her clever vivacious talk, so exactly justifying your description of her. She said she was going to write to you, her dear enchanted & enchanting "White Cat, who had opened your palace-doors to herself & her brother,"[1]—and I liked to hear of your "*galloping*" .. because that seemed stranger than the fairy tale even. Yet you are not well.! Ah yes, do get to Rome—do not run mortal risks in an unfavorable climate. Here, it is so cool as to be almost cold in the evenings & mornings—but I like the air, I like the sky & the hills, & the yellow Arno itself,— & I cant help *loving* places a little, when I like them a great deal. Robert says that he shall never get me away from Rome, there is such deep room there for the roots. In the meanwhile as you once sent me a diploma of tormentor general, I will ask you to write to me (now that you will be at Rome before us) any information you may collect about an apartment—it would be doing us a very great kindness. On the same kindness I rely, NOT[2] *to let me torment you really*, & trouble you when you are not well. We were promised a letter of introduction to Mr Crawford[3] before you named him, by Mr Powers the distinguished sculptor here, who is one of our very few acquaintances and one of the simplest, gentlest men of genius in the world. He is doing in the marble now, a most beautiful Eve, with that chaste purity of expression which people agree to call classical, yet free from the pedantry of the old forms. She holds the apple in her hand *untasted*, .. with the sin so near, that the first shade of sorrow has fallen upon her face- It is a very lovely work. So is his "Greek Slave", which is more celebrated. If you pass through Florence, do remember us, and let me be the happier for the sight of your dear kind face. Then, be sure that I must be ready to love everyone whom you love much .. it will not be hard, believe me.

For Rome, keep in mind that we would *rather* be away from the English quarter– The *Strada Giulia* has been talked of by us, & the Via *Gregoriana*[4] .. we dont mind any desolation of fashionable life. I am well, but not able to do much in the way of exertion just now– Whenever you write, just say how you are .. not that I would teaze you even for *that*, dearest Fanny. May God bless you & keep you as best He knows how.

Your most affectionate
Ba—

Think of my forgetting to thank you for the kindness of writing to M.[r] Colyar. Thank you– But if he is only learned in the English quarter, his information will not precisely meet our wants.— Oh, I should like so much to know if enclosures (such as this for instance) are paid for double at the Roman Office. A dreadful tradition of such a misfortune has reached us .. and we who have packets of letters, fold within fold, should not like it at all, I can assure you. MUST every letter be written on *one single undivided sheet*? Now dont think of writing to me till you are settled & inclined to write .. but when you do, just give me a *no* or *yes* to the above question.

Publication: None traced.
Manuscript: University of Texas.

1. Presumably an allusion to Mme. d'Aulnoy's 17th-century fairy tale *La Chatte Blanche*.
2. Underscored three times.
3. Thomas Crawford (1813?–57), an American sculptor, had been in Rome since 1835; his studio was in the Piazza Barberini. In 1844 Crawford married Louisa Cutler Ward (1823–97), sister of Julia Ward Howe. The Brownings later became acquainted with the Crawfords in Rome. Crawford completed a bust of John Kenyon in 1841 (see *Reconstruction*, H115 and H263).
4. Murray's *Handbook for Travellers in Central Italy* (1843), notes that "a good sitting-room, with three bedrooms and a kitchen, in the fashionable quarter, costs on the average from thirty to thirty-five scudi. In the streets which lie beyond the ordinary beat of English visitors, as in the Strada Giulia, the same accommodation may be obtained for less than half this sum" (p. 249); see letter 2691, note 2.

2703. EBB TO MARY RUSSELL MITFORD

[Florence]
[ca. 20 September 1847][1]

Ever dearest Miss Mitford, I am delighted to have your letter & lose little time in replying to it. The lost letter, meanwhile, does not appear.[2] The moon has it, to make more shine on these summer-nights,—if still one may say "summer" now that September is deep & that we are cool as people hoped to be when at hottest. Dearest friend, how glad you make me by this comforting account of yourself, of K's & the new gardener's[3] good conduct, & of the friends you are able to see without fatigue, & best of all, of the improvement in your walking. And yet, and yet, I dont like "the stick" and the "two or three miles only" a day; and cant understand why either a mere sprain or a mere rheumatic affection should produce a lasting effect of such a nature as you apprehend. Do you try warm baths? Pray take care & apply remedies, & let me see you as active as ever when we meet ... at Paris? is it to be? or at Reading? for we may reach England, I prophecy, before you reach France. *Settling* in England is different & more difficult .. but I long to see some dear, loving faces that glitter with a melancholy light in the distance!— yes, the faces, for instance, of my dear dearest sisters– If they did not write to me, I could not bear this absence. One set of affections does not exclude another, & that the oldest: it is the heart which grows larger rather, to take all in– I love my family, and my friends too, better than ever I did! Understand how that must be– Thank you, my dear friend, for caring to go & see my sisters whenever you shall go to London. You will be welcome to them, be sure, both for my sake & yours– As to Tennyson, I am sorry, I cant help being sorry, both for the two women as well as for him, and for all women as well as those two.[4] I am "spoilt as a judge," do you say .. but why, pray, am I spoilt as a judge? I throw my own case aside, which is exceptionally happy, I do believe, among wives of Tennysons or Thompsons, & so does not apply .. and I hold on general principles that it is better to be tormented by Apollo than left asleep in the sun by Marsyas,[5]—that it is better & nobler. You would feel it to be better—at the bottom of your soul you do!—and so would any woman, not prepared to accept the flats of life flatly– Then you know I never could believe that a poetry could come out of a man which never was in him, & that the artist was altogether separate from the individual & personal. Deep, deep, under the personal habits, may lie the poetical nature .. and black, black, with tobacco smoke & gin-fumes, may gather the personal habits—but that the poetical nature, the deep feeling, the noble sympathy, should not be *there*, in the poet, is what nothing could make me doubt, though the tongue of men & angels[6] should assert it. Remember that M[r] Harness professes not to understand Tennyson's poems:—he may understand Tennyson just as little– Do tell me your full thought of the Commonwealth of women.[7] I begin by agreeing with you as to his implied under-estimate of women: his women are too voluptuous, .. however of the most refined voluptuousness– His gardener's daughter,[8] for instance, is just a rose; and "a Rose" one might beg all poets to observe, is as precisely *sensual*, as fricasseed chicken, or even boiled beef & carrots. Did you read M[rs]

Butler's "Year of Consolation", & how did you think of it in the main?[9] As to Mr Horne's illustrations of national music,[10] I dont know .. I feel a little jealous of his doing well what very inferior men have done well .. men who could'nt write Orion, & the Death of Marlowe. Now, dearest dear Miss Mitford, you shall call him "tiresome" if you like, because I never heard him talk, and he may be tiresome for aught I know, of course .. but you SHANT say that he has not done some fine things in poetry– Now, you KNOW what the first book of Orion is! and Marlowe .. & Cosmo!—& *you* SHANT say that you dont know it, & that when you forgot it for a moment, I did not remind you. For the marriage, may it be very happy. Nineteen!—how young!—it had not struck me that she c.^d be so young– A great difference indeed! Still, marriages are happy on different principles, .. & some women like to be loved DOWN to, with fondness rather than sympathy, .. while some like the level ground of conformity of taste & character, so as to be nearest all ways. Still, nineteen is very young, & in the case of ordinary women & men, one might stand aghast at it. Poor Mrs Partridge, (you see, however) married without any such disparity, (in a worldly sense!—for I dare say there may be disparity enough at bottom) does not appear the happier for *that* even. I am sorry that she should seem so depressed, poor thing– If she had *children*, it would be an interest in life—but oh, I can understand how dreadful it must be to look round for an answering thought, word, smile, and find nothing. Resolute, sensible women shape themselves in time to this position,—but it must be a painful process—especially with such as have suffered their imagination to overflow into their actual life: for when the waters dry up, there is a desolate prospect then:—and she is a woman of that class, by your description. Did the Anglo-Saxon romance come to nothing?[11] Does she like gardening? Does she see you often? Tell me of Mrs Tyndal's[12] visit, which will be such a pleasure to two, of course .. saying nothing of Mr Tyndal's, who will know you then for the first time. I hope you may like him, & find her as joyous as you expect. Did I tell you that my cousin Arlette Butler has married Captain Reynolds with the approbation of the whole world, & that bride & bridegroom are on the point of setting off for Italy? We are to see them at Rome: but it is improbable that they should go to Naples according to their plan, the disturbances there having burst into full revolt.[13] It was our plan to leave Florence on the 21.st We stay however one month longer, half through temptation, half through reason—which is strongest, who knows?– We quite love Florence & have delightful rooms,—and then, though I am quite well now as to my general health, it is thought better for me to travel a month hence– So I suppose we shall stay.

In the meanwhile our Florentines kept the anniversary of our wedding day (& the establishment of the civic guard) most gloriously a day or two or three ago, forty thousand persons flocking out of the neighbourhood to help the expression of public sympathy & overflowing the city.[14] The procession passed under our eyes into the piazza Pitti, where the Grand Duke & all his family stood at the Palace window melting into tears, to receive the thanks of his people. The joy & exaltation on all sides were most affecting to look upon– Grave men kissed one another, & graceful young women lifted up their children to the level of their own smiles, and the children themselves mixed their shrill little '*vivas*' with the shouts of the people. At once, a more frenetic gladness & a more innocent manifestation of gladness were never witnessed. During three hours and a half the procession wound on past our windows—& every inch of every house seemed alive with gazers all that time—the white handkerchiefs fluttering like doves, .. and clouds of flowers & laurel leaves floating down on the heads of those who passed. Banners, too, with inscriptions to suit the popular feeling .. 'Liberty' .. the 'Union of Italy' .. the 'Memory of the martyrs', 'viva Pio nono' .. "viva Leopoldo secondo" .. were quite stirred with the breath of the shouters. I am glad to have seen that sight .. and to be in Italy at this moment, when such sights are to be seen. My wrist aches a little even now, with the waving I gave to my handkerchief, I assure you,—for Robert & I & Flush sate the whole sight out at the window, & would not be reserved with the tribute of our sympathy. Flush had his two front paws over the window sill, with his ears hanging down.—but he confessed at last that he thought they were rather long about it, particularly as it had nothing to do with dinner & chicken bones, & subjects of consequence. He is less tormented, & looks better,—in excellent spirits & appetite always .. & *thinner*, like your Flush.—& very fond of Robert, as indeed he ought to be. On the famous evening of that famous day I have been speaking of, we lost him—he ran away & stayed away all night, .. which was too bad, considering that it was our anniversary besides, & that he had no right to spoil it. But I imagine that he was bewildered with the crowd & the illumination—only as he *did* look so very guilty & conscious of evil on his return, there's room for suspecting him of having been very much amused, "motu proprio",[15] as our Grand Duke says in the edict. He was found at nine oclock in the morning at the door of our apartment, waiting to be let in.—mind, .. I dont mean the Grand Duke. Very few acquaintances, have we made at Florence, & very quietly lived out our days. M.r Powers the sculptor is our chief friend & favorite—a most charming, simple, straightforward, genial American .. as simple as the man of genius he has proved himself needs be. He sometimes comes to talk & take coffee with us, & we like him much. His wife is an amiable woman, & they have heaps of children from thirteen downwards, all except the eldest boy, Florentines[16]—and the sculptor has eyes like a wild Indian's, so black & full of light. You would scarcely wonder if they clave the marble without the help of his hands. We have seen besides the Hopner's, Lord Byron's friends at Venice, you will remember. And Miss Boyle, the niece of the Earl of Cork, & authoress & poetess on her own account, having been introduced once to Robert in London at Lady Morgan's, has hunted us out & paid us a visit. A very vivacious little person, with sparkling talk enough. Lord Holland has lent her mother & herself the famous Careggi villa where Lorenzo the Magnificent died, and they have been living there among the vines these four months. These and a few American visitors are all we have seen at Florence—we live a far more solitary life than you do, in your village & with the 'prestige' of the country wrapping you round. Pray give your sympathies to our Pope, & call him a great man. For liberty to spring from a throne, is wonderful, .. but from a papal throne, is miraculous– That's my doxy– I suppose dear M! Kenyon & M! Chorley are still abroad. French books I get at, but at scarcely a new one, .. which is very provoking. At Rome it may be better– I have not read 'Martin' ever since the first vol. in England, nor G Sand's 'Lucretia'—even.[17]

May God bless you. Think sometimes of
your ever affectionate
EBB–

Direct *Toscana* & not *Italia*—& bear in mind that we are here for one month longer.

Address, on integral page: Miss Mitford / Three Mile Cross / near Reading.
Publication: EBB-MRM, III, 219–224 (as [15? September 1847]).
Manuscript: Wellesley College.

1. Conjectural date provided by EBB's references to the Florentine celebrations on 12 September 1847, and to the delay in their plans to leave Florence on 21 September 1847.
2. EBB had referred to a "missing letter" a month earlier; see letter 2694.
3. In a letter to Lucy Anderdon Partridge, dated 28 August 1846, Miss Mitford described him as "a nice lad from Dinton proper," (Chorley, I, 227), but he was eventually replaced by Sam Sweetman (see letter 2642, note 2).
4. Most likely a reference to Charlotte Rosa Baring, an early romance and probably the inspiration for Amy of "Locksley Hall," (see letter 2694, note 11), and Emily Sellwood, who married Tennyson in 1850.
5. This comparison between Apollo and Marsyas, god of music and skillful challenger respectively, seems to echo EBB's previous contention that marriage should be based upon love and mutual interests and abilities, and not simply a matter of convenience, as Miss Mitford asserted; see letters 2206 and 2317.
6. Cf. I Corinthians 13:1.
7. In a letter to Miss Mitford on 28 May [1848], EBB professed "to be a good deal disappointed" in Tennyson's poem, *The Princess (EBB-MRM*, III, 240).
8. Rose was the name of the central figure in "The Gardener's Daughter," (1842).
9. See letter 2661, note 8.
10. We have been unable to trace any book or article by Horne to fit EBB's description. It may be that he had mentioned the possibility of such a work to Miss Mitford, which he never completed.
11. *Costanza of Mistra: a Tale of Modern Greece*, which appeared anonymously in 1839, is the only work known to have been published by Lucy Anderdon Partridge.

314   [ca. 20 September 1847]   No. 2703

12. Miss Mitford's friend Henrietta Harrison (d.1879) married Acton Tindal on 30 July 1846.
13. A pamphlet entitled *Protesta del popolo delle Due Sicilie* was published anonymously in Naples in 1847, in which the author, Luigi Settembrini (1813-76), criticized the King and his government in the harshest terms, inciting public demonstrations. Cf. *Casa Guidi Windows*, I, 1203-19.
14. See letter 2697, note 3, and letter 2701.
15. "Of his own accord."
16. See letter 2681, note 14. Nicholas (1835-1904) was the eldest child at this time. Both he and James had been born in Cincinnati.
17. *Lucrezia Floriani* was published in 1846. EBB had mentioned Sue's *Martin* a year earlier; see letter 2590, note 4.

2704. MARY RUSSELL MITFORD TO EBB

[Three Mile Cross]
[*Postmark:* 2 October 1847]

⟨★★★⟩ few books. The most interesting that I have ⟨r⟩ead for many years is Lamartine's Histoire des Girondins.[1] Do read that. Even at the Palace where they read so little they are all devouring those eloquent Volumes—the Queen & all. I would not have believed that Lamartine's prose could be so fine—but the prose of poets is often finer than their verse—witness Southey & Scott & Dryden- Do read that splendid work. The Author does injustice to Napoleon I think, & is over candid to Robespierre & many of the other Revolutionary Heroes—so that one wonders sometimes *who* was guilty—but still the book is charming.— Also I am reading Appert's Dix Ans à la Cour de Louis Philippe,[2] very pleasant esprit—& I have just finished Le Chien d'Alcibiade—a Tale of some cleverness although too close an imitation of Gerfaut.[3] It is wonderful how much the French novelists leave our's at a distance especially as to character. In Martin there is a physician who is charming, & much vividness & power—but the conclusion is unsatisfactory & altogether it is a falling off. Tell me if you hear of anything new by George Sand or Balzac or Eugène Sue or Victor Hugo—or any good French books. I see by the papers that poor Frederic Soulié is dead-[4] I was just reading a novel of his on the wars of La Vendée (Saturnine Fichet) which was interesting—only he had imitated a likeness between two persons from the old French Story of Martin Guerre, which story aforesaid—the actual story & name—Dumas had been using in Les Deux Diane—by the way I am reading 3 series by Dumas, Les Deux Diane—Les Memoires d'un Medecin & Le Batard de Mouléon & I believe there are two or three other works of the same sort besides-[5] Of English books I have been much pleased by M:r Jesse[']s Antiquities of London—very pleasant gossip—& S:t John[']s Wild sports of the Highlands a mixed Vol of Deerstalking & Natural History which is charming–⁶ Did I tell you of an article highly & justly praiseful of your poetry by Mʳ Gilfillan in Tait's Magazine,⁷ ⟨& of⟩ a very charming mention both of you & Mʳ Brow⟨ning⟩ in some letters to Mʳ Dickens upon Italy by some His⟨torian,⟩ which had appeared in The Daily News & have been sep⟨arately printed⟩ in a Volume.–⁸ What are you about dear ⟨...⟩ every thing for me to Mʳ Browning & believe me

ever most faithfully yours
M R M

Address, on integral page: La Signora Browning / Poste Restante / Firenze / Toscana / [and at left, below] Florence / Tuscany / Italy.
Docket, in EBB's hand: Miss Mitford's / autograph.
Publication: None traced.
Manuscript: Armstrong Browning Library.

1. Alphonse Lamartine's historical work appeared in March 1847.
2. *Dix Ans à la cour du roi Louis-Philippe et souvenirs du temps de l'Empire et de la Restauration* (1846) by Benjamin Nicolas Marie Appert (1797–1847).
3. A novel by Charles de Bernard, published in 1838; see letter 1650, note 3. *La Queue du chien d'Alcibiade* (1847) was a two-act comedy by Balzac's friend Léon Gozlan.
4. Frederic Soulié died on 23 September 1847.
5. *La Bâtard de Mauléon*, a collaborative work with Auguste Maquet, was published in 1846; *Les Deux Diane* was an historical romance that appeared from 1846 to 1847; and *Mémoires d'un Médicin: Joseph Balsamo* appeared as a feuilleton from 1846 to 1848.
6. *Short Sketches of the Wild Sports and Natural History of the Highlands* (1846) by Charles Saint John and *Literary and Historical Memorials of London* (2 vols., 1847) by J. Heneage Jesse.
7. In *Tait's Edinburgh Magazine* for September 1847, pp. 620–625; the author of the article was George Gilfillan (1813–78). For the complete text, see pp. 380–385.
8. *Facts & Figures from Italy. By Don Jeremy Savonarola, Benedictine Monk, Addressed during the last two winters to Charles Dickens, Esq.* (1847). Don Jeremy Savonarola was a pseudonym for Francis Sylvester Mahony, who also wrote under the pseudonym of Father Prout. The letter, dated "Rome, June 18 [1847]," contained a footnote by Mahony that "Browning and his newly-married wife, the gifted Elizabeth Barrett, have been wandering in Italy. May we look on the poetic couple as *par poetarum 'mox daturos,'* (if possible) *Progenium meliùs canentum!"* (p. 295). This footnote did not appear in the version of the letter as it originally appeared in *The Daily News* of 30 June 1847.

2705. RB TO ARABELLA & HENRIETTA MOULTON-BARRETT

[Florence]
Oct. 4, '47.

Ba has been writing a long letter to her dear Sisters,¹ who are also mine— and if I did not know that they love her as she loves them, I should make sure that nothing I could tell them would be listened to after her—for how I remember what her letters are!—but I also know that any little piece of news about the writer, will always be affectionately received by those of whom .. only yesterday .. I will tell you what she said: we had just got a note (of which, very likely, Ba's letter may speak) from Mrs. Jameson's niece—goodnatured and full of kind feeling, but rather abundant in sentimentalities about the Coliseum, St Peters &c– Upon which I remarked to Ba—"How much more it would interest you if she had described the dresses your sisters wore .. since she speaks of their calling at Ealing"– "Their dresses?"—said Ba—"what I would give to hear of their shoes!"– And, dear Henrietta and Arabel, be quite sure that she was entirely true in that, as in every other utterance she is capable of .. the longer I have the happiness of living with her, the more do I understand and venerate her perfectly loving nature—but all this you know, and my only chance of interesting you is in telling you what news I can. I hope and believe that at this moment Ba is better than she has been for some weeks, or even longer. She looked so decidedly better and stronger yesterday that we took advantage of the lovely weather—and walked out—with no ill effects. I must tell you, that she is the most *tractable and docile* creature in the world—keeping in the house, when fatigue seems properly avoided, and observing all regulations of diet &c just as if her own good were *not* concerned in it—as it certainly is not, in her thought. She always retains that sweetest of all imaginable sweet tempers, making it a blessing to be near her—and I see every day fresh reason to admire *your* generous kindness to me, who have taken such a blessing away from you—tho' only for a time, I trust, and to return it to you with increased powers both for your good and her own. I wonder if she tells you anything about her good looks—her rounded cheeks with not a little colour on them, and her general comparative .. shall I dare to write it .. plumpness? It surely is so, or my eyes are very faithless. She will have told you about our interrupted journey to Rome: I know it will be difficult, or, indeed, impossible for you to make yourselves *quite* easy about the dangers or inconveniences of our movements,—but you may rely upon one thing—that we do nothing without a great deal of deliberation,—and whatever poor human sagacity *can* foresee,—we endeavour not to miss seeing: but unluckily there is no plan, that we have yet hit on, without disadvantage in some degree, to counterbalance the advantage—to travel,—to stay still and be overtaken by the winter in a bad wintering place,—to stop short, with little fatigue, but in some city where the comforts are less certainly attainable,—or to go further, for the purpose of faring better, but with a great increase of trouble in the going,—all these considerations have to be weighed carefully. Depend on it, we shall do the best we can, trusting in providence that has hitherto interfered so signally in our behalf. Of one matter, which looks formidable in the English papers, you need have very little fear indeed. One would suppose, to read some of these accounts, particularly those extracted from the French gazettes, that we were in open insurrection, with all the horrors of mobs, riots, noises and dangers:[2] while there is not a symptom of anything of the kind—indeed, there *is* no mob in this admirably civilized country,—much less in this renowned city, where you two young ladies might walk alone in the evening without the least fear of an impertinent word or look. We certainly find it very delightful to be in Italy just at this time, when it is so thoroughly alive—and our pleasure will not be greatly diminished, if all those rumours operate as they are said to do in keeping away the flocks of travellers—however accounts differ, and we know nothing positively as yet. Meanwhile, we are ⟨as⟩ happy here as the day is long—and it will be no great misfortune if we are for⟨ced to⟩ take up our quarters in Florence for some six months longer. On another ⟨im⟩portant point, too, we have been reassured lately—there appears to be no ⟨cause⟩ to doubt that one of the Physicians here is an able and desirable man[3]—(unfortunately, this "one" is *not* Mrs Jameson's old friend, Herbert[4]—who may be getting *too* old a friend.) Mrs J., by the way, is a kind, good, sympathizing friend of ours—but dont take her notions of Florence, and the life there, without a little allowance—for she found Florence the gayest of gay cities, distracting from its routine of visits, given & received, &c. and gave us the notion of a place where we should be teazed to death .. quite a mistake; for (as I dare say it happens in most other gay cities)—you must seek out these dissipations or they will never seek out you—the world being quite able to amuse itself without either Mrs. J. or Mr & Mrs B: so that, where she felt unable to read or write for an hour by herself, we enjoy exactly as much solitude as we like—not receiving six visits in six months. I have got to the end of my piece of paper,—and what have I told you, after all? Whereas, what true, truest delight your affectionate congratulations gave me when Ba & I got your letters so fortunately the day *before* our great day!—for on the day itself it was impossible to go thro' the streets for the procession. God bless you both for your goodness to her and to me. Believe me ever with the deepest love and most earnest wishes for your happiness,

your RB

Address, on integral page: Miss Barrett.
Publication: TTUL, pp. 49–53.
Source: Transcript in editors' file.

   1. This letter was accompanied by a letter from EBB, no longer extant, in which she apparently referred to the possibility that she might be pregnant again. (In a letter to Miss Mitford dated 22 February [1848], EBB wrote that "the people about me, months & months ago, took the fact for granted, in spite of all I could say to the contrary" *EBB-MRM,* pp. 229–230). The Brownings' departure from Florence to Rome had been postponed for a month from 20 or 21 September 1847 (see letters 2701 and 2703) to about 19 October 1847 (see letters 2702 and 2703). Between the 4 October 1847 date of this letter, when the journey to Rome is only "interrupted," and shortly thereafter, the Brownings decided not to leave Florence at all during the winter of 1847–48, and began the search for alternate accommodations detailed in letter 2707 and later letters.

2. Although the revolutionary spirit was flourishing throughout Tuscany, the worst demonstrations at this time were, for the most part, limited to Leghorn (Harry Hearder, *Italy in the Age of the Risorgimento: 1790–1870*, 1983, pp. 80–81).

3. Thomas William Trotman (1810?–62), a physician and accoucheur, was recently established at "Via della Scala, 4280" (Murray's *Handbook for Travellers in Northern Italy*, 1852, p. 457).

4. See letter 2697, note 5.

2706. DANTE GABRIEL ROSSETTI TO RB

50 Charlotte Street
Portland Place
Oct 17 1847

Sir,

Being a most enthusiastic admirer of your works, I can no longer restrain myself from intruding upon you (though I feel that I do so at the risk of being considered presumptuous) with a question concerning them, which I have for some time been deliberating whether or not to venture on.

It is now two or three months ago that I met, at the British Museum, with a Poem published in 1833, entitled "Pauline, a Fragment of a Confession," which elicited my warm admiration, and which, having failed in an attempt to procure a copy at the publisher's, I have since transcribed. It seemed to me, in reading this beautiful composition, that it presents a noticeable analogy in style and feeling to your first acknowledged work, "Paracelsus": so much so indeed as to induce a suspicion that it might actually be written by yourself. Which doubt has ever since so haunted and perplexed me, that now, in taking this somewhat hazardous measure to rid myself of it, I am bold enough to hope that even should you look upon me as having no right to pretend to the solution so much desired, I may at least obtain your indulgent forgiveness.

Believe that I am, Sir,

Always,
Your distant respectful admirer,
Gabriel Rossetti[1]

R. Browning Esq.

Address: For / Robert Browning Esqre
Publication: Adrian, p. 538.
Manuscript: Huntington Library.

1. Dante Gabriel Rossetti (1828–82) was a painter and a poet, associated with the Pre-Raphaelite Brotherhood. He was admitted to the Royal Academy in 1846. For the copy of *Pauline* which he transcribed, see *Reconstruction*, B28.

2707. EBB TO HENRIETTA MOULTON-BARRETT

1881 Via Maggio. Florence
[20 October 1847][1]

My dearest Henrietta, your turn is it not? My ever dearest Henrietta, then .. I write to you in the first moment of *decision*, after having been cast to & fro like Sancho Panza in the blanket these many days. I really began to think that we never sh^d get settled again .. and as Robert neither eats nor sleeps when he is anxious, it was gradually growing to be more important to me, (this state of uncertainty,) than might seem to be reasonable. Oh, how you surprised me by your dear letter from Bognor![2] how astonished I was, & how glad! Because you see, Henrietta, it will do you good, all of you, & give you all better spirits in the long run .. that is, if you are wise, .. if my dearest Arabel is not "wonderfully imprudent" for instance, in bathing so late in the season, .. (for I am not quite easy about *that*, do assure her—) and if you use without abusing the opportunity of fresh air & change of scene. For the rest, I understand– I understand, Henrietta. But now do enjoy it as well as you can, every one of you, & tell me all about it– I am so glad that you brought Minny with you– It was quite right of her to consent to be brought, too, .. and it will be quite right if you all stay beyond the month to get properly *inspirited* for the winter. You wont regret it afterwards—yet *I* regret your not going away earlier in the year– How strange of dearest Papa!– But at the last, it was kind—and I thank him silently to myself for sending you. In the meanwhile, will the Peytons resist Arabel's conjuring? I sh^d not wonder if she effected her purpose– Now, above all, dont let dear Trippy delay going to you– The change would do her such great good that I thought of her with some of the first thoughts I had, in my pleasure to hear of Bognor. What rooms has she in Upper Glo[u]cester Street? As good & large as the former ones in Montagu St? Tell me all about it, & if the same landlady is in ascendent– And if the co-lodgers go with her?—and if she is pleased, dear thing, altogether? I meant to write to her this time; but as you bid me write in time to Bognor, why I am afraid to put off your letter any longer, and must choose another moment for hers. Moreover, Robert takes it into his head that my cheeks are flushed whenever I write (and he is not far wrong in saying so) & that therefore writing cant be good for me (and he *is* wrong there) which brings on me such a flood of reproaches that generally I yield the point (of the pen) just as if I wholly agreed with him, which I dont. Now let me tell you of ourselves– Believe or do not believe in our superhuman virtue (mine especially) but the truth is that we had really decided against Rome before Mr Jago's decision set the seal on ours– In the first place, Robert was frightened about the journey for me, which even in a private carriage (and he was actually trying hard to persuade himself that it w^d be the *cheapest* plan to buy a britska, a pair of horses and a coachman, to drive about Rome in after the completion of the journey) which even in this said easy britska, seemed to present certain risks– And in the second place we had the kindest letter from Fanny Dowglass who had taken all sorts of trouble for us & exhorted us to come & choose between various uncomfortable & dirty kinds of lodgment, at a high price– Now, as Robert said, here was I going to Rome to *pay* for being shut up in an uncomfortable way, just within reach of temptation—and to pay too for this discomfort, just when we were likely to want money & to want comfort more than usual– It seemed foolish of us altogether. It seemed wise to wait for the opportunity which God one day may give us, of going to Rome when we can enjoy it, see the wonders of it, & feel better fortified against the drawbacks– Florence is full of beauty which by putting out one's hand it is possible to touch, & full of luxuries too at the very cheapest rate. And as for the climate, why the objection is the liability to cold winds, which I, with my habits, would never think of going out in– The sun is Italian—and so is the weather generally—neither gloomy nor variable: and the winter is a short one. (If we chose to go on the Arno, it w^d be over-hot—and indeed I sh^d not dare to agree to taking an apartment for six months in that situation, lest Robert & Wilson sh^d both of them be laid up with bilious fever about April.) Therefore Florence seems to me a very safe residence for me as to climate, under certain conditions. It w^{dnt} be worth returning to Pisa, I think, on the mere ground of climate. Florence w^d be dangerous to *restless invalids* who, because they are in Italy, think it incumbent to go out everyday, & unnecessary to choose sheltered walks when they go—for the heat is so unequally distributed here, that one street seems a funnel for hot air, & another for cold, .. and the transitions, rushed upon, are of course fatal to chest-complaints where the owners are indiscreet & incautious– But I never go out at all on cold days .. I did not, you know, at Pisa .. and in going out, always I am satisfied with sheltered walks—though so "wonderfully imprudent", tell Arabel. I am not in the least afraid therefore of wintering here, & shall not take advantage of Mr Jago's permission to return to Pisa which as a residence is so inferior in all ways. It is the less worth while, that necessarily I may be more confined to the house this winter than usual—and Pisa disagreed with Wilson too! it is another consideration.

So resolving to remain at Florence we had to determine on an apartment—& first of all we had an idea of keeping on our grandiosity in Palazzo Guidi & very nearly came to an arrangement—& the padrone will repent his refusal of our terms, it seems to me, considering the length of our residence. It is very different to let rooms at high rates for three or four months, and for six– But no, we divided upon two scudi at last- After all it is better perhaps, for we sh^d have found it difficult to warm such immense rooms, and really we did'nt want to give balls or to receive forty people to dinner or anything of that especial sort. Well! Robert went from one side of Florence to another, & I lay on the sofa making all sorts of objections to every apartment he could find .. which sounds amiable of me, particularly as he neither ate nor slept in the interim as I explained before. You see it was rather serious to settle for six months, & to make (besides) what might prove an unpleasant transition from those rooms we liked so much—— The Arno-rooms were too hot & too high up .. with a splendid view of the river, said Robert; but oh, so hot, & oh so high! At last we had to hesitate between an apartment once occupied by the Garrows in the Piazza Santa Maria Novella, on the first floor, but somewhat dingy, & away from all the *festas* .. and a little baby-house kind of place in the Piazza Pitti close by .. Such tiny rooms! The drawing room with a sofa like a board, five little chairs, & one large comfortable one—& where to put the grand piano, (to say nothing of other grand ideas) was a problem. But the situation, .. nothing c^d be perfecter than the situation– Observe—three sides of this Piazza are filled by the Palace Pitti & at the bottom is the row of houses in question, for the most part having very small rooms. The only vacant apartment, this proposed one of ours .. a bad staircase, steep & narrow .. & on the second floor the people agreeing to take us for twenty scudi a month, that is four pounds, nine shillings– As nearly as possible we were to taking it, though very possibly we might have fallen there on a single spoon .. At least everything seemed scanty & over-simple– A champagne-glass was like a roc's egg.[3] So at last, we determined on an apartment in via Maggio (the same street as Palazzo Guidi's) where we settled yesterday[4]—an apartment on the first floor, the drawing room small, but pretty, everything most complete in the way of furniture & comforts,—even to cut-glass bottles for perfume & toilette pincushions. My room is faultless & the Princess of Wirtemburg performed her accouchement there to the general satisfaction.[5] Our padrone was courier to Prince Albert & the Duchess of Cambridge;[6] & his wife being a Frenchwoman, they understand the whole theory of "what is and should be," and nothing falls short– For this we pay what we paid at Pisa, five pounds, eleven shillings, (a month) much more than we meant to pay—and the drawback is that we shall not have much sun– Still, the double doors & closely fitting windows, & stoves, seem to promise a sufficient warmth. The provoking thing is that since we settled, our people at Palazzo Guidi have intimated that they were ready to accept our terms rather than part with us——and I dont like to say to Robert how provoked I am to think of it– He has been pressed enough as it is,—thinking never of himself, (as usual) & always of me & of my comfort in the whole arrangement. Besides, we shall do very well here I dare say—and presently we shant miss so much our terrace & the other attractions of our old domain. One advantage is that the nights are more silent—my bedroom looking into a courtyard- A spring sofa & two or three spring arm chairs, .. plenty of luxury of that sort- And now for the plan- Observe!⁷ The crosses (*) are windows, & the squares (□) doors- See plan. You see it is'nt as compact as our old apartment, though so much smaller. The drawingroom is pretty—a French clock (which really goes) and a chaise longue which draws out & was particularly recommended to my attention by the lady of the house. I have been trying to pull about the furniture into graceful disorder,—but must be contented at last with having the piano & the sofa wherever they please to stand. Since we came here & your last letter came to Florence, Robert has continually been talking of Arabel's coming .. wishing her to come .. & proving how without the least increase of expense (if she dared to think of *that*) we sh^d be able to have the advantage of her darling presence & companionship.

Ah—how Clara Lyndsay's kind proposal made my heart leap within me!⁸ Too tantalizing it was! Only we could not have let her go to Rome— she w^d have been forced to stay at Florence till we went ourselves—and what comfort, what consolation! But I suppose I might as well wish for an angel straight from Heaven in apocalypse, & therefore there's little use talking. I will tell you whom we have had instead .. *the Major's minor from Pisa*-⁹ The stars mix in these things, or I scarcely w^d have believed it- Do you remember my pet enemy & vis à vis who talked of Mrs Browning giving herself such wonderful airs & trying to buy her house over her head at any price demanded?. Mrs Loftus, remember! These Loftuses (whose maid by the by, is an acquaintance of Wilson's) came to Florence about the time we did, went away in the summer, & have returned for the winter & taken an apartment close at hand in the Piazza Pitti- Robert was calling on the Irvings & met all three, Major, wife, & daughter .. & to his surprise, two cordial hands were extended—"Having had the satisfaction of a letter from him" (much like the satisfaction of being shot through the head) "they *must* become acquaintances .. Mrs. Loftus meant to do herself the pleasure of paying a visit to Mrs Browning" .. &c &c.! So of course he c^d only say that we sh^d be glad to see them, & the whole three poured in about three mornings ago. The arch-enemy is a tall rather gaunt woman, with an unpleasant voice— the daughter quite young, only just introduced, & as little pretty as a very *petite* & young looking girl can be .. (it has grown to be a sort of proverb with Robert to say "as ugly as Miss Loftus", but I dont agree with him when he comes to extremities) and they have been used to good society, I sh^d say. Nothing c^d be more friendly than their manner, & I gave them a history of our adventures at Vallombrosa to break the ice. As to Mr Irving I do really like him—he comes very often to sit with us, and so does his son the young man, who is intelligent enough & in so sad a state of health that one is glad to enliven him now & then. Mrs Irving too is better than I set down at first .. Robert likes her: but they all return to Pisa in about ten days, much to the despair of the wife & son. As for Mr Irving himself he has a crotchet about Florence & pretends to abuse it—calls it as bad as Bath or Cheltenham .. which perhaps after all it may be to persons up to their neck in English society, who are forced to float with the stream. He told Robert the other day that Lady St Germains[10] had been enquiring about me with the deepest interest, & that Lady Caroline Cocks had said so & so, & that Lord Eastnor had passed through Florence- .. All in a breath!! Lady St Germains['] "deep interest" I can appreciate- You remember how rude she was to me one morning when I visited Lady Margaret at her house—but it all means, I suppose, that I have been thoroughly talked over—which does'nt so much please me- There's the worst of a congregation of one's beloved countrymen! Not that one need so very much mind. Poor Mr Surtees was here for a few days, & Wilson met him in the street looking altered & thin, she thought—& now he is gone back to Pisa with his daughter who is said to be better in health- Everything I ever heard for good of an Italian climate, my experience acquiesces in—it is all but divine, perfect, that is, .. & the very breathing of the air grows upon you like a luxury- Oh .. I always forget, so let me while I remember it "par exception"[11] say to Arabel about the loss of the broach that as nearly as possible I lost her hair out of my ring, but *did'nt* .. because when the glass was gone I became aware of the disaster & stopped its progress. For the broach, as far as it can [be] remedied, one day it shall. I am glad about Fanny Hanford,[12] liking her much for both her own sake & dear Mrs Martin's—but it is a melancholy prospect this going to Ireland for the approaching winter. Why could he not appoint a liberal & merciful agent, he who is rich? With weak health on his side & hers I do not think that the duty of residing there at such an obvious risk can be imperative. You wicked person, Henrietta .. you who "dont publish my letters," you say! How then, did Mrs Martin opine so & so? Tell her if you write, that we will take the sunniest rooms for her & Mr Martin, if they will but come to Florence directly. I am very well upon the whole, & have lost the sickness & recovered the power of eating which at one time quite went from me. Moreover I am obedient & lie on the sofa, & dont walk & dont do anything wrong indeed- There is a Dr Trottman whom Robert has heard wonders of, but for the present it w.^{d} be *quite absurd* to take advice, considering that I know everything advisable. Yes—Dr Cook said what I told you, to be sure—but then he said it because I had been plunged in the deepest innocense of ignorance, never lying down except when I could'nt sit up, & baking myself at the fire & burning myself with hot coffee & hot brandy & water as one might do in a fit of colic .. doing as wrong as could be because I did'nt know better.

Therefore it was that he said [']'If I had been called in sooner" &c &c. When he *was* called in, observe, he did nothing at all .. only abolished those errors of mine, & bade me lie still & keep the room cool– *Now*, what could all the Faculty do if we invoked their aid? Now, when there is nothing wrong, no spasm, no suffering worth speaking of, and, besides, *no ignorance*? ..– M.rs Browning herself admits that there does not seem much occasion for it– The single point is the opium—& you know, for experience has proved, that I cant do without it—and M.r Jago's opinion is worth the world's, seeing that *he* knows the necessities of my constitution in this respect better than any one else can. Now are you satisfied, wise people all of you? I have an egg at breakfast, & another beaten up in wine at twelve oclock– After dining at three, Robert takes me into my room & performs the operation of (as he calls it) "putting his baby to bed" .. shuts me up carefully to go to sleep, which I do as regularly as possible. At five Wilson comes with the medicine, and having taken it I go back to the drawingroom to drive him out to his walk– Between six & seven we have coffee—& at nine, supper– You see it is'nt a very laborious day– Wilson is quite well I am glad to say. Will the Reynolds's find us out, do you suppose in Florence? Of course they will stay here for a while to see the works of art, or they will be barbarians—and Robert took it into his fantasy that he actually met them in the lodging in the Pitti .. only *that* must have been pure fantasy. If they come I *should* like to see them certainly .. I should like to "realize" him, .. as the Americans say, though I do seem to know the man already. Perhaps they wont guess at our being here. It was wrong of Arlette (was'nt it?) not to take poor Anne [Gent] with her, after the hundred promises– Wrong, & perhaps foolish—it would have been a comfort to have with her one who was attached to her, & not mercenary: & really I shall not be altogether sorry if Arlette has occasion to regret it. Anne always calculated on being her own maid when she married. Oh, I wonder whether when Robert takes this letter to the post he will bring me back another– I long for Arabel's so, which she promised in the crossing of M.rs Martin's. Ask her to write a line to Nelly Bordman just to say that I am grateful for the advice & if possible, that Robert is more grateful than I .. & that we stay at Florence accordingly. I will write to her soon. Indeed Henrietta, she is full of excellence, & since for my sake you will like her, I am sure that for her own you will never learn to unlike– Thank you, dearest Henrietta. Do tell me of Arabella Bevan. I shall so gladly hear the good news–

We have had another great festa here, in honour of our Grand Duke who deserved it: five hundred waxen torches, each nearly as large as a tree, carried alight through the darkness– It was splendid, & the enthusiasm of the people, most moving. I have caught a taste for *festas* lately, .. & had to explain to Robert (who was really calculating on it as if it were my necessity

No. 2707 [20 October 1847] 325

of life & I could'nt live out of Piazza Pitti & the immediate neighbourhood accordingly) that after all I was not literally such a "baby" as the facts seemed to prove. Here in Via Maggio we are better situated for the festas than even in Palazzo Guidi .. (besides) .. & it was'nt needful to go into a drawer on the Pitti for such a cause as that– Lady Bolingbroke![13] She is good & kind– She will succeed perhaps in time– My love to your friends & mine– Mind you write, write, write, remembering that you cant do it often enough & that we are at Florence for six months! Mention Stormie.. Robert bids me be affectionate to the uttermost for him—& I am

your most attached
Ba–

Give the enclosed to dear Henry. His letter was a blessing to me. Love to all– Direct both Toscana & Italia.

Address, on integral page: Miss Barrett / Manor House / Bognor / Sussex.
Publication: Huxley, pp. 52–58 (in part).
Source: Transcript in editors' file.

1. The Brownings' move from Palazzo Guidi to Via Maggio occurred on 19 October, according to a "Memorandum" by RB (see *Browning Institute Studies*, 1, 21), and in this letter, EBB says they "settled yesterday" in that apartment.
2. According to EBB's cousin, Surtees Cook, the Barrett household had taken a house in the popular resort town of Bognor, in Sussex, for a month; they returned to London on 27 October 1847 (Surtees, 5 and 27 October 1847).
3. i.e., something rare or difficult to obtain.
4. A memorandum, in RB's hand, of the Brownings' tenancy at Palazzo Guidi formed part of lot 261 in *Browning Collections* (see *Reconstruction*, E551).
5. We have been unable to identify this "Princess"; however, this reference, taken together with the one to "her highness of Brunswick" at the end of letter 2711, despite EBB's evident confusion, seem to refer to the same person.
6. Augusta Wilhelmina Louise (1797–1889), 3rd daughter of Frederick, Landgrave of Hesse-Cassel, had married Aldolphus Frederick (1774–1850), Duke of Cambridge, in 1818.
7. On her drawing, besides identifying the various rooms and "via maggio," EBB has written: "Wilson will sit in the dining room—as it straggles away rather from us & as her bedroom is small."
8. Clara Sophia Lindsay (*née* Bayford, b. 1811) was EBB's cousin. She had married Martin Lindsay in 1846, and they were coming to Italy because of his poor health; evidently, she had offered to have Arabella accompany them. They visited the Brownings in Florence in 1849, shortly after the birth of Pen Browning.
9. See letter 2664, note 3. Miss Loftus was probably the older daughter, Mary Harriet Anne Loftus, who married George Augustus Cranley Onslow 11 July 1848.
10. Harriet (*née* Pole-Carew, d. 1877) was the wife of John Eliot, 1st Earl of St. Germans (1761–1823). *The Tuscan Athenæum* for 20 November 1847 noted that she was staying at the Quattro Nazioni (no. 4, p. 32). Lady Caroline Cocks and Lord Eastnor were friends from Hope End days. For a biographical sketch of Lady Margaret Cocks, see vol. 2, pp. 341–342.
11. "As an exception."
12. Fanny Hanford married William Lloyd of Farmley, co. Kilkenny, Ireland, on 18 November 1847.
13. See letter 2641, note 12.

2708. RB TO MARY LOUISA BOYLE

[Florence]
Monday, 3. p.m. [25 October 1847][1]

Dear Miss Boyle–

Thank you very truly for the kind trouble of the note– I called—(alone, for my wife is indisposed)—on Mlle de Fauveau,[2] and was shown the beautiful & *Cellinesque* Bells, by her mother–

I have to thank your Brother for a card yesterday. Will your own occasions never bring you near Via Maggio again?

Ever yours faithfully,
Robert Browning.

Publication: None traced.
Manuscript: Armstrong Browning Library.

1. Dating based on RB's reference to Via Maggio. The Brownings took rooms at 1881 Via Maggio on 19 October 1847, and remained there for ten days. The only Monday they were there was October 25th.
2. Félicie de Fauveau (1799–1886) was a French sculptress who was born in Florence. Romantic in style, her work was inspired by Dante and Walter Scott. She and her mother had been exiles in Italy since 1834 because of their Royalist sympathies. Mlle. Fauveau "worked in marble, in alabaster, and in silver, in many branches, brooches, clasps, and wings, which would have done no discredit to Benvenuto Cellini" (*Mary Boyle: Her Book*, ed. Sir Courtenay Boyle, 1901, p. 129).

2709. EBB TO FANNY DOWGLASS

Florence–
October 25. [1847][1]

It is grievous to have to put one's gratitude, let it be ever so warm, in the place of oneself, my dearest Fanny, as I feel to my cost in beginning to write this letter. Yours was the very kindest, *you* are the very best, as always you are .. and I thank you from my husband's heart & mine (he says "Do tell her how thankful I am") for all this trouble you have taken & for which after all I can but love you back, & thank you as I say, .. for thus the matter lies– We *cannot go to Rome at all this winter* .. I have had strict injunctions from my medical friend in England not to attempt such a journey, .. and, disappointed as we both are, I dare not resist & must make the best of the sunshine at Florence & take a house in a warm situation, & forgo you for the present– Through my self will & ignorance (the two together) I had an illness at Pisa .. a *miscarriage* .. which I tell you that you may understand my precise reasons now for being submissive & avoiding the risk of giving as much anxiety & pain as I did then. Otherwise you might wonder at our choice of this climate & of our making & unmaking our minds in the front of your good counsel. We offered to travel to Rome by twenty miles a day, & it was not agreed to by the medical authorities– And so I miss you once more my dear, dear friend– If we had known, I w^d [2] have seen you by some effort when you were in our neighbourhood .. but it seemed so certain that we should meet & be together in a few weeks!—as if anything could be certain while the earth turns round!– Well—but I may hope that God's providence will bring us face to face before long, though it must not be immediately– To the last we were hoping,—and I am very well: it is all pure precaution, observe .. & were it not that I behaved ill before, the temptation w^d be strong to behave ill now & to break these chains through the middle. As to the climate of Florence I am not myself afraid of it, because we shall be in the Piazza Pitti where a perpetual sun prevents the necessity of fires, and I shall never go out except on the mildest days, & then only to walk up & down in the sunshine before the door. For restless, impatient invalids, (less schooled than I have been) who pass from the funnel of hot air in one Florentine street to a funnel of cold air in another, I can understand how the place must be highly dangerous– For me I think it will be safe– I shall have the Florentine sun, & the *fear* of the shadow & the wind—and our three months of winter will soon go by—and I hear of consumptive persons who are the better for wintering here, having taken my precautions. So you wont shake your head— you are to imagine, too, how sedulously I am taken care of. It makes me ashamed sometimes– Just as if really I were worth it!– The consequence is that I begin to think it quite important not to run this risk or that risk, &, in such a way, make the kindest & dearest person in the world too much out of spirits– Our new apartment is made up of little sunshiny rooms & we give twenty scudi for it[3]—cheaper than your Rome, only that Rome is Rome—& who would not rather live at Rome & pay for it?– Still we shall be close to Raffael in the Pitti gallery, and Florence is beautiful—and, if God pleases, we shall be very happy here. Now I will tell you whom you will have at Rome instead of me, .. and more shame for me if I only say of it "A fair exchange" ... one ought to be humbler you will retort, if but for the appearance' sake. Clara Lyndsay (*late Bayford*) is on her way to Rome, my sisters write to me, with her invalid husband, & means to remain the winter there— & perhaps they may have arrived by the time you get this letter of mine. She married last year, and three months afterwards was almost a widow—he broke a blood vessel & stood at the very gates of death. A trial spared to her by the ineffable Mercy! He is well now, but is sent to Italy for the winter out of precaution. A good, kind Christian man I have heard him described[,] a widower with one child—and Clara is said to be no wise *quenched* by her marriage, but as joyous & full of jests as ever. I dont know whether she will like Italy as well as Scotland, but I am sure that to find you in Rome will be a great joy to her- Now I ought not to forget to tell you of Miss Boyle who wrote a very kind little note to Robert the other day to offer to come & sit with me & talk to me & help him to take care of me in all sorts of ways- Really it was very kind. She is settled with her family in a Florentine palazzo, & has left the Carreggi-[4] We know scarcely anybody here & shrink more than you may fancy, from the whole *idealogy* of the little white cards with corners turned down, which sometimes force you into social relation with persons with whom you cant sympathize if you try. Florence might be made detestable, yes, even Florence .. if you were floated fairly into the muddy stream of what is called here *society*——so different a thing from mental intercourse, .. so inferior a thing to Christian brotherhood! Yet I believe I ought to take care, having sinned much already (as I grew aware when my prison-door seemed shut fast for ever) against Humanity in God's likeness, by my preference of Humanity in *my own*- To send my rain on the just and unjust (.. viz on those like or unlike *me* forsooth!!) of old was as difficult to me as if I had a right idea of "justice!"- Poor creatures that we are (that *I* am!) to talk of *justice*. I should not be so happy, if justice had been measured out to me! My dearest friend, let me be comforted by a letter from you sometimes, & let it mention your health always—and I will faithfully remember those hateful rules of postage which put away double letters & single envelopes- Remember that I am to know your cousins one day,[5] & to be loved by you every day, precisely as if we had made use of your active kindness in our behalf—— May God bless you dearest Fanny- Robert asks you to accept his thankful regards from the hands of your

most affectionate Ba-

Address, on integral page: Alla Signora Dowglass / 93. Piazza di Spagna- / Roma.
Publication: None traced.
Manuscript: Huntington Library.

    1. Year provided by postmark.
    2. Underscored three times.
    3. After spending three months in Palazzo Guidi (20 July-19 October), the Brownings moved to 1881 Via Maggio for ten days before taking up residence in an apartment in the Piazza Pitti, where they stayed until May 1848.
    4. After a brief excursion to the baths at Casciano, the Boyles returned to Florence, where they took an apartment on the ground floor of the Casa Lagerschwerd. See *Mary Boyle: Her Story*, ed. Sir Courtenay Boyle, 1901, pp. 207-210.
    5. Presumably a reference to Dr. Pollock and his wife; see letter 2681, note 9.

2710. RB to Dante Gabriel Rossetti

Florence,
Nov 10, 1847

My dear Sir

I hope you will have attributed the delay in answering your very kind & flattering letter,[1] to the only cause which could occasion it,—my absence from England. You are quite right in your guess: I wrote the little poem you treat so goodnaturedly, in pursuance of a boyish plan, of which I soon found out the impracticability: the few copies printed have been long withdrawn from the publishers—& I believe that at the present moment scarcely half a dozen of my friends are aware that such a literary sin is chargeable to me— among these last it will be pleasant for me henceforth to consider one whose indulgent sympathy removes much of the irksomeness with which I usually revert to that poor little book. I may add, that, beside the faults for which the author is directly answerable, the misprints are portentous—I having made my first essay at the business of correcting the proof sheets, over Messrs Saunders & Otley's parlour-table, to avoid breaking my *incognito* by giving my address & receiving the copy at home! However, there is compensation in all things, and but little to regret in having written "Pauline," since I am indebted to that circumstance for the honor & pleasure of your note, & for the right which it gives me of esteeming myself,

My dear Sir,
Yours very truly
R_____ B_____

G .... R .... Esqr

Publication: Browning Institute Studies, 15 (1987), 87-88.
Source: Transcript in William Allingham's commonplace book, in the possession of Mark Samuels Lasner.

1. Letter 2706.

2711. EBB to Henrietta Moulton-Barrett

Florence.
November 23 & [2]4 [1847][1]

As it seems to be my most ungrateful & incredible habit to neglect thanking you for your letters, let this begin by a heap of thanks, my own dearest Henrietta, for the last dear one, & for the promise of Arabel's, with Mr Boyd's which I shall expect day by day. I cant understand how it was that I did not mention her letter & yours—but if either had *not* been received, you would have been sure to have heard of *that* 'in thunder lightning & in rain'–[2] As it is, I rather am apt to grumble. You dont write often enough—oh not half! Just consider that there are two of you, & that I am sometimes a whole month without a line– Is it fair? Now consider. Ought I to be longer than ten days at furthest without hearing? Henry too might write to me sometimes .. tell dear Henry that from me. When I think that he has written, it's a great comfort & joy. As to other things, Henrietta, it is like your affectionateness to say such & such words: but it is easier (forgive me) to SAY THEM, than to take them up as a creed as you expect me to do ... *if* you expect it. Many exceed me in much .. but I do pretend to know what love means—and I know that it does not mean a mere sunshiney aspect while a person happens to please you in everything– If you committed a murder & were sent to Newgate, I should be at your side the next hour, if the thing were possible—*that* is what I mean by loving you– Much more, if you chose to wear a peach coloured gown while I thought green more becoming to you, would I take your hand in the street as warmly as if you had chosen the green. Much more, if you had run against me in the dark, meaning not to hurt me, would I hasten to prove to you that I did not mean to give *you* pain by disbelieving your assertion to such an effect. So you see that whichever way some circumstances are considered, an obvious conclusion from them can scarcely be altered. Not that I shall refer further to it– Only *dont* misuse words, my own dear Henrietta. That *you* love me, has been most perfectly proved—and that I love them all in the house you live in, besides loving you, with a natural grateful love, I hope not to have disproved throughout my life .. not voluntarily at least, & with my eyes open persisting in the act– May God bless them all, & you! You do not mention Papa except incidentally. I want to know if he kissed you & Arabel when you went away & returned, so mind to tell me faithfully. Aunt Jane will have left England, I fear, before my letter can reach her. The "other trustee" is M: Arnould, the barrister—an intimate friend of Robert's. Oh, never mind the wills, dearest Henrietta!— nobody will die any sooner because of will-making, unless it is through being teazed into making it– What vexed me a little, was having to take a stranger (M: Chorley) as executor, when one of my brothers would have acted so much more naturally in a mere family matter—and if Henry's letter had come rather sooner .. but there's no use in this talking, & after all it's of no great consequence .. none, except as a matter of feeling. M: Kenyon is trustee, but declined the executorship on account of not being young enough. Now let me look about for something to tell you. Robert came in from his walk the other evening with an "Ah, ha! I have been kissed by somebody since I saw you last." I suppose he meant to make me dreadfully jealous; instead of which I was siezed with the most absurd, supernaturally absurd idea in the world, .. for actually it came into my head that you and Arabel

No. 2711   23–[2]4 November [1847]   331

were in Florence .. Arabel at any rate!—yes, I thought it was Arabel! Let that sublime touch of absurdity prove how much I think of you! Robert seeing me quite gasp for breath, hastened to explain that it was only his haunting friend, Father Prout,—who spending an hour or two in Florence on his road to Rome, of course met Robert, & *kissed him* in the street, mouth to mouth, a good deal to his surprise. Father Prout, always very cordial, enquired about me with solicitude, reiterated his regret at my veil being down at Leghorn, keeping from him the light of my countenance, & refreshed all Robert's regrets about Rome by explaining how he could have housed us with a purple cardinal for nothing & introduced us into any Italian society we pleased to select. Meanwhile he is to send us from Rome a letter of introduction to our Grand Duke's librarian of the Pitti, Count Groberg,[3] who is said to be a learned man & will give us access to men & books here. Father Prout was in too great haste, to go home with Robert & see his unveiled prophetess,—so Robert went with him into a coffee house & helped him into the diligence afterwards. Then we had a visit a few evenings since .. from Miss Boyle again. She came at half past eight & stayed till eleven .. keeping us up against all precedent[4] .. & was very agreeable & kind, and took sandwiches and offered (she also) Count Groberg, who is a friend of hers. I like her– She expresses her "high-breeding" with an amusing sort of restiveness. Robert who knows & remembers everything just at the right moment, quoted a passage out of a quaint work by Robert Boyle her famous ancestor,[5] & just stopped himself in time from a reference to the thieving propensities of her grandmother Lady Cork– She in the utmost goodhumour, caught up the abandoned hint & did not suffer us to languish over the said traditions, relating how her grandfather's horses & port were abstracted feloniously, with other interesting particulars– "Did you never know her, M.[r] Browning? I wonder you did'nt." Robert & Miss Boyle had the talking all their own way, and I the listening, which was better worth while.

So, Henrietta, you call me "sly" about Gerardine! Ah, but it was'nt my secret, observe, & then there has been such fuss & tribulation on the point up to this moment that I could'nt guess how it was to end. Gerardine when she travelled with us last year was only seventeen, & childish & unformed in many ways, though a most intelligent & quick-minded child, & from her education full of poetical taste & association. M.[rs] Jameson who adored her, complained of her in the same breath .. and Robert was given to making side-comments in my ear about that creature "as pure as the angels" who "could'nt be trusted to walk down a street by herself lest she should run away with the first man at the corner." In fact there were exaggerations in dear M.[rs] Jameson's thoughts about Geddie, .. who was just a pretty accomplished, gentle little girl, with some want of high motive & of comprehended duties .. thinking how to please herself, and loving "aunt Nina" in a sort of indolent fashion, (enough to wish to please her too, if it could be done without much exertion) .. but who was no more fitted to be what M?s Jameson desired, a *laborious artist*, than to fly up to heaven like a lark. For ever & ever there were discussions about Gerardine's indolence, who had been besought to do this drawing or that, instead of which she lay in bed in the morning & played with Flush at night– She is such a gentle, caressing little creature, that I felt myself drawn to her side; and I used to make heaps of excuses for her, for which she used silently to kiss my hands– And yet M?s Jameson was rightly displeased very often—and there was no concealing that after having devoted herself & her means to the education of this niece, .. bringing her out to Italy at her expense, & ministering to her enjoyment in all ways .. she had a claim to attention & obedience, even had her wishes been less reasonable than they were. But there was a want of steadiness in the management– If Gerardine looked pale, she was set on her pedestal directly & adored—and then when the colour came back, she was scolded a little .. & so on. M?s Jameson was like a fond mother–(Geddie at least ought to love her) and Robert took the liberty so often of telling her what he took to be the truth in a very blunt fashion, & also what "HE should do if he had the *misfortune* of having a wife like Gerardine" .. (which was'nt by any means an agreeable form of sympathy to M?s Jameson, though it gave Robert an occasion of showing a wonderful quantity of ferocity & savage determination) that I was half nervous with the discussion– Poor M?s Jameson used, then, to turn round into abrupt comments on her charming qualities, & observe how *three men out of every five would be in love with her forthwith* .. "Oh not *you*, Browning, of course! I am aware that under no possible circumstances, she could have been calculated to please *you*—I only speak of ordinary men &c &c"– Received in profound silence, & with a little push against me under the table, which meant "*Did you ever hear anything so absurd? no never*". And it *was rather* absurd to be sure, seeing that Gerardine is just pretty & no more at most .. only M?s Jameson's fond affection which is the root of all, is not a thing to smile at but to love her for– She feels like a mother. Well—they left us & went to Rome, and when on their return we had them as our visitors here at Florence, a catastrophe had taken place .. poor Geddie had completed her offences by falling in love with a bad artist,![6] an unrefined gentleman,!! a Roman catholic! (converted from Protestantism!) a poor man!! with a red beard!!! whatever Geddie could mean by it was what M?s Jameson in her agony could'nt divine. "The truth is," said she to me, "the dear child who never thought in her whole life before of love & marriage, had it all put into her head at once by the sight of your & Browning's happiness—oh I see it, I understand how it was". So Robert & I were to have the blame of Geddie's falling in love, observe. I opened my eyes in considerable embarrassment .. certainly it was'nt my "pattern in the mount"[7] which had been adopted by Gerardine, according to M^rs J's own description: but I agreed to "speak to Geddie", & I did my best. Only Geddie's reading was very different, of her hero's qualities. "So good & generous! & handsome too! and likely to be a good artist when he *tries* .. (draws very well already!)—likely to *turn back again* from being a Roman Catholic—left off smoking just to please Aunt Nina & was *very* firm." Geddie had made up her heart, it was plain, .. and the great scene we had, in the course of which I was very, very sorry both for her & Mrs Jameson, produced no practical effect whatever on either side. When they returned to England, first I heard that everything was broken off, "Geddie being considered much too young" by her parents,—and then came a letter from herself to say that all was right again & that she was very happy. Poor little thing, I do hope she may continue so with the best reasons. I have a strong opinion of course on the right & righteousness of a woman's abiding by her own choice in marriage—but then, Gerardine is, to my mind, scarcely a woman yet—has had no experience of men or women, & just gives herself away to the first asker, .. who may be a good man nevertheless, .. I say nothing to the contrary. Father Prout speaks well of him—only he is Father Prout's convert, & that's a matter of course therefore—& I do think with her refinement of habits & associations, it is rather surprising that she should have been attracted where, according to Mrs Jameson, there is no corresponding refinement. Mrs J. said that he was unpolished in his manners, & seemed unaccustomed to the society of women. Then a catholic convert is more objectionable than a catholic by birth—so it seems to me. Mind you repeat nothing of this—I wont be "sly" any more as you reproach me for it, but you mus'nt mention these things, nor appear to Mrs Jameson as if you had been told of them too particularly. He is of a good Scotch family, .. but as to present position, we fancy that he is rather a picture-dealer than an artist. Mrs J. says he never can be a good artist—she undervalues his abilities much & laments that "her child should be lost to her". "He never can be a friend of mine", she repeats. Altogether I am sorry—but it may turn out better than the outside promises. They have *broken gold*, & Geddie has sent him her picture—& next summer he goes to England to marry her & take her to live at Rome—

Tell me .. where are the Reynolds's? They must have passed through Florence, I should imagine, by this time. Neither of them nor of the Lyndsays have we seen the least sign—and oh, Henrietta, how could you send *me* that bag? It is quite too bad & too kind of you, and I shall have to put my head into it when I get it, to hide the blushes of shame. Dreadful, dreadful, about poor Mr Deffell![8] What selfishness there is, in a man's choosing to put himself beyond his cares by inhaling prussic acid, .. and what childishness to have such cares as those pitiable ones about money!– Tell me if you see the daughters. The sons seem not to feel it too much. Indecent, indeed! Perhaps the unfortunate mother & daughters may be now drawn a little together: it has struck me that the whole family are "somewhat to seek" in natural affectionateness– They stand off from one another like the points of a triangle. How different from .. the Bayfords, for instance! Quite delighted I am to hear of dearest Trippy's being so comfortably settled again– Kiss her dear cheeks for me, if you please, and the lips, too, .. and tell her that before I am spoilt on both sides like a thoroughly spoilt apple, I hope to do it myself. Robert was vexed a little with me for "telling all about the house"—and really all *he* thought about it was his fear & trembling lest I should be taken ill & die before we could tumble out of it fast enough. As to *reproaching me*, the idea of the possibility of such a thing never entered his mind. He is *perfect* to me .. that's the only word to be used. And if I were to tell you every little thing in prose & rhyme,[9] you could not understand the whole of what I mean when I say so, without standing by & seeing & hearing for yourselves. One of the happy results is, that I never am afraid of doing or saying what could by possibility displease him .. in other words, he cant be displeased by whatever I may do or say, .. so that I am at liberty to talk out aloud all the '*bêtises*'[10] that come into my head. I talk as I should to you .. or a little more freely if that be possible –. there is not the thinnest shadow of constraint between us– It is a great comfort to be able to think & speak together at every moment of the day, & when I remember how different it must be in most other tête à têtes of the kind between men & women, I hope I thank God for it, with some, however inadequate, gratitude. Such nonsense as is spoken in this room, to be sure,! Flush opens his eyes halfway & then shuts them & goes to sleep on the dignified conviction of being able to do it a little better if he tried!– I tell my dreams even, and have visions of letters in the candle according to Wilson's instructions—and now & then we take to a little sense by way of change .. only it seems to me that Robert would rather hear the nonsense, of the two, because he accepts *that* as a sign of my being in spirits, .. and then, the thing most delightful to him is the liberty between us .. the absence of embarrassment & restraint. If I wanted to offend him I should do something in the way of respect & obedience.—— Now I will tell you .. The other day he said to me .. (in relation to Flush or some equally weighty subject I think it was ..) "I do wish, Ba, you would'nt do *so or so*". To which I answered .. "Well—I wont do it any more". Was ever a more unexceptionable answer,?—yes, and it was meekly delivered too. But *he* did'nt like it at all, nevertheless, & cried out quite quickly— "DONT say such words to me, Ba"—"Why what ought I to say then?"—"Say that you will do as you please as long as you please to do it". So you see what a difficult position mine is .. you see!—— My vow of obedience is only appealed to on great occasions, such as finishing a mutton-chop, or cutting one more slice of bread & butter .. & it's almost a pity that so much good vowing should have gone for almost nothing. Oh, of course we shall be glad to see the Tulks untulked,[11] if they care to come to see us—only unless they live close by they must accept Robert's visits for mine. I hope Sophia may be more in the right about her husband than Mary Minto—&, by the way, give my love to Mary & ask her why she does'nt come to Florence at once as she talked of doing. M[rs] Minto would like Italy as well as she did France .. I mean there are no drawbacks such as she may fear; & I wonder they dont come at once. We would take rooms for them & cheaply. It surprises us a little that the Duke of Lucca's chamberlain should choose Florence as his retiring-place—he will not be popular with us Tuscans, .. of that he may be very sure.[12] We had a festa on last monday week, the day of St Leopold, the name-day of our Grand-Duke[13]—& our piazza was nearly brimming over with people. A beautiful sight, really! He had gracefully solicited the civic guard to replace for that day his usual military attendance,—and, as gracefully, the civic guard sent for this purpose all their *nobles*, .. so that the very sentinels on duty at the palace-doors were marquises or dukes— Graceful on both sides, was it not? The service extended of course to four & twenty hours, and the nobles armed themselves for the vigil with so many dozens of champagne, cakes &c—and at twelve at night, and at nine in the morning, the Duke paid them a visit. When they came to replace the military, the people who thronged the piazza shouted & clapped their hands— and that clapping of hands is a sound so full of life & mental affirmation to me, (it is'nt mere *animal* life) that it throbs and thrills through one. Then the band played, and a hymn in congratulation of the Grand Duke, was sung in grand chorus beneath his windows (they sent us a copy of the poem) after which he the Duchess & their children came out into the balcony and bowed their thanks to the people.[14] Think how we rejoiced in our situation all this time. I could sit with my feet on the fender & nod back to their Highnesses. We threw draperies of crimson silk, by the desire of the *padrone*, out of our five front windows, & only just escaped the glory of an illumination. So you argue with M[r] Kenyon about "spheres of usefulness", Henrietta! Depend on it, there's one usefulness of the sun & another of the moon.[15] Rolling stones which gather no moss do something else, I dare say. Some are workers in the shop & some in the field, you know—but you must know besides that we have'nt given up England & never shall—though it would be folly in us with our means & my health, to plant ourselves so deeply there that we could not fly before the winters. To winter in England when there is the least chance of escaping, would be most absurd at any time, I do think—and now the facilities of movement are everyday becoming greater & we shall have railroads through France very soon: and even without them, we both *like* travelling .. it is the pleasure of pleasures to us- Oh, we shall go to Jerusalem some day—but to London *first*. I dont like to fasten my soul to plans which the uncertainty of the future must render uncertain .. because the rending away would give too much pain, you see. I shut my eyes & open my mouth, like a child, waiting for happy providences. Meanwhile, I hold you in my heart of hearts—believe that of me—and if Robert were to meet & kiss you in the streets here instead of Father Prout, it would be an intense joy. I think they might, some of them, in some vacation have proposed coming down the Rhine, & come a little farther. So well I am, Henrietta, if I must'nt say *"too well"*—& dear Minny tells Wilson, I hear, that it is highly improper of me to say it, for various reasons. Today I was out, walked up & down in the broad sunshine of our piazza, & missed my parasol—we have the windows open every day—& I believe it will be my own fault, not the atmosphere's, if I am not able to walk out a little on most days throughout the winter. Wilson has made my black merino very well .. trimmed with black velvet & jet buttons .. and it wont be too warm for all my boastings. One goes out with furs *and a parasol*, quite in natural combination. As to the other house, I fear it is not let yet .. in which case we lose the whole of the three months. You know, if the people let it for five or six months, they promised to pay back the money .. but that's too good to be in the least probable. Oh, we have a complement of spoons here—of cups & saucers too, only of the plainest order. The linen is the best—fine sheets & good beds .. On the whole we do very well in this house, and although I behaved abominably in the whole matter I cant be sorry at our being here rather than in Via Maggio where her highness of Brunswick[16] must have suffered from every shade of blue devilrie, if she was in the least like my lowness in bodily & mental constitution. Is Lady Bolingbroke successful yet? does she advise? Give my love to S & S Cook- Give it too to Mrs Orme .. and to Lizzie. Write oftener, you & Arabel, to your own Ba--now *do write*. Love to all. How did George prosper on circuit?

    Is Crow quite well? & the children? Robert writes for himself.

Address, on integral page: Angleterre viâ France / Care of Miss Trepsack / (Miss Barrett) / 10 [*sic*, for 12]. Upper Gloucester Street / Gloucester Place / Portman Square / London / [and in unidentified hand] missent to Somers Town / JD.
Publication: Huxley, pp. 59–67 (in part).
Source: Transcript in editors' file.

    1. Year provided by postmark.
    2. Cf. *Macbeth*, I, 1, 2.
    3. According to *The Tuscan Athenæum* for 4 December 1847, "On Monday, Novr 29th, at 8 o'Clock in the evening, Count Jakob Gröberg de Hemsö departed this life at the age of 72. He had been confined to his house for six days previous, by an attack of the lungs. — He was born at Gannafre in the parish of Hemsö in the island of Gothland, on the 7th May 1776. ... In 1828 he came to reside in Tuscany, and, in 1836, was appointed Chamberlain to H.R.H. the Grand Duke, and in 1841 Librarian of the Palatine library. — He was the author of a great many valuable works, chiefly geographical and statistical" (no. 6, p. 52).
    4. Miss Boyle explains: "My visits to Casa Guidi were daily, or rather nightly, for my mother's health at this time compelled her to retire early to rest; and at the moment I had bidden her goodnight, I would fly to Casa Guidi and spend the early evening, or

prima sera, as the Italians call it, with my poets. How delightful were those moments— how swiftly they did pass! how rich was the wit, the wisdom, the knowledge, the fancy, in which I revelled with those dear companions! And then a ring would come at the bell just at the proper moment to save my sweet hostess from fatigue" (*Mary Boyle: Her Story*, ed. Sir Courtenay Boyle, 1901, p. 220).

    5. Robert Boyle (1627-91), son of the "great" Earl of Cork, was a philosopher and chemist. A complete Latin edition of his works was issued in Geneva in 1677 under the title *Opera Varia*, a copy of which sold as lot 416 in *Browning Collections* (see *Reconstruction*, A293; present location unknown). This volume was inscribed by RB on the title page: "Robert & E.B. Browning," and on the fly-leaf: "I bought this book on a stall *by the weight*, R.B. Florence."

    6. Robert Macpherson (d. 1873), grand-nephew of the poet James Macpherson, was an artist living and working in Rome, whom she married two years later.

    7. Cf. Hebrews 8:5.

    8. John Henry Deffell (1778?-1847), a merchant of Billiter Court, who lived at 38 Upper Harley Street, had become despondent in consequence of commercial difficulties. On 28 October 1847 he entered a chemist's shop in Whitecross Street and, posing as a doctor, asked for prussic acid, which he seized and drank. After a brief chase he was taken to Cripplegate Dispensary where he died. A verdict of "'Temporary Insanity" was given. Besides his wife of 42 years, Elizabeth (*née* Mackenzie), he left three sons and three daughters: John (40), Henry (38), Francis (20), Caroline (41), Justina (39) and Charlotte (32). Deffell, owner of Jamaican estates, including "Swansea" and "Saltsprings," was a Barrett family friend for many years and there were many connections between the families in business affairs—for example Deffell's nephew, Duncan Anderson of Mincing Lane, was a broker for EBB's father.

    9. Cf. *Paradise Lost*, I, 16.

    10. "Stupidities."

    11. Charles Augustus Tulk (1786-1849) and two of his daughters, together with their families, had decided to settle in Florence. One daughter was Louisa Susanna (1819?-1848) who married James Peard Ley in 1844; they had two children: Louisa and James. The other daughter was Sophia Augusta Tulk (1823-1909) who married Henry Cottrell (1811-71) on 25 September 1847. The Tulks were friends of the Barretts with whom there was a family connection as a result of the marriage of Tulk's eldest daughter, Caroline Augusta, to John Gordon. Gordon's sister Anne married EBB's uncle Samuel in 1833. For more information on the Tulk/Barrett and Cottrell/Browning relationship see "Sophia Cottrell's Recollections" by Scott Lewis, *Browning Society Notes*, 24 (1997), 17-49.

    12. Henry Cottrell had recently left his post as Chamberlain in the household of Charles Louis de Bourbon, Duke of Lucca. Cottrell was one of three Englishmen ennobled by the Duke who gave him the honorific title of Count. EBB is probably referring to the recent disturbances in Fivizzano. The Duke of Lucca had lately ceded his Duchy to his cousin, the Grand Duke of Tuscany, in exchange for funds to settle his debts. In any event, the Duchy of Lucca would have passed to the Grand Duchy of Tuscany after the death of the Duchess of Parma, but the Duke of Lucca's financial situation had led him to act hastily. However, when the Duchess of Parma died on 18 December 1847, and it became apparent that the Duke had altered terms of earlier agreements, and some of the outlying areas had been ceded to the Duke of Modena, the inhabitants of these areas were upset to find themselves subjects of unpopular rulers, and fighting broke out. The excitement was soon dispelled, but it left Tuscans, in particular, with even less friendly feelings toward the former Duke of Lucca than they already felt.

    13. The feast of St. Leopold the Good, an 11th-century Austrian prince, is celebrated on 15 November.

    14. Leopold's family at this time consisted of twelve children: three from his first marriage and nine from his second wife Maria Antonia. We have been unable to trace the poem referred to by EBB.

    15. Cf. I Corinthians 15:41.

    16. See letter 2707, note 5.

2712. RB TO ARABELLA & HENRIETTA MOULTON-BARRETT

Florence,
Nov. 25. [1847][1]

Thank both my dearest Sisters for their most affectionate letters: I had intended to write a proper answer—(i.e. proper as to length, for the feeling of it would be much the same, whether expressed briefly or otherwise)—but this last day allowed me, is formed to rather a bustling one for us quiet people—as I have to make some couple of journeys to the Post Office, besides calling on an American friend of Mr Kenyon's,[2] just arrived; so take in few words, instead of many, the repeated assurance of the great happiness and comfort which your sympathy gives me. I know we three have only one object at heart,—the good of Ba,—and it is the greatest comfort, as I say, that you two, who are away, should be so indulgent to me who am obliged to act according to the best of my poor judgment: but then you, who know Ba, must not believe all *she* believes about the wonderful kindness of getting out of a scrape when one has been goose enough to get into it—the taking that cold house was all my fault, for I ought to have known that no comfort makes up for the absence of the sun in this country whither we come precisely for the sun—never mind! it is well over, and we are here in little funny rabbit-hutch rooms,—but *so* warm, and cheerful! we shall do capitally, I have little doubt,—though Rome, with its deliciously *soft*—(not bracing and dry—) air would have been the proper wintering-place, had all circumstances proved propitious. Ba is very much better than she has ever been: she walked out with me yesterday for a good half hour in the blazing *November* sun(!)—and purposes doing the like this morning, when the weather seems finer than ever. She is always in the best of spirits, talking & laughing to heart's content, and (best of all) sleeping soundly after it: a letter from you makes her still happier, however,—so you must help me in that respect. If you could see her face when I come in from the Post with one in my pocket,—and perhaps try to look peculiarly grave and disappointed ... she sees thro' me in a moment!

I am sure Ba has told you of all the little nullities which pass for events in our life—and how the time passes swiftly by without our noticing it: I dare say she did justice to my sublime feelings on the occasion of the earthquake which I supposed to be merely poor Flush solacing himself by a hearty scratch![3] Does she tell you how the said Flush's faculties are developing themselves surprisingly—how he sits and *talks* in the oddest way, for minutes together? I dare say you know all our news. If you were here we would, however, try hard and amuse you better—not that there would be any great difficulty in this lovely city with its still lovelier neighbourhood: what a pity of pities that this may not be! still let us be thankful for what we have

No. 2713 8 December [1847] 339

got—in this restoration to health of Ba. I will not write more now—only this,—Be quite sure I will keep you well & constantly informed of whatever happens, as it happens. Ba, herself, writes more than is said to be good for her: but then she is so used to it, and it *so* gratifies her, that I hold my tongue— oftener than I ought, perhaps! Good-bye, dearest Henrietta & Arabella. God bless you ever–

RB.

Address, on integral page: Miss Barrett.
Publication: TTUL, pp. 53-55.
Source: Transcript in editors' file.

1. Year determined by RB's reference to the move from the "cold house" (the one in Via Maggio) to the one they have come to for "the sun" (the one in Piazza Pitti).
2. See note 10 in the following letter.
3. "A slight shock of Earthquake," as described in *The Tuscan Athenæum* of 20 November 1847, had occurred on 8 November (no. 3, p. 29).

2713. EBB TO MARY RUSSELL MITFORD

Florence.
Dec. 8. [1847][1]

Have you thought me long, my dearest Miss Mitford, in writing? When your letter came we were distracted by various uncertainties, torn by wild horses of sundry speculations,—& then, when one begins by delay in answering a letter, you are aware how a silence grows & grows. Also I heard OF you, through my sisters & Mrs Dupuy,[2] & THAT made me lazier still. Now dont treat me according to the Jewish law– An eye for an eye[3] .. no! but a heart for a heart, if you please: and you never can have reason to reproach mine for not loving you. Think what we have done since I wrote last to you. Taken two houses, that is, two apartments, each for six months, presigning the contract. You will set it down as excellent poets' work in the way of domestic economy: but the fault was altogether mine as usual—and my husband, to please me, took rooms which I could not be pleased by three days, through the absence of sunshine & warmth.[4] The consequence was that we had to pay heaps of guineas away, for leave to go away ourselves—any alternative being preferable to a return of illness .. and I am sure I should have been ill if we had persisted in staying there– You can scarcely fancy the wonderful difference which the sun makes in Italy. Oh .. he is'nt a mere "round O"[5] in the air, in this Italy, I assure you! He makes us feel that he rules the day[6] to all intents & purposes. So away we came into the blaze of him here in this piazza Pitti, precisely opposite the Grand Duke's palace, I with my remorse, & poor Robert without a single reproach– Any other man, a little lower than the angels,[7] would have stamped & sworn a little, for the mere relief of the thing—but as to *his* being angry with *me* for any cause except not eating enough dinner, the said sun would turn the wrong way first. So here we are on the Pitti, till April, .. in small rooms yellow with sunshine from morning to evening; and most days I am able to get out into the piazza & walk up & down for some twenty minutes, without feeling a shadow or breath from the actual winter. Also it is pleasant to be close to the Raffaels .. to say nothing of the immense advantage of the festa-days, when (day after day) the civic guard comes to show the whole population of Florence, their Grand Duke inclusive, the new helmets & epaulettes & the glory thereof– They have swords too, I believe, somewhere. The crowds come & come, like children to see rows of dolls: only the children would tire sooner than the Tuscans. Robert said musingly the other morning as we stood at the window—"Surely, after all this, they would USE those muskets". It's a problem—a "grand peutêtre".[8] I was rather amused by hearing lately that our civic heroes had the gallantry to propose to the ancient military, that these last should do the night-work i.e., when nobody was looking on & there was no credit .. as they found it dull & fatiguing. Ah—one laughs, you see—one cant help it now & then. But at the real & rising feeling of the people, by night & day, one does'nt laugh indeed– I hear & see with the deepest sympathy of soul, on the contrary. I love the Italians too, & none the less, that something of the triviality & innocent vanity of children, abounds in them.

A delightful & most welcome letter was the last you sent me, my dearest friend. Your bridal visit must have charmed you, & I am glad that you had the gladness of witnessing some of the happiness of your friend M.rs Acton Tindal, .. *you* who have such quick sympathies, & to whom the happiness of a friend is a gain counted in your own. The swan's shadow is something in a clear water–[9] For poor M.rs Partridge if she is really, as you say M.rs Tindal thinks, pining in an access of literary despondency, why *that* only proves to me that she is not happy otherwise, .. that her life & soul are not sufficiently filled for her woman's need. I cannot believe of any woman, that she can think of *fame first*. A woman of genius may be absorbed indeed in the exercise of an active power, .. engrossed in the charges of the course & the combat: but this is altogether different to a vain & bitter longing for prizes .. and what prizes, .. oh gracious Heavens? The empty cup of cold metal! *so* cold, *so* empty, to a woman with a heart. So if your friend's belief is true, still more deeply do I pity that other friend, who is supposed to be unhappy from such a cause. A few days ago, I saw a bride of my own family, M.rs Reynolds, Arlette Butler who married Cap.t Reynolds some five months since– I think I told you of that marriage, & I had a week or two of intercourse with her as she & her husband passed through Florence to Rome on their bridal tour. She seems happy & looks well, and it was very pleasant to be able to talk over & over the dear dear people in England whom she had parted from so lately. The warmth of my sisters['] lips & hands seemed to be on her's, & so it was natural that I should never have loved her so much before. Many were her exclamations at seeing me! She declared that such a change was never seen, I was so transfigured with my betterness! "Oh Ba, it is quite wonderful indeed." We had been calculated on, during her three months at Rome, as a "piece de resistance" .. and it was a disappointment to find us here, in a corner, with the salt. Just as I was praised, was poor Flush criticised. Flush has not recovered from the effects yet of the summer plague of fleas, and his curls, though growing, are not grown. I never saw him in such spirits nor so ugly! and though Robert & I flatter ourselves upon "the sensible improvement," Arlette could only see him with reference to the past when in his Wimpole Street days, he was sleek ⟨and f⟩at & she cried aloud at the loss of his beauty. Then we have had ⟨another⟩ visitor, M! Hillard,[10] an American critic, who reviewed me in the ⟨old w⟩orld & so came to *view* me in the new:—a very intelligent man, of a good, noble spirit. And Miss Boyle, ever & anon, comes at night, at nine oclock, to catch us at our hot chesnuts & mulled wine, & warm her feet at our fire—and a kinder, more cordial little creature, full of talent & accomplishment, never had the world's polish on it. Very amusing too, she is, & original, & a good deal of laughing she & Robert make between them. Did I tell you of her before, & how she is the niece of Lord Cork, & poetess by grace of certain Irish Muses?[11] Neither of us know her writings in any way, but we like her & for the best reasons—— And this is nearly all, I think, we see of the "Face divine"[12] masculine or feminine .. & I cant make Robert go out a single evening, not even to a concert, nor to hear a play of Alfieri's:—yet we fill up our days with books & music, (& a little writing has its share)[13] & wonder at the clock for gallopping. It's twenty four oclock with us, almost as soon as we begin to count. Do tell me of Tennyson's book—& of Miss Martineau's. I was grieved to hear a distant murmur of a rumour of an apprehension of a return of her complaint: somebody said that she could not bear the *pressure of dress*, & that the exhaustion resulting from her fits of absorption in work & enthusiasm on the new subject of Ægypt, was painfully great,—& that her friends feared for her.[14] I should think that the bodily excitement & fatigue of her late travels must have been highly hazardous—& that indeed throughout her convalescence, she should have more spared herself in climbing hills, & walking & riding distances. A strain, obviously, might undo everything. Still, I do hope that the bitter cup may not be filled for her again. What a wonderful discovery this substitute for æther-inhalations,[15] seems to be. Do you hear anything of it's operation in your neighbourhood? We have had a letter from M! Horne who appears happy & speaks of his success in lecturing on Ireland, & of a new novel which he is about to publish in a separate form after having printed it in a magazine.[16] We have not set up the types, even of our *plans* about a book, very distinctly—but we shall do something some day, & you shall hear of it the evening before. Being too happy does'nt agree with literary activity quite as well as I sh^d have thought; & then dear Mr Kenyon cant persuade us that we are not rich enough, .. so as to bring into force a lower order of motives. He talks of Rome still—— Now write, dear dearest Miss Mitford, & tell me of yourself & your health, & how K. gets on, & how the child is—& *do, do* love me as you used to do. Tell me of every little thing, that I may fancy I hear you talk. As to French books, one may swear, .. but you cant get a new publication, except by accident, at this excellent celebrated library of Vieusseux's,[17] & I am reduced to read some of my favorites over again, I and Robert together– You ought to hear how we go to single combat, ever & anon, with shield & lance. The greatest quarrel we have had since our marriage by the way, (always excepting my crying conjugal wrong of not eating enough!) was brought up by Masson's pamphlet on the Iron Mask & Fouquet. I would'nt be persuaded that Fouquet was "in it," and so "the anger of my lord waxed hot."[18] To this day he says sometimes .. "Dont be cross, Ba! *Fouquet was'nt the Iron Mask after all.*"

God bless you, Dearest Miss Mitford,

your ever affec^{te}
EBB.

We are here till April.

Address, on integral page: Miss Mitford / Three Mile Cross / near Reading.
Publication: EBB-MRM, III, 224–228.
Manuscript: Wellesley College.

1. Year provided by postmark.
2. Miss Mitford's friend, Mrs. J.P. (Sophia) Dupuy, lived near the Barretts at 31 Welbeck Street. In 1849 she moved to 37 Wimpole Street, just opposite the Barretts.
3. Cf. Exodus 21:24.
4. See letter 2709, note 3.
5. Unidentified.
6. Cf. Genesis 1:16.
7. Cf. Psalm 8:5.
8. "Great perhaps" (see letter 2698, note 4). EBB's description of the civic guard is echoed in *Casa Guidi Windows,* I, 744–758.
9. In a letter to Charles Boner, dated 11 October 1847, Miss Mitford wrote that the newly-married couple "spent four days at the 'Bear' in Reading ... I never saw a happier couple—both elegant, gracious and full of gaiety and sensibility; he is a fine athletic dark man of thirty-one or thirty-two, she a most sweet and lovely blonde of twenty-three or twenty-four. ... I have never seen two people so happy and so deserving of happiness" (*Mary Russell Mitford: Correspondence with Charles Boner and John Ruskin,* ed. Elizabeth Lee, 1914, p. 80).
10. George Stillman Hillard (1808–79), American lawyer, editor, and critic, was travelling in Italy at this time, and recorded: "I entered Florence on the twenty-second of November, and left on the thirteenth of December" (*Six Months in Italy,* Boston, 1853, I, 181). The review EBB refers to appeared in *The North American Review* of July 1842 (pp. 201–245); for that portion relating to EBB, see our vol. 6, pp. 373–379. Hillard's

No. 2714 [mid-] December [1847] 343

account of his travels includes his recollections of the Brownings; for the text, see pp. 408–409.
  11. EBB mentioned her to Miss Mitford in letter 2703.
  12. *Paradise Lost*, III, 44.
  13. EBB was probably working on a poem she called "A Meditation in Tuscany," which she submitted to *Blackwood's Edinburgh Magazine* in 1848, and which they returned asking her to supply notes. It was never printed in *Blackwood's*, but eventually it formed the first part of *Casa Guidi Windows*. RB was revising his earlier works for what would be the 1849 collected edition (see letter 2637, note 1).
  14. EBB's sources were evidently mistaken since Harriet Martineau seems to have been enjoying relatively good health at this time. She wrote an account of her travels in 1846–47, which was published as *Eastern Life, Present and Past* in the spring of 1848.
  15. A reference to the use of chloroform instead of æther as an anæsthetic (see letter 2654, note 15). In March 1847 James Young Simpson, a Scottish physician, "read a paper on chloroform to the Medico-Chirurgical Society of Edinburgh" (*EB*), and despite the initial controversy caused by his advocacy for the use of chloroform particularly in obstetrics, its use became wide-spread. EBB refers to both æther and chloroform in *Casa Guidi Windows*, I, 695.
  16. Horne's novel *The Dreamer and the Worker* had appeared as a monthly serial throughout 1847 in *Douglas Jerrold's Shilling Magazine*, thanks to Jerrold's generosity; however, the book was not published as a single title until 1851.
  17. According to Murray's *Hand-Book for Travellers in Northern Italy* (1847), "Vieusseux's, in the Palazzo Buondelmonti, Piazza S. Trinita, is excellent, but the subscription, about 10*s*. a month, is high. The collection of journals and newspapers of every country is very extensive and well chosen" (p. 474).
  18. Exodus 32:22. The editors of *EBB-MRM* suggest that this is a reference to the novelist Michel Masson; however, we have been unable to trace any work by him on the man in the iron mask. Nevertheless, one of his contemporaries, the novelist Jacob Paul La Croix, whom EBB mentioned in conjunction with Masson in letter 1774, was the author of *L'Homme au Masque de Fer* (1837), in which he argues that the masked prisoner was Nicolas Fouquet (1615–80), Finance Minister under Cardinal Mazarin from 1653 to 1661. Other investigators have identified the unknown prisoner as Count Matthioli, secretary to the Duke of Mantua, who had been arrested for treason. Despite claims for either, no one has ever proved with certainty who the man was. Evidently, RB remained curious about the subject. In a letter to Mrs. Fitzgerald, dated 8 November 1883, he explained that he had enquired of Don Carlos, the Bourbons claimant to the throne of Spain, if he knew the identity since it was supposed to be "transmitted from sire to son by the Royal family of France: he said he did not—neither did his uncle Chambord: the secret died with the little Dauphin in the Temple" (*Learned Lady: Letters from Robert Browning to Mrs. Thomas Fitzgerald, 1876–1889*, ed. Edward C. McAleer, Cambridge, Mass., 1966, p. 173).

2714. EBB & RB TO ANNA BROWNELL JAMESON

[In EBB's hand]   Florence.
[mid-] December [1847][1]

Indeed, my dear friend, you have a right to complain of *me*, whether or not *we* had any, in thinking ourselves 'deeply injured creatures by your last' silence. Yet when in your letter which came at last, you said "write directly" I *meant* to write directly– I did not take out my vengeance in a forgone malice, be very sure. Just at the time, we were in a hard knot of uncertainties, about

Rome & Venice & Florence, & a cold house & a warm house—for instance we managed (that is, I² did—for altogether it was my fault) to take two apartments in the course of ten days, each for a term of six months, .. getting out of one of them by leaving the skirts of our garments, RENT,³ literally, in the hand of the proprietor. You have heard most of this, I dare say, from M! Kenyon or my sisters. Now too, you are aware of our being in piazza Pitti, in a charmed circle of sunblaze. Our rooms are small but of course as cheerful as being under the very eyelids of the sun must make everything; and we have a cook in the house who takes the office of traiteur on him, & gives us English mutton chops at Florentine prices,—both of us quite well & in spirits, & (though you never will believe this) happier than ever. For my own part, you know I need not say a word if it were not true, and I must say to you who saw the beginning with us, that this end of fifteen months is just fifteen times better & brighter; the mystical "moon" growing larger & larger till scarcely room is left for any stars at all: the only differences which have touched me, being to more & more happiness. It would have been worse than unreasonable if in marrying I had expected one quarter of such happiness, and indeed I did not, to do myself justice—and every now & then I look round in astonishment & thankfulness together, yet with a sort of horror, seeing that this is not Heaven after all. We live just as we did when you knew us, just as shut-up a life– Robert never goes anywhere except to take a walk with Flush, .. which is'nt my fault as you may imagine: he has not been out one evening of the fifteen months: but what with music & books, & writing & talking, we scarcely know how the days go—it's such a gallop on the grass. We are going through some of old Sacchetti's novelets now: characteristic work for Florence, if somewhat dull elsewhere. Boccaccios cant be expected to spring up with the vines in rows, even in this climate. We got a newly printed addition to Savonarola's poems the other day⁴— very flat & cold—they did not catch fire when he was burnt. The most poetic thing in the book, is his face on the first page, with that eager, devouring soul in the eyes of it. You may suppose that I am able sometimes to go over to the gallery & adore the Raphaels—and Robert will tell you of the divine Apollino which you missed seeing in Poggio Imperiale,⁵ & which I shall be set face to face before, some day soon, I hope. I am looking so well that a cousin of mine lately married & on the usual tour, who came to visit us on her way through Florence, declared it was a case "past recognition"- We had parted in my room in poor Wimpole Street,—so of course she did see some difference. A summer in the open air, & half a winter with liberty of walking out a little most days, and unclouded happiness (except the *transalpine* clouds!) throughout all that time, may be supposed to have had an influence for good. In making people egotists .. you will say. Well—give me back my egotism, I only beseech of you. Let it be an I for an I, according to the strictest of the Jewish Law–[6] I want so much .. *we* want so much .. to hear every, the least & greatest thing, about you, dearest Madonna Nina, & of Geddie too. Thank her, by the way, for the letter she sent me, & which I shall answer in time, notwithstanding appearances. It was quite a surprise to me, who had received a contrary tradition just before, that her marriage should be a fixed thing, .. & fixed for so early a time. Oh, may God order it all for her happiness .. & for yours. I wonder & wonder in my head on the subject of your wonderful plans, which you just hint at, & which are interwoven, you say, with *ours*, .. & whether yours & Geddie's may not, or *must not* be of the same skein—as for ours, they are the merest cobweb at present, & not discussable beyond this flare of the pinewood .. Florence, I delight in: it combines art & nature, to say nothing of the conveniences of "l'homme policé",[7] which Robert classes roughly when he speaks of "a place where you may buy Toulon lozenges". (Is *that* the way to spell *Toulon*? I leave it to "l'homme policé" to spell right.) As to the society of Florence, we know nothing of it happily– Only M! Powers, & lively, clever Miss Boyle, & one or two passing Americans who come with or without letters of introduction, break on our tête à tête—& nobody at all thinks of tormenting us, as far as the "regular residents" are concerned. We do quite as well here as ever we did at Pisa in this respect of being untormented– All I complain of is, the want of new books– My dear French romances, Robert goes to hunt for me in vain– I have'nt read even Lucresia—nor Balzac's last but three.[8] Father Prout was in Florence for some two hours in passing to Rome, & of course, according to contract of spirits of the air, Robert met him, & heard a great deal of you & Geddie, (saw Geddie's picture, by the way, & thought it very like) .. was told much to the advantage of M! Macpherson,[9] & at the end of all kissed in the open street, as the speaker was about to disappear in the diligence. When you write, tell me of the *book*– Surely it will be out anon—and then you will be free, shall you not? Have you seen Tennyson's new poem—and what of it? Miss Martineau is to discourse about Ægypt, I suppose,—but in the meanwhile, do you hear that she forswears mesmerism, as M! Spenser Hall does,[10] according to the report Robert brings me home from the newspaper-reading– Now I shall leave him room to stand on & speak a word to you. Give my love to Gerardine & dont forget to mention her letter. I hope you are happy about your friends, & that in particular, Lady Byron's health is strengthening & to strengthen. Always my dear friend's

Most affectionate
EBB

[Continued by RB]

Dear Aunt Nina .. A corner is just the place for eating Christmas pies in, but for venting Christmas wishes, hardly! What has Ba told you, and wished you in the way of love? Because I wish you the same & love you the same—and Geddie being part of you, gets her due part. We are as happy as two owls in a hole, two toads under a tree-stump,—or any other queer two poking creatures that are let live after the fashion of their black hearts—only Ba is fat and rosy,—yes, indeed! Florence is empty and pleasant- Goodbye therefore till next year—shall it not be then we meet?

God bless you-
RB.

Address, in EBB's hand, on integral page: Mrs Jameson / Ealing.
Publication: LEBB, I, 354-356 (in part).
Manuscript: Wellesley College.

1. Year determined from postmark, and RB's Christmas wishes place this letter in mid to late December.
2. Underscored twice.
3. Cf. I Samuel 15:27.
4. *Poesie di Ieronimo Savonarola illustrate e pubblicate per cura di Andin de Rians* (Florence, 1847). The likeness of Savonarola, opposite the title-page, is an engraving of the portrait by Fra Bartolomeo, and depicts Savonarola in his monk's cowl (cf. *Casa Guidi Windows*, I, 273-276). Franco di Benci Sacchetti (1332?-1400), son of a prosperous and respected Florentine Guelph merchant, was the author of *Trecento novelle* (only 223 of the 300 stories have survived), which depicts the manners and customs of middle-class life in 13th-century Florence. Sacchetti's stories lack a frame-work like the *Decameron* of his more famous contemporary Boccaccio, and often conclude with a moral. A selection of these stories was published in Paris in early 1847 in *Tesoro dei Novellieri Italiani scelti dal decimoterzo al decimonono secolo*, and is possibly the edition which the Brownings read.
5. This 17th-century palace just outside the Porta Romana was built by the wife of Cosimo II, and, according to Murray's *Hand-Book for Travellers in Northern Italy* (1847), "in the dining room is a small statue of Apollo which is said to be the work of *Phidias*, and is of exquisite beauty. It was considered to be the finest statue in Florence, by Canova, who, whenever he was there, took his friends to see it" (p. 574).
6. Cf. Exodus 21:24.
7. "Civilized man."
8. See letter 2654, in which EBB mentions *Une Instruction criminelle* and *L'Envers de l'histoire contemporaine* as "new works" by Balzac. In letter 2703 (see note 17), EBB said she had not read Sand's *Lucrezia Floriani*.
9. According to the *DNB*, Father Prout was a frequent visitor to Mrs. Jameson when she was in Rome.
10. The Brownings' source for this is unknown. There is no evidence that Harriet Martineau or Spencer Timothy Hall ever denied their belief in mesmerism. In a letter to Mary Carpenter, dated 17 April 1866, Miss Martineau denied a belief in spiritualism, but affirmed that her position on mesmerism was "the same that it was twenty years ago" (*Harriet Martineau's Autobiography*, 1877, III, 421).

2715. JOSEPH ARNOULD TO RB

18 Victoria Square, Pimlico.
Dec. 19th/47

Very welcome, my dear Browning, was the sight of your hand writing once more, & truly on my part it ought to have been acknowledged earlier: but you live so constantly in our thoughts here; & you & yours are so often the subject of our words, that the only forgetfulness I can reproach myself with, in not writing, is that of not telling you how much we think & talk of you: it seems to me that yourself & Mrs Robert Browning are the most frequently & kindly talked of people, of any whose names are current in this great, jealous, & generally oblivious London society, as far at least as my little knowledge of it extends. It is impossible, at all events I find it so, not to envy you your life of study & repose in Florence, a city of all others I think, delightful, to those who will lead their own life in it, & let the noisy shallow stream of gossip & scandal, which there runs perpetually, foam away as it will without heeding it: you have air clear, though cold, libraries, stores of art, a cheerful smiling country, & silent streets, great churches, & cloudless moonlights for thought & that higher energy of creative invention, to expand in: well exchanged all this, to my mind, for the smoke & stir of this dim spot where with low thoughted cares we toil on after money, or power, or pleasure: I am still climbing, without much encouragement up the stubborn ascents of the Law: for rapid climbing in that direction, as in fact for rapid climbing anywhere, you want nimbleness & shiftiness of foot, hand & eye, which unluckily for me, I don't possess: all I can bring to the work is a certain toughness of sinew, strength of mind, & an indomitable resolution never to bate heart or hope: I believe I may say after 6 years that I am some few decided steps in advance, & only last week had my first opportunity, which I have long wanted, of making a speech in Court in a case of some importance to my client: wherein those who should be able to judge of such things tell me I acquitted myself not discreditably: then I am at length on the eve of publishing a Law Book[1] which has cost me (man of genius don't smile at such plodding) 4 years of the best labour & pains I could bestow on it & therefore, if I am not an absolute dolt, ought to do something for me: at all events therefore, my dear friend, to put an end to this egotism (strongest proof of my confidence in your friendship)—if I fail I shall have the satisfaction of knowing that to the best of my powers I have striven not to fail, & shall take failure as the just verdict of man on my want of ability.

We have been very quiet for some months' past: I know you will be sorry to hear that my dear wife has been for some time a great invalid; for the last year she had been complaining & (this is of course completely *entre nous*[2] as old friends) having at length prevailed upon her to undergo an examination it appeared that she had been for some long time labouring under that very distressing, but I believe not uncommon malady with women *prolapsus uteri*; which in all probability had for months if not years been producing that debility of which she at times used to complain: I sent her down immediately to the sea side where she has now been for 6 weeks & I am delighted to say appears completely renovated, & will, as I am assured by the first medical advice in London, get completely sound: I should hardly have told you all this thus explicitly were it not in order to account (what nothing but the Truth could explain) for the depression of health & spirits which has quite prevented her from seeing her friends, especially your sister & Mrs Browning, so often as she could have wished: I trust that, after Xmas, all this may be altered.

I have not heard from Domett since I wrote to you last, nor have I any positive information as to his present exact position with Governor Grey:[3] but this I know, that on Grey's first going out as governor, Domett was singled out by him in a very marked way; he took him in his company to Auckland (govt station in the North Island), talked a great deal & very confidentially about plans of government &c, which was very natural as Domett had been throughout advocating the very line of policy which Grey went determined to carry out. I think from all this it is most probable that our friend has ere this received some appointment, which will at all events enable him to live on there, until the opportunity offers of something more valuable: you know how little would suffice Domett; ship biscuit, a bed, a room, fire & grog when required. Meantime I am very anxiously looking for his next letter from which I shall learn something positive:

I see a great deal of Chorley, a valuable friendship which is not the least of the benefits for which I have to thank you: his life is one of the most desperate hard work—over work in fact: I wish he could only grasp one decided success: this he wants at present very much: besides his journalism he is doing a great deal just now in the translation of operas (chiefly French—the *Iphigenie* of "the Ritter Gluck" among the number) for Mons. Jullien,[4] who is giving English opera at Drury Lane: the work is lucrative, but laborious from the high pressure speed at which it is required to be done: his play, I was in great hopes .. was to have been acted at the Princesse's [*sic*], but Maddox, the manager, was it seems so disheartened at the result of the Philip Van Artevelde that he has declared finally against any more new plays: so that unless Miss Cushman takes the play with her elsewhere I fear it will not be brought out at all:[5] As to the Philip Van Artevelde the critics all pronounced it nought as an acting play:[6] I confess I could not agree in their verdict, for, though wanting in lightness & event, yet there was a nobleness & grandeur about the character of Philip as developed by Macready, & a power & interest about many of the scenes, which gave me, & seemed to me calculated to give any moderately cultivated audience, very high pleasure. Dickens, in the conduct of his present story, 'Dombey & Son'—seems to me sadly degenerating from the humourist of native English growth, into the sentimentalist of a half French, half German & to my mind wholly unsupportable school—the clear raciness of style & vigour of thought, as it seems to me, gone—& in it's stead melodramatic vehemence of action, alternating with most morbid anatomy of the inner men & women of his tale— a sense of unreality & effort in the whole business which when one recollects his old felicity & facility is painful:[7] Tennyson is on the eve of publication "The Princess—a Medley" & as you may imagine 'the Town' is on the tiptoe of expectation: My dear Browning do you know the German transcendental writers at all—especially *Fichte*?[8] an enterprising American bookseller here has been translating all his exoteric works i.e. all except his Formal System of Metaphysics—the titles will show you the nature of the Books[:] "The destination of Man" "The nature & vocation of the scholar" "Characteristics of the present age'['] Religion or the Holy life (last not yet published)- I have been reading them with that engrossing, rapt, concentrated attention which no book can command except one which speaks to the very soul of the reader: formalized in Fichte's books I find what has long been hovering vaguely before my own mind as truth: especially on Religion & Christianity. D<small>O READ THEM</small>—they are not costly[,] the price of the hitherto published is as follows *Characteristics of the Present Age* 7^s. *Vocation of the Scholar* 2^s. The *Destination of Man* 3^s. 6^d. *The Nature of the Scholar* 6^s.—in all 18^s. 6^d. May I send them to you: I am sure you would find grand food for thought in them: to my mind the most satisfactory word which has yet been spoken about that which is of supreme interest to all men: you will find yourself in that school where Carlyle evidently had been a most earnest student: the manner even closely resembling Carlyle in his loftier & graver moods; I mean when he does not give himself up to the grotesque whimsicality which he seems to have caught from Richter:[9] altogether I think *you* must read these books: tell me about it when you write next & my dear Browning, if not too exacting, let me ask for a letter soon; if you knew the pleasure your letters give me, I should not ask this in vain: I should so like you to give me the benefit of your thoughts on such great subjects as that of the Progress of the Race as developed after Fichte's theory in his book ⟨now⟩ named Characteristics of the Present age—which in ⟨re⟩ality contains his whole plan of world history: ⟨it⟩ would be an infinite refreshment to my mind if you would condescend occasionally to hold commune with it on such points & then too I think our letters, having some worthier end than mere gossip might be more frequent: I trust Mrs. Browning's health will continue improving: "Give my kindest regards to Browning & his wife when you write" were my wife's general orders—& will you take & give mine & Believe me your warmly attached Friend

J. Arnould

Publication: Smalley, pp. 96–98.
Manuscript: Pierpont Morgan Library, Gordon N. Ray Bequest.

    1. *A Treatise on the Law of Marine Insurance and Average: With References to American Cases, and the Later Continental Authorities* was published in 1848; subsequent editions appeared throughout the 19th and 20th centuries. In the preface to the sixteenth edition, published in 1981, the editors state that the work "is a masterpiece, in the forefront of the great writings on commercial laws in the English language: owing ... to the genius of its author" (p. vii).
    2. "Between us."
    3. See letter 2662, note 4. In 1848, Grey appointed Domett Colonial Secretary for the southern province of New Munster. In this position Domett was involved in a wide range of government activities; over the next few years, he would concentrate on policies related to education in the colony. (See *The Diary of Alfred Domett: 1872–1885*, ed. E.A. Horsman, 1953, pp. 22–25.)
    4. Louis Antoine Jullien (1812–60), French-born composer and conductor, had arrived in England in 1841, and had become a household name by this time. He was often featured in *Punch*, where he was referred to as "the Mons." According to *The New Grove Dictionary of Music and Musicians* (1980), "an ill-planned season of grand opera at the Drury Lane Theatre, beginning in December 1847 with Berlioz as conductor, caused his first bankruptcy in England" (9, 749). *Grove* lists translations of ten libretti of opera by Chorley, including Gluck's *Iphigénie en Tauride*; however, it was not performed until 1860. Jullien's failure caused Chorley to suffer "the loss, not only of all his labour, but the greater part of his remuneration" (*Henry Fothergill Chorley: Autobiography, Memoir, Letters*, ed. H.G. Hewlett, 1873, II, 92). While visiting in Rome in 1756, Gluck was created Knight of the Golden Spur by the Pope, hence the "Ritter."
    5. *Duchess Eleanor*, which Chorley had started working on in late 1846, was not performed until 1854, with Charlotte Cushman in the lead role (see letter 2642, note 8).
    6. Macready's adaptation of Henry Taylor's verse drama was produced by John Medex Maddox at the Princess Theatre from 22 November through 3 December 1847, but it was an immediate failure. In his diary entry for 22 November, Macready wrote: "Acted Philip Van Artevelde. Failed; I cannot think it my fault" (*The Diaries of William Charles Macready, 1833–1851*, ed. William Toynbee, 1912, II, 377). The following day, Macready noted that he "saw the papers, which—I should instance the *Times* and *Chronicle* as especially disgusting—did not raise my spirits" (II, 378). Macready blamed the rest of the cast; and, according to his biographer, "the critics were inclined to agree with him" (Alan S. Downer, *The Eminent Tragedian: William Charles Macready*, 1966, Cambridge, Massachusetts, pp. 282–283). Charlotte Cushman, who had offered to act the part of Adriana in the play, for whatever reasons ended up not acting in the play, but her sister Susan took the part of Clara. The review in *The Athenæum* for 27 November, while noting some problems with the cast, was more critical of Macready's adaptation, stating that the author, "while yet living, had the honour of having his work mutilated for the stage" (no. 1048, p. 1225).
    7. Arnould's opinion of Dickens's latest work was not dissimilar to that of Macready. In his diary entry for 30 November, in which he noted Maddox's decision to close *Philip Van Artevelde*, Macready wrote: "Read the December No. of *Dombey and Son*, which I did not like. I thought it obscure and heavy" (II, 379). Nor was Carlyle impressed; see the penultimate paragraph of letter 2682.
    8. Johann Gottlieb Fichte (1762–1814) was a German metaphysical philosopher. Several of his works, including the ones Arnould names here, were translated into English by

a Scottish actuary named William Smith (1816-96), and were published as single titles in "The Catholic Series" between 1845 and 1849 by John Chapman (1822-94), who was an agent for American publishers, which may explain Arnould's confusion. Smith's translations were collected as *The Popular Works of Johann Gottlieb Fichte, with a Memoir* (2 vols., 1848-49). There is no evidence that Arnould ever sent these works to RB, nor that RB ever acquired them. Fichte's ideas and writings, as indicated by Arnould, influenced Carlyle's works.

9. Carlyle was an admirer of the German novelist and philosopher Johann Paul Freidrich ("Jean Paul") Richter (1763-1825), whose works he translated and praised.

2716. EBB TO ARABELLA MOULTON-BARRETT

Florence.
Dec– 22-23 [1847][1]

Is it shameful of me not to have stamped out my last no-letter with a letter many days before this day? Forgive me my own dearest Arabel .. for I write to you this time as is fair .. forgive & shut your eyes close on my sins:— remembering besides that you yourselves might have written before if the whole world did as it should– Still, there is a dear letter to thank you for .. the one after M!˙ Boyd's—or did I write myself subsequent to it? Really I think I did. The weather has grown cold within these two days, & the touch of frost in the air seals me up into a state of do-nothingness—one does'nt feel up to anything but the fire. I find Robert in the drawingroom each morning when I come to breakfast—an extraordinary finding! Generally he finds *me* .. seeing that my dressing is quicker done than his shaving. But now in his unwearied kindness, he makes a point of getting up earlier by half an hour, that he may be first, & try to heap the pinewood & set in order the thermometer to prevent my suffering from the cold. He never has me out of his head, one way or another—there never was a woman, made such a fuss about, since Eve—and *she* made the fuss herself. The consequence is that I have come seriously to consider all other marriages as not to be named in the same sentence as any way comparable or analogous to mine—they seem something different, & it's an unfairness to talk of parallel lines. For instance, Arlette's .. I speak as far from myself as possible, in speaking of her's. She appears to me *quite happy*—indeed she told me that she was .. which she need'nt have done, for of course I put no question. She said that her husband was very amiable & kind, & that they "suited one another exactly"—and I observed with pleasure that she "would not be afraid of keeping the dinner waiting a little while" .. which is a definitive trait in a man of what I conceive to be Capt. Reynolds's nature. It proved that the rein was not held too tight after all. The first time she came to see me, she came alone: the second morning, she brought *him*—after which I never saw him, although she had the kindness (& I thought it really kind) to come to me almost every day of the short remainder of their stay in Florence. Now you bid me say my thoughts of Capt. Reynolds. Remember that I had only some ten minutes or fifteen, of his society, & that he has not much "abandon" in his conversation, to assist one out of this disadvantage. I was a good deal struck by his very *veteran* appearance—the twenty years difference between himself & his bride, which you seemed to see, being still more obvious to us. He looks to me nearer fifty than forty, much. Yet; life in India is a wearing thing, & as he said "he had had his fling in life altogether" .. which I did not at all doubt, .. he may look older than he is– In any case, if it is no objection to Arlette, it is of no consequence to anybody. For the rest, he is what would everywhere be called a *fine-looking man*—but as to being "handsome", .!!! I take the Apollo over the river[2] to witness that I open my eyes with wonder at the idea of any one's calling him so even by an eccentricity. It is a coarse face with a common expression– A good presence, though, with a certain air of military gentlemanliness– No remarkable polish, with all this– Robert who is a physiognomist, says that he believes him to be an amiable man & goodnatured; & when he (Capt Reynolds) asked me how I thought Arlette was looking, he did so with a glance of interest, which made me feel that he loved her. Reserved & shy he is .. and this is rare in a military man, & I dont like him the less for it upon the whole, .. but of course it shackles him terribly in conversation, & adds to the inconvenience of not really having much to say. What could have induced dear Arlette & him to set out for Italy, is a sort of riddle to me—it is quite curious how little interest they seemed to have in seeing anything.. Think of their being here a month, & never going to Fiesole![3] We tried to persuade them to go in vain– I even hinted to Arlette that it w.d be a sort of disgrace not to have been to Fiesole. Only an hour's drive, too– "But what is there to see?" asked Cap.t Reynolds– Milton's Fiesole, the Fiesole of the Romans, the Fiesole of the Etruscans, and "what to see"? Robert answered that there was a splendid "view", in any case– We thought they had resolved on going at last, but the weather "looked uncertain", and so, *that* came to an end. Moreover they did not see half nor a quarter nor a tenth of what was to be seen in Florence, & went to Rome the *shortest* way .. missing Perugia & all the interest & beauty. So strange it seemed to us, & would seem to you, I think: for why come to Italy at all if one does not care for the sights of Italy? Their travelling is done in the most expensive way possible, the courier who was with them persuading them to prefer the hotels to the private apartments, notwithstanding Arlette's inclination to the latter—& by what she told me, we are calculating that they must have spent from sixty to seventy pounds in the course of a month for just living. Not that she thought it at all dear—but in reality & according to Florentine prices

it was most extravagant: and then they were not particularly comfortable ..
complained of smells .. & were on a second floor, to boot- They did not
appear to use their carriage here- Arlette always walked to see me & came
by herself; & once Robert walked back with her, & once he & I did so together. I thought her looking very handsome- I never saw her looking so
well. Oh, I made her tell me about you, .. but she went away without telling
half I wanted to hear, & some things I did not dare to ask questions of, feeling too deeply for the possible answers. Dear Arlette! I quite loved her, do
you know? She seemed the representative of so much of the past & the absent. When she came into the room first, I was glad that Robert was out
walking, for he hates to see the tears in my eyes; & the emotion of receiving
her took me by surprise .. I never thought to cry at seeing Arlette, and the
tears came in spite of reason. Everything past came back at the sight of her
& was joined to the present—everything .. everybody—the poor dark room
in Wimpole Street, & your beloved faces & voices. Such a dream it seemed,
to meet in Florence, & *so*! She is to write to you, she says, to certify what
she thinks of my looks- She told me & Robert that the change was past
belief almost—meaning the change for the better. Well, now! shall you be
able to garble an extract from all these words, which may not displease
Bummy? She wrote to me at the first arrangement of the marriage, about the
bridegroom's beauty & talents, & the fairies only know what—so if she expects me to be "dazzled", nothing herein said can of course satisfy her—but
you must use tact & discretion & not get me into a scrape. Robert told me I
was inclined to be over-severe, & that his own impression was in favour of
the goodnature & amiability—& he is famous as a physiognomist I assure
you. They seem resolved on buying a house in London & living there &
Arlette thinks that the Bevans' plans are of a like colour. You know, Arabel,
M! Bevan is ten times more a man than this Capt Reynolds!—that is, to my
mind: infinitely his superior in intellect, & of a higher nature altogether.
Still, in his class & after his pattern, Capt Reynolds may be an excellent
person, .. & we must not deny that it is a class & pattern which many women
prefer. Only, Arabella will be elevated by her marriage, .. and Arlette NEVER
CAN. Not *by that means*, at least. Which brings me back to my preference
after all- How sorry I am that dear Bummy sh!d have returned to the same
house in the same place: nothing could be more unfortunate- I am sorry too
that she did not go to Tours:—it seems to me a pity altogether! Most of all
sorry I am that no letter should come today. Oh you wicked people!—and
Henrietta was beginning to have the influenza, when you wrote last, & I
hear that the newspapers talk of influenza .. influenza! Do take care of yourselves- Now, Arabel, you who go out at night, do you cover your chest &
throat up. Robert tells me two or three times a day that I dont love him, &

once with ever so many impromptu verses he said & sung it .. (did I tell you what an improvisatore he was?) said & sung that I did'nt love him ..

> "That I only deceive
> Beguile him and leave
> At the treason to grieve,
> While like fair mother Eve
> I laugh in my sleeve!"

& all because I object to turning him out of his chair, when my sofa is as near the fire .. or because I dont sit with a shawl over my head, or some such fantastical reason. Of course this cold weather .. why there is a sprinkling of snow in the piazza today .. affects my throat a little—and the fuss, oh, the fuss! I cant help laughing sometimes, though I could cry too, at, the dear dreadful look of anxiety in his eyes– "Now Ba, if you love me, you will think of something to do yourself good– Now, my love, I do beseech you to think of something—" But I cant think of anything except ordering out the sun, or a slight mizzle perhaps ... Oh, but he wont have me laugh– Because if I were to be ill .. what w^d become of the universe, I wonder? You are to understand, all this while, that I am NOT ill, my darling Arabel, nor with any inclination to illness: it is simply that my throat is a little hoarse, off & on .. (no losing of voice, mind!) with the sharper air, .. which is softening again. The snow vanishes while I write .. also there is no sign of frost on the windows. But Robert has taken to abuse poor Florence, .. somewhat unjustly, it seems to me, because we have had really wonderful weather until the last few days. Arlette thought poor Flush as much altered for the worse as I was for the better—but he improves rapidly & will soon recover his beauty, having an extraordinary appetite plainly with that design, the cold weather being favorable in another way. Now, Arabel, while the winter lasts & you go out at nights, mind to cover yourself up. If you were married to Robert, how you w^d quarrel to be sure, just on that subject of covering up .. just as you & I used to quarrel, when you would'nt put on a shawl or a boa or a something. I tell you that he reproaches me who am an innocent & do such things most obediently, precisely that you *may* understand how for love's sake *you* ought to behave– And there's Henrietta– Wetting her feet in walks to Hampstead I dare say. Tell me particularly about the influenza. My best love to dearest Trippy, & exhort her to take care, & keep by the fire & avoid catching colds & coughs. Dear thing, I think of her a good deal. Oh, how I think of you all– How I love you, my own darling Arabel, & long for the presence of you, which w^d be so much better than the summer!– You must say to Mr Stratten, with my true & grateful regards, that he always was better to me & kinder than I had a right to claim; and that, for my poetry, even if he were severe upon it, I hope I should try to use the opinion as a means of improvement,—

since, as an "occasion of discord," I never could. But instead of being severe, he is over-gentle,—& you must thank him for this as for the rest. It gives one courage to rub together the pieces of dry wood & try to strike a light in the darkness: and when it shall be light enough to see my face he will see it full of respect & esteem for him always. He has helped me in more important things than poetry itself. Arabel,—Why do you not mention poor M.ʳ Hunter? I see no sign of him in a letter of yours. Is it quarrel the nine hundred & ninetyninth, or what? I wish much to hear whether he is prospering in the pupil-plan, & how dear Mary likes Ramsgate, & her new duties- As to poor dear unfortunate Annie Hayes, I tremble to think or imagine. I hope you wrote to her affectionately & earnestly, for it is my strong conviction that *you may do something* .. at least, if you cannot, that no one else will care to try. Also it is not in sorrow & in sin, that human beings should be cold to & stand aloof from one another—though the world's maxims & experience are of a different complexion. Do not give her up, Arabel, whatever you hear. I am sorry that you did not see her in London. No one is ever compromised by another's ill conduct, except when ceasing to tell the truth unsparingly- I am sure you agree with me in this at the bottom—and I agree with *you*, of course, as to the painfulness of associations without sympathy. M.ʳ Hayes's conduct appears detestable, past believing almost, .. but if he acted on provocation & in sudden passion, what better c.ᵈ be expected from a coarse-minded man? I am full of regret that Annie sh.ᵈ have quarrelled with Papa- Oh miserable, miserable marriage! She had better have died before that hour. I have heard from M.ʳˢ Strutt[4] of her arrival in Rome & answered by desiring her to send her precious parcel to join Clara Lindsay's— writing by the same post to Clara that both sh.ᵈ be sent to me by the safest public conveyance, as I cant have patience to wait any more for "private hands." At first I was afraid of "risks"—but I cant have patience. I have had a very kind letter from Lady Margaret Cocks. So the Martins are gone to Pau? The other evening Miss Boyle brought her brother to us, celebrated for his Vandyke beauty.[5] A handsome man certainly, & with a beard to justify my predilections, besides the moustache—and such a melodious voice, such refined or over refined manners! A very charming person, really, & I dare say the hero of many a "grande passion". Lady Morgan says of him—"He never sh.ᵈ marry: he *belongs to all of us*!" Then we have had two American ladies,[6] pleasing & cultivated, but talking detestably, .. with that provincial enunciation of the vowels, which I never shall get over in the Americans. They brought letters of introduction from M.ʳˢ Sigourney. Ah—Christmas is coming! My heart flies across the mountains to you—may God bless you all! Tell me of Papa & all. It grieves me that you answer my questions so .. but I feared it. Severity is one thing, injustice another. On what grounds he continues that line of conduct, is past my power of guessing at. Poor Papa!

After all, it is most grievous for himself. I wonder if he & others will even think of me this Christmas. Robert says every now & then "We will have a merry christmas, Ba .. shant we?" and I say 'yes' & smile: but ⟨the⟩ truth is that these anniversaries are filled to me with bitter thoughts & that I shall ⟨be⟩ glad when they are over. Take care of dear Minny, that she does not tire her⟨self⟩ with Christmas work, so as to be ill again. My love to all my brothers. ⟨But o⟩ught'nt I to say particularly to dear Henry, after his kindness to me? Lov⟨e me⟩, Arabel! May God bless you for ever.

Your Ba–

The weather quite mild again.

Address, on integral page: To the care of Miss Tripsack / (Miss Arabel Barrett) / 10 [*sic*, for 12] Upper Gloucester Street / Dorset Square. / [and in another hand] Not known as directed / W Sidman / Try 12.
Publication: None traced.
Manuscript: Gordon E. Moulton-Barrett.

1. Year determined by EBB's references to the visit from her newly-wed cousin, Charlotte Mary "Arlette" Reynolds (*née* Butler).
2. Perhaps a reference to the "Apollino," in the Tribune of the Uffizi, which Murray's *Hand-Book for Travellers in Northern Italy* (1847) says is "considered one of the most valuable monuments that have reached us. It exhibits very high qualities of art" (p. 544).
3. *The Tuscan Athenæum* of 6 November 1847 announced the arrival of Captain Charles Reynolds during the week of 29 October to 5 November, first at the Albergo Reale and afterwards at the Albergo dell'Arno (no. 2, p. 16).
4. Presumably Elizabeth (*née* Byron, 1782–1867), wife of Jacob George Strutt (1784–1867), an English artist in Rome. He and their son, Arthur John Strutt (1819–88), are both described as "landscape painters" in *The Roman Advertiser* for 10 February 1849. Their studio was located at 52 Via del Babuino, which is the address recorded in EBB's earliest extant address book; see vol. 9, p. 387 under "Strull." Mrs. Strutt was the author of numerous books, including one entitled *The Feminine Soul: Its Nature and Attributes. With Thoughts upon Marriage, and Friendly Hints upon Feminine Duties* (1857). Writing about the "emancipation of women," she refers to EBB, claiming that it was "an idea which seems to have taken hold of the fancy of one of our most gifted poetesses; one to whom to wish 'unsexed,' would be to wish the disrobing of one of the gentlest, and most loving intellectual forms; yet who, strange to say has, amid much that is beautiful, much that is lofty, written two of the most absurd and most unpleasing sonnets in the English language, addressed to ... George Sand" (p. 215).
5. In *Mary Boyle: Her Book*, ed. Sir Courtenay Boyle (1901), she describes her brother Charles John (1806–85) as follows: "Yet the real, surpassing gift of beauty was reserved for my brother Charles. Ah! what a store of love and memory is connected with that dear name, and how well did the Greek epithet 'Kalos' become him, which implies in its melodious sound both moral and physical beauty. The term beautiful does not appear, perhaps, often applicable to a man, but it certainly was to Charles. In feature, colouring and expression he was the counterpart of our mother, the same soft brown hair, the same sapphire blue eyes, the same faultless outline of profile" (pp. 11–12). In 1849 he married Zacyntha Moore, whom he had met the preceding summer in Rome, where they had become engaged (pp. 205–206).
6. Unidentified.

APPENDIX I

Biographical Sketches of Principal Correspondents and Persons Frequently Mentioned

JAMES STRATTEN (1795-1872)

THE REV. JAMES STRATTEN was born on 26 May 1795 in Bradford-on-Avon, Wiltshire, and he spent his youth at nearby Holt. At the age of 17 he was accepted at Hoxton Academy, where he studied for four years. Before beginning his ministry at Paddington Chapel, a prosperous non-conformist congregation in Marylebone, London, he spent two years in Dublin. He was only 24 years old when he assumed the pastorship of Paddington Chapel in November 1818, which lasted for nearly 42 years.

On 7 May 1819 Stratten married Rebekah Wilson (1792?-1870), eldest daughter of Thomas Wilson of Maida Vale. She is described in *The Congregational Year Book* (1873) as "the pattern and model of a wife and mother, and daughter, and friend, and counsellor; a helper in the work of the ministry, and a bright and beautiful ornament to the Church of Christ." They had five children while residing at Clarendon Place, Maida Vale: Thomas Wilson (b. 1821-died in infancy), John Remington (1823-1905), Arthur Clegg (1828-1907), Frances Elizabeth (1831-55), and Charlotte Rebekah (1832-38). By the time the family moved to nearby Pine Apple Place in 1841, the eldest and youngest children had died.

When exactly the Barretts became acquainted with the Strattens is unknown. In all probability it was soon after he commenced his ministry at Paddington Chapel when his popularity as a preacher would have attracted them to his pulpit on one of the many visits the family members made to Elizabeth Moulton, EBB's grandmother, who lived in nearby Baker Street. The earliest reference to Stratten is in a letter from EBB's brother Samuel to their sister Henrietta, dated 30 October 1829, and written from Charterhouse, in which he relates his previous weekend visit to his grandmother which included attendance at Paddington Chapel; however, he did not hear Stratten preach on that occasion.

EBB's first reference to Stratten is in a letter to Hugh Stuart Boyd in December 1836, a year after the Barretts had settled in London at 74 Gloucester Place, a short walk from the chapel. She commented: "Mr. Stratten has just been here. I admire him more than I ever did, for his admiration of my doves. By the way, I am sure he thought them the most agreeable of the whole party,—for he said, what he never did before, that he could sit here an hour!" (letter 548).

In May 1843, EBB and her sister Arabella presented Mrs. Stratten with a "little work-table," the top of which was painted by Arabella (letter 1256). Arabella, who taught a Bible class for young women at the chapel, and Mrs. Stratten were close friends.

When EBB first mentioned Stratten to RB in August 1846, she described him as having "a heart of miraculous breadth & depth,—loving further than he can see ... having in him a divine Christian spirit." In the same letter, EBB indicates that at one time she considered engaging Stratten's assistance in her plans to marry RB: "once I could not help wishing to put our affairs into his hands to settle them for us—but *that* would be wrong because Papa would forbid Arabel's going to the chapel or communicating with his family, & it would be depriving her of a comfort she holds dear" (letter 2569).

Writing from Italy a few weeks after their marriage, EBB was concerned about Stratten's opinion of what she had done, and asked Arabella, "Does Mr. Stratten blame me much?" (letter 2624). EBB frequently enquired after him and his family when writing to her sister. By 1851, the Strattens had moved to 65 Hamilton Terrace, St. John's Wood.

As EBB's interest in Swedenborgianism developed, she was concerned that her ideas might not meet with Stratten's approval, and she asked Arabella not to "ruffle Mr. Stratten with any mention of Swedenborg" (12 April [1853]). A few months later EBB expressed how glad she was that he was "beginning to give a grave thought to this subject" (15 August [1853]). However, within several months she wrote that Stratten had "no right to conclude that *spiritual* communications mean perforce *Satanic* communications"([16-] 19 December [1853]). Eventually, EBB was convinced that Stratten was sympathetic to her own ideas about spiritualism, but that he was unwilling to acknowledge them from the pulpit. Evidently he hinted that he had felt the presence of his dead children, and EBB was sure that with the aid of a medium he would have succeeded in communicating with them. Referring to a sermon in 1855, she said, "He pleased me a good deal by his *spiritualism* in my sense—his references to angelic ministrations,—& to the probable ministration of departed spirits towards their friends surviving on the earth. I have thought several times that he is in advance (on this subject) of the great majority of pulpit teachers .. in fact in advance of the ordinary Christians of the day" ([20 September 1855]).

EBB had mostly praise for Stratten's preaching and his views in general. However, on one occasion she noted that he "quite displeased me yesterday by his sermon—view of the war [i.e., the Russo-Turkish War of 1845-55]—of our chosen island & enormous glory! & no word of the alliance [i.e., between England and France]" ([1 October 1855]). Several volumes of his sermons were published in his lifetime, as well as a collection of psalms and hymns which he

Rev. James Stratten

compiled; a work entitled *The Intermediate State, and Other Discourses* (1867) was in the Brownings' library (see *Reconstruction*, A2222).

Stratten had hoped that his older son, John Remington Stratten, would succeed him at the Paddington Chapel, but his son instead entered the Church of England and was ordained in 1849. On 23 September 1852, he married Augusta, daughter of Samuel Hope. They visited the Brownings in Florence in November 1854. EBB described him as "young & gentle-looking" but "inferior in picturesqueness of appearance & manner to his father" (26 November [1854]).

The Stratten's younger son, Arthur Stratten, was a stockbroker in the City of London, first at Bartholomew Lane, then at Old Broad Street. Barrett family papers indicate that both George and Arabella Moulton-Barrett consulted him on business matters.

Mrs. Stratten presented a book to Pen Browning before the Brownings left for Paris in October 1855, and Pen wrote a letter of acknowledgement, to which EBB appended a note to reiterate her consolation on the death of the Strattens' daughter Fanny the previous month.

Realizing the influence the Strattens had on her sister, EBB wrote to Mrs. Stratten before leaving England in autumn 1856 to "commend" Arabella to the Strattens' care "to prevent her over-exerting herself in the schools & when the weather gets cold, or even when weather is warm. She minds me no more than Balaam did his ass,—but if the angel spoke .. if dear Mr. Stratten would speak when the opportunity shall occur, .. it would be otherwise—and really sometimes she works beyond her strength, & over the limit of duty therefore" ([17 October 1856]).

When *Aurora Leigh* was published, EBB decided against giving a copy to Stratten, but she was curious about his opinion of her new work and asked her sister to "tell me what he says" (10-18 December [1856]). A copy of EBB's *Poems Before Congress* (1860), inscribed to "Mrs. Stratten with the affecte. love of A Barrett," is now at the Armstrong Browning Library (see *Reconstruction*, M61), and a copy of EBB's *Poems* (1844) was presented by EBB to Fanny Stratten (*Reconstruction*, C85).

Amongst the members of Stratten's flourishing congregation was John McIntosh, his wife Frances, and their six children, the youngest of whom was Charlotte. She married EBB's brother Octavius in 1859.

In late 1858 Stratten became ill, and this illness eventually caused him to resign as pastor of Paddington Chapel in March 1860. Letters from EBB to Arabella indicate that there was probably some friction between Stratten and the congregation's leaders over various matters, but he remained in the area and continued to preach at the chapel from time to time, and the friendship between Arabella and the Strattens endured for the remainder of their lives. Stratten's wife Rebekah died on 22 November 1870, and he died on 12 May 1872.

Appendix II

Checklist of Supporting Documents

IN EDITING THIS volume of the Brownings' collected correspondence, we have studied all known original items of Browningiana during the period it covers. Besides primary sources (listed in *The Browning Collections: A Reconstruction*) there exists an extensive body of significant secondary source material, most of it relating to the Barrett and Moulton-Barrett families.

These supporting documents have been invaluable in editing the correspondence, helping us assign dates and prepare notes to enhance the meaning of the letters. We have decided, therefore, to provide a listing of such items—thus sharing them with others contemplating in-depth Browning studies.

Listed below is the supporting material for the period covered by this volume. Subsequent volumes will carry similar appendices of material parallel to their primary-correspondence contents.

Relevant extracts are given where the material includes comments directly pertaining to EBB or RB, or comments impinging on events covered in the primary correspondence.

Following the practice established for our *Checklist*, in all cases where the writer, recipient, or any part of the date is conjectured, we give the first phrase, for positive identification. This is also done in cases where there are two letters of the same date to the same recipient. Location of the document is given, as a cue title or abbreviation, in square brackets at the right-hand margin.

SD1269] 21 September 1846. A.L.s. John Forster to Sarianna Browning. . . . *you cannot imagine the surprise with which I saw this morning's announcement. Not unmixed with a little pang, . . that I should have known it first through the strangeness of a newspaper.* . . . [Heydon]

SD1270] 21 September 1846. A.L.s. Anne Montague to Sarianna Browning. Relating to marriage of EBB and RB. [Heydon]

SD1271] 22 September 1846. A.L.s. Thomas Carlyle to Edward FitzGerald. . . . *Do you know Poet Browning? He is just wedded, as his card testifies this morning; the Mrs Browning still an enigma to us here.* . . . [Yale]

SD1272] 22–23 September [1846]. A.L. signed with initials. Anna Brownell Jameson to Lady Noel Byron. ... *I will not leave Paris if there be a possibility of my being of use or comfort to you– In the mean time a piece of Romance has come across my life which I must tell you because it will also, in some cases—modify my plans. Robert Browning, my poet, is here [Paris]—& with a wife he has run off with—& who, think you is this wife?—no other than Elizabeth Barrett—my poetess—a pretty pair to go thro this prosaic world together!—but there was nothing else to be done apparently—her life depended on her leaving England this winter—(at least all hope of health;)—her father would not hear of it—& Browning, in desperation—for he has long loved her, asserted the only right that could supersede that of a father—married her a week ago—& has brought her so far safely—but she has suffered much—she is nervous—frightened—ashamed[,] agitated[,] happy, miserable– I have sympathized, scolded[,] rallied, cried & helped—& now they want me to join them on the road to the South– I am quite willing to do so, for many reasons—but shall take no step till I hear from you and they will probably go on.... Wednesday— ... Robert Browning & his wife are now under the same roof with me & have a nice apartment– She had a feverish desire to go on on—as if there was to be neither peace nor health till she was beyond the Alps—she is now better—more quiet—& willing to rest here a few days—rest is indeed most necessary for her. ...* [Morgan]

SD1273] [ca. 23 Sept 1846]. A.L.s. Anna Brownell Jameson to Unidentified Correspondent. ... *I have also here a poet and a poetess—two celebrities who have run away and married under circumstances peculiarly interesting, and such as render imprudence the height of prudence. Both excellent; but God help them! for I know not how the two poet heads and poet hearts will get on through this prosaic world. I think it possible I may go on to Italy with them* ... Gerardine Macpherson, *Memoirs of the Life of Anna Jameson* (1878), pp. 228–229. [   ]

SD1274] 24 September [1846]. A.L. signed with initials. Anna Brownell Jameson to Lady Noel Byron. ... *yours of the 22d ... reached me today—it is a great relief* [.] ... *I have now decided on travelling Southwards–* ... *This charming fugitive pair of whom I told you, are a great interest & a great care*—she is in a most feeble state—but better certainly today than I have ever yet seen her– I really believe I have saved her life by persuading her to rest– R B. came down this morning to settle about our movements—& I shall go down the Rhone with them—the rest is uncertain—as to the step they have taken, I see that the sympathy & approval of all her relations is secure, except that of her father—& with him, the disapprobation—without deigning to give reason—seems like a madness. The deportment of both is perfect, but how the experiment is to end I know not– I have not faith in the poetical temperament as a means of permanent happiness tho, it may heighten the relish of sentiment—in short, I fear—even now I see what makes me fear, but I hope also—both are so good! ... Our road is thus arranged—28th to Chartres & Orleans—30 to Bourges—Oct 1 to Roanne & St Vallier—Oct 2 embark on the Rhone for Avignon[,] about the 4 leave Marseilles for Leghorn—about the 6th Pisa–* ... *There will be delays on the road perhaps—for E.B. can not travel fast—& we may make alterations.* ... [Morgan]

SD1275] 25 September 1846. A.L.s. Thomas Carlyle to John A. Carlyle. ... *Robt. Browning the Poet has suddenly married,—a Miss Barrett, Poetess, who lay lamed on a sofa for many years, but is now suddenly on her feet again. Good people both: I heartily wish them as happy a pilgrimage as can be had.–* ... [Scotland]

SD1276] 28–29 September [1846]. A.L. signed with initials. Anna Brownell Jameson to Lady Noel Byron. *We are preparing to leave Paris this Evening ... Orleans Sep. 29. I was interrupted by the cares of packing, paying, & thinking for myself & others—& employ an hour or two of rest here to tell you that we are so far on our* *journey, safe & well. ... While travelling with these friends I am obliged to put all my own convenience & all selfish projects out of the question– They have thrown themselves upon me with such an entire & undoubting confidence—that to have refused help & comfort—or even hesitated*[,] *would have been like a brute or a stone. I did* hesitate *in my own heart at first—partly on Gerardines account, but it has all turned out well & could* hardly *be better– Letters from her family met her here at Orleans—all full of comfort & approbation—one of* [them] *from Mr Kenyon her cousin—in which he uses the strongest expressions of sympathy & kindness & says that "while he appreciates the delicacy which prevented them from confiding in him or in* any *one—he must—if his advice had been asked*[—]*have advised just what they have done." There is no letter from her father—but she* hopes *he will relent—in short she is much comforted, & certainly gaining strength in spite of the exertion & fatigue—as yet there is not a trace of animal spirits, tho evidently a sense* [of] *deep happiness, gratitude & love—as to him— his joy & delight and his poetical fancies & antics, with every now & then the profoundest seriousness & tenderness interrupting the brilliant current of his imagination make him altogether a most charming companion— The deportment of both is in the best taste & Gerardine can only gain by all she sees & hears– we are five in company including her maid—six, including her pet dog—so you can conceive that we are rather a cumbersome party, & I am in constant dread about her—and not, I must confess, in very good spirits, but I am "in for it" as the phrase is and regret nothing—& so much for my biography, so far– ... We hope to reach Bourges some time tomorrow– Thence we go on to the Rhone by Nevers—& embark as I suppose at Lyons—it is of consequence to get EB on board the steam boat where she can lie down & be at rest– we shall, I* hope, *reach Marseilles by the 6th of October—& embark as soon as possible, by the first boat for Genoa & Leghorn & so reach Pisa about 10th or latest the 12th– can you now follow us in thought?—on the 5th you may fancy us at Avignon—& we have some thoughts of visiting Vaucluse if EB can stand the fatigue. ...* [Morgan]

SD1277] 28 September [1864]. A.L.s. John Kenyon to RB, Sr. ... *There is no man to whom on all these accounts I would rather have given a daughter of mine—if I had one. ... I have not heard from her father, who probably may consider me as cognisant of their intensions, with a wise delicacy she insisted that I should know nothing of it ...* [Heydon]

SD1278] 28 September 1846. A.L.s. Anne Benson Procter (*née* Skepper) to Unidentified Correspondent. ... *I am astonished at what you tell me about Miss Barrett– Six weeks since Mrs. Jameson was to introduce them to each other!—— Women love a "little artifice & ingenuity" but most men are above it– ...* [Yale]

SD1279] 29 September 1846. A.L.s. W. Deattry to A.G. Fyfe. With docket in hand of Edward Moulton-Barrett (father). [Eton]

SD1280] [ca. October 1846]. A.L.s. William Johnson Fox to Eliza Flower. ... *but the winters are colder* [at Florence] *than at Pisa. What say you to the latter, and arranging with the Brownings? You might remunerate them by the good offices of mediation and reconciliation which may be required. I wonder whether she is still angry with anybody that does not understand* Sordello? *She almost quarrelled with H. Martineau for her want of perception. Forster never heard of the Browning marriage till the proof of the newspaper notice was sent; when he went into one of his great passions at the supposed hoax, ordered up the compositor to have a swear at him, and demanded to see the* MS. *from which it was taken; so it was brought, and he instantly recognised the hand of Browning's sister. Next day come a letter from R. B. saying he had often meant to tell him or write of it, but hesitated between the two, and neglected both. She was better, and a winter in Italy had been recommended some months ago. ...* Garnett, p. 277.

[   ]

SD1281]　　2 October 1846. A.L.s. George Goodin Moulton-Barrett to the Editors of *Blackwood's Edinburgh Magazine. My Sister, who since her last communication with you, has married Mr. Browning, has left for Pisa, where she purposes passing the winter; it is therefore impossible for her to inspect the Proofs you have enclosed; and indeed she expressed no desire to have any, as she has great confidence in the accuracy of your Printers. The Messrs Duncun* [sic] *published for her in I think the year 1832 a translation of the 'Prometheus,' but all the unsold copies were by her directions consigned to the tomb some years back. I regret that I cannot now forward to you a copy, but I trust that I shall be able to do so upon my return to Town early in November. 'An account of the early Christian Poets,' and articles upon the English Poets published in the Athenæum in I think 1843, are the only prose compositions of my Sister that have been made public. Your very flattering note I will forward to Italy.*　　　　　　　　　　　　[Scotland]

SD1282]　　5 October [1846]. A.L.s. Henry Shirley to Edward Moulton-Barrett (father). *The enclosed having followed me* ... With enclosed letter dated 29 September 1846.　　　　　　　　　　　　　　　　　　　　　　　　　　　　　　　　　　[Eton]

SD1283]　　7–9 October [1846]. A.L. signed with initials. Anna Brownell Jameson to Lady Noel Byron. *We are so far on our long anxious journey—ten days since we left Paris—& only here* [*in Avignon*]*! but tedious as our progress has been, & even painful now & then—I rejoice every hour that I did venture on a step which seemed not without risks of many kinds– We have brought our poor invalid so far in safety—& without any* increase *of indisposition, or any return of her disorder, but the suffering has been very great—not only we have had to carry her fainting from the carriage but from her extreme thinness & weakness, every few hours journey has bruised her all over—till movement became almost unbearable—with her present feelings it is not perhaps great praise to say that all this has been endured with* patience—*but the unselfish sweetness of the temper—the unfailing consideration for others, I did not quite expect– He is most devoted & their mutual deportment has been marked by the most graceful propriety without any appearance of* gêne– *Gerardine has profited every way—by the example, by the sympathy—by the conversation*[,] *by all she has seen, seen, felt & heard, & has been very good. We came down the Rhone yesterday in a dirty confined steam boat*[,] *the rain pouring in torrents—& today we are resting here, EB on her bed in the hope of being able to go to Vaucluse tomorrow—Geddie*[,] *R.B. & myself have been running about, seeing as much as we could–* ... *There has been for these last days—as you can well suppose, cause of deep anxiety—but for pleasure of one kind a higher has been substituted– I have the feeling that I have been of some use to these dear people—whatever may be the issue—what has been done, has been well done & the rest remains with God—& "reason, virtue, time"—you know what follows—sometimes I have an inward trembling—& fear—but hope is stronger than fear—now I will say good night, & finish tomorrow——— Oct 9—We were at Vaucluse yesterday of which I spare you all description at present—but in some respects it was altogether different from what I had anticipated— the scenery more* savage *& barren—not like one of the southern vallies & the fountain a most tumultuous torrent——— On the whole a very pleasant day–* ... *It has just been settled that we embark from Marseilles at 5 oclock on Saty. (the 11th) on board "l'Ocèan"—a fine french steamer—& we hope to be at Leghorn early on Monday, & at Pisa a few hours afterwards– It does not seem certain whether we are to touch at Genoa— at Pisa I shall resign the sort of responsibility I have taken on myself—God send us safe there!——but in any case I have done right & you dearest friend—will not judge actions by the result—but by the motive— E.B. is tolerably well this morning—& there is no return of disease tho' occasionally much suffering–* ...　　　　　　　　　　　[Morgan]

SD1284]　　7–9 October [1846]. A.L.s. Anna Brownell Jameson to Charlotte Murphy. *I begin a scribble to you from hence to be finished when we have settled our* future *which is yet undecided. Our journey has been very tedious, very anxious, yet all things considered I would not but have made it for the world. Our poor invalid has suffered greatly, often fainting and often so tired that we have been obliged to remain a whole day to rest at some wretched place; to complete the tedium of our progress we had incessant rain down the Rhone from Lyons to Avignon, one perpetual deluge—so that we were reduced to a hot crowded cabin on board a daily Steamboat. This was the climax; but in spite of all, the journey has been a happy one and I can never repent it. Nothing could have been better for Gerardine; if it had been arranged on purpose as a perpetual lesson, it could not have been more effectual and she has been really very good and very efficient, considering. ... We spent the day in looking over the old palace of the Popes; poor E. B. obliged to spend the hours on her bed, but sympathising with us and full of sweetness and goodhumour, anxious that we should see everything and satisfied to hear that her husband had been amused with all he saw. She is really charming. Gerardine is going to write a full and particular account of our progress ... and what we are to do I will tell you to-morrow. ... Thursday 9th. We went yesterday to the far-famed fountain of Vaucluse, about 18 miles from the city; a pleasant day on the whole and E. B. got through it very well. Gerardine was in a state of enchantment, the dear child is certainly very good and very happy and very well. ... It is decided that we leave Avignon to-morrow to catch the French steamer which goes from Marseilles next day (the 11th) and on Monday morning about noon we hope to be in Pisa, where I hope to have letters. ... Anna Jameson: Letters and Friendships,* ed. Mrs. Steuart Erskine (1915), pp. 233–235. [ ]

SD1285] 8 October [1846]. A.L.s. Edward Moulton-Barrett (father) to Septimus Moulton-Barrett. ... *We are going on very slow, yet making progress, having papered Harry[,] Stormie, Henrietta & George's Rooms, with cheap, yet decent patterns– The Drawing Rooms, not begun yet, but on Monday we intend starting with them–* ...
[GM-B]

SD1286] 12 October 1846. File Copy of Letter. Edward Moulton-Barrett (father) to Henry Shirley. [Eton]

SD1287] 12 October 1846. A.L.s. George Prince of Wales (former slave) to Edward Moulton-Barrett (father). [Eton]

SD1288] 12 October 1846. A.L.s. William Wordsworth to Edward Moxon. ... *Miss Barrett, I am pleased to learn, is so much recovered as to have taken to herself a Husband. Her choice is a very able man, and I trust that it will be a happy union, not doubting that they will speak more intelligibly to each other than, notwithstanding their abilities, they have yet done to the Public.* ... [Huntington]

SD1289] 15 October [1846]. A.L. unsigned. Anna Brownell Jameson to Lady Noel Byron. *I had the comfort of finding your letter of the 3d. on my arrival here [Pisa] yesterday– We have brought our dear Invalid in safety to what she fondly calls her "home"—as they purpose spending the winter here– I wrote to you from Avignon, dear friend—& of our subsequent adventures have only to say that on the 11 we embarked at Marseilles—had a most stormy passage of 26 hours to Genoa—remained there (our boat stopping) a night & a day—a more stormy passage that night to Leghorn where we landed at 8. next morning—(the 14.) & came on here by the rail road as soon as possible– I suffered so dreadfully during the Voyage that I have not yet recovered– It is like your self to sympathize with me so kindly about my friends– They are really excellent— but with all the abundance of love, & sense & high principles—I have had now & then a tremour at my heart about their future—he is full of spirit & good humour & his unselfishness—& his turn for making the best of every thing & his bright intelligence & his rare acquirements of every kind rendered him the very prince of travelling companions—but—(always buts!!) he is in all the common things of this life the most impractical* *of men—the most uncalculating—rash—in short the worst* manager *I ever met with. She—in her present state—& from her long seclusion almost helpless—now only conceive the ménage that is likely to ensue & without* FAULT *on either side!—but no more of that——for the present our first care is to get her into some comfortable Lodging[—]no easy matter—when I have helped in this as far as I can, I shall consider that I have performed my undertaking—& shall either fix myself here or at Florence for a month—here if I can find masters & instruction in art for Gerardine—if not, at Florence—but mean time direct to Pisa ... I have just seen EB—looking wonderfully well—considering all the fatigue undergone—under her husband's influence & mine she is leaving off those medecines on which she existed[—]ether, morphine, &c & I am full of hope for her*[.] [Morgan]

SD1290] 16 October [1846]. A.L.s. Anna Brownell Jameson to Ottilie von Goethe. ... *we are just arrived in Pisa yesterday after a very long & very wearying journey—some dear & interesting friends (of whom I will tell you a great deal when we meet) joined us en route & the very feeble health of one friend has been a cause of delay—we had a dreadful voyage from Marseilles to Genoa—& yet a worse voyage from Genoa to Leghorn.* ... [Goethe]

SD1291] 27 October 1846. A.L.s. Anna Brownell Jameson to Lady Noel Byron. ... *We are in Pisa still as you see & likely to remain another fortnight—rain—rain—rain—every day– The Arno rushing past us, a turbulent flood—the waters out between this & Florence so that it is scarcely safe travelling—but I have occupation– Gerardine is happy, busy, interested & we are in no haste to part from our friends– They have settled themselves in a comfortable lodging—& all their arrangements are as sensible as if they had never spoken anything but prose in their lives & they are so happy!—& the quality of the happiness is so rare & so fine!– O if it may but last!– I wish you would buy a pamphlet published by Moxon—entitled Bells & Pomegranates No 8– It contains two pieces, poems in the Dramatic forms— "Luria" & "Souls Tragedy"—they might be called "Profession and Performance"—there is a quiet unconscious grandeur in the conception of the first—Luria—a depth of Irony in the last—& a vigour & beauty in both which enchant me– There is occasional obscurity of diction—if you do not like them at first—I wish you would read them twice—for my sake—& then tell me what you think– He—Browning, is preparing a second Edition of these—& of Paracelsus– I am glad that they are required—for I have often thought them rather too "Caviare" to be relished– I have a letter from Kenyon today in which he tells me that he considered her—with all her fine qualities of mind & heart as doomed to end her days in her sick room—he saw no escape for her from the peculiar despotism of her father & he says "it never occurred to his grosser sense that there was a man who could undertake the difficulties the constant slavery & anxiety attendant on the circumstances of her health" &c—what would he say if he saw B—carrying his wife up & down two flights of stairs—hanging over her as if she were something spared to him for a while out of heaven!—& she deserves his devotion & appreciates it. We are together every day & sometimes for nearly the whole day—never weary as it should seem of each other—& if I talk of going on to Florence,—such a shade comes over the countenance of both—I cannot but feel it—& Gerardine!– She will certainly be improved by all she hears—I would desire nothing better or higher for her just at this period of her life–* ... *My two friends are as poets, enthusiastic about Lord B. We went to see the Lanfranchi Palace which he inhabited when here—it is now the property of a rich & noble family, the Toscanelli & retains nothing to recall his memory except the Garden in which he walked & studied—as it is said– I had my own thoughts—more with you than* there—*it was all sad to me, tho' you do your best to put that feeling out of my mind–* ... Typescript at the Bodleian Library. [   ]

SD1292] 30 October 1846. A.L.s. Margaret Fuller to Evert A. Duyckinck. ... *Mr Mathews made me promise to write to him of those to whom he gave me letters, but I have seen none of them except Mr Horne and him only once, as he has been almost all the time in Ireland. Miss Barrett has just eloped with Browning; she had to elope, Mr Horne says, from a severe hard father. The influence of this father seems to have been crushing. I hope she may now be happy and well; perhaps I shall see them (i e her and Browning) in Italy. ...* [NYPL-Ms]

SD1293] [30 October 1846]. A.L.s. Edward Moulton-Barrett (father) to Septimus Moulton-Barrett. *I am glad at the arrangement made for your further stay at the Rectory, as we are still in a great state of confusion & dirt– After my expressed dislike to any one, staying at the Rectory, I certainly am much surprised & annoyed to find that you have had, & still have visitors; whatever you & others think of it, it is extremely improper, & shows how little you are to be trusted. It is contrary to all usage & highly improper, that young Men should be staying in my House in my absence. This as respects society, but I know not how to term conduct, so completely in opposition to my wishes. You appear to think, I make no exceptions, your duty to be to act so, as to place yourselves always in opposition to me, it is enough to find out what my wishes are, in order to obstruct them– Surely never was Parent so cursed by a family, one that should have been my comfort & the source of enjoyment, verily forms the only drawback to my happiness. It appears to me as if you were trying how much would drive me away, & make me take some desperate step– I have learnt to my disgust that Mr. Chapman has also been down, why here is a Man, you knew I would not have in my house here willingly, & yet he is invited down to stay– Such conduct is infamous, independent of its being the height of impropriety– Who was the Person that invited him, I know that you have been active, for Cook told me that you had written to him to come down– What right had you to ask any Man to live at my expence, without consulting me? Surely you cannot think that you have by your conduct earned the privilege*[.] [GM-B]

SD1294] [late October 1846]. A.L. signed with initials. Mary Russell Mitford to Charles Boner. ... *The great news of the season is the marriage of my beloved friend Elizabeth Barrett to Robert Browning. Do you know him? I have only seen him once many years ago. He is I hear from all quarters a man of immense attainment & great conversational power– As a poet, I think him overrated– The few things of his which are clear seem to me as weak as water, & those on which his reputation rests*[,] *Paracelsus & The Bells and Pomegranates are to me as so many riddles– I could as soon construe < ... > as the jargon in which they are written. I dread exceedingly for her the dreadful trial of the journey across France to Italy & the total change of life & habits– Mrs. Jameson & her niece joined them at Paris, but my last letter was from Moulins, & she then seemed much exhausted. God grant she be not quite worn out by that terrible journey to Pisa! ...* [Yale]

SD1295] 7 November 1846. A.L.s. Ralph Waldo Emerson to Frederic H. Hedge. ... *I found in town yesterday a precious piece of gossip from London,—that "Bells & Pomegrantes" is engaged to "Seraphine" or Miss Barrett,—who is you know the* divine bed-rid, *to whom Miss Martineau's "Invalid" Book was dedicated. ...* [RWEMA]

SD1296] 12 November [1846]. A.L.s. Anna Brownell Jameson to Lady Noel Byron. ... *I left Pisa with exceeding regret—or rather our friends there. The attachment on all sides seemed to gather strength daily & it was time to part—since our existence was to be of necessity divided– Not often have four persons so different in age, in pursuits—& under such peculiar circumstances been so happy—so harmoniously happy together—however here we are in beautiful Florence—very beautiful—very bright—but also very cold. I have seldom* suffered *more from cold—for these great Italian houses* *are wonderfully uncomfortable—I remember it was ever so—but had forgotten the discomfort & only rememberd the beauty– We are in a lodging in the Piazza Santa Croce—close to the church– Sir Charles Herbert & his family, old friends of my fathers, are here & are in every respect most kind, cordial & serviceable– The girls are good natured, musical, speak Italian like natives & are pleasant companions for Gerardine—& so far all is well—her genuine delight in the objects of beauty around us is very agreeable to me– I have to contend with some bad habits & some hereditary faults, but the sweetness of the temper & the exceeding quickness of perception render her a charming companion– I am a little afraid of her being led into some dissipation here—of course it depends on myself how far I shall allow it—& I will do my best for her– When we first arrived here, I went for a day to the Hotel d'York, where the Table d'hote is celebrated for the company & the viands—opposite to me was a lady who immediately fixed my attention—first by the extraordinary beauty & abundance of her hair & then by the strange contrast between this beautiful hair & her face which was oldish & with no pleasing expression—it was the Countess Guiccioli. ...* Typescript at the Bodleian Library. [   ]

SD1297] 17 November [1846]. A.L.s. Anna Brownell Jameson to Ottilie von Goethe. ... *I ought to have told you that we have only been in Florence for last week—we did not leave Pisa till the 7 or 8th.—being delayed by the friends we left there—of whom I will tell you all when we meet ...* [Goethe]

SD1298] 23 November [1846]. A.L.s. John Kenyon to RB, Sr. *I have long and satisfactory letters today from Pisa ...* [Heydon]

SD1299] 28 November 1846. A.L.s. Frances Hanford to Frances Parthenope Nightingale. ... *You know all about Mrs Browning do you not? We have just been to see them. I cannot tell you how wonderful it seemed to see her sitting up and talking like anybody else and talking too of having travelled all across France by Diligence. I felt a little doubtful whether to call fearing she might think it a bore but they met us with open arms talking much of the James Martins kindness and looking upon us in the light of a bit of them. Mrs Jameson travelled with them from Paris to this place and was exceedingly kind to her: she is now at Florence busy in preparing her new work "The Lives of the Saints as illustrated by Art." Paracelsus is very poetical looking with large black eyes and a pale complexion: he was very agreeable in conversation and not at all high flown or lackadaisical. ...* [Verney]

SD1300] 30 November 1846. A.L. unsigned. Joseph Arnould to Alfred Domett. *... I think the last piece of news I told you of was Browning's marriage to Miss Barrett—which I had then just heard of: she is, you know, or else I told you or ought to have told you, our present greatest living English "poetess." She had been for some years an invalid leading a very secluded life in a sick room in the household of one of those tyrannical, arbitrary, puritanical ra[s]cals who go sleekly about the world, canting Calvinism abroad, and acting despotism at home: under the iron rigour of this man's domestic rule she, feeble & invalided, had grown up to eight & thirty years of age in the most absolute & enforced seclusion from society: cultivating her mind to a wonderful amount of accomplishment, instructing herself in all languages, reading Chrysostom in the original Greek, & publishing the best metrical translation that has yet appeared of the Prometheus Bound—having also found time to write three volumes of poetry, the last of which, raised her name to a place second only to that of Browning and Tennyson, amongst all those who are not repelled by excentricities of external form from penetrating into the soul and quintessential spirit of poetry that quickens the mould into which the poet has cast it. Well[,] this lady so gifted, so secluded, so tyrannized over fell in love with Browning in the spirit, before ever she saw him in the flesh—in plain English loved the writer before she knew the man. Imagine, you who know him, the effect which his graceful bearing, high demeanour, & noble speech, must have had on such a mind when* *she first saw the man of her visions in the twilight of her darkened room. She was at once in love as a poet soul only can be: and Browning, as by contagion or electricity, was no less from the first interview wholly in love with her; this was now some two years back; from that time his visits to her have been constant; he of course wished to ask her of the Father openly[;] "if you do[,"] was her terrified answer[, "]he would immediately throw me out of window, or lock me up for life in a darkened room["]; there was one thing only to be done & that Browning did: married her without the Father's knowledge & immediately left England with her for Italy, where they are now living at Pisa in as supreme a state of happiness as you can fancy two such people in such a place[.] The old rascal Father of course tore his beard—foamed at the mouth & performed all other feats of impotent rage:—luckily his wrath is absolutely idle for she has a small independence of some £350 per ann. on which they will of course live prosperously. I heard from him a week back in which he mentions you most kindly & begged me to tell you all about him— he is a glorious fellow by God– Oh I forgot to say—that the soi-disante invalid of 7 years, once emancipated from the paternal despotism has had a wondrous revival, or rather, a complete metamorphosis, walks, rides, eats, & drinks like a young and healthy woman—in fact is a healthy woman of, I believe, some five & thirty—a little old—too old for Browning—but, then, one word covers all, they are in Love—who lends his own youth to everything. ...* [BL]

SD1301] 18 December 1846. A.L.s. Thomas Fothergill, Jr., to [?Octavius Moulton-Barrett]. *I regret I shall not have time ...* Nine stanzas of verse were added later by [?Octavius Moulton-Barrett]. [GM-B]

SD1302] 20 December 1846. A.L.s. W. Sharp to Edward Moulton-Barrett (father). [Eton]

SD1303] 21 December 1846. A.L.s. William Hamilton to Edward Moulton-Barrett (father). [Eton]

SD1304] 21 December 1846. A.L.s. Robert McDonagh to Edward Moulton-Barrett (father). [Eton]

SD1305] 30 December 1846. A.L.s. Edgar Allan Poe to Evert A. Duyckinck. ... *My object in enclosing the Scotch letter and the one from Miss Barrett, is to ask you to do me a favor which (just at this moment) may be of great importance. It is, to make a paragraph or two for some one of the city papers, stating the facts here given, in connexion with what you know about the "Murders in the Rue Morgue." If this will not give you too much trouble, I will be deeply obliged. If you think it advisable, there is no objection to your copying any portion of Miss B's letter. ...* [NYPL-Ms]

SD1306] [ca. 1847]. Printed Document. Admission pass for Septimus Barrett Moulton-Barrett to Middle Temple Library, signed by Edward Eldred, sub treasurer. [GM-B]

SD1307] 26 January 1847. A.L.s. P.B. Brodie to Septimus Barrett Moulton-Barrett. [GM-B]

SD1308] 1 February 1847. File Copy of Letter. Edward Moulton-Barrett (father) to William Hamilton. [Eton]

SD1309] 6 February 1847. A.L.s. S. Newdick to [Septimus Barrett Moulton-Barrett]. *I trouble you with this letter ...* [GM-B]

SD1310] [22 February 1847]. A.L.s. Mary Russell Mitford to Charles Boner. ... *I at Miss Barrett's wedding! Ah dearest Mr. Boner it was a runaway match—she at 38 & in her state of health—never was I so much astounded. He prevailed on her to meet him at Church with only the two necessary witnesses—they went by railway to Southampton—crossed to Havre—up the Seine to Rouen—to Paris by railway—there they were a week—happening to meet with Mrs. Jameson she joined them in their journey to Pisa—& accordingly they travelled by Diligence by railway by Rhone boat—anyhow—to Marseilles—*

thence took shipping to Leghorn & then settled themselves at Pisa for six months– She says that she is very happy– God grant it continue! But think of the shock & the shake, & his never getting her a carriage to travel in—she accustomed to the luxuries of a Princess! She has £350 per annum left her by an uncle– There is no chance I fear of the father being reconciled– I felt just exactly as if I had heard that Dr. Chambers had given her over when I got her letter announcing her marriage & found that she was about to cross France– I never had an idea of her reaching Pisa alive. She took her own maid & her Flush– I saw Mr. Browning once & remember thinking how exactly he resembled a girl drest in boy's clothes—& as to his poetry I have just your opinion of it. It is one heap of obscurity confusion & weakness. Let me add to this that many of his friends & mine— William Harness, John Kenyon, Henry Chorley speak very highly of him– I suppose he is an accomplished man & if he makes his angelic wife happy I shall of course learn to like him. But he ought not to have persuaded her to take such a step. This of course is quite between ourselves. Do you know him personally? Did you ever see him? I met him once as I told you when he had long ringlets & no neckcloth—& when he seemed to me about the height & size of a boy of twelve years old– Femmelette—is a word made for him. A strange sort of person to carry such a woman as Elizabeth Barrett off her feet. He is a great musician & so forth– But I come back to the conceit of writing book upon book all bad—& being at this point engaged in preparing a new edition of his works—the first edition of each having gone off in the form of waste paper.... [Yale]

SD1311] [ca. March 1847]. Mary Russell Mitford to Emily E. Jephson. *Did you hear that my beloved friend Elizabeth Barrett is married? Love really is the wizard the poets have called him; a fact which I always doubted till now. But never was such a miraculous proof of his power as her travelling across France by diligence, by railway, by Rhone boat—anyhow, in fact; and having arrived in Pisa so much improved in health that Mrs. Jameson, who travelled with them, says she is "not merely improved but transformed." I do not know Mr. Browning; but this fact is enough to make me his friend. He is a poet also; but I believe that his acquirements are more remarkable than his poetry, although that has been held to be a high promise.* ... L'Estrange (2), III, 204.

[   ]
SD1312] [ca. March] 1847. A.L.s. Mary Russell Mitford to Mrs. Ouvry. ... *The people who know Mr. Browning well seem to like him much. Mr. Kenyon, Mr. Chorley, Mr. Harness—and it is so much my interest to think well of him, and his dear wife writes of him so magnificently, that I hope in time to forgive even his stealing her away. I confess, however, quite between ourselves, that I can't make out his poetry. Do you ever meet in society a very charming young man, Mr. Ruskin, the author of some very fine works on art, by an Oxford graduate? He is quite delightful.* Chorley, II, 81–82.

[   ]
SD1313] 9 April 1847. Receipt. Thomas Purdue to Septimus Barrett Moulton-Barrett, for Expenses attending his call to the Bar. With Statement of Account.

[GM-B]
SD1314] 13 April 1847. A.L.s. Thomas Carlyle to John Kenyon. ... *The name of the American Lady, who claims welcome from the Brownings wherever they may meet, is (in case you should forget it) Margaret Fuller—a truly "distinguished female."*
...
[Duke]

SD1315] [26 April 1847]. A.L.s. Anna Brownell Jameson to Lady Noel Byron. ... *we have been 9 days on the road from Rome; but it was necessary to spend much time in visiting certain objects, necessary for my purposes—at Spoleto, at Sello—at that wonderful place Assisi, at Perugia, at Arezzo—we delayed more or less—the weather has*

been detestable, luckily we had one fine day at Assisi—but in general rain & gloomy—& the difference of climate when we got into the Apennines made us shiver—poor Geddie, never very efficient has been like a dead weight in my arms poor dear child—she has been happier here with her friend Mrs. Browning—but I rather dread the rest of our journey—As to plans—we leave Florence on Thursday the 29 ... Typescript at the Bodleian Library.
[   ]

SD1316]   4 May [1847]. A.L.s. John Kenyon to Hiram Powers. *A few weeks ago I forwarded a letter of introduction to you for my friend Robt. Browning, who married my dear friend & relative Eliz. B. Barrett, whose name & genius are known on yr side the water in the New World—as in ours. Browning has every quality of mind & moral excellence to make you like him & trust him—and with the sympathy which exists between men like you I know, desires to know you. Give him, first for my sake—then for his own & your own any local information and any information as to Art, which may be useful or agreeable to him.*
[Smithsonian]

SD1317]   8 May 1847. A.L.s. Henry Shirley to [Edward Moulton-Barrett (father)]. *As Mr Anderson, Civil Engineer is about to return home* ...
[Eton]

SD1318]   10 May 1847. A.L.s. George Long Duyckinck to Hiram Powers. *Florence / My dear Sir / I take great pleasure in the opportunity of making you acquainted with Mr & Mrs Browning, with whose distinguished literary reputation you are already familiar. / I am desirous to add to the pleasure they will derive from your works, that of a personal acquaintance with yourself. / I remain very truly yours / George L. Duyckinck.*
[Smithsonian]

SD1319]   10 May 1847. A.L.s. George Long Duyckinck to Hiram Powers. *Florence / My dear Sir / Since seeing you I have taken the liberty of giving Mr and Mrs Browning, of England, a letter to you. Mrs Browning, when Miss Barrett published several volumes of poetry, which have given her name the highest literary rank. In addition to this she is one of the finest and most thorough scholars of her own or any other age although for many years a confirmed invalid. / Mr Browning is also a man of high poetic reputation. It gives me pride, as an American, to be able to present them to one of such eminence in the "Sister Art," as yourself. / I wrote this because I could not delicately put it into a note of introduction and I was also desirous of showing you that I had commended to your kindness persons of no ordinary stamp. / Yours very truly / George L. Duyckinck.*
[Smithsonian]

SD1320]   21 May 1847. A.L.s. Frances Hanford to Frances Parthenope Nightingale. ... *We are just returned from Mr Powers where Mr & Mrs Browning were so kind as to take us. Of course you saw the fisherboy now exhibiting in London. Is it not lovely and so classically simple and graceful and the execution so beautiful? His Eve too is very fine. But I think on the whole not equal to the Greek slave. She has plucked the apple but has not yet eaten. To show however that the mischief is done, that it is the first step which is the important one, the tail of the serpent is made to encircle her feet.* ... *We paid a passing visit to the Pitti with the Brownings and it is so delightful to see her enjoyment, everything that is beautiful from sentiment or form or colour she seizes directly, but particularly in sentiment. His pleasure too in showing her the things and his care for her, are very nice.* ...
[Verney]

SD1321]   23 May 1847. A.L.s. Margaret Fuller to Evert A. Duyckinck. Rome. ... *Tell Mr Mathews that thus far I vainly seek Mr and Mrs Browning here in Italy; nobody seems to know where they are, and I console myself for not seeing them by the hope that they are in some solitude of Italian beauty and Italian leisure, enjoying themselves as none can who keep upon the beaten track of travel. Admirable as Browning's* *sketches of Italian scenery and character seemed before, they seem far finer now that I am close to the objects. The best representation of the spirit of Italy which our day affords.* [NYPL-Ms]

SD1322] 23 June 1847. A.L. (third person). Thomas Westwood to [Arabella Moulton-Barrett]. *7 Denmark St, Camberwell / Mr. Westwood presents his compliments to Miss Barrett, & ventures to request she will be kind enough to forward the enclosed note to her sister, when she writes next. Should the so doing however, be attended with the slightest inconvenience, if Miss Barrett will favour Mr. Westwood with Mrs. Browning's present address & will return the note to him, he will be most happy to forward it himself.*
[Berg]

SD1323] 3 July 1847. A.L.s. Henry Shirley to Edward Moulton-Barrett (father).
[Eton]

SD1324] 16 July 1847. A.L.s. Joseph Arnould to Alfred Domett. ... *Browning is spending a luxurious year in Italy—is at this present writing—with his poetess bride dwelling in some hermit hut in "Vallambrosa where the Etruscan shades high overarched embower:" he never fails to ask pressingly about you, and I give him all your messages. I would to God he would purge his style of obscurities—that the wide world and the gay world and even the less illuminated part of the thinking world might know his greatness even as we do. I find myself reading Paracelsus and the Dramatic Lyrics more often than any thing else in verse.* ... Transcript at the British Library. [   ]

SD1325] [31 July–6 August 1847]. Mary Russell Mitford to Charles Boner. ... *I wrote the other day to Mrs. Browning's sisters to ask her address lamenting the long time that had intervened without my hearing from her, & she wrote me word that she had just had a similar letter from her—so a letter has been lost one way or the other– She is pretty well & at Florence still.* ... [Yale]

SD1326] 3 August 1847. A.L.s. George Blyth and William Paxton Young to Edward Moulton-Barrett (father). [Eton]

SD1327] 10 August 1847. A.L.s. Henry Roberts to Edward Moulton-Barrett (father). [Eton]

SD1328] 14 August 1847. File Copy of Letter. Edward Moulton-Barrett (father) to Henry Roberts. [Eton]

SD1329] 17 August 1847. File Copy of Letter. Edward Moulton-Barrett (father) to Andrew Somerville. [Eton]

SD1330] 20 August 1847. A.L.s. Andrew Somerville to Edward Moulton-Barrett (father). [Eton]

SD1331] 19 September 1847. A.L.s. Joseph Arnould to Alfred Domett. ... *Browning and his wife are still in Florence: both ravished with Italy and Italian life; so much so that I think for some years they will make it the Paradise of their poetical exile. I hold fast to my faith in "Paracelsus." Browning and Carlyle are my two crowning men amongst the highest English minds of the day. Third comes Alfred Tennyson ... Bye the bye—did you have happen upon Browning's "Pauline"? a strange, wild, (in parts singularly magnificent) poet-biography: his own early life as it presented itself to his own soul viewed poetically: in fact, psychologically speaking, his "Sartor Resartus": it was written and published three years before Paracelsus when Shelley was his God.* ... Transcript at British Library. [   ]

SD1332] [29 September 1847]. A.L.s. Mary Russell Mitford to Lucy Olivia Partridge. ... *you must bring me the seeds when you come after Xmas. Mind that then you are to take a day ticket & dine here & spend as many hours as you can. It is what I used to do once a month to Elizabeth Barrett, & what many persons have done by me this summer.* ... *Mrs. Browning was nearly 4 months without writing to me!!!—& we used to* *write to each other two or three times a week—but I am not an adorer of Mr. Brownings & the tender friendship of 12 years seems to be forgotten. She does not seem to have seen a creature but her husband (you know the sort of dotage which a woman sometimes has for a man when she marries after the usual time)– They spent all the summer at that hot burning Florence except five days at Vallombrosa——& are to winter at Rome—& except for her husband, her maid, an English Doctor at Pisa & Mrs. Jameson she does not seem to have had any intercourse with anybody. Her seeing the Doctor was on account first of her poor maids illness whose health ruined by tremendous sea sickness in crossing from Marseilles to Leghorn at last totally failed—& then by her (Mrs. Browning) having a mishap at 5 months.– She said in one or two of her letters that there was absolutely no modern Italian literature that the only books since Ariosto Tasso &c were bad translations from bad french novels. ...* [Yale]

SD1333] 16 October 1847. File Copy of Letter. Edward Moulton-Barrett (father) to George Blyth and William Paxton Young. [Eton]

SD1334] 18 October 1847. RB, Sr., to Henry Ellis. *Bank of England / Dear Sir, / I should feel very much obliged to you, if you would grant me a ticket of admission to the Library of the British Museum for the next 3 Weeks. I can procure the most satisfactory reference if required, but I trust that the circumstance of my having been 44 years in the Bank, & being the father of R Browning, Author of Paracelsus, will be deemed sufficient. ...* [BL]

SD1335] 30 October 1847. Copy of Document. Thomas Wathen to John Altham Graham-Clarke and George Goodin Barrett Moulton-Barrett, relating to the marriage settlement of Leonard Graham Clark and Isabella Horatia Butler. [Eton]

SD1336] 5 November 1847. A.L.s. RB, Sr. to Henry Ellis. *Hatcham New Cross / Sir, / Being desirous of possessing the privilege of Reading in the British Museum Library, I beg the favor of a ticket of admission, which if you are so good as to send me, you may be assured I will not misuse.– I have been for many years a resident at Hatcham, and am well known to many respectable inhabitants in the place but it may perhaps be more satisfactory to you if I name William Smee Esqr chief accountant Banks of England & John Knight Esqr. Secretary, as friends of mine, either or both of whom will if you think proper to apply to them readily vouch for my character and position in society– I name these Gentlemen because I am told that the testimonials of two householders of respectability are required by you previous to issuing a Ticket of Admission to the British Museum Library ...* [BL]

SD1337] 8 November 1847. A.L.s. William Smee to Henry Ellis. *Bank of England / My dear Sir Henry, The Bearer of this Note Mr. Robert Browning of the Bank of England I have known for the last forty years as a very honorable Character, and worthy in every respect of having the Privilege of access to the Reading Room of the British Museum ...* [BL]

SD1338] 19 November 1847. A.L.s. William Paxton Young to Edward Moulton-Barrett (father). [Eton]

SD1339] 22 November 1847. A.L.s. William Wemyss Anderson to Edward Moulton-Barrett (father). [Eton]

SD1340] 15 December [1847]. A.L.s. Arthur Hugh Clough to Unidentified Correspondent. ... *Mr. Burbidge and myself wish to publish together: ... We thought that we might copy the example set by Mr. Browning in his Bells and Pomegranates and publish a series of cheap numbers, called "Myths and Monologues"—to be continued, according to their success. ...* [Harvard]

SD1341] [18 December 1847]. A.L.s. Mary Russell Mitford to Lucy Olivia Partridge. ... *I did not mean a literal young Poet my dear love—only a Poetess for a* *daughter—in the sense of Mrs. Acton Tindals or Mrs. Browning's offspring– I hear very seldom from Mrs. Browning now. She seems to care for none but his admirers & I am none of those. I fear that marriage much ...* [Yale]

SD1342] 19 December 1847. A.L.s. Charles John Barrett Moulton-Barrett to Henrietta Barrett Moulton-Barrett. [Altham]

Supporting Documents: Index of Correspondents
(References are to SD number, not page number.)

Anderson, William Wemyss, 1339
Arnould, Joseph, 1300, 1324, 1331
Barrett, Arabella Moulton-, 1322
Barrett, Charles John Moulton-, 1342
Barrett, Edward Moulton-, 1282, 1285–1287, 1293, 1302–1304, 1308, 1317, 1323, 1326–1330, 1333, 1338, 1339
Barrett, George Goodin Moulton-, 1281, 1335
Barrett, Henrietta Barrett Moulton-, 1342
Barrett, Octavius Moulton-, 1301
Barrett, Septimus Moulton-, 1285, 1293, 1306, 1307, 1309, 1313
Blackwood's Edinburgh Magazine, Editor of, 1281
Blyth, George, 1326, 1333
Boner, Charles, 1294, 1310, 1325
Brodie, P.B., 1307
Browning, Robert, Sr., 1277, 1298, 1334, 1336
Browning, Sarianna, 1269, 1270
Byron, Lady Noel, 1272, 1274, 1276, 1283, 1289, 1291, 1296, 1315
Carlyle, John A., 1275
Carlyle, Thomas, 1271, 1275, 1314
Clarke, John Altham Graham-, 1335
Clough, Arthur Hugh, 1340
Deattry, W., 1279
Domett, Alfred, 1300, 1324, 1331
Duyckinck, Evert A., 1292, 1305, 1321
Duyckinck, George Long, 1318, 1319
Eldred, Edward, 1306
Ellis, Henry, 1334, 1336, 1337
Emerson, Ralph Waldo, 1295
FitzGerald, Edward, 1271
Flower, Eliza, 1280
Forster, John, 1269
Fothergill, Thomas, Jr., 1301
Fox, William Johnson, 1280

Fuller, Margaret, 1292, 1321
Fyfe, A.G., 1279
Goethe, Ottilie von, 1290, 1297
Hamilton, William, 1303, 1308
Hanford, Frances, 1299, 1320
Hedge, Frederic H., 1295
Jameson, Anna Brownell, 1272–1274, 1276, 1283, 1284, 1289–1291, 1296, 1297, 1315
Jephson, Emily E., 1311
Kenyon, John, 1277, 1298, 1314, 1316
McDonagh, Robert, 1304
Mitford, Mary Russell, 1294, 1310–1312, 1325, 1332, 1341
Montague, Anne, 1270
Moxon, Edward, 1288
Murphy, Charlotte, 1284
Newdick, S., 1309
Nightingale, Frances Parthenope, 1299, 1320
Ouvry, Mrs., 1312
Partridge, Lucy Olivia, 1332, 1341
Poe, Edgar Allan, 1305
Powers, Hiram, 1316, 1318, 1319
Prince of Wales, George, 1287
Procter, Anne Benson, 1278
Purdue, Thomas, 1313
Roberts, Henry, 1327, 1328
Sharp, W., 1302
Shirley, Henry, 1282, 1286, 1317, 1323
Smee, William, 1337
Somerville, Andrew, 1329, 1330
Unidentified Correspondent, 1273, 1278, 1340
Wathen, Thomas, 1335
Westwood, Thomas, 1322
Wordsworth, William, 1288
Young, William Paxton, 1326, 1333, 1338

Appendix III

Contemporary Reviews of The Brownings' Works

RB AND EBB, understandably, showed much interest in the reviews—favourable and otherwise—which their works received. Frequently mentioned in their correspondence, the criticisms unquestionably influenced their subsequent writings. Because it is difficult to convey the full impact of the reviews through brief quotes, and since many of them would be hard for readers to locate, we here reproduce—in chronological order for each poet—all reviews we have traced for the period covered by this volume.

WORKS BY EBB

Poems (1844). *The Eclectic Review,* November 1846, pp. 573–585.

PEOPLE HAVE OFTEN asked, "What is poetry?" and have received replies more obscure than the inquiry—replies, that remind us of William Penn's test of the wisdom to be gleaned from asking questions, "*That,* friend, is as the answers may be." We shall not attempt any solution of the question, "What is poetry?" considered as a demand for definition. In that sense it has received one or two replies which the world will not easily see amended—and, as to present use, the faculty to apprehend a definition is not always a concomitant of the power to appreciate that to which it refers. But, to draw our remarks into a circle, by ending where they began; as Sir Walter Scott made it the test of a truthful painting, that it excited in its beholders emotions similar to those which the objects it sought to represent would call up, so we appeal to all thoughtful and feeling minds, by the emotions these volumes awaken, whether they be not poetry.

The varied opinions formed of Miss Barrett—the contrast between the degrees assigned to her on the scale of excellence, reminds one of what is said by John Foster, in his Journal, about truth,—that she may be likened to a beautiful statue seen by a crowd of spectators at many different angles and distances, and therefore appearing to each one differently to all the rest. In order to come near enough to what we would rightly behold, let us consider the aspect under which their author presents these poems to us; let us examine the preface; if it be true to its idea, *that* is a part which in no work should be overlooked, especially where, as in this case, it is the truthful voice of the writer—the very key to the objects and aims of the after pages. Listen, now, to what they are; of her expressed design in individual poems we may speak when we consider them. Now hear the views with which, as a poet, she speaks to the public:—

"If it were not presumptuous language on the lips of one to whom life is more than usually uncertain, my favourite wish for this work would be, that it be received by the public as a step in the right track, towards a future indication of more value and acceptability. I would fain do better,—and I feel as if I might do better: I aspire to do better. It is no new form of the nympholepsy of poetry, that my ideal should fly before me; and if I cry out too hopefully at sight of the white vesture receding between the cypresses, let me be blamed gently if justly. In any case, while my poems are full of faults, as I go forward to my critics and confess,

[375]

they have my heart and life in them,—they are not empty shelled. If it must be said of me, that I have contributed immemorable verses to the many rejected by the age, it cannot at least be said that I have done so in a light and irresponsible spirit. Poetry has been as serious a thing to me as life itself; and life has been a very serious thing: there has been no playing at skittles for me in either. I never mistook pleasure for the final cause of poetry; nor leisure, for the hour of the poet. I have done my work, so far, as work—not as mere hand and head work, apart from the personal being, but as the completest expression of that being, to which I could attain,—and as work I offer it to the public,—feeling its short-comings more deeply than any of my readers, because measured from the height of my aspiration,— but feeling also that the reverence and sincerity with which the work was done, should give it some protection with the reverent and sincere."—p. xii.

We feel that this preface spreads an Ægis over its writer; criticism, at least, may not touch her. We are, indeed, deeply moved, as the image glides before us of the solitary poetess, the love of her glorious art rising above her weakness and her weariness, "as a flame, tempest swayed,"—forgetting completely the toil of the way in its inspiring end, as the Persian Prince, for that his heart was full of the lady of his love, overlooked that it was a path of gold he trampled, in bounding to her. Well may we resolve against our indolence when we remember Elizabeth Barrett Barrett. We think upon the peaceful people whom warriors left unconquered because they could not fight where there was no resistance; of Cœur de Lion saying, as he turned his weapon from the Knight of the Leopard, "I cannot strike one who neither trembles nor strives"; of virgins unharmed by lions in their hunger; of Una, safe in her wanderings; of all images that figure to us the might of gentleness, the greatness of humility, as we read this aspiration and appeal. We must say one word on the allusion they contain,—and which is repeated in several of the poems,—to a circumstance necessary to be considered in forming a right appreciation of them,— the impaired health of the writer. There are few entirely unqualified to estimate how a weakened frame restrains the flights of mind; how thoughts, amid which, at other times, she moves as in her home, seem then to elude her grasp, or to stifle her with their greatness; to be unwieldy when she would pour them into the mould of language, and intangible when she would array them as a defence. Then, our very earnestness of desire to alter the exact idea, seems to call up a cloud of words that mock us, and we can only make our conception visible by marking off, as it were, what does not belong to it, that so the dweller within the boundary line may rise upon the thought of the reader. In carefully considering these poems, not abstractedly, but as a true reflection of the mind of their author, it appears to us, that their having been wrought through a mental strength somewhat borne down by bodily weariness, will explain, and win forbearance for those passages, which, compared with happier parts, seem laboured or perplexing. We do not forget that there are times when illness repays for long exhaustion, by intervals of power; when it seems to loosen instead of tightening the bonds of the flesh, and through the attenuation of the tenement, the spirit takes a wider range beyond it,—when the power to embody waits on the power to conceive,—when words are warmed through with the sunshine of feeling, and the felicities of language weave a transparent garb for the subtle thought. It is part of the law of compensation, and of such bright seasons these volumes afford proof; yet they may claim forbearance even while they command admiration, for the weight of indisposition is daily felt, and its periods of expansion are rare. We repeat, the strength of the mind is here far more striking than the weakness of the body; yet these volumes may be considered a remarkable psychological phenomenon as truly as Mozart's "Requiem," or Mrs. Hemans's "Antique Greek Lament." We cannot leave this subject without remarking the pure, vigorous, and cheerful tone of thought which distinguishes them. There is no repining; life, whether a sad or joyous season, is spoken of as given for exertion whose results end not with time,—nay, as being cheered by the toil that ennobles it, or, better still, as passed in peace through Him whose it is. If we are perplexed in choosing passages in proof, it is by their number, not their rareness. Perhaps we do not select the best evidence, but enough is found in this noble Sonnet on Work:—

> What are we set on earth for? Say, to toil.
> Nor seek to leave thy tending of the vines,
> For all the heat o' the day, till it declines,
> And death's mild curfew shall from work assoil.
> God did anoint thee with His odorous oil,
> To wrestle, not to reign; and he assigns
> All thy tears over, like pure crystallines,
> For younger fellow-workers of the soil
> To wear for amulets. So others shall
> Take patience, labour, to their heart and hands,
> From thy hands, and thy heart, and thy brave cheer.
> And God's grace fructify through thee to all.
> The least flower, with a brimming cup, may stand,
> And share its dew-drop with another near.

We have been surprised occasionally to hear persons infer from isolated sentences, as that quotation in the preface, "we learn in suffering what we teach in song," or those lines in the "Vision of Poets," "Knowledge by suffering entereth, and life is perfected by death," that Miss Barrett thinks mental power necessarily associated with pain,—that the vocation of a poet is one of much sadness. We think this might be sufficiently disproved by her poetic art having been her selected solace through all trial, (as she herself says in the dedication to her father, "if this art of poetry had been a less earnest object to me, it must have fallen from exhausted hands before this day"); by the self-evidence that one who can so sing must find pleasure in the song; but at least she must be believed to think nobly of her vocation, who says in her poem on The dead Pan:—

> What is true, and just, and honest,
> What is lovely, what is pure—
> All of praise that hath admonisht,
> All of virtue shall endure;
> These are themes for poet's uses,
> Stirring nobler than the Muses,
>   Ere Pan was dead.

Our space will permit but few remarks on the distinguishing characteristics of Miss Barrett's poetry. We must, however, observe that it is the utterance of a devout heart. The proof of this is, not that religion is the constant theme of these volumes; on the contrary, they take an unusually wide range of topics,—but that human passions, daily scenes, common interests, are viewed from a point which the religious mind alone can occupy. If, as Dr. Arnold said, the law of Christ should rule in such wide harmony in Christian souls, that no strange discrepancy should be felt in passing from a sick room to the work of every day, we may welcome another name among the writers, whose most earthly page moves no feeling discordant with those of an hour of sacred meditation. Some poets, whose writings we can hardly refuse to call beautiful, make for themselves a moral atmosphere, in which the forms traced glow with radiance and power; they claim from us unhealthy sensibilities, and disquiet the mind, as if its sense of beauty harmonised with two opposing types. We rejoice that Miss Barrett contrasts with these, and that she does not dwell exclusively on religious themes;— there is abundant store of works for those who seek expressly religious edification. It has been well said that the mission of a Christian poet, in this age, is more to the world than to the Church,—rather to speak of earthly things in a religious spirit than to explain sacred things to the devout; to show that godliness embraces all things rather than to mark the boundary of the inner court of the temple. Is it not part of the working of a general law, that in a day when Carlyle and others systematically speak of earthly energies by terms appertaining to powers that are not of the earth, we should have a Poet who paints the wide though passing interests of man in colours that harmonize with the light of the sanctuary? Miss Barrett's topics roam through a wide field; she treads it with a firm step, and from the height surveys an extended territory, won only by the strong-minded. But her foot-prints have a woman's delicacy of outline, however high they ascend. The union exhibited of clear and vigorous thought, of sense, which it were no compliment to call manly, with the fine feeling of beauty, the delicacy of apprehension which can pertain but to woman, we regard as one symptom among many less pleasing of *this* age. Having had first, in the Rosa Matilda or Della Cruscan school, the feminine fragility, and then, as if extremes evoked each other, the strong purpose without the grace of womanhood in Mary Wollstonecraft, we now behold the better parts of each united in—

"Perfect" women, "nobly planned
To warn, to comfort, and command;
And yet" spirits "still, and bright
With something of an angel light";

and are ready to say that if the wild weeds must precede "the bright consummate flower," we accept of all rather than resign the last.

The volumes before us are the *habitual* voice of the spirit—the breathing of the life of thought; not the result of occasional and strained imagination,—not done on a sudden call to answer a fitful purpose,—but, as their author says, "they have her heart and life in them,"—"they are the completest expression of her being to which she could attain." Perhaps this truth, this life-like emotion, is, with their variety of theme, the cause they every class of mind finds in them something which strikes its peculiar sympathies. In hearing these poems spoken of, we have found that almost every one of the shorter ones has intelligent admirers, who think it of unrivalled excellence,—others may be beautiful, but this superlative. Miss Barrett is sometimes accused of imitating Tennyson, but to our apprehension the contrast is far more striking than the resemblance. We have not time to point out instances in proof, but surely the likeness is, at most, but that of two who have studied in the same school; the tinge of colouring which, as in the case of the many dramatists of the Elizabethean age, clings, amid a thousand strongly marked differences to the writers of the same period.

We may surprise some by naming conciseness as one of Miss Barrett's distinguishing excellencies. We mean by conciseness fulness of meaning, conveyed in few and simple words: and if brevity is the soul of wit, it is no less the soul of the highest eloquence, the most touching pathos. We think, however, that the more careful is the inspection of Miss Barrett's writings, the more incontrovertible will this appear. These poems have two elements of conciseness, each in itself a great praise. First, their language is, as it were, twin with the thought; it is evidently constructed to express thought exactly as it exists in the mind of the writer,—to mark out and define the precise thing she means, in the precise aspect it wears to her,—not giving a vague and hazy outline of her design, but painting it out clear and individually so as to mark off the finest shade which distinguishes it from the most kindred thought. This is alike a result and cause of her originality,—"individuality *is* originality."

Let any one who doubts whether Miss Barrett possesses this power, express in fewer words, *leaving out no shade of meaning*, the greater part of the "Dead Pan," "Loved Once," "Crowned and Buried," &c.; or let him exert his power of compression on the "Fourfold Aspect," any half-stanza of which might be the motto for a long discourse. Deep feeling, no less than high thought, has left its trace on these wonderful lines,—the heat and light, inseparable elements in the fire of genius. "All deep things," says Carlyle, "are song."

In the next place, Miss Barrett's conciseness is caused by her skill in the use of symbols,—symbolic language being often the most condensed expression of thought. The analogies which her figurative language make apparent, perpetually give us the delight of surprise in the midst of familiarity. Unthought of resemblances are constantly developed from old figures,—

New, as if come from other spheres,
Yet welcome, as if loved for years.

It is of the similes in Coleridge's prose writings, especially the "Friend," more than any other, that Miss Barrett's have often reminded us. En passant, we may just mention a kindred power in another writer, which lately struck us. When employing an hour with the volume of our own George Herbert, we said internally, "What do these quaint but beautiful images recall to us?"—and after reading the Sabbath, the Elixir, Love Unknown, &c., (to which we appeal in favour of our judgment,) we replied, "It is certainly of something kindred in spirit, though widely unlike in form, in Miss Barrett's poems."

We must just mention this lady's excellence in sketching visible nature, and in painting human emotion. The former is perhaps the most remarkable, when we remember that for years she never put her foot on the green sward. How strongly and truly must the aspect of external nature have impressed her, to enable her to describe many of its more recondite and less noticeable graces, as she does! We have scarcely room for an example, which we choose for its brevity:—

What a day it was, that day!
Hills and vales did openly
Seem to heave and throb away,
At the sight of the great sky:

> And the silence, as it stood
> In the glory's golden flood,
> Audibly did bud—and bud!
>
> Through the winding hedgerows green,
> How we wandered, I and you—
> With the bowery tops shut in,
> And the gates that showed the view!
> How we talked there! Thrushes soft
> Sang our pauses out, or oft
> Bleatings took them from the croft.

Another of Miss Barrett's characteristics, is a spirit of generalization;—law, in the Platonic sense, ruling in her mind, and leading her to show that the causes which originate small and daily results, are the same which work among the large phenomena of the universe—or to draw a wide moral from a slight and passing circumstance—or to symbolize universal conditions of existence, or principles of action, by minute accidents: as in the meaning of the marble silence sleeping, in "Lady Geraldine's Courtship"; in the Sonnets on the "Seraph and Poet"; "Past and Future"; "Irreparableness"; "Tears"; "Perplexed Music"; "Patience taught by Nature"; or, as when in the "Romance of the Page," she makes us hear in the wood, by the slaughtered page, the convent bell tolling for the dead Abbess:—

> Dirge for abbess laid in shroud,
> Sweepeth over the shroudless dead,
> Page or lady, as we said,
> With the dews upon her head,
> All as sad, if not as loud!
>   *Ingemisco, ingemisco!*
> Is ever a lament begun
> By any mourner under sun,
> Which, ere it endeth, suits but *one?*

Miss Barrett's genius appears to us as incontrovertible in her slighter as in her greater productions—as the merest fragment of diamond which reflects a sunbeam is as truly a precious gem, as the "sea of light" on the brow of a sultan. But if called on for our weightiest proof of her genius, we should probably select her personification of Lucifer, in the Drama of Exile; though we admit the portrayment is of somewhat unequal merit, and,—but here the fault may lie in our own apprehension,—not in perfect keeping; at least his yearning lament for his Morning Star—his grief, even to tears, for his dethronement and her desertion, seem to us not in perfect keeping with the splendid passage we quote. We should premise that the "Drama of Exile" is the longest poem in the volumes, and represents, as its author says, "the new and strange experience of the fallen humanity, as it went forth from Paradise into the wilderness, with a peculiar reference to Eve's allotted grief, which, considering that self-sacrifice belonged to her womanhood, and the consciousness of originating the Fall to her offence, appeared to me imperfectly apprehended hitherto, and more expressible by a woman than a man. There was room, at least, for lyrical emotion in those first steps into the wilderness—in that first sense of desolation after wrath—in that first audible gathering of the recriminating 'groan of the whole creation'—in that first darkening of the hills from the recoiling feet of angels—and in that first silence of the voice of God. And I took pleasure in driving in, like a pile, stroke upon stroke, the Idea of Exile—admitting Lucifer as an extreme Adam, to represent the ultimate tendencies of sin and loss, that it might be strong to bear up the contrary idea of the heavenly love and purity." The belief of Lucifer that his original beauty is not all departed, lingering as an echo of its reality, making more visible the depth of evil which closes out all love and beauty from him, seems to us very fine; but it is useless to attempt an analysis of this personation, we leave it to the perception of our readers:—

> *Adam.* Perhaps a fallen angel. Who shall say!
> *Lucifer.* Who told thee, Adam?
> *Adam.*   Thou! The prodigy
> Of thy vast brows and melancholy eyes,
> Which comprehend the heights of some great fall.
> I think that thou hast one day worn a crown
> Under the eyes of God.
> *Lucifer.*   And why of God?
> *Adam.* It were no crown else! Verily, I think
> Thou'rt fallen far. I had not yesterday
> Said it so surely; but I know to-day
> Grief by grief, sin by sin.
> *Lucifer.*   A crown by a crown.
> *Adam.* Ay, mock me! now I know more than I knew.
> Now I know thou art fallen below hope
> Of final re-ascent.
> *Lucifer.*   Because?
> *Adam.*   Because
> A spirit who expected to see God,
> Though at the last point of a million years,
> Could dare no mockery of a ruined man
> Such as this Adam.   *   *   *
>   *   *
> *Eve.*   Speak no more with him,
> Beloved; it is not good to speak with him.
>   *   *   *   Being bereft,
> We would be alone. Go!
> *Lucifer.*   Ah! ye talk the same
> All of you—spirits and clay—go, and depart!
>   *   *   *
> And yet I was not fashioned out of clay.
> Look on me, woman! Am I beautiful?
> *Eve.* Thou hast a glorious darkness.
> *Lucifer.*   Nothing more?
> *Eve.* I think no more.
> *Lucifer.*   False heart, thou thinkest more!
> Thou canst not choose but think, as I praise God,
> Unwillingly but fully, that I stand
> Most absolute in beauty. As yourselves
> Were fashioned very good at best, so *we*
> Sprang very beauteous from the creant Word
> Which thrilled around us; God himself being moved,
> When that august work of a perfect shape,
> His dignities of sovran angel-hood,
> Swept out into the universe; divine
> With thunderous movements, earnest looks of
>   gods,
> And silver-solemn clash of cymbal wings.
> Whereof I was, in motion and in form,
> A part not poorest. And yet—yet, perhaps,
> This beauty which I speak of is not here,
> As God's voice is not here; nor even my crown—
> I do not know. What is this thought or thing
> Which I call beauty? Is it thought or thing?
> Is it a thought accepted for a thing?
> Or both? or neither? A pretext—a word?
> Its meaning flutters in me like a flame
> Under my own breath; my perceptions reel
> For evermore around it, and fall off,
> As if it were too holy.

Eve.   Which it is.
Adam. The essence of all beauty I call love.
The attribute, the evidence, and end,
The consummation to the inward sense,
Of beauty apprehended from without,
I still call love. As form, when colourless,
Is nothing to the eye; that pine-tree there,
Without its black and green, being all a blank;
So, without love, is beauty undiscerned
In man or angel. Angel! Rather ask
What love is in thee, what love moves to thee,
And what collateral love moves on with thee;
Then shalt thou know if thou art beautiful.
      *   *   *
Lucifer.   I scorn you that ye wail.
   *   *   *   Yet one cry
I, too, would drive up, like a column erect,
Marble to marble, from my heart to heaven;
A monument of anguish, to transpierce
And overtop your vapoury complaints,
Expressed from feeble woes!
Earth-Spirits! I wail, I wail!
   Lucifer. For, O ye heavens, ye are my witnesses
That *I*, struck out from nature in a blot,
The outcast and the mildew of things good,
   *   *   *
Was made by God like others.   *
   *   *   Ha! ye think,
White angels in your niches, I repent;
And would tread down my own offences, back
To service at the footstool! *That's* read wrong:
I cry, as the beast did, that I may cry—
Expansive, not appealing! Fallen so deep
Against the sides of this prodigious pit,
I cry—cry! dashing out the hands of wail,
On each side, to meet anguish everywhere;
And to attest it in the ecstacy
And exaltation of a woe sustained
Because provoked and chosen.
   *   *   *   *
My curse catch at you strongly, body and soul;
And *He* find no redemption, nor the wing
Of seraph move your way. And yet rejoice!
Rejoice! because ye had not set in you
This hate, which shall pursue you; this fire-hate,
Which glares without, because it burns within;
Which kills from ashes; this potential hate,
Wherein I, angel, in antagonism
To God and His reflex beatitudes,
Moan ever in the central universe,
With the great woe of striving against love;
And gasp for space amid the infinite,
And toss for rest amid the desertness,
Self-orphaned by my will, and self-elect
To kingship of resistant agony
Toward the good round me; hating good and love,
And willing to hate good and to hate love,
And willing to will on so evermore;
Scorning the past, and damning the to-come.
Go, and rejoice! I curse you!   [*Lucifer vanishes.*

The effect of this is injured by the impossibility of extracting the whole passage; yet here is not wholly lost the climax—the accumulation of scorn and woe, which reminds one of power of the same kind in the "Prometheus Bound" of Æschylus. We can give but one more extract from the "Drama of Exile,"—it is part of the address of Christ, when he appears in vision to reinstate Adam and Eve in their sovereignty over earth and its agencies:—

   *   *   Ponder it!
This regent and sublime humanity,
Though fallen, exceeds you. This shall film your
   sun;
Shall hunt your lightning to its lair of cloud;
Turn back your rivers, footpath all your seas;
Lay flat your forests; master, with a look,
Your lion at his fasting, and fetch down
Your eagle flying   *   *
   *   *   Therefore, over you,
Accept this sceptre; therefore be content
To minister with voluntary grace,
And melancholy pardon, every rite
And service in you to this sceptred hand.
Be ye to man as angels be to God—
Servants in pleasure, singers of delight;
Suggesters to his soul of higher things
Than any of your highest. So, at last,
He shall look round on you, with lids too straight
To hold the grateful tears, and thank you well;
And bless you when he prays his secret prayers,
And praise you when he sings his open songs,
For the clear song-note he has learnt in you,
Of purifying sweetness; and extend
Across your head his golden fantasies,
Which glorify you into soul from sense!
Go, serve him, for such price. That not in vain,
Nor yet ignobly ye shall serve. I place
My word here for an oath—mine oath for act
To be hereafter. In the name of which
Perfect redemption and perpetual grace
I bless you, through the hope and through the peace
Which are mine, to the love which is myself.

We must now say a few words on Miss Barrett's alleged faults. In the first place, a passage here and there,—as the conclusion of the song of the Nightingale, in the Drama of Exile, and part of that of the Morning Star, in the same poem, is pronounced perfectly unintelligible. We think it not unlikely that in future editions the author may make the ideas intended to be expressed, more perspicuous; in the mean time they are not to our apprehension, meaningless. Perhaps the excuse which Foster made for Coleridge, and which in the *Friend*, and the *Biographia Literaria* Coleridge makes for himself, is in some degree applicable to them; that there are ideas which dwell beyond the region assigned to language, and to which therefore language can furnish no full expression,—broken steps, the lamp which guides from one to another, being borne by the reader himself. Another complaint is directed against the occasional use of Greek words, which, in English composition is held inadmissible, or such as ought to be introduced rarely, and only on very special occasions. This rule is a sound one, and we are inclined to give judgment against our author for its violation. There is also fault found with her use of a few adjectives as if they included the meaning of both adjective and substantive, as "Human"—in the title of one of Miss Barrett's most generally acceptable poems, "The Cry of the Human." We presume this arises from her wish to give the most condensed form to a comprehensive idea;—where her power does not answer to her will, we can imagine her in her resolve for progressive excellence, regarding this and other difficulties, in the spirit of Penn's reply to his threateners with imprisonment, "Friend, thy strength shall never equal my patience."

Perhaps, however, the loudest complaint concerns the rhymes. We acknowledge that though some are of unsurpassed sweetness, they do not always pass muster either to eye or ear. One of the most faulty in this respect,—amusingly faulty we have heard it called,—"The Wine of Cyprus,"—has however, a magnificent and flowing rhythm, that seems to smile defiance at strictures; and bears us on, like a breeze over the billows,—though there are mingled with it touches of deep pathos, as if some way-mark of past suffering rose above the wave.

We hope again to meet Miss Barrett, when her aspirations for advance in her art have been more than realised; and when she has won a yet higher place among the imperishable names of her country. It is now more than two years since the volumes before us were published. Doubtless the time will come when that period for exertion, and we rejoice to learn, of amended health, will be nobly accounted for. If in our present parting we may venture to express a wish as to the future direction of her powers; it would be that some thrilling incidents of our History might be treated by one, so capable of "stirring the soul as by the sound of a trumpet"; and that whatever she may decide on this point,—she would present to the public more of her thoughts in the form of prose, a vehicle possessing facilities at least *different* to those of verse, and perhaps better than even verse adapted to some modes of lofty thought. We think this wish must be echoed by every one who can appreciate the graces of her exquisite preface,—which like her verse, presents a form of beauty undiscerned before.

It has occasionally happened to us to feel surprise at the temerity of critics, in composedly parcelling out blame to every quality of authors, the *coast* line of whose intellect, the entire extent of their own, would not fathom. How many spirited reviews would suffer total change if re-fashioned on the Platonic maxim,—"understand a man's ignorance before you attempt to judge his understanding!" But the effort to do justice to an author, sometimes involves presumption,—and in many cases we feel, that the mind, which from the height of its aspiration, looks down on all attained success, must yet perceive the lines of beauty it has designed with more exquisite appreciation than its critic. We shall, however, be not ill-satisfied if we succeed in suggesting these poems as a realm of thought, to those who may penetrate more deeply into its riches, than ourselves; and in any case, may know the joy of the humble,—reverence for the high,—for

> There is delight
> In praising, though the praiser sit alone
> And see the praised far off him, far above.

Poems (1844). Tait's Edinburgh Magazine, September 1847, pp. 620–625.

In selecting Mrs. Hemans as our first specimen of Female Authors, we did so avowedly, because she seemed to us the most feminine writer of the day. We now select Mrs. Browning for the opposite reason, that she is, or at least is said by many to be, the most masculine of our female writers.

To settle the respective spheres and calibres of the male and the female mind is one of the most difficult of philosophical problems. To argue, merely, that because the mind of woman has never hitherto produced a "Paradise Lost," or a "Principia," it is therefore for ever incapable of producing similar masterpieces, seems to us unfair, for various reasons. In the first place, how many ages elapsed e'er the *male* mind realised such prodigies of intellectual achievement? And do not they still stand unparalleled and almost unapproached? And were it not as reasonable to assert that man as that woman can renew them no more? Secondly, because the premise is granted—that woman *has* not—does the conclusion follow, that woman cannot excogitate an argument as great as the "Principia," or build up a rhyme as lofty as the "Paradise Lost?" Would it not have been as wise for one who knew Milton only as the Milton of "Lycidas" and "Arcades," to have contended that he was incapable of a great epic poem? And is there nothing in Madame De Stael, in Rahel the Germaness, in Mary Somerville, and even in Mary Wollstonecraft, to suggest the idea of heights, fronting the very peaks of the Principia and the Paradise, to which woman may yet attain? Thirdly, has not woman understood and appreciated the greatest works of genius as fully as man? Then may she in time equal them; for what is true appreciation but the sowing of a germ in the mind, which shall ultimately bear similar fruit? There is nothing, says Godwin, which the human mind can conceive, which it cannot execute; we may add, there is nothing the human mind can understand which it cannot equal. Fourthly, let us never forget that women, as to intellectual progress, is in a state of infancy. Changed as by malignant magic, now into an article of furniture, and now into the toy of pleasure, she is only as yet undergoing a better transmigration, and "timidly expanding into life."

Almost all that is valuable in Female Authorship has been produced within the last half-century, that is, since the female was generally recognised to be an intellectual creature; and if she has, in such a short period, so progressed, what demi-Mahometan shall venture to set bounds to her future advancement? Even though we should grant that woman, more from her bodily constitution than her mental, is inferior to man, and that man, having got, shall probably keep, his start of centuries, we see nothing to prevent woman overtaking, and outstripping with ease, his *present* farthest point of intellectual progress. We do not look on such productions as "Lear," and the "Prometheus Vinctus," with the despair wherewith the boy who has leaped up in vain to seize, regards ever after the moon and the stars; they are, after all, the masonry of men, and not the architecture of the gods; and if man may surpass, why may not woman, "taken out of his side," his gentle *alias*, equal them?

Of woman, we may say, at least, that there are already provinces where her power is incontested and supreme. And in proportion as civilization advances, and as the darker and fiercer passions which constitute the *fera natura* subside, in the lull of that milder day, the voice of woman will become more audible, exert a wider magic, and be as the voice of spring to the opening year. We stay not to prove that the *sex* of genius is *feminine*, and that those poets who are most profoundly impressing our young British minds, are those who, in tenderness and sensibility—in peculiar power, and in peculiar weakness, are all but females. And whatever may be said of the effects of culture, in deadening the genius of man, we are mistaken if it has not always had the contrary effect upon that of woman (where do we find a female Bloomfield or Burns?) so that, on entering on the far more highly civilised periods which are manifestly approaching, she will but be breathing the atmosphere calculated to nourish and invigorate, instead of weakening and chilling her mental life. Our admirable friend, Mr. De Quincey, has, we think, conceded even more than we require, in granting (see his paper on Joan of Arc) that woman can die more nobly than man. For whether is the writing or the doing of a great tragedy the higher achievement? Poor the attitude even of Shakespere, penning the fire-syllables of Macbeth, to that of Joan of Arc, entering into the flames as into her wedding suit. What comparison between the face inflamed of a Mirabeau or a Chalmers, as they thundered; and the blush on the cheek of Charlotte Corday, still extant, as her head was presented to the people? And who shall name the depicter of the death of Beatrice Cenci; or with Madame Roland, whose conduct on the scaffold might make one in "love with death?" If to die nobly demand the highest concentration of the moral, intellectual, and even artistic powers—and if woman has *par excellence* exemplified such a concentration, there follows a conclusion to which we should be irresistibly led, were it not that we question the minor proposition in the argument—we hold that man has often as fully as woman risen to the dignity of death, and met him, not as a vassal, but as a superior.

To say that Mrs. Browning has more of the man than any female writer of the period, may appear rather an equivocal compliment; and its truth even may be questioned. We may, however, be permitted to say, that she has more of the *heroine* than her compeers. Hers is a high heroic nature, which adopts for the motto at once of its life and of its poetry, "Perfect through suffering." Shelley says:—

Most wretched men
Are cradled into poetry by wrong;
They learn in suffering what they teach in song.

But wrong is not always the stern school-mistress of song. There are sufferings springing from other sources—from intense sensibility—from bodily ailment—from the loss of cherished objects, which also find in such poetry their natural vent. And we do think that such poetry, if not so powerful, is infinitely more pleasing and more instructive than that which is inspired by real or imaginary grievance. The turbid torrent is not the proper mirror for reflecting the face of nature; and none but the moody and the discontented will seek to see in it an aggravated and distorted edition of their own gloomy brows. The poetry of wrong is not the best and most permanent. It was not wrong alone that excited, though it unquestionably directed, the course of Dante's and Milton's vein. The poetry of Shakespere's wrong is condensed in his sonnets—the poetry of his forbearance and forgiveness, of his gratitude and his happiness, is in his dramas. The poetry of Pope's wrong (a scratch from a thorn hedge!) is in his "Dunciad," not in his "Rape of the Lock." The poetry of Wordsworth's wrong is in his "Prefaces," not in his "Excursion." The poetry of Byron's wrong is in those deep curses which sometimes disturb the harmony of his poems; and that of Shelley's in the maniacal scream which occasionally interrupts the pæans of his song. But all these had probably been as great, or greater poets, had no wrong befallen them, or had it taught them another lesson, than either peevishly to proclaim, or furiously to resent it.

Mrs. Browning has suffered, so far as we are aware, no wrong from the age. She might, indeed, for some time have spoken of neglect. But people of genius should now learn the truth, that *neglect* is not *wrong*; or if it be, it is a wrong in which they often set the example. Neglecting the tastes of the majority, the majority avenges itself by neglecting them. Standing and singing in a congregation of the deaf, they are senseless enough to complain that they are not heard. Or should they address the multitude, and should the multitude not listen, it never strikes them that the fault is their own; they ought to have compelled attention. Orpheus was listened to: the thunder is: even the gentlest spring shower commands its audience. If neglect means wilful winking at claims which are *felt*, it is indeed a wrong; but a wrong seldom if ever committed, and which complaint will not cure—if it means, merely, ignorance of claims which have never been presented or enforced, where and whose is the criminality?

To do Mrs. Browning justice, she has not complained of neglect nor of injury at all. But she has acknowledged herself inspired by the genius of suffering. And this seems to have exerted divers influences upon her poetry. It has, in the first place, taught her to rear for herself a spot of transcendental retreat, a city of refuge in the clouds. Scared away from her own heart, she has soared upwards, and found a rest elsewhere. To those flights of idealism in which she indulges, to those distant and daring themes which she selects, she is urged less, we think, through native tendency of mind, than to fill the vast vacuity of a sick and craving spirit. This is not peculiar to her. It may be called, indeed, the Retreat of the Ten Thousand; though strong and daring must be those that can successfully accomplish it. Only the steps of sorrow—we had almost said only the steps of despair—can climb such dizzy heights. The healthy and the happy mind selects subjects of a healthy and a happy sort, and which lie within the sphere of every-day life and every-day thought. But for minds which have been wrung and riven, there is a similar attraction in gloomy themes, as that which leads them to the side of dark rivers, to the heart of deep forests, or into the centre of waste glens. Step forth, ye giant children of Sorrow and Genius, that we may tell your names, and compute your multitudes. First, there is the proud thundershod Æschylean family, all conceived in the "eclipse" of that most powerful of Grecian spirits. Then follows the vast skeleton of "De Rerum natura," the massive product of the grief of Lucretius—

Who cast his plummet down the broad
Deep universe, and said, No God;
Finding no bottom, he denied
Divinely the divine, and died,
Chief poet upon Tiber side.
    Mrs. Browning.

There stalk forward, next in the procession, the kings, priests, popes, prelates, and the yet guiltier and mightier shapes of Dante's Hell. Next, the Satan of Milton advances, champing the curb, and regarding even Prometheus as no mate for his proud and lonely misery. Then comes, cowering and shivering on, the timid Castaway of Cowper. He is followed by Byron's heroes, a haughty yet melancholy troop, with *conscious madness* animating their gestures and glaring in their eyes. The Anciente Marenere succeeds, now fearfully reverting his looks, and now fixing his glittering eye forward on a peopled and terrible vacancy. And, lastly, a frail shadowy and shifting shape, looking now Laon, now like Lionel, and now like Prometheus, proclaims that Alastor himself is here, the Benjamin in this family of tears.

"Whither shall I wander," seems Mrs. Browning to have said to herself, "to-day to escape from my own sad thoughts, and to lose, to noble purpose, the sense of my own identity? I will go eastward to Eden, where perfection and happiness once dwelt. I will pass, secure in virtue, the far flashing sword of the cherubim; I will knock at the door and enter. I will lie down in the forsaken garden; I will pillow my head where Milton pillowed his, on the grass cool with the shadow of the Tree of Life; and I will dream a vision of my own, of what this place once was, and of what it was to leave it for the wilderness." And she has passed the waving sword, and she has entered the awful garden, and she has dreamed a dream, and she has, awaking, told it as a "Drama of Exile." It were vain to deny that the dream is one full of genius—that it is entirely original; and that it never once, except by antithesis, suggests a thought of Milton's more massive and palpable vision. Her paradise is not a garden, it is a flush on a summer evening sky. Her Adam is not the fair large-fronted man, with all manlike qualities meeting unconsciously in his full clear nature—he is a German metaphysician. Her Eve is *herself*, an amiable and gifted blue-stocking, not the mere meek motherly woman, with what Aird beautifully calls the "broad, ripe, serene, and gracious composure of love about her." Her spirits are neither cherubim nor seraphim—neither knowing nor burning ones—they are fairies, not, however, of the Puck or Ariel species, but of a new metaphysical breed; they do not ride on, but split hairs; they do not dance, but reason; or if they dance, it is on the point of a needle, in cycles and epicycles of mystic and mazy motion. There is much beauty and power in passages of the poem, and a sweet inarticulate infinite melody, like the fabled cry of mandrakes in the lyrics. Still we do not see the taste of turning the sweet open garden of Eden into a maze—we do not approve of the daring precedent of trying conclusions with Milton on his own high field of victory—and we are, we must say, jealous of all encroachments upon that fair Paradise which has so long painted itself upon our imaginations—where all the luxuries of earth mingled in the feast with all the dainties of the heavens—where celestial plants grew under the same sun with terrestrial blossoms, and where the cadences of seraphic music filled up the pauses in the voice of God. Far different, indeed, is Mrs. Browning's from Dryden's disgusting inroad into Eden—as different, almost, as the advent of Raphael from the encroachment of Satan. But the poem professed to stand in the lustre of the fiery sword, and this should have burnt up some of its conceits, and silenced some of its meaner minstrelsies. And all such attempts we regard precisely as we do the beauties of the Apocrypha, when compared to the beauties of the Bible. They are as certainly beauties, but beauties of an inferior order—they are flowers, but not the roses which grew along the banks of the Four Rivers, "or caught in their crimson cups the first sad drops wept at committing of the mortal sin."

"One blossom of Eden outblooms them all."

Having accepted from Mrs. Browning's own hand sadness, or at least seriousness, as the key to her nature and genius, let us continue to apply it in our future remarks. This at once impels her to, and fits her for, the high position she has assumed, uttering the "Cry of the Human." And whom would the human race prefer as their earthly advocate, to a high-souled and gifted woman? What voice but the female voice could so softly and strongly, so eloquently and meltingly, interpret to the ear of him whose name is Love, the deep woes, and deeper wants of "poor humanity's afflicted will, struggling in vain with ruthless destiny?" Some may quarrel with the title, "The Human," as an affectation; but, in the first place, if it be, it is a very small one, and a small affectation can never furnish matter for a great quarrel. Secondly, we are not disposed to make a man, and still less a woman, an offender for a word, and thirdly, we fancy we can discern a good reason for her use of the term. What is it that is crying aloud through her voice to Heaven? It is not the feral or fiendish element in human nature? That has found an organ in Byron—an echo in his bellowing verse. It is the human element in man—bruised, bleeding, all but dead under the pressure of evil—circumstances, under the ten thousand tyrannies, mistakes, and delusions of the world, that has here ceased any longer to be silent, and is speaking in a sister's voice to Time and to Eternity—to Earth and Heaven. The poem may truly be called a prayer for the times, and no collect in the English liturgy surpasses it in truth and tenderness, though some may think its tone daring to the brink of blasphemy, and piercing almost to anguish.

Gracefully from this proud and giddy pinnacle, where she had stood as the conscious and commissioned representative of the human race, she descends to the door of the factory, and pleads for the children inclosed in that crowded and busy hell. The "cry of the factory children" moves you, because it is no poem at all—it is just a long sob, veiled and stifled as it ascends through the hoarse voices of the poor beings themselves. Since we read it we can scarcely pass a factory without seeming to hear this psalm issuing from the machinery, as if it were protesting against its own abused powers. But, to use the language of a writer quoted a little before, "The Fairy Queen is dead, shrouded in a yard of cotton stuff made by the spinning-jenny, and by that piece of new improved machinery, *the souls and bodies of British children,* for which death alone holds the patent." From Mrs. Browning, perhaps the most imaginative and intellectual of British females, down to a pale-faced, thick-voiced, degraded, hardly human, factory girl, what a long and precipitous descent. But though hardly, she is human; and availing herself of the small, trembling, but eternally indestructible link of connexion implied in a common nature, our authoress can identify herself with the cause, and incarnate her genius in the person of the poor perishing child. How unspeakably more affecting is a pleading in behalf of a particular portion of the race, than in behalf of the entire family! Mrs. Browning might have uttered a hundred "cries of the human," and proved herself only a sentimental artist, and awakened little save an echo dying away in distant elfin laughter; but the cry of a factory child, coming through a woman's, has gone to a nation's heart of hearts.

Although occupied thus with the sterner wants and sorrows of society, she is not devoid of interest in its minor miseries and disappointments. She can sit down beside little Ella (the miniature of Alnaschar) and watch the history of her day-dream beside the swan's nest among the reeds, and see in her disappointment a type of human hopes in general, even when towering and radiant as summer clouds. Ella's dream among the reeds! What else was Godwin's *Political Justice*? What else was St. Simonianism? What else is Young Englandism?

And what else are the hopes built by many now upon *certain* perfected schemes of education, which, freely translated, just mean the farther sharpening and furnishing of knaves and fools; and now upon a "Coming Man," who is to supply every deficiency, reconcile every contradiction, and right every wrong. Yes, he will come mounted on the red-roan horse of sweet Ella's vision!

Shadowed by the same uniform seriousness are the only two poems of hers which we shall farther at present mention—we mean her "Vision of Poets," and her "Geraldine's Courtship." The aim of the first is to present, in short compass, and almost in single lines, the characteristics of the greater poets of past and present times. This undertaking involved in it very considerable difficulties. For, in the first place, most great poets possess more than one distinguishing peculiarity. To select a single differential point is always hazardous, and often deceptive. 2dly, After you have selected the prominent characteristic of your author, it is no easy task to express it in a word, or in a line. To compress thus an Iliad in a nutshell, to imprison a Giant genie in an iron pot, is more a feat of magic than an act of criticism. 3dly, It is especially difficult to express the differentia of a writer in a manner at once easy and natural, and picturesque, and poetical. In the very terms of such an attempt as Mrs. Browning makes, it is implied that she not only defines, but describes the particular writer. But to curdle up a character into one noble word, to describe Shakespere, for instance, in such compass, what sun-syllable shall suffice; or must we renew Byron's wish?—

> Could I unbosom and embody now
> That which is most within me; could I wreak
> My thought upon expression!
> * * * * * *
> And that one word were Lightning, I would speak;
> But as it is, I live and die unheard,
> With a most voiceless thought, sheathing it as a sword.

Accordingly, this style of portraiture (shall we call it, as generally pursued, the thumb-nail style?) has seldom been prosecuted with much success. Ebenezer Elliott has a copy of verses after this fashion, not quite worthy of him. What, for example, does the following line tell us of Shelly?

"Ill-fated Shelly, vainly great and brave."

The same words might have been used about Sir John Moore, or Pompey. Mrs. Browning's verses are far superior. Sometimes, indeed, we see her clipping at a character, in order to fit it better into the place she has prepared for it. Sometimes she crams the half of an author into a verse, and has to leave out the rest for want of room. Sometimes over a familiar face she throws a veil of words and darkness. But often her one glance sees, and her one word shows, the very heart of an author's genius and character. Our readers may recur to the lines already quoted in reference to Lucretius, as one of her best portraitures. Altogether this style, as generally prosecuted, is a small one, not much better than anagrams and acrostics—ranks, indeed, not much higher than the ingenuity of the persons who transcribe the "Pleasures of Hope" on the breadth of a crown-piece, and should be resigned to such praiseworthy personages. By far the best specimen of it we remember, is the very clever list involving a running commentary of the works of Lord Byron, by Dr. M'Ginn; unless, indeed, it be Gay's *Catalogue Raisonné* of the portentous poems of Sir Richard Blackmore. Who shall embalm, in a similar way, the endless writings of James, Cooper, and Dickens?

"Lady Geraldine's Courtship," as a transcript from the "red-leaved tablets of the heart"—as a tale of love, set to the richest music—as a picture of the subtle workings, the stern reasonings, and the terrible bursts of passion—is above praise. How like a volcano does the poet's heart at length explode! How first all power is given him in the dreadful trance of silence, and then in the loosened tempest of speech! What a wild, fierce logic flows forth from his lips, in which, as in that of Lear's madness, the foundations of society seem to quiver like reeds, and every mount of conventionalism is no longer found; and in the lull of that tempest, and in the returning sunshine, how beautiful, how almost super-human, seem the figures of the two lovers, seen now and magnified through the mist of the reader's fast-flowing tears. It is a tale of successful love, and yet it melts you like a tragedy, and most melts you in the crisis of the triumph. On Geraldine we had gazed as on a star, with dry-eyed and distant admiration; but when that star dissolves in showers at the feet of her poet lover, we weep for very joy. Truly a tear is a sad yet beautiful thing; it constitutes a link connecting us with distant countries, nay, connecting us with distant worlds. Gravitation has, amid all her immensity, wrought no such lovely work as when she rounded a tear.

From this beautiful poem alone, we might argue Mrs. Browning's capacity for producing a great domestic tragedy. We might argue it, also, from the various peculiarities of her genius—her far vision into the springs of human conduct—into those viewless veins of fire, or of poison, which wind within the human heart—her sympathy with dark bosoms—the passion for truth, which pierces often the mist of her dimmer thought, like a flash of irrepressible lightning—her fervid temperament, always glowing round her intellectual sight—and her queen-like dominion over imagery and language. We think, meanwhile, that she has mistaken her sphere. In that rare atmosphere of transcendentalism which she has reached, she respires with difficulty, and with pain. She is not "native and endued" into that element. We would warn her off the giddy region, where tempests may blow, as well as clouds gather. Her recent sonnets in Blackwood are sad failures,—the very light in them is darkness—thoughts, in themselves as untangible as the films upon the window pane, are concealed in a woof of words, till their thin and shadowy meaning fades utterly away. Morbid weakness, she should remember, is not masculine strength. But can she not, through the rents in her cloudy tabernacle, discern, far below in the vale, fields of deep though homely beauty, where she might more gracefully and successfully exercise her exquisite genius? She has only to stoop to conquer. By and bye we may—using unprofanely an expression originally profane—be tempted to say, as we look up the darkened mountain, with its flashes of fire hourly waxing fewer and feebler, "As for this poetess, we wot not what has become of her."

While we are venturing on accents of warning, we might also remind her that there are in her style and manner peculiarities which a wicked world will persist in calling affectations. On the charge of affectation, generally, we are disposed to lay little stress—it is a charge so easily got up, and which can be so readily swelled into a cuckoo cry; it is often applied with such injustice, and it so generally attaches to singularities in manner, instead of insincerities in spirit and matter. But why should a true man, or a true woman, expose themselves needlessly to such a charge? We think in general, that true taste in this, as in matters of dress and etiquette, dictates conformity to the present mode, provided that does not unduly cramp the freedom and the force of natural motions. There is, indeed, a class of writers who are chartered libertines—who deal with language as they please—who toss it about as the autumn wind leaves; who, in the agony of their earnestness, or in the fury of their excitement, seize on rude and unpolished words, as Titans on rocks and mountains, and gain artistic triumphs in opposition to all the rules of art. Such are Wilson and Carlyle, and such were Burke and Chalmers. These men we must just take as they are, and be thankful for them as they are. We must just give them their own way. And whether such a permission be given or not, it is likely to be taken. "Canst thou draw out Leviathan with a hook, or his tongue with a cord which thou lettest down? will he make many supplications unto thee? will he speak soft words unto thee? Will the Unicorn be willing to serve thee, or abide by thy crib? canst thou bind him with his band in the furrow? will he harrow the valleys after thee? wilt thou believe that he will bring home thy seed, and gather into thy barn?" No: like the tameless creatures of the wilderness—like the chainless elements of the air—such men obey a law, and use a language, and follow a path of their own.

But this rare privilege Mrs. Browning cannot claim. And she owes it to herself and to her admirers to simplify her manner—to sift her diction of whatever is harsh and barbarous—to speak whatever truth is in her, in the clear articulate language of men—and to quicken, as she well can, the dead forms of ordinary verbiage, by the spirit of her own superabundant life. Then, but not till then, shall her voice break fully through the environment of coteries, cliques, and Magazine readers, and fall upon the ear of the general public, like the sound sweet in its sublimity, simple amid its complex elements, earthly in its cause and unearthly in its effect upon the soul, of a multitude of waters.

At present she seems to have seated herself, like a second witch of Endor, in a cave of mystery and vaticination—her "familiar," her gifted husband, a spirit well worthy of holding high consultation with herself; and who, like the famuli of ancient magicians, is equally adapted for humorous sport, and for serious thought and enterprise. We have in spirit been visiting her cavern, and have come back in the mood of prophesying. She has, if not taught, confirmed on us impressions, in reference to the future progress of Poetry, which we may close this lucubration by expressing.

That Poetry, notwithstanding its present degraded and enfeebled conditon, is not extinct, nor ever shall be extinguished, we may at once assume. As long as the sky is blue, and the rainbow beautiful—as long as man's heart is warm and the face of woman fair—Poetry, like seed-time and harvest, summer and winter, shall not cease. Nay, may we not apply to it the words of Campbell, applied originally to hope—

> Eternal Art, when yonder spheres sublime
> Pealed their first notes to sound the march of time,
> Thy joyous youth began, but not to fade:
> When all the sister planets have decayed,
> When wrapt in fire the realms of ether glow,
> And heaven's last thunder shakes the world below,
> Thou undismayed shall o'er the ruins smile,
> And light thy torch at Nature's funeral pile.

But in two things especially we perceive a provision being made in the present day, for the sustenance of the Poetic spirit, and for the further development of the Poetic faculty. One is the advancement of scientific truth. This, so far from being, as in the vulgar notion, adverse, is favourable to the progress of Poetry. Poetry, as a true thing, must be furthered by the advance of every other section of truth. Poetry can rule by division as well as by multiplication. Poetry stands ever ready to pour her forces through the smallest breaches which science makes. Nay, all the sciences are already employed, and shall yet be more solemnly enlisted into the service of Poetry. Botany goes forth into the fields and the woods, collects her fairest flowers, and binds with them a chaplet for the brow of Poetry. Conchology from the waters and from the sea shores gathers her loveliest shells, and hark! when uplifted to the ear of Poetry, "pleased, they remember their august abodes, and murmur as the ocean murmurs there." Anatomy lays bare the human frame—so fearfully and wonderfully made—and Poetry breathes back a portion of the spirit which that cold clay has lost, and its dry bones and withered sinews begin to live. Chemistry leads Poetry to the side of her furnace, and shows her transformations scarcely less marvellous and magical than her own. Geology lifts, with daring yet trembling hand, the "veil that is woven with night and with terror," from the history of past worlds, of cycles of ruin and renovation of creations and destroyings, and allows the eye of Poetry to look down in wonder, and to look up in fire. And Astronomy conducts Poetry to her observatory, and enjoys her amazement at the spectacle of that storm of suns, for ever blowing in the midnight sky. In the progress of astronomy, indeed, we see opening up the loftiest of conceivable fields for the poet. Who has hitherto adequately sung the wonders of the Newtonian—how much less of the Herschellian heavens? In prose alone (excepting, indeed, some splendid passages of the "Night Thoughts")—prose often kindling into poetry; the prose of Chalmers and of Nichol have these themes been worthily treated. But who is waiting, with his lyre in his eager hand, to be ready to sing the steep-rising glories of the Rossian heavens? We have the "Night Thoughts," which are a century behind the present stage of the science; but who shall write us a poem on "Night," worthy, in some measure, of vieing with that solemn yet spirit-stirring theme? Sooner or later it must be done. The Milton of Midnight must yet arise.

Another security for the future triumphs of Poetry is to be found in the spread of the Earnest Spirit. That such a spirit is coming over the age, men feel as by a general and irresistible intuition. There are, besides, many distinct evidences, and in nothing more so than in the present state of Poetry. Its clouds, long so light and gay, are rapidly charging with thunder, and from that black orchestra, when completely filled, what tones of power and music may be expected. All the leading poets of our later day—Tennyson, Browning, Mrs. Browning, Emerson, and Bayley—are avowing and acting on their belief that Poetry is no child's pastime, but one of the most serious of all serious things. This fills us with hope and high expectancy. It recalls to us a past period, when the names of prophet and of poet were the same; when bards were the real rulers; when the highest truth came forth in melody; when rhyme and reason had never been divorced. It points us forward, with sunbeam-finger, to a future day, when, in Emerson's fine language, "Poetry shall lead in a new age, as there is a star in the constellation Harp, which shall yet, astronomers tell us, be the polar star for a thousand years." We are, however slowly nearing that star! And, when men have become more enlightened, more welded into unity, more penetrated with high principle, more warmed with the emotion of love—when the earth has become more worthy of shining between Orion and the Great Bear—between Mars and Venus—there shall break forth from it a voice of song, holier far than Amphion's; sweeter than all Orphean measures; comparable to that fabled melody, by which the spheres were said to attune their motions; comparable, say rather, to that nobler song, wherewith, when Earth, a stranger, first appeared in our sky, she was saluted by her kindred orbs—"when the morning stars sang together, and all the Sons of God shouted for joy."

[George Gilfillan]

Works by RB

Luria and *A Soul's Tragedy*. *The New Quarterly Review*, January 1847, pp. 350–352.

AMONG THE PSYCHOLOGICAL poets of the day, it is impossible to pass over Robert Browning. His last ventures claim our attention—"Luria," and "a Soul's Tragedy,"—both of them strongly touched with the style mystical, but more than usually intelligible nevertheless. There has always been, and probably always will be, an order of poets, who, not looking out on nature for themselves, nor mixing in society on the common terms of fellowship, withdraw to the study of poetry as an abstract art, and refining on its means and ends, devote their efforts to the metrical manifestation of their own separate individuality; and then claim to be original, simply because of the unwonted mode of their proceeding, and the obscurity of the results. To this order of mind belongs Mr. Browning. Not only, like Walter Savage Landor, does he aim at the peculiar in his mode of thinking out and executing his subjects, but he has also invented a symbol language exclusively his own, which requires interpretation. The latter, of course, has been a work of time. His innovations on, and additions to, the English language, were at first comparatively few, though then sufficient to make the ordinary reader wonder what he meant; gradually, they became more numerous, so as to baffle the understanding of initiate students themselves. Hence, in his mystical poem of "Paracelsus," there were gleams and glances of sweet and serene beauty, making up bright rents in "the blanket of the dark," through which, like Heaven they "peeped through," as if to cry out to the frantic poet, "Hold! hold!" and cease to darken knowledge in that way any longer! Our bard, however, disregarded the admonition; he felt evidently that to be intelligible would be an impeachment on his understanding. Who would write for the many? Who, then, for the few? Who, then, for any body but himself? "Paracelsus," at any rate, though generally dim, was still sometimes clear. Accordingly, Mr. Browning undertook the tragedy of "Strafford," written upon the principle of there being scarcely a completed sentence in the whole poem. Mr. Macready, nevertheless, did marvels with these *disjecta membra*. We recollect the occasion well. Scene after scene we listened, and seemed to understand the business that passed before our eyes; but of the dialogue, beyond the general impression that words were spoken in different tones of passion and emphasis, we could make nothing. Every now and then a phrase or two flashed on the mind with a mysterious significance; then again all was blank, or the mere interlocution of suggestive fragments. We were fain to attribute the strange sensation we consequently experienced to Mr. Macready's asthmatic style of elocution, and amiably supposed that he had indulged it more than usual on the evening in question. On our arrival at home, however, the tragedy itself lay on our table. We took it up eagerly—read here—read there,—all the same! It was not the actor's mannerism,—it was the author's caprice!

Somehow, nevertheless, we contrived to make out what we thought the writer meant. Then came "Sordello!"—that baffled every attempt. There has yet been found no mind able to comprehend the author's purpose. The detail of the story—the character of the persons—what they do, what they say, though an account of both seems to be rendered—every thing, save the first line and the last, is as inexplicable as the riddle of the sphynx. Yet is there something in the mass of obscurity so singularly piquant, that while we retain the book in our possession, we are prompted, as we have already related, once and again to look into it, in the forlorn hope that the enigma has a solution.

Mr. Browning redeemed himself in the first number of his "Bells and Pomegranates." *Pippa Passes* is a beautiful poem; addressed undoubtedly to the highest class of readers, and not without its difficulties both in subject and treatment; but still fascinating and charming, in a peculiar sense, to the poetic student. "King Victor and King Charles," the next number, was less felicitous: the theme was undramatically rendered, so far as it was removed by its style and structure from popular sympathy. "The Return of the Druses" has fine passages, but is liable to the same objection in a still greater degree. "The Blot on the 'Scutcheon," produced at Drury Lane, was a melo-dramatic theme, poetically treated. Never was subject more domestic, more easy of execution for the stage; scarcely ever was failure more signal. Whatever may be the merits of Mr. Browning's dramas, they are unsuited for the theatre. His "Colombe's Birth-day," lately published, is pleasant reading—(the second or third time, if on the first or second perusal one has come to understand the plot), but displays the author's usual perversities, both in sentiment and diction.

After what we have said, we are happy to record that the "Luria" and "the Soul's Tragedy," now published, are generally intelligible. Their aim, however, is not so high, nor their scope so wide, as with the best of Mr. Browning's pieces. We have in "Luria" a modern Coriolanus, illtreated by his adopted country, deprived of his triumph in the moment of success; yet gently, patiently yielding to his sentence, preferring suicide to revenge. "The Soul's Tragedy" consists of two parts: the first written in blank verse, the second in prose; each in harmony with its particular subject. We have first the patriot conceiving all manner of fine things in behalf of his kind,—sensitive and sentimental to a degree of maniac extravagance; and next the same man, in possession of temporary power, guilty of all the enormities against which his indignant eloquence had been previously directed. Both these are founded on notions obvious and familiar enough; but they may be read with facility, and this is something, where the composition is Mr. Browning's, to begin with. We have left ourselves no room for extracts; but it is not by extracts that Mr. Browning can be judged. They may mislead, but must fail to inform. He who would appreciate Mr. Browning's poetry, must first learn to admire. A hard condition! yet one which will amply repay the learner; for Mr. Browning, notwithstanding his perversity and obscurity, is in the first class of poets. He soars out of sight, indeed; but it is the spectator's weakness that he cannot follow him. Would the poet, mighty as he is, condescend to public appreciation, no man would be more successful. There is no doubt of Mr. Browning's genius; but genius, to be appreciated, should be amiable, in all the humility of true pride.

PARACELSUS; SORDELLO; AND BELLS AND POMEGRANATES. *Revue des Deux Mondes*, 15 August 1847, pp. 627–653.

LA CRITIQUE ANGLAISE applique parfois à la poésie des formules et des raisonnemens tout-à-fait propres à effaroucher les muses: elle s'est, par exemple, demandé compte, un beau matin, du discrédit où les poètes étaient tombés après avoir, durant les vingt-cinq premières années de ce siècle, joui d'une vogue et d'une popularité sans exemple. Cette révolution imprévue a été discutée tout aussi sérieusement et à peu de chose près de même qu'aurait pu l'être une crise tout à coup survenue dans le trafic des cotons ou des fers, «De 1800 à 1825, lisions-nous, il y a douze ans déjà, dans la *Revue d'Édimbourg*, il y avait pour la poésie des consommateurs en grand nombre et pleins d'ardeur. La demande excédait l'offre: la production était stimulée par un placement presque certain; car, bonne ou médiocre, toute poésie s'écoulait. Depuis la mort de Byron, cette branche du commerce national n'a fait que décroitre: elle est frappée maintenant d'une déplorable stérilité. Vainement le marché s'encombre, et les vers sont au rabais. Les transactions sont de plus en plus rares, les acheteurs de plus en plus froids. A qui la faute?»

La faute n'en est probablement à personne. Il y a dans la vie des peuples, comme dans celle des individus, un concours de circonstances qui les rendent plus ou moins sensibles à telle ou telle excitation de l'intelligence. La France, par exemple, tant que les événemens politiques ont eu quelque grandeur, n'a pas quitté du regard, d'abord les clubs tumultueux, puis les frontières toujours plus lointaines; l'éloquence révolutionnaire, les fanfares impériales, fermaient nos oreilles à toute pacifique harmonie. C'est à grand'peine que M. de Châteaubriand ou Mme de Staël triomphaient parfois de cette indifférence profonde que l'on témoignait pour les enseignemens ou les plaisirs littéraires. A la même époque, la Grande-Bretagne,—bien que profondément et sérieusement engagée dans les conflits européens,—devait à sa tranquillité intérieure un progrès très marqué, un élan très vif vers les nobles délassemens de l'esprit. C'est une chose merveilleuse à lire que les grandes *revues* anglaises pendant les premières années du xixe siècle. En 1803, tandis que l'invasion menaçante semble devoir ne laisser place à d'autres soucis que ceux de la prise d'armes nationale, les Aristarques d'Édimbourg débattent à loisir le mérite des poèmes de Delille, comparent l'*Amadis de Gaule* de Southey à l'*Amadis de Gaule* de Stewart Rose, étudient la prose capricieuse de Lichtenberg et discutent la biographie de Chaucer par William Godwin. De l'Europe en feu, de la France triomphante et de son altier capitaine, à peine en est-il question, çà et là, incidemment, lorsqu'il faut contredire quelques-uns des plus grossiers mensonges inventés contre nous par la presse tory. Plus tard, et en présence d'événemens qui bouleversent le monde, vous retrouvez la même indifférence pour les agitations extérieures. En 1814, s'ils daignent jeter les yeux de l'autre côté du détroit, ces fiers insulaires n'y voient d'intéressant que la correspondance littéraire et philosophique de Grimm et de Diderot.—Qui donc alors, si ce n'est un *reviewer* anglais, pouvait s'occuper de Diderot et de Grimm?—En Angleterre même, leurs grandes affaires étaient *le Corsaire* et *la Fiancée d'Abydos*, ou bien encore *le Clair de lune, la Fille du Doge, Ariadne*, chefs-d'œuvre oubliés de lord Thurlow. Cette apathie politique du peuple anglais, ce calme des esprits, cette attention profonde accordée aux poètes dans ce coin du monde, à l'heure même où Wellington et Castlereagh faisaient prévaloir l'intérêt britannique dans les grandes assemblées de la diplomatie européenne, forment, à notre avis, un contraste imposant et curieux.

C'en est un encore, en sens inverse, que le déclin de l'influence poétique dix ans plus tard, alors que la paix règne partout, que les événemens s'apaisent, que la vie politique est nulle et se révèle à peine, de temps à autre, par quelques commérages parlementaires. Ne semble-t-il pas que l'heure est alors favorable pour scander les strophes harmonieuses, et se livrer à tous les rêves de l'imagination? Platon luimême ne s'humaniserait-il pas en ce moment pour cette «chose légère, volage, sacrée,» qu'on appelle un poète? N'est-il pas permis, lorsque l'état est prospère, les lois obéies, l'armée au repos, de se laisser entraîner par cet aimant victorieux et divin, derrière lequel se forme la chaîne oblique «des danseurs, des chanteurs, des choristes, qui secondent les séductions de la Muse?» Mais, que voulez-vous? depuis vingt-cinq ans, on se tait, on écoute, on admire, et peut-on admirer, écouter, se taire éternellement? Après l'enthousiasme, la satiété, la satiété même injuste. Puis, l'admiration est-elle encore possible, lorsque, Walter Scott détrôné, Byron mort, les lakistes devenus vieux, il ne reste plus dans le ciel poétique que des astres secondaires, *stella minores*, beaux-esprits brillans et bien doués sans doute, mais sans excellence, sans originalité, sans génie: Rogers, Campbell, Barry Cornwall, Milman, et tant d'autres?

Cependant, si la poésie moderne avait eu un caractère plus précis, et si ses progrès avaient été du même ordre que ceux de la science, elle n'eût pas été sujette à ce triste retour. Par malheur, elle suivait une tendance directement opposée à la marche des esprits. Plus ceux-ci devenaient positifs et sérieux, plus ils se montraient épris de la vérité sous toutes ses formes, et plus il semblait que les poètes eussent à cœur de méconnaître cette vérité, de la remplacer par leurs caprices arbitraires, de substituer la violence, l'exagération, l'enivrement individuel et capricieux, aux lumineuses et sereines inspirations de la raison universelle. Tandis que les mœurs se calmaient, s'épuraient, les poètes faisaient appel aux emportemens furieux de la passion, aux excitations des sens. Le niveau des intelligences s'élevait rapidement: ils semblaient prendre à tâche de méconnaître ce glorieux phénomène et de s'abaisser, par l'abus des images matérielles, par l'énergie triviale du langage, par le mépris de toute grace et de tout raffinement, au niveau de leurs plus incultes et de leurs plus grossiers lecteurs. Leur incontestable talent ne servait qu'à évoquer des fantômes auxquels, pour quelques instans, ils savaient prêter l'éclat, le mouvement, la vie, mais dont l'illusoire splendeur s'éteignait, comme celle d'un rêve, aux premiers rayons du jour, au premier éveil de la réflexion. La nouveauté paradoxale de ces créations fantastiques excitait un facile enthousiasme, mais ne supportait pas l'examen. Ainsi s'explique leur vogue immense et le prompt soubresaut de l'opinion, lorsqu'elle s'est rendu compte des prestiges qui l'avaient égarée.

Dans la préface d'un drame remarquable, écrit en vue d'une réaction décisive, et par un poète qui s'est conquis un rang distingué dans le mouvement actuel de la poésie anglaise,* nous trouvons un jugement sévère sur ces monarques littéraires si brusquement découronnés.

«Ce qui les caractérise, c'est une fervente sensibilité, une grande prodigalité d'images, la vigueur et la beauté du style, la facilité, l'adresse de la versification, le talent de lui communiquer, par un rhythme accentué fortement, cette espèce de mélodie qui caresse le mieux l'oreille inexpérimentée. On trouve chez eux ce que la poésie a de plus attrayant: chaleur intérieure, ornementation brillante; et si l'admiration qu'ils excitaient n'avait pas eu pour résultat de rendre le public indifférent à des qualités plus hautes, plus sérieuses et plus variées, on n'aurait pu, sans injustice, la juger excessive; mais en s'abandonnant ainsi, sans aucun frein, à une poésie exclusivement voluptueuse, n'en était-on pas venu à méconnaître ce qu'il y a d'intellectuel et d'immortel dans cet art sublime? J'avoue que telle est ma pensée, et j'aurais peine à croire que le goût public n'ait dû subir une fâcheuse altération, lorsque les chefs-d'œuvre du passé se sont trouvés tout à coup sans lecteurs. Nous y revenons aujourd'hui; mais il a fallu vingt-cinq ans pour nous rendre ce culte proscrit.....»

M. Taylor poursuit en signalant les plus essentiels défauts des poètes modernes. Il leur reproche l'abus des images, l'absence d'observation et de sagesse expérimentale. Au lieu d'étudier la vie, ils planent dans des régions inhabitées qu'ils peuplent de leur orgueil insatiable, de leur personnalité ambitieuse. Tout ce qui est simple, vrai, raisonnable, leur demeure étranger. Entre leurs mains, la poésie n'agit plus guère que sur l'imagination et sur les sens. «Le langage même qu'ils parlent est en désaccord absolu avec les conditions morales où l'homme doit être placé pour faire usage de son libre entendement. Les réalités de la nature et ce qu'elles suggèrent d'idées justes, mêlées à cet impétueux courant de sentimens exaltés et de tableux surchargés de couleurs, choqueraient par leur froideur inopportune... Ces fantaisies ailées ne peuvent prendre pied sur la terre où nous marchons, ni respirer l'air qui fait vivre le commun des hommes.»

Il est naturel que toute émotion factice se dissipe promptement, que tout prestige dure peu. Lord Byron, avant d'avoir parcouru sa courte et orageuse carrière, était en quelque sorte las de lui-même, et ses succès,—

---

*Voyez la préface de *Philip van Artevelde*, drame de M. Henri Taylor.

pour lesquels il n'est pas certain qu'il ne méprisât point ses lecteurs,—lui avaient laissé une sorte de remords. Lord Byron cependant, s'il n'était pas un philosophe accompli, possédait à plus forte dose que beaucoup de ses successeurs les plus précieuses et les plus solides qualités de l'intelligence. Jamais sa logique ne lui fait absolument défaut; jamais il ne se laisse aller à ces aberrations fantastiques, qui trahissent à la fois l'ignorance profonde et la vanité sans remède de ses imitateurs les plus heureux. Sa misanthropie était plutôt une affectation qu'une faiblesse, une infirmité réelle; elle lui laissait une vive sympathie pour les hommes en général, et pour les idées qui font la force et la gloire des sociétés modernes. Ce talent, auquel, pour être complet, manquaient seulement les bases solides et une critique moins indulgente, aurait pu mûrir avec les années, et se transformer en s'élevant à des hauteurs qu'il n'a point touchées; tel qu'une mort prématurée l'a laissé, il a exercé une fatale influence sur la poésie contemporaine. Byron seul, il est vrai, n'avait pas fait tout le mal, et M. Taylor signale un autre brillant corrupteur du goût public:

«Imagination plus puissante et plus expansive, Shelley était inférieur à Byron par l'absence de ces qualités pratiques, de cette habileté littéraire, sans lesquelles,—n'en déplaise aux partisans de l'inspiration pure,—il ne peut guère exister, surtout à notre époque, de poésie achevée...Trahi par le désir de perfectionner les moindres détails, de donner à chaque vers isolé une valeur indépendante, à chaque mot une puissance, une splendeur particulières, Shelley s'efforçait d'ailleurs d'ôter toute réalité aux phénomènes naturels dont il se constituait le peintre, et de nous les montrer tels que jamais nos organes visuels ne les ont embrassés. Il écrivait ou semblait écrire d'après ce principe, que nul sujet ne saurait se prêter à la poésie, si, décomposé au préalable, déclassé, isolé de tous ses rapports ordinaires, enlevé à son ordre naturel, il n'arrivait devant le lecteur à l'état de vision et de chimère. Tout poète, à son gré, devrait être un voyant extatique, un fascinateur éblouissant... De là ces vers qui produisent sur l'imagination l'effet d'une liqueur enivrante, mais ne laissent après eux ni un souvenir distinct, ni une impression profonde. Contemplez dans tout son éclat, sur la fin d'un jour d'été, l'horizon embrasé par les derniers feux du soleil, ou lisez une de ces vagues et rayonnantes conceptions, l'enseignement et le profit seront les mêmes. Dès que vous fermez le livre, dès que l'astre a disparu, le prestige cesse, les fantômes s'effacent: l'impression produite sur la mémoire survit à peine à l'impression produite sur les sens.»

En somme, les principaux griefs de la critique et de l'opinion contre une école poétique dont le succès fut immense, et dont on commence à scruter les productions avec une sévérité inattendue, ces griefs, vivement formulés par M. Taylor, peuvent se résumer ainsi: peu de philosophie, peu de vérité; une exaltation factice; une grande richesse de formes servant à déguiser la pauvreté, la puérilité des sujets; nulle observation, nulle connaissance des hommes. Le talent employé à éblouir, à séduire, et non à faire prévaloir des idées justes, à communiquer la lumière d'une haute expérience, c'est là ce que reprochent à Byron, à Shelley, leurs successeurs moins illustres. N'y aurait-il pas dans ces jugemens sévères quelques leçons dont, chez nous, on peut déjà comprendre la portée? N'est-il pas curieux de voir se produire, chez nos voisins comme chez nous, la réaction du bon sens outragé de la raison méconnue, contre les triomphes passagers de l'imagination déréglée, du faux goût érigé en système?

En essayant d'apprécier Alfred Tennyson, nous avons indiqué pour ainsi dire le premier symptôme de cette rébellion, le début de la nouvelle génération poétique.* Cette génération cherche l'originalité dans le simple, elle n'admet que les idées les plus naturelles, et ne les veut relever que par les délicatesses du style. Par malheur, nous l'avons fait pressentir, Tennyson, à peu près nul comme inventeur, n'est artiste remarquable que par l'exquise élégance de son style. Il communique bien ainsi, par le choix, l'harmonie et la couleur des mots, une sorte de nouveauté aux idées les plus triviales, mais cette originalité spéciale ne lui appartient même pas tout entière. Il n'a pas découvert dans les entrailles du globe un métal inconnu. Fondeur habile, de plusieurs alliages anciens il a formé une composition nouvelle qui charme les connaisseurs par ses reflets et sa sonorité particulière. Quelquefois son style rappelle Wordsworth, quelquefois Leigh Hunt ou Charles Lamb, plus souvent Keats, et non-seulement Keats, mais les anciens rimeurs dont celui-ci avait été l'écho, Ben-Jonson et Spenser par exemple, ou bien encore Herrick et l'école métaphysique, et même, en quelques endroits, comme un involontaire hommage, lord Byron, tout détrôné qu'il est. Tel est le talent, nous n'oserions dire ce génie.

En 1835, c'est-à-dire cinq ans après que le succès de Tennyson eut attesté, chez le public anglais, la renaissance du goût poétique, deux nouveaux candidats firent appel à ce sentiment régénéré. L'un était Henri Taylor, dont nous venons d'indiquer les opinions et les doctrines; l'autre, Robert Browning, que nous voudrions aujourd'hui faire connaître.

Tous deux débutèrent par un drame, et tous deux par un drame conçu avec des idées et des proportions qui lui fermaient la scène. On a élevé, nous le savons, contre cet ordre de productions, des objections fort spécieuses. On l'a considéré comme un monstre hybride qui, créé pour ainsi dire à deux fins, ne saurait suffire ni à l'une ni à l'autre. Si vous voulez écrire un drame, pourquoi vous priver de la concision, de l'enchaînement logique, de l'intérêt puissant que cette forme possède lorsqu'elle se produit avec toutes les conditions d'existence, la vitalité scénique, le prestige de la déclamation, des costumes et du décor? Si c'est un poème, pourquoi vous charger d'entraves inutiles, pourquoi vous assujettir à ces divisions appropriées aux besoins du théâtre, à l'attention distraite du spectateur? Pourquoi renoncer à l'intervention directe du poète, qui, parlant en son nom, a toute liberté de conter et de décrire, tandis que les personnages fictifs n'ont, à cet égard, que des droits fort limités par la vraisemblance? «La poésie dramatique, a dit Bacon, est comme l'histoire réduite en tableaux,—*veluti historia spectabilis*.» Qu'est-ce qu'un drame composé pour des lecteurs?—A ces vigoureux argumens ne répondrait-on pas, au besoin, par des raisons équivalentes, et aussi par des précédens incontestables? Ne peut-on alléguer, par exemple, que les conceptions scéniques se refusent obstinément à montrer dans toute leur pompe, dans toute leur énergie, dans toute leur originalité, certains spectacles, certains faits essentiellement dramatiques? Ne peut-on supposer telle ou telle passion dont tout l'art du monde ne déguiserait pas l'horreur à mille auditeurs réunis dans un théâtre, et qui, sans doute, y soulèverait une tempête de réprobation, tandis que chacun de ces méticuleux spectateurs, rentré chez lui, seul â seul avec un drame écrit, en subira sans révolte la terrible influence? Serait-il trop hardi d'affirmer que, dans l'état actuel de notre civilisation, il existe deux publics très distincts: l'un, celui des théâtres, en garde contre toute innovation essentielle et dérouté par les moindres témérités; l'autre, en revanche, celui des salons et des bibliothèques, auquel le vaudeville, le drame de tous les jours, ne procurent aucune émotion? S'il en est ainsi, trouvez bon que, pour ce dernier public, le poète invente des plaisirs plus raffinés, plus composites, exigeant un autre degré d'instruction, un jugement plus libre, une attention plus intense. On a plus d'une fois tenté cette épreuve; on a réussi. Que répondre à ce simple fait?

Le *Paracelsus* de Browning est évidemment destiné à ces lecteurs d'élite; encore exige-t-il d'eux une abnégation particulière et un plus complet abandon de tout ce qui constitue la curiosité dramatique. Ce drame, en effet, qui remplit un volume, n'a guère qu'un acteur, en ce sens du moins que le très petit nombre de personnages inventés pour donner la réplique à ce héros solitaire n'ont aucune importance et ne détournent en rien l'attention qu'il commande. Cette attention n'a guère qu'un mobile, toujours le même. Nous assistons aux angoisses d'un homme, ou plutôt d'un être abstrait, qui aspire d'abord après la science, puis, désabusé d'elle, après l'amour, et, faute d'avoir à temps combiné ces deux grands principes de la force humaine, meurt sans avoir réalisé le vaste dessein d'éclairer et d'affranchir ses semblables.

Cette donnée admise, pourquoi le poète a-t-il choisi Paracelse? Pourquoi exalter aux proportions d'un philosophe régénérateur du monde ce médecin vagabond, ce chimiste aventureux dont l'*archæum magnum*, union symbolique de trois principes, est relégué depuis long-temps parmi les inventions les plus contestables de la philosophie mystique? Un poète moins décidé à faire abstraction complète de la réalité eût reculé devant les vulgarités de cette vie, qui fut celle d'un charlatan plutôt que celle d'un penseur et d'un philanthrope sublime. Paracelse, avec sa tunique rouge, son épée Azoth dans le pommeau de laquelle il cachait un démon familier, son ivrognerie bien constatée, ses fanfaronnades, ses déréglemens, résiste, ce semble, à l'idéalisation. Tout autre philosophe de la même époque,—Giordano Bruno, par exemple, Campanella, Jean Reuchlin ou Agrippa de Nettersheim,—se prêtait mieux à la singulière combinaison de Browning. Leur préférer un homme que le martyre a épargné, qui, après avoir capté l'admiration de la foule par de véritables tours de passe-passe, a mérité qu'elle désertât la chaire où il montait la tête alourdie par le vin, c'est affecter tout d'abord, ce nous semble, un trop complet dédain pour l'histoire; c'est tenir trop peu de compte de ce que chacun sait, de ce que l'on sait soimême, et se priver ainsi de la confiance qu'inspirent au lecteur un choix bien fait, une conception saine, une vue nette et claire du sujet que l'on veut traiter.

A part ce défaut capital, et en ne tenant compte du récit que comme d'un mythe à plaisir inventé, le personnage de Paracelse, moins sympathique, moins vrai que celui de Faust, est une création assez imposante. L'enthousiasme, le dédain, les anxiétés du doute, les joies de la certitude, le sentiment de la puissance intellectuelle, le désespoir qu'un grand esprit doit ressentir quand il se reconnaît au-dessous de la haute mission qu'il s'était donnée, voilà les péripéties de ce *monodrame* singulier, ses élémens de variété, ses moyens de soutenir l'intérêt. Or, il n'appartient qu'à un

---

*Voyez dans la livraison du 1ᵉʳ mai 1847 l'étude sur Alfred Tennyson.

vrai talent de dissimuler le défaut complet d'action, l'uniformité du thème, l'inévitable langueur de ces divagations égoïstes. Paracelse, traitant avec toute la rigueur didactique du professorat les sujets les plus ardus de la métaphysique, ne se fait pardonner l'aridité de ses définitions que par une extrême vigueur de style, et en multipliant les plus riches nuances sur la trame de ses interminables raisonnemens. Souvent même cette verve d'argumentation s'élève à une véritable éloquence, comme dans le discours que tient Paracelse à son confident Festus et à Michal, la fiancée de cet ami dévoué, lorsqu'ils veulent le dissuader de quitter Wurtzbourg. Tous deux l'ont accusé de mépriser le passé, de trop compter sur lui-même et sur sa force isolée de tout enseignement:

«Je comprends vos tendres craintes; mais ce n'est point à la légère que j'ai cessé de croire à ces trésors si haut prisés par vous, aux travaux, aux préceptes de l'antique sagesse. La vérité est en nous. Quoi que vous en puissiez croire, elle ne nous vient pas du dehors; il est un centre dans chacun de nous où elle séjourne splendide et complète. Notre chair grossière enserre de murailles massives et redoublées cette perception sincère et parfaite qui est le vrai. L'erreur est le résultat de ces liens de la matière qui la surchargent et l'aveuglent; savoir consiste plutôt à dégager, en lui ménageant une issue, cette lumière emprisonnée qu'à donner accès aux prétendues clartés du dehors. Guettez de près la démonstration, la naissance d'une vérité; vous remonterez aisément à cette source intime où se cache la lumière amoncelée, que le hasard en extrait rayon par rayon. Le hasard, dis-je, car si nous ignorons encore d'où ces rayons viennent, de même nous méconnaissons ce qui leur ouvre les portes du cachot obscur. Bien des hommes ont vieilli parmi les livres, et sont morts endurcis dans leur ignorance aveugle, dont l'insouciante jeunesse avait promis ce que n'ont pas tenu leurs labeurs presque séculaires. Et tout au contraire, il est arrivé souvent à tel promeneur d'automne, aussi libre d'esprit que les insectes bourdonnant au soleil, d'émettre une sublime vérité,—produit mystérieux, spontané, tel que le promontoire de nuages sorti tout à coup des vapeurs invisibles.*»

Ce passage est doublement remarquable en ce qu'il n'indique pas seulement l'ordre de pensées où nous transporte *Paracelsus*, mais semble faire partie du programme poétique de Browning. Lui aussi, contempteur hardi du passé, chercheur de formes nouvelles, lui aussi se fiera surtout à l'inspiration intérieure et dédaignera de la soumettre aux préceptes d'une rhétorique surannée. Bien décidé à se passer de lecteurs s'il n'en trouve pas dont la croyance en lui soit complète, il ne court pas au-devant de l'admiration, il ne brigue pas les suffrages, et, plutôt que de courtiser les vivans, il évoquera autour de lui un auditoire de spectres. C'est en effet par une évocation de fantômes qu'il débute, lorsque, mécontent peut-être de l'accueil fait à *Paracelsus*, il écrit son second poème intitulé *Sordello:*

«Quiconque le voudra bien peut entendre raconter l'histoire de Sordello. Histoire ou conte, qu'importe? Qui me croit sur parole verra cet homme suivre sa fortune, tout comme moi, jusqu'au bout. Vous n'avez pour cela qu'à me croire. Me croirez-vous?

Voici Vérone. Mais, avant tout, laissez-moi vous avertir que, libre dans mon choix, je n'aurais pas pris un rôle dans cette histoire qui pouvait être si bien contée par le héros lui-même, l'auteur s'effaçant de bonne grace et laissant à chaque auditeur le soin de compléter l'œuvre à son gré. En effet, si fier que je puisse être en voyant, au fond de ses vastes abîmes, le passé diviser ses flots écumeux pour laisser surnager, de tant de mémoires englouties, celle-ci, que ma prédilection aura sauvée, cependant, après ce premier triomphe, je prendrai grand plaisir à suivre, comme le plus inaverti des spectateurs, et sans savoir un mot de plus que vous, les phases de ce récit merveilleux. Il sied pourtant à quiconque risque un sujet nouveau, et crée de toutes pièces des hommes d'une race inconnue, de les produire lui-même, après avoir pris soin de crayonner le nom de chaque personnage à la bordure du costume qu'il porte, et de se tenir à côté d'eux, l'habit bariolé sur le dos, la longue baguette à la main, en bon et fidèle exhibiteur.

Donc, cette fois, me voici vous faisant face, amis appelés des quatre coins du monde, braves gens tombés du ciel ou vomis par l'enfer pour écouter l'histoire que je me propose de dire. Et, convenez-en, les poètes ont beau jeu à manier habilement la drague qui leur fournit, faute d'auditeurs vivans, les morts retirés du fin fond des ondes. On nargue ainsi le Destin, qui prétendrait vous imposer silence parce qu'il peut vous refuser de vrais yeux à faire briller, de vrais cœurs à torturer, de vrais fronts à dérider autour de vous. Je sais, pour ma part, quelque chose de ses rigueurs; mais il est un pays où il perd ses droits, où beaucoup de sympathies me sont acquises.—Beaucoup? me demande maint railleur.—Les voici, mécréant!—Admirez la foule que je rassemble; sur ces visages ranimés vous ne trouverez guère l'empreinte funeste du trépas. Il n'a rien moins fallu, toutefois, pour les décider à goûter encore l'air des vivans, que le désir bien naturel de voir leurs successeurs à l'œuvre.—Salut à mon auditoire défunt!—ils s'asseoient les uns près des autres, chaque spectre tâchant de paraître aussi peu mort que possible, frères et frères mêlant leur froide haleine. Critique à l'esprit subtil, je te vois d'ici près de….. Mais n'allons pas troubler un seul de ces miraculeux spectateurs, ni fâcher la Mort, qui me les prête à grand'peine.

Amis!—je parle aux vivans pour tout de bon,—n'allez pas, sur cette évocation funèbre, croire qu'un éloge judicieux me fâche, moi qui guetterai au contraire toute occasion d'exciter vos caressantes approbations, et cela, crainte de vous voir endormis.—Maintenant, Vérone, il est temps de te montrer, etc.*»

Rien ne donne mieux que cette entrée en matière, l'idée d'un parti pris audacieux, d'une indépendance hautaine, d'une fantaisie qui se proclame reine et maîtresse, dût-elle manquer de sujets et trôner dans la solitude. Faudrait-il néanmoins la prendre au mot? Un poète quelconque peut-il de bonne foi se montrer insensible à l'approbation contemporaine, se résigner à n'être applaudi que par des fantômes? Que d'autres l'admettent. Pour nous, après le mille sorties de nos poètes cavaliers, nous savons ce que valent ces apostrophes, ces airs dégagés, ces désintéressemens d'emprunt, étalés à grand bruit pour faire effet.

C'est encore une ressource de mise en scène que l'obscurité calculée. Browning en abuse quelquefois. Il l'a outrée dans *Sordello*. Nous ne saurions dire comment se passent exactement les choses chez nos voisins;

---

*I understand these fond fears just express'd, etc.
(*Paracelsus*, p. 36 et 37.)

*Who will, may hear Sordello's story told, etc.
(SORDELLO, *Book the first*.)

mais, dans ce bon pays de France, nous n'oserions garantir qu'il se trouvât six personnes, des plus curieuses et des plus alléchées par la difficulté, capables de s'appliquer à démêler, derrière les nuages dont il a pris plaisir à l'entourer, le roman décousu de Browning. A quoi vont, cependant, ces ténèbres volontaires? Et pour qui ces ombres multipliées à dessein? Le vulgaire, auquel le poète le plus sublime n'est pas dispensé de songer, s'arrête épouvanté devant une si longue énigme. Les connaisseurs, depuis long-temps au fait des artifices littéraires, savent bien que la force et la clarté, la pleine lumière et la sincère beauté, vont ordinairement de compagnie, que les natures incomplètes, les idées fausses, les drames invraisemblables, comme tout ce qui est suspect, douteux, de mauvais aloi, recherchent le demi-jour et ses illusions. Ceux-ci ne tomberont pas dans le piége. Restent, il est vrai, quelques *dilettanti* prétentieux qui, s'attachant volontiers aux choses bizarres, aux génies incompris, et tout fiers d'avoir un goût à eux, feignent de se passionner pour ce qui a rebuté le plus grand nombre des juges. Nous ne savons quel prix leurs suffrages peuvent avoir aux yeux de certains écrivains épris d'une gloire exceptionnelle, mais il nous paraîtrait sage de ne les briguer jamais. Tel applaudissement équivaut pour nous à une attestation de mauvais goût, et un homme bien avisé ne se consolera jamais de ces approbations à contresens.

L'époque choisie par Browning pour y placer son second récit semblerait présager un tableau violent des mœurs italiennes au moyen-âge. C'est le moment où l'empire allemand est aux prises avec les communes confédérées de l'Italie, combattant au nom du pape et de l'indépendance nationale. Chacun a pu se faire une idée de ces luttes acharnées entre guelfes et gibelins, où la bourgeoisie des villes, excitée par les évêques, guerroyait contre les nobles, tour à tour soutenus ou réprimés par leur impérial suzerain. On a lu, dans l'érudit ouvrage de Sismondi, sinon dans les vers de Gunther ou dans la chronique d'Otton de Frisingue, les horribles détails de ces révoltes populaires, de ces tyranniques vengeances, qui peu à peu avaient effacé partout l'idée du droit et donné toute licence au crime fier de sa force. En déplorant ces épouvantables vicissitudes, on ne peut en méconnaître le caractère vivant, animé, pittoresque. Ces cités qui marchent au combat, emmenant avec elles, en guise de palladium, leur *carroccio* surmonté de l'image du Christ en croix, et l'étendard de la ville entre deux voiles blanches; ces empereurs qui reviennent de la croisade, suivis de bandes sarrasines, et lancent les soldats de Mahomet contre les troupes du pape; Rome, s'efforçant de renaître à la vie républicaine, et plaçant un patrice à la tête du sénat; les noms même de tous ces prétendans qui se heurtent et se mêlent dans l'arène sanglante: Barberousse, Henri-le-Lion, Ezzelin-le-Féroce, donnent un cachet singulier à ces guerres acharnées. Ajoutez que tout alors est symbole, image, et amuse l'œil. Va-t-on réclamer justice, on se présente portant la croix. L'empereur, entrant en Italie, devait faire halte dans la plaine de Roncaglia: tous les chevaliers tenant fief de l'empereur, convoqués par le héraut de la cour, devaient se trouver dans la plaine autour d'un bouclier attaché à un poteau de bois; tous, ainsi que leurs feudataires nobles, devaient garder le prince pendant la première nuit. Le lendemain on faisait un appel, et quiconque avait manqué à ce devoir d'honneur était dépouillé de son fief. On n'en finirait pas à énumérer toutes les curiosités de ce temps; toutefois nous ne conseillerons jamais de les aller chercher dans Browning. Ce n'est pas qu'il les ignore: son érudition est au contraire surabondante; mais elle porte sur des minuties et,—ce qui est un grave défaut,—elle néglige toute sorte d'éclaircissemens, supposant à chaque lecteur une science spéciale qu'il est bien rare de rencontrer, même chez les plus instruits. C'est ainsi que dès le début, et en quelques vers seulement, Browning met en jeu une multitude de personnages, sans prendre garde que, faute de quelques explications nécessaires, ils n'auront aucun caractère ni aucun sens. Le comte de Saint-Boniface, seigneur de Vérone, Azzo d'Este, Taurello Salinguerra de Ferrare, Ezzelin Romano, l'empereur, le pape, la ligue lombarde, font irruption sur la scène, et c'est seulement avec le plus grand effort d'attention que l'on parvient à discerner leurs rapports d'alliance ou de guerre, leur rôle dans les discussions politiques de l'Italie. Avec cette méthode de donner tête baissée *in medias res*, on déroute la pénétration et la bonne volonté les plus dévouées. Ce cliquetis de noms inconnus, de faits oubliés ou nouveaux, emportés dans le courant d'un vers rapide, concis, sautillant, obscur, est vraiment effrayant. Si vous persistez, nonobstant ces premières difficultés, à chaque page vous rencontrerez de nouveaux personnages, de nouvelles allusions, de nouvelles énigmes, et pas une halte, pas un résumé, rien qui vous permette de reprendre haleine, de récapituler, de classer les élémens confus de cette épopée inextricable. Le style est à l'avenant du récit. Chaque phrase, prise à part, est comme un petit chaos où les nuages se pressent, passent les uns devant les autres, s'enchevêtrent, se brisent, s'effacent. L'architecture a eu jadis des caprices analogues: elle aimait à compliquer la distribution intérieure des maisons féodales, à cacher de sombres cabinets dans les détours de tortueux corridors, à creuser dans l'épaisseur obscure du granit des labyrinthes sans issue. Alors, du moins, ces fantaisies étaient en rapport avec les mœurs. La tyrannie avait besoin d'impénétrables recès, d'oubliettes aveugles; menacée et soupçonneuse, il lui fallait de secrètes issues pour se dérober aux assassins, de sonores réduits où les complots à voix basse avaient des échos imprévus. De nos jours, cependant, à quoi serviraient tant de précautions? Aussi ne songe-t-on guère qu'à se ménager l'air le plus pur, la plus abondante lumière, et l'art, selon nous, trouve encore assez de ressources dans la recherche savante du bien-être inconnu à nos devanciers. Pourquoi n'appliquerait-on pas à la poésie cette règle salutaire du progrès? Et ne lui doit-on pas de l'avertir quand on la voit se méprendre à ce point, qu'elle croit grandir dans les ténèbres, gagner en force ce qu'elle perd en simplicité, dominer parce qu'elle rebute?

Du reste, à propos de *Sordello*, Browning a reçu du public une leçon sévère. Ceux-là même qui avaient salué le plus volontiers les promesses de *Paracelsus* se refusèrent à en voir l'accomplissement dans un mélodrame prétentieusement rimé, qui avait pour mérite supérieur l'attrait d'un logographe en six chants. On avait lu vingt fois, plus clairement et plus agréablement écrite, l'histoire de cet enfant royal que l'on élève sous un faux nom pour le dérober aux dangers de sa naissance; heureux tant qu'il végète dans une favorable obscurité, misérable et frappé de mort quand les événemens l'arrachent à son humble fortune, à ses rêves de poète, pour le mêler aux terribles conflits de l'ambition politique. Il n'y avait ni dans ce sujet trivial, ni dans la bizarrerie des moyens employés pour le rajeunir, de quoi balancer les fatigues d'une lecture pénible. Ce poème n'obtint d'autre succès que de rallier autour de Browning une petite église de novateurs à tout prix, lesquels s'obstinèrent à voir en lui un descendant direct de Shakespeare, méconnu pour un temps, mais qu'il faudrait bien un jour, bon gré, malgré, accepter pour tel.

Leurs conseils sans doute agirent puissamment sur l'imagination du poète et lui donnèrent le change sur sa véritable vocation. L'auteur de *Sordello* tenta presque immédiatement le théâtre, où, plus que partout ailleurs, il devait échouer. Le théâtre, en effet, veut avant tout des conceptions claires, une imagination maîtresse d'elle-même, un esprit symétrique et méthodique. Autant le lecteur est patient, autant il met de zèle et d'humilité à suivre le poète partout où celui-ci le veut conduire,—dût-il en fin de compte juger qu'on lui a imposé des efforts inutiles et mal payés,—autant le spectateur va droit au fait et veut être immédiatement au courant de ce qui se passe. Avec lui, point de longues ambages, point de vaines et capricieuses excursions. Armé d'une logique bornée, mais rigoureuse, il n'admet de mystère que la dose voulue pour entretenir jusqu'au bout la curiosité nécessaire. Toute autre incertitude le décourage, l'impatiente et l'irrite. Les recherches du style lui doivent être cachées, et il est un art tout particulier de rendre supportables les plus belles effusions lyriques, dangereuses pour peu qu'on les prodigue. Or, Browning, on peut bien s'en douter déjà, n'était pas l'homme prudent et réfléchi que la scène demande. Confiant, osé, persuadé, à tort ou à raison, que son génie et son obstination prévaudraient sur toutes les résistances, il se crut probablement appelé à régénérer l'art dramatique, et ce ne fut pas trop d'une double épreuve pour lui ôter cette illusion.

Des deux pièces qu'il a fait représenter,—*Strafford*, tragédie historique, jouée à Covent-Garden, et *A Blot in the Scutcheon* (*une Tache sur l'Écusson*), drame romanesque joué à Drury-Lane,—la dernière surtout mérite de nous arrêter. C'est l'histoire d'une jeune fille noble, Mildred Tresham, restée après la mort de ses parens sous la tutelle de son frère Thorold. Un instant de faiblesse a fait d'elle la maîtresse du comte Mertoun; mais cette faute est secrète, et le déshonneur auquel les Tresham sont exposés si elle éclate, la *tache* qui souillerait alors leur noble *écusson*, peuvent encore être évités. Mertoun vient en grande pompe solliciter la main de Mildred; son rang, sa beauté, sa jeunesse, ses immenses domaines justifient cette demande, bien accueillie par Thorold. Il semble donc que l'hymen va tout réparer et couvrir de ses voiles sacrés la faute de la jeune fille; toutefois ce n'est là qu'un trompeur sourire de la destinée. Le vieux Gérard, serviteur de Tresham, garde un visage triste au milieu des fêtes qui se préparent. Il sait qu'il n'a qu'un mot à dire pour que le mariage projeté devienne impossible, et sa fidélité lui prescrit impérieusement de ne rien cacher à son maître. Lord Tresham, l'orgueilleux frère de Mildred, apprend donc que sa sœur, cet ange de pureté, cette hermine gardée de toute souillure, reçoit les visites nocturnes d'un jeune homme inconnu. Vainement il voudrait douter de cette vérité cruelle: Gérard est un irrécusable témoin, et d'ailleurs il offre la preuve de ce qu'il avance. Avant de sévir, lord Tresham veut avoir une entrevue avec sa sœur, l'amener à un aveu, sonder ce cœur perverti. A peine en peut-il croire ses oreilles lorsque Mildred, avertie par lui qu'il la sait coupable, se déclare prête à épouser le jeune comte. Il y a ici une absurdité tellement palpable et en même temps si peu facile à supposer,

qu'une citation textuelle devient nécessaire:

TRESHAM,—Dois-je me taire ou parler?
MILDRED.—Parlez!
TRESHAM.—Soit. Est-il une accusation que les hommes,... un homme du moins pût porter contre vous,... et que vous ayez voulu me cacher?... Je ne croirai jamais que le mensonge puisse avilir vos lèvres. Dites-moi seulement: Pareille accusation n'existe pas... et je vous croirai, fallût-il pour cela refuser de croire le monde entier,... un monde d'hommes meilleurs que je ne suis, de femmes telles que je vous suppose. Parlez! (Mildred se tait.) Rien? Expliquez-vous donc! que tout s'éclaircisse; ôtez quelque chose à ce poids sous lequel je descends plus bas que la tombe... Rien encore? Allégez, Mildred, allégez ce poids mortel. Ah! si je pouvais prendre sur moi de répéter ce qu'ils disent contre vous! Le dois-je, Mildred?... Toujours ce silence?... (Après une pause.) Est-il vrai que vous recevez un amant, chaque nuit, chez vous? (Après une nouvelle pause, et d'un ton plus bref.) Alors, son nom?... Jusqu'à présent, vous seule occupiez ma pensée. Maintenant, son nom!
MILDRED.—Cherchez, Thorold, une expiation à mon crime, si tant est qu'il puisse être expié. Faut-il vous dire que j'endurerai tout et vous bénirai, que mon âme appelle ce purificateur où ses souillures seront dévorées? Mais ne me rendez pas plus coupable encore. Assez d'infamie comme cela. Je ne puis révéler ce nom.
TRESHAM.—Jugez donc vous-même! Que dois-je faire? Prononcez..... Cette journée, de manière ou d'autre, s'achèvera pour nous deux; mais, demain, le comte se hâtera de venir... Hier, d'après votre désir, une lettre de moi lui a prescrit de se rendre ici. Cela dit tout; le reste se devine; «Sa demande a trouvé grace devant vous...» Maintenant dictez-moi la lettre qui doit démentir la promesse ainsi faite; trouvez les mots, dont je dois me servir.
MILDRED.—Mais, Thorold,—si je le recevais comme il s'attend à être reçu?
TRESHAM.—Le comte!
MILDRED.—Je suis prête à l'accueillir.
TRESHAM, se levant, indigné.—Holà! Guendolen!

(ENTRENT GUENDOLEN ET AUSTIN).*

TRESHAM.—Guendolen, et vous aussi, Austin, soyez les bien-venus. Regardez de ce côté. Vous voyez bien cette femme.
AUSTIN et GUENDOLEN, stupéfaits.—Quoi! Mildred...
TRESHAM.—Celle qu'on appelait Mildred autrefois, et maintenant une fille perverse qui chaque nuit,—lorsque les habitans de la maison paternelle sont livrés au sommeil,—reçoit, la perfide et l'infâme, le complice de ses plaisirs criminels ... oui, sous ce toit qui vous abrite, Guendolen, et vous, Austin, sous ce toit que tour à tour ont habité mille Tresham, dont aucun, Dieu merci, ne ressemblait à cette misérable.

Dans une situation pareille, en face d'une si violente accusation, victime d'un malentendu si évident et si facile à éclaircir, comprend-on que Mildred se taise? Il le faut cependant, car toute la pièce repose sur l'erreur où demeure Tresham. Du reste, ce n'est qu'une des mille invraisemblances à relever dans cette fable singulière. Ainsi Mildred, après l'étrange scène que

─────────
*Austin est le frère cadet de lord Tresham; lady Guendolen est leur cousine et l'amie de Mildred.

nous venons de lire, ne juge pas à propos de contremander Mertoun, qui, le soir même, doit se rendre secrètement chez elle. Expliquez-vous, si vous le pouvez, l'imprudence aveugle de ces deux amans, et le peu de souci que témoigne le comte pour l'honneur de celle qui, le lendemain même, va devenir sa femme; expliquez-vous encore que la rage de Tresham contre l'audacieux inconnu surpris par lui sous le balcon de Mildred ne s'apaise pas quelque peu lorsque, ce naïf séducteur venant à jeter son masque, il reconnaît le fiancé de sa sœur. Mais non: bien que la réparation de l'outrage fait au nom des Tresham soit assurée s'il laisse la vie à Mertoun, Thorold se croit tenu de provoquer et d'immoler ce pauvre jeune homme qui ne fait pas mine de vouloir sérieusement se défendre; après quoi le drame finit par le trépas du frère vengeur et de la sœur coupable, Austin et Guendolen restant seuls au monde pour que l'écusson si bien lavé dans ces flots de sang n'aille pas s'écarteler avec quelque autre blason moins illustre.

Browning n'a pas écrit moins de six autres pièces, tantôt pour la scène, tantôt pour la lecture, et qui ont été réunies par lui dans un recueil intitulé *Cloches et Grenades (Bells and Pomegranates)*.* A part l'une de ces pièces, *the King Victor and the King Charles*, qui roule sur l'abdication de Victor-Amédée de Savoie et sa malheureuse tentative pour reprendre ensuite la couronne (1730-31), toutes sont du ressort de la fantaisie, comme la plupart de celles qui composent *le Spectacle dans un Fauteuil* de M. Alfred de Musset. Cependant, à l'exception de deux petits proverbes rimés, *Pippa Passes* et *A Soul's Tragedy*, nous ne croyons pas nous tromper en affirmant qu'elles ont toutes été composées avec l'espoir et l'arrière-pensée de les produire sur le théâtre. L'une de ces comédies, *Colombe's Birthday*, pouvait s'y présenter au même titre que le *Hunchback*, la *Love-Chase* ou le *Woman's wit* de Sheridan Knowles. C'est, comme ces dernières, ce que nos ancêtres littéraires appelaient une comédie héroïque, c'est-à-dire une intrigue romanesque mêlée de quelques scènes destinées à faire sourire les spectateurs, et généralement dénouée à l'amiable, sans poison, ni blasphème, ni poignard. *Le Prince jaloux*, de notre Molière, et même *Amans magnifiques* (si vous en retranchez les dryades dansantes et les voltigeurs sautant sur des chevaux de bois), donneraient une assez juste idée du ton général de ces compositions, que certains écrivains de nos jours ont vainement essayé de réhabiliter.

Colombe de Ravestein est duchesse de Juliers et Clèves (arrangez ceci avec les annales du XVIIe siècle). Une année à peine s'est écoulée depuis qu'on est allé la chercher dans son couvent pour lui poser sur le front la couronne ducale, et déjà il lui est donné de connaître l'inconstance de la fortune. Le prince Berthold, appuyé par le pape, l'empereur, le roi d'Espagne et le roi de France, vient, en vertu de droits plus ou moins équivoques, revendiquer le duché, qu'il déclare usurpé par sa cousine Colombe. A peine ce formidable prétendant approche-t-il des frontières, que tous les courtisans de la jeune princesse, au lieu de prendre les armes, en champions galans, pour Dieu et leur dame, s'éclipsent prudemment l'un après l'autre. Elle resterait absolument seule et sans protection, si le hasard, et l'amour, volontiers de concert avec le hasard, ne lui suscitaient un généreux défenseur dans la personne de maître Valence, simple avocat de Clèves, chargé par ses concitoyens de porter leurs doléances à la princesse. Ébloui de sa beauté, touché de ses malheurs, indigné des trahisons qui l'entourent, Valence se dévoue, corps et ame, à la duchesse abandonnée. Il l'éclaire sur ses droits, il dirige ses démarches, il plaide sa cause, il soulèverait au besoin, pour elle, les bourgeois de Clèves, qui entreraient en campagne commandés par ce jeune et valeureux avocat. Son dévouement inattendu lui vaut la confiance entière, puis la reconnaissance attendrie de sa noble protégée. Ces deux sentimens font en elle de si rapides progrès, que, lorsque Berthold, ébranlé par les raisonnemens de Valence et séduit par la beauté de Colombe, se montre disposé à transiger, à l'aide d'un bon mariage, sur les droits respectifs de sa cousine et lui pourraient faire valoir, cet expédient si naturel révolte la princesse, comme un acte de monstrueuse ingratitude. Elle hésite cependant entre les deux rivaux, l'un qui semble lui faire grace en l'épousant, l'autre qui brûle silencieusement pour elle d'une flamme pure et discrète; mais tous les cœurs sensibles ont déjà pressenti son choix. L'amour désintéressé l'emporte sur les calculs ambitieux. Colombe, qui, pour son anniversaire, doit un présent à chacun de ses amis, fait à Valence le plus beau de tous: elle se donne elle-même à lui, laissant à Berthold la tranquille possession de son beau duché.

C'est presque au hasard, et de souvenir, que nous comparions les drames de fantaisie aux comédies héroïques d'autrefois. En y songeant mieux, il nous revient à la mémoire une scène des *Amans magnifiques* tout-à-fait semblable à celle où Valence porte à la princesse les propositions conjugales du duc Berthold. C'est la scène où le général Sostrate, chargé par le prince Iphicrate et le prince Démoclès d'expliquer leurs vœux à la princesse Ériphile, dont il est lui-même épris, remplit, à son grand ennui, cette délicate mission. Les curieux peuvent la relire et comparer.*

Ni le *Return of the Druses* ni *Luria* ne sauraient être pour nous l'objet d'une étude approfondie. Dans la première de ces tragédies, Browning a mis en scène un imposteur qui se fait passer pour prophète, afin de soulever une colonie druse, établie dans une des îles Sporades, contre les chevaliers hospitaliers de Saint-Jean. L'héroïne de la pièce est une jeune vierge du Liban, partagée entre l'amour affectueux qu'elle accorde à l'amour d'un des chevaliers chrétiens et l'éblouissante perspective d'épouser un homme investi par le ciel même d'un caractère sacré. Ce conflit de passions donne lieu à une scène dont l'idée est assez belle. Anael, la jeune enthousiaste fanatisée par les exhortations de Djabal, le faux prophète, a pénétré dans l'appartement du préfet des hospitaliers, et, croyant obéir à Dieu, elle l'a poignardé. Djabal, à qui ce meurtre était dévolu, arrive après qu'il est commis, et trouve sa complice encore couverte du sang qu'elle vient de répandre. Dans le

---

*Un mot sur ce titre bizarre. Browning prétend qu'il a voulu indiquer par là son désir «d'alterner ou de confondre la musique et l'éloquence, la mélodie et la pensée, le sens et le rhythme.—Ceci, ajoute-t-il, eût paru prétentieux à exprimer autrement; c'est pourquoi j'ai choisi la forme symbolique. Or, dans la langue des rabbins et des pères, les deux mots ci-dessus ont souvent le sens que je leur donne. Une autre acception est celle-ci: *la foi et les bonnes œuvres*. Laquelle des deux avait en vue Giotto quand il plaçait une grenade dans la main de Dante? et Raphaël, quand il couronnait des fleurs du grenadier (dans la *Camera della Segnatura*) le front de sa Théologie?»

Colombe's Birthday, act. IV, sc. IV.—*Les Amans magnifiques*, act. II, sc. IV, et act. IV, sc. VII.

trouble des premières explications, il lui laisse entrevoir qu'il n'est pas, comme elle le croit, un envoyé céleste, et l'innocente jeune fille se trouve alors en face d'un crime horrible, sans excuse, dont le poids l'écrase.

DJABAL.—Non, je ne suis pas Hakim.... Djabal est mon véritable nom. J'ai menti, et cet affreux malheur est venu de mes mensonges. Non... Écoute-moi, tu m'accableras ensuite de tes mépris... Aujourd'hui et pour toujours, ton crime est à moi... Pense un instant au passé.

ANAEL, se parlant à elle-même.—Ai-je frappé un seul coup?... ou deux coups? ou un plus grand nombre?

DJABAL—... J'étais venu pour ramener ma tribu vers ces lieux où dort, parmi les ténèbres, Bahumie le rénovateur. Anael.... quand je vis mes frères, je me dis: Il faudrait un miracle.... Et quand je t'eus vue: Le miracle se fera!

ANAEL, à elle-même.—La tête a frappé le seuil de la porte méridionale.

DJABAL.—.... Une ame pure ne suffisait pas à cette vaste entreprise. Peu à peu je m'engageai... Je croyais que le ciel serait avec moi.... J'affirmai qu'il s'était déclaré.

ANAEL.—Est-ce le sang versé qui fait germer tous ces rèves?... — Voyons, quelqu'un ne disait-il pas là, tout à l'heure, que tu n'étais pas Hakim? Mais tes miracles? mais ce feu qui se jouait, sans te blesser, autour de ton corps?... (Changeant tout à coup d'accent.) Ah! vous voulez m'éprouver... Vous êtes encore notre saint prophète?...

Après un moment de douloureuse attente, elle se jette dans les bras de Djabal, convaincue qu'il a voulu l'éprouver et honteuse des soupçons qu'il semble avoir conçus; mais il s'éloigne silencieusement d'elle, honteux lui-même de cette confiance si aveugle, si persistante. Le voile tombe alors des yeux d'Anael, qui maudit d'abord l'indigne artisan de tant de fraudes. Après ce premier élan de fureur, le dévouement reprend tout à coup son empire sur cette ame généreuse.

ANAEL.—Suis-moi, Djabal!
DJABAL.—Où faut-il te suivre?
ANAEL.—A la honte. Je la partagerai avec toi. Ne vaut-il pas mieux en finir d'un seul coup avec ces tortures? Qu'ils te raillent, ces frères si crédules! Que Loys lui-même t'insulte et te raille! Viens à eux, ta main dans ma main... Marchons.
DJABAL.—Où veux-tu m'entraîner?
ANAEL.—Où?—Devant ces Druses que tu as trompés. Maintenant que tu touches à ton but, avoue,—je t'aime encore,—avoue l'imposture dont tu t'es servi.—Peut-être ne t'ai-je jamais autant aimé.—Viens affronter l'infamie.—Oui, je t'aime, et te préfere à tous... J'accepte le déshonneur au lieu du triomphe; l'homme à la place du dieu.—Viens donc !*...

Djabal se sent incapable d'un si noble sacrifice. Anael s'éloigne, et, dénonçant ses projets, elle est sur le point de les faire avorter. Toutefois, au moment suprême, lorsqu'un mot de sa bouche peut détruire l'enthousiasme des Druses pour leur faux prophète, lorsqu'elle voit Djabal à sa merci, la pitié, l'amour, l'emportent. Elle s'est empoisonnée et tombe morte à ses pieds, après l'avoir proclamé Hakim. Les Druses voient dans le trépas d'Anael le châtiment de ses blasphèmes et la preuve manifeste de l'intervention divine en faveur de leur chef. L'occasion serait belle pour briser leur joug et les ramener au Liban; mais Djabal, renonçant à ses ambitieux projets, se poignarde sur le corps de la jeune fille morte pour lui.

Luria, comme Othello, est un capitaine more au service d'une république italienne. Florence, ingrate envers lui, n'en est pas moins l'objet de son entier dévouement. Tandis que cette démocratie soupçonneuse l'entoure d'espions, tandis qu'elle cherche à glisser la trahison jusque dans les baisers de sa maîtresse, tandis qu'elle lui prépare, au lieu du triomphe, un jugement et un trépas ignominieux, Luria, qui n'ignore aucune de ses perfidies, lui reste fidèle envers et contre tous, quitte à mourir, le cœur brisé, quand il aura fait triompher ses armes et vaincu les troupes de Lucques. C'est là son unique vengeance, c'est là aussi le dénoûment du drame, qui rappelle à certains égards les principales situations du *Carmagnola* de Manzoni.

A côté de ses tragédies et de ses comédies fantastiques, Browning a placé, dans son dernier recueil, ce qu'il appelle *Dramatic Lyrics*, c'est-à-dire de petites poésies, la plupart, en effet, reposant sur une action qui, développée, deviendrait un drame. La *Dolorida* de M. de Vigny, *Jeanne la Rousse* de Béranger, mais surtout certaines ballades allemandes, comme *le Chasseur sauvage* de Burger, *l'Infanticide* de Schiller, la *Lorelei* de Clément Brentano, *Dame Siègelinde* de Louis Uhland, *le Prince le plus riche* de Justin Kerner, donnent, avec des nuances bien différentes, une idée de ce genre mixte. C'est là qu'on peut le mieux, et aussi le plus favorablement, apprécier les qualités du jeune poète anglais. L'énergie soutenue de son style, pénible dans un drame de longue haleine, éclate dans un cadre plus resserré. L'effort laborieux, le manque de naïveté, s'aperçoivent moins; et, si Browning n'avait point fait de drames, on le jugerait, sur ces courtes ballades, doué de toutes les qualités qui font réussir au théâtre. *Le Laboratoire*, *le Confessionnal*, par exemple, sont des tragédies résumées, où la passion la plus délirante s'exprime avec une formidable violence. L'une nous transporte dans un cabinet d'alchimiste, où, masquée de verre et penchée sur le creuset fumant, une grande dame, que torture la jalousie, attend le poison destiné à sa rivale.

LE LABORATOIRE.

Il est avec elle; ils savent que je les sais ensemble. Ils s'imaginent que je verse des larmes, et ils rient; ils rient de moi, qu'ils croient priant pour eux dans les désertes profondeurs de l'église.—Mais je suis ici.

Broie, humecte, pétris tes pâtes! Bats, pile à loisir tes poudres! Est-ce que je suis pressée, moi? Assise à contempler ton étrange entourage, je m'y plais mieux qu'au milieu des hommes qui m'attendent pour danser au bal du roi.

Ce qui est dans ce mortier, tu l'appelles une gomme?— Ah! le bon arbre, d'où tombent ces larmes d'or! Et dans cette buire de cristal, cette liqueur d'un bleu si doux, qui promet une saveur exquise, est-ce du poison?

Hâtons-nous! As-tu fini?... Cette liqueur est trop sombre. Pourquoi n'a-t-elle pas l'aspect flatteur, attrayant, de l'autre breuvage? Il faut que le venin vengeur devienne plus brillant à l'œil, il faut qu'*elle* le contemple et l'admire, qu'*elle* l'essaie et s'y délecte, qu'*elle* le préfere et s'y arrête long-temps.

Rien qu'une goutte!—Songes-y, elle n'est pas frèle et petite comme moi.—C'est par là qu'elle l'a séduit.— Ceci ne suffira jamais pour ôter leur ame à ces grands

---
The Return of the Druses, acte IV, sc. I.

yeux pleins d'une mâle ardeur,—pour arrêter le sang magnifique qui va et vient dans ces puissantes veines.

Car la nuit dernière encore, tandis qu'ils se parlaient tout bas, j'ai tenu mes yeux sur elle, pensant que ce regard, si je pouvais le tenir sur elle durant la moitié d'une minute, la renverserait, flétrie, à mes pieds. Elle n'est pas tombée.—Et ceci suffirait?

Non que je veuille lui épargner la souffrance. La mort doit être lente et sa trace profonde. Mords, noircis, calcine ce corps si charmant. Certes il n'oubliera pas le visage de la mourante.

Est-ce fait?—Prends ce masque. Oh! va, ne crains rien; il doit la tuer; je ne m'exposerai pas à le perdre,—ce précieux poison acheté au prix d'une fortune.—D'ailleurs, s'il la tue, elle, peut-il me nuire?

Et maintenant, à toi tous mes joyaux, gorge-toi d'or à ton gré. Tu peux aussi, vieillard, tu peux, si cela te tente, baiser mon front, même baiser mes lèvres;... mais secoue de mes vêtemens ces cendres dont l'horreur trahirait ma vengeance.—Je serai bientôt au bal du roi.*

Ou nous nous trompons fort, ou *le Confessionnal* est emprunté à l'une de ces vifs saynètes dans lesquels l'auteur du *Théâtre de Clara Gazul* s'est plu à démonétiser l'inquisition. Seulement Browning a placé le récit de la trahison monacale dans la bouche de la femme même qui en est l'instrument et la victime;† cette femme raconte par quels artifices on lui a persuadé de dénoncer elle-même son amant, et comment elle l'a vu, sur l'échafaud, subir l'ignoble supplice de la *garote*. Puis, se livrant à sa fureur:

Mensonge, tout est mensonge! s'écrie-t-elle; leurs prêtres, leur pape, leurs saints, leur....., tout ce qu'ils redoutent, tout ce qu'ils espèrent, mensonges, infâmes mensonges!... Point de ciel avec eux; avec eux point d'enfer. Et sur terre, avec eux, pas un recoin, fût-ce l'horrible cachot où mon corps est prisonnier, si je n'y puis crier vers Dieu et les hommes:—ils mentent, ils mentent! Encore une fois ils mentent!**

Les plus longs de ces petits poèmes sont presque toujours des narrations, des légendes, et presque toujours aussi le poète s'y efface pour laisser parler un des personnages fictifs qu'il évoque. Par exemple, s'il veut raconter l'histoire de ce chevalier qui, sur l'ordre de sa dame, alla chercher le gant qu'elle avait jeté dans une fosse habitée par des lions, Browning n'hésitera pas à faire intervenir notre poète Ronsard, comme truchement, entre lui et ses lecteurs. Ces fictions multiplient pour le poète les chances de manquer aux convenances du sujet. Nous savons bien que peu

---

Dramatic Romances and Lyrics, p. 11.

†On peut comparer avec le poème de Browning le saynète du *Théâtre de Clara Gazul* intitulé *le Ciel et l'Enfer*.

**   It is a lie—their Priests, Their Pope,
           Their saints, their... All they fear or hope
           Are lies, and lies. . . . .
           . . . .
           No part in aught they hope or fear
           No Heaven with them, no Hell,—and here
           No Earth, not so much space as pens
           My body in their worst of dens
           But shall bear God and Man, my cry,—
           Lies,—lies, again,—and still, they lie!
              (*Dramatic Romances and Lyrics.*—
               Spain, the Confessional, p. 11.)

d'Anglais ont lu le poète vendômois, encore qu'il ait passé deux ans de sa vie au service de Jacques Stuart, et que l'infortunée reine Marie, qui se rappelait l'avoir eu à sa cour, envoyât des rosiers d'argent à celui qu'elle nommait «l'Apollon de la source des Muses;» mais enfin, la légende de Browning venant à passer sous les yeux de gens à qui l'ancienne poésie française n'est pas étrangère, on pourrait rapprocher avec quelque surprise cette muse

. . . . gâtant par son français
Des Grecs et des Latins les graces infinies

des vers que lui prête le poète anglais. Lisez l'ode *à la Rose*, ou *l'Institution pour l'adolescence de Charles IX;* puis, sans ménager la transition, passez à l'histoire du *Gant*, telle que Browning l'a rimée. Le contraste est vraiment gai.

Hélas! disait un jour en bâillant le roi François, l'éloignement donne du prix à tout. Qu'un homme ait mille affaires sur les bras, la paresse lui semble avoir de merveilleuses douceurs. Oui, mais une fois qu'il a tout loisir, il ne demande plus que de nouveaux soucis. A peine avons-nous la paix depuis quelques jours, et je me prends à songer que la guerre est le seul vrai passe-temps. Les vers m'expliqueront-ils ceci, maître Pierre? Voyons ce que vous aurez à nous dire.—Moi qui sans vanité ne suis guère en peine de citer mon Ovide:—Sire, répliquai-je, toute joie n'est que nuées, et les hommes sont autant d'Ixions abusés... —Ici le roi m'interrompt, en sifflant:—Laissons cela..., et allons voir nos lions.—Telle est la chance de quiconque se livre à son éloquence devant notre gracieux souverain.*

Jamais violon faux écorcha-t-il mieux vos oreilles que cette poésie familière, bavarde, légèrement ironique, se plaisant aux détails, et si peu grecque, si franchement anglaise? Browning peut, après tout, invoquer à sa décharge plus d'un illustre exemple. Le Beaumarchais de Goethe et la Jeanne d'Arc de Schiller sont tout aussi bizarrement accoutrés que le Pierre Ronsard du poète anglais.

La fuite d'une jeune duchesse allemande, qui, lasse de sa solitude orgueilleuse, se laisse enlever par une tribu de Bohêmes errans,† et l'histoire bien connue du *Preneur de rats de Hamelin*,—encore que nous préférions de beaucoup la ballade originale, si simple et si rapide,—prêtent moins à la critique, et cela par une raison très évidente: c'est que la fantaisie du poète, prenant ici ses coudées franches, se jouait dans cette région vague où tout est vraisemblable et facilement accepté. En revanche, le *David chez Saül* jure étrangement avec les traditions et le sentiment de la poésie biblique. C'est un air de cithare exécuté sur le cor anglais.

Certaines affectations nous gâtent le talent de Browning, en le montrant préoccupé de recherches puériles, toujours dédaignées de l'artiste qui voit en grand. Entre autres, nous citerons le mauvais goût qui lui fait si souvent placer deux tableaux dans le même cadre, comme si de cette juxtaposition il attendait les plus merveilleux effets, ou comme s'il voulait forcer le lecteur à trouver entre les deux poèmes ainsi rapprochés quelque lien mystérieux, quelque parenté philosophique. L'empoisonneuse et la blasphématrice, dont nous parlions tout à l'heure, sont aussi reliées, on ne

---

Bells and Pomegranates.—The Glove.

†*Bells and Pomegranates.*—The Flight of the Duchess.

sait vraiment pourquoi, sous ce titre commun: *la France et l'Espagne (ancien régime)*. Ailleurs nous avons *l'Italie en Angleterre et l'Angleterre en Italie*, c'est-à-dire les souvenirs d'un proscrit italien et ceux d'un voyageur anglais, tous deux racontant les impressions qu'ils ont reçues sous le ciel natal; ailleurs encore *le Camp et le Cloître*, brusque opposition entre le dévouement enthousiaste du soldat et les haines engendrées à l'ombre des retraites où croupit l'oisiveté monacale. Ici le jeune conscrit impérial vient en souriant mourir aux pieds de son général victorieux; là, parmi les fleurs et les parfums d'un riche jardin, un moine poursuit *in petto* d'imprécations venimeuses l'homme que la règle lui commande d'appeler «son frère.» Certes, il n'y a point là matière à graves reproches, et ces combinaisons arbitraires n'ont rien au fond que de très innocent; mais l'innocence même de ces moyens, et l'espèce de manie qu'ils indiquent, à quelque chose de mesquin, d'apprêté, d'artificiel, qui nous rappelle malheureusement nos futilités romantiques d'il y a vingt ans.

Quelquefois une originalité de meilleur aloi, celle de la pensée, distingue ces monologues lyriques. Dans la pièce intitulée *Madhouse Cells*, le poète nuance bien la folie religieuse et la monomanie jalouse. On lit aussi avec intérêt, nonobstant sa prolixité, le discours d'un prélat italien sur son lit de mort, où le tourmente la singulière ambition d'une magnifique sépulture. Il explique à ses héritiers pourquoi il tient tant à ces splendeurs posthumes. De tout temps, une rivalité d'orgueil exista, dit-il, entre lui et un de ses compatriotes. Ils aimèrent la même femme, ils poursuivirent la même carrière, ils reposeront dans le même temple. Or, l'évêque a toujours eu le dessus. Jeune homme, il épousa celle qu'ils aimaient; devenu veuf, il a devancé son émule dans les honneurs ecclésiastiques, et maintenant, maintenant encore, il le veut éclipser par les décorations de son mausolée.* Cette donnée, véritablement, n'est pas commune, et dérive d'une observation assez profonde, d'un coup d'œil assez juste jeté sur les étranges passions qui dominent l'homme. Voici une pièce, dans le même genre, dont nous essaierons de rendre l'aisance familière et l'horreur secrète. Un grand seigneur italien promène dans la galerie de son palais un officieux négociateur, venu pour conclure certaine affaire importante:

Vous voyez, peinte sur ce mur, ma défunte duchesse. C'est une image vivante, un ouvrage vraiment merveilleux. Fra Pandolfo y consacra toute une journée ses mains actives, et voilà une figure immortelle.—Asseyez-vous donc, et regardez tout à votre aise.—J'ai voulu, sur-le-champ, vous nommer Fra Pandolfo, car les étrangers comme vous ne contemplent jamais cette physionomie frappante, ce regard plein d'ardeur et de passion, sans se tourner aussitôt vers moi;—moi seul écarte le rideau qui cache cette peinture,—et tous me demanderaient, s'ils l'osaient, comment ce regard singulier se trouve là... Vous ne serez donc pas le premier à m'interroger ainsi, et je veux vous répondre sans attendre vos questions.

Ce n'était point la présence seule de son époux qui animait ainsi d'une lueur joyeuse le pâle visage de la duchesse. Que Fra Pandolfo vînt à dire: «Le manteau de madame cache un peu trop ses belles mains,» ou bien encore: «Le pinceau ne saurait rendre ces roses, reflets du sang, qui viennent mourir sur sa poitrine;»

certes, elle ne prenait point ces paroles pour autre chose qu'un éloge courtois, mais elle n'en rougissait pas moins de plaisir. Elle avait un cœur... comment exprimer ceci?... trop facilement ému de joie, et qu'un rien faisait trop tôt palpiter. Elle aimait tout ce que rencontraient ses yeux, et ses yeux erraient volontiers de toutes parts. Tout la frappait au même degré. Le présent dont j'ornais son sein, les lueurs décroissantes du couchant, le rameau chargé de fruits que lui portait au jardin quelque niais empressé, la mule blanche sur laquelle, autour des terrasses, elle galopait, tout lui était sujet de douces paroles, ou au moins de rougissante émotion. Elle rendait grace aux hommes... certes, rien de mieux... mais elle les remerciait avec des façons... je ne saurais trop les définir... comme si elle eût mis au même rang le don que je lui avais fait d'un nom honoré depuis neuf siècles, et l'offrande insignifiante du premier venu.

Qui s'abaisserait à blâmer sérieusement de pareils enfantillages? Eût-on toutes les délicatesses du langage,—et vraiment c'est de quoi je me pique le moins,—comment se faire comprendre à demi-mot d'une personne ainsi douée? Comment lui dire: «C'est ceci ou cela qui me choque en vous. Ici vous n'arrivez pas au but, ici vous le dépassez?» Alors même qu'elle accepterait humblement ces leçons et n'engagerait pas une lutte d'esprit, alors même qu'elle se bornerait à s'excuser..., ce serait encore un abaissement, et je n'ai jamais voulu m'abaisser. Oh! certes, elle souriait si je venais à passer près d'elle; mais qui passant, après moi, sans obtenir le même sourire? Les choses allaient s'aggravant. Je dus parler en maître. De ce moment, tous sourires disparurent à la fois... La voilà, ma duchesse, à croire qu'elle est vivante...

Si vous voulez maintenant vous lever, nous irons rejoindre en bas la compagnie. Je vous le répète, la munificence bien connue du comte votre maître me garantit amplement que toute prétention, raisonnable de ma part, quant à la dot, sera noblement accueillie. D'ailleurs, je vous l'ai déjà dit, c'est sa charmante fille que j'ambitionne avant tout. Nous descendrons ensemble, mon cher monsieur... Remarquez aussi ce Neptune apprivoisant un cheval marin. On l'estime un morceau rare, et Claus d'Inspruck l'a fondu en bronze pour moi seul.*

On ne niera pas, nous l'espérons, qu'il n'y ait dans ce drame domestique, si froidement raconté, devant le portrait de la victime, par l'involontaire meurtrier, quelque chose qui glace et fait mal. Tant de passion, de gaieté, de sympathies, d'émotions, de vie surabondante et heureuse, étouffées par un imperturbable et dédaigneux égoïsme;—cet éclat joyeux s'éteignant au sein d'une lourde atmosphère;—cette bienveillance universelle refoulée par un orgueil implacable;—le contraste est bien choisi, nettement exprimé; il prépare l'effet des derniers vers, où l'on entrevoit qu'une autre destinée, jeune et brillante, va venir se perdre à son tour dans l'abîme où fut engloutie la première.

Browning, qui se fait tour à tour Italien, Espagnol, Hébreu, Français même,—autant qu'il le peut, du moins,—a quelquefois aussi abusé de la fantaisie allemande. La tendance du génie germanique à traduire en personnifications bizarres les forces secrètes de la nature a-t-elle jamais inspiré de plus folles visions que celles-ci, par exemple?

---

*Bells and Pomegranates.—The tomb at St. Praxed's.

*Dramatic Lyrics.—Italy.

LE CLARET ET LE TOKAY.

I.

Mon cœur descendait tout à l'heure, avec notre flacon de claret,* sous les massifs glaïeuls qui servent de masque à la face noire de cet étang. Encore à présent, aux bords çà et là rompus de l'humide cavité, contemplant les bulles brillantes et l'onde émue, de l'oreille et des yeux je suis mon cœur.

A voir notre riant petit flacon lancé dans ces profondeurs de plus en plus noires et froides, ne dirait-on pas quelque aimable et coquette Française, les bras collés au flanc, les jambes raides et tendues, alors qu'enlevée au tourbillon léger de la vie elle tombe dans le silencieux océan de la mort?

II.

Le tokay grimpa lestement sur notre table, gardien-pygmée de quelque château fort, robuste et bien pris dans ses grêles proportions, son arroi et ses armes en bel ordre. Il regardait fièrement au nord, lorsque, tournant sur lui-même, il souffla dans son petit cor un défi hautain à la soif, d'un plumet d'ivrogne orna son chapeau rabattu, tourna son pouce dans sa moustache rouge, choqua et fit sonner ses grands éperons de fer, serra sa ceinture de Bude autour de sa taille, et avec une imperturbable impudence, secouant ses épaules de bossu, il semblait dire à tous venans que de vingt coquins pareils il se rirait, plus hardi que jamais. Puis, ramenant en avant la poignée de son sabre, et la main droite posée sur sa hanche, le petit homme d'Ausbruck s'en alla se pavanant.†

Vous avez reconnu le *Trinklied* fantastique. Vous vous rappelez ces inspirations du panthéisme d'outre-Rhin qui donnent à la vigne, au vin les instincts et le langage de l'homme,—comme la mythologie grecque leur donnait une existence divine.—Vous vous rappelez l'hymne de Kerner sur les souffrances du vin captif quand la vigne fleurit au dehors, quand la séve bout dans les rameaux.

Maintenant, quelle place assigner à ce talent que nous venons d'étudier dans ses manifestations diverses? De tous les poètes contemporains, Robert Browning est celui qui s'est le moins isolé de la tradition byronienne. Lui aussi on peut l'accuser de matérialiser la poésie, et d'en subordonner l'élément idéal au sensualisme des sons et des images. Lui aussi se préoccupe de communiquer des impressions plutôt que de propager des idées. Il est artiste avant d'être croyant, artiste avant d'être patriote, artiste avant d'être philosophe ou moraliste. Ses convictions politiques, d'ailleurs, sont saines et libérales. Nous en attesterions, au besoin, la belle imprécation intitulée *le Meneur perdu, the Lost Leader*, où il flétrit en termes énergiques l'apostasie d'un poète qu'il ne daigne pas nommer.** Browning se fait honneur d'être du peuple et pour le peuple, comme Milton, Shakespeare, Burns et Shelley,

Shakespeare was of us, Milton was for us,
Burns, Shelley, were with us.

---

*On sait que le mot *claret* désigne en Angleterre le vin de Bordeaux.

†*Dramatic Romances and Lyrics*, p. 20.

**   Just for a handful of silver he left us,
       Just for a ribband to stick in his coat,—etc.
           (*Dramatic Romances and Lyrics*, p. 8).

Si l'auteur de *Paracelsus* a pour religion suprême ce panthéisme volage qui s'éprend de tout spectacle, de toute musique, et la divinise pour l'heure même où il en subit l'influence, il ne faudrait pas néanmoins s'imaginer qu'il soit d'un naturalisme outré, comme Wordsworth, ou mystique à la façon de Coleridge et de Shelley; il est, avant tout, préoccupé de l'homme, de ses passions, du langage et des actes qu'elles produisent. Chez lui, la recherche métaphysique, l'étude des traditions, l'effort littéraire, convergent au même but, qui est le drame, le drame en récit, le drame en action, le drame en monologue, peu importe. Si, avec une prédisposition si marquée, il n'atteint pas à l'excellence dramatique, c'est que l'énergie d'un style nerveux et pittoresque, la connaissance des faits historiques, une certaine aptitude à innover dans l'observation et la peinture des caractères, ne suffisent point à l'homme qui écrit pour la scène. Il a besoin, surtout à notre époque, d'une science spéciale qui lui permette de faire valoir toutes ses autres facultés, et cette science spéciale, qui règle la distribution d'un ouvrage, ménage habilement l'action, taille les scènes à la mesure qu'elles doivent avoir, équilibre les rôles, prévient ou détruit toute objection, Browning ne l'a pas. Il ne l'a pas même autant que l'avait Shakespeare, à qui la pratique de la scène révéla, du moins en partie, les ressources de cette poétique à part. Il n'a pas non plus cette fougue du génie, cet essor lyrique, cette puissance de souffle, qui, vertus suprêmes du poète, lui tiendront toujours lieu des aptitudes et des connaissances secondaires. Tout imparfait qu'est son talent, nous pouvons cependant, sans attendre les progrès qu'il devra peut-être à une plus complète maturité, reconnaître à Browning parmi les poètes actuels de l'Angleterre une physionomie à part, un rôle distingué. Sa hardiesse nous plaît; son originalité, qui souvent lui coûte cher et ne vaut pas toujours ce qu'elle lui coûte, n'en est pas moins une qualité dont il faut savoir lui tenir compte. Enfin il a, ce qui suffirait à nous le recommander, le goût et la connaissance des littératures européennes. Dans ce temps où les écrivains anglais semblent mettre leur orgueil à s'isoler, à se rendre inaccessibles, et,—chose étrange,—à ignorer ce qui se passe hors de leur île, à s'abstraire du grand mouvement extérieur, on ne refusera point quelques éloges à celui qui cherche des ressources dans la communion la plus large des intelligences, n'excluant aucun modèle, ne dédaignant aucune inspiration, et modifiant par d'heureuses combinaisons ce que le génie national peut avoir de trop rigoureux, de trop entier, de trop asservi aux préjugés de lieux et de race.

L'écrivain chez Browning ne doit pas nous faire oublier l'homme. Aujourd'hui la critique se plaît à interroger la vie privée des poètes. On aime à soulever le demi-voile qui cache ces idoles inconnues; on aime à se rendre compte de tout ce qui peut expliquer le travail singulier de ces intelligences à part. On ne suivra donc volontiers sous les ombrages d'un de ces *cottages* fleuris qui se multiplient aux abords de Londres, retraites paisibles où se réfugient, par goût autant que par nécessité, les écrivains épris de la solitude et de ses féconds loisirs. C'est là que nous pourrions, admis chez Browning, le surprendre en tête-à-tête avec son crapaud favori, dont l'éducation fait partie de ses travaux. Ces goûts fantasques sont fréquens chez les littérateurs anglais. Tout le monde connaît l'ours et le chien de Byron; le singe brésilien de Thomas Hood et le corbeau de Charles Dickens ont aussi leur renommée.

Par un beau soir d'été, lorsque le dôme majestueux de Saint-Paul, perçant le brouillard qui enveloppe Londres, découpe sa silhouette sur la blancheur argentine du crépuscule, nous aimerions à errer avec l'auteur de *Paracelsus* sur les coteaux boisés qui entourent sa demeure, causant de cette Italie où il allait naguère, consciencieux artiste, étudier sa tragédie de *Luria*, ses petits drames de *Pippa Passes* et de *A Soul's tragedy*. Nous aimerions à le suivre encore dans son ermitage, maintenant embelli par la présence d'une femme d'élite associée aux travaux et à la destinée du poète;* mais ici doit s'arrêter, nous le sentons, notre curiosité. Quel droit aurions-nous d'insister sur ces innocentes indiscrétions lorsqu'elles n'auraient plus la valeur de renseignemens littéraires? Contentons-nous donc d'ajouter que Browning, estimé comme poète par un petit nombre d'esprits choisis, est, au demeurant, un des hommes les plus honorables de la littérature contemporaine. Sa vie est simple et sévère. Son art l'occupe à l'exclusion de tout autre intérèt, et il ne profite du droit qu'il aurait aux relations les plus distinguées que pour choisir dans le monde aristocratique des amities dignes de la sienne.

PAUL ÉMILE DURAND FORGUES.

*Browning a récemment épousé une digne émule de mistress Norton, de lady Stuart Wartley, de mistress Brookes et de tant d'autres muses qui foulent à cette heure les frais |poems| de la poétique Angleterre. Miss Eliza Barrett,—aujourd'hui mistress Browning,—a publié en 1833 une traduction d'Eschyle, et en 1841 une légende poétique intitules *le Roman du Page*.

BELLS AND POMEGRANATES. The British Quarterly Review, November 1847, pp. 490–509.

ROBERT BROWNING HAS conquered for himself a high rank amongst contemporary poets, and there are few persons, we presume, who pretend to an acquaintance with the literature of the day, to whom his name has an unfamiliar sound. If they have not read his poems, they have heard them praised; the chances are, that among their acquaintance, two or three are warm admirers; and in no scanty number of families may one hear energetic protests against the "affectation" of the title which it has pleased him to adopt as a collective name for the effusions of the last five years. "Bells and Pomegranates!" exclaims the testy objurgator, "what stuff! What is the sense of such an affected title?" Whereupon some admirer replies: "Bells and Pomegranates, sir, is a Rabbinical symbol, used by Mr. Browning to indicate an alternation of music with discoursing, sound with sense, poetry with thought." The testy old gentleman refuses to accept such an explanation, and closes the discussion by observing—"Rabbinical, indeed! we want English, not Hebrew, sir!"

Such an objection, such a discussion proves at least that Robert Browning has a place apart from and above the herd of implacable verse-writers, ambitious of demonstrating that poetry *is* a drug—ambitious of proving the truth of Göthe's sarcasm—

Wer treibt die Dichtkunst aus der Welt?
Die Poeten!

The objection proves that he has his place in our literature; otherwise, no one would trouble himself with a mere title. Accordingly, we think our duty as critics is calmly to consider his claims to renown; for whatever may be the opinion formed of his poetical powers, the very fact that such powers have in our day raised a man into reputation in a department where, since the giants who lately trod the stage have passed into silence, so few names have been heard above the crowd—this fact, we say, has a significance in it, which the future historian of literature will have to ponder on.

There is one distinction we would wish clearly to establish before proceeding further. Horace declares that a poet is *born*, not *made*. In some sense, this is not true. A poet must be made as well as born: he must live in a certain condition of circumstances: either his epoch must be favourable to the musical expression of great convictions, or his own education must be favourable to the acquisition and practice of his art. All this looks very much like a truism, we are aware; but it is not our fault if obvious considerations have been so long overlooked that we are forced to recur to them. What we mean to educe is this: unquestionably a poet must be born with certain faculties which no education can supply, without which all education is incapable of producing lasting poetry. In a tribe of savages there will be found one or two men in whom some uncontrollable impulse urges them to pour forth their feelings into a rude but rhythmic melody. There is a song in the mind of every true poet; and it is only as a singer that he *is* a poet. No *education* creates this impulse in the breast of the savage. Nature created him a Bard, and as such his tribe salutes him.

That which is indispensable in a tribe of savages is also indispensable in a civilized nation; but with some apparent qualifications. Poetry, in as far as it is a Song, cannot be learned; but in as far as it is an Art, it can be learned. In the productions of what are called real poets—*great* poets, whether they wrote epics, or mere lyrics—there is a vitality which is so charming that it makes us overlook a thousand faults; but, on the contrary, in the productions of those whom we may call poets *made*—mere imitators, clever arrangers—there is amidst all the splendour of ornament a want of life, of freshness, of conviction; so that we are never roused to rapture, we are never haunted by their strains till they become "familiar as household words;" and in them we are intolerant of the faults which in the works of real poets are passed over unheeded. The reason is plain: a rose is not the less a rose because it has many specks of dirt upon it; but one of those specks would ruin a piece of china. And by an instinctive justice in mankind it is always the poets *made* upon whom much criticism is exercised at the time of the appearance. The Singer is listened to; the Artist is criticised.

Among the poets to whom we should deny the name of Singers there are many of very remarkable pretensions; and their works show to what a height a man may raise himself who was made, not born, a poet. In fact, the born poets are extremely rare. The test to apply is to ask yourself—"Would Mr. —— have been a poet, if other poets had not written before him? Is the irresistible οἶστρος within him which would, in all conditions of life, have goaded him to that fine frenzy in which Song is speech?" If you have any sagacity, you cannot be long in determining this question.

The Singer is born according to the will of Nature; the Artist is made according to the accidents of the times, and of his own condition. The one is born in all ages, in all conditions; the other is only producible under certain conditions. It is impossible to predict the appearance of the one; but of the other we may confidently say, "such a time is favourable—such a time is unfavourable." And we have hammered away at this distinction in order that we might conclude with saying: The present moment is by no means favourable to poetry; a conclusion which the reader will long ago have drawn for himself, but which is here recorded, 1st, that we may explain *why* the present is unfavourable to poetry; and 2nd, that we may the better understand how Robert Browning has been able to reach the place he occupies.

The present moment is unfavourable to poetry, because there reigns an intellectual anarchy, and an exhaustive spirit of application, which prevent sympathy in any great convictions, and which pin us down to the present, by barricading us from the future. It is an age of application, rather than of invention. There is prodigious intellectual activity, but it is not employed in opening up new tracks of thought. Great ideas are in the process of incarnation; great changes are taking place within the womb of society; but it is a period of gestation, and we are not yet on the eve of a new birth. All the great epochs in the history of literature have been stirring, troubled epochs, when society was in travail, and the poet's song was either a song of jubilee for the coming era, or the last cry of despair over the departing. In such periods there is an excitement in the public mind favourable to literature—which is the expression of society—and particularly to poetry. A man gifted with a musical feeling, and strongly influenced by the tendencies of the age, will then rise up, and by uttering in articulate and beautiful tones the thoughts and aspirations which are agitating the dumb millions, be saluted as their Poet; but the very same man, thrown upon other times, would distinguish himself in some other way, so that men should never suspect that he had in him the material for a poet. In our day, we may observe how few men of remarkable powers have given any labour to poetry; and this is the more striking, because almost all our writers have "the accomplishment of verse;" so that if they do not throw their thoughts into poems, it is from an instinctive or reflective sense of the futility of such an employment of their energies. Let us take Macaulay as an example. No one will pronounce him a born poet; yet who will deny that he has greater talents than many men who in their day have been regarded as great poets? and if he had given up his days and nights to the practice of his art, he would assuredly have attained to mastery; but he would not have produced poems such as would rouse the enthusiasm of the public, and deserve the attention of posterity; simply because he would have no exalted aspirations, no great convictions, afforded him by his epoch as the inspiration of his song. Unable to reflect the Present, he would be forced to give some pale copy of the Past; to the Future no one turns his eyes. It is this sense of the age not being poetical—of its affording the Singer no song of triumph, no elegy of regret, which keeps men of the highest powers from the cultivation of the Muse. It is not that people, now-a-days, are indifferent to poetry. Those who declaim against the age as being too practical or too earnest for the indulgence of poetry, make the egregious mistake of confounding the public indifference to *their* poems with an indifference to poetry itself. The old poets were never more widely diffused, more thoroughly enjoyed, than at present. The men who had something to sing, and sung it, are still listened to; but the feeble variations of those airs, which our modern singers thrust upon the public, find no listeners, because they have no charm.

This, then, is the great obstacle to a poet's success in the present day: there is nothing for him to sing! Those who believe they are writing poems, do little more than vary the themes of those who have gone before them. Instead of a man being stung with a resistless impulse to utter something he has thought, or felt, or seen in this world, and to utter it in impassioned music, he stands up in the market-place, and with more of less skill declaims to you what he has gathered of the utterances of Byron, of Wordsworth, of Shelley, of Keats, or of Scott. You, having heard the original strain, decline listening to his murderous reminiscence; while he, draping himself in his neglect, tells you that you are "dead to the influence of poetry."

So inevitable is imitation, that not only are all the herd of verse-writers to be classed under various "schools,"—one belonging to the "school" of Byron—another to the "school" of Wordsworth, as if Poets were Pedagogues, instructing ingenious youth in the emotions they are to feel, in the opinions they are to hold, and in the things they are to observe!—but even such a distinguished Poet as Tennyson, perhaps the only one of our day who deserves the name of poet—even he submits to the necessity, and imitates Wordsworth. Having apparently put "all his sufferings into song," he took to copying Wordsworth, and then was wisely silent.

Another example of this imitative tendency, which is forced upon writers by the absence of any materials in the age itself, is afforded in the tragedy of the "*Patrician's Daughter*," by Mr. Marston. The author was convinced that dramatists are on the wrong scent in endeavouring on the stage to represent the Past. He felt that a dramatic poet should hold up to his age the very "body of the time." He knew that passions were as violent—tragedies as terrible—characters as strongly marked now as of old; and he determined to select a subject from the present age. Now, one would think that in a drama written, as it were, upon theory—written to prove the truth of such a proposition—the author would be careful to avoid all imitation, and still more careful to paint the age with accuracy. But it turned out that the author imitated both Bulwer and Knowles; and as to accuracy, if he had been so wide of the mark in an historical tragedy, the critics would have torn him to pieces. The actors were men in frock coats and white kid gloves—their language was full of Elizabethan idioms and phrases—and the manners were of *no* age. In fact, he had imposed upon himself a task greater than he was aware of: he had endeavoured to enfranchise himself from imitation—to see with his own eyes.

To be able to see for yourself, and to picture to others what you have seen, are the first great characteristics of genius. To ordinary eyes a flock of sheep present few indications of variety; one sheep is indistinguishable from another sheep. To the shepherd's eye each differs from each, and has its separate name: to him, a thousand minute appearances distinguish one from the other, because his practised eye sees at a glance that which the unpractised eye could with difficulty discern even when pointed out. In the same way the man of genius is endowed with vision so keen, that where ordinary men observe only the broad distinctions of character, he detects all the myriad shades of difference; he is enabled to individualize. In consequence of this faculty, he is enabled to see things in their truth, because he sees for himself. The greater part of mankind neither see for themselves nor think for themselves. And rare as it is for a man to have that clear intellectual vision, it is perhaps as rare for him to have such powers of expression that he shall be able to write out what he really means. Any one who has handled the pen must be sensible of the astonishing difficulty there is in resisting the temptation to set down the phrases which *memory* so readily brings forward as expressive of what is in the mind, rather than allow what is in the mind to shape its own expression. Hence the absence of spontaneity in style. Men neither write as they think, nor as they speak, but as they remember others to have written. Instead of regarding style as the incarnation of their own thoughts, and consequently striving to make it as personal and distinct as they can, they regard it as an ornamental dress in which they ought to clothe their thoughts, and are careful to clothe them according to the fashion. No wonder that there are few good writers! No wonder that it is rare to meet with a piece of writing, in prose or verse, which conveys any clear, distinct, truthful picture of the thing described.

It will be readily admitted, therefore, that imitation is the rock upon which almost all writers must split; because, except in the case of a man of genius, writers are unable to think for themselves, and to write out distinctly what is in their minds. Imitation is not here limited to the obvious parodying of one particular master—as in the case of a writer belonging to the "school" of Byron, or to the "school" of Wordsworth; this is the lowest, vulgarest form of imitation, and arises from a narrow view of the nature of poetry—arises, indeed, from a confusion of *success* with the *conditions* of success. But there is a less direct, less obvious imitation, which men fall into, and which consists in adopting the opinions and the language of certain writers who have been their study, and whom they are forced to repeat, because they cannot see for themselves, think for themselves, nor write for themselves. Among the sand-numerous productions which crowd upon the age, how few pages are there of which the writers can say "that is mine—emphatically mine; neither appropriated from another, nor dressed according to the fashion; but born within my own experience, and clothed by me after my manner."

If we descend from these preliminary considerations to the application of them to the subject before us, we shall easily point out how and why Robert Browning has attained his present position. He is assuredly not a great poet; he is not even a distinguished poet, whose works will be gathered into future collections; but he is nevertheless a man who stands out in relief from his contemporaries—he is a writer of whom one must speak with the respect due to originality. In an age more favourable to the production of poetry, he might have been conspicuous; for he is endowed with some portion of the great faculty which we may metaphorically call the "eye to see." Deficient in some of the great requisites of his art, he has that one primary requisite: the power of seeing for himself and writing in his own language. Robert Browning is Robert Browning—call him sublime or call him feeble, take any view you will of his poems, you must still admit that he is one standing up to speak to mankind in his speech, not theirs—what he thinks, not what they think. We do not say that there are no traces of other poets in his works: he is of his age, and no man can pretend to escape its influence; he has studied poetry, and no man can at all times separate in his mind the acquired from the generated; but we do say emphatically that he is, in our strict and narrow sense of the term, no imitator, but an original thinker and an original writer.

Unfortunately, this high praise demands some qualification, and we are forced to add, that he is neither a deep thinker nor a musical writer. So that, although his originality has created for him an eminent position amongst a race of imitators, he has never yet been able to charm the public—he has never produced anything like "Mariana at the Moated Grange," "Locksley Hall," "Ulysses," "Œnone," "Godiva," or the "Miller's Daughter," (we mention those least resembling each other,) with which Tennyson has built himself a name. Nor do we anticipate that he will ever do so. He has now been some years before the public, and in various characters. His first poem, which (unlucky circumstance!) is still regarded as his best, was *Paracelsus*. We well remember its appearance, and the attention it drew on the new poet, who, being young, was held destined to achieve great things. As a first work, it was assuredly remarkable. It had good thoughts, clear imagery, genuine original speech, touches of simple pathos, caprices of fancy, and a power of composition which made one hope that more experience and practice would ripen him into a distinguished poet. There were two objections, which occurred to us at the time. We did not lay much stress upon them, as the author was evidently young. Age and practice, we thought, would certainly remove them. They were the sort of faults most likely to be found in youthful works—viz., a great mistake in the choice of subject, and an abruptness, harshness, and inelegance of versification. It was pardonable in a young man to make a quack his hero; it looked a paradox, tempting to wilful and skilful ingenuity. On the other hand, it also betokened, or seemed to betoken, a want of proper earnestness and rectitude of mind—a love rather of the extraordinary than of the true. Paracelsus was not the hero a young man should have chosen; and yet one felt that he was just the hero a young man would choose. It seems to us that what this betokened has come to pass, and that in his subsequent works we have, if not the *same* fault, yet a fault which springs, we take it, from the same source. His conceptions are either false or feeble. In the work which succeeded "Paracelsus," we noted a repetition of the very error itself—viz., in the attempt to idealize into a hero that great but desperate Strafford, the "wicked earl," as he was called, and as his actions prove him. Meanwhile the other fault—that, namely, of harshness and abruptness—was carried almost to a ridiculous extent; language was spasmodic, and tortured almost into the style of Alfred Jingle, Esq., in *Pickwick*, as the Edinburgh Reviewer remarked at the time. Next, after an interval of two or three years, if our memory serves us, came *Sordello*. What the merit or demerit of conception in that poem may be, no one can presume to say; for except the author himself and the printer's reader (in the course of duty), no earthly being ever toiled through that work. Walking on a new-ploughed field of damp clayey soil, would be skating compared to it. Even his staunchest admirers could say nothing to *Sordello*. Great as is the relish for the obscure and the involved in some minds, there was no one found to listen to these Sybilline incoherences. Other dealers in the obscure have at least charmed the ear with a drowsy music, but Sordello's music was too grating and cacophonous to admit of the least repose. Whether Browning is to this day convinced of his mistake we know not, but to our ever-renewed surprise we often see *Sordello* advertised. That he has not burnt every copy he could by any means lay hands on, is to be explained only upon the principle which makes a mother cherish more fondly the reprobate or the cripple of her family.

This much, at any rate, is significant; he has ventured on no such experiment on the public patience since *Sordello*. The subsequent poems here collected, as *Bells and Pomegranates*, are always readable, if not often musical, and are not insults to our ears. But, as we hinted, the old objections still remain. He has not yet learned to take due pains with his subject, nor to write clearly and musically. It appears as if he sat down to write poetry without the least preparation; that the first subject which presented itself was accepted, as if any canvass was good enough to be embroidered upon. And respecting his versification, is appears as if he consulted his own ease more than the reader's; and if by any arbitrary distribution of accents he could make the verse satisfy his own ear, it must necessarily satisfy the ear of another. At the same time, he occasionally pours forth a strain of real melody, and always exhibits great powers of rhyming. One of the most evenly written of his pieces happens to be a great favourite of ours, and we quote it here for the sake of its manful, sorrowful reproaches.

THE LOST LEADER.

I.

Just for a handful of silver he left us,
   Just for a riband to stick in his coat—
Got the one gift of which fortune bereft us,
   Lost all the others she lets us devote;
They, with the gold to give, doled him out silver,
   So much was theirs who so little allowed:
How all our copper had gone for his service!
     Rags—were they purple, his heart had been proud!
We that had loved him so, followed him, honoured him,
   Lived in his mild and magnificent eye;
Learned his great language, caught his clear accents,
   Made him our pattern to live and to die!
Shakspeare was of us, Milton was for us,
   Burns, Shelley, were with us—they watch from their graves!
He alone breaks from the van and the freemen,
   He alone sinks to the rear and the slaves!

II.

We shall march prospering—not thro' his presence;
   Songs may excite us—not from his lyre;
Deeds will be done—while he boasts his quiescence,
   Still bidding crouch whom the rest bade aspire:
Blot out his name, then, record one lost soul more,
   One task unaccepted, one footpath untrod;
One more devil's triumph, and sorrow to angels,
   One wrong more to man, one more insult to God!
Life's night begins: let him never come back to us!
   There would be doubt, hesitation, and pain;

Forced praise on our part—the glimmer of twilight,
   Never glad confident morning again!
Best fight on well, for we taught him,—come gallantly,
   Strike our face hard, ere we shatter his own;
Then let him get the new knowledge and wait us,
   Pardoned in Heaven—the first by the throne!

There are some expressions here to which one might object, but the whole poem exhibits a strength, solidity, and sobriety uncommon in contemporary writing. There is no affectation of thought in it; there is none of the pretension which usually mars such poems. The feeling is true, and is manly in its sorrow; and if poets ever listened to the advice so liberally offered them by critics, we would counsel Robert Browning to spare us his caprices, and give us more such writing. He is still young, but he is old enough to have outlived the tendency which urges inexperienced poets into a fantastic and unreal region, simply because they have not sufficiently penetrated into the world of reality. For as Jean Paul, in his *Vorschule der Œsthetik*, admirably says, "the novelty of their feelings makes them suppose that the objects which excite them are also novel; and they believe that through the former they produce the latter. Hence they plunge either into the unknown and unnamed, in foreign lands and times; or, still more willingly, occupy themselves with the lyrical: for, in the Lyric, there is no other nature to be represented than that which the Lyrist brings with him."* This period Browning has outlived; and from him now, if ever, we ought to expect works that are the transcript of real experience.

But will he pardon us if we say, that we would more gladly meet him on the next occasion as a writer of prose? It may seem a strange compliment to pay a man who comes before us as a poet; yet a compliment it is. We could say the same to few of his rivals: mediocre as is their poetry, their prose we suspect would be detestable. By dint of assiduous study, "a reasonable good ear in music," and a fluent rhyming faculty, they produce verses which, if they do not touch the heart, nor stir the soul, do nevertheless, in some measure, gratify the ear. But if we pause for a moment to consider the *material* of their works, we shall find it so weak, vapid, common-place, or false, that to think of it in prose is alarming. They do not seem to have thought enough and seen enough to be able to be reasonable in prose. This is not the case with Browning. His works have many defects, but they have not that; they show a clear, open mind, prone to reflection; they show that he thinks for himself, and such a man is worth hearing. But he would be better worth hearing in prose than in verse, because, as Göthe said of the rhymers of his day, it is a pity to hear men attempt to *sing* what they can only *speak*.

Ihr Guten—grosser und Kleiner—
Ihr singt euch müde und matt;

---

*Die Neuheit ihrer Empfindungen muss ihnen als eine Neuheit der Gegenstände vorkommen; und durch die ersten glauben sie die letzten zu geben. Daher wirken sie sich Entweder ins Unbekannte und Unbenannte in fremde Läude und Zeiten ohne individualität; oder vorzüglick, auf das Lyrische; denn in diesem ist Keiner Natur nachzuahmen als die mitgebrachte.

Und singt doch keiner
Als was er zu sagen hat!

Browning is certainly not a born singer, and what is more, he has not caught the echo of another's music—he wants the melody and grace of which verse should be made. The sense of Beauty is not keen in him; and thoughts, however noble, conceptions, however grand, will not supply the place of beauty.

Pinxisti Venerem, colis, Artemidore, Minervam,
Et miraris opus displicuisse tuum?

asks Martial, and we may put the same question to Browning.

The exigences of prose would be beneficial to him, by curbing his capricious flights, and making him pay more attention to the ground plan than he now does. He will understand our meaning if we refer to *Pippa Passes*—one of the most admired of his "Bells and Pomegranates," and one that really contains some charming writing. What his purpose was, we know not; what the piece means, we have in vain asked ourselves and others. It opens with Pippa springing out of bed on New Year's Day, and in an irregular lyrical monologue informing us that she means to enjoy her holiday.

For am I not this day
Whate'er I please? Whom shall I seem to-day?
Morn, Noon, Eve, Night—how must I spend my day?

She then intimates her intention, though very vaguely, of personating several characters—

The brother,
The bride, the lover, and the mother—
Only to pass whom will remove—
Whom a mere look at half will cure
The Past, and help me to endure
The Coming .... I am just as great, no doubt,
As they! ...

At the conclusion of this very unintelligible monologue she enters the street, and the scene changes. We are then introduced to an adulteress and her paramour, who having just murdered the husband, are feverishly endeavouring in the assurances of their mutual love to drown their remorseful horror. This is a powerful scene, instinct with the true passion of the drama, and written with the vigour and somewhat of the licence of our Elizabethan dramatists. It also contains some fine lines of mere poetry. In the midst of their guilty triumph, as Ottima has bidden her lover to crown her as his queen,

Your spirit's arbitress
Magnificent in sin,

Pippa is heard singing without

The year's at Spring,
The day's at morn:
Morning's at seven,
The hillside's dew-pearled;
The lark's on the wing,
The snail's on the thorn,
God's in his heaven,
All's right in the world.

[Pippa passes.

The sound of this innocent voice at once arrests Sebald's guilty conscience, and in a paroxysm of remorse he slays his mistress and himself.

The scene then changes, and we have a new set of actors—young artists—and a new dramatic anecdote—which is closed in the same way, by a song from without, and the stage direction, *Pippa passes*. In this way throughout the piece Pippa is made, as it were, the conscience of the personages. The whole piece is but a collection of anecdotes or scenes, with that slender thread. At length we are conducted through this maze of writing to the final scene, which is Pippa's chamber. Her day is ended, and she returns home to favour us with some more unintelligible monologue. In the course of this she runs over the names of the personages introduced into the various scenes at which she *passed*, and she tells us that *she has been* these persons. Hear her:—

Ah, but—ah, but, all the same,
No mere mortal has a right
To carry that exalted air;
Best people are not angels quite—
While—not worst people's doings scare
The devils; so there's that regard to spare!
Mere counsel to myself, mind! for
I have just been Monsignor,
And I was you, too, mother,
And you, too, Luigi! How that Luigi started
Out of the turret—doubtlessly departed
On some love-errand or another—
And I was Jules the sculptor's bride.
And I was Ottima beside,
And now what am I? tired of fooling!

This is tolerably explicit, and further on she says:—

Now one thing I should like to really know:
How near I ever might approach all these
I only fancied being this long day.

From these indications we are led to suppose that all we have had passed before our eyes in the preceding scenes was but the pageant of a dream—a reflection of what was passing in the busy fancy of Pippa. If such was the poet's intention—and we can guess none other—he has very faintly in the piece indicated that which should have been clear as day; and he has, moreover, employed what appears to us a very clumsy and unsatisfactory machinery. Nor can we understand his purpose in giving us such a dream, or fancy-picture. Was it to show that even in the pure innocent soul of a young girl, there were contained the elements out of which (if thoughts were incarnated into acts) could be created the adulterer, the murderer, the egotistical artist, &c.? If so, he has not made out his case:—it is a paradox he has not made plausible.

But it is needless for us to multiply objections—none of his admirers have been able to tell us what was his intention in writing it; and, for ourselves, when we compare the passage wherein Pippa says, that the mere act of passing this bride, lover, and mother,

will remove
Whom a mere look at will half cure.
The past, and help me to endure
The coming ....

with her subsequent declaration that she *has been* these very persons, we are utterly bewildered. He may have had a purpose, and know what that purpose is, but he has failed to impart it to his readers.

To express in one sentence our disapproval of Browning's obscurity, we should say that it is not the obscurity which is suggestive, but the obscurity which is tiresome: it is not owing to the subtlety or profundity of the thoughts, but to the want of steadiness and clearness in the handling.

One ill consequence of his negligence in bringing out his purpose clearly, when he has one, is the transitoriness of the impression he leaves upon the mind. *The Blot on the 'Scutcheon* is a play we have read, and of which we otherwise have some knowledge, yet we have totally forgotten all about it, except that it seemed to us more Spanish than English in its feeling, and thoroughly false in the delineation of motives and passions. *The Flight of the Duchess* is a favourite with most readers, and contains some admirable writing; but surely never was a story worse told. In this singular poem we see Browning's merits and faults fully displayed. Its somewhat ostentatious luxuriance of rhyme has scarcely been surpassed by Butler, Pulci, or Byron; and some of the descriptive bits are admirable.

> Ours is a great wild country:
> If you climb to our castle's top,
> I don't see where your eye can stop;
> For when you've passed the corn-field country,
> Where vineyards leave off, flocks are pack'd;
> And sheep range yields to cattle tract,
> And cattle tract to open chase,
> And open chase to the very base
> Of the mountain, where, at a funeral pace,
> Round about, solemn and slow,
> One by one, row by row,
> Up and up the pine trees go,
> So, like black priests up, and so
> Down the other side again
> To another greater, wilder country,
> That's one vast red, drear, burnt-up plain,
> Branch'd thro' and thro' with many a vein
> Whence iron's dug, and copper's dealt;
> Look right, look left, look straight before,
> Beneath they mine, above they smelt
> Copper ore and iron ore,
> And forge and furnace, mould and melt,
> And so on, more and ever more,
> Till, at the last, for a bounding belt,
> Comes the salt and hoar of the great sea shore,
> And the whole is our Duke's country!

The Duke dies, and his "yellow Duchess" takes her infant abroad, where they remain many years, till the child had grown into a man:—

> And he came back the pertest ape
> That ever affronted human shape;
> Full of his travel, struck at himself—
> You'd say, he despised our bluff old ways
> —Not he! For in Paris they told the elf
> That our rough Northland was the Land of Lays,
> The one good thing left in evil days;
> For the Mid-Age was the Heroic Time,
> And only in wild nooks like ours
> Could you taste of it yet as in its prime,
> True Castles, with proper Towers,
> Young-hearted women, old-minded men,
> And manners now as manners were then.
> So, all the old Dukes had been, without knowing it,
> This Duke would fain know he was, without being it;
> 'Twas not for the joy's self, but the joy of his showing it,
> Nor for the pride's self, but the pride of our seeing it.
> He revived all usages thoroughly worn out,
> The souls of them fumed forth, the hearts of them torn-out:
> And chief in the chase his neck he perill'd;
> On a lathy horse, all legs and length,
> With blood for bone, all speed, no strength;
> —They should have set him on red Berold,
> With the red eye slow consuming in fire,
> And the thin stiff ear like an abbey spire!
>
> Well, such as he was, he must marry, we heard:
> And out of a convent, at the word,
> Came the lady, in time of spring,
> —Oh, old thoughts they cling, they cling!
> That day, I know, with a dozen oaths
> I clad myself in thick hunting clothes
> Fit for the chase of the urox or buffle,
> In winter-time when you need to muffle;
> But the Duke had a mind we should cut a figure,
> And so we saw the Lady arrive:
> My friend, I have seen a white crane bigger!
> She was the smallest Lady alive,
> Made, in a piece of Nature's madness,
> Too small, almost, for the life and gladness
> That over-filled her, as some hive
> Out of the bears' reach on the high trees
> Is crowded with its safe merry bees—
> In truth she was not hard to please!
> Up she look'd, down she look'd, round at the mead,
> Strait at the Castle, that's best indeed
> To look at from outside the walls:
> As for us, styled the "serfs and thralls,"
> She as much thanked me as if she had said it,
> (With her eye, do you understand?)
> Because I patted her horse while I led it;
> And Max, who rode on her other hand,
> Said, no bird flew past but she inquired
> What its true name was, nor ever seemed tired—
> If that was an eagle she saw hover,
> And the green and gray bird on the field was the plover?
> When suddenly appeared the Duke,
> And as down she sprung, the small foot pointed,
> On to my hand,—as with a rebuke,
> And as if his back bone were not jointed,
> The Duke stepped rather aside than forward,
> And welcomed her with his grandest smile;
> And, mind you, his mother all the while
> Chilled in the rear, like a wind to Nor'ward;
> And up, like a weary yawn, with its pullies
> Went, in a shriek, the rusty portcullis,
> And, like a glad sky the north-wind sullies,
> The Lady's face stopped its play,
> As if her first hair had grown grey—
> For such things must begin some one day!

This Duchess was an active, lively creature, who would have made an excellent chatelaine, but

> The Duke's plan admitted a wife at most
> To meet his eye with other trophies,
> Now outside the hall, now in it
> To sit thus, stand thus, see and be seen
> At the proper place in the proper minute,

And die away the life between.

She sickens and pines away, her health and spirit broken. The Dowager Duchess and the Duke always scolding and snubbing her; and when her husband sees her ailing, he swears it is done "to spite him."

> Well, early in autumn, at first winter warning,
> When the stag had to break with his foot, of a morning,
> A drinking hole out of the fresh tender ice
> That covered the pond till the sun, in a trice,
> Loosening it, let out a ripple of gold,
> And another and another, and faster and faster,
> Till, dimpling to blindness, the wide water rolled:
> Then it so chanced that the Duke, our master,
> Asked himself, what were the pleasures in season,
> And found, since the calendar bade him be hearty,
> He should do the Middle Age no treason
> In resolving on a hunting party.
> Always providing the old books showed the way of it.

With great pomp and preparation is this hunting party set on foot; and as the "old books" assigned a conspicuous place to the lady, it is of course resolved that the duchess is to fill that place with becoming state. To the duke's surprise, she refuses point blank. Her health would not allow of it. The duke is in a silent rage, and goes forth upon his expedition. A graphic description of gypsies is here introduced, for which we have no space. One of them, an old blear-eyed hag, comes forward to the duke—

> "She was come," she said, "to pay her duty
> To the new duchess, the youthful beauty:"
> No sooner had she named his lady,
> Than a shine lit up the face so shady;
> And its smirk returned with a novel meaning—
> For it struck him, the babe just wanted weaning;
> If one gave her a taste of what life is and sorrow,
> She, foolish to-day, would be wiser to-morrow;
> And who so fit a teacher of trouble,
> As this sordid crone, bent well nigh double?
> So, glancing at her wolf-skin vesture,
> (If such it was, for they grow so hirsute,
> That their own fleece serves for natural fur-suit.)
> He contrasted, 'twas plain from his gesture,
> The life of the lady, so flower-like and delicate,
> With the loathsome squalor of this helicat.
> I, in brief, was the man the duke beckoned
> From out of the throng; and while I drew near
> He told the crone, as I since have reckoned,
> By the way he bent and spoke into her ear
> With circumspection and mystery,
> The main of the lady's history,
> Her frowardness and ingratitude;
> And for all the crone's submissive attitude
> I could see round her mouth the loose plaits tightening,
> And her brow with assenting intelligence brightening,
> As though she engaged with hearty good will
> Whatever he now might enjoin to fulfil,
> And promised the lady a thorough frightening.
> And so just giving her a glimpse
> Of a purse, with the air of a man who imps
> The wing of the hawk that shall fetch the hernshaw,
> He bade me take the gypsy mother,
> And set her telling some story or other,
> Of hill or dale, oakwood or fernshaw,
> To while away a weary hour
> For the lady left alone in her bower,
> Whose mind and body craved exertion,
> And yet shrank from all better diversion.

The old gipsy has an interview with the duchess, and then, as far as we can make out the drift of some very obscure writing, she either entices the duchess away, inducing her to leave this wretched do-nothing life, and join the free roving gipsies, or else, by some necromantic spell, spirits her away. The upshot clearly is, that the duchess departs and returns no more.

It would have cost the poet very little trouble to have made all clear, which in this work is so obscure; but that little trouble he has not chosen to bestow. What is the consequence? The poem leaves no distinct impression. We have waded through columns of rhyme, sometimes pleased with a fine image, sometimes with a vigorous description, often with a strange sense of the writer's power; but we close the book with no desire to recur to it, with no picture on which to dwell. In a word, the substance of the poem has been sacrificed to the mere writing. This will appear idle criticism to our modern poets, no doubt; they only think of "passages," and if they have succeeded in writing here and there some dozen lines that will look well in extract, they believe they have written a poem. It is not so, however. A poem is not made out of "passages;" it is the musical embodiment of some strong emotion or some deep thought; and however necessary beauty may be to the expression, the thing to be expressed requires equal if not greater labour.

In bringing our rambling observations to a close, we should say that Robert Browning deserves his position from his originality; but although his name has a certain celebrity, he has not yet won for himself a niche in the temple of his nation's literature. He is rather a thinker than a singer; and yet cannot be accepted as a remarkable thinker. The general conception of his larger works is weak and wavering, but the details exhibit no common powers. Whatever merits he may possess, are, however, damaged by the eccentricity and want of beauty of his style. It is abrupt, harsh, full of familiar turns, and yet not familiar in its general structure; spasmodic in its vehemence, and obscure from mere negligence. We should be loath to charge him with affectation; but it does appear astonishing that any man so well read as Robert Browning, should play such tricks with his style, except for the purpose of aping originality and attracting attention. Originality lies not in being unlike the rest of mankind. That is eccentricity. What is true and beautiful, has always a direct parentage with everything else that is true and beautiful. Originality, therefore, will not be shown in startling the public with a novelty; but in producing that which is at once novel yet familiar: like many other things, and yet distinctly individual, and having such an air of ease and obviousness, that people will wonder it was never done before.

We have been sparing of extracts, as neither the novelty nor the costliness of the works warranted our occupying space with passages to support our opinions. As the effect of this has perhaps been somewhat unfavourable to the poet, we cannot do better than conclude with quoting his much-admired romance:—

HOW HE BROUGHT THE GOOD NEWS FROM GHENT TO AIX.

I.

I sprang to the stirrup, and Joris and He;
I galloped, Dirck galloped, we galloped all three.
"Good speed!" cried the watch, as the gate bolts undrew;
"Speed!" echoed the wall to us galloping through;
Behind shut the postern, the lights sank to rest,
And into the midnight we galloped abreast.

II.

Not a word to each other, we kept the great pace
Neck by neck, stride by stride, never changing our place;
I turned in my saddle and made its girths tight,
Then shortened each stirrup, and set the pique right,
Rebuckled the check-strap, chained slacker the bit,
Nor galloped less steadily Roland a whit.

III.

'Twas moonset at starting; but while we drew near
Lokeren, the cocks crew and twilight dawned clear;
At Boom, a great yellow star came out to see;
At Düffeld, 'twas morning as plain as could be;
And from Mecheln church steeple we heard the halfchime,
So Joris broke silence, with "Yet there is time!"

IV.

At Aerschot, up leaped of a sudden the sun,
And against him the cattle stood black every one,
To stare through the mist at us galloping past,
And I saw my stout galloper Roland at last,
With resolute shoulders, each butting away
The haze, as some bluff river headland its spray.

V.

And his low head and crest, just one sharp ear bent back,
For my voice, and the other pricked out on his track;
And one eye's black intelligence—ever that glance
O'er its white edge at me, his own master, askance!
And the thick heavy spume flakes, which aye and anon
His fierce lips shook upwards in galloping on.

VI.

By Hasselt, Dirck groaned, and cried Joris, "Stay spur!
Your Roos galloped bravely, the fault's not in her,
We'll remember at Aix"—for one heard the quick wheeze
Of her chest, saw the stretched neck and staggering knees,
And sunk tail, and horrible heave of the flank,
As down on her haunches she shuddered and sank.

VII.

So left were we galloping, Joris and I,
Past Looz and past Tongres, no cloud in the sky;
The broad sun above laughed a pitiless laugh,
'Neath our feet broke the brittle bright stubble like chaff;
Till over by Dalkem a dome spire sprang white,
And "Gallop!" gasped Joris, "for Aix is in sight!"

VIII.

"How they'll greet us,"—and all in a moment his roan
Rolled neck and croup over, lay dead as a stone;
And there was my Roland to bear the whole weight
Of the news which alone could save Aix from her fate,
With his nostrils like pits full of blood to the brim,
And with circles of red for his eye-sockets' rim.

IX.

Then I cast loose my buff coat, each holster let fall,
Shook off both my jack-boots, let go belt and all;
Stood up in the stirrup, leaned, patted his ear,
Called my Roland his pet name, my horse without peer;
Clapped my hands, laughed and sang, any noise, bad or good,
Till at length into Aix Roland galloped, and stood.

X.

And all I remember is, friends flocking round
As I sate with his head 'twixt my knees on the ground,
And no voice but was praising this Roland of mine,
As I poured down his throat our last measure of wine,
Which (the burgesses voted, by common consent)
Was no more than his due who brought good news to Ghent.

[G.H. Lewes]

Appendix IV

EBB's Letters to Her Sister Henrietta

LEONARD HUXLEY, IN his introduction to *Elizabeth Barrett Browning: Letters to Her Sister, 1846–1859* (1929), makes the following comment: "Henrietta lovingly preserved those [letters] which were written to her; in 1875, many years after her death, her husband reinsured their existence with no less care by copying them all into a set of quarto MS. books. His invaluable foreword and notes explain family history and allusions in a way possible only to one who still had personal knowledge of those concerned." Huxley did not prepare his edition of EBB's letters to Henrietta from the holographs, but worked from the transcripts made by Surtees, who edited out over two-fifths of their content. Huxley made further excisions, "many nursery details" and "passing references to persons and things that have no general interest," with the result that he published approximately half of the text.

Within a few months of the appearance of Huxley's work, the family was approached by a book dealer who acquired the original letters. They exchanged hands several times and eventually became an integral part of the private library of Arthur A. Houghton, Jr. While in his possession, Mr. Houghton graciously allowed the present editors to prepare full transcripts. The holographs remained with Mr. Houghton until 13 June 1979 when they sold at Christie's, London, as lot 66. Their present whereabouts are unknown.

The copies made by Surtees are still in family hands and have been used extensively by the present editors. We consider his introduction, written from an unique perspective, merits publication. We extend our gratitude to Mary V. Altham for permission to present it here.

Happy Years of Elizabeth Barrett Browning
by William Surtees Altham (*né* Cook)

Elizabeth Barrett (whose works the public are familiar with) was the daughter of Edward Barrett Moulton-Barrett of Hope End Herefordshire J.P. and Sheriff for the county in 1814. Her father was born 28.th of May 1785, was educated at Harrow, and at Trinity College Cambridge as a gentleman Commoner; and he died at his house 50 Wimpole Street, in London, 27.th of April 1857. The paternal name was, originally, Moulton; but in 1798, when minors, he and his brother Samuel Moulton-Barrett, (of Carlton Hall Yorkshire, M.P. for Richmond in that county, who died without issue,) on succeeding to the estates, in Jamaica, of their maternal grandfather, Edward Barrett of Cinnamon Hill, had the surname of Barrett conferred on them and their descendants, by licence from the Crown, in *addition* to that of Moulton. The name was, therefore, in reality, Moulton-Barrett, though the tendency was to drop the Moulton altogether. The Moultons were an old Royalist family. The Barretts were whigs.

Edward and Samuel Moulton-Barrett had rather a long minority. They started in life, on coming of age, each with a clear income of at least £12000 a year; but they of course felt the effects of the change of England's policy in Jamaica—the abolition of that evil thing slavery. Their hearts and consciences went with emancipation, but their purses suffered. Edward Moulton-Barrett, who by the way was never in Jamaica,[1] always maintained that the withdrawal of duty on slave grown sugar was the only grievance proprietors, if they were Christian men, could legitimately complain of. This he argued was unjust, a cowardly concession to mistaken clamour, and an encouragement to that slavery which we profess so to abominate. The slave owner might fairly urge that he cannot forego good income, and therefore must have slaves to work his plantations, IF the British consumer be allowed to plead that he cannot forego cheap sugar, and must buy from Cuba. The difference is only in degree. When the shoe pinches the world is apt to be inconsistent. Edward Moulton-Barrett's eldest surviving son (and present representative), when a very young man, once had the temerity to proclaim, in the generosity of his heart, at a festive board in Jamaica in 1839, to the dismay of his fellow guests, that he thought the compensation money allotted by Parliament ought not to have gone to the Landowners, but to the slaves as a compensation for their sufferings.

Hope End, the beautiful seat of Edward Moulton-Barrett, beneath the Malvern Hills, eventually passed to another family. We give a sketch of the mansion as it stood in 1832. A new proprietor has stamped out the Hope End where Elizabeth Barrett Browning passed her childhood and youth. An

---

1. Surtees has the following note: "R. Browning says he was brought from Jamaica to England as a small child, on the death of his father." For Edward Moulton-Barrett's childhood see our Volume 1, pp. 286–287. Charles Moulton, his father, did not die until 1819.

Hope End Mansion

Elizabethan edifice now appears in its place: but we hear it was hard work to pick to pieces the costly pile erected by Edward Moulton-Barrett; and it would seem, to the uninitiated, rather a capricious waste of substantial stone masonry. We might, at one time, almost have said, with another poet:–

> Here didst thou dwell, here schemes of pleasure plan,
> Beneath yon mountain's ever beauteous brow:
> But now, as if a thing unblest by man,
> Thy faery dwelling is as lone as thou!
> *Childe Harold.*

The mother of Elizabeth Barrett Browning of whom so little has been said, (and from whom so much sweetness of disposition, so much gentleness, goodness, beauty, permeated to her descendants,) was the daughter of John Graham-Clarke of Kenton Lodge, Northumberland, by Arabella daughter and co-heir of Roger Altham, who derived from Mark-hall in Latton, Essex. We are all proud of consanguinity to Elizabeth Barrett Browning. Beautiful in mind as in person, her mother was one whom to know, it was said, was to love. Edward Moulton-Barrett fixed his first, his earliest, his only affections, in this direction. His guardian, the first Lord Abinger, conceiving it to be a mere boyish passion that would pass away, would not, at first, yield consent. He had never seen the Lady, and it was artfully arranged that he should meet her at a dinner party, where it was contrived that he should escort to the dining room the very fascinating and beautiful young creature who had so charmed his ward. On being told who she was, he exclaimed, (so it has been handed down,) "I hold out no longer—she is far too good for him!" They were married on the 20th of May 1805, the bridegroom being under age. In conformity with Sir Bernard Burke's courteous custom, we do not give the date of birth, where ladies are concerned. She died Oct. 1. 1828; and the parents of Elizabeth Barrett Browning rest in peace, in one grave, in Ledbury Church, Herefordshire, the parish in which Hope End is situated, where a marble monument, by Lough, has been erected to their memory. A pleasant path on the southern side of a piece of water in Hope End park, where Mrs Moulton-Barrett was wont to take exercise in her last illness, used to be known, in the long years ago, as "Mrs Barrett's walk."

Of this marriage there were eight sons, of whom five survive; and three daughters. The eldest son, Edward, was drowned in 1839, with two other young men, by the capsizing of a small yacht, at Torquay, where he had gone, with his sister the poetess who had broken a small blood vessel, her delicacy of health proceeding from no other cause. This was the source of her long sorrow. They were the nearest in years, the "Bro and Ba" (pet names) who clung to each other with more than usual tenderness; and the terrible idea would possess her mind that, had he not gone to Torquay on her account, his young life might have been spared. We do not think the gloom of this sad event altogether passed away until her marriage with Robert Browning in 1846, when a new life sprung upon her, new hopes, more cheerful writing, effulgence, happiness, which may easily be perceived pervading her letters. Elizabeth Barrett Browning died at Florence on the 29th of June 1861, where she was buried. Her sisters were Henrietta Barrett, (to whom the letters were addressed,) who married in 1850, her second cousin William Surtees Cook, (late a Major in 83d Foot); she died in 1860: and Arabella who died unmarried, in 1868, at her residence of Delamere Terrace, London. How the three sisters cleaved to each other, in wondrous affection, the letters abundantly show.

We believe this is all that need be stated. A hope was once whispered, by a gentle spirit "gone before," that these letters might one day be submitted to the public. A new generation is cropping up that "know not Joseph"; and the hand may soon be still who alone is familiar with all the niceties, all the delicacy required in fulfilling the hope– It has been said that the letters, especially domestic letters, unguarded and unprepared, of Elizabeth Barrett Browning, were thrown off with such facility, and always so naturally, so happily and pleasantly expressed that they indicate a latent power in prose, which might, had she so selected, have equalled, if not surpassed in brilliancy her own poetry. The public will judge for themselves.

APPENDIX V

The Brownings in 1847

DURING THE EARLY months of their marriage the Brownings enjoyed a brief period of anonymity—"not receiving six visits in six months" (letter 2705). As interest in their personal life intensified, they were sought out and comments began to appear in private correspondence and print; but there is little available of this nature from which to draw referring to their early days in Italy.

One of the earliest callers on the Brownings was Father Prout who made a passing reference to them in a volume which appeared at the end of 1847 (see letter 2704, note 8). Another early visitor was Mary Boyle whose recollections appeared in 1901 (see letter 2698, note 2). Two Americans, George Stillman Hillard and George William Curtis, who called separately on the Brownings during the period covered by this volume, left brief records of their visits.

Hillard's account appeared in 1853. Subsequently, RB wrote to his sister Sarianna, 19 December 1853: "I see Murray is going to reprint an American book of travels in Italy by Mr Hillard we knew a few years ago—it having had a great success in the U. States—so much the worse for them, for it is really a very poor commonplace affair, far beneath what I should have judged the author capable of producing—see it however, if you can for the sake of the flaming account of 'the Brownings'" (MS at Lilly Library).

Curtis published his recollections of the Brownings on two occasions, the first following the death of EBB in 1861 and the second that of RB in 1889. The versions are markedly different, modified for the events that precipitated them.

To amplify the letters of 1847 we reprint Hillard's and Curtis's accounts in full.

I

by George Stillman Hillard
From *Six Months in Italy*, Boston, 1853, I, 177–178.

It is well for the traveller to be chary of names. It is an ungrateful return for hospitable attentions, to print the conversation of your host, or describe his person, or give an inventory of his furniture, or proclaim how his wife and daughters were dressed. But I trust I may be pardoned if I state, that one of my most delightful associations with Florence arises from the fact, that here I made the acquaintance of Robert and Elizabeth Browning. These are even more familiar names in America than in England, and their poetry is probably more read, and better understood with us, than among their own countrymen. A happier home and a more perfect union than theirs, it is not easy to imagine; and this completeness arises not only from the rare qualities which each possesses, but from their adaptation to each other. Browning's conversation is like the poetry of Chaucer, or like his own, simplified and made transparent. His countenance is so full of vigor, freshness, and refined power, that it seems impossible to think that he can ever grow old. His poetry is subtle, passionate, and profound; but he himself is simple, natural, and playful. He has the repose of a man who has lived much in the open air; with no nervous uneasiness and no unhealthy self-consciousness. Mrs. Browning is in many respects the correlative of her husband. As he is full of manly power, so she is a type of the most sensitive and delicate womanhood. She has been a great sufferer from ill health, and the marks of pain are stamped upon her person and manner. Her figure is slight, her countenance expressive of genius and sensibility, shaded by a veil of long brown locks; and her tremulous voice often flutters over her words, like the flame of a dying candle over the wick. I have never seen a human frame which seemed so nearly a transparent veil for a celestial and immortal spirit. She is a soul of fire enclosed in a shell of pearl. Her rare and fine genius need no setting forth at my hands. She is also, what is not so generally known, a woman of uncommon, nay, profound learning, even measured by a masculine standard. Nor is she more remarkable for genius and learning, than for sweetness of temper, tenderness of heart, depth of feeling, and purity of spirit. It is a privilege to know such beings singly and separately, but to see their powers quickened, and their happiness rounded by the sacred tie of marriage, is a cause for peculiar and lasting gratitude. A union so complete as theirs—in which the mind has nothing to crave nor the heart to sigh for—is cordial to behold and soothing to remember.

II
by George William Curtis
From "Editor's Easy Chair," *Harper's New Monthly Magazine*, September 1861, pp. 555–556.

Fourteen years ago this Easy Chair was sitting one day in his cool room in Florence—cool, although it was Italy and summer. A knock at the door was followed by the brisk entrance of one of the few men in Europe that Mr. Easy Chair then cared to see—Robert Browning. How delightful the hour that followed was, those at once know who know Robert Browning. It ended with a promise of meeting at Browning's tea-table that evening.

In the evening the same alert, robust, thoroughly English-looking man presented to his wife one of the thousand young Americans who had read with eager enthusiasm her then recently-published volumes, which had a more general and hearty welcome in the United States than any English poet since the time of Byron and Company, who were the poets of our fathers.

The visitor saw, seated at the tea-table in the great room of the palace in which they were living, a very small, very slight woman, with very long curls drooping forward, almost across the eyes, hanging to the bosom, and quite concealing the pale, small face, from which the piercing, inquiring eyes looked out sensitively at the stranger. Rising from her chair she put out cordially the thin, white hand of an invalid, and in a few moments they were pleasantly chatting, while the husband strode up and down the room, joining in the conversation with a vigor, humor, eagerness, and affluence of curious lore which, with his trenchant thought and subtle sympathy, make him one of the most charming and inspiring of companions.

A few days after the same party, with one or two more, went to Vallombrosa, where they passed two days. Mrs. Browning was still too much of an invalid to walk, but we sat under the great trees upon the lawn-like hill-sides near the convent, or in the seats in the dusky convent-chapel, while Robert Browning at the organ chased a fugue of Master Hugues, of Saxe-Gotha, or dreamed out upon twilight keys a faith-throbbing toccata of Galuppi's.

In all her conversation, so mild and tender and womanly, so true and intense and rich with rare learning, there was a girl-like simplicity and sensitiveness and a womanly earnestness that took the heart captive. She was deeply and most intelligently interested in America and Americana, and felt a kind of enthusiastic gratitude to them for their generous fondness of her poetry.

She had been married not a year, and since then she has lived almost exclusively in Italy. Few Italians, and certainly no foreigner, are so saturated with the very spirit of Italy as her husband; and few Italians and no foreigner have been more enthusiastically devoted than she to the political regeneration of that country. Her poems within a few years have been almost exclusively inspired by her Italian political sympathies, and have insensibly been much moulded in their expression by the style of her husband.

Without question or delay Elizabeth Barrett Browning must be counted among the chief English poets of this century, and unquestionably the first English poet of her sex. And her memorable excellence will be that she was not only a singer but a hearty, active worker in her way, understanding her time, and trying, as she could, to help it. It is a curious juxtaposition, that of "Don Juan" and "Aurora Leigh," and yet they are related in this that they are the two great poems of modern English social life as felt by a man of the world and a religious woman, who were both poets. On the other hand, the literature of love has had few additions since the *Vita Nuova*, the sonnets of Shakespeare, and of Petrarch (if you like him), so true and sweet and subtle as Mrs. Browning's "Sonnets from the Portuguese." And were they not repaid by the "One word more," the last poem in Browning's last volume?

Her public fame will make her widely mentioned. Literature mourns a loss. But the private grief to the many who loved her is a deeper pang. Her death changes Italy and Europe to how many! If you would know what she was, read Browning's "One word more." He made no secret of it; why should another?

"This I say of me, but think of you, Love!
This to you, yourself my moon of poets!
Ah! but that's the world's side—there's the
 wonder—
Thus they see you, praise you, think they
 know you,
There, in turn, I stand with them and praise
 you,
Out of my own self I dare to phrase it.
But the best is when I glide from out them,
Cross a step or two of dubious twilight,
Come out on the other side, the novel
Silent silver lights and darks undreamed of,
Where I hush and bless myself with silence."

III

by George William Curtis
From: "Editor's Easy Chair," *Harper's New Monthly Magazine*, March 1890, pp. 637–639.

It is more than forty years since Margaret Fuller first gave distinction to the literary notices and reviews of the New York *Tribune*. Miss Fuller was a woman of extraordinary scholarly attainments and intellectual independence, the friend of Emerson and of the "transcendental" leaders, and her critical papers were the best then published, and were fitly succeeded by those of her scholarly friend George Ripley. It was her review in the *Tribune* of Browning's early dramas and the "Bells and Pomegranates" that introduced him to such general knowledge and appreciation among cultivated readers in this country that it is not less true of Browning than of Carlyle that he was first better known in American than at home.

It was but about four years before the publication of Miss Fuller's paper that the Boston issue of Tennyson's two volumes had delighted the youth of the time with the consciousness of the appearance of a new English poet. The eagerness and enthusiasm with which Browning was welcomed soon after were more limited in extent, but they were even more ardent, and the devoted zeal of Mr. Levi Thaxter as a Browning missionary and pioneer forecast the interest from which the Browning societies of later days have sprung.

When Matthew Arnold was told in a small and remote farming village in New England that there had been a lecture upon Browning in the town the week before, he stopped in amazement, and said, "Well, that is the most surprising and significant fact I have heard in America."

It was in those early days of Browning's fame, and in the studio of the sculptor Powers in Florence, that the youthful Easy Chair took up a visiting card, and reading the name Mr. Robert Browning, asked, with eager earnestness whether it was Browning the poet. Powers turned his large, calm, lustrous eyes upon the youth, and answered, with some surprise at the warmth of the question:

"It is a young Englishman, recently married, who is here with his wife, an invalid. He often comes to the studio."

"Good Heaven!" exclaimed the youth, "it must be Browning and Elizabeth Barrett."

Powers, with the half-bewildered air of one suddenly made conscious that he had been entertaining angels unawares, said reflectively, "I think we must have them to tea."

The youth begged to take the card which bore the poet's address, and hastening to his room near the Piazza Novella, he wrote a note asking permission for a young American to call and pay respects to Mr. and Mrs. Browning, but wrote it in terms which, however warm, would yet permit it to be put aside if it seemed impertinent, or if for any reason such a call were not desired. The next morning betimes the note was despatched, and a half-hour had not passed when there was a brisk rap at the Easy Chair's door. He opened it, and saw a young man, who briskly inquired,

"Is Mr. Easy Chair here?"

"That is my name."

"I am Robert Browning." Browning shook hands heartily with his young American admirer, and thanked him for his note. The poet was then about thirty-five. His figure was not large, but compact, erect, and active; the face smooth, the hair dark; the aspect that of active intelligence, and of a man of the world. He was in no way eccentric, either in manner or appearance. He talked freely, with great vivacity, and delightfully, rising and walking about the room as his talk sparkled on. He heard, with evident pleasure, but with entire simplicity and manliness, of the American interest in his works and in those of Mrs. Browning, and the Easy Chair gave him a copy of Miss Fuller's paper in the *Tribune*. It was a bright, and to the Easy Chair, a wonderfully happy hour. As he went, the poet said that Mrs. Browning would certainly expect to give Mr. Easy Chair a cup of tea in the evening, and with a brisk and gay good-by, Browning was gone.

The Easy Chair blithely hied him to the Café Doné, and ordered of the flower girl the most perfect of nosegays, with such fervor that she smiled, and when she brought the flowers in the afternoon, said, with sympathy and meaning: "Eccola, signore! per la donna bellissima!"

It was not in the Casa Guidi that the Brownings were then living, but in an apartment in the Via della Scala, not far from the place or square most familiar to strangers in Florence—the Piazza Trinità. Through several rooms the Easy Chair passed, Browning leading the way, until at the end they entered a smaller room arranged with an air of English comfort, where at a table, bending over a tea-urn, sat a slight lady, her long curls drooping forward. "Here," said Browning, addressing her with a tender diminutive, "here is Mr. Easy Chair." And as the bright eyes but wan face of the lady turned toward him, and she put out her hand, Mr. Easy Chair recalled the first words of her verse he had ever known:

"'Onora, Onora!' her mother is calling.
She sits at the lattice, and hears the dew falling,
Drop after drop from the sycamore laden
With dew as with blossom, and calls home
  the maiden.
'Night cometh Onora!'"

The most kindly welcome and pleasant chat followed, Browning's gayety dashing and flashing in, with a sense of profuse and bubbling vitality, glancing at a hundred topics; and when there was some allusion to his "Sordello," he asked, quickly, with an amused smile, "Have you read it?" The Easy Chair pleaded that he had not seen it. "So much the better. Nobody understands it. Don't read it except in the revised form which is coming." The revised form has come long ago, and the Easy Chair has read, and probably supposes that he understands. But Thackeray used to say that he did not read Browning because he could not comprehend him, adding, ruefully, "I have no head above my eyes."

A few days later—

"O day of days! O perfect day!"—

the Easy Chair went with Mr. and Mrs. Browning to Vallombrosa, and the one incident most clearly remembered is that of Browning's seating himself at the organ in the chapel, and playing—some Gregorian chant, perhaps, or hymn of Pergolesi's. It was enough to the enchanted eyes of his young companion that they saw him who was already a great English poet sitting at the organ where the young Milton had sat, and touching the very keys which Milton's hand had pressed.

It was midsummer in Italy, but the high narrow streets of Florence stretch a protecting shade over the lingering pilgrim, and from such companionship as that of the Via della Scala even Venice long wooed in vain. But at last, reluctantly, although the fascinating way lay through Bologna and Ferrara, the journey began toward Venice; and in that city, so early and always dear to Browning, whose romantic life and story most deeply touched and stirred his imagination, and in which he lately died, the Easy Chair received from the poet a glimpse of his earliest impressions.

Writing from Casa Guidi, in Florence, on the 9th of August, 1847—Casa Guidi, upon which a tablet records that there Elizabeth Barrett and Robert Browning lived, and *Casa Guidi Windows*, *Sonnets from the Portuguese*, and *Aurora Leigh* were written—Browning says:

"The people of the house there [Via della Scala] told us honestly on the morning of your departure that they could only receive us for a single month, at the expiration of which were to begin certain whitewashings and repaintings. We continued our quest, therefore, and at last found out this cool, airy apartment, which we shall occupy for another month or six weeks, whatever be our subsequent plans, for Rome, or for the Venice you describe. ...

I spent a month of entire delight there some eight years ago, and tho' nothing I have since seen has effaced the impressions of my visit, yet your fresher feelings *bring out* whatever looks faint or dubious in them, as a gentle sponging might revive the gone glory of some old picture. (You must know I have seen an exquisite copy of a Giorgione, the original of which—so I was told—grew only visible and intelligible when thus wetted.) I am glad the railroad and gas-lighting do Venice no more wrong, and that you find all the old strange quietness, and—ought I to be glad of this, too?—depopulation; for of late years we have heard a great deal of the returning life and prosperity of the place; and Mr. Valery, I observe, retracts his earlier bodements of a speedy extinction of what little glimmer of light he still saw.

As for me, I remember that the accounts of the depreciation of the value of houses, coupled with the indifference of the inhabitants of them, were enough to set one dreaming (in one's gondola!) of getting to be as rich as Rothschild, buying all Venice, turning out everybody, and ensconcing one's self in the Doge's palace, among the dropping gold ornaments and flakes of what was lustrous color in Titian's or Tintoret's time, waiting for the proper consummation of all things and the sea's advent.

But do you really find the air so light and pure in this by right mephitic time of August, with those close *calles*, pestilential lagunes, etc., etc., and all that our informants frighten us with? Should a winter in Venice prove no more formidable in its way than it seems a summer does, why, we may have cause to regret our determination to give up our original plans. I am sure your kindness will tell us, should it be enabled, any good news of the winter and spring climate—if weak lungs may brave it with impunity." ... .

To this letter of Browning's, written in his young manhood—he was then thirty-five—about the Venice which always charmed him, may be well added the words of the Lady of Mura, written only a few weeks before the poet's death. Asolo is a sequestered town, which Browning said that he discovered, and in which he fell under the glamour of very Italy. In the prologue to his last volume, written in September before the letter that follows, the poet says:

"How many a year, My Asolo,
   Since—one step just from sea to land—
I found you, loved, yet feared you so—
   For natural objects seems to stand
   Palpably fire-clothed!"

The letter says:

"I have bought in ancient Asolo a narrow, tall tower, into which in the last century (very early) a house was built, and this curious place I have selected for villeggiatura when the scirocco is too strong in Venice for health or comfort. It was here that Browning fifty years ago was inspired to write 'Sordello' and 'Pippa Passes,' so to me it has that charm added to many others. It is such a rough and out-of-the-way little place that you may only know it by name. There is no hotel, no railway, no factory, no sign of modern civilization. It is on a hill, which has an ancient ruined fortress at the top, and was an old Roman settlement, with the usual Roman *mise en scène*, baths, amphitheatre, etc., in the days of Pliny, who somewhere mentions it.

Near my tower, which is built in the ancient wall of the mediæval town, is the tower of Caterina Cornaro, and one sees from most of my windows, so high are they, the whole Marca Trevigiana, with its tragic and dramatic associations of the early Middle Ages; the Eccelini, the Azzi, the incessant wars in which towns were treated by the tyrants like shuttlecocks in the game of battledoor.

Browning and his sister have been here for the last six weeks, and you may fancy how intensely the poet enjoys revisiting after so many years the scenes of his youthful inspirations. He was only twenty-five or six when he first discovered Asolo. ... Few young people are so gay and cheerful as he and his dear old sister." ... .

It is a pleasant last glimpse of Browning at Asolo, where the master-spell of Italy first touched his genius, and whither at the end he came—"*asolare*, to disport in the open air, amuse one's self at random"—at heart and in temper of the same unquenched and unquenchable vitality as on that summer day long ago when he sat where Milton had sat, and pressed, as Milton had pressed, the keys of the organ at Vallombrosa.

"Ah, did you once see Shelley plain?
   And did he speak to you?
And did you speak to him again?—
   How strange it seems and new!"

List of Absent Letters

DURING THE COURSE of our research in editing the Brownings' correspondence, brief references have been found, principally in sale catalogues, to additional letters. All attempts to locate these documents have failed. In addition, some letters are in known locations, but access to them has been denied. Following is a list of letters which, for such reasons, are absent from this volume. Those that are located and become available will be presented in a supplementary volume.

21 September 1846. Anna Dorothea & Basil Montagu to EBB & RB. 1 p., 8vo. In the private collection of Peter N. Heydon.

21 September [1846]. Robert Pauncefote to RB. *I have just thrown down the paper* ... . 2 pp., 8vo. In the private collection of Peter N. Heydon.

23 September 1846. John Hanmer to RB. 2½ pp., 8vo. In the private collection of Peter N. Heydon.

23 September 1846. John Westland Marston to RB. 2 pp., 8vo. In the private collection of Peter N. Heydon.

[24 September 1846]. Richard Monckton Milnes to RB. *Your mysterious card reached me yesterday* ... . 2 pp., 8vo. In the private collection of Peter N. Heydon.

25 September 1846. Frederick Oldfield Ward to RB. 4 pp., 8vo. In the private collection of Peter N. Heydon.

List of Collections

(References are to letter number, not page number.)

Armstrong Browning Library, Baylor University, Waco, Texas, 2644, 2690, 2704, 2708

Altham, Mary V., Babbacombe, England, 2619

Barrett, Gordon E. Moulton-, Mobe Sound, Florida, 2649, 2672, 2716

Berg Collection, The Henry W. & Albert A., The New York Public Library, Astor, Lenox and Tilden Foundations, 2620, 2624, 2640, 2645, 2655, 2656, 2660, 2668, 2680–2682, 2686, 2691, 2697

British Library, Department of Manuscripts, London, 2632, 2661, 2694, 2700

Fitzwilliam Museum, Cambridge, England, 2667

California State University, Hayward, California, 2659

Huntington Library, The Henry E., San Marino, California, 2696, 2698, 2706, 2709

Lilly Library, The, Bloomington, Indiana, 2639, 2658, 2674, 2695

Meredith, Michael, Eton, England, 2638, 2688

Morgan Library, The Pierpont, New York, 2616, 2623, 2636, 2637, 2715

New York Public Library, Manuscript Division, New York, 2675

Texas, University of, Harry Ransom Humanities Research Center, Austin, Texas, 2702

Trinity College, Cambridge, England, 2665

Turnbull Library, Alexander H., Wellington, New Zealand, 2662, 2685

Vaticana, Biblioteca Apostolica, Rome, Italy, 2646

Wellesley College Library, The English Poetry Collection, Wellesley, Massachusetts, 2617, 2622, 2625–2629, 2642, 2643, 2652–2654, 2669, 2671, 2676, 2679, 2687, 2692, 2703, 2713, 2714

Yale University, The Beinecke Rare Book and Manuscript Library, New Haven, Connecticut, 2666, 2683

List of Correspondents

(References are to letter number, not page number.)

Arnould, Joseph, 2623, 2637, 2662, 2685, 2715
Arnould, Maria, 2637
Barrett, Arabella Moulton-, 2620, 2621, 2624, 2630, 2631, 2640, 2645, 2655, 2656, 2660, 2663, 2668, 2672, 2673, 2680, 2681, 2686, 2690, 2697, 2701, 2705, 2712, 2716
Barrett, George Goodin Moulton-, 2616
Barrett, Henrietta Moulton-, 2621, 2630, 2631, 2641, 2647, 2650, 2655, 2663, 2664, 2670, 2673, 2678, 2684, 2689, 2690, 2701, 2705, 2707, 2711, 2712
Barrett, Septimus Moulton-, 2649
Boyd, Hugh Stuart, 2628, 2634, 2643, 2679
Boyle, Mary Louisa, 2699, 2708
Browning, Elizabeth Barrett Moulton-Barrett, 2616–2622, 2624–2630, 2632, 2634, 2636, 2638–2650, 2652–2656, 2658–2661, 2663, 2664, 2667–2672, 2674–2676, 2678–2681, 2684, 2686–2689, 2691, 2692, 2694–2704, 2707, 2709, 2711, 2713, 2714, 2716
Browning, Robert, 2618, 2623, 2631, 2633, 2635, 2637, 2651, 2653, 2655, 2657, 2659, 2662, 2663, 2665, 2666, 2673, 2677, 2682, 2683, 2685, 2687, 2688, 2690, 2693, 2705, 2706, 2708, 2710, 2712, 2714, 2715

Browning, Sarianna, 2639, 2658, 2674, 2695
Carlyle, Thomas 2677, 2682
Chorley, Henry Fothergill, 2651
Curtis, George William, 2693
Dowglass, Fanny, 2691, 2696, 2698, 2702, 2709
Duyckinck, George Long, 2675
Haworth, Euphrasia Fanny, 2683
Horne, Richard Hengist, 2618, 2635, 2636, 2688
Jameson, Anna Brownell, 2629, 2633, 2653, 2659, 2666, 2667, 2676, 2687, 2714
Lowell, James Russell, 2644
Martin, James, 2652
Martin, Julia, 2625, 2627, 2652, 2669, 2692
Mathews, Cornelius, 2648
Mitford, Mary Russell, 2617, 2622, 2626, 2642, 2654, 2671, 2694, 2703, 2704, 2713
Milnes, Richard Monckton, 2665
Moxon, Edward, 2657
Palmer, E.F.R., 2619
Rossetti, Dante Gabriel, 2706, 2710
Thomson, Anne, 2646
Westwood, Thomas, 2632, 2638, 2661, 2700

[415]

Index

(For frequently-mentioned persons not covered by the biographical sketches in Appendix I, or for places or topics frequently named, the principal identifying note, if in this volume, is italicized. If the principal identifying note occurs in a prior volume, its page reference is given in square brackets at the beginning of the entry.)

Adam, 236, 242
Adelaide, Queen, 305
Æsop
   Fables, 274
Africa, 184
Agnès de Méranie (Ponsard), 120
Aix, 24
Aladdin, 188
Alajnier, Mdme., 71
Albert, Prince, 321
Alfieri, Vittorio, 138, 229
   "Sonneto CXXXIV"
      quotation from, 42
Alps, The, 150, 267, 284
America, 86, 99, 117
American Anti-Slavery Society, The, 99
American Notes for General Circulation (Dickens), 281
Anacreon
   "Ad Cicadam" ("To the Cricket"), 45
Ancelot, Marguerite Virginie (*née* Chardon)
   Année à Paris, Une, 120
Angelico, Fra, 46
Année à Paris, Une (Ancelot), 120
Annunciata (maid), 258, 260, 303, 305
Apennines, The, 122, 198, 207, 215, 254, 290
"Apollino" (Phidias), 344
Apollo, 82, 174, 310, 352
"Apparent Failure" (RB), 18n
Appert, Benjamin Nicolas Marie
   Dix Ans à la cour du roi Louis-Philippe et souvenirs du temps de l'Empire et de la Restauration, 314
Arabian Nights, The
   "Story of Sinbad the Voyager, The," 198
Arezzo, 174, 179, 183, 282, 286
Aristotle, 120

Arlette, *see* Butler, Charlotte Mary
Arno (river), 21, 25, 43, 46, 64, 107, 110, 113, 133, 149, 174, 177, 183, 192, 207, 213, 229, 240, 243, 275, 286, 298, 301, 308, 320, 321
Arnould, Joseph, [vol. 6: 361-363]
   letters from, 20, 63, 74, 151, 249, 347
   letters to, 63, 347
   Treatise on the Law of Marine Insurance and Average, A, 347
   trustee to the Brownings' marriage settlement, 71, 74, 251, 330
Arnould, Maria (*née* Ridgeway), 20, 21, 21n, 152-153, 154, 250, 350
   health, 63, 347
   letter from, 63
Arnoulds, The, 240
Asciano, 42
Athenæum, The, 36, 67, 136, 139n, 150, 194n, 222n, 350n
   Westwood's contribution to, 67
Auckland, 348
Aunt Carry's Ballads for Children (Norton), 67
Aurora Leigh (EBB), 55n, 261n, 360, 411
Austria, 124, 231, 302
Aventures de Saturnin Fichet ou la Conspiration de la Rouarie, Les (Soulié), 116, 314
Avignon, 17, 23, 24, 45, 83, 89, 149

Babbage, Charles, [vol. 2: 293], 123
Bacchus, 192
Bacco in Toscana, (Redi), 86n
Bagni di Lucca, 122, 123, 146, 158, 160, 166, 167, 191, 204, 227, 269, 271, 285, 305, 306
Bailey, Philip James
   Festus, 67

[417]

Baillie, Joanna, [vol. 3: 269n], 88
Ballads and Other Poems (Howitt), 67, 117, 150
Balzac, Honoré de, [vol. 3: 114n], 19, 39, 82, 84, 116–117, 132, 314, 345
   César Birotteau, 116
   Comédie Humaine, La, 116, 118
   Dernière Fée, ou La nouvelle Lampe merveilleuse, La, 120
   Esther, 116
   Femme de soixante ans, La, 120
   Illusions perdues, 116
   Instruction Criminelle, Une, 116, 120
   L'Envers de l'histoire contemporaine, 120
   Recherche de l'absolu, La, 116
Baring, Rosa, 281
Barrett, Alfred Price Barrett Moulton- ("Daisy"), (brother), [vol. 1: 293–294], 72, 95, 96, 140, 162, 172, 180, 193, 244, 261, 268, 293
Barrett, Arabella Barrett Moulton- (sister), [vol. 1: 291], 3, 18, 30, 34, 44, 46, 75, 76, 77, 78, 85, 96, 97, 104, 108, 109, 114, 118, 150, 159, 162, 205, 206, 208, 209, 210, 213, 227, 241, 244, 245, 246, 247, 248, 266, 269, 272, 275, 282, 287, 310, 319, 320, 322, 323, 330–331, 339, 341, 344, 358, 360
   health, 107, 109, 193
   letters from, 14, 22, 47, 48, 50, 73, 74, 77, 87, 108, 109, 126, 139, 144, 157, 162, 184, 187, 195, 199, 203, 210, 223, 266, 304, 317, 324, 327, 338, 351
   letters to, 8, 13, 22, 23, 46, 48, 56, 70, 87, 121, 128, 139, 154, 168, 186, 194, 214, 223, 252, 270, 288, 300, 315, 338, 351
   likeness of, 187
Barrett, Charles John Barrett Moulton- ("Storm"/"Stormie"), (brother), [vol. 1: 292], 12, 17, 28, 50, 79, 95, 104, 105, 109, 124, 128, 133, 140, 193, 219, 220, 221, 231, 246, 260, 268, 293, 325, 365
   in Jamaica, 109, 128, 172, 180, 185
   letter from, 140
Barrett, Dulcibella (cousin), 96
Barrett, Edward Barrett Moulton- ("Bro"), (brother), [vol. 1: 289–290]
   death, 30
Barrett, Edward Barrett Moulton- (father), [vol. 1: 286–288], 2, 3, 12, 15, 17, 23, 27, 30, 32, 42, 44, 47, 49, 52, 53, 71, 76, 79, 80, 81, 83, 95, 96, 103, 104, 110, 114, 118, 124, 129, 133, 134, 140, 147, 158, 159, 172, 180, 190, 193, 208, 210, 214, 221, 233, 244, 246, 260, 266, 267, 268, 277, 293, 294, 319, 330, 355, 362, 367, 369, 370
   EBB's description of, 30, 33–34
   health, 282

   letters from, 13, 27, 30
   letters to, 3, 28, 247
   returns EBB's letters, 49, 247
Barrett, Elizabeth Barrett Moulton- ("Ba"), [vol. 1: xxvi–xxxiv], 64, 67, 152, 154, 236, 237, 250
   health, 1, 5, 24, 31–32, 34, 54, 76, 165, 168, 171, 174, 176, 179, 191, 239, 272, 282, 362, 363
   improvement of, 3, 7, 23, 36, 38, 45, 49, 56, 59, 60, 63, 66, 70, 92, 99, 107, 126, 151, 164, 174, 187, 195, 196, 201, 204, 215, 240, 266, 270, 272, 316, 338, 341, 346, 349
   medical consultants, *see* Chambers, William Frederick; Cook, Francis; Jago, Francis Robert
   miscarriage, 155, 157, 158, 159, 160, 183, 213, 272, 282, 326
   use of opiates, 15, 76, 87, 106, 126–127, 143, 155, 157, 160, 165, 255, 324
   likeness of, 24
   marriage settlement, 63, 190, 210, 217–218, 251
   marriage to RB, 3, 4, 6, 7, 14, 20–21, 53
   wedding anniversary, 266–267, 285, 288, 300, 311–312
   will, 190
   works
      Aurora Leigh, 55n, 261n, 360, 411
      "Bertha in the Lane"
         quotation from, 377–378
      "Book of the Poets, The," 364
      Casa Guidi Windows, 18n, 121n, 248n, 262n, 307n, 342n, 343n, 346n, 411
      "Change on Change," 38
      "Confessions," 36n
      "Crowned and Buried"
         review of, 377
      "Cry of the Children, The," 99
         review of, 382
      "Cry of the Human, The"
         reviews of, 379, 382
      "Dead Pan, The"
         quotation from, 376
         review of, 377
      "Dead Rose, A," 38
      "Drama of Exile, A"
         quotations from, 378–379, 382
         reviews of, 378, 379, 382
      "Fourfold Aspect, The"
         review of, 377
      "Heaven and Earth. 1845"
         review of, 383
      "Hector in the Garden," 38
      "Irreparableness"
         review of, 378
      "Lady Geraldine's Courtship"
         quotation from, 83
         reviews of, 378, 383

Index

"Lay of the Brown Rosary, The"
  quotation from, 411
"Life"
  review of, 383
"Love"
  review of, 383
"Loved Once"
  review of, 377
"Man's Requirements, A," 38
"Maud's Spinning," 38
"Meditation in Tuscany, A," 343n
"Mountaineer and Poet"
  review of, 383
"Past and Future"
  review of, 378
"Patience Taught by Nature"
  review of, 378
"Perplexed Music"
  review of, 378
Poems (1844), 135, 141
  reviews of, 67, 375-385
Poems (1850), 211n
Poems Before Congress, 360
"Poet, The"
  review of, 383
"Portrait, A," 97
Prometheus Bound (1833), 364, 368, 397
Prometheus Bound (revised), 28, 124
"Prospect, The"
  review of, 383
"Reed, A," 38
"Romance of the Swan's Nest, The"
  review of, 382
"Romaunt of the Page, The," 397
  quotation from, 378
  review of, 378
"Runaway Slave at Pilgrim's Point, The," 86, 86n, 99, 117
"Seraph and Poet, The"
  review of, 378
"Some Account of the Greek Christian Poets," 364
Sonnets from the Portuguese, 411
"Tears"
  review of, 378
"To George Sand. A Desire," 356n
"To George Sand. A Recognition," 356n
"Two Sketches"
  review of, 383
"Vision of Poets, A"
  quotation from, 381
  reviews of, 376, 383
"Woman's Shortcomings, A," 38
"Work"
  quotation from, 376
Barrett, George Goodin Barrett Moulton- (brother), [vol. 1, 292-293], 12, 13, 16, 17, 27, 28, 30, 49-50, 51, 72, 73, 74, 75, 95, 109, 112, 124, 128-129, 133, 134, 141, 147, 180, 192-193, 208, 221, 234, 244, 260, 268, 276, 277, 293, 336, 360, 365
  letters from, 13, 17, 102, 129
  letter to, 1
  practising law, 172
Barrett, Georgiana Elizabeth ("Lizzie"), (cousin), [vol. 9: 89n], 97, 110, 133, 134, 147, 221, 234, 260, 269, 336
  letter from, 124
Barrett, Henrietta Barrett Moulton- ("Addles" or "Harry"), (sister), [vol. 1: 290], 3, 8, 12, 18, 22, 26, 27, 30, 34, 35, 44, 72, 88, 89, 114, 118, 125, 133, 141, 147, 162, 169, 172, 190, 191, 192, 193, 217, 221, 225, 234, 252, 256, 261, 272, 275-277, 282, 287, 288, 289, 293-294, 310, 339, 341, 344, 357, 365
  health, 353
  letters from, 14, 22, 47, 48, 50, 73, 126, 139, 144, 157, 162, 176, 184, 187, 199, 203, 210, 220, 234, 266, 288, 294, 304, 317, 319, 322, 327, 329, 338
  letters to, 13, 28, 48, 56, 73, 93, 105, 121, 154, 158, 176, 188, 194, 203, 223, 241, 266, 270, 300, 315, 319, 329, 338
Barrett, Henry Barrett Moulton- ("Henny"), (brother), [vol. 1: 293], 54, 95, 124, 172, 180, 193, 208, 221, 231, 244, 268, 293, 307, 330, 356, 365
  letters from, 325, 330
  letter to, 325
Barrett, Octavius Butler Barrett Moulton- ("Occy"/"Occyta"/"Joc"), (brother), [vol. 1: 295-296], 95, 109, 110, 124, 172, 180, 193, 244, 293, 360
Barrett, Samuel Barrett Moulton- (brother), [vol. 1: 290-291], 357
Barrett, Samuel Goodin (cousin), [vol. 8: 100n], 96, 125, 130, 268
Barrett, Septimus James Barrett Moulton- ("Set"/"Sette"), (brother), [vol. 1, 294-295], 95, 109, 172, 180, 193, 244, 293
  letters from, 102, 108, 111, 124
  letters to, 102, 112
Barrett, Susanna Maria (née Bell), (cousin), 96, 125, 130, 268
Barry, Charles, 172
Bartolo da Sassoferrato, 164
Bâtard de Mauléon, La (Dumas, père), 314
Bate, Gerardine ("Geddie"), [vol. 13: 7n], 17, 38, 47, 48, 59, 60, 88, 94, 113, 114, 138, 139, 166, 174, 176, 178, 180, 183, 199, 225, 263-264, 316, 331-333, 345, 346, 363, 364, 365, 366, 367, 371
  engagement, 333
  letter from, 345
  likeness of, 345
  travels with the Brownings, 11, 19, 23, 24, 25, 83, 331

Bath, 323
Battle of Life, The (Dickens), 100
Bayfords, The, 334
Bayley, Sarah, [vol. 10: 325–327], 89, 234
   letters from, 92, 208
Belgium, 298
Belisarius, 150
Bell, Matilda, 96
Bell, Matthew, 75, 88, 96
Bell, Robert (chemist), 71, 87
Belle Assemblée, or Court and Fashionable Magazine, La, 123
Bellosguardo, 246
Bells and Pomegranates (RB), 67, 367, 373
   expenses of, 141
   reviews of, 385–404
   revisions of, 64
Benedictines, 257
Bentley, Richard (publisher), 116
Bernard, Charles de, [vol. 9: 50n]
   Gentilhomme campagnard, Le, 183
   Gerfaut, 314
   Queue du chien d'Aliciade, La, 314
Bevan, Arabella (*née* Hedley), (EBB's cousin), [vol. 13: 10n], 52, 71–72, 75, 134, 162, 181, 186, 189, 205, 242, 244–245, 289, 324, 353
Bevan, James Johnstone, 52, 71–72, 75, 96, 134, 181, 189, 205, 220, 231, 244, 269, 289, 353
Beyle, Marie Henri, *see* Stendhal (Marie Henri Beyle)
Bezzi, Giovanni Aubrey, 267
Bible, The, 93
   quotations from, 5, 6, 8, 19, 23, 36, 38, 43, 45, 80, 82, 100, 131, 143, 175, 193, 200, 217, 237, 280, 284, 295, 332, 335, 339, 342, 344
Blackwood's Edinburgh Magazine
   EBB's contributions to, 28, 38, 44, 83, 124, 134, 142
Blizzard, Mrs., 71
Blot in the 'Scutcheon, A (RB)
   reviews of, 385, 391, 402
Boboli Gardens, 224, 258, 263, 290, 292
Boccaccio, Giovanni, 344
Bognor, 319
Bolingbroke, Isabella Charlotte Antoinette Sophia, [vol. 13: 297n], 80, 96, 325, 336
Bologna, 131, 138, 150, 153, 158, 164, 165–166, 167
Bonser, Betsy, 53, 80, 95
"Book of the Poets, The" (EBB), 364
Bordman, Eleanor Page, [vol. 3: 177n], 15, 76, 86, 87, 157, 213, 324
   letters from, 15, 53, 157, 231
   letters to, 53, 155
Bourbon, Charles Louis, Duke of Lucca and afterwards Duke of Parma, 287, 335
Bourbon, Ludwig, 290

Bourges, Cathedral of, 17, 23, 45
Boyd, Hugh Stuart, [vol. 2: 339–341], 17, 53, 88, 89, 173, 193, 222, 228, 234, 244, 260
   health, 109, 133
   letters from, 87, 157, 162, 211, 329, 351
   letters to, 44, 60, 85, 211, 293, 358
Boyle, Carolina, 305
Boyle, Carolina Amelia (*née* Poyntz), 305, 306
Boyle, Charles John, 326, 355
Boyle, Edmund, 8th Earl of Cork, 305, 313, 341
Boyle, Mary Louisa, 295, *296n*, 305–306, 308, 313, 331, 345
   letters from, 297, 326, 328
   letters to, 297, 305, 326
   visits the Brownings, 305, 331, 341, 355
Boyle, Robert, 331
Briareus, 67
Brick Court, 151
British Museum, The, 123, 318
British Quarterly Review, The, 397–404
Browning, Christiana (half-aunt), 163
Browning, Elizabeth Barrett (*née* Moulton-Barrett), *see* Barrett, Elizabeth Barrett Moulton- ("Ba")
Browning, Jane (*née* Smith), (step-grandmother), 163
Browning, Jane Eliza (half-aunt), 163
Browning, Jemima Smith (half-aunt), 163
Browning, Louisa (half-aunt), 163
Browning, Margaret Morris (aunt), 163
Browning, Mary (half-aunt), 163
Browning, Reuben (half-uncle), 163
Browning, Robert, [vol. 1. xxiv–xxvi], 6, 281, 282, 283, 284, 285, 290, 384
   health, 24
   likenesses of, 24, 274
   literary opinions
      of Balzac's works, 116
   marriage settlement, 63, 190, 210, 217–218, 251
   marriage to EBB, 1, 2, 3, 4, 5, 14, 53, 201
   wedding anniversary, 266–267, 285, 288, 300, 311–312
   will, 190
   works
      "Apparent Failure," 18n
      Asolando
         quotation from, 412
      Bells and Pomegranates, 67, 118, 366, 367, 373
         expenses of, 141
         reviews of, 385–404
         revisions of, 64
      Blot in the 'Scutcheon, A
         quotation from, 391
         reviews of, 385, 391, 402
      "Camp"
         review of, 395

Index

"Claret and Tokay"
  review of, 396
"Cloister, The"
  review of, 395
Colombe's Birthday
  reviews of, 299, 385, 392
"Confessional, The"
  quotation from, 394
  review of, 393-394
Dramatic Romances and Lyrics, 118, 372
  quotation from, 394
  review of, 393
"Flight of the Duchess, The"
  quotations from, 402, 403
  reviews of, 394, 402
"France and Spain"
  review of, 395
"Glove, The"
  review of, 394
"How They Brought the Good News from Ghent to Aix"
  quotation from, 404
"Incident of the French Camp"
  review of, 395
"Italy and France"
  review of, 395
King Victor and King Charles
  reviews of, 385, 392
"Laboratory, The"
  review of, 395
"Lost Leader, The"
  quotations from, 396, 400
  review of, 396
Luria, 118, 366
  reviews of, 385-386, 392, 397
"Madhouse Cells"
  review of, 395
"Memorabilia"
  quotation from, 412
"My Last Duchess"
  review of, 395
"One Word More. To E.B.B."
  quotation from, 410
Paracelsus, 318, 367, 372, 373
  quotation from, 249
  reviews of, 385-386, 387-397, 399
  revisions of, 64, 135, 366
Pauline, 318, 329, 372
"Pied Piper of Hamelin, The"
  review of, 394
Pippa Passes
  EBB's comments on, 114
  quotation from, 401
  reviews of, 385, 392, 397, 401
  revisions of, 135
Poems (1849), 65n, 83, 86, 97, 99, 114, 122, 135, 142, 193

Return of the Druses, The
  quotation from, 393
  reviews of, 385, 392
"Saul"
  review of, 394
"Soliloquy of the Spanish Cloister"
  review of, 395
Sordello, 363, 411
  reviews of, 385-397, 399, 400
Soul's Tragedy, A, 118, 366
  reviews of, 385-386, 392, 397
Strafford
  reviews of, 385, 391
"Tomb at St. Praxed's, The"
  review of, 395
Browning, Robert, Sr. (father), [vol. 3: 307-309], 15, 69, 137, 163, 197, 251, 285
  drawings, 196
  letter from, 70
Browning, Robert (grandfather), 163
Browning, Robert Wiedemann Barrett ("Pen"), (son), 360
Browning, Sarah (half-aunt), 163
Browning, Sarah Anna (*née* Wiedemann), (mother), [vol. 3: 309-310], 65, 69, 136, 137, 153, 186, 196, 197, 247, 251, 284, 285, 348
  health, 64, 70, 169, 251
Browning, Sarianna (sister), [vol. 3: 310-311], 15, 20, 21, 63, 64, 65, 89, 97, 122, 138, 164, 169, 186, 233, 240, 251, 348, 363
  letters from, 136, 196, 220
  letters to, 69, 136, 196, 284
  likenesses of, 197, 240
Browning, Thomas (half-uncle), 163
Browning, William Shergold (half-uncle), [vol. 3: 113n], 163
Brunynge, Robert, 169
Buckingham, Mr., 6
Bummy, *see* Clarke, Arabella Sarah Graham- (aunt)
Butler, Charlotte Mary ("Arlette"), (EBB's cousin), [vol. 1: 222n], 52, 95, 141, 162, 173, 175, 181, 186, 190, 205-206, 220
  see also Reynolds, Charlotte Mary
Butler, Frances (*née* Graham-Clarke), ("Fannie"), (EBB's aunt)
  health, 124
Butler, Frances Anne (*née* Kemble), ("Fanny"), 47, 100, 113, 118
  Year of Consolation, A, 150, 311
Butler, Louisa Charlotte (EBB's cousin), 95
Butler, Pierce, 118
Butler, Richard Pierce (EBB's uncle), [vol. 1: 199n], 125
Butlers, The Thomas, 181, 190
Byron, Lady, 88, 345

422 Index

Byron, Lord, 62, 101, 228, 239, 313, 366
  Beppo
    quotation from, 250
  Corsair, The
    quotation from, 273
  Letters and Journals of, 226

Cadiz, Duke of, 124, 132, 184
Café Doney, 239, 260
Calabria, 306
Camaldoli, 243, 255
Cambridge, Duchess of (Princess Augusta Wilhelmina Louise of Hesse-Cassel), 321
Cambridge, 95
"Camp" (RB)
  review of, 395
Campo Santo, 21, 43, 45, 62, 149
Canova, Antonio
  "Venus," 217
Canterbury, 190, 245
Carlyle, Jane Baillie (*née* Welsh), 202, 237
Carlyle, Margaret (*née* Aitken), 237
Carlyle, Thomas, [vol. 5: 365-368], 53, 86, 242, 245, 349, 372
  comments on RB's work, 53
  letters from, 202, 236, 242, 277, 282, 291, 299
  letters to, 200, 236
  Oliver Cromwell's Letters and Speeches, 236
  Sartor Resartus, 372
Carmichael, Louisa Charlotte (*née* Butler), (EBB's cousin), 205
Casa Guidi, *see* Palazzo Guidi
Casa Guidi Windows (EBB), 18n, 121n, 248n, 262n, 307n, 342n, 343n, 346n, 411
Cascine, 199, 207, 215, 216, 224, 232
Catholics/Catholicism, Roman, 90, 189, 205, 231, 296
Cavalieri di Santo Stefano (church), 138
Cavendish Square, 224
Centofanti, Francesco, 205, 221, 226, 227, 228, 229, 252, 258, 259
Centofanti, Mme., 227, 231
Cerutti, Angelo, 138
  New Italian Grammar, A, 138
  Vita di Angelo Cerutti, 138
Cervantes, Miguel de
  Don Quixote
    quotation from, 26
César Birotteau (Balzac), 116
Chambers, William Frederick, [vol. 11: 327-328], 32, 370
Champs Élysées, Les, 11
"Change on Change" (EBB), 38
Chapman, Maria Weston, 99
Chapman, Palmer ("Despair"), 54, 367
"Charles I when Prince of Wales" (Velázquez), 38

Chartres, 11
Chartres, Cathedral of, 11
Chateaubriand, François René de, 193
Chaucer, Geoffrey, 61, 281
Chelsea, 237, 291
Cheltenham, 216, 323
Chiswick, 259
Chorley, Henry Fothergill, [vol. 8: 325-328], 21, 64, 65, 81, 89, 117, 138, 250, 267, 313, 348, 370
  Duchess Eleanour, 83, 114, 118, 348
  executor to EBB's will, 330
  letters from, 36, 39, 74, 81, 117, 152, 232
  letter to, 110
  translates Gluck's operas, 348
  trustee to the Brownings' marriage settlement, 71, 74, 81
Christ, Jesus, 96, 105, 140, 230, 246
Christianity, 96, 105
Chrysostom, St. John, 255, 368
Church of England, 105, 131, 191, 219, 250, 306
Church of Scotland (Leghorn), 131, 219
Cinderella, 203
"Claret and Tokay" (RB)
  review of, 396
Clarke, Arabella Sarah Graham- ("Bell"/ "Bummy"), (EBB's aunt), [vol. 1: 297-298], 41, 52, 71, 72, 75, 89, 94-95, 124, 133-134, 141, 162, 173, 190, 206, 225, 233, 242, 244, 277, 306, 353
  letters from, 71, 72, 134, 141, 205
  letters to, 15, 27, 36, 52, 220
Clarke, Isabella Horatia Graham- (*née* Butler), (EBB's cousin), [vol. 13: 160n]
  death of, 54, 124
Clarke, John Altham Graham- (EBB's uncle), [vol. 1: 297], 206
Clarke, Leonard Edmund Graham- (EBB's cousin), 27, 54, 124, 134
Clarke, Mary Frances Graham- (EBB's cousin), 124, 134
Clésinger, Jean Baptiste Auguste, 184
"Cloister, The" (RB)
  review of, 395
Cobden, Richard, 174, 184
Cocks, Caroline Margaret, 323
Cocks, Lady Margaret Maria, [vol. 2: 341-342], 323, 355
Coleridge, Samuel Taylor
  Christabel
    quotation from, 22
  Rime of the Ancient Mariner, The
    quotation from, 262
Coliseum, 316
Colle, 127, 138, 164, 165
Collegio Ferdinando, 26, 36, 38, 45, 46, 62, 149, 164, 178
Collyer/Colyar, Mr., 309

Index

Collyer/Colyar, Mrs., 226, 227, 271, 286
Colombe's Birthday (RB)
   reviews of, 385, 392
Comédie Humaine, La (Balzac), 116, 118
"Confessional, The" (RB)
   review of, 393-394
"Confessions" (EBB), 36n
Cook, Elizabeth (*née* Surtees), (EBB's cousin), 221, 306
Cook, Francis, 87, *91n*, 106-108, 110, 114, 117, 121, 126, 130, 139, 143, 144, 155-156, 157, 158, 159, 160-161, 167, 168, 171, 172, 174, 176, 179, 182, 264, 323, 373
Cook, Mrs. Francis, 109, 133
Cook, Susan (EBB's cousin), 77, 96, 109, 124, 163, 172, 181, 193, 209, 221, 242, 269, 306, 336
Cook, William Surtees (EBB's cousin), [vol. 12: 363-368], 27, 49, 54, 71, 72, 77, 96, 124, 140, 163, 172, 181, 193, 209, 221, 231, 260, 269, 276-277, 306, 336, 367
   "Happy Years of Elizabeth Barrett Browning," 405-407
Cooks, The, 260
Cork, Lady (Mary Monckton, Countess of Cork and Orrery), 331
Cornwall, Barry (pseud.), *see* Procter, Bryan Waller
Corsica, 42
Cosmo de' Medici (Horne), 311
Cottrell, Henry, 335
Cottrell, Sophia Augusta (*née* Tulk), 335
Cowper, William
   "Task, The"
      quotation from, 150
Cracow, 124, 164
Crawford, Thomas, 308
Creswells, The, 179
Crimes Célèbres (Dumas, père), 117
Cromwell, Oliver, 100, 202
Crow, Elizabeth, *see* Treherne, Elizabeth (*née* Crow)
"Crowned and Buried" (EBB)
   review of, 377
"Cry of the Children, The" (EBB), 99
   review of, 382
"Cry of the Human, The" (EBB)
   reviews of, 379, 382
Curradi, Francesco
   "Madonna di sotto gli Organi," 127
Curtis, Burrill, 252
Curtis, George William, 247, 248, *249n*, 252
   "Editor's Easy Chair," 409-412
   letter from, 278
   letter to, 278
Curzon, George Henry Roper-, [vol. 2: 189n], 79
Cushman, Charlotte Saunders, [vol. 11, 23n], 110, 114, 118, 348
Cushman, Susan, 110

Custine, Astolphe Louis Léonard, Marquis de
   Russie en 1839, La, 112, 115
Cyprus, 213
Cyprus wine, 85, 213, 228

D'Aulnoy, Marie Catherine, Comtesse
   Chatte Blanche, La, 308
D'Azeglio, Massimo Tapparelli
   Niccolò de' Lapi, 47
Daily News, The, 315
   announcement of the Brownings' marriage, 7
Dante Alighieri, 204, 230, 286
   Inferno
      quotation from, 236
   tomb of, 199
Darley, George, [vol. 4: 264]
   death, 84
David Lyon (ship)
   EBB's shares in, 141
Davis, John (dyer), 144
"Dead Pan, The" (EBB)
   review of, 377
"Dead Rose, A" (EBB), 38
Death of Marlowe, The (Horne), 311
Deffell, John Henry, 333
Delle vite de più eccelenti pittori, scultori, ed architettori (Vasari), 114
Demosthenes, 175
Dernière Fée, ou La nouvelle Lampe merveilleuse, La (Balzac), 120
Deux Diane, Les (Dumas, père), 314
Devonshire, 221
Devonshire Place, 125, 205
Dickens, Charles ("Boz"), 47, 62, 193, 349
   travels, 100
   works
      American Notes for General Circulation, 281
      quotation from, 281
      Battle of Life, The, 100
      Dombey and Son, 237, 349
      Facts & Figures from Italy, 315
      Pictures from Italy
         quotation from, 62
Disraeli, Benjamin
   Tancred: or, the New Crusade, 237
Dix Ans à la cour du roi Louis-Philippe et souvenirs du temps de l'Empire et de la Restauration (Appert), 314
Dombey and Son (Dickens), 237, 349
Domett, Alfred, [vol. 4: 315-317], 64, 152, 249, 348
Dowglass, Frances J. ("Fanny"), [vol. 5: 296n], 7, 226, 227, 305, 306
   letters from, 269, 305, 308, 320, 326
   letters to, 270, 285, 295, 305, 308, 326
Dowson, Christopher, Jr., [vol. 3: 124n], 21, 152, 250

Dowson, Mary (*née* Domett), 250
"Drama of Exile, A" (EBB)
   reviews of, 378, 379, 382
Dramatic Romances and Lyrics (RB), 372
   review of, 393
Dreamer and the Worker, The (Horne), 341
Drury Lane Theatre, 348
Dryden, John, 314
Duccio di Buoninsegna, 113
Duchess Eleanour (Chorley), 83, 114, 118, 348
Dudevant, Amantine Lucile Aurore (*née* Dupin), *see* Sand, George.
Dudevant, Solange (afterwards Clésinger), 184
Dumas, Alexandre (père), 82, 116, 117, 184
   trial of, 183
   works
      Bâtard de Mauléon, La, 314
      Crimes Célèbres, 117
      Deux Diane, Les, 314
      Hamlet (translation of), 184
      Kean: Désordre et génie, 117
      Mémoires d'un Médicin: Joseph Balsamo, 314
      Reine Margot, La, 184
      Speronare, Le, 183, 184
Dupuy, Sophia (Mrs. J.P.), [vol. 3: 182n], 339
Duyckinck, George Long, *198n*
   letter from, 197
   letter to, 197
Dyce, Juliana (*née* LeFevre), 206

Ealing, 316
Eastnor, Lord, [vol. 2: 79n], 323
Eclectic Review, The, 67, 192, 375–380
Eden, 298
Edinburgh, 28, 67
"Editor's Easy Chair" (Curtis), 409–412
Egidio, Father, 254, 256, 257
Egypt, 100, 341, 345
Elijah, 43
Emerson, Ralph Waldo, [vol. 5: 292n], 192
   Poems (1847), 67
Enfield, 66
England, 30, 37, 38, 41, 45, 52, 53, 57, 62, 65, 66, 68, 70, 72, 76, 77, 79, 81, 83, 85, 86, 89, 93, 94, 99, 100, 102, 106, 107, 110, 111, 114, 115, 116, 122, 123, 125, 126, 127, 133, 135, 138, 143, 146, 148, 149, 150, 153, 162, 164, 175, 176, 178, 180, 183, 188, 189, 201, 202, 208, 210, 215, 219, 220, 224, 229, 244, 246, 256, 265, 267, 270, 272, 279, 282, 291, 298, 301, 304, 305, 306, 310, 313, 326, 329, 330, 333, 335, 340
English, Jemima Georgiana (*née* Carden), 54, 191, 204

English, The, 94, 104, 113, 123, 146, 153, 231, 300
Esau, 71
Esther (Balzac), 116
Euganean Hills, 109
Europe, 207
Eve, 232, 351, 354
"Eve Tempted" (Powers), 216, 246, 308
Examiner, The, 88, 135, 136, 193, 298

Facts & Figures from Italy (Dickens), 315
Fauveau, Félicie de, 326
Femme de soixante ans, La (Balzac), 120
Ferdinand I (de Medici), 26
Ferrucci, Caterina Francesca (*née* Franceschi), 50, 51
Ferrucci, Michele, 36, *37n*, 43, 47, 50, 51, 59, 85, 104, 113, 114, 123
Festus (Bailey), 67
Fichte, Johann Gottlieb, 349, 350n
   Popular Works of Johann Gottlieb Fichte, with a Memoir, The, 349
Fiesole, 167, 192, 260, 290, 352
Fig Tree Court, 151
Fisher, Harriet, [vol. 4: 106], 109, 177, 321
"Fisher Boy, The" (Powers), 208, 216, 246, 264
"Flight of the Duchess, The" (RB)
   reviews of, 394, 402
Florence, 38, 42, 43, 46, 59, 62, 78, 82, 88, 92, 94, 95, 104, 113, 115, 117, 131, 137, 138, 139, 142, 144, 145, 146, 149, 150, 153, 154, 158, 160, 161, 162, 163, 164, 165, 166, 167, 168, 172, 173, 174, 175, 176, 177, 179, 180, 182, 183, 184, 187, 189, 191, 192, 195, 196, 197, 198, 199, 203, 204, 205, 212, 213, 215, 216, 219, 220, 221, 224, 226, 227, 228, 234, 240, 244, 245, 246, 248, 252, 257, 258, 259, 261, 262, 263, 265, 267, 268, 271, 272, 273, 275, 282, 283, 284, 285, 286, 287, 290, 291, 292, 294, 295, 297, 298, 300, 302, 305, 306, 308, 309, 311, 312, 313, 317, 320, 321, 322, 323, 324, 325, 326, 327, 328, 331, 332, 333, 335, 340, 344, 345, 346, 347, 352, 353, 354
   see also specific places and streets
Florence, Archbishop of, *see* Minucci, Ferdinando
Florence, Cathedral of (Duomo), 199, 205, 213, 217, 230, 231, 296, 301
   baptistery, 204
   campanile, 229
Flossy (Westwood's dog), 66, 150, 299
Flush (EBB's dog), 5, 9, 17, 19, 24, 26, 39, 45, 46, 54, 66, 70, 72, 86, 91, 97, 100, 110, 118, 126, 128, 139, 142, 143, 145,

149, 150, 173, 187, 192, 209, 212–213, 215, 216, 230, 243, 253–254, 260, 272, 274, 282–283, 290, 294, 297, 299, 303–304, 312, 332, 334, 338, 341, 344, 354, 370
  eating habits, 232
  health, 209, 210, 232, 282, 312, 341
  misdeeds, 72
Flush (Miss Mitford's dog), 312
Foggo, Catherine Clare St. George, *see* Horne, Catherine Clare St. George
Forgues, Paul Émile Durand, 397
Forster, John, [vol. 11: 329–331], 88, 298, 363
  letters from, 193, 199, 232, 281
  letter to, 363
Fouquet, Nicolas, 342
"Fourfold Aspect, The" (EBB)
  review of, 377
Fox, Henry Edward, 296n, 306, 313
France, 3, 123, 125, 144, 163, 207, 282, 283, 310, 335
"France and Spain" (RB)
  review of, 395
Freeman, Augusta (*née* Latilla), 226
French, The, 24, 100, 124, 300
French language & literature, 16, 26, 47, 51, 82, 93, 104, 115–116, 117, 150, 183, 205, 283, 313, 342, 345
Fuller, Margaret, 99, 202, 238, 370

Gabriel, Archangel, 147
Galignani's Messenger, 39, *40n*, 84, 138
Galileo Galilei, 90, 246
"Gardener's Daughter, The" (Tennyson), 310
Garrow, Joseph, 109, 177, 321
Garrow, Theodosia (*née* Abrams), 109, 177, 321
Garrow, Theodosia (afterwards Trollope), [vol. 4: 105n], 94, 109, 177, 208, 321
Geddie, *see* Bate, Gerardine
Geneva, 104
Genoa, 22, 23, 24, 131, 146, 149
Genoa, Cathedral of, 22
Gent, Anne, 95, 324
Gentilhomme campagnard, Le (Bernard), 183
Gentleman's Magazine, The, 125
George Lovell (Knowles), 136
Georgia, 153
Gerfaut (Bernard), 314
German language & literature, 163
Germany, 39, 201
Gibson, John, 175
Gibson, Susanna Arethusa Milner- (*née* Cullum), 240
Giles, Eliza Wilhelmina (*née* Cliffe), [vol. 2: 250n], 221, 233
Giles, George, 234

Gilfillan, George, 315, 385
Giorgione (Giorgio Barbarelli), 278
"Glove, The" (RB)
  review of, 394
Gluck, Christoph Willibald
  Iphigénie en Tauride
    Chorley's translation, 348
God, 48, 156, 159, 217, 219, 233, 234, 237, 247, 265, 272, 273, 274, 281, 286, 288, 289, 302
Goethe, Ottilie von, 113
Gorgona, 42
Gosset, Arabella Sarah (*née* Butler), (EBB's cousin), [vol. 1: 21n], 125
  health, 134
Great Western Railway, 293
"Greek Christian Poets, Some Account of the" (EBB), 364
"Greek Slave, The" (Powers), 216, 246, 309
Greeks, The, 300
Greene, Henry, 130, 131, *134n*
Greenough, Horatio, 269, 269n
Greenough, Louisa Ingersoll (*née* Gore), 269
Gregory, St., *see* Nazianzen, St. Gregory
Greville, Robert Northmore, 28
  Poetic Prism, or, Original and Reflected Rays from Modern Verse, Sacred and Serious, The
    EBB's contribution to, 28
Grey, George, 152, 250, 348
Gröberg, Jakob (Count de Hemsö), 331
Groeme, Mr., 123
Groemes, The, 123
Guerre, Martin, 314
Guiccioli, Countess Teresa (*née* Gamba), 101
Guizot, François Pierre Guillaume, 124, 132, 140

Hall, Spencer Timothy, 345
Hamlet (translation by Dumas, père), 184
Hampstead, 303, 354
Hand-Book for Travellers in Northern Italy (1847), (Murray), 212
Hanford, Compton John, *44n*, 173, 180, 190, 210, 216, 217, 233, 260, 273, 277
  letter to, 180
  witness to the Brownings' marriage settlement, 210, 217, 277
Hanford, Frances ("Fanny"), 43, *44n*, 112, 173, 180, 190, 210, 216, 217, 233–234, 247, 260, 273, 323
  letter to, 180
"Happy Years of Elizabeth Barrett Browning" (Cook), 405–407
Harfleur, 169
Harness, William James, 281, 310, 370
Hatcham, 21, 63, 97, 137, 153, 250, 251, 284

Haworth, Euphrasia Fanny, [vol. 3: 314–315], 136
  letters from, 137, 239
  letter to, 239
  St. Sylvester's Day, 239
Hayes, Ann Henrietta (*née* Boyd), [vol. 2: 339], 147, 172, 242, 355
Hayes, Henry William, 172, 355
"Heaven and Earth. 1845" (EBB)
  review of, 383
"Hector in the Garden" (EBB), 38
Hedley, Jane (*née* Graham-Clarke), (EBB's aunt), [vol. 1: 299–300], 11, 41, 52, 71, 75, 95, 162, 189, 289, 330
  letters from, 41, 71, 72, 112, 141
  letters to, 15, 36, 41, 52, 75, 330
Hedley, Robert (EBB's uncle), 71, 109, 112, 133, 189
  letter to, 52
Hedleys, The, 41, 52, 72, 109, 133, 162, 175, 181, 189, 220, 233, 289
Heine, Heinrich
  Reisebilder, 42
Hemans, Charles Isidore
  The Roman Advertiser, 113
Heraud, John Abraham, 192
Herbert, Charles Lyon, 291, 306, 317, 368
Herefordshire, 43
Hillard, George Stillman, 338, 341
  "Six Months in Italy," 408–409
Histoire des Girondins (Lamartine), 314
Hodgson's Bookshop, 223–224
Holland, Lord, *see* Fox, Henry Edward
Holloway, Thomas, 306
Hood, Frances Freeling ("Fanny"), 68, 150
Hood, Jane (*née* Reynolds), 68
  death of, 68
Hood, Thomas (1799–1845), 68, 150
Hood, Thomas (1835–74), 68
Hope, Samuel, 359
Hoppner, Miss, 226
Hoppner, Marie Isabelle (*née* May), 226–227, 228, 239, 252, 286, 313
Hoppner, Richard Belgrave, 226–227, 239, 252, 286, 313
Horace (Quintus Horatius Flaccus)
  Epistles
    quotation from, 105
Horne, Catherine Clare St. George (*née* Foggo), 242, 265–266, 280
Horne, Richard Hengist, [vol. 4: 317–320], 67, 311, 367
  Cosmo de' Medici, 265, 311
  Death of Marlowe, The, 311
  Dreamer and the Worker, The, 341
  letters from, 7, 39, 60, 61, 280, 341
  letters to, 60, 61, 265, 280
  marriage, 242, 265, 280, 311
  Orion, 265, 311
Hotel de la Ville de Paris, 10, 19
Hotel du Nord (Florence), 177
Hotel Messagerie (Paris), 9, 10
Hotel Peverada (Le tre Donzelle), (Pisa), 25
Hotel Rouen, 9
Houndsditch, 237
Howitt, Mary (*née* Botham), [vol. 4: 41n], 118, 298
  Ballads and Other Poems, 67, 117, 150
Howitt, William, [vol. 7: 263n], 118, 298
Hoxton Academy, 357
Hugo, Victor, 193, 314
  Notre-Dame de Paris, 83
Hunt, James Henry Leigh, 62
Hunter, George Barrett, [vol. 3: 315–316], 79, 124, 140, 147, 193, 221, 234, 244, 355
Hunter, Mary, [vol. 3: 87n], 124, 141, 147, 193, 221, 244, 355

Illusions perdues (Balzac), 116
"Incident of the French Camp" (RB)
  review of, 395
India, 352
Instruction Criminelle, Une (Balzac), 116, 120
Intermediate State, and Other Discourses, The (Stratten), 359
Iphigénie en Tauride (Gluck)
  Chorley's translation, 348
Ireland, 100, 190, 323, 341
  famine in, 153
"Irreparableness" (EBB)
  review of, 378
Irving, James (1792–1855), 53, 54, 55n, 80, 91, 104, 133, 142–143, 190, 291, 322, 323
Irving, James (1822–56), 54, 142–143, 322, 323
Irving, Judith (*née* Nasmyth), 53, 104, 142, 322, 323
Isabella II, Queen of Spain, 124, 132, 184
Italian language & literature, 26, 47, 51, 54, 70, 82, 92, 93, 104, 126, 150, 164, 205, 221
Italy, 5, 6, 10, 21, 23, 27, 32, 33, 36, 41, 42, 47, 52, 53, 62, 65, 66, 71, 72, 83, 91, 92, 95, 98, 100, 104, 105, 107, 109, 110, 113, 115, 117, 121, 122, 123, 125, 127, 131, 133, 135, 142, 144, 145, 147, 148, 150, 161, 162, 164, 165, 166, 171, 174, 176, 179, 180, 182, 189, 191, 197, 198, 200, 201, 207, 219, 220, 224, 225, 226, 227, 229, 231, 232, 236, 237, 243, 244, 246, 267, 268, 269, 270, 272, 290, 296, 298, 300, 301, 302, 306, 311, 312, 317, 320, 327, 332, 335, 339, 352
"Italy and France" (RB)
  review of, 395
Italy and Its Comforts: The Manual of Tourists ("Valery"), 278

Jacob, 71, 82
Jago, Francis Robert, [vol. 5: 124n], 15, 53, 71, 104, 157, 319, 320, 324, 326
  letters to, 143, 155
Jamaica, 53, 95, 109, 125, 130, 133, 185, 220, 244, 246, 268
James I, King, 169
Jameson, Anna Brownell (*née* Murphy), [vol. 4: 320–323], 9, 10, 11, 16, 17, 23, 25, 27, 36, 38–39, 42, 76, 87, 88, 97, 131, 144, 146, 168, 174, 175, 176, 178–179, 180, 183, 184, 187, 190, 191, 207, 224, 225, 232, 316, 317, 331-333, 363, 367, 369, 373
  health, 25
  Legends of the Madonna, 180
  letters from, 46, 82, 88, 92, 94, 125, 131, 138, 343
  letters to, 46, 58, 113, 137, 165, 167, 198, 262, 343
  Sacred and Legendary Art, 11, 38, 150, 180, 183
  sketch of the Brownings, 24
  travels with the Brownings, 9, 11, 16, 19, 22, 23, 24, 36, 62, 83, 100, 149
  visits the Brownings, 174
Janin, Jules Gabriel, 123
  Voyage en Italie, 112
Jean Cavalier (Sue), 83
Jerusalem, 100, 109, 114, 237, 245
Jesse, J. Heneage
  Literary and Historical Memorials of London, 314
Jesuits/Jesuitism, 286
Johnstone, Edward, 242
Jordan, 282, 298
Juif Errant, Le (Sue), 83
Jullien, Louis Antoine, 348, 350n

K., *see* Kerenhappuch
Kean: Désordre et génie (Dumas, père), 117
Kemble, Adelaide, 100
Kenyon, Edward (EBB's cousin), [vol. 3: 229n], 244, 267
Kenyon, John (EBB's cousin), [vol. 3: 316–318], 3, 4, 15, 23, 31, 32, 35, 39, 47, 51, 63, 64, 65, 70–71, 72, 77, 81, 89, 93, 100, 102, 117, 124, 133, 135, 138, 152, 158, 190–191, 218, 221, 227, 228, 234, 244, 262, 267, 268–269, 275, 282, 284, 313, 335, 338, 342, 344, 363, 370
  letters from, 14, 18, 35, 47, 59, 123, 138, 144, 200, 202, 208, 226, 291
  letters to, 74, 156, 157, 159
  trustee to the Brownings' marriage settlement, 63, 74, 210, 218, 330
Kerenhappuch ("K."), (Miss Mitford's maid), [vol. 5: 62n], 82, 118, 280, 293, 310

King Victor and King Charles (RB)
  reviews of, 385, 392
Kinnersley Castle, 220
Kirby, Ben, 280
Knight, Charles
  Pictorial Edition of the Works of Shakespeare, The, 282
Knight, John, 373
Knowles, James Sheridan
  George Lovell, 136
Kock, Charles Paul de, 82

L.E.L., *see* Landon, Letitia Elizabeth
L'Envers de l'histoire contemporaine (Balzac), 120
La Verna, 243, 255
"Laboratory, The" (RB)
  review of, 393
"Lady Geraldine's Courtship" (EBB)
  reviews of, 378, 383
Lamartine de Prat, Alphonse Marie Louis de, 314
  Histoire des Girondins, 314
Landon, Letitia Elizabeth, 118
Landor, Walter Savage
  letter from, 208
  "To Robert Browning," 193
  quotation from, 380
Le Havre, 5, 8, 11, 15, 26
Leamington, 233
Leaning Tower (Campanile, Pisa), 26, 36, 38, 45, 46, 62, 90, 92, 104, 149, 164, 183, 211, 212, 213, 253
Leeds, 38
Leghorn, 25, 83, 115, 181, 203, 207, 219, 229, 286, 331
Lely, Peter, 202
Leopoldo II, Grand Duke of Tuscany, 50, 113, 207, 229, 231, 246, 258, 259, 275, 290, 298, 300, 302, 312, 324, 331, 335, 339, 340
Lewes, George Henry, 404
"Life" (EBB)
  review of, 383
Life in the Sick-Room (Martineau), 367
"Light of Love" (Anon), 174, 179, 183
Lindsay, Clara Sophia (*née* Bayford), (EBB's cousin), 322, 325n, 327, 333, 355
Lindsay, Martin, 327, 333
Literary and Historical Memorials of London (Jesse), 314
Little Bookham, 17, 22, 27, 29, 54
Lizzie, *see* Barrett, Georgiana Elizabeth
"Locksley Hall" (Tennyson), 281
Loftus, Harriet Margaret (*née* Langrishe), 161, 170, 171, 322
Loftus, Mary Harriet Anne, 322
Loftus, William Francis Bentinck, 161, 171, 322

London, 11, 14, 21, 28, 31, 41, 47, 64, 75, 76, 92, 103, 125, 140, 142, 145, 152, 153, 162, 169, 173, 178, 183, 190, 203, 205, 208, 212, 216, 221, 232, 233, 236, 237, 239, 240, 242, 244, 245, 246, 247, 251, 280, 293, 294, 295, 301, 305, 310, 313, 335, 347, 348, 353, 355
   see also specific places and streets
"Lost Leader, The" (RB)
   review of, 396
Louvre, The, 11, 19
"Love" (EBB)
   review of, 383
"Loved Once" (EBB)
   review of, 377
Lovejoy, George, 118
Lovejoy, Pattie, 118
Lowell, James Russell, [vol. 5: 373–374]
   letter from, 99
   letter to, 86
Lowth, Robert
   Select Psalms in Verse, 45
Lucca, Duke of, *see* Bourbon, Charles Louis
Lucca, 59, 81, 122, 136, 138, 160, 164, 166
Lucréce (Ponsard), 120
Lucretia: or the Children of the Night (Bulwer-Lytton), 67
Lucrezia Floriani (Sand), 313, 345
Luisa Fernanda, Infanta of Spain, 124, 132, 184
Lungarno (Florence), 229
Lungarno (Pisa), 114
Luria (RB), 366
   reviews of, 385–386, 392, 397
Luther, Martin, 96
Lyons, 17, 19, 23
Lytton, Edward George Bulwer-, 192
   Westwood's comments on, 67
   Lucretia: or the Children of the Night, 67

Macaulay, Thomas Babington, 68
McIntosh, Charlotte, 360
McIntosh, Frances, 360
McIntosh, John, 360
Macpherson, Robert, 332, *337n*, 345
Macready, William Charles, 348
Maddox, John Medex, 348
"Madhouse Cells" (RB)
   review of, 395
"Madonna del Gran' Duca," (Raphael), 217
"Madonna della Seggiola," (Raphael), 217
"Madonna di sotto gli Organi" (Curradi), 127
Madrid, 163
Mahony, Francis Sylvester ("Father Prout"), 206–207, *211n*, 286, 331, 333, 336, 345
Maîtres Mosaïstes, Les (Sand), 83
Malvars, Marianne, 227
Malvern, 253
Malvern Hills, 253

"Man's Requirements, A" (EBB), 38
Man in the Republic: A Series of Poems (Mathews), 99
Manchester, 192
Manilius
   Astronomica
      quotation from, 291
Mannyng, Robert, 173n
Manzoni, Alessandro, 47
Marcus Aurelius Antoninus
   statue of, 287
Maremma, 199
Margary, Emma (*née* Russell), 260, 269, 293
   see also Monro, Emma (*née* Russell)
Margary, Peter John, 193, 208, 209, 293
"Mariana" (Tennyson), 67
Marseilles, 11, 24, 27, 36, 45, 52, 111, 117, 149
Marston, John Westland, 67
Marsyas, 310
Martin, James, [vol. 2: 342–343], 29, 35, 36, 37, 43, 109, 175, 273, 274, 323
   health, 208, 277
   letters from, 89, 108, 111, 112
   letter to, 111
Martin, Julia (*née* Vignoles), [vol. 2: 342–343], 17, 27, 108, 124, 125, 180, 260, 323
   letters from, 37, 40, 111, 112, 324
   letters to, 29, 40, 111, 173, 273
Martin ou l'enfant trouvé (Sue), 313, 314
Martineau, Harriet, [vol. 4: 325–327], 38, 118, 237, 245, 341, 345, 363
   letters from, 282, 291, 298
   Life in the Sick-Room, 367
   travels, 100
Martineau, James, 48
Martins, The, 89, 109, 208, 217, 355
Masaccio, Tomasso
   frescoes of the life of St. Peter, 216
Masson, Michel, 342
Mathews, Charles, 197
Mathews, Cornelius, [vol. 6: 363–364], 371
   letters to, 98, 197
   Man in the Republic: A Series of Poems, 99
   Poems on Man, 99
Matteucci, Carlo, 147, 170
Matteucci, Robinia Elizabeth (*née* Young), 147, *148n*, 169–170, 172
"Maud's Spinning" (EBB), 38
Maule, Fox, 163
May, George, 280
Mayfair, 152
Mazzini, Giuseppe, 104
Medici, Cosimo de, 61, 62
Medici, Lorenzo de' (Lorenzo the Magnificent), 295, 297, 305, 313
Medici, The, 123, 177, 189

"Meditation in Tuscany, A" (EBB), 343n
Mediterranean Sea, 109
Mémoires d'un Médicin: Joseph Balsamo (Dumas, père), 314
Mendelssohn, Felix, 169
Metternich, Prince Clemens von, 302
Michaelangelo Buonarroti, 172, 174, 176, 182, 196, 213, 216, 217, 239, 264
"Pietà," 217
Milan, 183, 199, 244
Miller, Mr. (baker), 304
Miller, Mrs. (baker's wife), 304
Miller, Jane, 53, 86, 214, 244
Milnes, Richard Monckton, [vol. 4: 29n]
letters from, 36, 39, 164
letter to, 164
Milton, John, 214, 246, 298, 352
"Lycidas"
quotation from, 83
Paradise Lost
quotations from, 205, 215, 334, 341
"Sonnet XI"
quotation from, 153
Minny, *see* Robinson, Mary
Minto, Mary, 335
Minto, Mary Eliza, 335
Minucci, Ferdinando, Archbishop of Florence, 212, 215
Mitford, Mary Russell, [vol. 3: 319-321], 245, 293
health, 293
letters from, 4, 15, 18, 37, 81, 114, 125, 245, 279, 309, 314, 339, 340
letters to, 4, 18, 37, 44, 81, 115, 182, 279, 309, 339
Monro, Emma (*née* Russell), 147, 209, 221
see also Margary, Emma (*née* Russell)
Monro, Theodore, 209, 293
Montagu Square, 228
Montagu Street, 319
Montepulciano wine, 85
Montpensier, Duke of, 124, 132, 184
Moore, John, 96
Moore, Thomas, 84
"St. Senanus and the Lady"
quotation from, 212
Morgan, Lady (Sydney Owenson), [vol. 3: 250n], 305, 306, 308, 313, 355
Moscow, 112, 114, 115
Mother Puss (Browning family cat), 70
Moulton, Elizabeth (*née* Barrett), (EBB's grandmother), [vol. 1: 285], 357
"Mountaineer and Poet" (EBB)
review of, 383
Moxon, Edward, [vol. 4: 328-330], 122, 141, 142
letter from, 135
letter to, 135

Murray's *Hand-Book*, *see Hand-Book for Travellers in Northern Italy* (1847)
Museum of Natural History (Florence), 292
"My Last Duchess" (RB)
review of, 395
Mystères de Paris, Les (Sue), 83, 116

Nankivell, Charles Benjamin, 26, *29n*, 264
Naples, 191, 204, 205, 234, 246, 306, 311
Napoleon I, Emperor, 314
New Cross, 77, 97
New Italian Grammar, A (Cerutti), 138
New Quarterly Review, The, 385-386
New Zealand, 152
New Zealand Company, 250
Newgate, 330
Newman, John Henry, 16, 105, 153
Nice, 24, 95, 189
Nicholas I, Czar, 126
Normanby, Lord, *see* Phipps, Constantine Henry, 1st Marquis of Normanby
Northumberland House, 259
Norton, Caroline Elizabeth Sarah (*née* Sheridan)
Aunt Carry's Ballads for Children, 67
Norwood, 140
Notre Dame, 45
Notre-Dame de Paris (Hugo), 83

Occy, *see* Barrett, Octavius Butler Moulton-
O'Connell, Daniel, 95, 175, 184, 219
Odessa, 112
Oliver Cromwell's Letters and Speeches (Carlyle), 236
Orion (Horne), 311
Orleans, 4, 5, 6, 10, 11, 13, 14, 15, 18, 23, 27, 28, 304
Orme, Charlotte (*née* Searman), [vol. 1: 115n], 191, 234, 269, 336
Oxford, 245
Oxford Street, 224

Paddington Chapel, 357, 358, 359, 360
Palace of the Doge (Venice), 278
Palazzo Guidi (Casa Guidi), 258, 263, 288, 320, 321, 325
Palazzo Lanfranchi (Palazzo Toscanelli), 62, 101
Palazzo Pitti, 202, 259, 275, 312, 321, 331, 339
Palatine Gallery, 210, 216, 217, 327
Palazzo Vecchio, 224
Palermo, 306
Pall Mall, 21, 164
Palmer, E.F.R., *8n*
letter from, 7
Palmerston, Henry John Temple, 140, 153
Panizzi, Antonio, 123

Paracelsus (RB), 318, 367, 372, 373
   reviews of, 385–386, 387–397, 399
   revisions of, 64, 135, 366
Paris, 5, 8, 9, 10, 11, 13, 15, 16, 19, 21, 23, 36, 38, 41, 45, 47, 52, 62, 71, 76, 100, 108, 109, 120, 124, 133, 144, 145, 149, 175, 178, 183, 184, 189, 193, 205, 310
   see also specific places and streets
Parliament
   House of Lords, 172
Partridge, Lucy Olivia Hobart (*née* Anderdon), 283, 311, 340
Pasquin, Antoine Claude ("Valery")
   Italy and Its Comforts: The Manual of Tourists, 278
"Past and Future" (EBB)
   review of, 378
"Patience Taught by Nature" (EBB)
   review of, 378
Patten, Martha, 95
Pau, 43, 109, 112, 189, 274, 355
Pauline (RB), 318, 329, 372
Pelago, 252, 254, 262, 274
People's Journal, The, 299
"Perplexed Music" (EBB)
   review of, 378
Perseus, 199
Perugia, 267, 271, 275, 282, 286, 352
Pescia, 164
Petrarch (Francesco Petrarca), 17, 45, 97, 100, 149, 193
Peverada, Sig., 123, 124
Peyton, Eliza (*née* Griffith), [vol. 2: 149n], 50
Peyton, Elizabeth Rosetta ("Rosa"), 43
Peytons, The, 43, 319
Phidias
   "Apollino," 344
Philip van Artevelde (Taylor), 348
Phipps, Constantine Henry, 1st Marquis of Normanby, 11
Piazza del Gran Duca (Piazza della Signoria), 191, 199, 224
Piazza Pitti, 174, 263, 290, 300, 303, 312, 321, 322, 324, 325, 327, 335, 336, 339, 340, 344
Piazza Santa Croce, 368
Piazza Santa Maria Novella, 174, 204, 228, 229, 321
Piazza Santa Trinità, 260
Pictorial Edition of the Works of Shakespeare, The (Knight), 282
"Pied Piper of Hamelin, The" (RB)
   review of, 394
"Pietà" (Michelangelo), 217
Pippa Passes (RB)
   EBB's comments on, 114
   reviews of, 385, 392, 397, 401
   revisions of, 135

Pisa, 3, 5, 10, 11, 16, 17, 19, 20, 21, 25, 26, 30, 32, 33, 36, 38, 39, 42, 43, 45, 46, 57, 58, 59, 62, 63, 64, 66, 75, 76, 78, 90, 92, 93, 94, 99, 100, 104, 109, 113, 117, 122, 123, 126, 127, 133, 137, 138, 142, 143, 149, 150, 152, 161, 164, 171, 172, 173, 174, 177, 178, 180, 183, 187, 188, 191, 195, 196, 197, 199, 204, 207, 210, 212, 213, 219, 220, 224, 225, 232, 239, 258, 264, 271, 272, 287, 291, 305, 320, 321, 322, 323, 326, 345
   see also specific places and street
Pisa, Cathedral of (Duomo), 26, 36, 38, 43, 45, 62, 75, 81, 88, 90, 91, 92, 104, 125, 127, 130, 131, 133, 136, 137, 140, 145, 149, 212, 213
   baptistery, 149
   campanile ("Leaning Tower"), 26, 36, 38, 45, 46, 62, 90, 92, 104, 149, 164, 183, 211, 212, 213, 253
Pisa, University of, 85, 133
   library, 36, 43, 51, 114
Pistoia, 138, 164, 165, 166, 191
Pius IX, Pope ("Pio Nono"), 85, *86n*, 112, 153, 164, 175, 231, 274, 287, 290, 298, 302, 312, 313
Plutarch
   Parallel Lives
      quotation from, 252
Poe, Edgar Allan, 100
   Raven, The, 67, 100
Poems (1844), (EBB), 135, 141
   reviews of, 67, 375–385
Poems (1847), (Emerson), 67
Poems (1849), (RB), 65n, 83, 86, 97, 99, 114, 122, 142
Poems (1850), (EBB), 211n
Poems Before Congress (EBB), 360
Poems on Man (Mathews), 99
Poesie di Ieronimo Savonarola iluustrate e pubblicate per cura di Andin de Rains (Savonarola), 344
"Poet, The" (EBB)
   review of, 383
Poetic Prism, or, Original and Reflected Rays from Modern Verse, Sacred and Serious, The (Greville)
   EBB's contribution to, 28
Poggio Imperiale, 344
Poland Street, 207
Pollock, James Edward, 227, 286
Ponsard, François
   Agnès de Méranie, 120
   Lucrèce, 120
Pope, Alexander
   Essay on Criticism, An
      quotation from, 125

Popular Works of Johann Gottlieb Fichte, with a Memoir, The (Fichte), 349
"Portrait, A" (EBB), 97
Powers, Elizabeth (*née* Gibson), 232
Powers, Hiram, 192, *194n*, 208, 216, 239, 252, 264, 291, 308, 312, 345
"Benjamin Franklin," 291
"Eve Tempted," 216, 232, 246, 308
"Fisher Boy, The," 208, 216, 246, 264
"Greek Slave, The," 208, 216, 246, 309
Prato, 138, 164, 165, 191
Presbyterianism/Presbyterians, 219
Presse, La, 199
Price, Robert, 268
Princess, The (Tennyson), 193, 281, 298, 310, 345, 349
Princess's Theatre, 348
Pritchard, James, 152
Procter, Bryan Waller ("Barry Cornwall"), 36, 135
letter from, 59
Prometheus Bound (1833), (EBB), 364, 368, 397
Prometheus Bound (revised version), (EBB), 28, 124
"Prospect, The" (EBB)
review of, 383
Prospero, 42
Prout, Father (pseud.), *see* Mahony, Francis Sylvester
Provence, 45
Pump Court, 151
Puritans/Puritanism, 169
Pusey, Edward Bouverie, 16, 105, 245
Puseyism/Puseyites, 91, 96, 105, 153

Queue du chien d'Aliciade, La (Bernard), 314

Rabelais, François
quotations from, 295, 340
Rachel, 82
Ramsgate, 355
Raphael (Raffaello Sanzio), 11, 176, 182, 196, 201, 210, 217, 264, 298, 327, 340, 344
"Madonna del Gran' Duca," 217
"Madonna della Seggiola," 217
Raven, The (Poe), 67, 100
Ravenna, 166, 183, 199
Reading, 310
Recherche de l'Absolu, La (Balzac), 116
Recoaro, Baths of, 131, 138, 166, 167, 262
Redi, Francesco, 85
Bacco in Toscana, 86n
"Reed, A" (EBB), 38
Reine Margot, La (Dumas, père), 184
Reisebilder (Heine), 42
Retreat Penn, 129

Return of the Druses, The (RB)
reviews of, 385, 392
Revue des Deux Mondes, 386–397
Reynolds, Charles William, 175, 190, 206, 225, 241, 269, 289, 311, 340, 351, 352, 353
Reynolds, Charlotte Mary (*née* Butler), ("Arlette"), (EBB's cousin), 225, 241, 242, 244, 277, 289, 311, 324, 340, 341, 351, 352, 353, 354
see also Butler, Charlotte Mary ("Arlette"), (EBB's cousin)
Reynoldses, The, 260, 289, 290, 306, 324, 333
Rhine (river), 109, 221, 244, 336
Rhone (river), 3, 17, 19, 23, 25
Ricardo, Harriet (*née* Mallory), 204
Richter, Johann Paul Freidrich ("Jean Paul"), 349
Robespierre, François Maximilien Joseph de, 314
Robinson, Mary ("Minny"), [vol. 1: 47n], 12, 16, 27, 52, 53, 71, 74, 80, 95, 110, 133, 145, 163, 173, 181, 188, 193, 222, 232, 234, 243, 247, 261, 319, 336, 356
health, 27, 124, 306
letter from, 231
Rolandi, Pietro, 6
Roman Advertiser, The, 113
"Romance of the Swan's Nest, The" (EBB)
review of, 382
"Romaunt of the Page, The" (EBB), 397
review of, 378
Rome, 36, 38, 42, 59, 88, 92, 94, 100, 112, 113, 114, 115, 125, 131, 138, 146, 149, 150, 164, 174, 175, 179, 180, 183, 184, 191, 204, 205, 207, 225, 226, 227, 228, 234, 241, 244, 245, 260, 262, 267, 271, 272, 273, 274, 275, 278, 282, 285, 286, 288, 289, 290, 292, 294, 297, 298, 299, 302, 304, 305, 308, 309, 311, 313, 316, 319, 320, 322, 326, 327, 331, 332, 333, 338, 340, 341, 342, 344, 345, 352, 355
see also specific places and streets
Roper-Curzon, *see* Curzon, Roper-
Rossetti, Dante Gabriel, *318n*
letters from, 318, 329
letter to, 329
Rossini, Gioacchino Antonio, 131, 158
Rothschild, House of, 163, 218, 247, 278
Rothschild, Lionel Nathan, 25
Rouen, 8, 184
Rouge et le Noir, Le (Stendhal), 117
Rousseau, Jean Jacques, 132
Rubempré, Lucien, 116
"Runaway Slave at Pilgrim's Point, The" (EBB), 86, 86n, 99, 117
Ruskin, John, 370
Russell, John, 68

Russell, Mary Anne, 125
Russia, 169
Russie en 1839, La (Custine), 112

Sacchetti, Franco di Benci, 344
Sacred and Legendary Art (Jameson), 11, 150
St. Anthony, 257, 297
St. Bartholomew's Fair, 237
St. George the Martyr (English Church in Pisa), 130
St. Germans, Lady (Harriet Eliot, *née* Pole-Carew), 323
St. John the Baptist, 229
Saint John, Charles
  Short Sketches of the Wild Sports and Natural History of the Highlands, 314
St. Joseph, 255
St. Lawrence, 199, 219, 281
St. Leopold, 335
St. Marylebone (church), 3, 14, 35, 52
St. Mary-le-Bow, Cheapside, 66
St. Paul's (cathedral), 236
St. Peter, 239
St. Peter's (basilica), 316
St. Petersburg, 112, 250
St. Senanus, 297
San Felice (church), 259, 267, 275, 294
San Giovanni, 226, 229, 230
San Gualberto, 257, 263, 274, 275, 281
San Ranieri, 96, 160, 196
San Torpes, 90, 96
Sancho Panza, 319
Sand, George (Amantine Lucile Aurore Dudevant, *née* Dupin), 116, 184, 221, 314
  Lucrezia Floriani, 313, 345
  Maîtres Mosaïstes, Les, 83
Santa Croce (church), 213
Santa Croce (piazza), 368
Santa Maria Novella (church), 228
Santa Maria Novella (piazza), 174, 204, 228, 229, 321
Santa Trinità (bridge), 260
Santa Trinità (piazza), 260
Sardinia, King of, 153
Sartor Resartus (Carlyle), 372
Satan, 257
Saul, 35
"Saul" (RB)
  review of, 394
Saunders & Otley, Messrs., 329
Savonarola, Girolamo
  Poesie di Ieronimo Savonarola iluustrate e pubblicate per cura di Andin de Rains, 344
Scotland, 150, 237, 327
Scott, Walter, 47, 314
Seine (river), 3, 5
Select Psalms in Verse (Lowth), 45

"Seraph and Poet, The" (EBB)
  review of, 378
Sette, *see* Barrett, Septimus Barrett Moulton-
Shakespeare, William, 93, 174, 179, 183, 184, 199, 282
  works
    As You Like It
      quotation from, 152
    Hamlet
      quotations from, 133, 305
    Macbeth
      quotations from, 188, 275, 330
    Merchant of Venice, The
      quotation from, 132
    Othello
      quotation from, 204
    Richard III
      quotation from, 204
    "Sonnet 116"
      quotation from, 20
Shelley, Mary Wollstonecraft (*née* Godwin), 226
Shelley, Percy Bysshe, 62, 226, 227, 232, 372
  "Julian and Maddalo"
    quotation from, 20
Short Sketches of the Wild Sports and Natural History of the Highlands (Saint John), 314
Siècle, Le, 93, 116, 150
Siena, 38, 113, 114, 122, 127, 132, 138, 150, 164, 165, 166, 167, 191
Sigourney, Lydia Howard (*née* Huntley), 355
Silverthorne, James, [vol. 13: 358n], 3, 35
  health, 136
Sindbad, 198
Sistine Chapel, 174, 184
"Six Months in Italy" (Hillard), 408–409
Smee, William, 373
Smith, Mary Anne (*née* Clarke), [vol. 4: 8], 213
Snare, John, 39
"Soliloquy of the Spanish Cloister" (RB)
  review of, 395
Sombre, David Ochterlony Dyce-, 206
Sonnets from the Portuguese (EBB), 411
Sordello (RB), 363, 411
  reviews of, 385–397, 399, 400
Sorrento, 191
Soul's Tragedy, A (RB), 366
  reviews of, 385–386, 392, 397
Soulié, Frédéric, 116, 314
  Aventures de Saturnin Fichet ou la Conspiration de la Rouarie, Les, 116, 314
Southampton, 5, 207
Southey, Robert, 314
Speronare, Le (Dumas, père), 183, 184
Spohr, Ludwig, 169
Spring, Rebecca (*née* Buffum), 53

Index

letter from, 53
Statira (ship), 109
Stendhal (Marie Henri Beyle), 117
   Rouge et le Noir, Le, 117
Stisted, Clotilda Elizabeth, 94, *97n*, 287
Storm/Stormie, *see* Barrett, Charles John Barrett Moulton-
Strafford (RB)
   reviews of, 385, 391
Stratten, Arthur Clegg, 357, 359
Stratten, Augusta (*née* Hope), 359
Stratten, Charlotte Rebekah, 357
Stratten, Frances Elizabeth, 357, 360
Stratten, James, 27, 53, 79, 147, 162, 169, 170, 188, 219, 233, 234, 261, 354
   biographical sketch, 357-360
   Intermediate State, and Other Discourses, The, 359
Stratten, John Remington, 357, 359
Stratten, Rebekah (*née* Wilson), 53, 357, 358, 360
Strattens, The, 294
Strutt, Elizabeth (*née* Byron), 355
Sue, Eugène, 47, 93, 116, 314
   Jean Cavalier, 83
   Juif Errant, Le, 83
   Martin ou l'enfant trouvé, 313, 314
   Mystères de Paris, Les, 83, 116
Surrey, 97
   Zoological Gardens, 261
Surtees, Elizabeth, 104, 142
Surtees, Margaret Caroline, 104, 142, 143, 246, 323
Surtees, Robert, [vol. 13: 181], 25, 80, 91, 104, 142, 246, 323
Swedenborg, Emanuel, 358
Swedenborgians/Swedenborgianism, 358
Swiss, The, 300
Switzerland, 100, 221, 227, 305, 306

Tait's Edinburgh Magazine, 315, 380-385
Tancred: or, the New Crusade (Disraeli), 237
Tantalus, 182
Tarpeian rock, the (Rome), 282, 285, 286, 292
Taunton, 54, 96, 193, 209
Taylor, Henry
   Philip van Artevelde, 348
"Tears" (EBB)
   review of, 378
Temple, The, 152
Tennyson, Alfred, [vol. 7: 385-388], 150, 193, 281, 298, 310, 368, 372
   travels, 100, 150
   Westwood's comments on, 67
   works
      "Gardener's Daughter, The," 310
      "Locksley Hall," 281
      "Mariana," 67

Princess, The, 193, 281, 298, 310, 341, 345, 349
Terni, 282, 286
Teynham, Lord, *see* Curzon, George Henry Roper-
Thackeray, William Makepeace
   Vanity Fair, 237
Thomson, Anne, [vol. 10, 327-328], 209
   letters from, 92, 208
   letter to, 92
Thomson, James, 209
   Castle of Indolence, The
      quotation from, 42
Tilbury & Co., Edward, 77
Times, The, 67, 97n, 136, 150, 242, 248n, 265
Tindal, Acton, 311
Tindal, Henrietta (*née* Harrison), 311, 340, 374
Tintoretto, Jacopo Robusti, 278
Titian (Tiziano Vecellio), 278
   "Venus of Urbino," 248
"To George Sand. A Desire" (EBB), 356n
"To George Sand. A Recognition" (EBB), 356n
"To Robert Browning" (Landor), 193
Toby (Boyd's dog), 86
"Tomb at St. Praxed's, The" (RB)
   review of, 395
Tonbridge, 294
Torlonia and Co., Messrs., 299
Torquay, 191
Toulon, 345
Tours, 189, 220, 233, 353
Tower of London, The, 169
Tractarians, 105
Trafalgar Square, 228
Treatise on the Law of Marine Insurance and Average, A (Arnould), 347
Treherne, Elizabeth (*née* Crow), [vol. 4: 80n], 54, 80, 97, 133, 231, 261, 306, 336
Treherne, Ellen, 133, 231
Treppy, *see* Trepsack, Mary
Trepsack, Mary ("Trep"/"Trippy"), [vol. 1: 301-302], 12, 15, 17, 28, 54, 72, 77, 80, 89, 96, 110, 124, 134, 142, 144, 157, 163, 172, 181, 186, 210, 221, 233, 247, 248, 257, 260, 294, 301, 306, 319, 334, 354
   letters from, 142, 163, 306
   letters to, 15, 26
Trollope, Frances (*née* Milton), [vol. 3: 68n], 94, 192
Trotman, Thomas William, 317, 323
Tulks, The, 335
Turgot, Anne Robert Jacques, 294n
Turkey, 164
Turner, Mrs., 80, 110, 162, 170, 172
Tuscans, The, 231, 335, 340
Tuscany, 163, 165, 224, 231, 258, 302
Tuscany, Grand Duchess of (Maria Antonia), 335

Tuscany, Grand Duke of, *see* Leopold II
"Two Sketches" (EBB)
  review of, 383
Tyrol, The, 150, 204, 221

Uffizi Gallery, 216, 217, 224
  Tribune, 248

Valery (pseud.), *see* Pasquin, Antoine Claude
Vallombrosa, 212, 213, 214, 216, 220, 221, 224, 225, 226, 227, 228, 230, 234, 239, 240, 243, 244, 246, 250, 252, 253, 255, 256, 258, 259, 260, 261, 262, 271, 274, 275, 281, 282, 285, 287, 291, 295, 297, 298, 299, 322, 372, 373
Van Dyck, Anthony, 355
Vanity Fair (Thackeray), 237
Vasari, Giorgio, 26, 38, 45, 62, 99, 149
  Delle vite de più eccelenti pittori, scultori, ed architettori, 114
Vaucluse, 17, 19, 24, 28, 45, 88, 89, 100, 149, 150, 193
Vauxhall, 237, 261
  Gardens, 261
Velázquez, Diego Rodriguez de Silva, 39
  "Charles I when Prince of Wales," 38
Venice, 42, 76, 92, 99, 112, 117, 131, 133, 138, 139, 145, 150, 151, 158, 164, 166, 167, 172, 183, 190, 191, 199, 204, 221, 226, 227, 244, 262, 264, 278, 286, 313, 344
  see also specific places
Venus, 174
"Venus" (Canova), 217
Venus de Medici, 173, 182, 187, 192, 212, 213, 217, 248
"Venus of Urbino" (Titian), 248
Vergil (Publius Vergilius Maro), 27
Verona, 138, 150, 151, 158, 167
Via della Scala, 278
Via delle Belle Donne, 263
Via Giulia, 309
Via Gregoriana, 272, 309
Via Maggio, 321, 325, 326, 336
Vicenza, 131, 138
Victoria, Queen, 208, 314
Vienna, 244, 267
Vieusseux's reading room (Florence), 342
Villa Careggi, 295, 297, 305, 306, 313, 328
Villa Catalani, 153

Villa Cresci, 153
"Vision of Poets, A" (EBB)
  reviews of, 376, 383
Vita di Angelo Cerutti (Cerutti), 138
Volterra, 114, 122, 127, 132, 136, 138, 150, 164, 165, 166, 167, 191
Voyage en Italie (Janin), 112

Walm's Well, 253
Wanstead, 21
Waterloo House, 274
Wesley, John, 153
West Indies, 293
Westmorland, 282
Westwood, Miss, 66
Westwood, Mary, 66
Westwood, Thomas, [vol. 5: 375–376]
  letters from, 58, 65, 245
  letters to, 54, 58, 148, 297
Wilson, Elizabeth, [vol. 13: 381–387], 3, 6, 8, 10, 11, 12, 14, 16, 18, 19, 24, 25, 26, 35, 48, 51, 53, 59, 60, 72, 76, 78, 80, 88, 91, 94, 96, 110, 117, 126, 127, 132, 133, 142, 145, 155, 156, 159, 160–161, 162, 170, 177, 178, 179, 180, 186, 188, 191, 192, 203, 204, 205, 210, 215, 224, 227, 228, 230, 231, 232, 234, 243, 245, 247, 248, 253–254, 255, 257, 258, 261, 262, 264, 267, 272, 281, 282, 289, 290, 291, 297, 303, 304, 305, 306, 320, 322, 323, 324, 334, 336, 370, 373
  health, 25, 106–108, 111, 114, 117, 121–122, 126, 130, 139, 143, 144, 155, 157, 160, 173, 179, 191, 221, 291–292, 306, 324
Wilson, Frances ("Fanny"), 53, 191, 247
Wimpole Street, 17, 29, 34, 44, 51, 52, 53, 66, 71, 72, 74, 97, 107, 108, 133, 148, 150, 217, 224, 233, 244, 246, 258, 276, 277, 290, 299, 341, 344, 353
"Woman's Shortcomings, A" (EBB), 38
Wordsworth, William
  "Ode: Intimations of Immortality"
    quotation from, 20
Wyatt, Richard James, 175

Year of Consolation, A (Butler), 150, 311
Young, Mary (*née* Ancrum), 147, 169, 170, 171, 172, 221, 271